To Connu, a
dear and old
friend from the
Big City.

John

URBAN AMERICA
CONFLICT AND CHANGE

URBAN AMERICA
CONFLICT AND CHANGE

J. JOHN PALEN AND KARL H. FLAMING, *EDITORS*
University of Wisconsin–Milwaukee

HOLT, RINEHART AND WINSTON, INC.
New York Chicago San Francisco Atlanta
Dallas Montreal Toronto London Sydney

Reproduced on the cover: ESTATE *by Robert Rauschenberg*, 1963. Oil and Printer's Ink, 96 x 70 inches. Philadelphia Museum of Art: Given by the Friends of the Philadelphia Museum of Art.

Given Alfred North Whitehead's statement that "the actual world is a process," it is critical to ask how one makes meaning out of this process. We believe that the evolutionary perspective provides one answer. This book, therefore, encompasses a general approach to the theoretical and historical perspective on sociocultural change. The appeal of this approach to the study of urban change is that it links our frontier past to the industrial present and the postindustrial future.

The focus of *Urban America* is thus on the evolution and development of American urban society, rather than on a cross-cultural overview of cities in general. Within the evolutionary perspective, this book offers to the student a systematic introduction to writings on urbanism and urbanization in America. While not all social change has been truly evolutionary, most crucial social trends are both linear and cumulative and do over time transform organized social life.

The volume has three general objectives: to suggest a conceptual framework for organizing and discussing American urban development; to provide a selection of the best materials available on urban America; and to integrate these selections within our framework.

The readings, in conjunction with our comments, are designed to give the student some insight into the developing social and spatial patterns of American urban areas. Our teaching experience has convinced us that introductory students or those in the first section of advanced urban courses possess a natural interest in the trends in their own society. Thus, we believe it fruitful to cultivate this natural curiosity rather than swamp students with comparative materials. Pedagogically speaking, knowledge of their own society better prepares students to appreciate the rich cross-cultural materials available.

In selecting the readings for this volume we have tried to avoid being overly sectarian or strenuously biased in favor of one discipline. We have included what we feel to be excellent writings without regard to the author's professional affiliation, our sole purpose being to communicate both a basic framework and a coherent body of knowledge.

In terms of format, the book is divided into five sections, each of which includes an introductory essay and overview by the editors. These essays are designed to aid the student in integrating the articles within the general theme of the book. To stimulate further exploration of crucial issues, each section closes with a basic annotated bibliography.

Section One provides a sociological analysis of historical materials on the early growth and development of North American cities. The seven readings examine the significance of population growth, technology, and natural environment on the evolution of urban social organization. Here, our emphasis is on the city as a locus of change. This section presents a wide spectrum of urban historical literature, which illustrates some of the antecedents of the contemporary American city. Hopefully, this literature will sensitize the reader to long-term trends within his own societal framework. Historical material, reinterpreted from a sociological perspective, can offer a comprehensive description of how change has come about in our own society. Historical materials also provide a baseline for interpreting cross-cultural trends.

Having laid the historical groundwork, Section Two presents a sociological examination of current patterns of urbanism and urbanization—particularly the morphology or structure of cities. The seven readings emphasize evolving urban structure. The metropolitan and intermetropolitan setting is viewed as the product of such processes as competition, adaptation, and selectivity. These articles range from the most significant ground-breaking contributions of the Chicago School to contemporary empirical work on questions such as city-suburban changes and the existence of megalopolis. The section analyzes, at the macro- or large-aggregate level, the distribution of the American urban population and discusses changes in patterns of urban spatial distribution and form.

The central emphasis of Section Three is on issues concerning the organization of urban life styles. This micro-level analysis examines how and why life styles change or resist change over time. A micro- or interactional-level analysis of the social structure and organization found within cities complements the macro-level focus of Section Two. Materials range from studies of the Brahmins of Boston to the Vice Lords of Chicago. Special attention is given to theory and research on urbanism as an emerging way of life.

Section Four discusses a variety of contemporary urban problems that have recurred throughout American history:

for example, the political system, housing, urban education, racism, poverty, and urban violence. Special attention is given to the problem of violence because of its frequency in contemporary urban life. Also discussed is the theoretical controversy concerning the role violence plays in urban change.

Section Five is concerned with mechanisms for bringing about change within the urban setting. The readings in this section illustrate the variety of different solutions to urban problems, including the strategies of traditional political theorists, the techniques of activists, the proposals of professional planners, and the visions of utopianists.

We would like to thank George Hesslink and Charles Tilly for their thorough editing of this manuscript. The volume is immeasurably stronger because of their efforts. Jan Carr and Jeanette Ninas Johnson of Holt, Rinehart and Winston provided extremely valuable editorial assistance. Special thanks to our typists Mary Annoi and Susan Schaeffer for their willingness to work with rough copy. Finally, we wish to thank our wives Karen and Nancy for their patience and understanding.

Addis Ababa, Ethiopia   J.J.P.
Milwaukee, Wisconsin   K.H.F.
January 1972

CONTENTS

SECTION TWO
EVOLVING URBAN STRUCTURES

SECTION THREE
EMERGING LIFE STYLES IN THE URBAN SETTING

SECTION FOUR
THE URBAN CRISIS

SECTION FIVE
PLANNING FOR THE URBAN CRISIS

URBAN AMERICA
CONFLICT AND CHANGE

The concept of the evolutionary development of social change intrigues and frustrates many sociologists. Contemporary usage of the term *evolution* sometimes is still confused with the deterministic version of the past century. Lest there be any misunderstanding, the term as used by contemporary evolutionists does not imply the naïve corollaries that accompanied the nineteenth-century conception of social evolution. Specifically, it does not imply: (1) inevitable social progress; (2) unilinear development along one and only one track; (3) the idea of fixed stages through which all societies must progress; (4) any form of social determination or universalism that suggest certain changes are inevitable and beyond human control.* Sociocultural evolution as used here is an approach or perspective to the study of social change.

Two general assumptions underlie this approach to social change. Often, but not always, technological change precedes social organizational change. The invention of the automobile, for example, greatly expanded the perimeters of cities, but governmental social organization has not kept pace with this technological advance.

Second, evolution is cumulative. It is possible for the process to be reversible on a small scale, but over the long term there is increasing complexity, differentiation, and integration of social organization. The result of this process is a more efficient utilization of energy. In the factory system, for example, the creation of specialization through division of labor caused interdependency, which, in turn, caused greater productivity. In no case, however, should efficiency be confused with valuative concepts such as social progress.

While sociocultural evolution provides a general approach to the study of change, it does not identify specific variables in change. However, the concept of the ecological complex, as developed by Otis Dudley Duncan, does specify the major classes of variables most used by social evolutionists. The ecological complex as a scheme for identifying significant classes of variables emphasizes the interrelated properties of life in urban settings and illustrates how each class of variables contains implications for the others.

The ecological complex identifies the relationship among four classes of variables: population, social organization, environment, and technology. This set of relationships can be illustrated as follows:

*See Marvin Olsen, *The Process of Social Organization*. New York: Holt, Rinehart and Winston, 1968, p. 264.

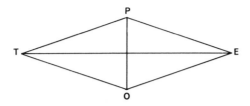

These categories can be remembered by using the mnemonic acronym of P.O.E.T. The four classes of variables (P.O.E.T.) are general and somewhat arbitrary categories, which means that the line of demarcation between them is sometimes cloudy. This is particularly true of the line between technology and social organization.

Population, technology, and environment operate singly and jointly in the development and modification of urban social organization. A growing population, for example, requires technological changes in order to more efficiently exploit the environment, a relationship that has been graphically brought to our attention as a consequence of the pollution crisis. Of course the chain does not stop here, for new levels and forms of urban social organization reflect back upon the influence of population, environment, and technology.

The evolutionary perspective directs one's attention to the interplay between these four categories. Which variables the social scientist chooses as the dependent variable (the effect to be explained) and which he treats as the independent variables (the ones producing the effect) reflect the particular interest, concern, and perspective of the individual. In this book major emphasis is on patterns of social organization and how they change at the aggregate level. Such an approach necessarily gives less attention to the role played by the discrete individual; an area which has been developed by social psychologists.

Before reading any of the sections we strongly suggest that you first read the short article by Otis Dudley Duncan which spells out the ecological complex and gives an example of its application. Duncan's article which immediately follows this introduction applies the systemic approach to the study of urban phenomena by drawing on the four categories of population, organization, environment, and technology. He argues that these four elements of the ecosystem are interdependent. Using the example of smog in Los Angeles he suggests that as transportation technology changed, the environment, the population, and the social organization of Los Angeles also changed. Duncan's illustration reminds us that man, even urban man, not only influences his environment, but that his environment imposes significant parameters on his behavorial and technological options.

The development of North America always has been closely tied to its cities. Today, three quarters of the United States population resides in urban places and the future of North America is clearly urban. However, the dimensions and quality of this future are far from obvious. As Arthur Schlesinger, Sr., once said, *the city is the frontier*.

FROM SOCIAL SYSTEMS TO ECOSYSTEM

OTIS DUDLEY DUNCAN

Levels and Systems

All science proceeds by a selective ordering of data by means of conceptual schemes. Although the formulation and application of conceptual schemes are recognized to entail, at some stage of inquiry, more or less arbitrary choices on the part of the theorist or investigator, we all acknowledge, or at least feel, that the nature of the "real world" exercises strong constraints on the development of schemes in science. Some schemes, used fruitfully over long periods of time, come to seem so natural that we find it difficult to imagine their being superseded. One type of scheme is deeply ingrained by our training as social scientists, to wit, the organization of data by *levels*. Kroeber is only voicing the consensus of a majority of scientists when he writes:[1]

> The subjects or materials of science . . . fall into four main classes or levels: the inorganic, organic, psychic, and sociocultural. . . . There is no intention to assert that the levels are absolutely separate, or separable by unassailable definitions. They are substantially distinct in the experience of the totality of science, and that is enough.

MacIver gives substantially the same classification, but instead of using the relatively colorless term "levels," he chooses to segregate the several "nexus of causation" into "great dynamic realms."[2]

It is significant that scientists, insofar as they do accept the doctrine of levels, tend to work *within* a level, not *with* it. The scheme of levels does not itself produce hypotheses; it can scarcely even be said to be heuristic. Its major contribution to the history of ideas has been to confer legitimacy upon the newer scientific approaches to the empirical world that, when they were emerging, had good use for any kind of ideological support.

Quite another type of conceptual scheme, the notion of *system,* is employed by the scientist in his day-to-day work. Conceptions of interdependent variation, of cause and effect, or even of mere patterning of sequence, derive naturalistically) manifests itself in collections of elements with more than from the idea that nature (using the term broadly for whatever can be studied nominal properties of unity.

From Otis Dudley Duncan, "From Social Systems to Ecosystem." Originally published in Vol. 31, No. 2 (Spring 1961) of *Sociological Inquiry*. Reprinted by permission.

No doubt there are many kinds of system, reflecting the kinds of elements comprising them and the modes of relationship conceived to hold among these elements. The point about this diversity that is critical to my argument is this. When we elect, wittingly or unwittingly, to work *within* a level (as this term was illustrated above) we tend to discern or construct—whichever emphasis you prefer—only those kinds of system whose elements are confined to that level. From this standpoint, the doctrine of levels may not only fail to be heuristic, it may actually become anti-heuristic, if it blinds us to fruitful results obtainable by recognizing *systems that cut across levels.*

One such system, probably because it is virtually a datum of immediate experience, is rather readily accepted by social scientists: personality. Manifestly and phenomenologically an integration of nonrandomly selected genetic, physiologic, social, and psycho-cultural elements, personality has a kind of hard reality that coerces recognition, even when it can be related to other systems only with difficulty or embarrassment. If I am not mistaken, however, the concept of personality system enjoys a sort of privileged status. We do not so readily accede to the introduction into scientific discourse of other sorts of system concept entailing integration of elements from diverse levels. The resistance to such concepts is likely to be disguised in charges of "environmental determinism" or "reductionism." An example: The working assumption of some human ecologists that the human community is, among other things, an organization of activities in physical space is criticized (though hardly refuted!) by the contention that such a conceptual scheme is contrary to "essentially and profoundly social" facts, i.e., "conscious choice of actors who vary in their ends and values."[3] We must resist the temptation to comment here on the curious assumption that the "essentially and profoundly social" has to do with such personal and subjective states as "ends and values," rather than with objective relations among interdependent living units. (Surely the latter is the prior significance of the "social," in an evolutionary if not an etymological sense.) The point to emphasize at present is, rather, that such a reaction to ecological formulations is tantamount to a denial of the crucial possibility that one can at least conceive of systems encompassing both human and physical elements. The "dynamic realm" of the psycho-social has indeed become a "realm," one ruled by an intellectual tyrant, when this possibility is willfully neglected or denied.

The Ecosystem

Acknowledged dangers of premature synthesis and superficial generalization notwithstanding, ecologists have been forced by the complexity of relationships manifested in their data to devise quite embracing conceptual schemes. The concept of ecosystem, a case in point, has become increasingly prominent in ecological study since the introduction of the term a quarter-century ago by the botanist, A. G. Tansley. "The *ecosystem*," according to Allee and collaborators, "may be defined as the interacting environmental and biotic system."[4] Odum characterizes the ecosystem as a "natural unit . . . in which the exchange of materials between the living and nonliving parts follows circular paths."[5] The first quotation comes from an enlightening synthesis of information now available on the evolution of ecosystems; the second prefaces an exposition of principles concerning the operation of "biogeochemical cycles" in ecosystems. Social scientists whose acquaintance with general ecology is limited to gleanings from the essays of Park[6] or the polemic by Alihan[7] might do well to inform themselves concerning current developments in ecological theory by consulting such sources as these. Even more readily accessible is the statement of Dice:[8]

> Ecologists use the term ecosystem to refer to a community together with its habitat. An ecocystem, then, is an aggregation of associated species of plants and animals, together with the physical features of their habitat. Ecosystems . . . can be of any size or ecologic rank. . . . At the extreme, the whole earth and all its plant and animal inhabitants together constitute a world ecosystem.

Later in his text (ch. xv) the same author undertakes a classification of "human ecosystems." This classification presents in elementary fashion much material familiar to social scientists; but it also conveys an unaccustomed emphasis on the "diverse relationships" of human societies "to their associated species of plants and animals, their physical habitats, and other human societies."[9]

Popularization of the ecosystem concept is threatened by the felicitous exposition by the economist, K. E. Boulding,[10] of "society as an ecosystem." The word "threatened" is well advised, for Boulding uses "ecosystem" only as an analogy, illustrating how human society is "something like" an ecosystem. His ecosystem analogy is, to be sure, quite an improvement over the old organismic analogy. But ecosystem is much too valuable a conceptual scheme to be sacrificed on the altar of metaphor. Human ecology has already inspired a generation of critics too easily irritated by figures of speech.

If the foregoing remarks suggest that general ecologists have come up with cogent principles concerning the role of human society in the ecosystem, then the discussion has been misleading. Actually, the writing of Dice is exception as a responsible attempt to extend general ecology into the human field. Most biological scientists would probably still hold with the caution of Clements and Shelford, that "ecology will come to be applied to the fields that touch man immediately only as the feeling for synthesis grows."[11] There is abundant evidence in their own writing of the inadvisability of leaving to biological scientists the whole task of investigating the ecosystem and its human phases in particular. As a discipline, they clearly have not heeded the plea of the pioneer ecologist, S. A. Forbes, for a "humanized ecology":[12]

> I would humanize ecology . . . first by taking the actions and relations of civilized man as fully into account in its definitions, divisions, and coordinations as those of any other kind of organism. The ecological system of the existing twentieth-century world must include the twentieth-century man as its dominant species—dominant, that is, in the sense of dynamic ecology as the most influential, the controlling member of his associate group.

Symptomatically, even when discussing the "ecology of man," the biologist's tendency is to deplore and to exhort, not to analyze and explain. The shibboleths include such phrasings as "disruption," "tampering," "interference," "damage," and "blunder," applied to the transformations of ecosystems wrought by human activities. Such authorities as Elton, Darling, and Sears state very well some of the dilemmas and problems of human life in the ecosystem.[13] They evidently need the help of social scientists in order to make intelligible those human behaviors that seem from an Olympian vantage point to be merely irrational and shortsighted. Insofar as they recommend reforms —and surely some of their suggestions should be heeded—they need to be instructed, if indeed social science now or ultimately can instruct them, in "The Unanticipated Consequences of Purposive Social Action."[14] If social science falls down on its job, a statement like the following will remain empty rhetoric: "Humanity now has, as never before, the means of knowing the consequences of its actions and the dreadful responsibility for those consequences."[15]

Illustration

Now, it is all very well to assert the possibility of conceptual schemes, like ecosystem, ascribing system properties to associations of physical, biological, and social elements. But can such a scheme lead to anything more than a disorderly collection of arbitrarily concatenated data? I think the proof of the ecosystem concept could be exemplified by a number of studies, ranging from particularistic to global scope, in which some such scheme, if implicit, is nevertheless essential to the analysis.[16] Instead of reviewing a sample of these studies, however, I would like to sketch a problematic situation that has yet to be analyzed adequately in ecosystem terms. This example, since it is deliberately "open-ended," will, I hope, convey the challenge of the concept.

The framework for the discussion is the set of categories suggested elsewhere[17] under the heading, "the ecological complex." These categories, population, organization, environment, and technology (P, O, E, T), provide a somewhat arbitrarily simplified way of identifying clusters of relationships in a preliminary description of ecosystem processes. The description is, by design, so biased as to indicate how the human elements in the ecosystem appear as foci of these processes. Such an anthropo-centric description, though perfectly appropriate for a *human* ecology, has no intrinsic scientific priority over any other useful strategy for initiating study of an ecosystem.

The example is the problem of air pollution, more particularly that of "smog," as experienced during the last two decades in the community of Los Angeles. Southern California has no monopoly on this problem, as other communities are learning to their chagrin. But the somewhat special situation there seems to present a configuration in which the role of each of the four aspects of the ecological complex, including its relation to the others, is salient. I have made no technical investigation of the Los Angeles situation and have at hand only a haphazard collection of materials dealing with it, most of them designed for popular rather than scientific consumption. (The personal experience of living through a summer of Los Angeles smog is of value here only in that it permits sincere testimony to the effect that the problem is real.) The merit of the illustration, however, is that ramifying influences like those postulated by the ecosystem concept are superficially evident even when their nature is poorly understood and inadequately described. I am quite prepared to be corrected on the facts of the case, many of which have yet to come to light. I shall be greatly surprised, however, if anyone is able to produce an account of the smog problem in terms of a conceptual scheme materially *less* elaborate than the ecological complex.

During World War II residents of Los Angeles began to experience episodes of a bluish-gray haze in the atmosphere that reduced visibility and produced irritation of the eyes and respiratory tract (E→P); it was also found to damage growing plants (E→E), including some of considerable economic importance, and to crack rubber, accelerating the rate of deterioration of automobile tires, for example (E→T). In response to the episodes of smog, various civic movements were launched, abatement officers were designated in the city and county health departments, and a model control ordinance was promulgated (E→O). All these measures were without noticeable effect on the smog. At the time, little was known about the sources of pollution, although various industrial operations were suspected. By 1947, a comprehensive authority, the Los Angeles County Air Pollution Control District, was established by action of the California State Assembly and authorized to conduct research and to exercise broad powers of regulation. Various known and newly developed abatement devices were installed in industrial plants at the insistence of the APCD, at a cost of millions of dollars (O→T).

Meanwhile, research by chemists and engineers was developing and confirming the "factory in the sky" theory of smog formation. Combustion and certain other processes release unburned hydrocarbons and oxides of nitrogen into the atmosphere (T→E). As these reach a sufficiently high concentration and are subjected to strong sunlight, chemical reactions occur that liberate large amounts of ozone and form smog. In particular, it was discovered that automobile exhaust contains the essential ingredients in nearly ideal proportions and that this exhaust is the major source of the contaminants implicated in smog formation. It became all the more important as a source when industrial control measures and the prohibition of household open incinerators (O→T) reduced these sources (T→E). Also implicated in the problem was the meteorological situation of the Los Angeles Basin. Ringed by mountains and enjoying only a very low average wind velocity, the basin frequently is blanketed by a layer of warm air moving in from the Pacific. This temperature inversion prevents the polluted air from rising very far above ground level; the still air hovering over the area is then subject to the afore-mentioned smog-inducing action of Southern California's famous sunshine (E→E).

The problem, severe enough at onset, was hardly alleviated by the rapid growth of population in the Los Angeles area, spreading out as it did over a wide territory (P→E), and thereby heightening its dependence on the already ubiquitous automobile as the primary means of local movement (T↔O). Where could one find a more poignant instance of the principle of circular causation, so central to ecological theory, than that of the Los Angelenos speeding down their freeways in a rush to escape the smog produced by emissions from the very vehicles conveying them?

A number of diverse organizational responses (E→O) to the smog problem have occurred. In 1953 a "nonprofit, privately supported, scientific research organization, dedicated to the solution of the smog problem," the Air Pollution Foundation, was set up under the sponsorship of some 200 business enterprises, many of them in industries subject to actual or prospective regulatory measures. The complex interplay of interests and pressures among such private organizations and the several levels and branches of government that were involved (O→O) has not, to my knowledge, been the subject of an adequate investigation by a student of the political process. Two noteworthy outcomes of this process merit attention in particular. The first is the development of large-scale programs of public health research and action (O→P, E) concerned with air pollution effects (E→P). Comparatively little is known in this field of epidemiology (or as some research workers would say nowadays, medical ecology), but major programs have been set up within the last five years in the U.S. Public Health Service (whose interest, of course, is not confined to Los Angeles) as well as such agencies as the California State Department of Public Health. Here is a striking instance of interrelations between medical ecology and the ecology of medicine illustrating not merely "organizational growth," as studied in conventional sociology, but also an organizational response to environmental-demographic changes. Second, there has been a channeling of both public and private research effort into the search for a "workable device," such as an automatic fuel cutoff, a catalytic muffler, or an afterburner, which will eliminate or reduce the noxious properties of automobile exhaust. California now has on its statute books a law requiring manufacturers to equip automobiles with such a device if and when its workability is demonstrated (O→T).

Some engineers are confident that workable devices will soon be forthcoming. The Air Pollution Foundation has gone so far as to declare that the day is "near when Los Angeles' smog will be only a memory." Should the problem be thus happily resolved, with reduction of pollution to tolerable levels, the resolution will surely have to be interpreted as the net result of an intricate interaction of factors in the ecological complex (P, O, T→E). But if the condition is only partially alleviated, how much more growth of population and increase in automobile use will have to occur before even more drastic technological and organizational changes will be required: redevelopment of mass transit, introduction of private electric automobiles, rationing of travel, limitation of population expansion, or whatever they may be? What will be the outcome of experience with increasing air polution in other communities, whose problems differ in various ways from that of Los Angeles? And the question of questions—Is the convulsion of the ecosystem occasioned by smog merely a small-scale prototype of what we must expect in a world seemingly destined to become ever more dependent upon nuclear energy and subject to its hazards of ionizing radiation?

Conclusion

I must assume that the reader will be kind enough to pass lightly over the defects of the foregoing exposition. In particular, he must credit the author with being aware of the many complications concealed by the use of arrows linking the broad and heterogeneous categories of the ecological complex. The arrows are meant only to suggest the existence of problems for research concerning the mechanisms of cause, influence, or response at work in the situation so sketchily portrayed. Even the barest account of that situation, however, can leave no doubt that social change and environmental modification occurred in the closest interdependence—so close, in fact, that the two "levels" of change were *systematically* interrelated. Change on either level can be comprehended only by application of a conceptual scheme at least as encompassing as that of ecosystem.

The reader's imagination, again, must substitute for documentation of the point that smog, though a spectacular case and full of human interest, is no isolated example of how problems of human collective existence require an ecosystem framework for adequate conceptualization. I do not intend to argue, of course, that sociologists must somehow shoulder the entire burden of research suggested by such a conceptualization. Science, after all, is one of our finest examples of the advantages of a division of labor. But labor can be effectively divided only if there is articulation of the several sub-tasks; in scientific work, such articulation is achieved by employment of a common conceptual framework.

Sociologists may or may not—I am not especially optimistic on this score—take up the challenge to investigate the social life of man as a phase of the ecosystem, with all the revisions in their thought patterns that this kind of formulation will demand. If they shirk this responsibility, however, other disciplines are not unprepared to take the leadership. Anthropology of late has demonstrated its hospitality to ecological concepts.[18] Geography, for its part, cannot forget that it laid claim to human ecology as early as did sociology.[19]

Of even greater ultimate significance may be the impending reorientation of much of what we now call social science to such concepts as welfare, level of living, and public health. Programs to achieve such "national goals" (to use the former President's language), like the studies on which such programs are based, are finding and will find two things: first, each of these concepts is capable of almost indefinite expansion to comprehend virtually any problem of human collective life; and, second, measures or indicators of status or progress in respect to them must be multi-faceted and relational. Public health, to take that example, is surely some sort of function of all elements in the ecological complex; it is observable in any sufficiently comprehensive sense only in terms of interrelations of variables located at all levels of the ecosystem. Extrapolation of current trends over even a short projection period is sufficient to suggest the future preoccupation of the sciences touching on man with much more macroscopic problems than they now dare to set for themselves. It is perhaps symptomatic that spokesmen for the nation's health programs now declare that the "science of health is a branch of the wider science of human ecology,"[20] and that expositions of the problem of economic development have come to emphasize the necessary shift "From Political Economy to Political Ecology."[21] Even the literati proclaim that the "fundamental human problem is ecological."[22] (Cf. the similar remark of Kenneth Burke: "Among the sciences, there is one little fellow named Ecology, and in time we shall pay him more attention."[23]) If one holds with

Durkheim that the basic categories of science, as well as the interpretive schemes of everyday life, arise from the nature and exigencies of human collective existence, it cannot be long before we are forced to conjure with some version of the ecosystem concept. The question is whether sociology will lead or lag behind in this intellectual movement.

NOTES

1. A. L. Kroeber, "So-Called Social Science," ch. vii in *The Nature of Culture* (Chicago: University of Chicago Press, 1952), pp. 66–67.
2. R. M. MacIver, *Social Causation* (Boston: Ginn & Co., 1942), pp. 271–72.
3. Arnold S. Feldman and Charles Tilly, "The Interaction of Social and Physical Space," *American Sociological Review,* 25 (December, 1960), p. 878.
4. W. C. Allee, Alfred E. Emerson, Orlando Park, Thomas Park, and Karl P. Schmidt, *Principles of Animal Ecology* (Philadelphia: W. B. Saunders Co., 1949), p. 695.
5. Eugene P. Odum, *Fundamentals of Ecology* (Philadelphia: W. B. Saunders Co., 1953), p. 9.
6. Robert E. Park, *Human Communities: The City and Human Ecology* (Glencoe, Ill.: The Free Press, 1952).
7. Milla Aïssa Alihan, *Social Ecology: A Critical Analysis* (New York: Columbia University Press, 1938).
8. Lee R. Dice, *Man's Nature and Nature's Man: The Ecology of Human Communities* (Ann Arbor: University of Michigan Press, 1955), pp. 2–3.
9. *Ibid.,* pp. 252–53.
10. Kenneth E. Boulding, *Principles of Economic Policy* (Englewood Cliffs, N.J.: Prentice-Hall, Inc.,1958), pp. 14–16.
11. Frederic E. Clements and Victor E. Shelford, *Bio-ecology* (New York: John Wiley & Sons, 1939), p. 1. Cf. F. Fraser Darling, "Pastoralism in Relation to Populations of Men and Animals," in *The Numbers of Man and Animals,* edited by J. B. Cragg and N. W. Pirie (Edinburgh: Oliver & Boyd, 1955).
12. Stephen A. Forbes, "The Humanizing of Ecology," *Ecology,* 3 (April, 1922), p. 90.
13. Charles S. Elton, *The Ecology of Invasions by Animals and Plants* (London: Methuen & Co., Ltd., 1958); F. Fraser Darling, *West Highland Survey: An Essay in Human Ecology* (Oxford: Oxford University Press, 1955); Paul B. Sears, *The Ecology of Man,* "Condon Lectures" (Eugene: Oregon State System of Higher Education, 1957). See also, F. Fraser Darling, "The Ecology of Man," *The American Scholar,* 25 (Winter, 1955–56), pp. 38–46; Donald F. Chapp, "Ecology—A Science Going to Waste," *Chicago Review,* 9 (Summer, 1955), pp. 15–26.
14. Title of an early essay by Robert K. Merton, *American Sociological Review,* 1 (December, 1936), pp. 894–904; a recent statement, pertinent to ecology, is Walter Firey's *Man, Mind and Land: A Theory of Resource Use* (Glencoe. Ill.: The Free Press, 1960).
15. Sears, *op. cit.,* p. 50.
16. The following are merely illustrative: A. Irving Hallowell, "The Size of Algonkian Hunting Territories: A Function of Ecological Adjustment," *American Anthropologist,* 51 (January–March, 1949), pp. 34–45; Laura Thompson, "The Relations of Men, Animals, and Plants in an Island Community (Fiji)," *American Anthropologist,* 51 (April–June, 1949), pp. 253–76; Edgar Anderson, *Plants, Man and Life* (Boston: Little, Brown & Co., 1952); Fred Cottrell, *Energy and Society* (New York: McGraw-Hill Book Co., 1955); Harrison Brown, *The Challenge of Man's Future* (New York: Viking Press, 1954).
17. Otis Dudley Duncan, "Human Ecology and Population Studies," ch. xxviii in *The Study of Population,* edited by Philip M. Hauser and Otis Dudley Duncan (Chicago: University of Chicago Press, 1959).
18. Marston Bates, "Human Ecology," in *Anthropology Today,* edited by A. L. Kroeber (Chicago: University of Chicago Press, 1953); J. G. D. Clark, *Prehistoric Europe: The*

Economic Basis (New York: Philosophical Library, 1952); Julian H. Steward, *Theory of Culture Change* (Urbana: University of Illinois Press, 1955).

19. H. H. Barrows, "Geography as Human Ecology," *Annals of the Association of American Geographers,* 13 (March, 1923), pp. 1–14; William L. Thomas, Jr., editor, *Man's Role in Changing the Face of the Earth* (Chicago: University of Chicago Press, 1956).

20. President's Commission on the Health Needs of the Nation, *America's Health Status, Needs and Resources. Building America's Health,* vol. 2 (Washington: Government Printing Office, 1953), p. 13.

21. Title of an essay by Bertrand de Jouvenel, *Bulletin of the Atomic Scientsts,* 8 (October, 1957), pp. 287–91.

22. Aldous Huxley, *The Devils of Loudon,* "Torchbook edition" (New York: Harper & Bros., 1959), p. 302.

23. Kenneth Burke, *Attitudes toward History,* Vol. I (New York: The New Republic, 1937), p. 192.

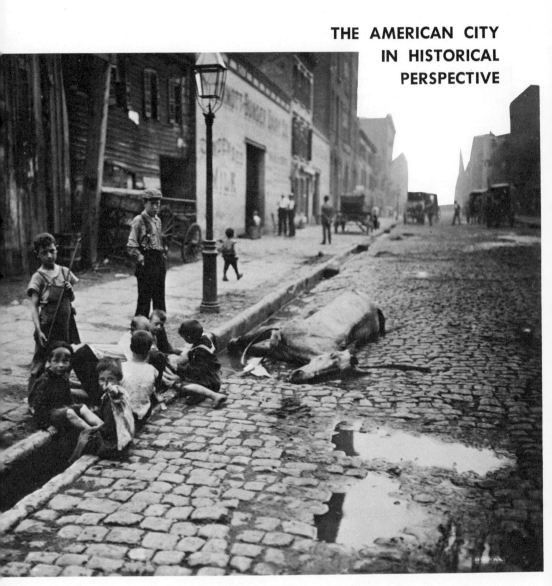

(Above) From the collections of the Library of Congress. (Top right) Congestion on Orchard Street, New York City. Photo by Lewis W. Hine. Courtesy George Eastman House. (Bottom right) Broadway north from Courtlandt Street and Maiden Lane, New York City. Photo by J. J. Fogerty, c. 1880. Courtesy of the New York Historical Society.

1.1 INTRODUCTION:
NORTH AMERICAN HISTORY
FROM A SOCIOLOGICAL PERSPECTIVE*

There was no indigenous evolution of the city in precolonial America. Prior to the European immigration, there were no cities as we know them north of the Rio Grande. Population growth was restricted by the physical environment and limited technology. North America's Indian population numbered less than a million and was nomadic or resided in agricultural villages. They were not city builders. Even the largest settlements, such as Cahokia, were not truly urban. The whole idea of the city, with its advanced technology and forms of social organization, was imported from Europe.

Today, the North American continent has a higher proportion of its population in large urban areas than any other continent (Breese, 1969:32). Obviously, considerable changes have taken place in North America since the arrival of the first colonists.

It is impossible to understand the characteristics and problems of the contemporary urban scene without some knowledge of what preceded our era. For example, contemporary problems such as urban violence, housing, pollution, and flight from the central city have complex historical antecedents. To understand the social changes accompanying American urbanization we must develop an historical perspective, because most American cities are not physically or socially products of the twentieth century. We cannot comprehend the contemporary situation in a vacuum.

However, it is no simple task to reconstruct the urban social history of North America from available sources. Most historical materials encompassed a very limited descriptive perspective. A popular form among past writers was the didactic urban biography containing a wealth of precise detail on obscure events and places. While they performed a very valuable function, these early urban historians unfortunately did not as a rule attempt to place their observations within any theoretical framework. As a result, their material is best viewed as a data source (yet one all too frequently overlooked by sociologists).

We have selected a variety of representative historical materials, which, when viewed through a conceptual framework, will give the reader some insight into and feeling for the development of early American cities. Since

*We would like to thank Ted Brown for his comments on an earlier version of this article.

these pieces were written for many different reasons and have no common theoretical theme, we will review some selected aspects of American urbanization from the vantage point of our own conceptual framework before discussing the articles. In particular, our perspective is that the city has been a major determinant in the emergence of new spatial, cultural, and social organizational forms.

Emerging Patterns

North American development has been largely urban development ever since the arrival of European colonists during the mid-seventeenth century. The New World was not particularly attractive either to the established English nobility or to the rural peasants—the former because they were already economically advantaged and the latter because they were tied to their land. More likely to migrate were "gentlemen" of lesser wealth and standing: artisans, shopkeepers, and day laborers, whose economic and cultural roots, whether English or Dutch, lay for the most part in the rising middle class of the Old World (Bridenbaugh, 1938:5). The early colonists thus tended to be the more urban of their home-country contemporaries, and they came for a variety of reasons. Some, such as the Puritans, came to establish their communal utopias (a new social organization form); others, like the French, to establish a commercial empire.

New England was from the outset an area of towns. The settlers of New England were largely English Puritan or Pilgrim religious dissenters, groups that contained many urban tradesmen, mechanics, and artisans. (For a discussion of the relationship of Puritanism to rationality, science, and industry, see Merton, 1957:574–606). Neither the Dutch who founded New Amsterdam nor the French Huguenots who filtered into the colonies following the revocation of the Edict of Nantes (1685) were basically agriculturalists. Both these groups chiefly entered commerce. Likewise, the Catholics who established Maryland as a religious haven and the Quakers who under Pitt settled Pennsylvania were not typically rooted to the soil. William Penn's "Holy Experiment" was from its inception to be an *urban* society built around a great "city of brotherly love" (Glaab, 1963:5). Even Virginia, which was unique among the major colonies in that it founded no major cities of note (Williamsburg never achieved more than local influence), was not isolated from essentially urban ideas and fashions. To the contrary, the tidewater aristocrats were bound by disposition and economics more to European and northern colonial cities than to Virginia's own Piedmont region, a fact bitterly resented by the colony's frontier farmers. Virginia's lack of towns was early recognized as an economic and social liability. A seventeenth-century clergyman opined that, "The only way of remedy for *Virginia's* disease (without which all other help will only palliate not cure) must be by procuring Towns to be built." Until such time as an ordered, rational Christian life could be established, Virginia would "continue under the curse of God" (Glaab, 1963:5).

Perhaps if the earliest settlers had been small farmers, the deprivations of the early years would not have been as severe or the loss of life as catastrophic. Experienced farmers, for example, would probably have had the good sense to shun such initial settlement sites as swampy Jamestown or stern, inhospitable Plymouth Rock.

Later site selections evidenced better judgment. The location of major centers generally reflected planning and design rather than happenstance. Cities were located on sites that showed a clear command of trading advantages. Considerations such as good harbors, control of avenues of trade and communication, and access to a productive hinterland were crucial determinants of a town's location (Bridenbaugh, 1938:3).

Emerging Growth Patterns

The P.O.E.T. framework illustrates clearly that the physical environment played a most significant role in the development of indigenous cities. Within the English colonies, five cities soon came to dominate colonial life. The northernmost city was Boston. Eleven hundred miles separated Boston from the newer and much smaller settlement of Charles Town (Charleston) in South Carolina. In between were Newport in Providence Plantations of Rhode Island, New Amsterdam, which became New York in 1664, and William Penn's Philadelphia. All these budding centers were washed by or had direct access to the Atlantic. New Amsterdam enjoyed the finest natural harbor on the continent; its site was the deliberate choice in 1625 of the Dutch West Indian engineer, Cryn Fredricksen. Boston, Newport, and Charles Town also enjoyed fine harbors, while the Quaker settlement of Philadelphia used the Schuylkill and Delaware rivers for access routes to world trade and markets.

The environmental advantages of these five cities helped establish their early domination of American economic life. As of 1700 the five cities contained only nine percent of the total colonial population, yet they already dominated the colonies' economic, political, and social life. The cities were the countryman's gateway to the markets and finished products of Europe. The officials of the Crown and the seats of colonial assemblies were located here. (The practice of sequestering state legislatures in otherwise remote and obscure interior hamlets was a later rural reaction to this pattern of urban dominance.) Governmental institutions, social amenities, and colonial political consciousness all developed in the larger towns.

However, more than favorable physical environment is required for the emergence of an urban center. For example, Montreal remained for years a frontier trading post, and Quebec, center of government and the Church, grew slowly—and yet both were superbly located on the St. Lawrence River. Quebec in 1665 contained only 550 Frenchmen, and one-quarter of these were religious. As Count Frontenac remarked, there were but two kinds of business in New France: conversion of souls and conversion of beaver (Morison, 1965:103). Neither Quebec nor Montreal had sufficient population size or diversity to permit complex forms of social organization to emerge.

In spite of the influence of colonial American cities, most colonists were not urban residents. Of the four million enumerated at the time of the first census in 1790 only 5 percent lived in towns of 2500 or more.* Due to the restrictions of the environment, towns were rarely far from the coast. By 1800, although the original thirteen states had extended their territory to the Mississippi, two-thirds of the population still lived within fifty miles of the Atlantic Ocean (Petersen, 1961:22). The Appalachian range was still a formidable barrier to centrifugal development. Of the four P.O.E.T. factors, physical environment still played the major role in the early nineteenth century. The statistical dominance of the rural population should, however, be kept in perspective. In 1790 England and Holland were the only nations on the globe that were over 10 percent urban. Philadelphia was possibly the second largest city in the English-speaking world with 42,000 inhabitants, followed by New York with 33,000.

Philadelphia by 1800 had grown to 70,000, New York to 60,000, and Boston to 25,000. These seaboard cities served largely as entrepots exchanging the produce of the hinterland for the finished manufactures of Europe. Not until after the War of 1812 did these cities really develop manufacturing interests. By this time, interior towns such as Louisville, Pittsburgh, Cincinnati, and Lexington, Kentucky, were beginning to acquire the manufacturing and social amenities to qualify them as true urban places. All but Lexington were located on major rivers, and all but inland Lexington were destined to be major metropolises. The effect of a limited physical hinterland can be seen in the case of Newport, which had been one of the five largest colonial cities. By 1800 its hinterland had been truncated by the expanding influence of Boston, and Newport was already declining as a major port of commerce.

New York rather than Philadelphia or Boston, was to become *the* American metropolis. A combination of natural topographic advantage, entrepreneurial skill, organizational enterprise, and a judicious application of graft all contributed to New York's rise. A major technological achievement, the spectacularly successful Erie Canal, plus an early recognition of the importance of the railroad, also gave New York open access to the riches of the West, and the city was fast to exploit this advantage. By the Civil War, New York handled two-thirds of the country's imports and one-third of its exports (Glaab, 1963:67).

Boston did not fare as well. Contrary to Charles Adams' assertion in Article 1.3, Boston failed to appreciate the overwhelming importance of the railroad. By the time Boston's merchants and civil leaders had convinced themselves that the railroad was not just a fad and launched their first cautious line across the Berkshires, it was too late. Thus, a sluggish system of social organization that failed to apply technology to expanding its hinterland environment meant Boston's commercial future was determined well before the Civil War. (For the ossification of Boston's social system, *see* Article 3.6

---

*Since the first settlements were towns, the subsequent development and growth of agricultural hinterlands meant the percentage of the total population living in towns actually *decreased* from the settlement of Jamestown until after the Revolutionary War. For example, in 1690 almost 10 percent of the American colonists lived in what could be classified as urban places; 100 years later only 5 percent of the new American republic's population was classified as urban. Not until 1830 was the urban percentage up to where it had been in 1690 (Glaab and Brown, 1967:25–26).

in Section Three.) Several decades later St. Louis similarly underrated the importance of technological innovations. Chicago did not.

A number of areas of urban life showed instances of deliberate planning and organization. In the design of towns, for example, planning was quite evident. In Charles Town and Philadelphia, the laying of the streets preceded the erection of dwellings. Both cities conformed to the basic gridiron pattern. Charles Town, which was laid out in 1672 according to Lord Ashley's instructions, formed when completed a narrow trapezoid four squares wide fronting on the Cooper River (Bridenbaugh, 1938:12–13). Similarly, Philadelphia was surveyed in 1682 according to the plans of the founder. Interestingly enough, Philadelphia is presently trying to renovate its central city and recapture the benefits of the colonial spatial pattern.

As a side note, one should not confuse planning with gracious living. Only occasionally were city streets paved; they commonly alternated between dustbowls and quagmires. Sanitation methods were primitive. Garbage was "collected" by scavenging hogs, dogs, and sometimes geese. In fact, Charles Town passed an ordinance protecting vultures because of the public service they performed in cleaning the remains of dead animals (Glaab, 1963:115). Technology in the cities was obviously limited.

In providing municipal services, Boston took the lead. In 1666 it forbade casting any filth or dirt into the street, directing the inhabitants to "bury ye same," while "all garbidge, beasts, enralls &c" were to be thrown from the drawbridge into the Mill Creek (Bridenbaugh, 1938:18). Many American municipalities still dispose of their refuse in this manner. Philadelphia laid the first water system in the 1700s, and soon after New York began to lay wooden pipes. Philadelphia at this time had the distinction of having the only streetlights, and only it and New York had sidewalks.

New Spatial and Social Forms

Competition for trade, industry, and influence reflected the lively interplay among population growth, technology, environment, and the development of social organizational forms that could capitalize on the other variables. By the latter half of the nineteenth century the increasing tempo of urbanization, plus newly billowing industrialization and bureaucratization, foretold a new social context, one whose ultimate development has yet to be realized. (See Webber (2.7) and Seeley (5.7) in this text.) During the nineteenth century, cities contended with each other and with rural areas for control of the nation's political and economic development.

"The lusty urban growth," to quote Schlesinger, "created problems which taxed human resourcefulness to the utmost" (Schlesinger, 1949:225). The problems of growth can be illustrated using the example of suburbanization. Movement from city to suburb is not solely a twentieth-century phenomenon. It began in the early part of the eighteenth century, and thus clearly cannot be attributed to declining property values due to nonwhite occupancy patterns. Even in the 1700s there were complaints of noise, dirt, pollution, crime, and lack of green space. Ben Franklin, townsman *par excellence,* moved from Philadelphia's High Street, grumbling that "the din of the

Market increases upon me; and that, with frequent interruptions, has made me say some things twice over" (Bridenbaugh, 1955:24).

Going hand in hand with the establishment of suburbs were complaints over the problems they created. As early as the seventeenth century, Bostonians were complaining about the failure of suburbanites to pay their way. Nor was the problem limited to established eastern cities. The Lexington, Kentucky, assessor in 1813 reported difficulty collecting taxes from those living on the edge of town. A few years later, Cincinnati officials complained that those on the town periphery did not contribute "their quantum of taxes." In 1829 the St. Louis city council voiced the same complaint and with remarkable prophecy stated "that although the evil is now in its infancy it promises to increase greatly in a few years and produce much evil" (Wade, 1959:306–307).

Even though the number and sizes of cities grew, at the termination of the Civil War the nation was still predominantly agrarian. Only fifty-five years later, a majority of the population would be urban. This interim saw the nation undergo a fantastic transformation. No longer were American cities invariably ports strung out along a coast or river. The technological breakthrough of the railroad had changed all that. Writing in 1885, Josiah Strong noted:

> In the Middle States the farms were the first taken, then the town sprang up to supply its wants, and at length the railway connected it with the world; but in the West the order is reversed—first the railroad, then the towns, then the farms. Settlement is, consequently, much more rapid, and the city stamps the country, instead of the country stamping the city. It is the cities and towns which will frame state constitution, make laws, create public opinion, establish social usages, and fix standards of morals in the West. (Strong, 1885:206)

As Richard C. Wade has put it, "the towns were the spearheads of the frontier" (1959:1).

The year 1880 marked a major milestone. For the first time less than half the occupied males were in agriculture. In absolute numbers, the urban population grew seven times during the half century following the Civil War, while the rural population merely doubled. Whatever the quality of life in cities, there was no disputing their quantitative growth. Industrialization was reworking the physical and social face of even the older mercantilist cities.

At the close of the Civil War, the population of New York exceeded one million—including the then-separate city of Brooklyn. By 1910, New York—with its five boroughs—totaled about five million. Chicago passed a million and became the "second city" in 1890; its World Columbian Exposition in 1893 dazzled the world. The nation's largest cities experienced their greatest population expansion during this period. In fact, of the ten largest cities in the United States in the 1960 census, only Los Angeles and Houston are really products of the twentieth century. All the others are, in physical terms, essentially nineteenth-century cities.

Social and institutional changes in the cities more than matched their phenomenal nineteenth-century growth. Following the Civil War a new social invention, the corporation, facilitated the transformation from a mercantilist to an industrial economy. The late nineteenth-century city came to reflect the economic domination of the local robber-barons just as the medieval city had reflected the power and personality of the ruling prince or doge.

At times, the domination of these captains of industry went far beyond the economic sphere. The totally planned town of Pullman, just south of Chicago, was an attempt to provide a controlled environment in which all needs would be met by the employer. Social disorganization, crime, vice, and strikes were to be abolished by fiat. Elected government with its inefficiency and corruption was "no longer necessary," for as George Pullman put it: "As long as the town of Pullman is owned by one association, there is little necessity of agitating the subject of its control by any municipal government" (Buder, 1967:107). This dream of a model town where all change was controlled was rudely shattered by the Pullman strike of 1894 in which the National Guard was called out to suppress the workers. Clearly the problems growing out of rapid urbanization and industrialization were not to be easily solved.

Exacerbating the problem was the massive influx of foreign immigrants to the cities. Prior to 1880 the bulk of immigrants had come largely from northern and western Europe. By the 1890s the stream was dominated by southern and eastern Europeans: Slavs, Italians, and Jews. The earlier northern European immigrants had not really entered without strain—the Germans, for example, were at first viewed as radicals. However, by the time the southern and eastern Europeans began arriving in large numbers, the early northern European immigrants were well on their way to being considered true Americans. The Irish, for example, had encountered tremendous hostility. Not only were they unrepented Papists, but they also fought back.* In the 1840s, for example, when mobs with semiofficial support burned Catholic churches in Philadelphia, Bishop John Hughes of New York issued a warning that makes contemporary militants appear mild-mannered. The good Bishop publicly promised that "if a single Catholic church is burned in New York, the city will become a second Moscow" (Hassard, 1866:276). Apparently the threat to burn the city to the ground had some effect, for not a single church was touched. By the turn of the century, the Irish and Germans were beginning to be thought of as natives. The eastern and southern Europeans pouring into the large cities had replaced them as "the foreigners."

Between 1901 and 1910 alone almost nine million immigrants inundated American cities. The reaction all too frequently was one of fear and revulsion. Native-born America suddenly became aware of the fact that 40 percent of the total 1910 population was of foreign stock: immigrants or the offspring of immigrants (Bogue, 1969:178).

Writers such as Josiah Strong and Lincoln Steffens portrayed the inner

---

*The Irish who had fled the famine in Ireland in the late 1840s were long regarded as inferior even to Negroes—a fact they bitterly resented, as evidenced by the anti-Negro draft riots of 1863 in New York. In 1854, the anti-immigrant, anti-Catholic, anti-Irish Know-Nothing Party elected the governor, all state senators, and 347 of 355 state representatives in Massachusetts (Cole, 1963:36). Several decades later, the Irish had become the state's dominant urban political force.

city as a series of ghettoes teeming with foreign (and possibly anarchist) hordes controlled by corrupt political machines. Most educated Americans of that time agreed with Andrew D. White's assertion that "with very few exceptions the city governments of the United States are the worst in Christendom . . . the most expensive, the most inefficient, and the most corrupt" (Bryce, 1890:25). The WASP native American, however, believed these problems to be clearly the fault of the immigrants who lived in the central-city ghettoes. Municipal reform, on the other hand, was associated with the Anglo-Saxon city periphery and its growing upper- and upper-middle-class suburbs.

As reinterpreted by the sociologist, the urban manifestation of the early twentieth-century Progressive movement was a middle-class attempt to do something about the "problem" of the inner city and its minority groups. Reforms included projects such as settlement houses to teach Americanism and city-manager systems to put local government back in the hands of non-ethnic groups. Others, espousing salvation-by-brick-and-mortar, lobbied for stricter building laws and construction of model tenements, an approach still found in urban renewal laws.

The census of 1920 tolled the demise of the rural era by indicating that over half the nation's population now resided in urban places. By the 1920s, it was no longer possible to accurately characterize the United States as anything but an urban nation.

Urban Imagery

The preceding materials have examined interrelationships among population, organization, technology, and environment. We will now concentrate on the variable of social organization—in particular, on ideology as a basic component of any pattern of social organization.

American cities have frequently been the victims of ideological lag. While nineteenth-century America experienced rapid urban population growth, new forms of urban social organization, and the emergence of an industrial technology, its attitudes regarding the growing cities frequently reflected the rural ideology of an earlier age. America has never been neutral about her great cities. They have been either exalted as the vital commercial heart and creative soul of the nation or denounced as behavioral sinks of crime, vice, and moral corruption. Certainly the city was distrusted by many of the founding fathers, who contrasted the idealized life of the yeoman with the corruption of urban places. They perceived that, as cities increased in population, deviation from established norms also increased.

To many colonial Americans, the cities of old Europe were archetypical of the evils that might befall the pristine new nation. Thus Thomas Jefferson advised against sending a young man to European schools, for once there "He acquires a fondness for European luxury and dissipation and a contempt for the simplicity of his own country." Not too surprisingly, Jefferson's conception of the perfect society bore a remarkable resemblance to eighteenth-century Virginia, with its limited population size, technology, and simple hierarchical social organization.

Over the years, the virtues of tilling the soil have become ingrained in

American culture. Even urbanists at times have felt compelled to adopt the rhetoric of the rural myth. Hofstadter, in discussing this agrarian myth, notes that even an opponent of rural interests such as Alexander Hamilton found it politic to concede that the "cultivation of the earth . . . has intrinsically a strong claim to pre-eminence over every other kind of industry" (Hofstadter, 1955:27). Alexis de Tocqueville, a most famous French observer of America also agreed that farm and village life were more natural. In his classic, *Democracy in America,* he condemned cities as the instruments by which the liberties known in the country are largely overturned.

Of course, policies and practice did not always coincide. America's most famous cosmopolite, Ben Franklin, stated that agriculture was "the only honest way to acquire wealth . . . as a reward for innocent life and virtuous industry;" interestingly enough, he did not engage in agriculture himself.

Thomas Jefferson's 1784 *Notes on Virginia* certainly indicates his antipathy to urban life, and his famous 1800 letter to Dr. Benjamin Rush went so far as to see some virtue in epidemics, arguing that: "The yellow fever will discourage the growth of great cities in our nation and I view great cities as pestilential to the morals, the health, and liberty of men" (Glaab and Brown, 1967:55). Less well publicized are Jefferson's practical proposals to prevent the spread of yellow fever. Even Schlesinger in his landmark article (1.2), leaves the picture incomplete by failing to note Jefferson's change of attitude toward the War of 1812. Always the pragmatist, Jefferson decided that for the nation to endure and prosper,

> We must now place the manufacturer by the side of the agriculturalist. . . .
> He, therefore, who is now against domestic manufacture, must be for reducing us either to dependence on that foreign nation, or to be clothed in skins, and to live like wild beasts in dens and caverns. I am not one of these; experience has taught me that manufactures are now as necessary to our independence as to our comfort. (Letter to Benjamin Austin on January 9, 1816, as cited in Ford, 1904:503–504)

Despite the fact that the nation officially became more than half urban with the 1920 census and is today three-quarters urban, the myth of a nation of self-reliant farmers has not died easily. It is still virtuous to have dirt on one's hands, particularly if one is in the public eye and/or running for political office. Occasionally a politician's attempts to identify with the supposedly plain folks has unintended overlays. For example, Calvin Coolidge during the 1920s posed for a campaign photo showing him as the simple farmer haying in Vermont. However, the photo conveys far more than was intended—the President's overalls are fresh, his shoes polished, and his Pierce Arrow with secret servicemen on the running boards can be made out in the background, clearly ready to rush him back to the city (Hofstadter, 1955:31). More recently, former U.S. Secretary of State Dean Acheson, the epitome of the eastern urban establishment, publicly referred to himself as "a simple country boy." Pity the poor city slicker.

This discrepancy between our simple imagery, which reflects an ideological commitment to a rural past, and the incontestable fact that an increasing proportion of the population resides in urban places has affected the ability of social institutions to cope with existing realities. For example, the failure of social institutions to keep pace with population growth resulted in colonial New York having only four out of twenty-seven council represen- tatives. Today, as in the past, the commitment to the agrarian myth continues to strongly influence many state legislatures, although farmers now constitute less than 5 percent of the employed labor force in the United States.

Article Overview

The materials that follow detail the urban character of North American development since the arrival of European colonists in the seventeenth cen- tury. As Schlesinger states in the next article (1.2), "the American city . . . marched westward with the outposts of settlement, always injecting exotic elements into pioneer existence, while in the older sections it steadily extended its dominion over politics, economics, and all other interests of life." The American city was an idea as well as a physical entity. Schlesinger's argu- ment is consistent with our general theme that the city has been a major factor in the emergence of new spatial, social, and cultural forms.

This article provides a broad historical overview of the development of the North American city. Schlesinger argues that the role of the city in North America has been grossly underestimated by historians. His is the classic—and little heeded—plea for an urban reinterpretation of American history.

Schlesinger discusses the effects of population growth (from five million in 1790 to 210 million today), environment (fertile open lands, nearness to rivers and lakes, and so on), and technology (industrialism, railroads, steam- boats) in producing social organizational changes. He states that cities from the very beginning influenced the urban way of life. Urban centers contrib- uted to a higher standard of living by providing hardware, firearms, medicine, and education in exchange for farm produce and the goods of extractive industries. Cities also were vitally involved in the emerging mechanisms of governance, control, and change. Urban interests clearly were influential in the framing and ratification of the Constitution.

Finally, Schlesinger argues that the organization of North American society was influenced by cities and their technology. In the competition for the trade of the hinterland, the cities fostered and financed the most ad- vanced forms of transportation. Toll roads, the Erie canal, and the locomotive all had urban sponsors. The form and structure of North American society came from the cities.

The selection (1.3) by Charles Francis Adams, the son of one President and the grandson of another, portrays urban growth as a result rather than as a cause of new forms of social organization. According to Adams, Boston's population growth failed to keep pace with the booming western metropolis of Chicago because the latter had developed a superior technology and, more importantly, had the flexible social organization to exploit it fully. Chicago provided a setting more congenial to the use of new approaches and tech- nology. Its growth was rapid, progressive, and creative; Boston's was sluggish, traditional, and hampered by the past. This harsh judgment is interesting, given Adams' position as a charter member of the Boston elite.

Adams also stresses the influence of environment in determining urban growth patterns. In this emphasis he is far from alone, for much of the nineteenth-century writing on cities stressed the importance of geographical advantages in fixing the fate of cities—that is, Cincinnati or St. Louis or Kansas City would be the fastest growing city in the west because of its location on the X river or lake and its surrounding fertile hinterland. By the last half of the nineteenth century, writers of that day had moved from environmentalism to stressing technological development as the prime cause of urban growth. It became the roar of the locomotive that was to boom the town. And sometimes, of course, it did.

Our national fixation has been on the growth of the frontier. However, the fact is that during the nineteenth century the major population growth was actually in cities. This growth was closely tied to the willingness of the cities to innovate with new technological forms such as railroads and corporations. As Adams' article indicates, those most willing to innovate were those most likely to experience the greatest growth and success in dominating the hinterlands. As we stated earlier, European settlers in the New World were by and large town-oriented; commerce and trade dominated agriculture from the very beginning. Even American farmers approached agriculture from an urban rather than a peasant perspective. The farmer from the beginning was tied to the cash economy of the city market. Today the farmer is also bound into the farm equipment industry, the university-business-agricultural technology system, and the federal taxing system. The modern farmer and his successor, possibly the manager of a multimillion-dollar agribusiness venture, are as urban as industrial managers.

The emergence of large cities was accompanied by numerous growing pains. Internal problems were exacerbated by a growing rural hostility to and distrust of the city. This antiurban sentiment can be easily documented by the unwillingness of the nineteenth-century and even twentieth-century rural-dominated state legislatures to address themselves to urban problems. Even today, the political powers of the largest cities do not match their economic strength. The selections from Josiah Strong (1.4) and Jacob Riis (1.5) provide descriptive accounts of specific aspects and problems of urban life. These articles illustrate patterns of urban change and provide colorful insights into life styles.

Josiah Strong's article gives a nineteenth-century moralist's view of the city. From Strong's perspective the city was a potential menace to civilization. Population growth (particularly of foreign-born Catholics) and technology were the causes of unwanted social organizational changes such as political machines and low church attendance. While Strong does not use sociological concepts, he appears to be saying that as population increases variation and deviance from established norms also increase, particularly among certain subcultures. In this respect, he foreshadowed Louis Wirth (see Section Three, 3.2). Strong's writings are important in that they mirror the view of the city held by nineteenth-century Protestant rural America. His book, Our Country, from which the "Perils: The City" excerpt is taken, sold over 175,000 copies, a phenomenal number at that date.

A second view of the "Gay Nineties" era is provided by the social reformer Jacob Riis, whose book, How the Other Half Lives, paints a vivid portrait of life in the tenements of New York. Riis believes that the dismal and desperate life of the turn-of-the-century urban poor was due to the limitations of the physical environment: that is, slum housing. Poverty, squalor, and misery are seen as an inevitable consequence of the interplay between human nature and the nature of the city. Thus, in the best muck-raking tradition, he attempts to bring pressure on the existing political power structure to legislate changes in the physical environment. While we can forgive him for thinking that the social ills of the time would be cured by improving slum housing, it is difficult to understand how this simplistic approach still has its adherents today; for example, present public-housing programs passed by Congress still reflect the nineteenth-century salvation-by-brick-and-mortar rationale.

The articles by W. Lloyd Warner (1.6) and Stephen Thernstrom (1.7) should be read as a set. Warner's late 1930s research on *Yankee City* (Newburyport, Mass.) represents what is still one of the most extensive and elaborate community studies ever done in this country. In terms of our general orientation, it is clear that Warner perceives a rigidification of the social structure as a result of technological changes. He hypothesizes a decrease in social mobility among the working class and attributes it to the change from craft to mass industrial production.

Thernstrom's article is an empirical critique of this position. He maintains that Warner's well-known picture of the Yankee City historical stratification system was seriously flawed by its lack of historical accuracy. In particular, Thernstrom argues that his own research indicates that the amount of social mobility in the past was far less than had been assumed by Warner. Thernstrom's research illustrates the necessity of accurately understanding our urban past in order to better interpret the present. In reading these two pieces keep in mind that Warner's selection was written twenty years before Thernstrom's critique. Obviously, the fact that Warner's work still stirs scholarly debate establishes it as a landmark study.

Given the brief period of urban America in the history of man's urban life, it is difficult to make definitive statements about the cumulative and directive aspects of changing growth patterns. Such questions of general cumulative change cannot be empirically answered in terms of the short time period of North American urban development. Nevertheless, major changes in population, social organization, environment, and technology do raise the possibility of emerging evolutionary development. While historical data cannot confirm or test an hypothesis regarding such developmental change, they do provide some insight into the characteristics and problems of the contemporary urban scene.

A number of themes, issues, and problems seem to stand out when one examines the historical material from the P.O.E.T. evolutionary perspective. Most obvious is the fact that North American development from the very beginning has been urban with respect to population characteristics and evolving social organizational forms. From the earliest colonial period to the present day it has been impossible to separate the growth and development of the American city from that of the nation itself, a point powerfully made by Schlesinger (1.2). The social organization of large aggregates in North America has from the first revolved around towns and cities.

From the first, environment has been a major influence on the American city, although its relationship to development has changed through time. For example, in the colonial period site selection was paramount. With the development of transportation technology, intercity competition for extended hinterlands developed. Today the question is how to ecologically accommodate large, densely settled populations within a spatially limited environment.

The literature also indicates that there has been for some time an incongruous gap between our imagery on ideal life styles and the realities of an urban existence. Americans idealize the family farm, but less than one-twentieth of the population is still employed in agriculture. We think rural, but clearly choose to live urban.

Population growth accompanied by technological change has resulted in continual problems of social organization as is illustrated by Strong, Riis, and Warner. An historical perspective protects one from naïvely assuming that problems of suburbanization, sanitation, crime, and out-of-date political structures, and all the rest are strictly unique contemporary phenomenon.

REFERENCES

Bogue, Donald J. (1969) *Principles of Demography*. New York: Wiley.

Breese, Jerald, ed. (1969) *The City in Newly Developing Countries: Readings of Urbanism and Urbanization*. Englewood Cliffs, N.J.: Prentice-Hall.

Bridenbaugh, Carl. (1938) *Cities in the Wilderness*. New York: Ronald.

———. (1955) *Cities in Revolt*. New York: Knopf.

Bryce, James. (1890) *Forum*, Vol. X, p. 25.

Buder, Stanley. (1967) *Pullman*. New York: Oxford.

Cole, Donald B. (1963) *Immigrant City*. Chapel Hill, N.C.: University of North Carolina Press.

Ford, P. L. (1904) *Works of Thomas Jefferson*. New York: Putnam.

Glaab, Charles N. (1963) *The American City*. Homewood, Ill.: Dorsey.

Glaab, Charles N., and Theodore Brown. (1967) *A History of Urban America*. New York: Macmillan.

Hassard, John R. (1866) *Life of the Most Reverend John Hughes*. New York: Appleton.

Hofstadter, Richard. (1955) *The Age of Reform*. New York: Knopf.

Merton, Robert. (1957) *Social Theory and Social Structure*. New York: Free Press.

Morison, Samuel Eliot. (1965) *The Oxford History of the American People*. New York: Oxford.

Petersen, William. (1961) *Population*. New York: Macmillan.

Schlesinger, Arthur M. (1949) *Paths to the Present*. New York: Macmillan.

Strong, Josiah. (1885) *Our Country: Its Possible Future and Its Present Crisis*. New York: Baker & Taylor.

Tocqueville, Alexis de. (1899) *Democracy in America*. New York: M. Walter Dunne.

Vidich, Arthur J., and Joseph Bensman. (1958) *Small Town in Mass Society*. New York: Doubleday (Anchor).

Wade, Richard C. (1959) *The Urban Frontier*. Cambridge, Mass.: Harvard University Press.

1.2 THE CITY IN AMERICAN HISTORY

ARTHUR M. SCHLESINGER

"The true point of view in the history of this nation is not the Atlantic Coast," declared Frederick Jackson Turner in his famous paper of 1893, "it is the Great West." Professor Turner had formed his ideas in an atmosphere of profound agrarian unrest; and an announcement of the superintendent of the census in 1890 that the frontier line could no longer be traced impelled him to the conclusion that "the first period of American history" had closed.[1] His brilliant essay necessitated a fundamental reappraisal of the springs of national development. Today, however, it seems clear that in his zeal to correct older views he overlooked the antithetical form of social organization which, coeval with the earliest frontier, has played a significant and ever-enlarging part in American life. Turner himself wrote in a private letter in 1925, though with evident misgiving, "There seems likely to be an urban reinterpretation of our history."[2]

A reconsideration of American history from the urban point of view need not lead to the distortion which Professor Turner feared. It should direct attention to a much neglected influence and, by so doing, help to illumine the historian's central problem: the persistent interplay of town and country in the evolution of American civilization. Recent historical writings reveal an increasing interest of scholars in the role of the city. It seems desirable, if only in broad outline, to develop certain of the larger implications of these studies and to indicate some of the further possibilities of the general subject for scholarly investigation.

Though agriculture occupied the vast bulk of the colonists, many of them, through personal liking or for economic reasons, preferred town life.[3] Usually the first object upon reaching the Atlantic shore was to found an urban community which might serve as a means of companionship and mutual protection and as a base from which to colonize the neighboring country. In time these towns did duty as business centers, assembling the agricultural products of the adjacent regions for export and paying for them with imported wares. Without access to English-made goods—hardware, tools, firearms, house furnishings, medicines, books, and the like—life in the colonies might easily have approached that of the savages.

From Arthur M. Schlesinger, "The City in American History," *Mississippi Valley Historical Review,* XXVII (June 1940), pp. 43–66. Reprinted by permission of the Organization of American Historians.

Small as these places seem by modern standards, they compared favorably in size and wealth with English provincial cities before the Industrial Revolution began to pile up their populations. As the larger American towns gained in corporate consciousness, they reached out for dependent territories and engaged in contests with one another for economic dominion. Much of colonial history might be rewritten in terms of these activities. Boston, the first to enter the race, possessed special trading advantages which enabled her for nearly a century to maintain a position of primacy, with New York, Philadelphia, and lesser centers hardly more than commercial satellites. These other towns, however, strove for their share of ocean-borne traffic and briskly cultivated their own local trading areas. Thus, the New Yorkers bitterly fought the proposal of the East New Jersey proprietors to erect a rival port at Perth Amboy, and for a time prevailed upon the provincial legislature to tax and otherwise shackle the commerce of Boston with eastern Long Island.[4] Incidentally, the intense application of New York, Philadelphia, and Charleston to the fur trade acted as a powerful stimulant to westward exploration.

As the eighteenth century progressed, Boston's rivals, helped by the occupation of their back-country districts, securely established their independent right to existence. New York completed her sway over western Connecticut and eastern New Jersey as well as over her own hinterland, while Philadelphia held in thrall western New Jersey, Pennsylvania, Delaware, and northern Maryland. It is evidence of the energy and enterprise of urban business that the chambers of commerce of New York and Charleston, formed respectively in 1768 and 1774, antedated all others in English-speaking lands. Beneficial as were the relations of these towns to their dependent areas, urban dominance bred jealousies and resentments which were to reach critical intensity in the later history of the nation. The ascendant city of a given district became a symbol of deception and greed. "A Connecticut Farmer," venting his spleen against New York in the *New-London Gazette,* August 17, 1770, expressed the fervent hope that "the plumes of that domineering city may yet feather the nests of those whom they have long plucked."

From the outset the inhabitants of the towns were confronted with what would today be called "urban problems." The conditions of living in a circumscribed community forced attention to matters of common concern which could not be ignored even by a people individualistically inclined. Lighting, fire protection, the care of streets, crime prevention, sewage disposal, water, community health, marketing facilities—such needs as these evoked remedial efforts which, if primitive in modern eyes, matched those of English cities of comparable size. In some places public-spirited citizens for a time maintained night watches out of their own purses, or else the towns required persons to serve their turns on penalty of fines. Sooner or later, however, policing after dark was accepted as a regular charge on the taxpayers. The removal of garbage generally devolved on roving swine and goats, while drainage remained pretty much an unsolved problem, though in a few communities householders laid private sewers. The fire hazard early stirred the municipal authorities to impose regulations as to the construction of chimneys and the keeping of water buckets. Civil spirit in the eighteenth century supplemented official efforts with the formation of volunteer fire companies which, long after the colonial period, continued to be the principal agency of fire fighting. The pressure of urban needs also fostered American inventiveness, producing Franklin's lightning rod and the fireplace stove.

As these illustrations suggest, the people of the cities evolved a pattern of life increasingly unlike that of the countryside or the frontier. The necessary concern with the general welfare contravened the doctrine of individualism and nourished a sense of social responsibility. This training in collective action, constantly reenforced by the everyday contact of the citizens in less formal undertakings, assumed a commanding importance as the Revolution approached. Happily for the future independence of America, the new policy of the British government, begun in 1763–1764, struck deeply at the roots of urban prosperity. The business classes rallied promptly to the defense of their interests and, heedless of the possible political consequences, enlisted the support of the artisan and mechanic groups. Throughout the decade of controversy the seaport towns set the pace of colonial resistance, furnishing most of the high-pressure leaders, staging turbulent demonstrations at every crisis, and laboring to mobilize rural support for the cause. Even in agricultural commonwealths like Maryland and Virginia, the most effective steps of opposition were taken when the colonists assembled at the provincial capitals for legislative purposes. Boston's preeminence in such exertions may well have been due to the fact that, having recently fallen behind Philadelphia and New York as an emporium, she was resolved at any cost to stay the throttling hand of the British government. With the assembling of the first Continental Congress the direction of the patriot movement shifted to Philadelphia, where presently the first capital of the new republic was established.

It would be a misconception, however, to consider the colonial town merely as an expression of political or economic energies. The city, then as now, was a place where men found a variety of outlets for their special talents, an opportunity to cultivate the art as well as the business of living. Ports of entry for European settlers and goods, the larger places were also ports of entry for European ideas and standards of taste. In nearly every respect city life had a transforming effect on all who came within its orbit. A knowledge of the "three R's" was more widely diffused there than among rural inhabitants. The urban monopoly of the printing presses, newspapers, and bookstores insured both the preservation and the extension of knowledge at many levels. In such an atmosphere men took time for thought while stirred to mental activity. The resulting spirit of innovation expressed itself in intellectual as well as commercial undertakings. It was city folk who took the lead in founding schools and colleges. The protected battle to establish inoculation as a preventive against smallpox was fought out in the towns. The first great victory for freedom of the press greeted the efforts of a Philadelphia lawyer defending a New York editor.

The man whom a recent biographer has called "the first civilized American" was a product of not one but many cities. Boston, Philadelphia, London, and Paris, each contributed to Franklin's intellectual growth and social understanding. Few elements of modern American culture but are indebted to his fostering care: printing, publishing, *belles-lettres,* journalism, education, the postal service, applied science. All these achievements rested, in final analysis, on that interest, encouragement, and financial support which a populous community alone could provide. How sedulously Franklin utilized these advantages appears in his autobiography, which reveals the care with which he educated his fellow Philadelphians to the need of such projects as a lending library, a hospital, and the formation of the American Philosophical Society. Yet Franklin with all his many-sidedness was less "civilized" than urban society as a whole. His range of interests did not include the theater, concerts, the improvement of architecture, or an active concern with art. In all these lines the pre-Revolutionary city, with the increase of wealth and leisure, showed a growing maturity.

It would be folly to deny that the city, both in its internal life and its external relations, played a role of critical importance in colonial society. Just as the biologist learns about complex organisms from studying the simpler forms, so the historical student may enrich his understanding of the later implications of urbanism by a better knowledge of colonial conditions. Though only Philadelphia contained as many as 30,000 people on the eve of Independence, and though less than one out of every twenty-five Americans lived in places of eight thousand or more, these towns revealed in embryo the shape of things to come.

If it be true that the percentage of townsfolk temporarily declined during the troubled years of war and the Confederation,[5] this fact merely accentuates the pivotal influence of urban leadership in the movement for a stronger federal government. [As Professor Beard has shown, the adoption of the Constitution signalized the triumph of the business and creditor classes, largely domiciled in the cities, over the debtors and small farmers of the back country.] The initial Congress under the Constitution was promptly greeted with petitions for tariff protection from Philadelphia, New York, Boston, and Baltimore. This event foreshadowed a conflict of interest in the new government between city and country, which led directly to the formation of the first national parties. Hamilton's so-called financial plan was designed to implement the purposes of the urban capitalists. Jefferson, imbued with physiocratic notions and himself an agriculturist, disapproved the trend of Federalist policy. "For the general operations of manufacture," he declared, "let our workshops remain in Europe." He perceived good even in the yellow-fever epidemic as a means of discouraging the growth of great cities.[6] The contrasting social ideals and economic motives reflected in this early alignment of parties engendered divergent views as to constitutional interpretation and produced recurrent clashes over specific measures. From that day to this the chief business of American politics has been to reconcile these interests in the service of the national welfare.

The spectacular size of the westward movement beginning shortly after the Revolution has obscured the fact that the city not only soon regained its relative position in the total population, but after 1820 grew very much faster than the rural regions. In 1790 one out of every thirty Americans lived in places of eight thousand or more; in 1820 one out of twenty; in 1840 one out of twelve; and in 1860 nearly one in every six.[7] The explanation of this apparent paradox is to be found in a number of factors, not the least of which is the success of the trans-Appalachian country in breeding its own urban communities. These raw western towns at first served as distributing points for commodities between the seaboard and the interior; but they soon became marts where the local manufacturer and the country dweller plied a trade to mutual advantage. Pittsburgh early began to branch out into manufactures; already by 1807 her atmosphere was described as choked with soot. Two years later Cincinnati possessed two cotton mills. Up and down the Ohio Valley many a rude settlement sought to emulate their example; the ambition to become a city dazzled nearly every cluster of log huts. The Indiana pioneers, for instance, hopefully named their tiny hamlets Columbia City, Fountain City, Saline City, Oakland City, and Union City or, flaunting their ambitions more daringly, called them New Philadelphia, New Paris, and even New Pekin.[8]

Meanwhile, in the East, scores of new cities sprang into being, generally at the fall line of the rivers, where water power was available for utilizing the industrial secrets which sharp-witted Americans had recently filched from Britain. It has often been remarked of the early days of New England manufacturing that the farmers' daughters went to the mill towns while their brothers sought the fertile West. But it is clear that, in this section as well as in the Middle Atlantic states, many a farm lad also joined the urban procession; for, long before the great foreign immigration of the forties, the leading cities began to increase rapidly in size. To such places went young men gregarious in temperament, or of a mechanical bent, or ambitious of gain, or fond of book learning. Much study remains to be given this early movement from country to town and to the related subject of the migration from city to city. As Professor Albion has shown, newcomers from New England dominated the business activities of New York City from about 1820 to the Civil War. "It is a singular fact," wrote a New Yorker in 1863, "that a foreign-born boy, or one from the New England States, will succeed in this city, and become a partner in our largest firms, much oftener than a born New York boy."[9]

With the settlement of the trans-Appalachian hinterland, New York, Philadelphia, and Baltimore engaged in a mighty struggle with one another for the conquest of western trade. Content no longer with near-by tributary districts, they sought to carve out economic dependencies and spheres of influence in the more distant country. This conflict of urban imperialisms was most strinkingly evidenced in the rivalry for transportation routes connecting with the West. It is unnecessary here to do more than recall the main weapons with which this prolonged contest was waged—first with turnpikes, then with canals and, finally, with the all-conquering steam railroad. Meanwhile middle-western cities, inspired by the eastern example, entered upon a somewhat similar struggle for power, each seeking to enlarge its orbit of trading operations at the expense of rivals and to benefit from the new ties with the seaboard. With a view to the commercial possibilities of the farther West, Chicago, St. Louis, Memphis, and New Orleans pushed competing plans for the construction of a Pacific railroad, a maneuvering for position which had important national political repercussions, notably in the Kansas-Nebraska Act.

This protracted strife for transportation facilities in the pre-Civil-War era determined the trend of future urban growth in all parts of the North. The

Erie Canal, reenforced by the later railroad construction, established conclusively the preeminence of New York on the seaboard and in the nation. As the new lines of communication penetrated Middle America, they expedited settlement and energized cities into being; oftentimes the railroad ran through the main street.[10] The rise of populous centers increased the market for foodstuffs, accelerated the invention of labor-saving implements such as the steel plow and the reaper, and thus furthered commercial agriculture, which in turn contributed to city growth. Chicago, though still far behind New Orleans, St. Louis, and Cincinnati in size and wealth, had by 1860 already acquired the economic sinews which would make her New York's chief rival before the century closed.

If the urban advance be measured in terms of the size of cities abroad, it is instructive to recall that in 1800 London, the largest European city, possessed around 800,000 people, Paris somewhat more than a half million. Philadelphia, then America's chief center, had less than 70,000, New York only 60,000. Though both London and Paris trebled in size by 1860, New York with 800,000 inhabitants (not counting Brooklyn) ranked as the third city of the Occidental world, while Philadelphia with nearly 565,000 surpassed Berlin. Six other American cities contained more than 100,000, four of them west of the Appalachians.

To master the new intricacies of metropolitan living called for something more than the easy-going ways of colonial times. Yet the municipal authorities, loath to increase taxes, usually shouldered new responsibilities only at the prod of grim necessity. It required the lethal yellow-fever epidemics of the 1790's to induce Philadelphia to set the example of installing a public water system. But with the speeding up of urban concentration after 1820 improvements came thick and fast. Over a hundred municipal water works were introduced before the Civil War, though in every case ignorance of the germ theory of disease necessarily centered attention on clear water rather than pure water. In 1822 Boston inaugurated gas lighting, and the following year she installed the first public-owned sewerage system. About the same time, regular stagecoach service was begun on the streets of New York, to be followed in the next decade by the introduction of horse-car lines. The primitive system of fire fighting by volunteer companies, however, continued everywhere until Boston in 1837 established a paid municipal department.

These civic advances were, of course, unevenly distributed. The smaller cities felt less keenly the pressure for change, while even the larger ones tended to subordinate community need to ulterior considerations. Thus, New York and Philadelphia, daunted by the political power of the volunteer companies, delayed the creation of fire departments until 1865 and 1870. Nor did any city try to combat the evil of slums which began to flourish along the seaboard in the 1840's as a result of the enlarging influx of immigrants. Recruiting their strength from the slum dwellers, the criminal classes, and the fire companies, political machines came into being, trafficking in franchises for the new municipal services and preparing the way for the notorious misrule of cities after the Civil War. The use of municipal offices for partisan purposes long antedated the introduction of the spoils system into state and national politics.

Despite such deterrent influences, it was from the cities that issued most of the humanitarian impulses of the pre-Civil-War period. The compactness of living dramatized all inequalities of condition, facilitated the banding together of the tender-hearted, and sometimes enlisted the support of wealthy philanthropists. The Tappan brothers of New York spread their largess over a wide variety of reform causes. From the cities came the effective energies behind the establishment of free public education, the more humane treatment of the insane, penal reform, the beginning of free public libraries, and the woman rights' movement. Such places also exerted an important influence on the struggle for manhood suffrage, the effort to abolish war, and the anti-slavery cause.

In the cities, too, were felt the first stirrings of the labor movement. For the increasing numbers of urban wage-earners the so-called safety valve of the frontier failed to work. "The wilderness has receded," declared an eastern observer in 1840, "and already the new lands are beyond the reach of the mere laborer, and the employer has him at his mercy."[11] In self-protection the workingmen early in the 1830's organized trade unions, first along the seaboard and then in such inland cities as Buffalo, Pittsburgh, Cincinnati, and St. Louis; and for a time the principal centers combined in a national federation of labor. Though the depression beginning in 1837 shattered most of the unions, the hard times turned men's thoughts to other schemes for curing the "diversities of extreme poverty and extreme wealth"[12] which city life rendered so glaring. Some fared forth into experimental communities where, by grace of Fourier, they hoped to demonstrate the practicability of just and humane living conditions.[13] Others like George H. Evans and his group proposed to drain off the excess urban inhabitants by means of free homesteads. This thought figured prominently in the early discussions of the subject in Congress.[14] Evans' suggestion of providing free transportation for settlers failed to gain support, however, and soon the whole homestead question became enmeshed in the slavery controversy.

The determined purpose of the city reformers to employ the power of government to remove social inequalities heightened the contrast between urban and frontier conceptions of democracy; the lag of the rural sections in cultural achievements marked an even wider gap between the two ways of life. The enlargement and multiplication of urban centers not only insured a greater appreciation and patronage of arts and letters, but immensely broadened the field for the recruitment of talent. To such communities were drawn many of the best minds of the countryside, for, as Dr. Holmes remarked, every considerable town had its "intellectual basin, or *suction-range*," as well as its economic gravitation field.[15] The people in the cities, too, were the first to feel the stimulating impact of new currents of European thought.

A varied and vital intellectual life resulted, of which any nation might be proud. Magazines proliferated until every taste and interest was regaled; newspapers became legion; publishing houses sprang up to supply the unprecedented demand for books. The story of this richly creative period in American letters can be told almost wholly in terms of Boston and its environs and of New York. Imaginative literature, however, also had its devotees in Cincinnati, St. Louis, and other inland cities. In the related arts the urban record showed less distinction; yet, apart from architecture, American civilization made fresh advances. Architecture suffered because the mushroom growth of cities required new construction at a rate that caused utility and pretentiousness to overshadow aesthetic considerations. Progress in music consisted chiefly in the broadening of musical appreciation, though in Stephen C. Foster Pittsburgh supplied a composer of genius. The theater became firmly established as an urban institution, and players like Charlotte Cushman and Edwin Booth won a repute in England as well as at home. Painters no longer felt the urgent need of seeking inspiration and support abroad. Their prestige was high, the products of their brush found a ready market, and, with the formation of the National Academy of Design in 1826, New York became the nation's art center.

Whatever the benefits accruing to the higher life, the waxing importance of the city occasioned increasing fear and resentment among country dwellers. This was especially true of the years from 1820 to 1860, which saw the urban population grow elevenfold. Country ministers denounced big cities, "cursed with immense accumulations of ignorance and error, vice and crime"; farm journals exhorted young men not to sacrifice their independence in order to "cringe and flatter, and . . . attend upon the wishes of every painted and padded form of humanity."[16] The printing press poured forth books, such as Clement Robbins' *Vampires of New York* and the anonymous paper-back series published by C. H. Brainard on the *Tricks and Traps* of New York, New Orleans, St. Louis, and Chicago. Writers of popular fiction, sensing the sales possibilities, eagerly embroidered upon the theme. George Lippard's melodramatic novel, *The Quaker City . . . . A Romance of Philadelphia Life, Mystery and Crime* (1844), ran through twenty-seven editions in five years.[17] Whether the net effect was to lessen or enhance urban fascination would be difficult to say. Byron, it will be recalled, wrote of "Saint Augustine in his fine Confessions, which make the reader envy his transgressions."

Politics also reflected the deepening rural distrust of city domination. The western opposition to the second United States Bank sprang largely from alarm at the control of credit facilities by the branch banks at Boston, New York, Philadelphia, and Baltimore. Likewise, the widening breach between South and North rested in considerable part on differences between rural and urban ways of life. The South, possessing few sizable towns and believing itself yoked to agriculture by slavery, became increasingly isolated from the currents of civilization flowing through the northern cities. It did not join in establishing free public schools; it feared and misunderstood the social experimentation rampant in the urban North; and, lacking the necessary nerve centers for creative cultural achievement, it fell far behind in arts, science, and letters. Moreover, southern economic life lay under constant tribute to northern urban enterprise. "It is a hopeless task," affirmed William Gregg, "to undertake to even approximate to the vast sums of wealth which have been transferred from the South to the North by allowing the Northern cities to import and export for us."[18] For twenty years before the war southern commercial conventions sought ways and means to escape this subordination, but their hope of building their own trading centers had no chance for success so long as lands and Negroes held a superior attraction for capital.

Historians might fell give greater attention to the question of the extent to which southern secession was a revolt against the urban imperialism of Yankeedom. The grievance of the planting elements seems clear; and the bitter comment of the *Charleston Mercury,* May 20, 1858, that "Norfolk, Charleston, Savannah, Mobile, are only suburbs of New York," suggests the rankling resentment of the population centers.[19] As Professor Russel's researches show, the southern towns and cities gave their powerful support to the movement for separation. Even New Orleans, despite its large admixture of northerners and foreign born, chose twenty secessionists and only four unionists to the state convention. According to the Missourian, John B. Henderson, the business class of Charleston believed that, once outside the Union, "Charleston in the course of ten years will become a New York. The merchants of Savannah . . . the merchants of Mobile and the merchants of New Orleans have the same opinion."[20] It is significant that one of the early acts of the Confederate and state authorities was to outlaw the accumulated indebtedness of many millions owing to northern merchants, bankers, and manufacturers.[21]

The years following the Civil War ushered in the modern era of cities.[22] In the East and the Middle West urbanization proceeded apace. By 1890 New York-Brooklyn with nearly two and a half million people rivaled Paris, and Chicago and Philadelphia with more than a million each ranked as the sixth and seventh cities of the Occident. Hardly less significant was the rise of cities in the Far West and the New South. If most of them seemed small by the new yardsticks of urban magnitude, their rate of growth was spectacular, and even their size would earlier have gained them respect. Thus, Los Angeles jumped from less than 5000 in 1860 to more than 100,000 in 1900, and Denver from nothing at all to 134,000, while Memphis with 23,000 in the earlier year exceeded 100,000 in the later. In the nation as a whole, the proportion of people living in towns of eight thousand or more grew from one out of every six persons in 1860 to about one out of four in 1880 and by 1900 to one in every three. Moreover, of this increasing horde of urban dwellers, considerably more than half resided in places of twenty-five thousand or more.

The city had at last become a national rather than a sectional institution. This development rested on the occupation of the Great West and the economic rehabilitation of the post-war South and, in all sections, on an application of business enterprise to the exploitation of natural resources such as the world had never known. To recount this material transformation at length would be to recite an oft-told tale. The urban dynamic, grotesquely magnified, was the governing force. Railroads, industrial combinations, financial power, legislative favors, formed the instruments of conquest. A complex of city imperialisms arose, each scheming for dominion, each battling with its rivals for advantage, and each perforce yielding eventual tribute to the lord of them all. "Every produce market, every share market," declared James Bryce, "vibrates in response to the Produce Exchange and Stock Exchange of New York."[23]

As urban centers grew in size and wealth, they cast an ever-stronger enchantment over the mind of the nation. Walt Whitman, returning after a short absence to New York and Brooklyn in September, 1870, hymned the "splendor, picturesqueness, and oceanic amplitude and rush of these great cities." Nature's triumph lay in her mountains, forests, and seas, but he observed, "The work of man too is equally great . . . in these ingenuities, streets, goods, houses, ships—these hurrying, feverish, electric crowds of men."[24] Little wonder that young men and women yielded to the potent allure. "We cannot all live in cities," wrote Horace Greeley in the *New York Tribune,* February 5, 1867, "yet nearly all seem determined to do so. Millions of acres . . . solicit cultivation . . .; yet hundreds of thousands reject this and rush into the cities."

Historians in their preoccupation with the dispersion of settlers over the wide expanse of the public domain have given little attention to this countermovement which even more profoundly altered the tissue of American life. In many parts the pull of the city depopulated the countryside. Over two-fifths of the townships of Pennsylvania, three-fifths of those of New England, and more than two-thirds of New York's suffered depletion between 1880 and 1890,[25] while the cities in these states grew by leaps and bounds. Similar rural losses occurred in the Middle West, though there the attraction of free homesteads doubtless played a larger part. The rapid dwindling of the open frontier during this decade came with little shock to a people who for many years had shown an increasing preference for city life and an eagerness to avail themselves of its social amenities and expanding economic opportunities. From 1790 to 1890 the whole population of the republic had grown 16-fold, the urban population 139-fold. The historic announcement of the superintendent of the census in 1890 was significant less as marking the end of an old America than as a long-overdue admission of the arrival of a new one.

If, as Walt Whitman thought, the city was the most comprehensive of the works of man, its lusty growth created problems which tried to the utmost the resourcefulness of the inhabitants. In some measure European experience furnished a guide, but to an increasing extent, notably in rapid transit, lighting, and communication, America pointed the way for the Old World. The record is extraordinary. Hardly had New York undertaken the first elevated railway in 1868 than San Francisco contrived the cable car, and hardly had this new means of conveyance begun to spread than Richmond demonstrated the superiority of the electric trolley system, and presently Boston added the subway. The need for better lighting led to the invention of Brush's outdoor arc-light and of Edison's incandescent bulb for indoors. Still another application of electric power, the telephone, laced the urban population into the texture of a neighborhood. By means of the multicelled department store, cities simplified the problem of shopping; and by means of the steel-framed skyscraper, they economized ground space by building their business districts upward.

This civic advance, however, entailed a shocking degradation of political standards. Americans had gained their experience in self-government under rural conditions; they had yet to learn how to govern concentrated populations. Preyed upon by self-interested men eager to exploit the expanding public utilities, municipal politics became a saturnalia of corruption. As Francis Parkman wrote, "Where the carcass is, the vultures gather together."[26] The Tweed Ring in New York was the symptom of a disease that afflicted Chicago, St. Louis, Minneapolis, San Francisco, and other communities as well. In Andrew D. White's measured opinion of the conditions, "With very few exceptions, the city governments of the United States are the worst in Christendom—the most expensive, the most inefficient, and the most corrupt."[27]

Against the entrenched forces of greed and graft the reformers fought undismayed. Defeated at many points, they at least awakened the nation to the growing problems of social maladjustment and human misery which the teeming cities exhibited. Through a concerted attack on the slum evil they induced the New York legislature to adopt a series of laws for better housing, though the results proved disappointing. They replaced the indiscriminate alms-giving of early times with scientific principles of charity, and established social settlements and playgrounds. Organized religion, harking to the need, responded with slum missions, institutional churches, and the preaching of the social gospel. In the cities, too, the modern labor movement was born, wresting concessions from the employing class through sheer bulk of numbers, joining with the humanitarians in securing factory legislation, and organizing labor's strength on an intercity, nationwide basis. Occasional voices speaking with a foreign accent cried up the advantages of socialism or anarchism, while Edward Bellamy, appalled by the ever-greater contrast between wealth and want in urban life, produced an American version of communism in his fanciful description of Boston as it would be in the year 2000.

The increasing tension of city life was reflected in a variety of ways. Hordes of people habituated to a rural environment had suddenly to adapt themselves to the frantic pace of urban communities. To this circumstance is to be attributed the startling growth of nervousness or neurasthenia, designated by one contemporary as "the national disease of America."[28] A New York medical authority, writing in 1881, descanted learnedly on the effects on the human organism of the heightened speed of movement, the constant struggle for survival, the discordant sounds of the streets, and the ceaseless mental excitements and endless distractions.[29] It was from this swelling number of nerve-racked urban folk that Mary Baker Eddy secured most of her converts to the new religion of Christian Science. It was partly due to the same reason that city dwellers for the first time turned to the systematic development of organized sports. If flabby muscles kept most of them from direct participation, each year saw greater throngs seeking an anodyne for their cares while watching professional contests.

Urban communities, however, made their greatest contribution as a cultural force. The larger cities now rounded out their cultural equipment. The establishment of art museums, the multiplication of public libraries, the increase of publishing houses, the founding of art schools, conservatories of music, and new universities—these were signs of urban maturity which deeply affected all who came in contact with them. Statistical studies, concerned in considerable part with men who won note during these years, merely confirm what has already been evident as to the relation of urban birth to leadership in fields of achievement. Based on analyses of *Who's Who in America, American Men of Science,* and similar compilations, these investigations show conclusively the advantages resulting from concentrated wealth, superior educational and cultural opportunities, the friction of mind on mind, and the encouragement given to arts and letters. One student found that towns of eight thousand or more produced nearly twice as many persons of distincton as their proportionate share.[30] In particular fields, such as science, literature, art, and engineering, the urban differential was far greater. Such findings, however, understate the significance of the city, for they leave out of consideration the countless gifted individuals who, born in rural districts or in other nations, found in the urban world their Promised Land.

Statistical generalizations suggest the broad base of the city's cultural pyramid rather than its height. Only a full historical survey could disclose the emergence of towering figures in nearly every field of science, learning, arts, and letters during these years. Suffice it to say that the present generation gladly attests its indebtedness to the creative efforts of such men as Simon Newcomb in astronomy, J. Willard Gibbs in physical chemistry, Lester F. Ward in sociology, Charles W. Eliot in education, Augustus Saint-Gaudens in sculpture, H. H. Richardson in architecture, Edward A. Mac-Dowell in music, and William Dean Howells in literature.

As the city forged ahead, imposing its economic fiat on the rest of the nation, developing ever more sharply its special way of life and opening new vistas of civilization, the rift between town and country reached threatening proportions. This antagonism has generally been conceived by historians in broad geographic terms. An accredited scholar, writing in the 1890's, saw the issue with clearer eyes. The "new sectionalism," he affirmed, is geographic only "in so far as the East is the section of the cities, while the South and West are the sections containing the bulk of the farmers." The decisive difference everywhere, he asserted, lay between urban and rural communities. "The people on the farms and in the villages in the East have shared no more in the advancing wealth of the past quarter of a century than the people on the farms and in the villages of the South and West." He estimated the average wealth of urban families at nearly three times that of rural families.[31]

If the typical country dweller had little conception of these larger economic factors, the passage of years brought him a growing sense of deprivation in his daily round of living. Contrasted with the rewards of urban life, he felt cheated of his due share of opportunities, comforts, and pleasures. Herbert Quick, looking back on his childhood days in Iowa, spoke particularly of the farm women, "pining for neighbors, for domestic help, for pretty clothes, for schools, music, art, and the things tasted when the magazines came in."[32] Though many of the younger generation escaped to the cities, this rendered life all the more irksome for those who, unable to leave or preferring the land, believed themselves saddled with unfair handicaps. Undoubtdly the farmer accepted too readily the urban estimate of his calling. That opinion had changed with the increasing dominance of cities. In the words of a contemporary, "The tiller of the soil, who in the days of our fathers was the embodiment of economic independence," is now the "stock figure . . . only of the humorist . . . The 'sturdy yeoman' has become the 'hayseed.' "[33]

To this rural feeling of inferiority, this deepening sense of frustration, the historian must look for the basic explanation of the recurrent agrarian uprisings. Tangible economic grievances, particularly in times of agricultural depression, merely stirred the smoldering embers into blaze. Such grievances assumed a variety of forms, but all of them represented extensions of urban imperialism at the cost of rural welfare. Farm leaders likened the big cities to giant cuttlefish running out their suckers into the blood stream of the countryside. It was left to the greatest of the agrarian champions, addressing the Democratic convention of 1896, to hurl the ultimate challenge to urban pretensions. "Burn down your cities and leave our farms," he cried, "and your cities will spring up again as if by magic; but destroy our farms and the grass will grow in the streets of every city in the country."[34] In the election that followed, the great cities of the North and West responded by casting decisive majorities against Bryan and free silver.[35]

Few persons in 1900 could have forseen the trends of urban development which the twentieth century has brought forth. These attest the vast recuperative powers of American society. One of the most notable advances has been the concerted effort to bridle the predatory forces which, in James Bryce's phrase, had made municipal government "the one conspicuous failure of the United States."[36] To this end, four hundred and fifty cities have adopted the commission-manager plan. A radical departure from the clumsy nineteenth-century form which had been based on the analogy of state governments, the new system seeks to apply to complex urban communities the principles of expert management rendered familiar by business corporations. Along with this change have occurred the first systematic and sustained attempts to substitute forethought for drift in the development of cities. Dating from 1905, the movement has spread in every direction, yielding rich dividends for community welfare and civic sightliness. In its wider consequences city planning has stimulated interest in county planning and state planning, and helps to account for the recent emphasis on regional and national planning.

The new municipal ideals, operating with varying intensity in different parts of the nation, made progress in face of the continued headlong rush into the cities both from the countryside and from foreign lands. With a third of the people living in places of eight thousand and upward in 1900, approximately half did so by 1930.[37] In the latter year nearly a third of the population resided in centers of one hundred thousand or more. During the three decades the country population gained less than eleven and a half million while the city population leaped more than thirty-five million. In reality, urban preponderance was bigger than these figures indicate, thanks to the rise of great metropolitan districts in all parts of the nation. These supercommunities had begun to form in the nineteenth century as swifter means of transportation and communication flung the population outward into the suburbs. But it was the coming of the automobile and the motor truck that raised them to their paramount position in the national economy. The census of 1930 disclosed ninety-six metropolitan districts, composed of one or more central cities with peripheral towns and rural communities, each district comprising a territory united by common social, industrial, and financial interests. The metropolitan areas of New York City lay in three states, embracing a region twice the size of Rhode Island and containing 272 incorporated communities. Greater Chicago in 1930 included 115 incorporated places, and greater San Francisco, 38.

These urban provinces, new to the American scene, possess greater economic, social, and cultural unity than most of the states. Yet, subdivided into separate municipalities and often lying in more than one state, they face grave difficulties in meeting the essential needs of the aggregate population. Some students of local government, despairing of any other solution, have proposed separate statehood for the largest metropolitan districts without regard to existing state lines.[38] It is clear that new and unanticipated strains are being placed on the federal system framed by the Fathers for a simple agricultural economy.

Of all the new trends in urban development, however, none has had such profound effects on American civilization as the altered relationship between country and city. Historians usually ascribe the subsidence of the agrarian revolt of the nineties to the discovery of fresh sources of gold supply. But perhaps a more fundamental explanation lies in the amelioration of many of the social and psychological drawbacks of farm life. The last decade of the century beheld an ampler provision of rural educational facilities, a rapid extension of the good-roads movement due to the bicycle craze, the penetration of the countryside by an increasing network of interurban trolley lines, the introduction of rural free delivery, and the spread of farm telephones following the expiration of the basic Bell patents. All these events helped to break down the ancient isolation and loneliness, and lent a new attraction to country existence.

Yet these mitigations seem small, compared with the marvels which the present century has wrought. The automobile has shortened all distances, while the radio and the movie have brought urbanizing influences to nearly every rural home. At the same time the tractor and other labor-saving devices have lightened the drudgery of the day's task.[39] Between 1900 and 1935 the mechanical power used in agriculture grew nearly eight-fold. Moreover, both the state and national governments have increasingly employed their powers to improve the economic and social status of the farmer. Some of the farthest reaching New Deal policies, such as the Tennessee Valley development, the triple-A effort, and the rural-electrification program, have had this as a major purpose. Though many inequalities remain, the country has achieved a position in American society of which his Populist forebears could not have dreamed.

While the farmers have shared more richly in advantages once confined to townsfolk, urban life in turn has become increasingly ruralized. Parks, playgrounds, and tree-lined boulevards have multiplied far out of proportion to the growth of population, while enlarging numbers of city workers have used the new means of transit to go farther and farther into the rustic suburbs. Retail trade has also felt the centrifugal pull, and even factories have shown a tendency to move outward into villages where taxes are low, and food and rent cheap. The extension of giant power will doubtless accelerate this diffusion and afford an increasing number of wage-earners a chance to work and live in semi-rural surroundings.

When the city encroaches sufficiently on the country and the country on the city, there will come an opportunity for the development of a type of civilization such as the world has never known. The old hard-and-fast distinction between urban and rural will tend to disappear, and a form of society take its place which, if America is to realize her promise, will blend the best features of the two traditional modes of life.

From humble beginnings in the early days of settlement the city has thus traced a varied course. In Europe the urban community emerged by imperceptible stages out of the town economy and culture of the Middle Ages; by comparison the American city leaped into being with breath-taking suddenness. At first servant to an agricultural economy, then a jealous contestant, then an oppressor, it now gives evidence of becoming a comrade and cooperator in a new national synthesis. Its economic function has been hardly more important than its cultural mission or its transforming influence on frontier conceptions of democracy. A force both for weal and woe, the city challenges the attention of scholars who will find in its ramifying history innumerable opportunities for rewarding research.

NOTES

1. Frederick J. Turner, *The Frontier in American History* (New York, 1920), 3, 38.

2. Letter to A. M. Schlesinger, dater Madison, Wisconsin, May 5, 1925.

3. Recent works concerned with urban aspects of American colonial history include Carl Bridenbaugh, *Cities in the Wilderness, The First Century of Urban Life in America, 1625–1742* (New York, 1938); Ernest S. Griffith, *History of American City Government. The Colonial Period* (New York, 1938); Virginia D. Harrington, *The New York Merchant on the Eve of the Revolution* (New York, 1935); Michael Kraus, *Intercolonial Aspects of American Culture on the Eve of the Revolution with Special Reference to the Northern Towns* (New York, 1928); and Leila Sellers, *Charleston Business on the Eve of the Revolution* (Chapel Hill, 1934).

4. Curtis P. Nettels, *The Money Supply of the American Colonies before 1720* (Madison, 1934), 108–109, 117–118.

5. *A Century of Population Growth* (Washington, 1909), 15.

6. Paul L. Ford, ed., *The Works of Thomas Jefferson* (New York, 1904–1905), IV, 86, IX, 147.

7. W. S. Thompson and P. K. Whelpton, *Population Trends in the United States* (New York, 1933), 20. Secondary works helpful for an understanding of urban history from 1783 to 1860 include Robert G. Albion, *The Rise of New York Port, 1815–1860* (New York, 1939); Lewis E. Atherton, *The Pioneer Merchant in Mid-America* (Columbia, 1939); Charles A. Beard, *An Economic Interpretation of the Constitution* (New York, 1913); Beverley W. Bond Jr., *The Civilization of the Old Northwest, 1788–1812* (New York, 1934), chaps. xii–xv; E. Douglas Branch, *The Sentimental Years, 1836–1860* (New York, 1934); R. A. East, *Business Enterprise in the American Revolutionary Era* (New York, 1938); James Ford et al., *Slums and Housing with Special Reference to New York City* (Cambridge, Mass., 1936), I, 54–149; Bessie L. Pierce, *A History of Chicago* (New York, 1937–), I (to 1848); Sidney I. Pomerantz, *New York: An American City, 1783–1803* (New York, 1939); and Robert R. Russel, *Economic Aspects of Southern Sectionalism, 1840–1861* (Urbana, 1924).

8. Note also Burns City, Cambridge City, Clay City, Coal City, Lincoln City, Hartford City, Michigan City, Monroe City, Rome City, Shirley City, and Switz City, not to mention numerous place names ending in "town," "burg," "port," and "ville," and the designation of the capital of the state as Indianapolis. Few of these "cities" ever attained the minimum census definition of a city (2500 inhabitants). In J. K. Paulding's novel, *Westward Ho!* (New York, 1832), II, 179, Zeno Paddock, coming upon one of these aspiring midwestern settlements, found "on the very spot where the court-house stood on the

map, a flock of wild turkeys gobbling like so many lawyers . . . . but the founder of New Pekin swore it was destined to be the great mart of the West, to cut out St. Louis, Cincinnati, and New Orleans, and to realize the most glorious speculation that was ever conceived by the sagacity or believed by the faith of man."

9. J. A. Scoville (Walter Barrett, *pseud.*), *The Old Merchants of New York City* (New York, 1863), I, 194, cited with other evidence in Albion, *Rise of New York Port,* 241–252.

10. "With the exception of such cities as Chicago, St. Louis and Cincinnati, settlers can hardly be said to have chosen their own localities," wrote Anthony Trollope, *North America* (New York, 1862), 441.

11. Orestes A. Brownson, "The Laboring Classes," *Boston Quarterly Review,* III, 1840, p. 372.

12. E. H. Chapin, *Humanity in the City* (New York, 1854), 20.

13. For a vigorous indictment of urban "incoherence and waste," see Albert Brisbane, *The Social Destiny of Man* (Philadelphia, 1840), chap. vii.

14. Fred A. Shannon, "The Homestead Act and the Labor Surplus," *American Historical Review* (New York), XLI, 1935–1936, pp. 641–643.

15. Oliver Wendell Holmes, *The Autocrat of the Breakfast Table* (Boston, 1892), *The Works of Oliver W. Holmes,* I, 127.

16. Quoted in Harold F. Wilson, *The Hill Country of Northern New England* (New York, 1936), 70–72.

17. George A. Dunlap, *The City in the American Novel, 1789–1900* (Philadelphia, 1934), 67.

18. William Gregg, "Southern Patronage to Southern Imports and Domestic Industry," *De Bow's Review* (New Orleans), XXIX, 1860, p. 82.

19. For the means employed by New York in "enslaving the cotton ports," see R. G. Albion, *Square-Riggers on Schedule* (Princeton, 1938), chap. iii.

20. Russel, *Economic Aspects of Southern Sectionalism,* 184, 239–243, 251, 284–286.

21. Contemporary estimates of the amount varied from forty to four hundred million dollars. John C. Schwab, *The Confederate States of America, 1861–1865* (New York, 1901), 110–123.

22. Allan Nevins, *The Emergence of Modern America, 1865–1878* (New York, 1927), and Arthur M. Schlesinger, *The Rise of the City, 1878–1898* (New York, 1933), Arthur M. Schlesinger and Dixon R. Fox, eds., *A History of American Life,* VIII, X, explore many aspects of the new role of the city.

23. James Bryce, *The American Commonwealth* (2 vols., London, 1888), II, 692.

24. Walt Whitman, *Democratic Vistas* (London, 1888), 13–14. Dr. Holmes, weary of hearing sentimentalists quote Cowper's line, "God made the country, and man made the town," retorted, "God made the *cavern* and man made the *house!* What then?" Holmes, *Works,* V, 303.

25. Josiah Strong, *The New Era* (New York, 1893), 167.

26. Francis Parkman, "The Failure of Universal Suffrage," *North American Review* (Boston), CXXVII, 1878, p. 20.

27. Andrew D. White, "The Government of American Cities," *Forum* (New York), X, 1890–1891, p. 357.

28. Edward Wakefield, "Nervousness: the National Disease of America," *McClure's Magazine* (New York), II, 1894, pp. 302–307.

29. G. M. Beard, *American Nervousness* (New York, 1881).

30. F. A. Woods, "City Boys versus Country Boys," *Science* (Cambridge, Mass.), N. S., XXIX, 1909, pp. 577–579. S. S. Visher, *Geography of American Notables* (Bloomington, 1928), *Indiana University Studies,* XV, no. 79, an illuminating analysis, lists other important studies in the footnotes to pages 7–8. Frederick J. Turner's discussion of "The Children of the Pioneers" in *The Significance of Sections in American History* (New York, 1932), chap. x, fails to distinguish between midwestern notables of rural birth and those born in the towns and cities.

31. Charles B. Spahr, *An Essay on the Present Distribution of Wealth in the United States* (New York, 1896), 44–49. He drew the line between country and city at towns of 4000 inhabitants.

32. Herbert Quick, "Women on the Farms," *Good Housekeeping* (New York), LVII, 1913, pp. 426–436, esp. 427.

33. Anon., "The Political Menace of the Discontented," *Atlantic Monthly* (Boston), LXXVIII, 1896, p. 449.

34. William J. Bryan, *The First Battle, A Story of the Campaign of 1896* (Chicago, 1896), 205.

35. *Nation* (New York), LXIII, November 12, 1896, p. 358.

36. Bryce, *American Commonwealth*, I, 608. Recent works shedding light on the twentieth-century city include Harlan P. Douglass, *The Suburban Trend* (New York, 1925); Murray H. Leiffer, *City and Church in Transition* (Chicago, 1938); William P. Ogburn, *Social Characteristics of Cities* (Chicago, 1937); Roderick D. McKenzie, *The Metropolitan Community* (New York, 1933); Thompson and Whelpton, *Population Trends in the United States;* and Urbanism Committee of National Resources Committee, *Our Cities, Their Role in the National Economy* (Washington, 1937).

37. By using the census definition of a city as a place of 2500 or more, 51.4 per cent of the people instead of 43.8 may be regarded as urban dwellers in 1920, and 56.2 per cent instead of 49.1 in 1930. The back-to-the-land movement, which affected perhaps a million persons during the years 1930–1933, seems to have been only a temporary effect of the Great Depression.

38. Howard W. Odum and Harry E. Moore, *American Regionalism* (New York, 1938), 127.

39. E. G. McKibben and R. A. Griffin, *Changes in Farm Power and Equipment: Tractors, Trucks, and Automobiles* (Philadelphia, 1938).

1.3 BOSTON VERSUS CHICAGO

CHARLES FRANCIS ADAMS

It was only thirty-three years ago on the 4th of last October,—exactly the lifetime of one generation of men,—that a regular *battue* took place close to what is now the centre of the great city of Chicago. On the morning of that day, in 1834, a large black bear had been shot in the woods just behind the little town, and its inhabitants, stimulated by so auspicious a commencement, sallied out for a day's sport; and before night they had killed forty wolves within what are now the limits of the city. Chicago now has a population somewhat larger than that of Boston, and performing far greater functions in the economy of the continent. What will be the relative position of the two cities thirty years hence can, perhaps, be imagined. Without indulging in prophecy, however, there is sufficient matter for observation and reflection in the history and relative growth of the two during the last thirty years, and it is matter from which, if sufficiently considered, both cities perhaps, and Boston at any rate, may derive some useful lessons. So far as Chicago is concerned, those thirty-three years include the story of a lifetime. Physically, it is a history of opportunities improved, energies developed, and difficulties overcome,—so overcome that the conquerors have grown to take a boastful pride and almost pleasure in the conflict. Though for Boston this period has not been equally eventful, yet for that city too it has produced its long list of changes, and of changes such as perhaps are not usually imagined, nor always, when realized, sources of satisfaction.

A comparative retrospection could not begin from a more distinctive date than that of 1837. Just three decades ago that year came, like the year 1867, in a period of depression, anxiety, and paper money. Mr. Van Buren was President of the United States, and Edward Everett was Governor of Massachusetts. Boston, a thriving city of eighty thousand inhabitants, was, relatively to the whole country, a much more important place than at present.

In its physical aspect the city has certainly changed since then. Its proper limits were necessarily much the same then as now, but its appearance was more picturesque and old-fashioned. The commercial centre of the town was still its business centre. The manufacturer as well as the merchant clustered around State Street—once King Street—and the old wharves and warehouses of Colonial times. Those, too, were the days of old-fashioned, roomy houses,

From Charles Francis Adams, "Boston," *North American Review* (January 1868).

before the "seventeen-foot front" came in. Not yet had the increasing volume of the business community, bursting its limits, sent its tide of granite fronts, like a destroying flood of lava, over the quiet, shady streets, pretty gardens, and substantial square, court-enclosed residences, the last of which have only just disappeared. The place has grown larger, but, unlike New York or Chicago, it is still the same place. For notwithstanding many local and individual changes, streets which were fashionable in 1837 are fashionable now; the same families not seldom live in the same houses; the wealthy names then are wealthy names still, and the men of note then are men of note now. The change has been simply the comparatively slow change of growth and expansion: it has been the change neither of creation nor of revolution.

The moral, social, and political questions agitating that community in 1837 were curiously the same with those still matters of earnest discussion. Railroads had begun to produce their effects, and the whole country was speculating,—speculating not in coppers or oil mines or gold mines, but in what answered the purpose quite as well,—in Western lands, in produce, in imports, in manufactures, and in exports. In 1837, as well as in 1867, the papers and society rang with a universal outcry against the absurdly high prices of the day, and the enormous cost of living. The whole world was making short cuts to fortune, and heaping up great wealth in paper dollars. In that same year came the crash; the banks suspended, the merchants were ruined, and provincial Boston was large enough to report one business failure a day during a period of six months; gold was at ten per cent premium, and the newspapers teemed with plans for the resumption of specie payments. In the Legislature the questions then discussed were curiously the same with those discussed in the same halls in 1867. The temperance question had begun to loom up, the fifteen-gallon law was passed, and the bar-rooms were for the first time closed on Sundays. Then, too, a novel experiment was tried,—a hotel (the Marlborough) was established "on temperance principles." The repeal of the usury laws was discussed, as also the expediency of passing a law regulating the hours of labor, known as the "Ten-Hour Law." In literature, also, the Athens of America still sounds the old harp-strings. In the year 1837 R. W. Emerson delivered a Φ. B. K. oration, as he did in 1867; Caleb Cushing declined to address the societies of Dartmouth College, and Mr. George S. Hillard took his place. Dr. O. W. Holmes brought out a little volume of poems, and the second volume of an interminable History of America, by George Bancroft, was published.

Commercially, Boston was for that time a city of great foreign trade and enterprise. Ships unloaded at her wharves from China, from Calcutta, from the African coast and the Mediterranean, from Russia, South America, and the Pacific coast. Only two years before the house of Sturgis had originated the California trade by sending out the Alert, with the author of "Two Years before the Mast" in her forecastle. Then and for years after Boston was considered the natural American terminus of the Liverpool trade, and Train's "Diamond Line" of fast Liverpool packets, which ran successfully for fifteen years, and transported one hundred and forty thousand passengers, was not originated until 1844. Since those days the population within the city limits has more than doubled, and has overflowed those limits into every suburban town. The industrial increase has been eightfold. In 1866 the money value of the manufactures of the city was returned at eighty-six millions of dollars, against less than eleven millions, the return of 1837, and exactly equalling the return of the whole State for that year. Its wealth has increased fourfold since that time. Its debt has increased more than sevenfold. Its rate of taxation has increased threefold, but its foreign commerce has not increased at all in the same ratio. Until within the last dozen years the foreign trade of the city flourished satisfactorily; but hidden causes must have been at work, for the crisis of 1857 seems to have given it a shock from which it has never recovered. Between 1836 and 1855, the yearly foreign entrances and clearances of the port of Boston rather more than doubled, and the gross numbers of each have not materially declined to the present time; but the character of the commerce has changed.[1] Though nominally foreign, nine tenths of those clearances and entrances are of vessels engaged in the coasting trade in everything but the name. They are not stately ships, rich in the association of the distant lands, bringing teas and spices from the East and wines and silks from Europe, to return laden with corn and gold and oil; they are Down-East coasters, averaging somewhat more than a hundred tons' measurement each, and carrying on a thriving business in facilitating the exchange of coal and firewood, fish, rags, and timber, the staples of the Provinces, for the ready-made boots and furniture, the butter, molasses, and manufactured tobacco, the produce of New England.[2] Thus, though the same number of sails as in 1855 now enter and leave Boston Harbor, in the course of each year, from or for foreign ports, yet in 1862–63, as compared with the earlier year, their aggregate tonnage had decreased ten per cent, and the value of their imports, having fallen off fifty per cent, had almost sunk to the level of 1836; while their exports, though double the value of those of 1836, had also fallen away one half in ten years.

 Not so New York. Her commerce has never ceased to grow. Entering and clearing in 1836 less than double the tonnage of Boston, and scarcely more than doubling it in 1855,—for Boston yet held her own bravely,—in 1862–63 her tonnage was fourfold that of Boston; and while her trade with the American foreign ports of the North Atlantic was little if at all larger than that of Boston, her traffic beyond the seas was nine times as great.[3] The trade of Boston with the British Provinces was during those years more than twice that of New York; with Great Britain the trade of New York was more than ten times that of Boston.[4] The same rule of change holds in the value of the commerce. In 1836 New York imported and exported, as compared with Boston, in about the ratio of five to one; in 1855 the ratio was as less than four to one, but in 1862–63 it stood at ten to one, and during the last three years (1864–1866), while the New York imports as compared with those of Boston have held the ratio of seven to one, her exports have stood as thirteen to one.[5] A relative importance reduced from one fourth to one tenth, and an absolute loss of some fifty per cent, is a result singularly suggestive as the lesson drawn from the experience of a single decennium.

 To return, however, to the decade of 1830–1840. A new era then opened on the world, for steam was working out its application to locomotion on land and to ocean navigation. The race was open to all; it was almost a clear field without favor. At that time Boston enjoyed several advantages. In 1837 she possessed the best developed germ of a railroad system in all America. She sent out ten trains a day on her finished lines to Lowell, Providence, and Worcester. Already her plan of great railroad extension was matured. The present Western Railroad was projected, and, in projecting it, the men of those days seem to have risen to an equality with the occasion; for, in the language of 1837, this road was "to extend from Worcester to the Connecticut River, at Springfield, and thence to the boundary line of the State of New York, where it will connect with railroads now in progress,—one leading to Albany, another to Hudson, and a third to Troy. From Albany a railroad line to the westward is already completed as far as Utica, and its continuation is projected through the State of New York to Buffalo, thence through the northern part of Pennsylvania, Ohio, and Indiana, across Illinois, to the Mississippi." Such a scheme speaks well for the day of small things.

As late as 1840 Boston was also the best balanced commercial city in America. When the Cunard line was established in that year, it naturally fixed its terminus in Boston. "The reasons for this choice were,—nearness to and convenience of access from the lower British Provinces and Lower Canada; a shorter distance from Europe; and superiority of harbor and wharf accommodations. The railway system of New England, also, although in its infancy, had already attracted attention in Europe. . . . . The establishment of a regular line of first-class steamships between Liverpool and Boston hastened the construction and extension of the railroads which had been commenced, and led to the projection of others. As a consequence Boston was for a few years possessed of a combination of railway and steamship facilities such as no other city on the seaboard could boast of. During this period, New York, although larger in wealth and in population, was to a consideration degree dependent upon Boston for its communication with the Old World." This state of affairs lasted until 1848. Before that year the great Boston houses had begun to establish selling agencies in New York. The Skinners went there in 1846, the Lawrences in 1851, and other houses of necessity followed. Then came the California trade, which gave such an immense commercial impetus to New York, and from that epoch the fate of Boston seemed sealed. It was not that her growth was to stop. She was to grow and will grow yet more,—grow, in all probability, quite as fast as growth is healthy,—but the nature of that growth was to change. It was not to be of varied nature and of well-balanced elements; the merchant and the manufacturer were no longer to move forward with equal steps; henceforth the city was to be more and more lop-sided; she was to become, in comparison with great, commercial, cosmopolitan New York, what Manchester was to London, or Lowell to herself. Her own children seemed to have lost their enterprise and their system, or rather to have transferred those qualities with grand results to other fields. They seemed to unite their energies to diminish her resources, or to cripple her strength. They built great railroads throughout the West, and managed them with incomparable skill, but those roads did not lead to Boston. They hurried their great selling agencies in hotter and hotter competition to New York, until the firm names alone remained in Boston, and seven eighths of their business was done by the branch houses; the steamships followed the business, and the shipping followed the steamships, and the wharves would have followed both, had they not, fortunately for Boston, been firmly planted in the rapidly rising mud of the harbor.

Still one channel of reviving prosperity was open to the city. The railroad system, once the most promising in the country, remained to it; Boston might yet be convenient and accessible, a ready place of import and export; and then general trade could hardly fail, some day, to revisit it. This, the one chance of salvation, was the chance most neglected of all. While New York was building railroad upon railroad, enlarging canals, ever opening fresh channels through which the wealth of the newly-developed West could be poured into her lap, Boston, with a lack of perception, a want of foresight, an absence of enterprise, and a superabundance of timidity, in sad contrast with great promise of an earlier and brighter day, was satisfied with that single line of railroad track directly connecting her with the overflowing West, which she had with an enterprise of a wholly different character boldly constructed in 1837. The result need not be dwelt upon. Boston proved herself not worthy of success in the race, and she lost the prize. She did all she could to limit the field of her enterprise,—to encourage her customers to go elsewhere,—to prevent them from coming to her. Success in such efforts is not difficult to attain. That she has grown and prospered is evident; so have Lowell and Providence, and probably Newport and Salem. So also have New York and Chicago. Here are two kinds of growth. One commercial, well-balanced and cosmopolitan, the other manufacturing, unequal, and provincial. Boston has increased and flourished, but its increase has been provincial. It is now the first, or perhaps second, city of the Lowell and Providence type in America, while thirty years ago, with less wealth and fewer inhabitants, what growth it had was the cosmopolitan growth of New York and London. So much for Boston thirty years since and now.

Meanwhile how has it fared with Chicago? Thirty years ago the Indians had just been carted away across the muddy prairie, and Chicago was a Western city of four thousand inhabitants. They were a sort of amphibious creatures, living in their prairie swamp on the shores of Lake Michigan, now wallowing in mud and now smothering in dust; without a railroad, without any particular trade, accumulating large imaginary fortunes by successful operations in corner lots, and suffering from attacks of chills and fever. It was a city of the Cairo or Eden style. But in the year 1837 corner lots were down; Chicago was dead, perhaps the deadest place in the whole broad land. The Chicagonese did not fail at the rate of one a day during those depressing six months, as did the business firms of Boston, because they all failed at once, and had it over. They did not sacrifice corner lots at a ruinous loss, simply because no one could be induced to buy them at any price. The city was bankrupt; the State was bankrupt; work on the canals and railroads was suspended, and corner lots were valueless. Such in 1837 was the condition of the Queen of the West. At length the dawn of revival broke upon this dark night of depression. In 1838 the Chicago wheat trade began with a well-known transaction covering thirty-nine double bushels. In 1839 her cattle trade amounted to three thousand creatures; in 1840 the city had revived enough to finish the canal which connects the Chicago River with the Illinois, and which had been begun in 1836. In 1850 the city had a population of thirty thousand inhabitants, and at last was the fortunate centre of a railroad system comprising forty-two miles, all in successful operation. In 1853 came the crisis of her fate. In that year the Chicago and Galena Railroad, then open to Elgin, paid a dividend of eleven per cent, and "the truth took possession of the whole mind of Chicago, and became its fixed idea, that every acre with which it could put itself in easy communication must pay tribute to it forever. From that time there has been no pause and no hesitation; but all the surplus force and revenue of Chicago have been expended in making itself the centre of a great system of railroads and canals. . . . . The railroad system of which Chicago is a centre now includes eight thousand miles of track, and the railroad system of which Chicago is *the* centre embraces nearly five thousand miles of track."

Here then are two material records leading to two results. How different those results are any man can see who will glance over the columns of the daily press of the two cities, and observe the exultant tone of the one and the deprecatory tone of the other. The mystery of the difference is not difficult of solution. The one city has been in close sympathy with the material development of the age, the other has not. Both were surrounded by eager rivals; but while the one realized the value of the prize contended for, the other reposed, though not in content, on the laurels of earlier days. The material destiny of Chicago is now fixed. "Her vocation is to put every good acre in all that region within ten miles of a railroad, and to connect every railroad with a system of ship-canals terminating in the Mississippi and the Atlantic Ocean. That is, has been, and will be for many a year to come Chicago's work." Thus the young city of the West has instinctively appreciated the position and necessity of the country and the age; she has flung herself, heart, soul, and body, into the movement of her time; she has realized the great fact that steam has revolutionized the world, and she has bound her whole existence up in the great power of modern times. But for this, St. Louis might well have proved to her what New York has proved to Boston.

Not so Boston. That city, in spite of her wealth and prestige, her intrinsic worth and deserved reputation, her superficial conceit and real cultivation, failed to solve the enigma,—did not rise to the height of the great argument. The new era found her wedded to the old, and her eyes, dimmed with experiences of the past, could not credit the brilliant visions of the future. She promised well, but her career failed to come up to her promise. Her commerce has not increased. She no longer sends out her ships to every quarter of the globe. The warerooms of her manufacturers do not swarm with buyers from every part of the land. She has not opened new channels of intercourse with the West. She is not better known. She does not bear that proportional influence with the country now that she did then. She has lost much of her influence and all of her prestige. That steam intercourse with Europe which was planted with her twenty-five years ago has by no means flourished and waxed strong. Time now more than ever before is money, and Boston is still and must ever remain twenty-four hours nearer to Liverpool than is New York. A passage already quoted has shown how and why New York was through years to a degree dependent on Boston for her communications with Europe. Yet not ten, nor six, nor four steam packets for the Old World leave her docks now for one which did so twenty years ago. It is very well to explain this by vague reference to the operations of natural laws, and the principles of demand and supply. Do not those laws and those principles apply as well to Liverpool as to Boston? Boston once had a hold—not so strong a hold, but still a hold—on the Liverpool trade, as Liverpool had on the American trade. The principles of trade and the operation of general laws have not drawn Liverpool to London, as they have drawn Boston to New York. The reason is obvious. Liverpool has remained convenient and accessible, and Boston has not. The American trade with Great Britain is more than one third of the whole foreign trade of this country, and Boston seems likely soon to lose the remnant of it which she still retains. Not so Liverpool. Her steam navigation with America has not passed to London. In the month of March, 1867, she cleared thirty-one steamers for America; and often on a single day fifteen ocean steamers will clear from New York, while Boston, until the present year, has still continued to receive and send out, as in 1847, her two Cunarders a month.

Sadly as Boston has failed in rising to an equality with the occasion, much as her sagacity has been at fault, little as she has appreciated her own situation amid the material movements of the day, she has not seen herself distanced in the race without abundance of lamentation. The whole country has witnessed her frantic efforts to recover lost ground,—the superabundance of infallible remedies suggested as cures for her troubles,—the spasmodic efforts with which she has partially followed out these abortive schemes. Most citizens of Boston can run over in memory since 1848 a long list of futile enterprises, the projectors of which promised from them wealth to themselves and a renewed commercial eminence to their city. The Western men, and the seductions necessary to be held out to induce them to flock to Boston rather than to gay New York, have for years been the favorite theme of the city press, and furnished strong argument for endless subscription lists. In 1852 the Western purchaser must have a theatre to beguile away his evenings, or he would not come to Boston. Forthwith an enormous barn was built, which Boston fills a dozen times a year, and ruins endless managers in doing it. Then, the theatre having failed to beguile the Western man from his New York haunts, trade-sales were hit upon. The denizen of the prairie could not resist the temptation of great auctions. This lasted a year or two, and then was heard of no more. Then came up the Southern man in place of the Western man, and lines of steamers were established to run to Richmond, to Charleston, to Savannah, to New Orleans, and every other Southern port,—with what success the stockholders probably remember. Then a Grand Junction Railway was built to accommodate an export trade which could not exist, and it rotted away in hopeless bankruptcy. Then public meetings were held, and the principles of freedom abjured by venal orators in the vain desire to propitiate the cotton-lord. Then came the confused jumble of railroad schemes and oceanic steamer schemes and mammoth hotel schemes and harbor schemes, and even schemes to relax morals and the prohibitory liquor law in favor of that Western purchaser so earnestly longed for and so rarely seen. The simple fact being that Boston for years has not shown, nor does she now seem likely to show, in her commercial relations, either wisdom or instinct, either quickness or perseverance; her policy has been all flounder and spasm.

NOTES

1. Clearances. 1836: 1,358; tons, 204,334. 1855: 2,944; tons, 687,825. 1862–63 (average), 3,110; tons, 623,411. Entrances. 1836: 1,381; tons, 224,684. 1855: 3,144; tons, 707,924. 1862–63 average), 3120; tons, 662,008.

2. During 1862–63 Boston averaged each year 3,110 foreign clearances, aggregating 623,411 tons; of these, 2,256, aggregating 320,921 tons,—that is, more than half of all the clearances from Boston, measured by tonnage,—cleared for the British Provinces; and during the same period, of a yearly average of 3,120 entrances, aggregating 662,008 tons, 2,162, or 281,074 tons, were from the same quarter. The trade of Boston beyond the seas during the same period averaged yearly 400 each of entrances and clearances, aggregating 240,000 tons,—a decrease, estimated in tonnage, of forty per cent from the return of 1856.

3. For ports beyond the seas, New York in 1862–63 cleared yearly 2,601 sail, aggregating 1,858,939 tons, and entered yearly from the same 2,548 sail, aggregating 1,939,212 tons, against 388 clearances from Boston, aggregating 207,585 tons, and 469 entrances, aggregating 280,673 tons.

4. In 1862–63 Boston cleared for the British Isles on a yearly average 76 sail, aggregating 89,631 tons, and entered from them 100 sail, aggregating 151,071. New York cleared 1,327 sail, aggregating 1,202,957 tons, and entered 1,115, aggregating 1,118,205 tons.

5. The foreign commerce of Massachusetts, almost wholly through Boston, at the periods referred to, was as follows:—Imports, 1836, $25,681,462; $45,113,774; 1862–63 (average), $29,545,041; 1864–1966 (average at Boston only), $36,676,214. The exports were, 1836, $5,267,160; 1855, $28,190,925; 1862–63 (average), $19,653,267; 1864–1866, (average at Boston only) $19,417,856. Of New York, and almost wholly through the port of New York, the imports were,—1836, $118,253,416; 1855, $164,-776,511; 1862–63 (average), $223,353,864; 1864–1866 (average at port of New York alone), $249,827,121. The exports were, 1836, $29,000,000; 1855, $113,731,238; 1862–63 (average), $238,375,185; 1864–1866 (average at New York only), $245,388,233.

JOSIAH STRONG

The city is the nerve center of our civilization. It is also the storm center. The fact, therefore, that it is growing much more rapidly than the whole population is full of significance. In 1790 one-thirtieth of the population of the United States lived in cities of 8,000 inhabitants and over; in 1800, one twenty-fifth; in 1810, and also in 1820, one-twentieth; in 1830, one-sixteenth; in 1840, one-twelfth; in 1850, one-eighth; in 1860, one-sixth; in 1870, a little over one-fifth; and in 1880, 22.5 per cent, or nearly one-fourth.[1] From 1790 to 1880 the whole population increased twelve fold, the urban population eighty-six fold. From 1830 to 1880 the whole population increased a little less than four fold, the urban population thirteen fold. From 1870 to 1880 the whole population increased thirty per cent, the urban population forty per cent.[2] During the half century preceding 1880, population in the city increased more than four times as rapidly as that of the village and country. In 1880 there were only six cities in the United States which had a population of 8,000 or more. In 1880 there were 286, and in 1890, 437.[3]

The city has become a serious menace to our civilization, because in it, excepting Mormonism, each of the dangers we have discussed is enhanced, and all are focalized. It has a peculiar attraction for the immigrant. Our fifty principal cities in 1880 contained 39.3 per cent of our entire German population, and 45.8 per cent of the Irish. Our ten larger cities at that time contained only nine per cent of the entire population, but 23 per cent of the foreign. While a little less than one-third of the population of the United States was foreign by birth or parentage, sixty-two per cent of the population of Cincinnati was foreign, eighty-three per cent of Cleveland, sixty-three per cent of Boston,[4] eighty per cent of New York, and ninety-one per cent of Chicago.[5] A census of Massachusetts, taken in 1885, showed that in 65 towns and cities of the state 65.1 per cent of the population was foreign by birth or parentage.

Because our cities are so largely foreign, Romanism finds in them its chief strength.

For the same reason the saloon, together with the intemperance and the liquor power which it represents, is multiplied in the city. East of the

From Josiah Strong, *Our Country,* Revised Edition (New York: Baker & Taylor, 1891), Chapter 11.

Mississippi there was, in 1880, one saloon to every 438 of the population; in Boston, one to every 329; in Cleveland, one to every 192; in Chicago, one to every 179; in New York, one to every 171; in Cincinnati, one to every 124. Of course the demoralizing and pauperizing power of the saloons and their debauching influence in politics increase with their numerical strength.

It is the city where wealth is massed; and here are the tangible evidences of it piled many stories high. Here the sway of Mammon is widest, and his worship the most constant and eager. Here are luxuries gathered—everything that dazzles the eye, or tempts the appetite; here is the most extravagant expenditure. Here also, is the *congestion* of wealth the severest. Dives and Lazarus are brought face to face; here, in sharp contrast, are the *ennui* of surfeit and the desperation of starvation. The rich are richer, and the poor are poorer, in the city than elsewhere; and, as a rule, the greater the city, the greater are the riches of the rich and the poverty of the poor. Not only does the proportion of the poor increase with the growth of the city, but their condition becomes more wretched. The poor of a city of 8,000 inhabitants are well off compared with many in New York; and there are hardly such depths of woe, such utter and heart-wringing wretchedness in New York as in London. Read in "The Bitter Cry of Outcast London," a prophecy of what will some day be seen in American cities, provided existing tendencies continue: "Few who will read these pages have any conception of what these pestilential human rookeries are, where tens of thousands are crowded together amidst horrors which call to mind what we have heard of the middle passage of the slave-ship. To get into them you have to penetrate courts reeking with poisonous malodorous gases, arising from accumulations of sewage and refuse scattered in all directions, and often flowing beneath your feet; courts, many of them which the sun never penetrates, which are never visited by a breath of fresh air. You have to ascend rotten staircases, grope your way along dark and filthy passages swarming with vermin. Then, if you are not driven back by the intolerable stench, you may gain admittance to the dens in which these thousands of beings herd together. Eight feet square! That is about the average size of very many of these rooms. Walls and ceiling are black with the accretions of filth which have gathered upon them through long years of neglect. It is exuding through cracks in the boards; it is everywhere. . . . Every room in these rotten and reeking tenements houses a family, often two. In one cellar, a sanitary inspector reports finding a father, mother, three children, and four pigs. . . . Here are seven people living in one underground kitchen, and a little dead child lying in the same room. Elsewhere is a poor widow, her three children, and a child who had been dead thirteen days.[6] Her husband, who was a cabman, had shortly before committed suicide. . . . In another apartment, nine brothers and sisters, from twenty-nine years of age downward, live, eat, and sleep together. Here is a mother who turns her children into the street in the early evening, because she lets her room for immoral purposes until long after midnight, when the poor little wretches creep back again, if they have not found some miserable shelter elsewhere. Where there are beds, they are simply heaps of dirty rags, shavings, or straw; but for the most part these miserable beings find rest only upon the filthy boards. . . . There are men and women who lie and die, day by day, in their wretched single room, sharing all the family trouble, enduring the hunger and the cold, and waiting, without hope, without a single ray of comfort, until God curtains their staring eyes with the merciful film of death."[7] Says the writer: "So far from making the most of our facts for the purpose of appealing to emotion, we have been compelled to tone down everything, and wholly to omit what most needs to be known, or the ears and eyes of our readers would have been insufferably outraged. Indeed, no respectable printer would print, and certainly no decent family would admit, even the driest statement of the horrors and infamies discovered in one brief visitation from house to house." Such are the conditions under which many tens of thousands live in London. So much space is given to this picture, only because London is a future New York, or Brooklyn, or Chicago. It gives a very dim impression of what may exist in a great city side by side with enormous wealth. Is it strange that such conditions arouse a blind and bitter hatred of our social system?

Socialism centers in the city, and the materials of its growth are multiplied with the growth of the city. Here is heaped the social dynamite; here roughs, gamblers, thieves, robbers, lawless and desperate men of all sorts, congregate; men who are ready on any pretext to raise riots for the purpose of destruction and plunder; here gather foreigners and wage-workers who are especially susceptible to socialist arguments; here skepticism and irreligion abound; here inequality is the greatest and most obvious, and the contrast between opulence and penury the most striking; here is suffering the sorest. As the greatest wickedness in the world is to be found not among the cannibals of some far-off coast, but in Christian lands where the light of truth is diffused and rejected, so the utmost depth of wretchedness exists not among savages who have few wants, but in great cities, where, in the presence of plenty and of every luxury men starve. Let a man become the owner of a home, and he is much less susceptible to socialistic propagandism. But real estate is so high in the city that it is almost impossible for a wage-worker to become a householder. In 1888 the Health Department of New York made a census which revealed the fact that there were then in the city 32,390 tenement houses,[8] occupied by 237,972 families, and 1,093,701 souls. Investigation in 1890 showed that the tenement houses had increased in two years about 5,000. If there were an average of 33.76 to each house, as in 1888, the tenement house population in 1890 was nearly 1,260,000. The law in New York requires a juror to be owner of real or personal property valued at not less than two hundred and fifty dollars; and this, the Commissioner says, relieves seventy thousand of the registered votors of New York City from jury duty. Let us remember that those seventy thousand voters represent a population of two hundred and eighty thousand, or fifty-six thousand families, not one of which has property to the value of two hundred and fifty dollars. "During the past three years, 220,976 persons in New York have asked for outside aid in one form or another."[9] Said a New York Supreme Judge, a few years ago: "There is a large class—I was about to say a majority—of the population of New York and Brooklyn, who just live, and to whom the rearing of two or more children means inevitably a boy for the penetentiary, and a girl for the brothel."[10] "When an English Judge tells us, as Mr. Justice Wills did the other day, that there were any number of parents who would kill their children for a few pounds' insurance money, we can form some idea of the horrors of the existence into which many of the children of this highly favored land are ushered at their birth."[11] Under such conditions smolder the volcanic fires of a deep discontent. . . .

These dangerous elements are now working, and will continue to work, incalculable harm and loss—moral, intellectual, social, pecuniary. But the supreme peril, which will certainly come unless there is found for existing tendencies some effectual check, and must probably be faced by many now living, will arise, when, the conditions having been fully prepared, some great industrial or other crisis precipitates an open struggle between the destructive and the conservative elements of society. As civilization advances, and society becomes more highly organized, commercial transactions will be more complex and immense. As a result, all business relations and industries will be more sensitive. Commercial distress in any great business center will the more surely create wide-spread disaster. Under such conditions, industrial paralysis is likely to occur from time to time, more general and more prostrating than any heretofore known. When such a commercial crisis has closed factories by the ten thousand, and wage-workers have been thrown out of employment by the million; when the public lands, which hitherto at such times have afforded relief, are all exhausted; when our urban population has been multiplied several fold, and our Cincinnatis have become Chicagos, our Chicagos New Yorks, and our New Yorks Londons; when class antipathies are deepened; when socialistic organizations, armed and drilled, are in every city, and the ignorant and vicious power of crowded populations has fully found itself; when the corruption of city governments is grown apace; when crops fail, or some gigantic "corner" doubles the price of bread; with starvation in the home; with idle workmen gathered, sullen and desperate, in the saloons; with unprotected wealth at hand; with the tremendous forces of chemistry within easy reach; then with *the opportunity, the means, the fit agents, the motive, the temptation to destroy, all brought into evil conjunction,* THEN will come the real test of our institutions, then will appear whether we are capable of self-government.

NOTES

1. Compendium of the Tenth Census, Part 1, pp. xxx and 8. The Eleventh Census has not yet given us the urban population in 1890.
2. Mr. William S. Springer in *The Forum,* December 1890, estimates from reports and semi-official data that the increase of rural population from 1880 to 1890 was only eight per cent, while that of the urban population was more than 57 per cent.
3. The first official count. The final official count will doubtless make some change in this number.
4. The State Census, taken in 1885 showed 67 per cent.
5. "Foreign by birth or parentage" includes those, only one of whose parents was foreign. Their number is comparatively small and even less important than they might seem, because in a large proportion of instances the native parent was of foreign parentage.

The Tenth Census gives the number of persons, foreign-born, in each of the fifty principal cities, but does not give the native-born population of foreign parentage. We have, however, tolerable satisfactory data for computing it. The parentage of the populations of twenty-eight states, seven territories and the District of Columbia was tallied according to a highly complicated form in order to secure the desired ratios. On this basis the Census Office made an elaborate estimate of those who were foreign by birth or parentage in the whole country and placed the number at 24,995,943. The whole number of the foreign-born was ascertained to be 6,679,943. The former number contains the latter 2.238 times; that is, the foreign-born population multiplied by 2.238 gives the population foreign by birth or parentage. It should be observed, however, that this ratio varies in different states, due doubtless to the preponderance of different races in different sections of the country. For instance, in Massachusetts those of foreign parentage were in 1880 almost exactly twice as many as those of foreign birth. Accordingly for any city in that state we multiply the number of foreign-born by two, which gives the total of the foreign-born and the native-born of foreign parentage, provided the ratio beween the two is the same in the cities as in the whole state, which must be assumed as long as there is no evidence to the contrary. In Wisconsin, the Census showed that those of foreign parentage were 2.34 times the number of the foreign-born, while in Missouri the ratio was 2.63 to one.

Accordingly, in order to estimate the number of those foreign by birth or parentage in a given city in any one of the thirty-five states and territories in which the above tally was made, we multiply the number of the foreign born in that city by the number which the census showed to be the ratio between those of foreign parentage and those of foreign birth in the state in which the city is located. If the city is in a state in which the tally was not made, as for instance, Pennsylvania, Ohio or Illinois, the best we can do is to multiply by the number which is the average for the whole country, viz., 2.238.

We hear it objected that one does not see in our cities any such proportion of foreigners as is indicated by the above figures. It should be remembered that of the population foreign by birth or parentage, five-ninths were born in the United States; and at least one quarter of the foreign-born came to this country in childhood, so that six-ninths or two-thirds of this population though it remains largely foreign in ideas, becomes thoroughly Americanized in speech and appearance.

Accordingly if twenty-one per cent of the population of Boston *appear* foreign, we must not be surprised to learn that sixty-three per cent are foreign by birth or parentage.

6. The investigations here reported were made in the *summer*.

7. The Bitter Cry of Outcast London, pp. 3, 4, 10.

8. In New York under the law of 1887, a tenement house is one occupied by three or more families, living separately. The above census did not include the better class of apartment houses.

9. Mrs. J. S. Lowell, in *The Christian Union,* March 26, 1885.

10. Henry George's Social Problems, p. 98.

11. In Darkest England, p. 65.

1.5 THE TENEMENTS
OF NINETEENTH-CENTURY NEW YORK

JACOB RIIS

The Battle with the Slum: What the Fight Is About

The slum is as old as civilization. Civilization implies a race to get ahead. In a race there are usually some who for one cause or another cannot keep up, or are thurst out from among their fellows. They fall behind, and when they have been left far in the rear they lose hope and ambition, and give up. Thenceforward, if left to their own resources, they are the victims, not the masters, of their environment; and it is a bad master. They drag one another always farther down. The bad environment becomes the heredity of the next generation. Then, given the crowd, you have the slum ready-made. . . .

Put it this way: you cannot let men live like pigs when you need their votes as freemen; it is not safe. You cannot rob a child of its childhood, of its home, its play, its freedom from toil and care, and expect to appeal to the grown-up voter's manhood. The children are our to-morrow, and as we mould them to-day so will they deal with us then. Therefore that is not safe. Unsafest of all is any thing or deed that strikes at the home, for from the people's home proceeds citizen virtue, and nowhere else does it live. The slum is the enemy of the home. Because of it the chief city of our land came long ago to be called "The Homeless City." When this people comes to be truly called a nation without homes there will no longer be any nation. . . .

The Children of the Poor

Who and where are the slum children of New York to-day? That depends on what is understood by the term. The moralist might seek them in Hell's Kitchen, in Battle Row, and in the tenements, east and west, where the descendants of the poorest Irish immigrants live. They are the ones, as I have before tried to show, upon whom the tenement and the saloon set their stamp soonest and deepest. . . .

The first excerpt on this page is taken from Riis' *The Battle with the Slum,* New York, The Macmillan Company, 1902. Selections following are from Riis' *The Children of the Poor,* New York, Charles Scribner's Sons, 1892.

The worst old rookeries fall everywhere in this city to the share of the immigrants from Southern Italy, who are content to occupy them, partly, perhaps, because they are no worse than the hovels they left behind, but mainly because they are tricked or bullied into putting up with them by their smarter countrymen who turn their helplessness and ignorance to good account. Wherever the invasion of some old home section by the tide of business has left ramshackle tenements falling into hopeless decay, as in the old "Africa," in the Bend, and in many other places in the down-town wards, the Italian sweater landlord is ready with his offer of a lease to bridge over the interregnum, a lease that takes no account of repairs or of the improvements the owner sought to avoid. The crowds to make it profitable to him are never wanting. The bait he holds out is a job at the ash-dump with which he connects at the other end of the line. The house, the job, and the man as he comes to them fit in well together, and the copartnership has given the Italian a character which, I am satisfied from close observation of him, he does not wholly deserve. . . .

I have in mind one Italian "flat" among many, a half underground hole in a South Fifth Avenue yard, reached by odd passage-ways through a tumbledown tenement that was always full of bad smells and scooting rats. Across the foul and slippery yard, down three steps made of charred timbers from some worse wreck, was this "flat," where five children slept with their elders. How many of those there were I never knew. There were three big family beds, and they nearly filled the room, leaving only patches of the mud floor visible. The walls were absolutely black with age and smoke. The plaster had fallen off in patches and there was green mould on the ceiling. And yet, with it all, with the swarm of squirming youngsters that were as black as the floor they rolled upon, there was evidence of a desperate, if hopeless, groping after order, even neatness. The beds were made up as nicely as they could be with the old quilts and pieces of carpet that served for covering. In Poverty Gap, where an Italian would be stoned as likely as not, there would have been a heap of dirty straw instead of beds, and the artistic arrangement of tallow-dips stuck in the necks of bottles about the newspaper cut of a saint on the corner shelf would have been missing altogether, fervent though the personal regard might be of Poverty Gap for the saint. The bottles would have been the only part of the exhibition sure to be seen there. . . .

The cleaning out of a Mulberry Street block left one lop-sided old rear tenement that had long since been shut in on three sides by buildings four stories higher than itself, and forgotten by all the world save the miserable wretches who burrowed in that dark and dismal pit at the bottom of a narrow alley. Now, when the fourth structure goes up against its very windows, it will stand there in the heart of the block, a survival of the unfittest, that, in all its disheartening dreariness, bears testimony, nevertheless, to the beneficent activity of the best Board of Health New York has ever had—the onward sweep of business. It will wipe that last remnant out also, even if the law lack the power to reach it.

Shoals of Italian children lived in that rookery, and in those the workmen tore down, in the actual physical atmosphere of the dump. Not a gunshot away there is a block of tenements, known as the Mott Street Barracks, in which still greater shoals are—I was going to say housed, but that would have been a mistake. Happily they are that very rarely, except when they are asleep, and not then if they can help it. Out on the street they may be found tumbling in the dirt, or up on the roof lying stark-naked, blinking in the sun—content with life as they find it. If they are not a very cleanly crew, they are at least as clean as the frame they are set in, though it must be allowed that something has been done of late years to redeem the buildings from the reproach of a bad past. The combination of a Jew for a landlord and a saloon-keeper—Italian, of course—for a lessee, was not propitious; but the buildings happen to be directly under the windows of the Health Board, and something, I suppose, was due to appearances. The authorities did all that could be done, short of tearing down the tenement, but though comparatively clean, and not nearly as crowded as it was, it is still the old slum. It is an instructive instance of what can and cannot be done with the tenements into which we invite these dirty strangers to teach them American ways and the self-respect of future citizens and voters. There are five buildings—that is, five front and four rear houses, the latter a story higher than those on the street; that is because the rear houses were built last, to "accommodate" this very Italian immigration that could be made to pay for anything. Chiefly Irish had lived there before, but they moved out then. There were 360 tenants in the Barracks when the police census was taken in 1888, and 40 of them were babies. How many were romping children I do not know. The "yard" they had to play in is just 5 feet 10 inches wide, and a dozen steps below the street level. The closets of all the buildings are in the cellar of the rear houses and open upon this "yard," where it is always dark and damp as in a dungeon. Its foul stenches reach even the top floor, but so also does the sun at mid-day, and that is a luxury that counts as an extra in the contract with the landlord. The rent is nearly one-half higher near the top than it is on the street-level. Nine dollars above, six and a half below, for one room with windows, two without, and with barely space for a bed in each. But water-pipes have been put in lately, under orders from the Health Department, and the rents have doubtless been raised. "No windows" means no ventilation. The rear building backs up against the tenement on the next street; a space a foot wide separates them, but an attempt to ventilate the bed-rooms by windows on that was a failure.

1.6 EFFECTS OF INDUSTRIALISM
IN ''YANKEE CITY''

W. LLOYD WARNER

Introduction

During the field research a great strike broke out. All the workers in the shoe factories quit their jobs, joined a union, and through union intervention defeated management. To find out the meaning and significance of what happened in this crisis, we studied the structure of the factories and corporate enterprise. Research was done on the history of the city's economic life from the early 1600's until the strike. Special attention was given to the development of the great shoe corporations and the loss of local control to the big cities. The breakdown of the skill hierarchy and the effect of this on the workers and the city became apparent. The movement of the city's separate life into the larger American society and the loss of part of its autonomy are reported in the next several chapters. The emergence of what appears to be the great society which includes all of America is indicated.

The Industrial History of Yankee City

When we explore the social and industrial history of Yankee City, moving back through the years marked by the beginning of industrial capitalism and through the brilliant years of the clipper ship era to the simple folk economy of the earliest community—noticing how an earlier phase of the constantly changing society limits and molds the succeeding ones—it becomes certain that some of the knowledge necessary for explaining the strike can be, and must be, obtained by this scientific process. Furthermore, we see very clearly the times when certain necessary factors which explain the strike appear in the life of the town and how, in conjunction with other causes, their gradual evolution made the strike inevitable. It also becomes abundantly clear that the Yankee City strike was not a unique event but must be treated as representative of a type and that this type is almost certainly worldwide in its importance and significance. . . .

From a simple and undifferentiated society, there developed in Yankee City the type of economic life with which standard histories of New England

From W. Lloyd Warner, *Yankee City* (New Haven, Conn.: Yale University Press, 1963). Copyright © 1963 by Yale University. Reprinted by permission.

have made us familiar. During the era of shipbuilding, shipping, and fishing, a great number of handicrafts also developed. These included such primary industries as wood-carving, cordage-making, carpentering, blacksmithing, and sail-making. During the winter months the fishermen of Yankee City, as of other New England towns, made shoes. The women manufactured wool and cotton garments within the household. During the nineteenth century, numerous other independent crafts appeared, such as silversmithing, comb-making, leather-tanning, and carriage-building. The most important industry in view of its later development, however, was the manufacture of shoes.

Apprenticeship functioned in the handicraft system of the eighteenth and most of the nineteenth centuries as our trade, engineering, art, and professional schools do in our industrial system today. It was society's educational device for transforming its youth from the "green," unproductive stage to the stage of full economic maturity as master craftsmen. . . .

The Strike and the Evolving Social and Economic Systems

Before we ask ourselves what this economic history has told us about the causes of the strike, let us re-assess our findings. We have spoken of an economic history. However, we do not have one history but several—at least six histories can be traced. We can conveniently divide the technological history of Yankee City's shoe industry into five phases (see Fig. 1.6A). At least two important stories are to be found here; the tools change from a few basic ones entirely hand-used to machines in an assembly line, and the product from a single pair of shoes to tens of thousands in mass production.

The changes in the form of division of labor are another story of the utmost importance. (The sequences in the vertical columns of Fig. 1.6A are exactly ordered; the horizontal interrelations are approximations and indicate basic trends.) In the beginning, the family made its own shoes, or a high-skilled artisan, the cobbler, made shoes for the family. In time, several families divided the high-skilled jobs among themselves, and later one man assigned the skilled jobs to a few men and their families. Ultimately, a central factory developed and the jobs were divided into a large number of systematized low-skilled jobs. The history of ownership and control is correlated with the changes in the division of labor. In early days, tools, skills, and materials were possessed by the family; eventually, the materials were supplied by the owner-manager, and soon he also owned the tools and machines. The sequence of development of producer-consumer relations tell a similar story. The family produced and consumed its shoes all within the circle of its simple unit. Then, the local community was the consumer-producer unit, and ultimately the market became national and even worldwide. Worker relations changed from those of kinship and family ties to those of occupation where apprenticeship and craftsmanship relations were superseded and the individual unit became dominant in organizing the affairs of the workers. The structure of economic relations changed from the immediate family into a local hierarchy and the locally owned factory into a vast, complex system owned, managed, and dominated by New York City.

With these several histories in mind (and with the help of Fig. 1.6A),

FIGURE 1.6A. The History of the Differentiation of the Yankee City Shoe Industry

	Technology	Form of Division of Labor	Form of Ownership and Control	Producer–Consumer Relations	Worker Relations	Structure of Economic Relations
IV **The Present** **(1920–1945)**	*Machine tools:* mass production, assembly line methods	Nearly all jobs low skilled; a very large number of routinized jobs	*Outside* ownership and control of the factory (tools leased)	Very few retail outlets; factory merely one source of supply for a chain of shoe stores	Rise of industrial unions, state supervised. No (or weak) unions	Center of dominance New York. Very complex financial, producer, and retail structure. Local factory not important in it
III **Late Intermediate Period (approximately to World War I)**	*Machine tools:* machines predominate; beginning of mass production through use of the machine (McKay)	A central factory with machines; still high degree of skill in many jobs	First small and later large *local* men of wealth own or lease the tools and machines	National market and local capitalist; many outlets	Craft and apprenticeship (St. Crispin's Union)	Center of dominance local factory; complex hierarchy in local factory system
II **Early Intermediate Period (approximately to the Civil War)**	*Machine tools:* few machines, first application (Elias Howe, etc.)	One man assigns highly skilled jobs to few men; highly skilled craftsmen ("letting-out" system)	Small, locally controlled manufacturers; tools still owned by workers, materials and market controlled by "owner"	Owner and salesmen to the consumer regional market	Informal, apprenticeship and craft relations	Simple economic, no longer kinship; worker subordinate to manager
	Hand tools: increasing specialization and accumulation of hand tools	Specialization among several families; a few highly skilled jobs	*Local control:* not all shoemakers need own all tools; beginning of specialization	Local buyer from several producer families sells products (no central factory)	Kinship and neighbors among workers	Semi-economic but also kinship and neighborliness
I **The Beginning (early 1600's)**	*Hand tools:* few, basic, and simple	All productive skills in the family, including making of shoes; a few cobblers for the local market	*Local control:* skills, tools, and materials owned and controlled by each family; or by the local cobbler	The family produces and consumes shoes and most other products	Largely kinship and family relations among workers	Very simple non-economic; the immediate family

let us ask ourselves what would have happened if the strike had taken place in each of the several periods. In period one, with a family-producing and consuming economy, it is obvious that such a conflict would have been impossible. The social system had not evolved to sufficient complexity; the forces had not been born which were to oppose each other in civil strife. In the second phase, several families in a neighborhood might have quarreled, but it is only in one's imagination that one could conceive of civil strife among the shoemakers.

In the third phase, however, there appears a new social personality, and an older one begins to take on a new form and assume a new place in the community. The capitalist is born and during the several periods which follow he develops into full maturity. Meanwhile the worker loses control and management of his time and skills and becomes subordinate in a hierarchy. There are, thus, distinct and opposing forces set up in the shoemaking system. What is good for one is not necessarily good for the other, but the interdependence of the two opposing groups is still very intimate, powerful, and highly necessary. The tools, the skills, and the places of manufacture belong to the worker; but the materials, the place of assembly, and the market are now possessed by the manager. Striking is possible but extremely difficult and unlikely.

In the fourth period, full capitalism has been achieved; the manufacturer is now the owner of the tools, the machines, and the industrial plant; he controls the market. The workers have become sufficiently self-conscious and antagonistic to machines to organize into craft unions. Industrial warfare still might prove difficult to start, although it did occur, because in a small city where most people know each other the owner or manager more often than not knows "his help" and they know him. The close relation between the two often implies greater compatibility and understanding, which cut down the likelihood of conflict. But when strikes do occur the resulting civil strife is likely to be bitter because it is in the confines of the community.

In the last period, the capitalist has become the supercapitalist; the workers have forgotten their pride in their separate jobs, dismissed the small differences among themselves, and united in one industrial union with tens and hundreds of thousands of workers throughout the country combining their strength to assert their interests against management. In such a social setting strikes are inevitable. . . .

The Strike and the Break in the Skill Hierarchy

We believe that the break in the skill hierarchy contributed importantly to the outbreak of the strike, to the course it took, and, in particular, to the coming of the union. The hierarchy of crafts which once organized the relations of the workers and provided a way of life for the shoe workers was really an age-grade system. Youngsters served their hard apprenticeship and, as neophytes, learned their task; even more importantly, they were taught to respect the skills they had learned and those they looked forward to learning. Above all, they acquired respect and admiration for the older men above them who had acquired the skills and who occupied the proud positions of journeymen and master craftsmen. These youngsters aspired to achieve for themselves a similar high position and respect. Each young man, in direct face-to-face interaction with those above him, imitated and learned a way of life while being highly motivated by the strong desire to escape the irksome limitations of his present low position and to attain the higher place where he would have the satisfaction of making his own decisions and possess the prestige and pay consequent to such great eminence. By the time he had learned how to do the things needed to equip himself for advancement, enough time had passed to mature him sufficiently to act the part of a man. There can be little doubt that age factors as well as those of skill determined the time for advancement.

During this preliminary period he learned that he was a craftsman, with a particular place in the whole system, and that there were responsibilities and obligations he had to learn which would give him certain rights and privileges. Thus, while he internalized this behavior and all its values and their many subtleties and learned what he was as a man, he became an inextricable member of the honorable fraternity of those who made, and who knew how to make, shoes. In this system, workers and managers were indissolubly interwoven into a common enterprise, with a common set of values. In this system the internal personal structure of workers and managers was made up of very much the same apparatus, and their personalities were reinforced by the social system of shoemaking.

In learning to respect the skill of the master craftsman, the apprentice learned to respect himself. He had security in his job, but he had even greater personal security because he had learned how to respect his job. And because he was a member of an age-graded male fraternity made up of other men like himself who had the knowledge and necessary skills to make shoes, he possessed that feeling of absolute freedom and independence and of being autonomous that comes from being in a discipline. He spent his life acquiring virtue, prestige, and respect, learning as he aged and climbed upward, and at the same time teaching those who were younger than he and who aspired to be like him.

Slowly this way of life degenerated and the machine took the virtue and respect from the worker, at the same time breaking the skill hierarchy which dominated his occupation. There was no longer a period for young men to learn to respect those in the age grade above them and in so doing to become self-respecting workers. The "ladder to the stars" was gone and with it much of the structure of the "American Dream."

When the age-grade structure which organized the male aborigines of Melanesia and North America into a hierarchy of prestige and achievement was broken under the impact of white civilization in many of these societies, the frustrations suffered by those who had once known respect for themselves and others crystallized into aggressive movements or into attempts to abolish the new ways and to retreat into the old and cherished ways of the past. There are many resemblances between what happened to these simple, non-European societies and what happened to the craft hierarchy of Yankee City.

The parallel between Yankee City's age-grade structure and theirs cannot be pushed too far, but certainly the two share obvious characteristics.

In the earlier days of the machine, the Knights of St. Crispin was organized and attempted to stop the further introduction of machinery. Most of the members longed for the good old days when there were no machines—when a trained hand and eye did the whole job. These attempts failed and the organization collapsed because it was not adaptive and could not stop the inevitable advance of industrial technology.

When the whole age-grade structure of craftsmanship had almost entirely collapsed and the American shoe worker was thereby denied his share of the American Dream, he and his kind were ready for any mass movement which would strike at those they charged, in their own minds, with the responsibility for their present unhappy condition. Much of this behavior was not conscious. Much of it was feeling rather than thought, as indeed it had been in the mass movements of the aboriginal Melanesians and North American Indians. It seems certain, however, that American workers, taught from childhood that those who apply themselves to their craft and practice the ethics of the middle class would be rewarded by achievement and success, would rebel and strike back out of sheer frustration when they found out that the American Dream no longer was attainable for them and that the hard facts belied the beautiful words they had been taught. It seems even more likely that the effects of the break in the skill hierarchy were potent forces which contributed their full share to the workers' striking and the union's becoming their champion.

1.7 "YANKEE CITY" REVISITED:
THE PERILS OF HISTORICAL NAÏVETÉ

STEPHEN THERNSTROM

It is easy enough to nod agreement at E. H. Carr's remark that "the more sociological history becomes, and the more historical sociology becomes, the better for both."[1] But in truth, unhappily, the mutually-enriching dialogue between history and sociology that Carr calls for has barely begun; so far, communication between the two disciplines has largely been in the form of a monologue, with history on the receiving end. Sociologists and social anthropologists have been eager to suggest how their brethren in the most traditional and least theoretical of the social sciences might broaden their horizons and deepen their insights into man's behavior in the past. It is clear, from a number of recent books and articles, that this advice has not gone entirely unheard.[2] What seems to have been neglected, however, is that if historians have much to learn from their colleagues in sociology, the converse of this proposition is also true. Carr's remark cuts both ways. Sociological work based on erroneous historical assumptions can be as superficial as sociologically primitive history, and it is no less common.[3] Close scrutiny of an influential specimen of contemporary social research which is particularly vulnerable to this charge may help to clarify why an accurate sense of historical perspective is indispensable to students of modern society.

One of the richest and most inviting sources of knowledge about modern American life is the *genre* that includes such books as *Black Metropolis, Caste and Class in a Southern Town, Streetcorner Society, Elmtown's Youth,* and *Middletown.* Maurice Stein has recently urged the relevance of these works to the student of 20th-century America in his stimulating study, *The Eclipse of Community: An Interpretation of American Studies.*[4] Stein, himself a sociologist, is surely correct in urging that the community studies conducted by American sociologists and anthropologists in the past 50 years are an exceptionally rich source of knowledge about the history of American civilization. But these works must be approached with a large measure of caution and critical reserve, for too many of them have been built upon shaky historical foundations. In particular, W. Lloyd Warner's famous

From Stephen Thernstrom, " 'Yankee City' Revisited: The Perils of Historical Naïveté," *American Sociological Review,* Vol. 30 (April 1965), pp. 234–242. Reprinted by permission of the author and the American Sociological Association.

"Yankee City" series well illustrates the distortions that historical ignorance and naïveté can produce.

The "Yankee City" series, five bulky volumes reporting on field research conducted in "an old New England community" in the 1930's, made W. Lloyd Warner the most influential American student of social stratification.[5] The first Yankee City publication, *The Social Life of a Modern Community* (1941), was widely praised, and the subsequent volumes and a host of other books by Warner and his students served to establish members of "the Warner school" as leading interpreters of American community life. In recent years, it is true, the techniques of social analysis pioneered in the Yankee City study have been severely criticised, but the abundant literature on the Warner school does not include a detailed analysis of the mistaken historical assumptions out of which so many of Warner's errors grew.[6] Future investigators of social stratification in American communities will no doubt avoid the methodological blunders tellingly exposed by Mills, Lipset and Bendix, Pfautz and Duncan, and other sociological critics; that glaring misinterpretations and distortions can stem from failure to utilize relevant historical data is less widely understood.

What follows is in no sense a full and balanced appraisal of the five Yankee City volumes or of Lloyd Warner's contributions to an understanding of American society. Such an appraisal would pay Warner the tribute he deserves as a pioneer in his field—for having gathered a wealth of interesting material about a subject that had been too little studied, and for having inspired an enormous amount of further research and controversy. It would applaud certain fruitful insights and note that Warner had the gift for social portraiture of a lesser social novelist; portions of the Yankee City volumes display some of the virtues of the novels of John P. Marquand, a writer who dealt with the same New England community. Such an assessment would be more appreciative, in short, and perhaps it is overdue. That, however, is a different task than the one undertaken here, and a larger one. These critical observations focus on what Warner failed to see about the community he studied so intensively in the 1930's and particularly on what he failed to see because of his misconceptions about the community's history.

That community was Newburyport, Mass., a city whose social and economic history I have been studying for the past five years. Like many another sociological field worker, Warner made evaluation and criticism of his work more difficult by obscuring the identity of the community studied with a pseudonym. The usual justification for this step is that it protects the identity of local informants. Whatever the merits of this argument, it seems clear that a latent function of this device is to lend an aura of typicality to the community in question: "Yankee City" is manifestly a place of more universal significance than Newburyport, Mass., "Jonesville" is more truly American than Morris, Ill. To say this is not to endorse the familiar criticism that cities like Newburyport were "unrepresentative" of the larger society. With respect to the problems that interested Warner, Newburyport was much more "representative" than his critics have allowed—though it is admittedly difficult to discern this from Warner's distorted and idealized description of the city.[7] The point is rather that Warner *assumed* Newburyport's representativeness without any critical examination of the issue, and that he made it difficult for others to think critically about the question by disguising the identity of the community.

The Uses of the Past

The Yankee City project was carried out on a scale that can only be described as prodigious. It still ranks as the most intensive, exhaustive, and expensive survey ever made of a small American city. The five published volumes occupy more than 1700 pages, with 208 tables, charts, and maps. The field work extended over a period of several years, and required the labor of some 30 research assistants. The amount of data collected was staggering. Warner at one point refers to "the millions of social facts" recorded; the study is replete with comments like this: "All of the types of social structures and each of the thousands of families, thousands of cliques, and hundreds of associations were, member by member, interrelated in our research." "Social personality cards" were compiled for all 17,000 members of the community, and interviews with local citizens occupied thousands of hours. Aerial photographs were made of Newburyport and environs; detailed questionnaires were administered at gas stations and lunch stands along the highway to discover what transients had stopped in the city and why; the plots of plays performed by students and various social organizations were collected and subjected to content analysis (which yielded the illuminating conclusion that they all "clearly conformed to the standards of the local group"). An observer was stationed at the movie house to "see who attended the pictures and with whom they attended," and newstands were closely scrutinized to see how actual purchases conformed to professed reading preferences. (One must sympathize with the haunted "upper upper" of Warner's Newburyport seeking furtively to pick up his monthly *Esquire* under the cool stare of a Radcliffe graduate student in sociology.) Death itself brought the citizen no more than partial respite from surveillance: "All the names of those persons buried in the several cemeteries were gathered and compilations were made of the members of several ethnic groups."[8]

Virtually every aspect of Newburyport life was probed by the Yankee City team—every aspect but one. Early in the first volume of the series the authors casually commented: "To be sure that we were not ethnocentrically biased in our judgment, we decided to use no previous summaries of data collected by anyone else (maps, handbooks, histories, etc.) until we had formed our own opinion of the city."[9] This was a remarkable and revealing utterance. To consult the historical record would be to fall victim to the biases and preconceptions of the historian, a man necessarily "unscientific," "culture-bound," "ethnocentric."

How, then, were Warner and his associates to form their "own opinion" about the Newburyport past? At times Warner was inclined to speak as if the past was simply irrelevant. He was contemptuous of the historical school in anthropology; the merely "ethnological or temporal aspects of social behavior" were of much less interest to him than "the scientific problems of explanation of the facts by classification and their interpretation by the formulation of laws and principles."[10] "The facts," in this context, meant the facts visible in the present.

It was quite impossible, however, for the Yankee City researchers to avoid making assumptions about what Newburyport had been like prior to their arrival on the scene; the reasons they gave for selecting Newburyport as a research site included a host of historical assumptions. They sought a small community which was "above all a well-integrated community." It was to be self-contained, as insulated as possible from "disruptive" influences emanating from large cities undergoing "rapid social change." Its population was to be "predominantly old American," and it was to have "developed over a long period of time under the domination of a single group with coherent tradition." Newburyport, Warner took for granted, was such a city, one whose "Puritan tradition" remained "unshattered," one whose "social superstructure remained very much what it had been at the end of the War of 1812."[11]

How did Warner decide that Newburyport met this rather unusual set of specifications? He found out "scientifically," by direct observation of the image of the past held by present members of the community. This seemed a plausible procedure for men determined to "use the techniques and ideas which have been developed by social anthropologists in primitive society in order to obtain a more accurate understanding of an American community."[12] Warner came to Newburyport after three years of observing a tribe of Australian aborigines, a people without a written history. In a community without written records, the dead exist only in the minds and deeds of the living; there history survives only as tradition, ritual, myth, "remembered experiences . . . newly felt and understood by the living members of the collectivity."[13]

Rarely is the student of a primitive community able to find sources that allow him to penetrate beneath this tissues of myths; much of the past is irrevocably lost. The modern social investigator, however, need not remain entirely at the mercy of such subjective data. He may ask not only "what is remembered of things past?" but also "what was the actual past?"[14] The historical record available to him, it need hardly be said, is not pure, disembodied Truth; even the simple factual information it contains was gathered by men whose interests and passions colored their perceptions, men who were "culture-bound." The point to be underscored, though, is that this record may be read in a way that allows us to discriminate, at least to some degree, between the mythic past and the actual past.

Warner eventually became aware of this crucial distinction. The last of the Yankee City volumes, published long after the others (1959), includes a lengthy and perceptive analysis of the image of the Newburyport past presented in the pageants staged during the tercentenary celebration of 1935. By utilizing historical sources Warner was able to detect and interpret some interesting discrepancies between the real past and the "history" portrayed in the pageants, which was what community leaders "now *wished* it . . . were and what they wished it were not. They ignored this or that difficult period of time or unpleasant occurrences or embarrassing group of men and women; they left out awkward political passions; they selected small items out of large time contexts, seizing them to express today's values."[15]

Regrettably, however, a similar indictment must be returned against the first four volumes of Warner's own study. "Where truth ends and idealization begins cannot be learned," the authors of *The Social System of the Modern Factory* tell us.[16] This was not a limitation imposed by the absence of historical evidence; it was the result of Warner's own methodological commitments. In this instance and in many others his interpretations rested on assumptions about the past which were demonstrably false. Warner's unwillingness to consult the historical record and his complete dependence on materials susceptible to anthropological analysis—the acts and opinions of living members of the community—served to obliterate the distinction between the actual past and current myths about the past. Thus, the Yankee City investigators' determination to escape the ethnocentric biases of culture-bound history led them to accept uncritically the community's legends about itself—surely the most ethnocentric of all possible views.

The ahistorical predilections of Warner and his associate produced a number of glaring misconceptions about the character of the community they studied. The static old "Yankee" city whose "social superstructure remained very much what it had been at the end of the War of 1812" was largely a creation of Warner's imagination. Every investigator admittedly sees the community he studies from a particular, limiting perspective; a degree of subjectivity is perhaps inescapable in treating a complex social object. But, whatever the bounds of legitimate subjectivity, the Yankee City series far exceeds them. As late as the 1930's, according to Warner, the "Puritan tradition" of Yankee City remained "unshattered," for the community's population was happily still "predominantly old American." But in point of fact the population of Newburyport had ceased to be predominantly "old American" more than half a century before the Yankee City team began its labors! The effects of mass immigration, the high birth rate of the newcomers, and the heavy migration of old residents from the community produced radical changes in the composition of the Newburyport population during the 1850–1880 period. By 1885, first- and second-generation immigrants constituted almost half of the city's population; their decendants and later immigrants together made up the overwhelming majority of the Newburyport population at the time of the Yankee City study. Furthermore, only a small minority of the "Yankee" families remaining in the community in 1880 were actually from old Newburyport families. A comparison of local city directories for 1849 and 1879 provides a precise measure of the extent of this devastating change: little more than a *tenth* of the family names recorded in the directory of 1879 could be located in the first local directory 30 years before. The economic and social transformation the community underwent midway in the 19th century, when it became a bustling manufacturing city, effectively shattered the social structure of preindustrial Newburyport. The Federalist ethos lingered on in a few old families, but the dominant values in this city of mobile newcomers bore no resemblance to Warner's description. It is true that the community's economic growth slowed after the Civil War, and that its total population was little larger in 1930 than it was in 1855, but to infer from these facts that Newburyport was a static, old Yankee community sealed off from the larger society was utterly mistaken.[17]

These misconceptions about the community become more comprehensible when we realize that the key concepts of the study—class and ethnicity—were both based entirely on the opinion of Warner's local respondents, and were defined so as to render difficult any systematic study of the relations between subjective opinion and objective social reality. An "ethnic," for example, was said to be a Newburyport resident who "considered himself or was considered by" others to be an "ethnic" and who "participated in the activities" of an "ethnic" association; any citizen who did not fulfill these two criteria, amazingly, Warner classified a "Yankee." Thus, a community in which immigrants, their children and grandchildren were an overwhelmingly majority could become, in Warner's mind, a city whose population was "predominantly old American."[18]

Not only did the Yankee City investigators accept uncritically the opinions of informants living in the community at the time; they tended to accept the opinion of informants from a particular social group with very special biases—Yankee City's "upper uppers." This group fascinated Warner; he devoted an inordinate amount of space to them, despite the fact that they constituted less than 2 per cent of the Newburyport population. The upper uppers were the few dozen prominent old Yankee families who presumably had enjoyed high status in the community for more than a century. In fact Warner overestimated the continuity and rootedness of even this tiny elite, as they themselves were wont to do; while each of his vivid "composite drawings" of upper uppers depicted a family that had resided in the community for several generations, Warner's own questionnaires showed that at the time of the study fewer than 60 per cent of this group had been born in or near Newburyport, and that almost a quarter of them had been born outside of New England entirely.[19] These were the Yankee City families whose sense of subtle prestige distinctions was translated into Warner's famous theory that the community was stratified into six discrete prestige classes; this was the "single group with a coherent tradition" whose eagerness to equate Newburyport history with their own history led Warner to believe that the community's "social superstructure . . . remained very much what it had been at the end of the War of 1812" and to attribute the apparent stability of the Newburyport social order to the fictitious dominance of the "Yankee."[20]

Industrialization and the Blocked Mobility Theory

The American class system was becoming "less open and mobility increasingly difficult for those at the bottom of the social heap," Warner wrote in 1947. "The evidence from Yankee City and other places in the United States," it seemed to him, "strongly" indicated that both manual laborers and their children enjoyed fewer opportunities to rise than was common in the 19th century; on the expanding frontier and in the idyllic craft structure of the 19th-century city, social mobility had been "certain," but the spread of the factory system had degraded the worker and had blocked the "ladder to the stars."[21] On the basis of his interpretation of "the industrial history" of Newburyport in *The Social System of the Modern Factory,* Warner concluded that the "traditional" American open class structure was becoming increasingly rigid; the "blue print of tomorrow" drawn up in Yankee City included the growing likelihood that America would soon see "revolutionary outbreaks expressing frustrated aspirations."[22]

The historical event that inspired these dark forebodings was the strike which closed all the shoe factories of Newburyport in 1933 and eventually resulted in management recognition of the shoe worker's union. Warner portrayed this strike as a dramatic success, and argued that such a radical departure from the community's tradition of social peace and labor quiescence required elaborate explanation. The initial field interviews, Warner admitted, revealed that Newburyport citizens tended to think of the strike as a struggle over economic grievances provoked by the depression: "Each man, owner, and worker, and townsman, spoke his own brand of economic determinism." But Warner found these answers superficial; there had been depressions, wage cuts and the rest in the city before, he observed, yet this was the first "successful" strike. There had to be some "secret" as to "why the Yankee City workers struck and . . . why men in other cities strike." That secret, Warner decided, lay "beyond the words and deeds of the strike;" it could only be ferreted out by probing deeply into the evolution of the community's productive system.[23] A knowledge of history, he now seemed to concede, could supply deeper insight into an event in the present.

Warner began his excursion into the Newburyport past with a hymn to the Golden Age of the craftsman, when every youngster became an apprentice and every apprentice a master. The local youth was gradually trained in the complex skills of his calling, and eventually became "an inextricable member of the honorable fraternity of those who made, and who knew how to make, shoes." In this system, presumably, "workers and managers were indissolubly interwoven into a common enterprise, with a common set of values."[24] To strike was unthinkable. The workman held a respected place in the community, and there was little social distance between him and the men for whom he worked. Economic power was concentrated at the local level, and the age-graded skill hierarchy of the craft assured maximum social mobility opportunities.

One day, however, the serpent "mechanization" entered this Eden:

> The machine took the virtue and respect from the worker, at the same time breaking the skill hierarchy which dominated his occupation. There was no longer a period for young men to learn to respect those in the age grade above them and in so doing to become self-respecting workers. The "ladder to the stars" was gone and with it much of the structure of the "American Dream."[25]

The shoe industry, Warner argued, underwent a technological revolution that shattered the craft order and destroyed local economic autonomy. The Newburyport laborers' sudden decision that a union was necessary to defend their rights was an inescapable consequence of this revolution. The growth of giant factories controlled by absentee owners opened up a vast social gulf between worker and manager. The steady encroachment of the machine rendered all manual skills useless; there resulted a sharp "break in the skill hierarchy." The status of all laboring jobs became equally degraded, and opportunities to rise into supervisory and managerial posts were eliminated. The "secret" behind the upsurge of union support in 1933 was thus a series of fundamental changes in the productive system, which separated the shoe workers from the community, blocked the mobility opportunities they had once enjoyed, and inspired a new sense of labor solidarity and class consciousness.

This portrait of a community in crisis, of course, represents a stunning reversal of the image of Newburyport presented in earlier volumes of the Yankee City series. The reader may well wonder if there were *two* Yankee Cities; the research for *The Social System of the Modern Factory* might almost have been conducted in another community. The placid New England town Warner selected for investigation because of its extraordinary continuity and stability suddenly became the site of a study in social disorganization and class conflict.[26]

Warner's new interest in historical change and his determination to present a dynamic analysis of the impact of larger social forces on Yankee City was commendable. Unhappily, however, his account of the evolution of Newburyport from "the simple folk economy of the earliest community" to the 1930's grossly distorted the city's actual history; it is a classic example of the old American habit of judging the present against a standard supplied by a romantic and sentimental view of the past. The sweeping conclusions about the American class structure he drew from this case study are not in accord with the Newburyport evidence, nor do they square with the findings of recent mobility studies conducted in other communities.

As an attempt to explain the shoe strike of 1933, *The Social System of the Modern Factory* can be quickly dismissed. This strike did not in fact represent as radical a departure from community traditions as Warner believed. "Everyone in management and labor agreed that the strike could not have happened" in the good old days, Warner reports, but strikes *had* taken place in Newburyport—in 1858, in 1875, and a good many times since.[27] The strike of 1933 was distinctive only in that it was more successful than previous strikes, and not very much more successful at that. As Handlin pointed out, the union asked for a closed shop and a 10 per cent wage increase, but it won simple recognition and no raise. And within three years the union had lost out in one of the two factories still open.[28] The events of 1933, therefore, were not unprecedented, and massive changes in the community need not be invoked to explain them.

Even if this be doubted, Warner's explanation of the strike is wholly unsatisfactory, because the causes to which he attributed the supposedly drastic changes of the 1930's were fully operative in Newburyport several decades before the events they presumably explain. Once upon a time, the Newburyport economy was organized along craft lines; labor was content, social mobility was "certain," to strike was unthinkable. Warner was exceedingly vague as to the actual dates of this idyllic craft age, but he assumed that memories of it were alive in the minds of the strikers of 1933, and one chart made it appear that craft and apprenticeship relations prevailed in local shoe production until "approximately World War I."[29] The vagueness is not accidental, for the craft order portrayed in this volume was but a Never Never land conjured up by the author. Not a shred of evidence pertaining to Newburyport itself is cited in support of this account; none could be. If one goes back as far as 1800, one can indeed find evidence of a well-integrated craft order in Newburyport, but its outstanding features were not equality and mobility but hierarchy, religiously-sanctioned elite rule, and institutionalized deference of the lower classes.[30] And, in any case, the craft order had virtually disappeared in Newburyport and industrial cities like it long before the 19th century drew to a close without producing a powerful union movement, much less "revolutionary outbreaks expressing frustrated aspirations."

Well before 1880 the Newburyport economy was dominated by large textile and shoe firms. Production was highly mechanized in both industries; all of the textile mills and some of the shoe factories were already controlled by absentee owners.[31] Factory laborers found no inviting "ladder to the stars" before them; in the substantial sample of workers and their sons I studied for the 1850–1880 period, there was not a single instance of mobility into the ranks of management or even into a foreman's position! Since Warner failed to present any quantitative evidence to substantiate his assertions about the supposed decline in mobility rates, no detailed comparison of mobility rates in Newburyport in the 1850–1880 period with those in the 1930's can be made.[32] Extensive comparisons between my own findings concerning the intra-generational and intergenerational occupational mobility of unskilled laborers in 19th-century Newburyport and mobility rates in several other 20th-century American communities, however, provide no support at all for Warner's claim that to rise "from the bottom of the social heap" has become increasingly difficult in modern America. Instead, both types of upward mobility seem to have become somewhat less difficult over the past century.[33]

Nor is Warner's stress on the importance of absentee ownership confirmed by the history of the community. Several of the Newburyport plants were controlled by outside capitalists in this early period; this was a common pattern in many American industries from the very beginning of industrialization. And, more important, labor-management relations in the firms still in local hands were not in fact characterized by the happy solidarity Warner attributed to them, local mythology to the contrary notwithstanding. Whether the Yankee Protestant mill-owner lived on High Street or in Boston could have mattered little to his Irish-Catholic employees, whose willingness or unwillingness to strike was governed by more tangible and impersonal considerations.

The clue to these errors, I believe, lay in the fact that Warner's new-found appreciation of history did not lead him to any critical awareness of what constituted historical *evidence*. Though he cited a few secondary historical accounts that were tangentially relevant to his analysis, Warner derived the main outlines of his romantic interpretation of "the industrial history of Yankee City" from his informants in the community in the 1930's. That this set of myths flourished in the city is indeed a social datum of great interest (though one might well be skeptical about how widespread these attitudes really were, given Warner's initial admission that most local residents viewed the strike as a simple and familiar contest over wage grievances). To comprehend the function of myths like these in the social struggles of the present, however, is impossible when they are taken for an accurate description of past social reality and used as the foundation for an ambitious theory of social change in industrial society.

The distortions that pervade the Yankee City volumes suggest that the student of modern society is not free to take his history or leave it alone. Interpretations of the present requires a host of assumptions about the past. The real choice is between explicit history, based on a careful examination of the sources, and implicit history, rooted in ideological preconceptions and uncritical acceptance of local mythology.

NOTES

1. Edward Hallett Carr, *What is History?* New York: Knopf, 1962, p. 84.

2. For a useful discussion of the impact on historical writing of some recent developments in the social sciences, see two essays by H. Stuart Hughes: "The Historian and the Social Scientist," *American Historical Review*, 66 (October, 1960), pp. 20–46; "History, the Humanities, and Anthropological Change," *Current Anthropology*, 4 (April, 1963), pp. 140–145. Both of these have been reprinted in Hughes' book, *History as an Art and as a Science*, New York: Harper and Row, 1964.

3. For a powerful critique of ahistorical social science, see Barrington Moore, Jr., *Political Power and Social Theory: Six Studies*, Cambridge: Harvard University Press, 1958, esp. Ch. 4. For an excellent case study written from a similar point of view, see E. R. Leach, *Political Systems of Highland Burma: A Study in Kachin Social Structure*, Cambridge: Harvard University Press, 1954. Carl Degler's "The Sociologist as Historian. A Look at Riesman, Whyte and Mills," *American Quarterly*, 15 (Winter, 1963), pp. 483–497, raises some of the issues considered below, though I believe Degler's substantive conclusions to be mistaken.

4. Princeton: Princeton University Press, 1960; Harper Torchbook paperback edition, 1964.

5. The five Yankee City volumes were published as follows: Vol. I, W. Lloyd Warner and Paul S. Lunt, *The Social Life of a Modern Community*, New Haven: Yale University Press, 1941; Vol. II, W. Lloyd Warner and Paul S. Lunt, *The Status System of a Modern Community*, New Haven: Yale University Press, 1942; Vol. III, W. Lloyd Warner and Leo Srole, *The Social Systems of American Ethnic Groups*, New Haven: Yale University Press, 1945; Vol. IV, W. Lloyd Warner and J. O. Low, *The Social System of the Modern Factory*, New Haven: Yale University Press, 1947; Vol. V, W. Lloyd Warner, *The Living and the Dead: A Study of the Symbolic Life of Americans*, New Haven: Yale University Press, 1959. A one-volume abridgement of the series has recently been published by Yale University Press under the title *Yankee City* (1963). For a guide to other publications by Warner and his students, and to the critical literature as of 1953, see Ruth Rosner Kornhauser, "The Warner Approach to Social Stratification," in Reinhard Bendix and Seymour M. Lipset, *Class, Status and Power: A Reader in Social Stratification*, Glencoe, Ill.: The Free Press, 1953, pp. 224–254.

6. See, however, the penetrating reviews by historians Oscar Handlin and Henry F. May. Handlin reviewed Vols. I and II of the Yankee City series in the *New England Quarterly*, 15 (September, 1942), pp. 554–557; Vol. III in the *New England Quarterly*, 18 (September, 1945), pp. 523–524; and Vol. IV in *The Journal of Economic History*, 7 (June, 1947), pp. 275–277. May reviewed Vol. IV for the *New England Quarterly*, 21 (June, 1948), pp. 276–277.

7. For a discussion of Newburyport's representativeness and the controversy provoked by Warner's claims, see Thernstrom, *op cit.*, pp. 192–206.

8. Warner and Lunt, *The Status System of a Modern Community*, p. 13; *Social Life of a Modern Community*, p. 90. These are but a few examples to suggest the monumental scale of the Yankee City venture. For a full account of "The Field Techniques Use and the Materials Gathered," see *Social Life*, pp. 38–75.

9. *Social Life*, p. 400.

10. *Ibid.*, Ch. 2.

11. *Ibid.*, pp. 1–5, 38–39; Warner and Low, *The Social System of the Modern Factory*, p. 2.

12. *Social Life*, p. 14.

13. Warner, *The Living and the Dead*, p. 4.

14. Cf. Robert Bierstedt, "The Limitations of Anthropological Methods in Sociology," *American Journal of Sociology,* 54 (January, 1948), pp. 22–30; Handlin, review of Vols. I and II of the Yankee City series, *op. cit.*

15. *The Living and the Dead*, p. 110.

16. *Social System of the Modern Factory*, p. 139.

17. See Thernstrom, *op. cit.*, pp. 84–86, 167–168, 195–196.

18. Warner and Srole, *The Social Systems of American Ethnic Groups*, p. 28. In his excellent study of Burlington, Vt., Elin L. Anderson found a similar myth, particularly among the upper classes. Anderson was unwilling to accept their claims without investigation, and discovered that in fact the "pure" Yankee stock made up less than a third of the population; *We Americans: A Study of Cleavage in an American City*, Cambridge: Harvard University Press, 1937, Ch. 3. For a similar finding in another Vermont community, see the unpublished study by Martin and Margy Ellin Meyerson described in David Riesman, *Faces in the Crowd: Individual Studies in Character and Politics*, New Haven: Yale University Press, 1952, p. 274.

19. *Social Life*, p. 209. "Composite drawings" of "fictive persons" play a crucial role in the Yankee City volumes. They occupy much space, and are often referred to in support of subsequent analyses. In these narrative sketches of local residents, "no one actual individual or family in Yankee City is depicted;" instead, "the lives of several individuals are compressed into that of one fictive person." Warner did not hesitate to "exclude all material which might identify specific persons in the community, and . . . included generalized material whenever necessary to prevent recognition. The people and situations in some of the sketches are entirely imaginary." *Social Life*, p. 129.

These sketches often seem illuminating. But have they any value as evidence? As the example cited in the text indicates, the method gives free rein to any biases and preconceptions the social scientist brings to his subject. Warner assures us that all the liberties taken with the original evidence were checked to see that "the essential social reality" was not impaired. This is a commendable effort, but is it an adequate substitute for the ordinary safeguards which the historian imposes upon himself by guiding the critical reader to the body of evidence on which he bases his interpretation? *Quis custodiet ipsos custodes?* Warner's desire to "protect" his subjects and to tell his story "economically" is understandable, but he paid a rather heavy price to satisfy these requirements. All too rarely in the Yankee City series is the ordinary reader able to check the assertions of a composite drawing against data of genuine probative weight.

20. *Social Life*, p. 5; *Modern Factory*, p. 2. John P. Marquand's savage lampooning of Warner as the "Malcolm Bryant" of *Point of No Return* should not be allowed to obscure the fact that the two men viewed the community from a very similar perspective. Marquand appears to have felt that Warner betrayed the confidence placed in him by Marquand himself and other upper-class respondents. Whatever the merits of this accusation, Warner's image of the community seems to have been shaped by this group to a striking degree.

21. *The Social System of the Modern Factory*, pp. 182–185, 87–89.

22. *Ibid.*, Ch. 10.

23. *Ibid.*, pp. 4–7.

24. *Ibid.*, p. 87.

25. *Ibid.*, pp. 88–89.

26. A possible explanation of this startling shift in Warner's image of the community would be that events in Newburyport since the publication of the early volumes had given the Yankee City researchers a different perspective. The actual chronology of

the series, however, does not support this suggestion. The strike took place in 1933; the volumes stressing the harmony of social relations in what was supposedly "above all a well-integrated community" (*Social Life,* p. 38) appeared in the early 1940's; the factory study, whose dark fears of "revolutionary outbreaks expressing frustrated aspirations" (*Modern Factory,* p. 185) were allegedly inspired by the 1933 strike, was published in 1947. A better explanation may be that Warner, though he never replied to his critics overtly, was stung by the charge that the Yankee City he portrayed was static, "trendless," and thus entirely unrepresentative of changing industrial America. Certainly this criticism could never be made of *The Social System of the Modern Factory,* for here Warner pursued trends with a vengeance, elaborating not only the national but the "world implications" of the dramatic changes he now perceived taking place in Newburyport.

27. *Modern Factory,* p. 5.

28. Handlin, *op. cit.*

29. *Modern Factory,* chart i, p. 65.

30. See Thernstrom, *op. cit.,* pp. 34–42, for a discussion of the craft order of pre-industrial Newburyport. In the Middletown volumes, Robert and Helen Lynd offered a more convincing sketch of the craft order and a more sophisticated version of the blocked mobility theory. For some critical reflections on their analysis, see *ibid.,* pp. 214–216.

31. It is ironic that Warner, in discussing the idyllic craft order in shoe manufacturing, alludes to the efforts of the Knights of Crispins to preserve stringent apprenticeship requirements and to prevent the use of "green hands" in the post-Civil War decade. Not only had the Knights everywhere lost this crucial struggle more than half a century before the "successful" Newburyport strike; it was precisely in Newburyport that the craft order was so weak as to permit capitalists from the great shoe center, Lynn, to set up "runaway shops" as a means of avoiding "Crispin trouble."

32. In *The Social Systems of American Ethnic Groups* Warner did attempt to supply quantitative data about social mobility in Newburyport, and his effort to analyze historically the occupational and residential mobility patterns of local ethnic groups was not completely unfruitful. But because he believed that the essence of class was *prestige,* Warner was too predisposed against objective indices to use them properly. See Thernstrom, *op. cit.,* pp. 336–238, for a detailed critique of the mobility study reported in *The Social Systems of American Ethnic Groups.*

33. See Thernstrom, *op. cit.,* pp. 202–203, 216–221.

Bridenbaugh, Carl. (1938) *Cities in the Wilderness*. New York: Ronald; and (1955) *Cities in Revolt*. New York: Knopf.

These are the definitive scholarly works on colonial and revolutionary American cities, and they provide an overwhelming abundance of detail. The fledgling urbanist should read these volumes selectively, lest trends become buried under minutiae.

Callow, Alexander, B., Jr. (1969) *American Urban History: An Interpretive Reader with Commentaries*. New York: Oxford.

A solid reader containing some forty-four articles. The opening and closing sections emphasize the concerns historians should have, while the middle sections document the types of things actually done.

Glaab, Charles N. (1963) *The American City*. Homewood, Ill.: Dorsey.

A documentary history containing a considerable number of fascinating excerpts and first-person vignettes on American urban life. Materials are organized temporally with no attempt at theoretical integration. Strongest on urban location, transportation, and rivalry. Somewhat weaker on the role of social class and the immigrants.

————, and A. Theodore Brown. (1967) *A History of Urban America*. New York: Macmillan.

A good general overview of the American city, with particular emphasis on nineteenth and early twentieth-century developments.

Green, Constance McLaughlin. (1965) *The Rise of Urban America*. New York: Harper & Row.

This short volume provides the neophyte with an introduction and overview of the growth of cities. Considerable attention is given to colonial cities.

Lynd, Robert S., and Helen M. (1956) *Middletown*. New York: Harcourt.

The first application of a social-scientific approach to the study of the life and life styles of a total community. Middletown (Muncie, Indiana) was main-street America of the 1920's. The Lynds' empirical findings remarkably parallel the artistic insights of Sinclair Lewis in *Babbitt*.

McKelvey, Blake. (1963) *The Urbanization of America: 1860–1915*. New Brunswick, N.J.: Rutgers University Press; and (1968) *The Emergence of Metropolitan America: 1915–1966*. New Brunswick, N.J.: Rutgers University Press.

A solid, two-volume history of American cities since the Civil War. Recommended.

Sjoberg, Gideon. (1960) *The Preindustrial City*. New York: Free Press.

A discussion of the spatial and social dimensions of nonindustrial urban life.

Thernstrom, Stephen, and Richard Sennett. (1969) *Nineteenth-Century Cities*. New Haven, Conn.: Yale University Press.

A reader of twelve essays on nineteenth-century cities (eight American) with major focus on the dimensions of mobility and stability of the social structures.

Vidich, Arthur J., and Joseph Bensman. (1960) *Small Town in Mass Society*. New York: Doubleday (Anchor).

The reaction of rural-oriented small towners to urbanization of their lives. Major attention is devoted to the questions of class, power, and religion. The volume is particularly strong in its discussion of the rural imagery of the urban world.

Wade, Richard C. (1959) *The Urban Frontier*. Cambridge, Mass.: Harvard University Press.

Documents the development of cities west of the Appalachians between 1790 and 1830. Provides information on the changing social structure and the emergence of urban problems as well as data on demographic and economic growth.

Weber, Ada Ferrin. (1899) *The Growth of Cities in the Nineteenth Century*. Ithaca, N.Y.: Cornell University Press.

A monumental study, and still the most complete and systematic statistical study of city growth. Also included is some extremely interesting material on urban values.

White, Norton, and Lucia. (1962) *The Intellectual Versus the City*. Cambridge, Mass.: Harvard and M.I.T. Press.

A discussion of how America's intellectuals from Jefferson to Frank Lloyd Wright have viewed the American city. As the title indicates, the major intellectual reaction to urbanism has not been one of love. This is a pioneer and valuable work, but it has been subjected to criticism for its oversimplification.

(Far left) New York City. Photo courtesy Pan American World Airways, Inc. (Above) Freeways at Los Angeles. Photo courtesy American Airlines. (Left) Freight and suburban facilities of the Illinois Central Railroad in Chicago are shown against a backdrop of skyscrapers along Michigan Boulevard. Courtesy Illinois Central Railroad.

2.1 INTRODUCTION: THE GROWTH AND DEVELOPMENT OF URBAN AREAS

Up through the mid-twentieth century we have seen the population move to large metropolitan areas and then decentralize or suburbanize within these same metropolitan areas. The question is, will these trends continue or will future urban settlements take radically new forms? At least one of the contributors to this section thinks the latter is the case. According to Melvin Webber (2.7), "We are passing through a revolution that is unhitching the social processes of urbanization from the locationally fixed city and region. . . . the glue that once held the spatial settlement together is now dissolving and the settlement is dispersing over ever widening terrains."

The question of the evolution of urban life revolves around the organization of America's expanding metropolitan areas. Existing institutionalized mechanisms of community and societal integration are the outgrowth of population adaptation to earlier city-hinterland settlement patterns. These early patterns reflected an era that did not have mass media, high powered transportation, or centralized economic and social institutions. We are now in an era of restructuring, which may result in a societal structure of a very different order.

To help us understand the general process of urban restructuring, let us consider some models of how urban spatial patterns change. The emphasis is on the dynamics of social change with particular attention given to the role played by technology. Next, we will analyze and discuss the readings in this section and their relevance to the above theme. Finally, we will explore the implications of contemporary theory and research in order to enhance our understanding of the growth and development of urban areas.

Spatial structure has long been a sociological concern, particularly within the area of the discipline known as human ecology. It was during the 1920s that American sociologists, particularly at The University of Chicago, developed the study of urban ecology. Booming commercial Chicago was in many respects a natural laboratory for studying a growing urban population. The Chicago sociologists recognized that the allocation of land use was related to population changes and technological development, especially the development of transportation technology. They stressed the importance of the uses of physical terrain, particularly as such land use reflected the expanding commercial, industrial, and social life of the metropolis. More than attempting a simple description of patterns (important as that is to the understanding of history), these sociologists sought to provide explanations of urban development. Thus, the early work of Robert E. Park, Ernest W. Burgess, and their students and disciples at The University of Chicago clearly influenced the developing field of human ecology. For Park, human ecology was not simply a mapping exercise of where things were, but rather a study of how the sociological, psychological, emotional, and moral experiences of living in the city were reflected in its spatial or physical organization. As Robert McKenzie put it, human ecology "deals with the spatial aspects of the symbiotic relations of human beings and human institutions" (R. D. McKenzie, 1931:314). The human ecologist focuses on the dynamic inter-play among population, organization, environment and technology (P.O.E.T.). Ecologists tend to study urban growth patterns in terms of changes within the ecosystem, with particular interest in industrialization, bureaucratization, and centralization insofar as these organizational processes influence the growth and development of the ecosystem. If the ecologist is also an evolu-tionist, he emphazies the extent to which the basic sustenance requirements of the population are exceeded, so that collective efforts can be devoted to other activities and goals (Olsen, 1968:266). Thus, access to resources is a key factor, as illustrated by Charles Adams' comparative analysis of the development of Boston and Chicago in Section One (1.3).

Probably the best known early example of the ecological approach is the Burgess concentric zonal hypothesis, first presented in 1924. Over the years the concentric zonal hypothesis model has been misused, being repre-sented as a static picture of city structure. This misrepresentation is unfor-tunate, for what Burgess was positing was a model, and only a model, of how cities developed spatially over time as a result of competition for space. Thus, Burgess hypothesized that the reorganization of spatial patterns re-sulted from urban *growth,* and changed accordingly.

In his theory of the growth of the metropolis, Burgess used the ecolog-ical processes of competition, segregation, invasion, and succession. He noted that factories, homes, and retail shops were not randomly distributed within the urban area. Rather, a process of sorting by economic and social factors produced a concentration of similar-type populations and land uses. Compe-tition for space resulted in a patterned distribution of persons, organizations, and institutions within the urban environment. Further, he suggested there was a clear pattern of evolving land usage, with a major determinant being population growth, particularly through in-migration. This process of segre-gation therefore resulted in areas of automobile rows, racial ghettos, apart-ment houses, high-income single-family neighborhoods, and warehouse districts. The Chicago sociologists called these "natural areas," in that they were the results of natural ecological processes rather than planning or the conscious creations of any government unit. In fact, early zoning laws gen-erally recognized such natural areas by drawing their boundaries so as to reinforce existing land-use patterns. This example illustrates how social processes, even in the absence of formal planning, can determine land-use patterns.

The processes that Burgess identified are still at work, although they have become considerably more complex. Intrusion of a new usage into an area is called *invasion*. The history of the American city is the story of the invasion of one land use by another. The end result is *succession*, when one group or function finally takes the place of another. Burgess stressed succession of land usages. Speaking of the zone of transition, he stated: "The present boundaries of deterioration were not many years ago those of the zone now inhabited by independent wage-earners, and within memories of thousands of Chicagoans contained the residences of the 'best families'" (Burgess, 1925:501).

Burgess hypothesized that the metropolitan area, in the absence of counteracting forces, grew through radial expansion from the center through a series of concentric rings or zones. He divided the metropolis into five zones, which frequently took on the characteristics of natural areas. The first area was Zone I, the Central Business District (CBD): Historically this was the center of the city—not necessarily geographically, but certainly in terms of converging transportation routes and maximum accessibility to key activities. The heart of the zone was the retail shopping district, with major department stores, theaters, hotels, banks, and central offices of economic, political, legal, and civic influentials. Consumption-oriented commercial activities tended to locate at the very core of the CBD, while the outer fringes contained the wholesale business district, with its market, warehouses, and storage buildings.

Zone II, the Zone of Transition: Its inner edge included older factory complexes, many from the previous century. Immediately beyond was an outer ring of retrogressing neighborhoods, an area of high crime rates and social disorganization. This area was where the immigrant, be he nineteenth-century Irish or twentieth-century Negro, Puerto Rican, or Mexican, received his first glimpse of the city. The immigrants settled here because they could not compete economically for more desirable locations. Thus, as a result of symbiotic processes, rather than by conscious design, a nonrandom spatial pattern emerged. In Burgess' day, the deterioration of the Zone of Transition was due to the fact that the land was owned speculatively with minimum maintenance in expectation of the CBD eventually expanding into the area. However, expansion of the CBD to this zone never occurred, for reasons we will shortly discuss, and today many of these same slums remain, while others were only recently destroyed by urban renewal.

Zone III, the Zone of Workingmen's Homes: This area was settled by the children of the immigrants. Physically it was (at least in Chicago, Burgess' model) a neighborhood of attached or two-family homes rather than tenements or single-family homes. The residents lived within a short commuting distance of their place of work. Typically, the father of the family had a blue-collar job, and his children hoped to live in Zone IV or a Levittown-type suburb. (For a discussion of life styles in working-class suburbs, see Bennett Berger in Section Three (3.7).)

Zone IV, the Zone of Better Residences: This ring comprised the area beyond the neighborhood of the second-generation immigrants. This was the zone of the great middle class: small business and professional people, salesmen, and those holding white-collar jobs. However, even in the 1920s this zone was changing from a community of single family homes to apartment buildings and residential hotels (that is, invasion of new land-use patterns).

Zone V, the Commuter Zone: In the early 1920s this area was composed of the upper-middle and upper-class WASP dormitory suburbs. Here were the classic suburban life patterns: husband leaving in the morning for the city and returning in the evening, while wife was left to raise the children, maintain the home, and participate in civic affairs.

By the late 1930s Burgess' concentric zonal model was encountering heavy criticism. Among the attacks, Alihan (1938) noted the difficulty of precisely delineating the zonal boundaries and Firey (1945) stressed the importance of the omitted nonecological factors such as sentiment and symbolism.

Alternative theories were not long in developing. Homer Hoyt in the late 1930s suggested that growth took place most rapidly along main transportation arteries and where there was the least economic resistance. He thus posited a sector theory in which growth radiated out in sectors from the central core. The pattern of developing land use in a particular sector was an extension of the predominant type of land use found near the center in that sector. Thus, an industrial sector might radiate in one direction from the core, high-income housing in another direction, and low-income housing in a third (Hoyt, 1939).

The 1940s produced a third hypothesis, the multiple-nuclei theory, by Chauncey Harris and Edward Ullman. The multiple-nuclei theory held that land-use patterns developed around several originally independent nuclei, rather than around a single center. Four factors were held to account for the rise of the nuclei and the differentiation of land usage:

1. Certain activities required specialized facilities. Retailing, for example, required a high degree of accessibility while manufacturing needed ample land and railroad service.
2. Like activities grouped together for mutual advantages, as in the case of the central business district.
3. Some unlike activities were mutually detrimental or incompatible with one another. For example, it was unlikely that high-income or high-status residential areas were located close to heavy industry.
3. Some uses such as storage and warehousing facilities, which had a relatively lower competitive capacity to purchase good locations, were able to afford only low-rental areas. (Harris and Ullman, 1945:7–17)

These various hypotheses posit ways in which different populations adapt to the natural and social environment through organization and technology.

When viewed from an evolutionary framework all of these models have common limitations. They assume that the city is industrial-commercial in nature, containing factories, warehouses, wholesale areas, and so on. They also assume heterogeneity of income, ethnic, and racial groups (*see* Quinn, 1950), characteristics not always found in the cities of other cultures. The concentric zonal and other models do not necessarily describe non-North American, nonindustrial cities. This point is documented by studies ranging from Hansen's (1934) study of Merida in Mexico to Gist's (1957) study of Bangalore, India.

Leo Schnore, after examining spatial changes in Latin American cities, hypothesized an evolutionary sequence of development from preindustrial to industrial models. He suggested that the "traditional Latin American land use pattern of high-income groups near the center rather than at the periphery as the concentric zonal model suggests, might have been typical of North American cities of an earlier era . . . . [This led him to ask] do the residential structures of the city evolve in a predictable direction?" (Schnore, 1965:371). If the answer to this question is yes, the otherwise chaotic events of urban development begin to fit into a meaningful evolutionary pattern.

Over the long range, the Burgess zonal hypothesis and its successors seem destined to become a less and less accurate reflection of patterns of urban change. This is, as we stated earlier, because they were developed just when technological innovation was about to change the spatial configuration of America. At the very time that the thesis of urban growth from center through intermediate points to the periphery was being developed, the automobile was beginning to seriously modify the pattern.

Patterns of Urbanization and Technology

The ecosystem approach stresses technological and environmental as well as population factors as determinants of evolving land-use patterns. The real importance of these factors can be seen in the historical development of American urban areas. The compactness of the nineteenth-century North American city, for example, was accentuated by the technology of industrialization. Boston was still a walking city in 1850, with dense settlement found only within a two-mile radius of the center. The urban core was reserved for the elite, for example, Beacon Hill. The horse-drawn streetcar pushed urban occupancy out to four miles from city hall by 1887. In the early 1890s, electrification pushed the area of convenient transportation out to six miles (Glaab and Brown, 1967:155). The limiting factor of transportation meant that workers had to remain in close proximity to the industrial plants, thus encouraging rows of overcrowded tenements. Steam power was by nature centripetal; it encouraged population concentration and the proximity of factory and power supply.

The street railroad permitted outward residential expansion. The first operational electric streetcar was put into service in Richmond, Virginia, in 1888. However, such outward movement could never get too far laterally from the all-important rails. Railroads enabled the hinterland directly adjacent to the rails to develop.

The advent of the automobile meant a great reduction in the friction of space—the time and cost of overcoming distance. As a result, the city exploded outward. Urban growth was now centrifugal. No longer was it necessary for place of work and place of residence to be contiguous. The interstitial areas between the railroad spokes became available for residential settlement. The first to abandon the central city were the upper class, who, bypassing the intermediate zones, went to the suburban periphery. Today the most affluent of a metropolitan area's residents usually are found clustered in selected fringe suburbs or in exurbia, rather than the city center. With some notable exceptions, the city core has increasingly become the residence of the black, the brown, and the poor white.

The automobile also afforded the opportunity for middle-class and finally even working-class groups to join the exodus to suburbia (see Gans (3.3) and Berger (3.7) in Section Three). In the period following World War II, low land costs, mass look-alike developments, and less-rigid building codes meant that the periphery, rather than the central city, was the cheapest place for new residential development. The relevant question in the contemporary metropolitan area is not "how far out do they live?" but "how long does it take to get there?"

Businesses, as well as residences, have leapfrogged the intermediate zones. Rather than expand into already occupied and costly city properties, firms are increasingly choosing to locate in peripheral areas where costs are lower. Today a company's market is usually national rather than local, and having direct access to the interstate highway system is far more useful than an inner-city location with access to the central city. Rapid truck transportation also makes the inner-city storage facilities far less necessary. When delivery times were long, large warehouses were required for storage; but today the question is increasingly not spatial but temporal: not "where is it?" but "how soon can it be delivered?"

Thus the technological changes of the car and truck did far more than simply extend the boundaries of the city; these changes also accelerated the development of a new urban form, the metropolitan community. Until this time, the American city resembled a preindustrial town at least insofar as it was a compact city composed of ethnic, economic, occupational, and racial communities (see Sjoberg, 1955). The new form of spatial structure was to be a supercommunity composed of cities. According to McKenzie:

> By reducing the scale of local distance, the motor vehicle extended the horizon of the community and introduced a territorial division of labor among local institutions and neighborhood centers which is unique in this history of settlement. . . . The metropolitan community, therefore, comprises a cluster of constellations of centers. Smaller cities and towns tend to group themselves around larger ones as planets group themselves around the sun. (McKenzie, 1933:6, 71)

Thus many of the smaller communities declined as they began to perform specialized functions for the larger emerging metropolitan area. Smaller communities became satellite cities. In the suburbs directly abutting the central city, political and economic considerations pulled in contradictory directions: While the suburbs were becoming more economically bound to the central city, they also were becoming politically autonomous units that could effectively resist annexation. From the 1920s onward, the central cities began to exhibit growth rates below those of their suburban rings. At the same time that the economic facilities of the suburbs were expanding, the central city's political power was decreasing. It is ironic that often the most "cosmopolitan" citizens of a metropolitan area reside in suburban enclaves.

During the early years of the twentieth century, American cities quickly enveloped surrounding towns and competed with each other for the control of contiguous hinterlands. The development of modern transportation and communication technology during this period further increased the likelihood of one city's sphere of influence overlapping that of other metropolises. But today this urban-rural dichotomy no longer adequately describes what is occurring in the total urban area. Rather, the focus is on city-city and city-hinterland relationships.

As improved technology has further reduced the significance of space, the phenomenon of megalopolis has emerged. These gigantic metropolitan areas are not always governed by the older patterns of central-city dominance. In fact, some ecologists, such as Melvin Webber (*see* 2.7), argue that the supremacy of the central city is a thing of the past. One thing seems certain: old models are no longer adequate, and we must rethink the dynamics of the urban ecosystem. The readings in this section suggest some contemporary approaches to the problem.

Article Overview

The readings in this section indicate how contemporary theorists and researchers attempt to deal with problems concerning the dynamics of urban ecosystems.

Article 2.2 by Paul Meadows approaches the question of the relationship between the city and technology from a broad theoretical perspective. As a theorist, Meadows focuses on the persistent problem of sorting out patterns from events. Since it is difficult to make sense of events taken one at a time, we search for meaning by identifying types of classes of things and ask how these classes relate to other classes. For example, Meadows provides a theoretical perspective within which one can examine the functions of the city in society. He argues that the

> . . .central concern has been less the phenomena within the city than the developmental and other regularities to be noted in the relationships between cities and their cultures, between cities and the cultures of many eras and areas—in other words, cities as intercultural phenomena.

Several of the selections (2.3, 2.4, and 2.5) describe the organization of American cities at the aggregate level. It may be useful at this point to alert the reader to some standard terms that are used to describe metropolitan areas. The Bureau of the Census, for example, has developed two basic urban area definitions: the Urbanized Area and the Standard Metropolitan Statistical Area (S.M.S.A.). The *urbanized area* consists of a central city of 50,000 inhabitants or more plus its surrounding incorporated places and unincorporated suburban territory meeting urban density criteria (1000 persons per square mile). Approximately four-fifths of the nation's population today resides in urbanized areas. The second definition, the *Standard Metropolitan Statistical Area,* uses territory as the building block. It is a county or group of counties having a central city of at least 50,000 inhabitants and adjacent counties that are essentially metropolitan in character and socially and economically integrated with the central city.

Urbanized areas, then, are based upon population density and have boundaries that change from census to census, while the S.M.S.A.'s are based upon the counties that are economically integrated with the central city. In 1960, the S.M.S.A. definition was modified to include super-S.M.S.A.'s called *Standard Consolidated Areas*. New York-northeastern New Jersey and Chicago–northwestern Indiana were the only standard consolidated areas in 1960; the 1970 census added two new ones: the Los Angeles and San Francisco S.C.A.'s.

The first empirical article (2.3), by Robert Weller, is an examination of the interdependence between larger metropolitan areas, a theme used by Meadows. Weller asks if there is actual evidence of merging megalopolises. He concludes that:

> . . . there is but limited evidence of increasing economic interdependence among the metropolitan areas of Megalopolis. If anything, their labor forces have become more homogeneous. One must therefore question the validity of concepts like Megalopolis as representing a new community form and consider them as clusters of large, contiguous cities until some evidence is made available to support the Megalopolitan concept.

One decade is, of course, too short a time span to make any but tentative conclusions. Weller's own data, contrary to his analysis, shows some megalopolitan area activities have increased while others have decreased in scale. As Scott Greer has noted, one consequence of the increasing scale in society is that a growing proportion of jobs are in making, processing, and distributing messages and services (Greer, 1962:42). Weller's analysis in Table 2.3C indicates that telecommunications and trucking, both examples of jobs having to do with processing and distributing messages and goods, appear to be on the increase in the megalopolitan labor force. Other service and knowledge activities on the increase include finance, insurance, real estate, business, and education. Thus if the emergence of new metropolitan forms is governed by the principles identified by Greer, then Weller's data could be interpreted to support the thesis that megalopolis is an emerging social form in large-scale urban societies.

Receiving even more attention than the emergence of megalopolises has been the spectacular growth of suburbs since World War II. Suburbs are commonly assessed to have higher socioeconomic status levels than the central cities they surround. Palen and Schnore (2.4) empirically examine this question of suburban advantage by ranking income, educational, and occupational income for 180 urban areas. Their findings generally indicate that population size has a considerable impact on predicting city-suburban status differentials. Palen and Schnore empirically demonstrate that the accepted generalizations of higher suburban income, education, and occupation levels are an accurate reflection of the nation's larger and older urbanized areas, but not of newer urbanized areas. They further show that, for the black population, Northern city-suburban status differentials approximate the white pattern, but this has not been the case for Southern urban areas. In the South, the 1960 data indicate no clear relationship between Negro socioeconomic status and city or suburban residence. Preliminary 1970 census data suggest that the suburbanization of the middle-class black population even in the South is now following the white pattern.

Herbert Gans, in his discussion of suburbanization (2.5), makes two principle observations. First, he believes that "further suburban growth is practically inevitable. . . ." This continuing out-migration reflects the desire of most suburbanites to have "a half acre or more of land and all their favorite urban facilities within a short driving distance from the house."

Second, Gans contends that the effects of suburbanization are mixed. He believes, on the basis of sociological studies, that the suburbs, contrary to the popular intellectual litany, are at least as conducive to mental stimulation as the city. A major criticism of suburbanization which Gans does find credible concerns "an ever-increasing class and racial polarization of city and suburb." However, he quickly notes that suburbanization is not the sole cause of class and racial polarization since the same pattern also goes on in the central city.

Though more explicit than Meadows (or Webber in 2.7), Jane Jacobs also examines general issues concerning the making of the city (2.6). Her discussion of the generators of diversity examines in more concrete terms Meadows' general proposition that the city itself is a "tool" and an independent entity in the ecosystem which affects the urbanization process. Jacobs illustrates this general principle in her examination of the diversity and proliferation of economic enterprises in the city when she proposes that

> . . . big cities *are* natural generators of diversity and prolific incubators of new enterprises and ideas of all kinds. Moreover, big cities are the natural economic homes of immense numbers and ranges of small enterprises.

This process is at a minimum, a result of the dependence of smaller enterprises on an environment that provides many varied supplies and skills.

Jacobs' focus on the value of diversity, which is but one dimension of urbanization, reflects her general commitment to the city. She equates city and civilization, in spite of Webber's (2.7) conviction that this era is a "post-city age."

The significance of enduring issues tends to be made more dramatically visible by efforts to predict the future. In Article 2.7 Melvin Webber attempts to project the future of the city as we enter the postindustrial age. Webber argues that "a new kind of large-scale urban society is emerging that is increasingly *independent* of the city." If so, this raises many questions: What are the likely characteristics of this new, emerging society? What is likely to be the basis for its social organization? What types of communities are likely to be found? What will the "physical city" look like? What problems are likely to dominate the urban scene?

Webber's answer to these macro- or aggregate-level concerns is general rather than specific. He points out that we need to develop better and more adequate concepts. As he says, "We still have no adequate descriptive terms for the emerging social order, and so we use perforce, old labels that are no longer fitting." He also suggests that the solution calls for cultural innovation, following the style of the new cosmopolites who are the producers of the information and ideas that stimulate societal development.

Our major problems, Webber observes, are transitional in nature, reflecting a "rapidly developing society-economy-and-polity whose turf is the nation." Poverty, crime in the streets, riots, and other urban problems transcend any single city or the city in general. Since they are national problems, Webber concludes that we must develop strategies at the societal level if these problems are to be solved.

Conclusion

Though cities have existed for at least 7000 years, it is only recently that they have become integrated into more inclusive social systems. Cities have become elements of larger social systems in ways not possible in any previous time in history. The contemporary scene, we believe, is one of empiricism in need of a powerful theory to challenge. Anachronistic concepts are no longer adequate for understanding today's world. As Scott Greer has pointed out:

> The crisis of the city is thus, in the beginning at least, an intellectual crisis. The inherited images are no longer applicable; they are partial and based upon assumptions about the total society that are unexamined and frequently outmoded. (Greer, 1962:21)

There is no simple model of change that can adequately explain the dynamics of the contemporary scene. This conclusion makes the ecosystem framework with its emphasis on an evolutionary development all the more valuable. Webber has put the issue well when he states that we now face transitional problems at the societal, rather than the local, level. The search for intellectual as well as for practical solutions transcends the city. Concepts must be developed that are interurban in scope. Pollution, race, population growth, and educational crises in the 1960s and 1970s have transcended any single city or group of cities. It is an exciting and challenging prospect to live in an era that calls for new ideas, new concepts, new models, and new images.

REFERENCES

Alihan, Milo A. (1938) *Social Ecology*. New York: Columbia University Press.
Burgess, Ernest W. (1925) "The Growth of the City," in R. Park, *The City*. Chicago: University of Chicago Press.
Firey, Walter. (1945) "Sentiment and Symbolism as Ecological Variables," *American Sociological Review*, Vol. 10, pp. 140–148.
Gettys, Warner E. (1940) "Human Ecology and Social Theory," *Social Forces*, Vol. 18, pp. 469–476.
Gist, Noel P. (1957) "The Ecology of Bangalore, India," *Social Forces*, Vol. 35, pp. 356–365.
Glaab, Charles N., and A. Theodore Brown. (1967) *A History of Urban America*. New York: Macmillan.
Greer, Scott. (1962) *The Emerging City: Myth and Reality*. New York: Free Press.

Hansen, Assel T. (1934) "The Ecology of a Latin American City," in Edward B. Reuter, *Race and Culture Contacts*. New York: McGraw-Hill.

Harris, Chauncey D., and Edward L. Ullman. (1945) "The Nature of Cities," *Annals of the Americas,* Academy of Political and Social Science, Vol. 242, pp. 7–17.

Hoyt, Homer. (1939) "The Structure and Growth of Residential Neighborhoods in American Cities." U.S. Federal Housing Administration, Washington, D.C.: U.S. Government Printing Office.

McKenzie, R. D. (1931) "Human Ecology," *Encyclopedia of Social Sciences,* Vol. 5, New York: Macmillan.

———. (1933) *The Metropolitan Community*. New York: McGraw-Hill.

Olsen, Marvin E. (1968) *The Process of Social Organization*. New York: Holt, Rinehart and Winston.

Quinn, James A. (1940) "The Burgess Zonal Hypothesis and Its Critics," *American Sociological Review,* Vol. 5, pp. 210–218.

———. (1950) *Human Ecology*. Englewood Cliffs, N.J.: Prentice-Hall.

Schnore, Leo F. (1965) "On the Spatial Structure of Cities in the Two Americas," in Philip Hauser and Leo Schnore, *The Study of Urbanization*. New York: Wiley.

Sjoberg, Gideon. (1955) "The Pre-Industrial City," *American Journal of Sociology,* Vol. 60, pp. 438–445.

2.2 THE CITY, TECHNOLOGY, AND HISTORY

PAUL MEADOWS

The Approach through Intra-Urbanism

Over two decades ago a leading United States urban sociologist, Professor Niles Carpenter, opened a discussion of urban sociology with this statement: "Recent trends in the field of sociology might be epitomized in a four-word phrase—'the quest for data.' "[1] In retrospect, one might, while accepting the importance of this empirical bent, still ask the elementary question, data about what? So far as urban sociology is concerned, it is perfectly obvious that so long as it is data about some relationship concerning social life within the American city—whether trend, stage, cause-effect, fact-implication, problem-policy—which is to be discovered, nothing else has ever seemed to count. Urban sociology has been and is yet literally (and without reservation apparently) the sociology of life *within* the city.

This approach to urban sociology, which we may designate as the sociology of intra-urbanism because of the manner in which social phenomena are interpreted solely in terms of the city itself, has been characterized by both purely intellectual as well as markedly pragmatic interests. As an intellectual curiosity, urban sociology represents the emergence of the city as in itself a legitimate object of sociological study. The city is *sui generis:* hence, the sociology of city life. This perspective was proclaimed in an extraordinarily influential volume of papers published by the University of Chicago Press in 1924: *The City,* edited by R. E. Park, E. W. Burgess, and R. D. McKenzie. The theoretical position taken by these authors is indicated in the initial paper by Professor Park: "The City: Suggestions for the Investigation of Human Behavior in the Urban Environment." The subsequent ecological, personality, and institutional investigations of a generation of urban sociologists are foreshadowed in some of the other papers in this volume: McKenzie's "The Ecological Approach to the Study of the Human Community," Park's "The Mind of the Hobo," and his famous paper on the metropolitan daily newspaper. Since then, the classroom texts in urban sociology[2] follow rather closely this thematic organization of this field. The much later, masterful essay by Professor Louis Wirth, summarizing and organizing the theory of a sociology

From Paul Meadows, "The City, Technology, and History," *Social Forces,* Vol. 36 (December 1957), pp. 141–147. Reprinted by permission of University of North Carolina Press.

95

devoted to the study of intra-urbanism and significantly titled "Urbanism as a Way of Life,"[3] has been one of the most commonly quoted and cited papers in U.S. sociology.

However, this intellectual curiosity about the city was complemented by another kind of interest, one which perhaps was not so welcome among the ranks of theoreticians, but nonetheless widespread and popular. This pragmatic interest grew out of the necessity felt by many urban leaders to find more adequate solutions to human problems in the city. Prompted by social workers, municipal administrators, and institutional managers, teams of sociologists and other social scientists, armed with questionnaires, notebooks and maps, invaded city streets and engaged in comprehensive social surveys and social anthropological studies of U.S. cities. This monumental quest of empirical facts has been described by a number of writers, notably by Pauline Young in her *Scientific Social Surveys and Research*.[4] Besides yielding up great quantities of data, this practical search for the policy-relevant fact served to highlight the enormous vitality of the city along with the tragic loss of human values occurring in the disorder uncouthly hardened, as Lewis Mumford has observed, "in metropolitan slum and industrial factory district,"[5] and in the widening circles of social derangement accompanying the residential and commercial exodus into the urban fringes. Urban sociologists in the United States owe a huge debt to these students of urban disorganization, a debt being slowly paid off in the form of newer patterns of community organization and municipal policy.

However, it is a contention of this paper that the prodigious empiricism of this double-barrelled investigation of urban life during the interwar and postwar years in the United States was an incomplete venture. Indeed, incompleteness marks any scientific enterprise, for investigation is a function of problems, and problems are unfortunately, even among scientists, a function of perspective. To be specific (but not exhaustive), consider the following limitations on any urban sociology which is content to be only a sociology of intra-urbanism.

In the first place, such an approach cannot possibly formulate universals and cannot, therefore, achieve universalism. It is no accident, for example, that some of the most popular sociological texts in the United States are emphatically American in scope, as even their titles indicate.[6] And even when their titles omit this fact, the contents do not.[7] There is, methodologically speaking, nothing amiss in the use of urban data which happen to be at hand. But the methodologists of science are constantly bewailing the failure, among many fields of scientific inquiry, to formulate problems which can lead to the development of trans-cultural or cross-cultural generalizations. This failure to arrive at arresting and provocative generalities cannot be compensated for by the abundance of attractive and stimulating, even limitedly useful, particularities.

In the second place, these American intra-urbanists have, following Wirth's crystallization of the conceptual field, worked with a very limited set of variables. For Wirth, urban social phenomena are a function of such variables as size and density of population, heterogeneity and mobility of population, secondariness and anonymity of population. This is a strictly sociologistic approach, eminently correct; but this merit does not—or should not—blind us to the narrowness of this circumscription of the field. Surely urbanism is not entirely a function of merely this handful of social variables operating neatly within the confines of the city boundary! Surely there are historic urbanisms—non-Western and non-industrial in character[8]—in which these variables are perhaps not even relevant! Moreover, it should be noted that the quality or state of social life which Wirth called the urban way of life seems to have little relationship to the historian's perception of the city as synonymous with civilization, and the artist's observation of the city as a qualitatively unique world which separates the urbanite from the primitive and the peasant in any era or area.

Fully appreciative of the importance and of the necessity of an intra-urban sociology, this paper proposes, however, to examine some of the work of urban sociologists (and others, mainly others) for whom the central concern has been less the phenomena within the city than the developmental and other regularities to be noted in the relationships between cities and their cultures, between cities and the cultures of many eras and areas—in other words, cities as intercultural phenomena. This second approach to the city, which does not deny but supplements the first, we may call, for want of a better name, an inter-urban sociology.

The witticism which states that sociology is what sociologists do is quite far off the mark as a description of urban sociology in this latter sense. For the plain fact is that some of the most valuable urban sociology has come from the pens of persons not usually identified with sociology—from historians, anthropologists, economists, and architects, among others. At least what they have written is sociology if one is sufficiently tolerant to conceive of the data of this field as consisting of invariant, or at least relatively stable, relationships between and among social and other phenomena. For these observers of the urban scene and role have been tremendously impressed by the abiding importance of (a) the relationship between technology and society, on the one hand, and the emergence and development of urbanism, on the other; and (b) the opposite relationship—that between urbanism and the emergence and development of technology and society. What we are really formulating here is in fact a reversible functional equation which sees these variables as functions of one another:

1. urbanism $= f$ (technology and society); and
2. technology and society $= f$ (urbanism).

It is proposed to explore during the remainder of this paper various aspects of these formulas, and to do so in terms of a major proposition, which reads as follows: *Urbanization represents the process by which urbanism emerges and develops out of the interaction of technology and society.* This proposition will then be restated and discussed: *Change and development in technology and society occur in and through urbanism.* Expressed as questions and not as assertions, this basic thought may be put thus: How do technological and social change encourage the rise of urbanism (urbanization)? Conversely, how does urbanization affect the processes of technological and social change?

Urbanism as a Function of Technology and Society

It might be helpful to state at this point the general theory of urbanism which expresses what is styled here the "inter-urban" approach to the sociology of the city. This theory may be formulated in a set of functional propositions somewhat as follows:

1. urbanization = f (economic surplus);
2. economic surplus = f (technology of surplus);
3. urbanization = f (technology of surplus).

Hence also:

4. the volume and rate of urbanization = f (the development and expansion of technology of surplus); and
5. great periods and epochs of urbanization = f (cycles of technological and social development).

The most perceptive—and probably the original—statement of the functional relationship between urbanization and technology-society was made by V. Gordon Childe, Australian-born professor of prehistoric archaeology, in his volume, *Man Makes Himself* (London, 1937). Subsequently, American historian Ralph Turner published his two-volume *The Great Classical Traditions,*[9] in which the Childe thesis receives further development and documented elaboration in terms of other culture situations. Together, these volumes constitute a full restatement of urban sociology in the direction of a theory of inter-urbanism.

The Childe-Turner discussions stipulate three major revolutions in history —the food-producing, the urban, and the industrial revolutions. Clearly, each is in point of fact a technological revolution, for each involves the development of skills and tools (techniques and technics) by which environmental resources are converted into economic goods and services. The nature of this conversion process is, of course, a function of the society and the technology, such that the type of economic organization and the level of technical theory (technology) determine the type, the rate, the volume, and the direction of resource utilization.[10]

Cities emerge historically when a technological complex (tools, skills, and theory) creates an economic surplus. The routes and scope of this exchange of the economic surplus develop an everwidening network of communities, and with the growth of trade and transportation there is a corresponding increase in the size and complexity of the urban net which contains and utilizes the surplus. Cities become linked with cities, cities in different cultures are related by trade and culture contacts generally with each other; the city becomes a cross-cultural emergent. Turner has expressed the relationships involved here in this manner:

> Since urban cultures appeared only with the formation of an economic surplus, they advanced largely as the economic surplus increased. In general, it is evident in the development of the ancient-oriental urban cultures, such increase has been brought about in three different ways: (1) by technological advances, such as the introduction of irrigation and metal-working,

(2) by the expansion of economic enterprise, such as the Babylonian and Egyptian penetration of Syria, and (3) by the development of new forms of economic administration, such as gang slavery and the estate system of cultivation.[11]

It is clear from their accounts of the great ancient and classical empires of the Mediterranean and Middle East that Childe and Turner do not adhere to any simple technological interpretation of urbanization, particularly of technology conceived of in limited terms. This point is well demonstrated in Turner's concept of a natural history of urbanism. Throughout, he indicates two variables in urban change and development, technology and social interaction. Stated as a formula, his conception might read thus: urbanization $= f$ (technology, interaction). Examining his depiction of urban cultural development stage by stage, we may note schematically, the correlatives as presented in Table 2.2A.

Acknowledging in passing the Spenglerian pessimism of this natural history conception,[12] one may observe that this scheme furnishes an excellent instance of the interpenetration of technology and society which an economic realism has always insisted is characteristic of any form of social organization. It spotlights the symbiotic dependence, the vital interdependence, which denotes the functioning of any urbanism. Urbanism depends upon the appearance and growth of an economic surplus. But that growth is clearly the

TABLE 2.2A. Schematic Presentation of Turner's Concept of a Natural History of Urbanism

Phase	Technology	Interaction
I. Emergence of Urban Culture	Agricultural and handicraft technics; appearance of economic surplus.	Primary social specialization: a power-holding group, and industrial group.
II. Social Specialization and Integration	New lands, new tools higher productivity; new raw materials.	Distinction in power-group: secular-military and priestly sections; compact work groups.
III. Internal Crisis	Systematic application of wealth-producing technics; new tools; resources; expansion of transportation technology; intensified craft specialization.	Acculturation with outgroups; intergroup struggle to control economic surplus; ascendance of the military.
IV. Urban Imperialism	Commitment of wealth to arms; military utilization of technology for greater resources.	Byzantine pattern of social organization; slavery; network of intercity contacts; new leadership unbound by tradition; conspicuous waste.
V. Decline	Failure of integration of masses possessing technical skills with markets; hence, loss of productivity and production innovations.	Political regimentation; lack of interest among power group in technological innovations; wasteful exploitations of resources and organization through war, etc.

function of interactional forces formulating and executing social policy with respect to the direction of the dominant technology and the disposition of the economic surplus. The fate of urbanism is bound up with the resolution of this problem.

Implicit in this reconstruction of the urban history of early periods is a Ricardian principle which further underscores the symbiotic dependence of urbanization on the interplay of technology and social interaction. The Ricardian principle of diminishing returns has been the setting of a number of discussions by the noted American author and urbanist, Lewis Mumford.[13] There are, he holds, the physical limits on the city of water supply, sewage disposal, traffic control, physical distance. There are the economic limits of increasing costs, frozen "price-pyramids" of land rents and mortgages, civic depletion, urban blight. There are the social limits of population density, complexity of organization, loss of social control, institutional impoverishment, and negative vitality. Here again the functional dependence of the city, in this case of the modern industrial city, is seen against the limited possibilities of a given stage of social interaction and technological development.

It is helpful to recall at this point that Mumford's own classification of the stages of modern industrial urbanism was based on this lively interplay of technological and social forces.[14] The fast shift which occurred in Western urbanization under the impact of industrialization Mumford ascribes to the changing pattern of productive technics and productive relations. Eotechnical," "paleotechnical," and "neotechnical" urbanisms represent for Mumford emergent cultural styles in which the transforming city is seen as an intricate and complex inter-urbanism—literally, if a new term may be permitted, an "urbanicism"[15]—of tools and institutions.

Technology and Society as Functions of Urbanism

Up to this point this discussion has focussed on the view that the city is an *organon*—literally a tool, an implement, or instrument—of a given technology and society. From this point of view the city is the creature and creation of technological and social processes. This thought has perhaps never been more eloquently phrased than by Mumford himself, who, though mindful of the fact that the city is an integral part of a larger functioning unity, nonetheless sees the city as the stage setting of a great and magnificent drama.

> The city, as one finds it in history, is the point of maximum concentration for the power and culture of a community. It is the place where the diffused rays of many separate beams of life fall into focus, with gains in both social effectiveness and significance. The city is the form and symbol of an integrated social relationship: it is the seat of the temple, the market, the hall of justice, the academy of learning. Here in the city the goods of civilization are multiplied and manifolded; here is where human experience is transformed into visible signs, symbols, patterns of conduct, systems of order. Here is where the issues of civilization are focussed; here, too, ritual passes on occasion into the active drama of a full differentiated and selfconscious society.[16]

However, the inter-urban approach to the sociology of the city also sees it as an independent variable shaping, fashioning, limiting, directing and otherwise influencing the total culture of which it is a part, and indeed of many other cultures. To bring out some of the salient themes of this theory of urbanism, it is proposed here to refer to some of the contrasts between peasant and urban cultures; to note the impact of urbanization on the social and technical processes; and to suggest something about the role of the city in the future development of the now "underdeveloped" areas of the world.

Inter-urban sociology, holding that the city is itself an independent variable in the functional nexus described by the terms technology and society, finds the urban revolution to be a major shaping force in the ascendancy of the technical order (to use at this point the excellent analysis provided by anthropologist Robert Redfield).[17] The city, with its occupational and technological interests subordinating the earlier kinship organization of social life, presents us with the social reality which is indeed civilization itself. Here in the city the tools and the institutions which constitute the apparatus of civilized living are coordinated, rationalized, and integrated. Urban and civilized, urbanism and civilization: these are, one discovers, interchangeable terms. The city is the matrix and the carrier, the mirror and the stage of that form and level of organized social living which historically may be recognized as civilization.

The city, then, may be said to have an index value, indicating, measuring, and summarizing the civilization. Childe suggests this theme when he notes the typical traits of urban societies, all of them characteristics of civilized life, and most of them plainly denoting the technical order. The traits he points to include: (1) the great increase in the size of the settlement (the material equipment for human association becomes far larger); (2) the institution of tribute or taxation with resulting accumulation of capital; (3) monumental public works; (4) the art of writing; (5) the beginning of such exact and predictive sciences as arithmetic, geometry, and astronomy; (6) developed economic institutions making possible a greatly expanded foreign trade; (7) full-time technical specialists, as in metal-working; (8) a privileged ruling class; (9) the state. Following Redfield, then, we may say that the urban setting provides the facilities, the impetus, the spirit for the emergence and perfection of the formalized institutional status systems which signalize the transformation of folk cultures into civilizations. The city thus becomes one pole in a continuum which has as its center the peasant village and culture and at its other extreme the primitive tribal community. With the emergence of the urban culture the old pre-urban society in which the technical order is subordinated within the moral order is shaken, often destroyed, always to some extent transformed by the new urbanism in which the moral order is embedded in the technical order, is seldom distinct from it, and often attains a superb adaptation to it. In fact, the mixing and mingling of many moral orders through trade and communication in the emporium which is the city usually subordinates (where it does not negate) the moral to the technical order. Meantime, the outward push of the city as the nucleus of the new world-order transforms country people into peasants: they become, as Redfield has suggested, part-societies with part-cultures, maintaining a tenuous autonomy in uneasy dependence on the city.

The historic novelty of this new order of things which the urban culture in fact is, which civilization indeed is, may be represented in many ways. Perhaps the most startling, certainly one of the most provocative, depictions of urbanism was drawn by the late Professor H. A. Innis, Canadian historian and political economist, who identified the central theme of civilization—of urbanism—with the conquest and monopoly of time.[18] By means of the symbolic and technical skills which the technology of economic surplus made available and concentrated in the city, human beings in many an early historic civilization fashioned their controls over time, resulting, in the course of time, in agricultural and craft technologies, public administration and military regimentation, and all the arts and skills of production and economy. State clashed with Church for the control of time, and ultimately into the interstices of weak control of time by the State came an invading industry which slowly became, in the industrializing cities of the West, "the first among equals" in the competition for the control of time. Time sits enthroned in the city, which links the ever-extending past with the ever-widening present and foreshadows relentlessly the future. Thus it is that a technological order in which social time is standardized, mechanized, packaged, priced, and merchandised in the strictest possible conformity to the time-patterned demands of the engineer and the accountant describes contemporary industrial urbanism in the West, an urbanism which promises to achieve, fairly soon, a universalism the scope of which no other historic urbanism has ever been able to approximate.

The historic novelty and uniqueness of the city as the collective utility and symbol which we call civilization is often misunderstood and misinterpreted as a result of the confusion created by two quite contradictory modes of thought about urbanism. There is, on the one hand, the tendency, as in the case of cultural primitivism, to treat the city as if it were a diabolic contrivance, stifling, corrupting, distorting the supernal moral and social values of a pristine social order identified with the primitive or peasant way of life. Thus, indigenous primitive or peasant cultures are often fervently acclaimed as good and fair beyond words; civilization is then earnestly dismissed as bad and deteriorating. This dichotomic moralism, which often passes for science in the hands, for example, of an eager anthropology or a subservient agricultural extension service, has often led, as George Dixon has observed,[19] to the interesting conclusion that " 'essentially human' social behavior is a function of the least 'civilized' social structures. 'Civilization' and social change . . . are invested with an inherited predisposition to engender 'problems.' " The Rousseauan cast of this view is unmistakable; its ideological or propagandistic values unmeasurable.

An equally misleading view of urbanism, glamorizing and glorifying the city with the same intemperateness and zeal with which the preceding view debases and discounts it, may be thought of as the heroic theory of the city. Here the city is seen as an abstract culture hero, creating, sustaining, elaborating, refining, often rescuing fundamental, significant human values. In its more academic guise this view regards the city as the dominant center in a gradient of power and influence extending out into the hinterland, touching and influencing even the land beyond the hinterland, the spacious and formless "Yonland." Urban sociologists, economists, and geographers in the United States have been and still are fascinated by this aspect of urbanism, which bureaucratizes for an entire society the social order within which these academic specialists do their daily work. Indeed, the tentacular bureaucracy of the city, whether medieval or modern, industrial or pre-industrial, provides considerable evidence for the scholarly heroism which invests the city with incredible—but unquestionably measurable—power and prestige.

Equally academic but less romantic is an entrepreneurial school of thought which argues that enterprise—any kind of collective enterprise: dynastic, ecclesiastical, military, political, industrial—is by its very nature a community-building phenomenon. The city becomes an important, indeed an essential, agent of enterprise, as we see in such familiar cases as the temple city, the fortress city, the shrine city, the capital city, the resort city, and so on. Moreover, as productive enterprise shifts from animate to inanimate sources of power, as it moves from low-energy to high-energy technology,[20] the urban aggregation of men, materials, and machines becomes ever larger, more technically subdivided, more intricately coordinated. A network of communication, control, decision-making and decision-enforcing binds these ever larger segments of humanity into a common life. Vast and complex multifunction cities mirroring the vastness and complexity of an evolving industrial technology, sometimes typifying in their uniformity the standardization of a machine technology, sometimes in their novelty and individuality the specialization and creativity of the machine—such is one perspective at least of the contemporary urbanism which is identified with a technology called industrialism.

It is not easy to maintain a balanced view of the city in the presence of these conflictive versions of the role of the city in history. A helpful moderation may perhaps be found in the ripe historical scholarship of Professor Childe in his closing comment on his survey of "man's progress through the ages":

> But just because tradition is created by societies of men and transmitted in distinctly human and rational ways, it is not fixed and immutable: it is constantly changing as society deals with ever new circumstances. Tradition makes the man, by circumscribing his behavior within certain bounds; but it is equally true that man makes the tradition. And so, we can repeat with deeper insight, "Man makes himself."[21]

NOTES

1. In L. L. Bernard (ed.), *Fields and Methods of Sociology* (New York: Long and Smith, 1934), p. 328.

2. For example, compare Nels Anderson and E. C. Lindeman, *Urban Sociology* (New York: F. S. Crofts, 1930) and T. L. Smith and C. A. McMahon, *The Sociology of Urban Life* (New York: Dryden Press, 1941).

3. *American Journal of Sociology*, 44 (July 1938), pp. 1–25.

4. Reference here is to Chapters I, II in Young's volume (3rd ed.; Englewood Cliffs, New Jersey: Prentice-Hall, 1956).

5. Lewis Mumford, *The Culture of Cities* (New York: Harcourt, Brace, 1938), p. 7.

6. Cf. S. A. Queen and D. B. Carpenter, *The American City* (New York: McGraw-Hill, 1953), or W. C. Hallenbach, *American Urban Communities* (New York: Harper, 1951).

7. For example, after a brave attempt at a global presentation, Professor Rose Hum Lee's *The City* (Philadelphia: J. B. Lippincott, 1954) settles down into familiar national grooves.

8. In this connection see the valuable paper by Gideon Sjoberg, "The Pre-Industrial City," *American Journal of Sociology*, 50 (March 1955), pp. 438–455.

9. Ralph Turner, Vol. I, *The Ancient Cities*, Vol. II, *The Classical Empires* (New York: McGraw-Hill, 1941).

10. The conceptual distinctions employed at this point are developed by the present writer in *La Tecnologia y el Orden Social*, Biblioteca de Ensayos Sociologicos, Instituto de Investigaciones Sociales, Universidad Nacional Mexico, 1956.

11. Turner, *op. cit.*, Vol. I, p. 279.

12. The idea of a natural history of urbanism is not necessarily so pessimistic. Compare the following: Lewis Mumford, "The Natural History of Urbanization," 382–400, in W. L. Thomas, Jr., *Man's Role in Changing the Face of the Earth* (Chicago: University of Chicago Press, 1956) with J. H. Seward, "Cultural Evolution: A Trial Formulation of the Development of Early Civilizations," *American Anthropologist*, 51, (1949), pp. 1–27.

13. Reference here is made especially to his *Culture of Cities*, p. 235.

14. Cf. his *Technics and Civilization* (New York: Harcourt Brace, 1935).

15. A term suggested by Professor J. O. Hertzler, colleague of the present writer, in a conversation about this subject. "Urbanism" might thus refer to the intraurban society, "urbanicism" to the inter-urban society in which city is part of a system of things, interrelated, interacting, and functioning as a unity.

16. Mumford, *Culture of Cities*, p. 3.

17. Cf. *The Primitive World and Its Transformations* (Ithaca, New York: Cornell University Press, 1953).

18. *The Bias of Communication* (Toronto: University of Toronto Press, 1951).

19. George I. J. Dixon, Cultural Primitivism, unpublished doctoral dissertation in sociology, University of Nebraska, 1954.

20. On this particular theme, cf. the original and provocative work by Fred Cottrell, *Energy and Society, the Relation between Energy, Social Change, and Economic Development* (New York: McGraw-Hill, 1955).

21. *Man Makes Himself* (New York: Mentor edition, 1951), p. 188.

2.3 AN EMPIRICAL EXAMINATION
OF METROPOLITAN STRUCTURE

ROBERT H. WELLER

Recently, the emergence of a new community form has attracted considerable attention. Gottman has written of the "megalopolis" in referring to the urbanized Atlantic seaboard from southern New Hampshire to northern Virginia.[1] Megalopolis is conceptualized as a chain of contiguous metropolitan communities bound together by a web of variegated interrelationships. Its major feature is a vast concentration and variety of people, things and functions; and it is viewed as the economic hinge of the nation, linking the North American continent and the foreign markets accessible by the Atlantic Ocean. Thus, Megalopolis is viewed as a functional entity, a super-metropolis, whose parts are interdependent and whose activities dominate the American economy.[2] And this concept is not without adherents. In a discussion of American urbanization, Friedmann and Miller have written: "The older established centers, together with the intermetropolitan peripheries that envelop them, will constitute the new ecological unit of America's post-industrial society that will replace the traditional concepts of the city and metropolis. This basic element of the emerging spatial order we shall call the urban field. . . ."[3]

If we are to understand the nature of urbanization in an industrialized society characterized by constantly shrinking spatio-temporal barriers, it seems necessary to determine empirically whether a new community form actually is emerging. At the outset, it is acknowledged that the areas designated by Gottmann as Megalopolis undoubtedly are the commercial and economic dominants of America. This report focuses, rather, on whether or not there is an increasing intermetropolitan division *within* Megalopolis. If so, this concept does identify a supercommunity; if not, Megalopolis is a mere configuration of metropolises which share a common geographic area.

Background

The concept of the metropolitan community is itself a relatively recent development. The classic presentation of this concept occurred when Gras published his *Introduction to Economic History*.[4] His basic theme was that

From Robert H. Weller, "An Empirical Examination of Metropolitan Structure," *Demography,* Vol. 4 (1967), pp. 734–743. Reprinted by permission of the Population Association of America.

with each stage of technological development, man has simultaneously developed a community organization "suitable to the techniques of wresting a livelihood from the resources of nature."[5] Gras collated information about the technological progress of man through recorded history with comparable information about his economic and social organization and presented a five-stage classification of community organization on a continuum. The metropolis represents the last of these ideal types. Each stage is distinguished by the function that the community performs for the population of an area or for a given group of people. Thus, what distinguishes a metropolis from a city is not size or shape, but the economic function of commercial dominance over a wide area.[6]

The concept of the metropolitan unit—comprised of both the metropolitan city and the surrounding countryside—as the ecological dominant of a technologically advanced society was further advanced by McKenzie through methods quite different than those of Gras. McKenzie concluded that the development of the metropolis had been made possible by greatly improved transportation, which multiplied the avenues of contact within an area and brought formerly independent communities into a single functioning unit. And he asserted that the economic unity of the metropolitan area is based on territorial differentiation and specialization of parts functionally integrated into a balance of spatial and temporal relations.[7] Bogue, influenced by the conceptual structure of both Gras and McKenzie, published *The Structure of the Metropolitan Community*,[8] in which the principal concern is the interrelationships between the metropolitan center and its hinterland.

Thus, considerable attention has been devoted to the assertion that the metropolis is a form of social organization that represents an adaptive response of man to his physical, socio-cultural, and technological environment and that this community form is the commercial and economic dominant of American society. It has also been suggested that there is an intermetropolitan division of labor and an interrelationship based on the functional specialization of metropolises in various types of economic activity. This analysis, then, is directed towards answering the question of whether the so-called "megalopolitan structure" is an example of intermetropolitan interdependence or whether it is simply what it most obviously appears to be—a number of contiguous metropolitan areas whose extremities have begun to overlap.[9]

Three major types of economic activity are necessary for the survival of any community: (1) that which is required for the maintenance of the physical community; (2) the services, including trade, necessary to maintain the population at a given level of living; and (3) manufacturing activity for local consumption.[10] Subsumed under these are the various types of occupational and industrial activity.[11] In any community the configuration of the established economic system must be such that any goods and services that cannot be produced locally will be imported from other areas. This can be effected only through local production of surpluses in some commodities to be exchanged for those items not produced locally. The community can export these commodities in two ways—it can ship out the product or service, or it can temporarily attract consumers from other areas. This is called export activity.[12]

Of course, cities are not self-sufficient entities but carry on exchanges both with their hinterland and with other cities through the indirect medium of the market, which serves to relate intercommunity needs among them. A functionally specialized city, then, is one whose export activity is quite different from that of the average city.[13]

The development of functional specialization between cities has been made possible largely by the general contraction of space and time produced by improvements in transportation and communication with the resulting fluidity of products and people, combined with the development of extremely large cities, itself made possible by these and other technological advances. Since specialization in an activity by a particular population aggregate is indicative of interdependence with other populations, the patterning of functional specialization may be used to examine the pattern of interdependence which exists among the various components of an urban system.[14]

It should be noted that all cities perform virtually all economic functions (for example, wholesale trade), but that they do so to varying degrees, with some cities becoming specialized in one or more types of activity and exporting the product of this activity to other areas and communities. But, since functional specialization of one area implies interdependence with another, any functional interrelationships existing within a system of metropolitan areas should be evident through an examination of employment statistics by industry. Consequently, if there is an intermetropolitan division of labor within Megalopolis, this should be revealed by a pattern of complementary functional specialization among the various metropolitan units. Further, this pattern should have increased temporally as the resultant of the process of differentiation of economic activity and the continued development of the intermetropolitan division of labor.

Unless such a pattern exists among the metropolitan areas of Megalopolis and unless the intensity of this pattern has increased through time, it is difficult to conceive of Megalopolis as anything other than a grouping of contiguous metropolises sharing a common geographic area.

Methods

The units selected for this analysis are the thirty-one metropolises within the area designated by Gottmann as Megalopolis. These were classified as Standard Metropolitan Areas in 1950 and Standard Metropolitan Statistical Areas in 1960.[15] Whether or not a given metropolis is functionally specialized in a particular type of activity has been determined through the use of location quotients, given in the ratio p_i/P_i, where p_i is the proportion of some labor force engaged in a particular activity, and P_i is the proportion of some base or standard population engaged in that activity. The usual inference drawn is that a ratio equal to unity indicates that local production is sufficient to satisfy local consumption, so that the community neither imports nor exports the products of that activity. Accordingly, a ratio greater than unity indicates export of the particular commodity, and a ratio less than unity implies the community cannot satisfy local consumption demands and must import the product to meet this deficiency.[16]

There are two types of export activity in which a metropolis can engage and which produce two conceptually distinct types of functional specialization —that between metropolitan city and hinterland and that between metropolises. Since our concern is intermetropolitan interdependence, that which exists between city and hinterland should be controlled. While in the present analysis this has been attempted through the selection of the base population, in other analyses, the conventional procedure has been to use the United States labor force as the base. This, however, certainly would include the effects of metropolitan-hinterland specialization, large numbers of nonmetropolitan workers and consumers, and interregional diversity of consumption and demand patterns. The base population used in this report is the collective labor force of the thirty-one metropolitan units of analysis. If the pattern of metropolis-hinterland interdependence were the same for all metropolises, this procedure would in fact control for that relationship and any differences would represent intermetropolitan exchanges. While this is not strictly the case, it is felt that a general similarity in this respect exists among metropolitan areas, that any errors incurred will not be cumulative from metropolis to metropolis, and that the effect of these errors will be similar in 1950 and 1960.

Two procedures have been followed to assess the existence of increasing differentiation between the various metropolitan areas. Location quotients for each activity have been determined and the variance of these ratios computed at each point of time. If differentiation occurred during the intercensal period, the variances should be larger in 1960 than in 1950. The second procedure has been to form ratios of the standard deviation of the location quotients in each activity to that in retail food, on the assumption that retail food activity basically represents nonexported activity. Therefore, variation in retail food activity between metropolitan areas can be regarded as approximately the amount of variation that can be expected by chance. If these ratios are not greater than unity, little support for interdependence is present. Further, the change in the 1950–60 period can be measured by summing these ratios at each point of time and comparing the two statistics. If, on the one hand, the aggregate 1960 statistic is larger than the 1950 measure, it seems safe to assert that the process of differentiation toward an intermetropolitan division of labor occurred. On the other hand, if the 1960 statistic is not larger than in 1950, little support is present for the notion that a new community form is emerging.

Results and Conclusions

The labor force profiles in the broad industrial groups are presented in Table 2.3A. Little change occurred in the overall distribution during this period. The largest increases occurred in the categories, "professional services" and "other industries." (The increase in the last was primarily attributable to an increase in the category of "industry not reporting.") The largest decreases occurred in the categories "personal services" and "retail food." These industrial categories declined by about 20 per cent over the respective 1950 portions of the labor force.

As a result of this stability, there was little change in the means of the

TABLE 2.3A   Industrial Characteristics of the Metropolitan Labor Force, 1950 and 1960

Industry	Percent of Total Labor Force		$\frac{1950}{1960}$
	1950	1960	
Construction	5.625	4.985	.886
Manufacturing	32.319	30.899	.956
Utilities, transportation and communication	8.349	7.198	.862
Wholesale trade	4.197	3.867	.921
Retail food	6.552	5.379	.821
All retail trade	15.696	13.737	.875
Finance, insurance and real estate	5.358	5.780	1.079
Business and repair services	2.746	2.969	1.081
Personal services	6.248	5.109	.818
Professional services	10.062	12.832	1.275
Public administration	6.032	6.221	1.031
Other industries[a]	3.345	6.403	1.914

[a]Includes nonurban activities, such as agriculture, forestry and fisheries, and mining, and industry not reported.
SOURCE: All data in this report are computed from the United States Census of Population, Table 35, "Economic Characteristics of the Population by Sex, for Standard Metropolitan Areas, Urbanized Areas, and Urban Places of 10,000 or More: 1950," and Table 75, "Industry Group of Employed Persons and Major Occupational Group of Unemployed Persons, by Sex, for Standard Metropolitan Statistical Areas, Urbanized Areas, and Urban Places of 10,000 or More: 1960."

location quotients (Table 2.3B). When the standard deviations of the location quotients are examined, the only large increase in variability occurs in the category "business and repair services." Since decreases in variability occur in most of the other general categories of economic activity, it appears that metropolitan areas have become more alike rather than more differentiated in this respect.[17] When ratios are formed of the standard deviation of the lo-

TABLE 2.3B   Location Quotients of General Types of Industrial Activity, 1950 and 1960

INDUSTRY	Mean of Location Quotients			Standard Deviation of Location Quotients			Standard Deviation of LQ_i to LQ in Retail Food		
	1950	1960	$\frac{1960}{1950}$	1950	1960	$\frac{1960}{1950}$	1950	1960	$\frac{1960}{1950}$
Construction	.995	1.042	1.047	.228	.190	.833	1.318	1.080	.819
Manufacturing	1.215	1.213	.998	.377	.337	.894	2.179	1.915	.879
Utilities, transportation and communications	.811	.813	1.002	.259	.213	.822	1.497	1.210	.808
Wholesale trade	.707	.745	1.054	.200	.182	.910	1.156	1.034	.894
Retail food	.897	.946	1.055	.173	.176	1.017	1.000	1.000	1.000
All retail trade	.942	.996	1.057	.115	.109	.948	.665	.619	.931
Finance, insurance, and real estate	.639	.708	1.108	.374	.319	.853	2.162	1.813	.839
Business and repair services	.814	.762	.936	.180	.226	1.256	1.040	1.284	1.235
Personal services	.862	.897	1.041	.456	.398	.872	2.636	2.261	.858
Professional services	.902	.924	1.024	.178	.171	.961	1.029	.972	.945
Public administration	.873	.891	1.021	.894	.776	.868	5.167	4.409	.853
Total							19.849	17.597	.887

cation quotients in each activity to that of retail food, there is a cross-sectional evidence of interdependence at each point of time, but there is *no* evidence of increasing interdependence except in "business and repair services." When a summary statistic is formed by summing these ratios, this figure drops from 19.85 in 1950 to 17.60 in 1960—a decline of 11 percent.

On the basis of these broad categories of economic activity, there is little empirical evidence for the notion of an increasing economic differentiation among the thirty-one metropolitan areas included in this study. Since it is possible that these more general types of activity might conceal more detailed interdependence, the additional step has been taken of performing a similar analysis using more detailed industry groups. (See Table 2.3C.)

TABLE 2.3C   Detailed Industrial Characteristics[a] of the Metropolitan Labor Force, 1950 and 1960

Industry	Percent of Total Labor Force		$\frac{1950}{1960}$
	1950	1960	
Construction	5.625	4.985	.886
Durable processing	2.429	2.201	.906
Durable fabricating	11.411	12.935	1.134
Nondurable processing	9.412	7.466	.793
Nondurable fabricating	9.066	8.297	.915
Railroads	1.741	1.009	.580
Trucking	1.219	1.247	1.023
Other transportation	2.445	2.124	.869
Telecommunications	1.445	1.505	1.042
Utilities and sanitary services	1.500	1.312	.875
Wholesale trade	4.197	3.867	.921
Retail food	6.552	5.379	.821
Other retail sales	9.145	8.359	.914
Finance, insurance, and real estate	5.358	5.780	1.079
Business services	1.342	1.866	1.390
Repair services	1.404	1.104	.786
Private household	2.787	2.249	.807
Other personal services	3.460	2.860	.827
Entertainment	1.101	.810	.736
Hospitals, welfare, and other professional services	5.749	7.445	1.295
Educational services	3.212	4.576	1.425
Public administration	6.032	6.221	1.031
Other industries	3.345	6.403	1.914

[a] With the exception of manufacturing activity, these categories follow those of the condensed classification of the United States Census, with the following alterations. The 1950 categories, "hotels and lodging places" and "other personal services," have been combined to equal the 1960 category, "other personal services." The 1950 categories, "medical and other health services" and "other professional and related services," have been combined to correspond with the 1960 category, "hospitals, welfare and other professional services," which consists of "hospitals," "welfare, religious and nonprofit membership organizations," and "other professional and related services." "Educational services, government" and "educational services, private" have been collapsed into "educational services." Retail food is the combination of "food and dairy products stores, and milk retailing" and "eating and drinking places." Manufacturing activity has been divided into four types, following the scheme presented in Otis D. Duncan *et al., Metropolis and Region* (Baltimore: The Johns Hopkins Press, 1960), pp. 57-8.
SOURCE: See Table 2.3A.

TABLE 2.3D   Location Quotients of Detailed Industrial Activities, 1950 and 1960

INDUSTRY	Mean of Location Quotients			Standard Deviation of Location Quotients			Standard Deviation of LQ_i to LQ in Retail Food		
	1950	1960	$\frac{1960}{1950}$	1950	1960	$\frac{1960}{1950}$	1950	1960	$\frac{1960}{1950}$
Construction	.995	1.042	1.047	.228	.190	.833	1.318	1.080	.819
Durable processing	1.522	1.353	.889	1.642	1.149	.700	9.491	6.528	.688
Durable fabricating	1.188	1.237	1.041	.908	.698	.769	5.249	1.966	.756
Nondurable processing	1.575	1.451	.921	1.207	.924	.766	6.977	5.250	.752
Nondurable fabricating	.793	.923	1.164	.450	.575	1.278	2.601	3.267	1.256
Railroads	1.070	1.019	.952	.886	.854	.964	5.121	4.852	.947
Trucking	.937	1.016	1.084	.222	.339	1.527	1.283	1.926	1.501
Other transportation	.515	.454	.882	.290	.292	1.007	1.676	1.659	.990
Telecommunications	.735	.831	1.131	.322	.279	.866	1.861	1.585	.852
Utilities and sanitary services	.966	1.026	1.062	.194	.237	1.222	1.121	1.347	1.202
Wholesale trade	.707	.745	1.054	.200	.182	.910	1.156	1.034	.894
Retail food	.897	.946	1.055	.173	.176	1.017	1.000	1.000	1.000
Other retail sales	.975	1.028	1.054	.009	.008	.889	.052	.045	.865
Finance, insurance, and real estate	.639	.708	1.108	.374	.319	.853	2.162	1.813	.839
Business services	.560	.596	1.064	.327	.380	1.162	1.890	2.159	1.142
Repair services	1.057	1.043	.987	.172	.177	1.029	.994	1.006	1.012
Private household	.785	.839	1.069	.480	.489	1.019	2.775	2.778	1.001
Other personal services	.925	.942	1.018	.629	.561	.892	3.636	3.188	.877
Entertainment	.813	.778	.957	.393	.325	.827	2.272	1.847	.813
Hospitals, welfare, and other professional services	.852	.890	1.045	.223	.167	.749	1.289	.949	.736
Educational services	1.024	1.004	.980	.249	.253	1.016	1.439	1.438	.999
Public administration	.873	.891	1.021	.894	.776	.868	5.167	4.409	.853
Total							60.530	53.126	.878

When this is done, the labor force profile is not quite as stable as when the more general categories are used. The standard deviations of the location quotients show that substantial increases occurred in four activities during the 1950–60 period: "nondurable fabricating," "trucking," "utilities and sanitary services," and "business services." (See Table 2.3D.) There is also considerable cross-sectional evidence of interdependence, as indicated by the ratio of the various standard deviations to that of retail food. However, there is only evidence of substantial increased differentiation or interdependence in the four types of activity mentioned above, while in twelve of the industry groups there is evidence of *decreased* interdependence. In this case, the aggregate statistic declines from 60.53 in 1950 to 53.13 in 1960—a decrease of 12 percent.

To sum up: there is but limited evidence of increasing economic interdependence among the metropolitan areas of Megalopolis. If anything, their labor forces have become more homogeneous. One must therefore question the validity of concepts like Megalopolis as representing a new community form and ecological unit and consider them as clusters of large, contiguous cities until some evidence is made available to support the Megalopolis concept.

NOTES

1. Jean Gottmann, *Megalopolis: The Urbanized Northeastern Seaboard of the United States* (New York: Twentieth Century Fund, 1961).
2. For instance, Gottmann (*ibid.,* p. 100) writes, "Despite the lively competition between the cities and the efforts at decentralization of various overcrowded activities, a specialization worked itself out, establishing *a new division of labor not only between groups of people but also between sections of the region, between places in "Megalopolis."* Elsewhere ("Megalopolis or the Urbanization of the Northeastern Seaboard," *Economic Geography,* XXXIII [1957], 189–200) after stating that "megalopolis" is of Greek origin and means a very large city, Gottmann refers to this region as an urban system. See also, Howard J. Nelson, "Megalopolis and the New York Metropolitan Region: New Studies of the Urbanized Eastern Seaboard," *Annals of the Association of American Geographers,"* LII (1962), 307–10.
3. John Friedmann and John Miller, "The Urban Field," *Journal of the American Institute of Planners,* XXXI (1965). See also, Christopher Tunnard, "America's Super-Cities," *Harper's Magazine* (August, 1958), pp. 59–65.
4. Norman S. B. Gras, *An Introduction to Economic History* (New York: Harper and Brothers, 1922). For an excellent summary, see Donald J. Bogue, *The Structure of the Metropolitan Community: A Study of Dominance and Subdominance* (Ann Arbor: University of Michigan Press, 1950), pp. 7–8.
5. Bogue, *ibid.*
6. Gras, *op. cit.,* p. 184.
7. R. D. McKenzie, *The Metropolitan Community* (New York: McGraw-Hill Book Company, 1933).
8. *Op. cit.*
9. Thus, Jerome Picard writes in "Urban Regions of the United States" (*Urban Land,* XXI, 4 [April, 1962], 3): "A popular misconception has led to calling this a 'city 500 miles long.' It most definitely is *not* a single city, but a region of concentrated urbanism—a continuous zone of metropolises, cities, towns and exurban settlement within which one is never far from a city."
10. Otis D. Duncan and Albert J. Reiss, Jr., *Social Characteristics of Urban and Rural Communities, 1950* (New York: John Wiley and Sons, Inc., 1956), p. 216.
11. For a study linking the occupational and industrial composition of a community, see Omer R. Galle, "Occupational Composition and the Metropolitan Hierarchy: The Inter- and Intra-Metropolitan Division of Labor," *American Journal of Sociology,* LXIX (1963), 260–69.
12. For a sophisticated handling of the dichotomy between maintenance and export activities, see Albert J. Reiss, Jr., "Functional Specialization of Cities," in *Cities and Society: The Revised Reader in Urban Sociology,* ed. Paul K. Hatt and Albert J. Reiss, Jr. (Glencoe: The Free Press, 1957), pp .555–76; and Gunnar Alexandersson, *The Industrial Structure of American Cities* (Lincoln: University of Nebraska Press, 1955).
13. Duncan and Reiss, *op. cit.,* p. 217. For a brief discussion of the European origins of the concept of functional specialization, see Alexandersson, *op. cit.,* p. 20.
14. This notion is stated explicitly by Noel P. Gist and Sylvia Fleis Fava (*Urban Society* [5th ed.; New York: Thomas Y. Crowell Company, 1964], 248), who write, "To the extent that specialization within a region occurs, to that extent there must be interdependence of the parts one on another." This is also a recurring theme in Amos H. Hawley, *Human Ecology: A Theory of Community Structure* (New York: The Ronald Press Company, 1950), especially in Chapter 12. Conceptually distinct approaches to measuring systematic interdependence, or in testing for interdependence to ascertain whether a system exists, may be found in Walter Isard and Robert Kavesh, "Economic Structural Interrelations of Metropolitan Regions," *American Journal of Sociology,* LX (1954), 152–62; and in Ralph W. Pfouts, "Patterns of Economic Interaction in the Crescent," in *Urban Growth Dynamics in a Regional Cluster of Cities,* ed. F. Stuart Chapin, Jr., and Shirley F. Weiss (New York: John Wiley and Sons, Inc., 1962), pp. 31–58.
15. There were 39 SMSA's in this area in 1960. Under 1950 definitions, however, many of the eight additional SMSA's would not have qualified as SMA's. For a discussion of

the differences in definition between SMA's and SMSA's as well as changes in boundary and title occurring to various SMSA's between 1950 and 1960, see Office of Statistical Standards, *Standard Metropolitan Statistical Areas* (Washington, D.C.: Government Printing Office, 1961). It was felt that analysis should be limited to units for which comparable data are available, at the same time recognizing that the process of economic differentiation implied by Megalopolis and similar concepts should foster the rise of new metropolitan areas specialized in particular types of economic activity. The places included in this study, by their 1950 SMA designations, are: Albany–Schenectady–Troy; Allentown–Bethlehem–Easton; Atlantic City; Baltimore; Boston; Bridgeport; Brockton; Fall River; Harrisburg; Hartford; Lancaster; Lawrence; Lowell; Manchester; New Bedford; New Britain–Bristol; New Haven; Philadelphia; Providence; Reading; Scranton; Springfield–Holyoke; Stamford–Norwalk; Trenton; Washington; Waterbury; Wilkes-Barre–Hazleton; Wilmington; Worcester; and York. The New York–New Jersey Standard Consolidated Area was used in 1960 because of its correspondence to the 1950 New York–Northeastern New Jersey SMA. For an appraisal of the extent to which SMA's correspond to communities, see Allan G. Feldt, "The Metropolitan Area Concept: An Evaluation of the 1950 SMA's," *Journal of the American Statistical Association*, LX (1965), 617–36.

16. Obviously, these arguments rest on a number of assumptions which may or may not be tenable in a given case. For a discussion of this problem, see John M. Matilla and Wilbur Thompson, "The Measurement of the Economic Base of the Metropolitan Area," *Land Economics*, XXXI (1955), 215–28; and George H. Hildebrand and Arthur Mace, Jr., "The Employment Multiplier in an Expanding Industrial Market: Los Angeles County, 1940–1947," *Review of Economics and Statistics*, XXXII (1950), 241–49. An earlier statistic from which the location quotient has been developed may be found in the "coefficient of localization," in A. J. Wensley and P. Sargent Florence, "Recent Industrial Concentration," *Review of Economic Studies*, VII (1940), 139–58.

17. An increase in homogeneity of economic activity should not be entirely surprising. Relatively advantageous locations for a given type of economic activity are dependent upon more favorable accessibility to basic industry inputs from regional and national sources and to regional and national markets. Basic industry inputs would include intermediate factors such as a skilled labor force, economies of scale, industry linkages, and so on, as well as the basic resources. As transportation and communication networks continue to improve within a region, any given point within that region will have better access both to the input factors and to the existing markets. Eventually this would reduce variance in accessibility for different points within the region. Further, the various metropolitan areas within the megalopolitan region have been experiencing population growth, which enlarges existing markets and creates new ones. These two factors, combined with the market orientation of the regional economy, are conducive to ubiquity of production and economic activity, and would lead to homogeneity of labor force profiles for the various metropolitan communities contained within the megalopolitan region. For a treatment of the consequences of variations in access characteristics, see Harvey S. Perloff *et al., Regions, Resources and Economic Growth* (Lincoln: University of Nebraska Press, 1960).

2.4 COLOR COMPOSITION
AND CITY-SUBURBAN STATUS DIFFERENCES[1]

J. JOHN PALEN and LEO SCHNORE

The junior author of the present report has recently demonstrated that city-suburban status differences in larger Urbanized Areas are just the opposite of those seen in smaller areas.[2] In the older and larger areas, he found, the suburbs had higher socioeconomic status than their central cities, but this was progressively less true of smaller areas. In small Urbanized Areas, the status of city residents tends to be higher than that of suburbanites. His research, however, was based upon a series of "Advance Reports" that did not break down population characteristics by color. It was therefore impossible to examine the possible effect that city-suburban differences in color composition might have had on city-suburban status differentials. This was unfortunate because nonwhites are heavily concentrated within the nation's large cities; rather few live in the "suburbs," however the latter may be defined.[3] There are also well-known differences between the major color groups in socioeconomic status. Since more complete data are now available, it is clearly desirable to re-examine city-suburban status differences while controlling for color.

In our replication of the earlier study it was hypothesized that the *white* population would show city-suburban status differences similar to those found for the total population. It was expected that population size and age of city would still be rather important factors: the larger and older the urban area, we expected, the higher the socioeconomic status of the white suburban population in comparison to that of the central city. For the *nonwhite* population, we anticipated no clear-cut relationship between the size and the age of the urban area, on the one hand, and city-suburban status differentials, on the other, since suburban communities have been so successful in excluding nonwhite residents.

In the original study it was possible to make city-suburban comparisons in 200 of the 213 Urbanized Areas officially delineated in conjunction with the 1960 Census of Population and Housing. For the present study such comparisons could be made for 180 areas using the white population, and for only 131 areas using the nonwhite population.[4] In each of these cases, we have determined whether the city or the suburban area was higher in socioeconomic

From J. John Palen and Leo Schnore, "Color Composition and City-Suburban Status Differences," *Land Economics,* Vol. 41 (February 1965), pp. 87–91. Copyright © by The Regents of The University of Wisconsin. Reprinted by permission.

status, using three traditional variables (income, education, and occupation). Income was operationally defined as median *family* income. The educational measure was the per cent of the population aged twenty-five years or over with four years high school or more. The occupational measure was the per cent of the employed labor force engaged in white-collar occupations.

City-suburban Status Differentials by Size and Color. An examination of Table 2.4A indicates that the *white population* shows the expected pattern of association between city size and the direction of socioeconomic status differentials. The larger the size, the greater the per cent of Urbanized Areas having higher status suburbs than central cities. The income data, for example, show that in Urbanized Areas with over 500,000 inhabitants there are no cases in which the central cities surpass their suburbs in median family income, while over half the cities do so in the smaller areas (under 150,000 inhabitants). When occupation is used as the status measure however, the suburban advantage in the larger Urbanized Areas is no longer as definite; and in the smaller areas the city plainly has the advantage. There is thus a clear association between size and the direction of city-suburban differentials in white socioeconomic status. Another point worth noting is that the various proportions shown for the white population are generally lower than the comparable figures for the total population. This can be attributed to the well-known concentration of nonwhites in the central city. Removing the low status nonwhites from the city figures tends to raise the white city population's status in relation to the white population of the suburbs.

The data for *nonwhites* are not nearly as clear-cut as those for whites. The figures in Table 2.4A for nonwhite income, education, and occupation show a weak pattern of relationship between the size of urban area and status

TABLE 2.4A   City-Suburban Differentials in Socioeconomic Status by Size of Urbanized Area and Color

Size of Urbanized Area (1960)	Per Cent of Urbanized Areas with Higher Suburban Median Family Income			Per Cent of Urbanized Areas with Higher Suburban Per Cent Completing High School			Per Cent of Urbanized Areas with Higher Suburban Per Cent in White-Collar Occupations			Number of Areas		
	Total	Non-white	White	Total	Non-white	White	Total	Non-white	White	Total	Non-white	White
1,000,000+	100.0	75.0	100.0	100.0	50.0	93.8	87.5	25.0	75.0	16	16	16
500,000–1,000,000	100.0	59.1	100.0	100.0	54.5	90.9	86.4	50.0	54.5	22	22	22
250,000–500,000	79.3	60.7	75.9	75.9	53.6	69.0	55.2	46.4	48.3	29	28	29
150,000–250,000	72.1	62.1	67.5	62.8	44.8	57.5	48.8	41.4	37.3	43	29	40
100,000–150,000	70.3	68.4	47.1	64.9	42.1	55.9	40.5	42.1	20.6	37	19	34
50,000–100,000	56.6	64.7	46.2	49.1	29.4	48.7	30.2	35.3	20.5	53	17	39
All Areas	74.0	64.1	67.2	68.5	46.6	64.4	50.5	41.2	37.8	200	131	180

SOURCES: United States Bureau of Census, *U.S. Census of Population: 1960, General Social and Economic Characteristics,* Final Report PC (1), Chapter "C" for individual states (Washington, D.C.: United States Government Printing Office, 1962), Tables 73, 74, 76, 77, and 78.

differentials. Moreover, the 16 Urbanized Areas of over a million are especially "deviant" cases. This is particularly true of the occupational data; in the largest size class only one out of every four areas has status differentials favoring the suburbs. This is despite the fact that the comparable income data favor the suburbs over the central city in three out of every four large areas. At best, there is a very weak association between city size and the direction of socioeconomic status differentials among nonwhites. Perhaps the most striking finding for nonwhites is that the results of city-suburban status comparisons depend so heavily upon the measure used.

City-suburban Status Differentials by Age and Color. As in the earlier study, the "age" of the Urbanized Area was determined by counting the number of intercensal decades that has passed since the central city first reached a population of 50,000 persons. Looking at Table 2.4B, the columns for the *white* population indicate that age of the central city and higher suburban socioeconomic status are positively associated. The older the city, the larger the proportion of suburbs holding the status advantage over the central city. For whites, the measure of occupational status again tends to favor the central city more than do the measures of income and education. The *nonwhite* population fails to show any clear relationship between a city's age and the relative status of city-dwellers and suburbanites. When occupation is used as the measure of status, status differentials are associated with city age only if one ignores the very oldest group of cities, i.e., those which first reached 50,000 between 1800 and 1860, and one would hardly recommend such a procedure.

Regional Variations. What accounts for the highly dissimilar city-suburban status differentials found in the two color groups? The most obvious factor that might influence the above results is regional location, which was not taken into account in the earlier study. This is especially likely to be true in the case of the nonwhite population. We therefore re-examined

TABLE 2.4B   City-Suburban Differentials in Socioeconomic Status by Age of City and Color

Census Year in Which City (or Cities) First Reached 50,000 Inhabitants	Per Cent of Urbanized Areas with Higher Suburban Median Family Income			Percent of Urbanized Areas with Higher Suburban Per Cent Completing High School			Percent of Urbanized Areas with Higher Suburban Per Cent in White-Collar Occupations			Number of Areas		
	Total	Non-white	White	Total	Non-white	White	Total	Non-white	White	Total	Non-white	White
1800–1860	100.0	71.4	100.0	100.0	57.1	100.0	100.0	21.4	85.8	14	14	14
1870–1880	100.0	92.9	100.0	100.0	64.3	93.3	100.0	64.3	86.7	17	14	15
1890–1900	86.1	78.3	87.1	75.0	47.8	71.0	58.3	52.2	48.4	36	23	31
1910–1920	75.0	50.0	76.1	75.0	50.0	69.6	54.2	43.7	34.8	48	32	46
1930–1940	71.9	50.0	50.0	56.3	35.0	53.1	31.3	35.0	18.8	32	20	32
1950–1960	50.9	60.7	33.3	47.2	35.7	40.5	24.5	32.1	14.3	53	28	42
All Areas	74.0	64.1	67.2	68.5	46.6	64.4	50.5	41.2	37.8	200	131	180

SOURCES: Same as Table 2.4A.

city-suburban differences in status while "controlling" crudely for region. As anticipated, Southern and non-Southern cities were most unlike. For convenience we shall refer to these areas as being either in the "South" or in the "North and West."[5]

An examination of Table 2.4C indicates that the previously-observed association between size and the direction of city-suburban status differences continues to hold generally for the white population regardless of region, though it is more marked in the South. In both broad regions the larger Urbanized Areas have suburbs possessing higher socioeconomic levels than their central cities. The most striking regional differences for the white population occur in the smallest areas. The status differentials in the South overwhelmingly favor the city proper, while this does not occur in the North and West.

The nonwhite patterns were, as expected, considerably different for Southern and non-Southern cities. *The nonwhite population of Urbanized Areas in the North and West show a clear association between city size and city-suburban differentials in socioeconomic status.* Nonwhites in these areas thus resemble the white population. *In contrast, Urbanized Areas in the South generally fail to show an association between size and city-suburban differentials in socioeconomic status.* In fact, the income data for Southern nonwhites in Table 2.4C show a perfect reversal of the pattern of association shown by the data for whites.

In Table 2.4D, the white population again exhibits the expected association between age of the city and city-suburban status differentials *in both broad regions.* The nonwhite figures for income and education show a rough association between city age and the direction of city-suburban status differ-

TABLE 2.4C   City-Suburban Differentials in Socioeconomic Status by Size of Urbanized Area, Color, and Region

Region and Size of Urbanized Area, 1960	Per Cent of Urbanized Areas with Higher Suburban Income			Per Cent of Urbanized Areas with Higher Suburban Education			Per Cent of Urbanized Areas with Higher Suburban Occupation		
South	Total	Non-white	White	Total	Non-white	White	Total	Non-white	White
500,000+	100.0	38.5	100.0	100.0	30.8	92.3	92.3	15.4	53.8
250,000–500,000	60.0	40.0	50.0	70.0	40.0	60.0	60.0	40.0	50.0
150,000–250,000	64.7	73.3	52.9	52.9	40.0	35.3	35.3	33.3	17.6
100,000–150,000	92.3	83.3	46.2	53.9	50.0	38.5	46.2	41.7	7.7
50,000–100,000	52.9	90.0	18.8	29.4	40.0	18.8	23.5	30.0	6.3
All Areas	72.9	65.0	52.2	58.6	40.0	46.4	48.6	31.7	24.6
North and West	Total	Non-white	White	Total	Non-white	White	Total	Non-white	White
500,000+	100.0	80.0	100.0	100.0	64.0	92.0	84.0	52.0	68.0
250,000–500,000	89.5	72.2	89.5	79.0	61.1	73.7	52.6	50.0	42.1
150,000–250,000	76.9	50.0	78.3	69.2	50.0	73.9	57.7	50.0	52.2
100,000–150,000	58.3	42.9	47.6	70.8	28.6	66.7	37.5	42.9	28.6
50,000–100,000	58.3	29.6	65.2	58.3	14.3	69.6	33.3	42.9	30.4
All Areas	74.6	63.4	76.6	73.9	52.1	75.7	51.5	49.3	45.0

SOURCES: Same as Table 2.4A.

TABLE 2.4D. City-Suburban Differentials in Socioeconomic Status by Age of City, Color, and Region

Region and Census Year in Which City (or Cities) First Reached 50,000 Inhabitants	Per Cent of Urbanized Areas with Higher Suburban Income			Per Cent of Urbanized Areas with Higher Suburban Education			Per Cent of Urbanized Areas with Higher Suburban Occupation		
South	Total	Non-white	White	Total	Non-white	White	Total	Non-white	White
1800–1880	100.0	60.0	100.0	100.0	40.0	100.0	100.0	0.0	80.0
1890–1900	100.0	75.0	100.0	87.5	37.5	62.5	87.5	50.0	50.0
1910–1920	70.6	58.8	70.6	70.6	47.1	58.8	64.7	29.4	29.4
1930–1940	76.5	60.0	47.1	47.1	33.3	41.2	23.5	40.0	11.8
1950–1960	60.9	86.7	18.2	39.1	40.0	22.7	30.4	26.7	9.1
All Areas	74.3	68.3	53.6	58.6	40.0	46.4	48.6	31.7	24.6
North and West	Total	Non-white	White	Total	Non-white	White	Total	Non-white	White
1800–1880	100.0	87.0	100.0	100.0	65.2	93.8	100.0	52.2	87.5
1890–1900	82.1	80.0	82.6	71.4	53.3	73.9	50.0	53.3	47.8
1910–1920	77.4	40.0	79.3	77.4	53.3	75.9	48.4	60.0	37.9
1930–1940	66.7	20.0	53.3	66.7	40.0	66.7	40.0	20.0	26.7
1950–1960	43.3	30.8	50.0	53.3	30.8	60.0	20.0	38.5	20.0
All Areas	73.8	60.6	75.7	73.8	52.1	75.7	51.5	49.3	45.9

SOURCES: Same as Table 2.4A.

entials in the North and West, but no noticeable association was found in the South on any of the three measures.

Conclusions

Our first hypothesis—that the white population would show city-suburban status differentials similar to those of the total population—was confirmed by the data. Within the *white* population there was a definite and regular association between the age and size of the urbanized area, on the one hand, and the direction of city-suburban status differentials, on the other. The older and larger areas were much more likely to have high status suburban populations, while in the newer and smaller areas the city itself was most likely to enjoy the status advantage.

The second hypothesis, to the effect that the *nonwhite* population would not show the same relationships, was only partially confirmed. It was discovered that there was another important factor in addition to city age and size. That factor was the regional location of the Urbanized Area. Looking at the nonwhite data, without respect to region, there is practically no relationship between size and age on the one hand, and the direction of city-suburban variation on the other. When region is controlled, however, such relationships do tend to appear in the North and West. City-suburban status differentials among nonwhites in the North and West are generally similar to those shown by the white population in both broad regions. In contrast, the nonwhite data for Southern areas do not reveal any clear and consistent set of associations between *either* (a) the age *or* (b) the size of the Urbanized Area and (c) the direction of city-suburban status differences.

Why does the Southern nonwhite population fail to show such consistent relationships? We can only speculate at this point. Some of the unusual features of the Southern nonwhite findings are probably due to the effects of housing segregation, which recent research shows to be increasing in that section of the country while decreasing in the North and West.[6] However, the most probable reason why the Southern nonwhites fail to show the usual city-suburban status differences is that in the South, as opposed to the North, the poorer and less advantaged nonwhite residents traditionally lived on the periphery of the city.[7] Although there are indications that this pattern is changing, there still exist many nonwhite areas at the *edges* of Southern cities, large and small, old and new. This "historical survival" of low status neighborhoods on the Southern city's periphery, as well as in its central core, may be confounding the pattern of city-suburban status differentials found in other populations. The Southern nonwhite population, in short, may be in a state of transition between the traditional residential pattern of the Old South and the contemporary American urban pattern seen in both white and nonwhite neighborhoods in the rest of the country.[8]

NOTES

1. For a detailed report, see J. John Palen, *The Effect of Color Composition on City-Suburban Status Differentials,* unpublished M. S. thesis, Department of Sociology, University of Wisconsin, 1963, pp. v, + 29.

2. Leo F. Schnore, "The Socio-Economic Status of Cities and Suburbs," *American Sociological Review,* February, 1963, pp. 76–85.

3. See Leo F. Schnore and Harry Sharp, "Racial Changes in Metropolitan Areas, 1950–1960," *Social Forces,* March, 1963, pp. 247–253.

4. Nonwhite Urbanized Area or central city figures were not available in 20 cases. Since the *white* figures were obtained by subtracting the appropriate *nonwhite* figures from the *total* figures, the absence of nonwhite statistics made it impossible to determine the characteristics of the white population. The nonwhite sample was further reduced by excluding any Urbanized Area containing less than seventy "suburban" nonwhite residents. In every other respect, the study summarized here was an exact replication of the earlier research, including a multiple correlation analysis not reported here.

5. Urbanized Areas were assigned to regions according to the state location of their principal central cities. The "South" was identified according to traditional census practice, i.e., as consisting of the District of Columbia and the following states: Maryland, Delaware, West Virginia, Virginia, North Carolina, South Carolina, Kentucky, Tennessee, Georgia, Florida, Alabama, Mississippi, Arkansas, Louisiana, Oklahoma, and Texas. Among the 200 Urbanized Areas studied by Schnore, 70 were in the South and 130 were in the North and West. White population data were available for 69 of these areas in the South and for 111 in the North and West. Nonwhite population data are reported here for 60 of the Urbanized Areas in the South and for 71 in the North and West.

6. Karl E. Taeuber, "Negro Residential Segregation, 1940–1960: Changing Trends in the Large Cities of the United States," a paper read at the 1962 meetings of the American Sociological Association.

7. Rudolf Heberle, "Social Consequences of the Industrialization of Southern Cities," *Social Forces,* October 1948, pp. 29–37.

8. The junior author's subsequent research has taken two directions, *viz.,* (a) refining the comparisons of socioeconomic status and (b) using a finer areal grain in comparing various parts of the larger urban complex. In a paper delivered at the 1963 meetings

of the Population Association of America (Philadelphia, Pennsylvania, April 27, 1963), some very detailed comparisons of educational status differences between city and suburban whites and nonwhites were reported; this paper was published as "Urban Structure and Suburban Selectivity," *Demography*, 1 (1964), pp. 164–176. A preliminary report on another study, using a tract-based analysis of 25 Southern and non-Southern cities, was given at the 1963 meetings of the American Association for the Advancement of Science (Cleveland, Ohio, December 27, 1963) under the title "The Segregation of Nonwhites in Metropolitan Centers." Forthcoming in *Demography*, 2nd Volume. The finer areal grain permitted by the use of census tracts leads to sounder inferences than those based upon gross city-suburban comparisons, such as reported in this paper. Nevertheless, these two follow-up studies do not contradict any of the conclusions stated above.

2.5 THE WHITE EXODUS
TO SUBURBIA STEPS UP

HERBERT J. GANS

In this unpredictable world, nothing can be predicted quite so easily as the continued proliferation of suburbia. Not only have American cities stopped growing for more than a generation, while the metropolitan areas of which they are a part were continuing to expand lustily, but there is incontrovertible evidence that another huge wave of suburban home building can be expected in the coming decade.

Between 1947 and about 1960, the country experienced the greatest baby boom ever, ending the slowdown in marriages and childbirths created first by the Depression and then by World War II. Today, the earliest arrivals of that baby boom are themselves old enough to marry, and many are now setting up housekeeping in urban or suburban apartments. In a few years, however, when their first child is two to three years old, and the second is about to appear, many young parents will decide to buy suburban homes. Only simple addition is necessary to see that by the mid-seventies, they will be fashioning another massive suburban building boom, provided of course that the country is affluent and not engaged in World War III.

The new suburbia may not look much different from the old; there will, however, be an increase in the class and racial polarization that has been developing between the suburbs and the cities for several generations now. The suburbs will be home for an ever larger proportion of working-class, middle-class and upper-class whites; the cities, for an ever larger proportion of poor and nonwhite people. The continuation of this trend means that, by the nineteen-seventies, a greater number of cities will be 40 to 50 per cent nonwhite in population, with more and larger ghettos and greater municipal poverty on the one hand, and stronger suburban opposition to open housing and related policies to solve the city's problems on the other hand. The urban crisis will worsen, and although there is no shortage of rational solutions, nothing much will be done about the crisis unless white America permits a radical change of public policy and undergoes a miraculous change of attitude toward its cities and their populations.

Another wave of suburban building would develop even if there had

From Herbert J. Gans, "The White Exodus to Suburbia Steps Up," *The New York Times Magazine*, January 7, 1968. © 1968 by The New York Times Company. Reprinted by permission.

been no post-World War II baby boom, for American cities have always grown at the edges, like trees, adding new rings of residential development every generation as the beneficiaries of affluence and young families sought more modern housing and "better" neighborhoods. At first, the new rings were added inside the city limits, but ever since the last half of the 19th century, they have more often sprung up in the suburbs.

Although these trends may not be so apparent to New Yorkers, who live in a world capital rather than in a typical American city, both urban and suburban growth have almost always taken the form of single-family houses, first on large lots and later, as less affluent city dwellers could afford to move out, on smaller lots. Even inside most American cities—again, other than New York and a few others—the majority of people live in single-family homes.

Moreover, studies of housing preferences indicate that the majority of Americans, including those now living in the city, want a suburban single-family house once they have children, and want to remain in that house when their children have grown up. This urge for suburban life is not limited to the middle class or just to America; the poor would leave the city as well if they could afford to go, and so would many Europeans.

The only people who clearly do not want to live in the suburbs are the single and some of the childless couples, and that handful of urban middle-class professionals and intellectuals living in New York and a few other cosmopolitan cities. For everyone else, suburbia means more housing space at less cost, a backyard and an up-to-date community—all of which make raising children significantly easier for the mother, more compatible neighbors, cleaner air, a chance to leave the dirt and congestion behind and, in recent years, a chance also to escape the expansion of Negro and poor neighborhoods. Even some of the dedicated urbanites move to the suburbs when their children are young, although they—but only they—miss the cultural facilities of the big city and are often unhappy in suburbia.

Obviously, the popular antisuburban literature, which falsely accuses the suburbs of causing conformity, matriarchy, adultery, divorce, alcoholism and other standard American pathologies, has not kept anyone from moving to the suburbs, and even the current predictions of land shortages, longer commuting and urban congestion in the suburbs will not discourage the next generation of home buyers. Most, if not all, metropolitan areas still have plenty of rural land available for suburban housing. Moreover, with industry and offices now moving to the suburbs, new areas previously outside commuting range become ripe for residential development to house their employees. Thus, for several years now, more than half the suburbanites of Nassau County have been commuting to jobs inside Nassau County; in the next decade, they will probably be joined by new commuters living in Suffolk County. Of course, all this leads to increasing suburban congestion, but most suburbanites do not mind it. They do not leave the city for a rural existence, as the folklore has it; they want a half acre or more of land and all their favorite urban facilities within a short driving distance from the house.

In some metropolitan areas, or in parts of them, land may indeed be too scarce and thus too expensive to permit another round of old-style suburbanization. There, people will move into "townhouses" and semidetached houses, which have less privacy than single-family houses, but still provide private yards and a feeling of separateness from the next-door neighbors. The recent failure of Reston, Va., the much praised new town near Washington, D.C., suggests, however, that the exquisitely designed communal recreational areas cannot substitute for private space. Most home buyers do not seem to want that much togetherness, and Reston's townhouses, which lacked front or back-yards, sold too slowly.

It goes without saying that almost all the new suburbanites—and the developments built for them—will be white and middle-income, for, barring miracles in the housing industry and in Federal subsidies, the subdivisions of the seventies will be too expensive for any family earning less than about $7,500 (in 1967 dollars). Thus, even if suburbia were to be racially inte-grated, cost alone would exclude most nonwhites. Today, less than 5 per cent of New York State's suburban inhabitants are nonwhite, and many of them live in ghettos and slums in the small towns around which suburbia has de-veloped.

Nevertheless, the minuscule proportion of nonwhite suburbanites will increase somewhat in the future, for, if the current affluence continues, it will benefit a small percentage of Negroes and Puerto Ricans. Some of them will be able to move into integrated suburban communities, but the majority will probably wind up in existing and new middle-class ghettos.

If urban employment is available, or if the ongoing industrialization of the South pushes more people off the land, poverty-stricken Negroes will con-tinue to come to the cities, overcrowding and eventually enlarging the inner-city ghettos. Some of the better-off residents of these areas will move to "outer-city" ghettos, which can now be found in most American cities; for example, in Queens. And older suburbs like Yonkers and Mount Vernon will continue to lose some of the present residents and attract less affluent new-comers, as their housing, schools and other facilities age. As a result of this process, which affects suburbs as inevitably as city neighborhoods, some of their new inhabitants may be almost as poor as inner-city ghetto residents, so that more and more of the older suburbs will face problems of poverty and social pathology now thought to be distinctive to the city.

That further suburban growth is practically inevitable does not mean it is necessarily desirable, however. Many objections have been raised, some to suburbia itself, others to its consequences for the city. For example, ever since the rise of the postwar suburbs, critics have charged that suburban life is culturally and psychologically harmful for its residents, although many socio-logical studies, including my own, have shown that most suburbanites are happier and emotionally healthier than when they lived in the city. In addition, the critics have charged that suburbia desecrates valuable farm and recreation land, and that it results in "suburban" sprawl.

Suburbia undoubtedly reduces the supply of farm acreage, but America has long suffered from an oversupply of farmland, and I have never under-stood why allowing people to raise children where other people once raised potatoes desecrates the land. Usually, the criticism is directed to "ugly, mass-produced, look-alike little boxes," adding a class bias to the charges, as if people who can only afford mass-produced housing are not entitled to live where they please, or should stay in the city.

Suburban developments sometimes also rise on recreational land, although state and Federal funds are now available to save such land for public leisure-time use. Even so, I find it difficult to believe that child raising and the at-home recreation that goes on in a suburban house is a less worthy use of land than parks, which people only visit during part of the year. Furthermore, there is no reason why we cannot have both suburbia *and* parks, the latter built farther out, with high-speed expressways and mass transit to bring them closer to visitors.

Suburban sprawl scatters residential developments over large areas be-cause single-family houses take up so much more acreage than multiple dwell-ings. As a result, highways, transit systems, utility lines and sewers must be longer and therefore more expensive. These added costs are not a steep price for affluent suburbanites; they want low-density housing more than economy, and they do not care that sprawl looks ugly to the trained eye of the architect. There may even be somewhat less sprawl in the future, partly because of town-house developments, partly because high land costs at the far edges of the suburbs may induce builders to fill up vacant land left in the existing sub-urban rings during earlier periods of residential construction. Moreover, the next wave of suburbia may finally generate sufficient political support for the building of high-speed mass transit systems, now languishing on the plan-ners' drawing boards, to connect the parts of the sprawling area.

The harmful effects of suburbia on the city are a more important crit-icism. One charge, made ever since the beginning of suburbanization in the 19th century, is that the suburbs rob the city of its taxpaying, civic-minded and culture-loving middle class. Actually, however, middle-class families are often a tax liability for the city; they demand and receive more services, par-ticularly more schools, than their taxes pay for. Nor is there any evidence that they are more civic-minded than their non-middle-class neighbors; they may be more enthusiastic joiners of civic organizations, but these tend to de-fend middle-class interests and not necessarily the public interest. Moreover, many people who live in the suburbs still exert considerable political influence in the city because of their work or their property holdings and see to it that urban power structures still put middle-class interests first, as slum organiza-tions, whose demands for more antipoverty funds or public housing are regu-larly turned down by city hall, can testify.

The alleged effect of the suburbs on urban culture is belied by the vast cultural revival in the city which occurred at the same time the suburban exodus was in full swing. Actually, most suburbanites rarely used the city's cultural facilities even when they lived in the city, and the minority that did continues to do so, commuting in without difficulty. Indeed, I suspect that over half the ticket buyers for plays, art movies, concerts and museums, particularly outside New York, are—and have long been—suburbanites. Besides, there is no reason why cultural institutions cannot, like banks, build branches in the suburbs, as they are beginning to do now. Culture is no less culture for being outside the city.

A much more valid criticism of suburbanization is its effect on class and racial segregation, for the fact that the suburbs have effectively zoned out the poor and the nonwhites is resulting in an ever-increasing class and racial polarization of city and suburb. In one sense, however, the familiar data about the increasing polarization are slightly misleading. In years past, when urban census statistics showed Negroes and whites living side by side, they were actually quite polarized socially. On New York's Upper West Side, for example, the big apartment buildings are *de facto* segregated for whites, while the rotting brownstones between them are inhabited by Negroes and Puerto Ricans. These blocks are integrated statistically or geographically, but not socially, particularly if white parents send their children to private schools.

Nor is suburbanization the sole cause of class and racial polarization; it is itself an effect of trends that have gone on inside the city as well, and not only in America. When people become more affluent and choose where they want to live, they choose to live with people like themselves. What has happened in the last generation or two is that the opportunity of home buyers to live among compatible neighbors, an opportunity previously available only to the rich, has been extended to people in the middle- and lower-middle-income brackets. This fact does not justify either class or racial segregation, but it does suggest that the polarization resulting from affluence would have occurred even without suburbanization.

Class and racial polarization are harmful because they restrict freedom of housing choice to many people, but also because of the financial consequences for the city. For one thing, affluent suburbia exploits the financially bankrupt city; even when payroll taxes are levied, suburbanites do not pay their fair share of the city's cost in providing them with places of work, shopping areas and cultural facilities and with streets and utilities, maintenance, garbage removal and police protection for these facilities.

More important, suburbanites live in vest-pocket principalities where they can, in effect, vote to keep out the poor and the nonwhites and even the not very affluent whites.

As a result, the cities are in a traumatic financial squeeze. Their ever more numerous low-income residents pay fewer taxes but need costly municipal services, yet cities are taking in less in property taxes all the time, particularly as the firms that employ suburbanites and the shops that cater to them also move to the suburbs. Consequently, city costs rise at the same time as city income declines. To compound the injustice state and Federal politicians from suburban areas often vote against antipoverty efforts and other Federal funding activities that would relieve the city's financial troubles, and they also vote to prevent residential integration.

These trends are not likely to change in the years to come. In fact, if the present white affluence continues, the economic gap between the urban have-nots and the suburban haves will only increase, resulting on the one hand in greater suburban opposition to integration and to solving the city's problems, and on the other hand in greater discontent and more ghetto rebellions in the city. This in turn could result in a new white exodus from the city, which, unlike the earlier exodus, will be based almost entirely on racial fear, making suburbanites out of the middle-aged and older middle-class families who are normally reluctant to change communities at this age and work-ing-class whites who cannot really afford a suburban house. Many of them will, however, stay put and oppose all efforts toward desegregation, as indi-cated even now by their violent reaction to integration marches in Milwaukee and Chicago, and to scattered-site public housing schemes which would locate projects in middle-income areas in New York and elsewhere.

Ultimately, these trends could create a vicious spiral, with more ghetto protest leading to more white demands, urban and suburban, for repression, resulting in yet more intense ghetto protests, and culminating eventually in a massive exodus of urban whites. If this spiral were allowed to escalate, it might well hasten the coming of the predominantly Negro city.

Today, the predominantly Negro city is still far off in the future, and the all-Negro city is unlikely. Although Washington, D.C.'s population is already about 60 per cent Negro, and several other cities, including Newark, Gary and Richmond, hover around the 50 per cent mark, recent estimates by the Center for Research in Marketing suggest that only five of the coun-try's 25 largest cities and 10 of the 130 cities with over 100,000 population will be 40 per cent or more Negro by 1970. (New York's Negro population was estimated at 18 per cent in 1964, although in Manhattan, the proportion of Negroes was 27 per cent and of Negroes and Puerto Ricans, 39 per cent.)

Moreover, these statistics only count the nighttime residential population, but who lives in the city is, economically and politically, a less relevant sta-tistic than who works there, and the daytime working population of most cities is today, and will long remain, heavily and even predominantly white.

Still, to a suburbanite who may someday have to work in a downtown surrounded by a black city, the future may seem threatening. A century ago, native-born WASP's must have felt similarly, when a majority of the urban population consisted of foreign-born Catholics and Jews, to whom they attrib-uted the same pejorative racial characteristics now attributed to Negroes. The city and the WASP's survived, of course, as the immigrants were incorporated into the American economy, and suburban whites would also survive.

Today's nonwhite poor play a more marginal role in the urban economy, however, raising the possibility that if the city became predominantly Negro, many private firms and institutions, which hire relatively few Negroes, would leave to build a new downtown elsewhere, a phenomenon already developing on a small scale in Arlington, Va., just outside Washington, D.C., and in Clayton, Mo., just outside St. Louis. If this trend became widespread, some-day in the distant future only public agencies and low-wage industries, which boast integrated work forces, would remain in the present downtown area.

Many white suburbanites might welcome this development, for it would cut their remaining ties to the city altogether. Some Negroes might also pre-fer a predominantly black city, partly because they would be able to move into the good housing left by whites, and partly because they would take over political control of the city, thus promising the rank-and-file ghetto resi-dent more sympathetic if not necessarily better treatment than he now gets from the white incumbents of city hall.

Nevertheless, the predominantly black city is undesirable, not only be-cause it would create apartheid on a metropolitan scale, but because it would be a yet poorer city, less able to provide the needed public services to its low-income population and less likely to get the funds it would need from a predominantly white Federal Government.

Unfortunately, present governmental policies, local, state and Federal, are doing little to reverse the mounting class and racial polarization of city and suburb. Admittedly, the strong economic and cultural forces that send the middle classes into the suburbs and bring poor nonwhite people from the rural areas into the city in ever larger numbers are difficult to reverse even by the wisest government action.

Still, governmental policies have not been especially wise. The major efforts to slow down class and racial polarization have been these: legislation to achieve racial integration; programs to woo the white middle class back to the city; plans to establish unified metropolitan governments, encompassing both urban and suburban governmental units. All three have failed. None of the open housing and other integration laws now on the books have been enforced sufficiently to permit more than a handful of Negroes to live in the suburbs, and the more recent attempt to prevent the coming of the predominantly black city by enticing the white middle class back has not worked either.

The main technique used for this last purpose has been urban renewal, but there is no evidence—and, in fact, there have been no studies—to show that it has brought back a significant number of middle-class people. Most likely, it has only helped confirmed urbanites find better housing in the city. The attractions of suburbia are simply too persuasive for urban renewal or any other governmental program to succeed in bringing the middle class back to the city.

Even most older couples, whose children have left the suburban house empty, will not return; they have just paid off their mortgage and are not likely to give up a cheap and familiar house for an expensive city apartment, not to mention their gardens, or the friends they have made in the suburbs. At best, some may move to suburban apartments, but most American cities other than New York have too few downtown attractions to lure a sizable number of people back to the center.

Metropolitan government is, in theory, a good solution, for it would require the suburbs to contribute to solving the city's problems, but it has long been opposed by the suburbs for just this reason. They have felt that the improvements and economies in public services that could be obtained by organizing them on a metropolitan basis would be offset by what suburbanites saw as major disadvantages, principally the reduction of political autonomy and the loss of power to keep out the poor and the nonwhites.

The cities, which have in the past advocated metropolitan government, may become less enthusiastic as Negroes obtain greater political power. Since the metropolitan area is so predominantly white, urban Negroes would be outvoted every time in any kind of metropolitan government. Some metropolitanization may nevertheless be brought about by Federal planning requirements, for as Frances Piven and Richard Cloward point out in a recent *New Republic* article, several Federal grant programs, particularly for housing and community facilities, now require a metropolitan plan as a prerequisite

for funding. Piven and Cloward suggest that these requirements could dis-
franchise the urban Negro, and it is of course always possible that a white
urban-suburban coalition in favor of metropolitan government could be put
together deliberately for this purpose. Under such conditions, however, metropolitan government would only increase racial conflict and polarization.

What, then, can be done to eliminate this polarization? One partial solution is to reduce the dependence of both urban and suburban governments
on the property tax, which reduces city income as the population becomes
poorer, and forces suburbs to exclude low-income residents because their
housing does not bring in enough tax money. If urban and suburban governments could obtain more funds from other sources, including perhaps the
Federal income tax, parts of the proceeds of which would be returned to
them by Washington, urban property owners would bear a smaller burden in
supporting the city and might be less opposed to higher spending. Suburbanites would also worry less about their tax rate, and might not feel so impelled
to bar less affluent newcomers, or to object to paying their share of the cost
of using city services.

Class polarization can be reduced by rent- or price-supplement programs
which would enable less affluent urbanites to pay the price of suburban living
and would reduce the building and financing costs of housing. But such measures would not persuade the suburbs to let in Negroes; ultimately, the only
solution is still across-the-board residential integration.

The outlook for early and enforceable legislation toward this end, however, is dim. Although election results have shown time and again that
Northern white majorities will not vote for segregation, they will not vote for
integration either. I cannot imagine many political bodies, Federal or otherwise, passing or enforcing laws that would result in significant amounts of
suburban integration; they would be punished summarily at the next election.

For example, proposals have often been made that state and Federal
governments should withdraw all subsidies to suburban communities and
builders practicing de facto segregation, thus depriving the former of at least
half their school operating funds, and the latter of Federal Housing Authority
(F.H.A.) insurance on which their building plans depend. However desirable
such legislation is, the chance that it would be passed is almost nil. One can
also argue that Washington should offer grants-in-aid to suburban governments which admit low-income residents, but these grants would often be
turned down. Many suburban municipalities would rather starve their public
services instead, and the voters would support them all the way.

The best hope now is for judicial action. The New Jersey Supreme Court
ruled some years back that builders on F.H.A. insurance had to sell to
Negroes, and many suburban subdivisions in that state now have some Negro
residents. The United States Supreme Court has just decided that it will rule
on whether racial discrimination by large suburban developers is unconstitutional. If the answer turns out to be yes, the long, slow process of imple-
menting the Court's decisions can at least begin.[1]

In the meantime, solutions that need not be tested at the ballot box
must be advanced. One possibility is new towns, built for integrated populations with Federal support, or even by the Federal Government alone, on

land now vacant. Although hope springs eternal in American society that the problems of old towns can be avoided by starting from scratch, these problems seep easily across the borders of the new community. Even if rural governments can be persuaded to accept new towns in their bailiwicks and white residents could be attracted, such towns would be viable only if Federal grants and powers were used to obtain industries—and of a kind that would hire and train poorly skilled workers.

Greater emphasis should be placed on eliminating job discrimination in suburban work places, particularly in industries which are crying for workers, so that unions are less impelled to keep out nonwhite applicants. Mass transit systems should be built to enable city dwellers, black and white, to obtain suburban jobs without necessarily living in the suburbs.

Another and equally important solution is more school integration—for example, through urban-suburban educational parks that will build up integrated student enrollment by providing high-quality schooling to attract suburban whites, and through expansion of the busing programs that send ghetto children into suburban schools. Although white suburban parents have strenuously opposed busing their children into the city, several suburban communities have accepted Negro students who are bused in from the ghetto; for example, in the Boston area and in Westchester County.

And while the Supreme Court is deliberating, it would be worthwhile to persuade frightened suburbanites that, as all the studies so far have indicated, open housing would not mean a massive invasion of slum dwellers, but only the gradual arrival of a relatively small number of Negroes, most of them as middle-class as the whitest suburbanite. A massive suburban invasion by slum dwellers of any color is sheer fantasy. Economic studies have shown the sad fact that only a tiny proportion of ghetto residents can even afford to live in the suburbs. Moreover, as long as Negro workers lack substantial job security, they need to live near the center of the urban transportation system so that they can travel to jobs all over the city.

In addition, there are probably many ghetto residents who do not even want suburban integration now; they want the same freedom of housing choice as whites, but they do not want to be "dispersed" to the suburbs involuntarily. Unfortunately, no reliable studies exist to tell us where ghetto residents do want to live, but should they have freedom of choice, I suspect many would leave the slums for better housing and better neighborhoods outside the present ghetto. Not many would now choose predominantly white areas, however, at least not until living among whites is psychologically and socially less taxing, and until integration means more than just assimilation to white middle-class ways.

Because of the meager success of past integration efforts, many civil-rights leaders have given up on integration and are now demanding the rebuilding of the ghetto. They argue persuasively that residential integration has so far benefited and will in the future benefit only a small number of affluent Negroes, and that if the poverty-stricken ghetto residents are to be helped soon, that help must be located in the ghetto. The advocates of integration are strongly opposed. They demand that all future housing must be built outside the ghetto, for anything else would just perpetuate segregation.

In recent months, the debate between the two positions has become bitter, each side claiming only its solution has merit.

Actually there is partial truth on both sides. The integrationists are correct about the long-term dangers of rebuilding the ghetto; the ghetto rebuilders (or separatists) are correct about the short-term failure of integration. But if there is little likelihood that the integrationists' demands will be carried out soon, their high idealism in effect sentences ghetto residents to remaining in slum poverty.

Moreover, there is no need to choose between integration and rebuilding, for both policies can be carried out simultaneously. The struggle for integration must continue, but if the immediate prospects for success on a large scale are dim, the ghetto must be rebuilt in the meantime.

The primary aim of rebuilding, however, should not be to rehabilitate houses or clear slums, but to raise the standard of living of ghetto residents. The highest priority must be a massive antipoverty program which will, through the creation of jobs, more effective job-training schemes, the negative income tax, children's allowances and other measures, raise ghetto families to the middle-income level, using outside resources from government and private enterprise and inside participation in the planning and decision-making. Also needed are a concerted effort at quality compensatory education for children who cannot attend integrated schools; federally funded efforts to improve the quality of ghetto housing, as well as public services; some municipal decentralization to give ghetto residents the ability to plan their own communities and their own lives, and political power so that the ghetto can exert more influence in behalf of its demands.

If such programs could extend the middle-income standard of living to the ghetto in the years to come, residential integration might well be achieved in subsequent generations. Much of the white opposition to integration is based on stereotypes of Negro behavior—some true, some false—that stem from poverty rather than from color, and many of the fears about Negro neighbors reflect the traditional American belief that poor people will not live up to middle-class standards. Moreover, even lack of enthusiasm for integration among ghetto residents is a result of poverty; they feel, rightly or not, that they must solve their economic problems before they can even think about integration.

If ghetto poverty were eliminated, the white fears—and the Negro ones —would begin to disappear, as did the pejorative stereotypes which earlier Americans held about the "inferior races"—a favorite 19th-century term for the European immigrants—until they achieved affluence. Because attitudes based on color differences are harder to overcome than those based on cultural differences, the disappearance of anti-Negro stereotypes will be slower than that of anti-immigrant stereotypes. Still, once color is no longer an index of poverty and lower-class status, it will cease to arouse white fears, so that open-housing laws can be enforced more easily and eventually may even be unnecessary. White suburbanites will not exclude Negroes to protect their status or their poverty values, and many, although not necessarily all, Negroes will choose to leave the ghetto.

Morally speaking, any solution that does not promise immediate integration is repugnant, but moral dicta will neither persuade suburbanites to admit low-income Negroes into their communities, nor entice urbane suburbanites to live near low-income Negroes in the city. Instead of seeking to increase their middle-income population by importing suburban whites, cities must instead make their poor residents middle-income. The practical solution, then, is to continue to press for residential integration, but also to eliminate ghetto poverty immediately, in order to achieve integration in the future, substituting government anti-poverty programs for the private economy which once created the jobs and incomes that helped poorer groups escape the slums in past generations. Such a policy will not only reduce many of the problems of the city, which are ultimately caused by the poverty of its inhabitants, but it will assure the ultimate disappearance of the class and racial polarization of cities and suburbs.

There is only one hitch: This policy is not likely to be adopted. Although white voters and their elected officials are probably more favorable to ghetto rebuilding than to integration, they are, at the moment, not inclined or impelled to support even the former. They lack inclination to rebuild the ghetto because they do not want to pay the taxes that would raise ghetto incomes; they are not so impelled because neither the problems of the ghetto nor even its rebellions touch their lives directly and intimately. So far, most of them still experience the ghetto only on television. Until many white Americans are directly affected by what goes on in the ghetto, they will probably support nothing more than a minuscule anti-poverty program and a token effort toward racial integration.

NOTE

1. The Supreme Court did declare discrimination by large suburban developers unconstitutional. And after the assassination of Martin Luther King, Congress passed legislation banning discrimination in a large part of the housing stock.——ED.

2.6 THE GENERATORS OF DIVERSITY

JANE JACOBS

Classified telephone directories tell us the greatest single fact about cities: the immense numbers of parts that make up a city, and the immense diversity of those parts. Diversity is natural to big cities.

"I have often amused myself," wrote James Boswell in 1791, "with thinking how different a place London is to different people. They, whose narrow minds are contracted to the consideration of some one particular pursuit, view it only through that medium . . . But the intellectual man is struck with it, as comprehending the whole of human life in all its variety, the contemplation of which is inexhaustible."

Boswell not only gave a good definition of cities, he put his finger on one of the chief troubles in dealing with them. It is so easy to fall into the trap of contemplating a city's uses one at a time, by categories. Indeed, just this—analysis of cities, use by use—has become a customary planning tactic. The findings on various categories of use are then put together into "broad, overall pictures."

The overall pictures such methods yield are about as useful as the picture assembled by the blind men who felt the elephant and pooled their findings. The elephant lumbered on, oblivious to the notion that he was a leaf, a snake, a wall, tree trunks and a rope all somehow stuck together. Cities, being our own artifacts, enjoy less defense against solemn nonsense.

To understand cities, we have to deal outright with combinations or mixtures of uses, not separate uses, as the essential phenomena. We have already seen the importance of this in the case of neighborhood parks. Parks can easily—too easily—be thought of as phenomena in their own right and described as adequate or inadequate in terms, say, of acreage ratios to thousands of population. Such an approach tells us something about the methods of planners, but it tells us nothing useful about the behavior or value of neighborhood parks.

A mixture of uses, if it is to be sufficiently complex to sustain city safety, public contact and cross-use, needs an enormous diversity of ingredients. So the first question—and I think by far the most important question—about planning cities is this: How can cities generate enough mixture among uses—

enough diversity—throughout enough of their territories, to sustain their own civilization?

It is all very well to castigate the Great Blight of Dullness and to understand why it is destructive to city life, but in itself this does not get us far. Consider the problem posed by the street with the pretty sidewalk park in Baltimore, which I mentioned back in Chapter Three. My friend from the street, Mrs. Kostritsky, is quite right when she reasons that it needs some commerce for its users' convenience. And as might be expected, inconvenience and lack of public street life are only two of the by-products of residential monotony here. Danger is another—fear of the streets after dark. Some people fear to be alone in their houses by day since the occurrence of two nasty daytime assaults. Moreover, the place lacks commercial choices as well as any cultural interest. We can see very well how fatal is its monotony.

But having said this, then what? The missing diversity, convenience, interest and vitality do not spring forth because the area needs their benefits. Anybody who started a retail enterprise here, for example, would be stupid. He could not make a living. To wish a vital urban life might somehow spring up here is to play with daydreams. The place is an economic desert.

Although it is hard to believe, while looking at dull gray areas, or at housing projects or at civic centers, the fact is that big cities *are* natural generators of diversity and prolific incubators of new enterprises and ideas of all kinds. Moreover, big cities are the natural economic homes of immense numbers and ranges of small enterprises.

The principal studies of variety and size among city enterprises happen to be studies of manufacturing, notably those by Raymond Vernon, author of *Anatomy of a Metropolis,* and by P. Sargant Florence, who has examined the effect of cities on manufacturing both here and in England.

Characteristically, the larger a city, the greater the variety of its manufacturing, and also the greater both the number and the proportion of its small manufacturers. The reasons for this, in brief, are that big enterprises have greater self-sufficiency than small ones, are able to maintain within themselves most of the skills and equipment they need, can warehouse for themselves, and can sell to a broad market which they can seek out wherever it may be. They need not be in cities, and although sometimes it is advantageous for them to be there, often it is more advantageous not to. But for small manufacturers, everything is reversed. Typically they must draw on many and varied supplies and skills outside themselves, they must serve a narrow market at the point where a market exists, and they must be sensitive to quick changes in this market. Without cities, they would simply not exist. Dependent on a huge diversity of other city enterprises, they can add further to that diversity. This last is a most important point to remember. City diversity itself permits and stimulates more diversity.

For many activities other than manufacturing, the situation is analogous. For example, when Connecticut General Life Insurance Company built a new headquarters in the countryside beyond Hartford, it could do so only by dint of providing—in addition to the usual working spaces and rest rooms, medical suite and the like—a large general store, a beauty parlor, a bowling alley, a cafeteria, a theater and a great variety of games space. These facilities are inherently inefficient, idle most of the time. They require subsidy, not because they are kinds of enterprises which are necessarily money losers, but because here their use is so limited. They were presumed necessary, however, to compete for a working force, and to hold it. A large company can absorb the luxury of such inherent inefficiencies and balance them against other advantages it seeks. But small offices can do nothing of the kind. If they want to compete for a work force on even terms or better, they must be in a lively city setting where their employees find the range of subsidiary conveniences and choices that they want and need. Indeed, one reason, among many others, why the much-heralded postwar exodus of big offices from cities turned out to be mostly talk is that the differentials in cost of suburban land and space are typically canceled by the greater amount of space per worker required for facilities that in cities no single employer need provide, nor any one corps of workers or customers support. Another reason why such enterprises have stayed in cities along with small firms, is that many of their employees, especially executives, need to be in close, face-to-face touch and communication with people outside the firm—including people from small firms.

The benefits that cities offer to smallness are just as marked in retail trade, cultural facilities and entertainment. This is because city populations are large enough to support wide ranges of variety and choice in these things. And again we find that bigness has all the advantages in smaller settlements. Towns and suburbs, for instance, are natural homes for huge supermarkets and for little else in the way of groceries, for standard movie houses or drive-ins and for little else in the way of theater. There are simply not enough people to support further variety, although there may be people (too few of them) who would draw upon it were it there. Cities, however, are the natural homes of supermarkets and standard movie houses *plus* delicatessens, Viennese bakeries, foreign groceries, art movies, and so on, all of which can be found co-existing, the standard with the strange, the large with the small. Wherever lively and popular parts of cities are found, the small much outnumber the large.[1] Like the small manufacturers, these small enterprises would not exist somewhere else, in the absence of cities. Without cities, they would not exist.

The diversity, of whatever kind, that is generated by cities rests on the fact that in cities so many people are so close together, and among them contain so many different tastes, skills, needs, supplies, and bees in their bonnets.

Even quite standard, but small, operations like proprietor-and-one-clerk hardware stores, drug stores, candy stores and bars can and do flourish in extraordinary numbers and incidence in lively districts of cities because there are enough people to support their presence at short, convenient intervals, and in turn this convenience and neighborhood personal quality are big parts of such enterprises' stock in trade. Once they are unable to be supported at close, convenient intervals, they lose this advantage. In a given geographical territory, half as many people will not support half as many such enterprises spaced at twice the distance. When distance inconvenience sets in, the small, the various and the personal wither away.

As we have transformed from a rural and small-town country into an urban country, business enterprises have thus become more numerous, not only in absolute terms, but also in proportionate terms. In 1900 there were 21 independent nonfarm businesses for each 1,000 persons in the total U.S. population. In 1959, in spite of the immense growth of giant enterprises during the interval, there were 26½ independent nonfarm businesses for each 1,000 persons in the population. With urbanization, the big get bigger, but the small also get more numerous.

Smallness and diversity, to be sure, are not synonyms. The diversity of city enterprises includes all degrees of size, but great variety does mean a high proportion of small elements. A lively city scene is lively largely by virtue of its enormous collection of small elements.

Nor is the diversity that is important for city districts by any means confined to profit-making enterprises and to retail commerce, and for this reason it may seem that I put an undue emphasis on retail trade. I think not, however. Commercial diversity is, in itself, immensely important for cities, socially as well as economically. Most of the uses of diversity on which I dwelt in Part I of this book depend directly or indirectly upon the presence of plentiful, convenient, diverse city commerce. But more than this, wherever we find a city district with an exuberant variety and plenty in its commerce, we are apt to find that it contains a good many other kinds of diversity also, including variety of cultural opportunities, variety of scenes, and a great variety in its population and other users. This is more than coincidence. The same physical and economic conditions that generate diverse commerce are intimately related to the production, or the presence, of other kinds of city variety.

But although cities may fairly be called natural economic generators of diversity and natural economic incubators of new enterprises, this does not mean that cities *automatically* generate diversity just by existing. They generate it because of the various efficient economic pools of use that they form. Wherever they fail to form such pools of use, they are little better, if any, at generating diversity than small settlements. And the fact that they need diversity socially, unlike small settlements, makes no difference. For our purposes here, the most striking fact to note is the extraordinary unevenness with which cities generate diversity.

On the one hand, for example, people who live and work in Boston's North End, or New York's Upper East Side or San Francisco's North Beach-Telegraph Hill, are able to use and enjoy very considerable amounts of diversity and vitality. Their visitors help immensely. But the visitors did not create the foundations of diversity in areas like these, nor in the many pockets of diversity and economic efficiency scattered here and there, sometimes most unexpectedly, in big cities. The visitors sniff out where something vigorous exists already, and come to share it, thereby further supporting it.

At the other extreme, huge city settlements of people exist without their presence generating anything much except stagnation and, ultimately, a fatal discontent with the place. It is not that they are a different kind of people, somehow duller or unappreciative of vigor and diversity. Often they include hordes of searchers, trying to sniff out these attributes somewhere, anywhere.

Rather, something is wrong with their districts; something is lacking to catalyze a district population's ability to interact economically and help form effective pools of use.

Apparently there is no limit to the numbers of people in a city whose potentiality as city populations can thus be wasted. Consider, for instance, the Bronx, a borough of New York containing some one and a half million people. The Bronx is woefully short of urban vitality, diversity and magnetism. It has its loyal residents, to be sure, mostly attached to little bloomings of street life here and there in "the old neighborhood," but not nearly enough of them.

In so simple a matter of city amenity and diversity as interesting restaurants, the 1,500,000 people in the Bronx cannot produce. Kate Simon, the author of a guidebook, *New York Places and Pleasures,* describes hundreds of restaurants and other commercial establishments, particularly in unexpected and out-of-the-way parts of the city. She is not snobbish, and dearly likes to present her readers with inexpensive discoveries. But although Miss Simon tries hard, she has to give up the great settlement of the Bronx as thin pickings at any price. After paying homage to the two solid metropolitan attractions in the borough, the zoo and the Botanical Gardens, she is hard put to recommend a single place to eat outside the zoo grounds. The one possibility she is able to offer, she accompanies with this apology: "The neighborhood trails off sadly into a no man's land, and the restaurant can stand a little refurbishing, but there's the comfort of knowing that . . . the best of Bronx medical skill is likely to be sitting all around you."

Well, that is the Bronx, and it is too bad it is so; too bad for the people who live there now, too bad for the people who are going to inherit it in future out of their lack of economic choice, and too bad for the city as a whole.

And if the Bronx is a sorry waste of city potentialities, as it is, consider the even more deplorable fact that it is possible for whole cities to exist, whole metropolitan areas, with pitifully little city diversity and choice. Virtually all of urban Detroit is as weak on vitality and diversity as the Bronx. It is ring superimposed upon ring of failed gray belts. Even Detroit's downtown itself cannot produce a respectable amount of diversity. It is dispirited and dull, and almost deserted by seven o'clock of an evening.

So long as we are content to believe that city diversity represents accident and chaos, of course its erratic generation appears to represent a mystery.

However, the conditions that generate city diversity are quite easy to discover by observing places in which diversity flourishes and studying the economic reasons why it can flourish in these places. Although the results are intricate, and the ingredients producing them may vary enormously, this complexity is based on tangible economic relationships which, in principle, are much simpler than the intricate urban mixtures they make possible.

To generate exuberant diversity in a city's streets and districts, four conditions are indispensable:

1. The district, and indeed as many of its internal parts as possible, must serve more than one primary function; preferably more than two.

These must insure the presence of people who go outdoors on different schedules and are in the place for different purposes, but who are able to use many facilities in common.

2. Most blocks must be short; that is, streets and opportunities to turn corners must be frequent.

3. The district must mingle buildings that vary in age and condition, including a good proportion of old ones so that they vary in the economic yield they must produce. This mingling must be fairly close-grained.

4. There must be a sufficiently dense concentration of people, for whatever purposes they may be there. This includes dense concentration in the case of people who are there because of residence.

The necessity for these four conditions is the most important point this book has to make. In combination, these conditions create effective economic pools of use. Given these four conditions, not all city districts will produce a diversity equivalent to one another. The potentials of different districts differ for many reasons; but, given the development of these four conditions (or the best approximation to their full development that can be managed in real life), a city district should be able to realize its best potential, wherever that may lie. Obstacles to doing so will have been removed. The range may not stretch to African sculpture or schools of drama or Rumanian tea houses, but such as the possibilities are, whether for grocery stores, pottery schools, movies, candy stores, florists, art shows, immigrants' clubs, hardware stores, eating places, or whatever, they will get their best chance. And along with them, city life will get its best chances.

In the four chapters that follow, I shall discuss each of these four generators of diversity, one at a time. The purpose of explaining them one at a time is purely for convenience of exposition, not because any one—or even any three—of these necessary conditions is valid alone. *All* four in combination are necessary to generate city diversity; the absence of any one of the four frustrates a district's potential.

NOTE

1. In retail trade, this tendency has been growing stronger, if anything. Richard Nelson, the Chicago real estate analyst, examining the postwar trend of retail sales in some twenty city downtowns, has discovered that the large department stores have typically lost trade; the chain variety stores have stayed about even; and the small and special stores have increased their business and usually have also increased in number. There is no real competition outside the cities for these small and various city enterprises; but it is relatively easy for the big and standardized, in their natural homes outside the city, to compete with what is big and standardized within. This happens, incidentally, to be exactly what has occurred in the neighborhood where I live. Wanamaker's, the big department store formerly located in Greenwich Village, has gone out of business here and established itself in a suburb instead, at the same time that small and special stores in its immediate former vicinity have increased by the score and flourished mightily.

2.7 THE POSTCITY AGE

MELVIN M. WEBBER

The pragmatic traditions in American political life have led us to attack the manifest problems of the moment with heavy commitment, but to avoid the longer-term confrontation of underlying issues. The several governmental attempts to undertake long-range problem analysis, forecasting, and planning have never succeeded. We have yet to implant a counter-tradition in America that, by exploring the future, would inform a national development policy. This failing reflects, in part, the current status of the social sciences, which have not developed adequate predictive theory in most fields of national concern. It is sobering that no sociologist predicted the magnitude of the Negro Revolt, that no prewar urbanist anticipated the postwar development patterns in American cities, and that, most troubling of all, no one has yet written systematic alternative futures seeking to chart the possible course of events in these fields.

As one consequence of our political traditions and our inadequate theory, we tend to overreact to events of the day. When a curve turns upward, we expect that it will go off the top of the chart; when it turns down, we despair that it will fall off the bottom. A decade ago we were all assured that America was floating serenely in middle-class affluence and that things could only get better. Then we suddenly changed our national self-image when we discovered a large lower-class population and large-scale poverty. The demonstrations of the past five summers have alternatively been read as signs of a new egalitarianism in America or an impending *apartheid*. We had thought our public school system was unexcelled, until Sputnik shocked us into wholesale reform. We believed that suburban development was going to provide decent homes for all, and now we believe that nothing short of immediate reconstruction of the old cities can save them from disaster.

There can be no doubt about the imperatives for confronting the current crises that are associated with the contemporary city. The outcries from the Negro ghetto must be answered humbly, humanely, and immediately; and that will call for huge investments of intellectual capital and federal money. The scale of the current building and rebuilding enterprise in the

From Melvin M. Webber, "The Postcity Age." Reprinted by permission from *Daedalus,* Journal of the American Academy of Arts and Sciences, Boston, Massachusetts, Vol. 97, No. 4 (Fall 1968), pp. 1091–1110.

cities is unprecedented. We shall have to double the size of our physical plant during the next thirty-five years; and that, too, must command full-scale commitment of our intellectual and financial resources. It now appears as though these investments will be forthcoming, largely because the current crisis has captured the nation's conscience and partly because it is our style to respond to emergencies in force.

But it will be an unfortunate mistake, another repetition of our traditional propensities, if we pour our resources into the manifest problems without also dealing with the less visible underlying issues. A deep-swell is shaping those curves on our month-to-month charts—a large historical change that may reshape the character of urban society in the developed world. This, too, must command our attention, for the coming changes may so inhibit future social mobility that our present short-run, ameliorative programs could prove ineffective in retrospect. If so, we had better try to anticipate those changes and then modify our action programs to conform.

Urbanization beyond the City

We are passing through a revolution that is unhitching the social processes of urbanization from the locationally fixed city and region. Reflecting the current explosion in science and technology, employment is shifting from the production of goods to services; increasing ease of transportation and communication is dissolving the spatial barriers to social intercourse; and Americans are forming social communities comprised of spatially dispersed members. A new kind of large-scale urban society is emerging that is increasingly independent of the city. In turn, the problems of the city place generated by early industrialization are being supplanted by a new array different in kind. With but a few remaining exceptions (the new air pollution is a notable one), the recent difficulties are not place-type problems at all. Rather, they are the transitional problems of a rapidly developing society-economy-and-polity whose turf is the nation. Paradoxically, just at the time in history when policy-makers and the world press are discovering the city, "the age of the city seems to be at an end."[1]

Our failure to draw the rather simple conceptual distinction between the spatially defined city or metropolitan area and the social systems that are localized there clouds current discussions about the "crisis of our cities."[2] The confusion stems largely from the deficiencies of our language and from the anachronistic thoughtways we have carried over from the passing era. We still have no adequate descriptive terms for the emerging social order, and so we use, perforce, old labels that are no longer fitting. Because we have named them so, we suppose that the problems manifested inside cities are, therefore and somehow, "city problems." Because societies in the past had been spatially and locally structured, and because urban societies used to be exclusively city-based, we seem still to assume that territoriality is a necessary attribute of social systems.

The error has been a serious one, leading us to seek local solutions to problems whose causes are not of local origin and hence are not susceptible to municipal treatment. We have been tempted to apply city-building instruments to correct social disorders, and we have then been surprised to find that they do not work. (Our experience with therapeutic public housing, which was supposed to cure "social pathologies," and urban renewal, which was supposed to improve the lives of the poor, may be our most spectacular failures.) We have lavished large investments on public facilities, but neglected the quality and the distribution of the social services. And we have defended and reinforced home-rule prerogatives of local and state governments with elaborate rhetoric and protective legislation.

Neither crime-in-the-streets, poverty, unemployment, broken families, race riots, drug addiction, mental illness, juvenile delinquency, nor any of the commonly noted "social pathologies" marking the contemporary city can find its causes or its cure there. We cannot hope to invent local treatments for conditions whose origins are not local in character, nor can we expect territorially defined governments to deal effectively with problems whose causes are unrelated to territory or geography. The concepts and methods of civil engineering and city planning suited to the design of unitary physical facilities cannot be used to serve the design of social change in a pluralistic and mobile society. In the novel society now emerging—with its sophisticated and rapidly advancing science and technology, its complex social organization, and its internally integrated societal processes—the influence and significance of geographic distance and geographic place are declining rapidly.

This is, of course, a most remarkable change. Throughout virtually all of human history, social organization coincided with spatial organization. In preindustrial society, men interacted almost exclusively with geographic neighbors. Social communities, economies, and polities were structured about the place in which interaction was least constrained by the frictions of space. With the coming of large-scale industrialization during the latter half of the nineteenth century, the strictures of space were rapidly eroded, abetted by the new ease of travel and communication that the industrialization itself brought.

The initial counterparts of industrialization in the United States were, first, the concentration of the nation's population into large settlements and, then, the cultural urbanization of the population. Although these changes were causally linked, they had opposite spatial effects. After coming together at a common place, people entered larger societies tied to no specific place. Farming and village people from throughout the continent and the world migrated to the expanding cities, where they learned urban ways, acquired the occupational skills that industrialization demanded, and became integrated into the contemporary society.

In recent years, rising societal scale and improvements in transportation and communications systems have loosed a chain of effects robbing the city of its once unique function as an urbanizing instrument of society. Farmers and small-town residents, scattered throughout the continent, were once effectively removed from the cultural life of the nation. City folks visiting the rural areas used to be treated as strangers, whose styles of living and thinking were unfamiliar. News of the rest of the world was hard to get and then had little meaning for those who lived the local life. Country folk surely knew there was another world out there somewhere, but little understood it and were affected by it only indirectly. The powerful anti-urban traditions in early American thought and politics made the immigrant city dweller a suspicious character whose crude ways marked him as un-Christian (which he sometimes was) and certainly un-American. The more sophisticated urban upper classes—merchants, landowners, and professional men—were similarly suspect and hence rejected. In contrast, the small-town merchant and the farmer who lived closer to nature were the genuine Americans of pure heart who lived the simple, natural life.[3] Because the contrasts between the rural and the urban ways-of-life were indeed sharp, antagonisms were real, and the differences became institutionalized in the conduct of politics. America was marked by a diversity of regional and class cultures whose followers interacted infrequently, if ever.

By now this is nearly gone. The vaudeville hick-town and hayseed characters have left the scene with the vaudeville act. Today's urbane farmer watches television documentaries, reads the national news magazines, and manages his acres from an office (maybe located in a downtown office building), as his hired hands ride their tractors while listening to the current world news broadcast from a transistor. Farming has long since ceased to be a handicraft art; it is among the most highly technologized industries and is tightly integrated into the international industrial complex.

During the latter half of the nineteenth century and the first third of the twentieth, the traditional territorial conception that distinguished urbanites and ruralites was probably valid: The typical rural folk lived outside the cities, and the typical urbanites lived inside. By now this pattern is nearly *reversed.* Urbanites no longer reside exclusively in metropolitan settlements, nor do ruralites live exclusively in the hinterlands. Increasingly, those who are least integrated into modern society—those who exhibit most of the attributes of rural folk—are concentrating within the highest-density portions of the large metropolitan centers. This profoundly important development is only now coming to our consciousness, yet it points up one of the major policy issues of the next decades.

The Participants in the High-Scale Society

Cultural diffusion is integrating immigrants, city residents, and hinterland peoples into a national urban society, but it has not touched all Americans evenly. At one extreme are the intellectual and business elites, whose habitat is the planet; at the other are the lower-class residents of city and farm who live in spatially and cognitively constrained worlds. Most of the rest of us, who comprise the large middle class, lie somewhere in-between, but in some facets of our lives we all seem to be moving from our ancestral localism toward the unbounded realms of the cosmopolites.

High educational attainments and highly specialized occupations mark the new cosmopolites. As frequent patrons of the airlines and the long-distance telephone lines, they are intimately involved in the communications networks that tie them to their spatially dispersed associates. They contribute to and consume the specialized journals of science, government, and industry, thus maintaining contact with information resources of relevance to their activities, whatever the geographic sources or their own locations. Even though some may be employed by corporations primarily engaged in manufacturing physical products, these men trade in information and ideas. They are the producers of the information and ideas that fuel the engines of societal development. For those who are tuned into the international communications circuits, cities have utility precisely because they are rich in information. The way such men use the city reveals its essential character most clearly, for to them the city is essentially a massive communications switchboard through which human interaction takes place.[4]

Indeed, cities exist *only* because spatial agglomeration permits reduced costs of interaction. Men originally elected to locate in high-density settlements precisely because space was so costly to overcome. It is still cheaper to interact with persons who are nearby, and so men continue to locate in such settlements.[5] Because there *are* concentrations of associates in city places, the new cosmopolites establish their offices there and then move about from city to city conducting their affairs. The biggest settlements attract the most long-distance telephone and airline traffic and have undergone the most dramatic growth during this era of city-building.

The recent expansion of Washington, D.C. is the most spectacular evidence of the changing character of metropolitan development. Unlike the older settlements whose growth was generated by expanding manufacturing activities during the nineteenth and early-twentieth centuries, Washington produces almost no goods whatsoever. Its primary products are information and intelligence, and its fantastic growth is a direct measure of the predominant roles that information and the national government have come to play in contemporary society.

This terribly important change has been subtly evolving for a long time, so gradually that it seems to have gone unnoticed. The preindustrial towns that served their adjacent farming hinterlands were essentially alike. Each supplied a standardized array of goods and services to its neighboring market area. The industrial cities that grew after the Civil War and during the early decades of this century were oriented to serving larger markets with the manufacturing products they were created to produce. As their market areas widened, as product specialization increased, and as the information content of goods expanded, establishments located in individual cities became integrated into the spatially extensive economies. By now, the large metropolitan centers that used to be primarily goods-producing loci have become interchange junctions within the international communications networks. Only in the limited geographical, physical sense is any modern metropolis a discrete, unitary, identifiable phenomenon. At most, it is a localized node within the integrating international networks, finding its significant identity as contributor to the workings of that larger system. As a result, the new cosmopolites belong to none of the world's metropolitan areas, although they use them. They belong, rather, to the national and international communities that merely maintain information exchanges at these metropolitan junctions.

Their capacity to interact intimately with others who are spatially removed depends, of course, upon a level of wealth adequate to cover the dollar costs of long-distance intercourse, as well as upon the cognitive capacities associated with highly skilled professional occupations. The intellectual and business elites are able to maintain continuing and close contact with their associates throughout the world because they are rich not only in information, but also in dollar income.

As the costs of long-distance interaction fall in proportion to the rise in incomes, more and more people are able and willing to pay the transportation and communication bills. As expense-account privileges are expanded, those costs are being reduced to zero for ever larger numbers of people. As levels of education and skill rise, more and more people are being tied into the spatially extensive communities that used to engage only a few.

Thus, the glue that once held the spatial settlement together is now dissolving, and the settlement is dispersing over ever widening terrains. At the same time, the pattern of settlement upon the continent is also shifting (moving toward long strips along the coasts, the Gulf, and the Great Lakes). These trends are likely to be accelerated dramatically by cost-reducing improvements in transportation and communications technologies now in the research-and-development stages. (The SST, COMSAT communications, high-speed ground transportation with speeds up to 500 m.p.h., TV and computer-aided educational systems, no-toll long-distance telephone service, and real-time access to national computer-based information systems are likely to be powerful ones.) Technological improvements in transport and communications reduce the frictions of space and thereby ease long-distance intercourse. Our compact, physical city layouts directly mirror the more primitive technologies in use at the time these cities were built. In a similar way, the locational pattern of cities upon the continent reflects the technologies available at the time the settlements grew.[6] If currently anticipated technological improvements prove workable, each of the metropolitan settlements will spread out in low-density patterns over far more extensive areas than even the most frightened future-mongers have yet predicted. The new settlement-form will little resemble the nineteenth-century city so firmly fixed in our images and ideologies. We can also expect that the large junction points will no longer have the communications advantage they now enjoy, and smaller settlements will undergo a major spurt of growth in all sorts of now-isolated places where the natural amenities are attractive.

Moreover, as ever larger percentages of the nation's youth go to college and thus enter the national and international cultures, attachments to places of residence will decline dramatically. This prospect, rather than the spatial dispersion of metropolitan areas, portends the functional demise of the city. The signs are already patently clear among those groups whose worlds are widest and least bounded by parochial constraints.

Consider the extreme cosmopolite, if only for purposes of illustrative cartooning. He might be engaged in scientific research, news reporting, or international business, professions exhibiting critical common traits. The astronomer, for example, maintains instantaneous contact with his colleagues around the world; indeed, he is a day-to-day collaborator with astronomers in all countries. His work demands that he share information and that he and his colleagues monitor stellar events jointly, as the earth's rotation brings men at different locales into prime-viewing position. Because he is personally committed to their common enterprise, his social reference group is the society of astronomers. He assigns his loyalties to the community of astronomers, since their work and welfare matter most to him.

To be sure, as he plays out other roles—say, as citizens, parent, laboratory director, or grocery shopper—he is a member of many other communities, both interest-based and place-defined ones. But the striking thing about our astronomer, and the millions of people like him engaged in other professions, is how little of his attention and energy he devotes to the concerns of place-defined communities. Surely, as compared to his grandfather, whose life was largely bound up in the affairs of his locality, the astronomer, playwright, newsman, steel broker, or wheat dealer lives in a life-space that is not defined by territory and deals with problems that are not local in nature. For him, the city is but a convenient setting for the conduct of his professional work; it is not the basis for the social communities that he cares most about.

Indeed, we may not be far from the time when the vernacular meaning of "community" will be archaic and disappear from common usage. It has already lost much of its traditional meaning for a great many of those on the leading edge of the society. If it is retained, it may be restricted to the provisions of children and of those adults who have not gained access to modern society.

The demise of the city is associated with far more subtle and powerful changes than the expansion of market areas for firms and the collaboration among scientists in distant nations. Behind these developments lies the internationalization of society generated by the knowledge explosion.

By its very nature, knowledge is specific to neither cities nor nations. An overriding, largely unanticipated consequence of science is its internationalizing effect—its introduction of common understandings, common libraries of information, common bases for valuation and validation, and, indeed, a common culture for men located in all parts of the world. The same consequences emanate from developments in technology, commerce, the arts, theater, literature, and virtually all areas of creative endeavor. Save for those, like Lyzenko, who hold to certain specialized epistemologies or ideologies, new discoveries and inventions are readily accepted, irrespective of their geographic origins. By now there is a large class of persons around the world who share in the world culture, while simultaneously participating in the idiosyncratic local cultures special to their regions of residence. Their range of opportunity is far larger and far more diverse than the most powerful and wealthy man of past eras could have imagined.

Knowledge is also cumulative; its store can only get larger, and the effects it generates are one-directional. We now know that the recent expansion of knowledge has triggered a rapid explosion of life-space—both geographically and cognitively. We can expect that explosion to continue, further bursting the barriers of geography and ignorance for larger proportions of the population. The counterpart of expanding life-space has been the contracting role of the cities and the nations as the organizing frameworks of societies. This is, of course, a revolutionary development. As Kenneth Boulding has synoptically put it, it portends the end of "civilization" as the culture of the *civitas*.[7] To be sure, the end of civilization has been in sight for a long time; through a telling etymological trick we have become accustomed to speaking of national citizenship, and we even describe some people as "world citizens." This usage is far more prophetic than we had realized.

Although the intellectual and business elites are undoubtedly still a minority among us, the vast middle class is rapidly adopting their styles and their capabilities, and lower-class persons are aspiring to them. About 40 per cent of American youth are now going to college, and the proportion will soon be over half. (In California it is now about 80 per cent.) Television has already supplied a window to a seamless world, a world that the present generation is actively exploring firsthand. If we ever succeed in using television creatively, it could become a more powerful educational force than the public schools have been—extending the classroom to every house and the spectrum of accessible knowledge far beyond the present bounds. Americans may already be consuming more books per capita, more magazines per capita, more music, more lectures, and more art than any population in the world—certainly far more than any peoples in the past. They are traveling widely for recreational and educational purposes; and in the course of their travels, they are absorbing information, ideas, and attitudes, even as they are seeding their own along their paths.

The nationals of other countries are, of course, engaged in the same set of activities. Western Europeans may be the next most-mobile people in the world, although the Japanese probably outpace even them in the rate at which they have been scouting the planet, absorbing and then exploiting the world's knowledge. The signs of this internationalization are clear: the rise of the international business firm, the near-instantaneous diffusion of fashion in dress and the arts, the spectacular spread of the hippie culture, the new international architecture, the Europeans' sense of personal loss at the assassinations of John F. Kennedy, Martin Luther King, and Robert F. Kennedy, the acceptance of the common market idea, and the new-found racial pride among mutually supportive colored peoples.

We have little reason to doubt that the accumulation and dispersion of knowledge will continue, bringing further dissolution of local differences. The economy is expanding in precisely those service industries that demand high educational attainment and sophistication: education, research and development, health, and the information services. Concomitantly, the traditional loci of growth that marked the industrial stage of national development are already on the decline. During the past twenty years, there has been almost no expansion in manufacturing employment in the U.S.; we may soon be seeing an actual decline, despite the fantastic expansion of output. Unskilled jobs are fast disappearing, and physically exhausting work may before long be completely consigned to machines.

The processes have been mutually reinforcing. The service occupations that require high skill have been able to expand because a highly educated labor force has been developing. In turn, these occupations, particularly those within the knowledge industries, have been reproducing their own next-generations of better trained persons and their own next-generations of new knowledge. Thus, we have been riding a rising spiral that is turning the economy upside down, converting it from one in which workers produce physical products to one in which they produce services. Many of the new services are concerned with the management of information, and the information content of most of the new physical products is rising rapidly. (Compare, for example, the information content of a transistor radio with that of a trainload of coal.) In the process, the emphasis on knowledge and information has been increasing dramatically. Already the number of Americans working full time as teachers is over two million. We may now be fast approaching the day, long heralded by the ancient Greek philosophers, when our major occupation will be learning for its own sake.

The Bypassed Preindustrial Locals

As the scale of the society has been rising, carrying the bulk of the national population into the dimly seen post-industrial era, a large segment of the population is being left further and further behind. A short time ago, many of these people were living in rural areas, a high proportion in the southern and Appalachian states; the migration to the cities during the past twenty-five years has by now relocated nearly all of them. Today, they are city dwellers, residing in the most dense sections of the metropolitan areas, but still living in the folk cultures their grandparents knew. Here in the Harlems and South Sides of the nation are some of the last viable remnants of preindustrial societies, where village styles are most nearly intact. Here the turf is the city block, and teenage gangs wage war in its defense. Here in the slum blocks of the central cities may be the only pure place-based social neighborhoods we have left.

American cities have always been magnets for preindustrial migrants searching for access into contemporary society. Like those who preceded them from Europe, the recent migrants are being both pushed by the hardships of their present life and pulled by the promise of opportunities that the city has traditionally held out. And yet the recent migrations occur in a very different setting. Those who now come must bridge a cultural gap far wider than the one their predecessors faced, one that is widening at an exponential rate.

Despite the suffering that accompanied nineteenth-century migration and acculturation, the stage was well set; the paths to social mobility were short and easily traversed. The new manufacturing industries called for large numbers of workers who could easily be trained to perform the standardized tasks. In turn, jobs made for income security that provided relief from the hazards of everyday life, thus fostering a non-fatalistic world-view through which future opportunities could be seen. The physical structure of the city permitted the various ethnic and national groups to settle in colonies within the cities. The transplanted old-world life styles of the ethnic ghettos eased the transition for the adult newcomers, while their children gradually introduced them to the new urban ways. The democratic institutions and the legal rules for acquiring citizenship and voting rights permitted the newcomers to control and then to use local governments instrumentally in accelerating their own development. For some, politics and government provided an important route to social mobility.

Free public schools served as an open doorway through which immigrants' children found access to semiskilled and skilled occupations and thus to higher social status than their parents enjoyed. The public schools, the free public colleges, the free libraries, the availability of free or cheap medical services, and the public life of the street became the major acculturating media. By living the city-based life, the second- and third-generation Americans acquired the social and cognitive skills and the internal psychic compentencies that modern urbanism demands. In the school, on the street, and frequently in illicit enterprises, the immigrants' children learned to use the money and credit economy, to defer gratification, to anticipate future problems and opportunities, to cope with crises, and to deal with multiple options. The city was, in effect, a school where peasant migrants learned with incredible speed to be urbanized Americans. Within single generations, groups that had followed the four-hundred-year-old peasant styles of life and thought were catapulted into a society of a vastly different kind and scale. Most of them landed on their feet; some of them shot to the forefront of the society and then led it on to its next stages of development.

The setting for the massive European and Asian migrations to the city was fortuitous. They arrived just when the national economy was embarking upon unprecedented industrial development, and they came into a social system constrained by few immovable barriers of social class. In a time when small capitalization was sufficient, some succeeded in establishing small, family-based businesses; in the milieu of a rapidly expanding economy, some of these soon became big businesses. Others entered the professions, government, and the large corporations where they established themselves as leaders among the intellectual elites.

The way out of the ghetto was fast and easy for a few groups of immigrants. For many Eastern European Jews, the departure from the immigrant ghetto areas in the slums occurred very quickly. Many of the Jews were culturally urbanized when they came here; in Europe the legal prohibition against their owning land kept them in towns where many were small merchants or traders. The relatively unstructured and open-ended character of their religious doctrines led them as a group to place high value on scholarship and individual achievement, to adopt a typically critical intellectual attitude, and to be concerned with the consequences of future events. These characteristics, coupled with a solidly cohesive family structure, served them well when they reached the United States. The Chinese and Japanese, with their cohesive, patriarchal family structure and high cultural value on intellectual achievement, were also among the most upwardly mobile groups.

In contrast, mobility has come slower to the Irish, southern Italian, and Polish immigrants, whose peasant heritage had few of these urbanizing attributes. Only within the past generation or two have their children been going to college in large numbers, leaving the ethnic ghetto and the working-class world-view behind them. The rigidity of traditional practices and beliefs and the emphasis on discipline and conformity exerted by the Catholic Church had previously discouraged exploration of wider conceptual worlds than those of the ethnic neighborhoods.

Whatever innate and cultural attributes may have sped social mobility for some of the early migrants to America's cities, their success was just as surely a consequence of the nation's stage of development at the time they arrived. Uneducated migrants to cities were not very far behind those who had arrived long before them. Those of quick mind could master the tasks required by the new factories speedily and then move beyond into the managerial and professional roles.

The Central Policy Issue

A far more difficult setting faces the migrants to the cities today. The explosive progress in the arts, sciences, and technologies has triggered an unprecedented rise in the scale of the national society, one marked by ever finer division of labor, calling for ever higher levels of education and training; by the shift from extractive and manufacturing industries to service industries that require long periods of preparation; by increasingly complex organization of the economy and polity; and by the expansion of the spatial and cognitive fields within which human interaction and economic transaction take place. Specialization, interdependence, and integration are the definitive traits of today's urbanism. This new scale of complexity distinguishes modern urbanism from earlier forms and is setting the policy agenda that the nation must now address.

Although it is still easy to migrate to the cities, the demands of large-scale society are making it more and more difficult for newcomers to gain entry into the new urban society. Those city dwellers who are presently least integrated into modern society are facing a series of hurdles far higher than the ones the earlier migrants found. The Appalachians, Negroes, Puerto Ricans, and Mexican Americans now concentrated within the central ghettos of metropolitan areas are not just the most recent wave of newcomers to those districts, as some scholars have suggested. The others were able to pass through, but today's residents could fail to make it.

The editors of *The Economist* saw the situation more clearly from London than did the American commentators who wrote in the days right after the Watts riot. In a brilliant editorial, they observed that Los Angeles symbolizes the frontier of modern society, with the technologically most advanced industries, the large numbers of research-and-development establishments, high-quality public services, and the most widespread distribution of the affluent, modern style of life. With no surprise that the first major riot should occur in Southern California, rather than Chicago or New York, they perceptively interpreted the outcry as a measure of the perceived gap between two juxtaposed populations at widely different stages of development. The Watts rioters were not striking out at the city. After all, the quality of the physical environment in south-central Los Angeles is far superior to that in the metropolitan ghettos of the East. These people were striking out at their plight—at the widening social distance that separates them from their visible neighbors and at the widening differentials in opportunity. The immediate objects of hostility in Watts and in the subsequent riots were whitey's policemen and the physical city. The police and the city were, however, merely convenient symbols of the rioters' frustrating sense of powerlessness and of the many handicaps keeping them from bridging the social gap. They were surely not the real objects of their anger.

By now the message of Watts, Newark, Memphis, and the other violent outcries is beginning to be heard in critical circles, reinforcing the earlier underlying theme of the civil rights movement. Too often the meanings are interpreted simplistically—as racial conflicts between blacks and whites, as rebellion against discriminatory practices, or as protests against the filth and depravity of the slum. The rioters are saying all these things—and more. Their docket of indictments is long and righteous; their dramatic moral censure of American society has by now provoked a crisis of conscience forcing the nation to confront the plight it had been silently ignoring for so long. The nation's response with the new civil rights legislation, new housing programs, and new policing practices is admirable and right; yet none of these is enough. The problems of the poor Negro Americans are not unique to them in America. To be sure, race has been an important exacerbating factor in retarding their progress, but preindustrial status is not a distinctive condition of Negroes. Large Mexican American, Puerto Rican, and domestic Caucasian populations are living in quite similar status, and we should not be surprised when they, too, stage revolts like those of the past three years. If disparities in stages of development are behind the current urbanization crisis, that crisis is far more deep-seated and touches far more people than the current debates recognize. It would then require a much more encompassing effort, one aimed at accelerating the urbanization of all groups whose social mobility has been retarded.

Toward an Urbanization Policy

As the scale of the society has risen, our governmental system has been slowly adapting to it. Almost without deliberate intention, the federal system has been modified to conform to the rise of the nation-state as successor to the city-state. Without an explicit policy decision, the national government has assumed responsibility for confronting the urbanization problems and opportunities, albeit often in the language of localism and home-rule.

The shift in the locus of policy-making in education clearly mirrors this important change. Education has traditionally been one of the most jealously guarded provinces of local governments. People care about their children's educational opportunities and have willingly supported public education through local taxation that permitted local control. And yet when accounted within a larger-system framework, the investment strategies have not always proved prudent. Unlike investments in roads, investments in people are easily lost because, unlike roads, people are movable. Thus, the northern and eastern cities become the beneficiaries of the poor schooling accorded Negro children in the southern states. Similarly they may attract graduates of southern colleges with few direct returns to the southern culture and economy.

Population mobility has raised a difficult dilemma for governments that were initially structured to serve geographically stable peoples. Our adaptive response has been to redistribute revenues and expenditures among geographic regions. Because only the least territorially-bounded of our governments can perform the redistributive function, we have been creating new roles for the federal government and a new set of functional relationships among our various public governments.[8]

At the same time we have been building a vast network of nonpublic organizations having a governmental character and self-assigned responsibilities. Each is organized upon an interest base, rather than a territorial one. Thus, trade associations effectively exert governmental constraints upon their corporation members, and professional associations govern the conduct of physicians, engineers, lawyers, and the rest. Trade unions, churches, and recreational groups have been similarly structured to serve the special interests of their members. All these groups are governments in the essential meanings of that term; they are regulative agencies with power to exert sanctions and enforce control. Increasingly, they have come to have nationwide realms for they have arisen as manifestations of a society rapidly moving into the post-industrial, post-city stage of its development. Combined with the thousands of "public governments," they contribute to a complex network of policy and decision centers.

With so complex a governing apparatus in this country, it is not possible to formulate a unitary set of policies for national development or a unitary mutually reinforcing set of programs. Nor is it possible to erect a unitary set of controls guided from a central command post. Goals for the nation are surely as pluralistic and competitive as the diverse groups that might formulate them. And yet there may be a national consensus that would permit us to pursue some common objectives in a directed and deliberate fashion. The complexity of contemporary society leaves no group independent of the others, and the welfare of any one group is now unavoidably bound up with the welfare of the others.

The United States has not until recently sensed the need for a national strategy that would accelerate economic and human development, for we have prospered well without one. Moreover, such a development policy has seemed to require far more centralization of authority and control than is tolerable or possible in this nation. Nevertheless, although the nation has prospered, all its members have not. If the left-behinds are to find access to modern society, we are going to have to launch as concerted a programmatic effort as the Latin American attempts to accelerate the social mobility of their *marginalidad*. We now have a considerable intellectual capability for developmental planning that we have so far been exporting. By exploiting those capabilities, while operating within the framework of our contemporary pluralistic governmental system, we should be able to increase the odds that the transition to the post-industrial age can be eased. If we can but use our available intelligence, we should be able to accelerate the social mobility of those who might otherwise never catch up.

"The city" can no longer serve as the central organizing idea behind such a planning effort. The next stage of urbanization planning will be guided by the concept of selective development—by the formulation of tactical programs that conform to strategic plans aimed at bringing the left-behind groups into contemporary urban society.

Some of the programmatic imperatives can be read in the very character of post-industrialism and suggest investment strategies for that human-development effort. The nation is surely rich enough to raise all incomes above the poverty line, and the means for doing so are now being invented at a rising rate. Family allowances and guaranteed minimum incomes appear to be economically feasible.

New jobs are needed in large volumes, particularly for those who are presently the least skilled. The need is most likely to be satisfied in the service occupations, and a wave of social invention under way suggests possibilities for creating new subprofessional careers that carry dignity and status—careers that might serve the recent migrants to cities as the earlier industrial jobs served the earlier arrivals. The poor quality of housing need no longer be the norm for the metropolitan centers. Again some imaginative new schemes are being devised that would merge public and private enterprises in mutually profitable and potentially productive house-building ventures—inside the cities and elsewhere. There is no imperative of the emerging new society so demanding as high-quality educational services, from prekindergarten to postdoctoral levels. Although the nation is now spending heavily in this sector of the economy, large expansion is needed. In parallel, the spectrum of public recreational services—ranging from parks and other outdoor facilities to high-brow museums and low-brow pool halls—are becoming near-necessary attributes of the new style of life. Medical and health services have never been adequate to the standards of health to which we have aspired, so a massive new effort is being aimed at planned improvement of people's physical and mental well-being, whether they live in cities or not.

The designs for such a strategy for national development can never be fitted into coherent and mutually reinforcing wholes. The pluralistic structure of American society would never permit that. Moreover, the dangers are likely to exceed the advantages, and it is wholly unlikely that we would ever know enough even to make such an attempt anyway. Some general policy guides, however, are both economically possible and politically feasible.

NOTES

1. The phrase is Don Martindale's; it closes his "Introduction" to Max Weber's *The City* (New York, 1962), p. 67. The theme is being sounded in many quarters nowadays. See especially, Scott Greer, *The Emerging City* (New York, 1962); Kenneth Boulding, *The Meaning of the Twentieth Century* (New York, 1965); York Willburn, *The Withering Away of the City* (Tuscaloosa, 1964); and Janet Abu-Lhughod, "The City Is Dead—Long Live the City" (Center for Planning and Development Research, University of California, Berkeley, 1966, mimeo.).
2. John Friedman presents a crisp clarification of the distinction in "Two Concepts of Urbanization," *Urban Affairs Quarterly,* Vol. 1, No. 4 (June, 1966), pp. 78–84.
3. Richard Hofstadter, *The Age of Reform* (New York, 1955) and *Anti-Intellectualism in America* (New York, 1963). Morton and Lucia White, *The Intellectuals Against the City* (Cambridge, 1964).
4. Richard L. Meier, *A Communications Theory of Urban Growth* (Cambridge, 1962).

5. I have elaborated this thesis in "Order in Diversity: Community Without Propinquity," in Lowdon Wingo, Jr. (ed.), *Cities and Space* (Baltimore, 1963), pp. 23–54.

6. For example, the first-generation jet airplanes, like the first railroads, accelerated the growth of the largest settlements. The big jets could land at only those airports with long runways and specialized facilities. The second- and third-generation jets are fast equalizing accessibility among settlements, recapitulating the accessibility effects of the railroads and then the highways.

7. Boulding, *The Meaning of the Twentieth Century*.

8. See Morton Grodzin's classic essay "The Federal System," in *Goals for Americans: The Report of the President's Commission on National Goals* (Englewood Cliffs, 1960), pp. 265–84.

ANNOTATED BIBLIOGRAPHY

Breese, Gerald. (1969) *The City in Newly Developing Countries.* Englewood Cliffs, N.J.: Prentice-Hall.
   A reader on the growth and development of cities in newly developing countries. The book contains provocative pieces on the current status of world urbanization, the role of the city in economic growth and social change in developing countries.
Greer, Scott. (1962) *The Emerging City: Myth and Reality.* New York: Free Press.
   As the title implies, Scott Greer examines the city as a part of the broader society. Greer provides an imaginative perspective that is bound to excite the theoretically oriented student.
Hauser, Philip M., and Leo F. Schnore. (1965) *The Study of Urbanization.* New York: Wiley.
   An interdisciplinary overview of urbanization as seen through the eyes of seventeen leading urban scholars. The fourteen articles appear to represent a state-of-the-art report for the various disciplines.
Jacobs, Jane. (1961) *The Death and Life of Great American Cities.* New York: Random House.
   A fascinating polemic against contemporary urban planning and planners, and what they are doing to bleed the city of vitality, diversity, and life.
Reissman, Leonard. (1964) *The Urban Process.* New York: Free Press.
   Reissman proceeds from describing the views of the city held by such men as Ebenezer Howard, Frank Lloyd Wright, Louis Mumford, and Robert Redfield, to the specification of the requirements for urban theory. The approach is cross-cultural and compares historical industrial development in Western nations with urban growth in the developing nations today.
Stein, Maurice R. (1960) *The Eclipse of Community.* New York: Harper & Row.
   Describes, discusses, and interprets "classic" community studies such as those done by Park and the Chicago School, the Lynds in *Middletown,* and Warner in *Yankee City.* The title of the volume gives the basic premise.
Theodorson, George A. (1961) *Studies in Human Ecology.* New York: Harper & Row.
   A collection of readings that is particularly strong in detailing the historical development of the field from the early classical position to contemporary neo-orthodox and sociocultural approaches. A good follow-up to Thomlinson's *Urban Structure* volume.
Thomlinson, Ralph. (1969) *Urban Structure.* New York: Random House.
   An ecologist's very readable description of the social and spatial character of cities, with particular emphasis on theories of distribution of inhabitants within cities and relationships between cities and their environs. The student in urban ecology should start his reading with this volume, since it provides a comprehensive overview of what has been done to date.
Vidich, Arthur J., and Joseph Bensman. (1968) *Small Town in Mass Society.* Princeton, N.J.: Princeton University Press.
   A descriptive study of how a small upstate New York town responds to the

circumstances of its essential powerlessness in dealing with modern mass industrial society. The revised edition also contains considerable discussion of the methods, theory, and implications of community studies.

Warren, Roland L. (1963) *The Community in America.* Skokie, Ill.: Rand McNally.

This book examines in a systematic way the common characteristics of American community life. For the student who is interested in the urban region as a community, this is an excellent book.

Weber, Max. (1958) *The City,* ed. and trans. by Don Martindale and Gertrud Neuwirth. New York: Free Press.

The classic treatment of ancient and medieval occidental cities. This is a "must read" work, but probably is most valuable if read after the student has a basic exposure to the extent and nature of contemporary urbanization.

SECTION THREE

EMERGING LIFE STYLES IN THE URBAN SETTING

(Above) An individualist builds a home to be shared by other members of his commune. Photograph by Dennis Stock. (Right) Suburban Los Angeles. Photo by Rotkin, P.F.I., Los Angeles.

3.1 INTRODUCTION: DIVERSITY AND URBAN LIFE STYLES

Historically, the city has been the meeting place as well as the working place for people of different cultures, races, interests, skills, and needs. In the city, diversity is both tolerated and rewarded; the city provides the milieu in which people with varied backgrounds can coexist. As Louis Wirth makes clear in Article 3.2, the city "has brought together people from the ends of the earth *because* they are different and thus useful to one another, rather than because they are homogeneous and likeminded." In the article, Wirth's point of departure is that:

> Since the population of the city does not reproduce itself, it must recruit its migrants from other cities, the countryside, and—in this country until recently—from other countries. The city has been the melting-pot of races, peoples, and cultures, and a most favorable breeding-ground of new biological and cultural hybrids. It has not only tolerated but rewarded individual differences.

Three general propositions related to diversity in urban areas are contained in the Wirth's observation. First, immigration has brought diverse people, activities, and cultures to the city, thereby serving as a mechanism of cultural diffusion. Second, the city has been an incubator of new sociocultural forms through sociocultural innovation. Third, the city is more than the place where new forms are introduced; it provides a setting in which established diverse forms can be successfully transmitted from generation to generation.

As a general setting for social life, the city provides the conditions for a unique and distinctive way of life called *urbanism*. Modes of life in urban communities are reflected in how people dress and speak, their beliefs about the social world, the things they consider worth achieving, what they do for a living, where they live, whom they associate with, and the reasons for their interactions with other people. Sometimes these ways of life are fleeting, but sometimes they continue through time as subcultures of the larger social system. In either case, sociologists in this section emphasize the organization of social behavior at the micro-level, where the largest unit of analysis is the neighborhood or local community. We generally want to know how and under what conditions different modes of life evolved through time within the urban setting with its neighborhoods, social organization, and social institutions.

As indicated in Section Two, the study of localized areas within the city has been a major interest of sociologists since the 1920s. Sociologists have been particularly concerned with documenting the impact of urban industrial technology on the life styles of groups new to the city. Probably the most influential of these sociologists was Louis Wirth. His 1938 article, "Urbanism as a Way of Life," was a significant contribution to the understanding of evolving urban life patterns. As Herbert Gans illustrates in Article 3.3, Wirth's study has been the starting point for untold numbers of dissertations and scholarly papers on the nature of interpersonal relations among urban inhabitants. In spite of its age, Wirth's article is still the subject of considerable debate, a mark of a classic piece.

Because of the influence of Wirth's contribution and because of the scope of his general argument, we have chosen for this section a number of articles that reflect on, develop, and criticize his observations on the urban way of life. According to Wirth, "a city may be defined as a relatively large, dense, and permanent settlement of socially heterogeneous individuals." Wirth suggests that urbanization and its components of size, density, and heterogeneity are the independent variables that are the determinants of urbanism. He then goes on to say:

> The central problem of the sociologist of the city is to discover the forms of social action and organization that typically emerge in relatively permanent compact settlements of large numbers of heterogeneous individuals. . . . Thus the larger, the more densely populated, and the more heterogeneous a community, the more accentuated the characteristics associated with urbanism will be.

Wirth was aware of the relationship between population and social organization. In his words,

> . . . increasing the number of inhabitants in a settlement beyond a certain limit will affect the relationships between them and the character of the city. Large numbers involve . . . a greater range of individual variation.

Urban population growth results in distinctive modes of life. The characteristics of this emerging urban way of life, as suggested by Wirth's study are:

1. An extensive division of labor and specialization; the craftsman no longer participates in every phase of manufacturing.
2. Weakening bonds of kinship and the decline of the family (increase of divorce, and so on). Family functions are transferred to specialized institutions outside the home (for example, health, educational, recreational).
3. Breakdown of primary groups and ties (neighborhood) and substitution of secondary contact and formal control mechanisms (police), leading to social disorganization. Traditional bases of social solidarity are undermined.
4. Relations with others as players of segmented roles rather than as whole persons; utilization of others as means to ends; utilitarian rather than affective relationships. Social contacts are impersonal, superficial, transitory, and segmented.

5. Emphasis on achievement over ascription; social mobility is both possible and expected.
6. Diversity of views, decline of cultural homogeneity, diversity of social values, emergence of subcultures.
7. Spatial segregation by color, ethnicity, religion, status, and so on.
8. Autonomy, alienation, rationality, sophistication, cosmopolitanism.

Sociologists during the 1920s and 1930s tended to view the city dweller as an autonomous individual subject to diverse stimuli, who found it difficult to maintain an integrated personality. They thought that increasing urbanization led to calculated sophistication, which replaced feeling and meaningful relationships. There is great similarity between this view of the city and that taken by Thomas Jefferson, Josiah Strong, and Jacob Riis in Section One.

Wirth built on the proposition that:

> As long as we identify urbanism with the physical entity of the city, viewing it merely as rigidly delimited in space, and proceed as if urban attributes abruptly ceased to be manifested beyond an arbitrary boundary line, we are not likely to arrive at any adequate conception of urbanism as a mode of life.

He was asking how life is lived in the city, rather than where people and institutions are located in urban space.

The idea that the city possesses a characteristic mode of life that is universal to all urban places is not unique to Wirth. "Weber, Simmel, and Spengler all assumed the characteristics of city culture—the large impersonal bureaucracies, the rule of rational exchange and rational law, the lack of warm personal contact between city men—to be qualities that pertain to the city *as a whole*" (Sennet 1969:12). The city is more than a politically delineated densely populated settlement.

Sociocultural Innovation and Diversity

In evaluating Wirth's thesis the reader should keep in mind that he developed it just after the high tide of foreign immigration, when the effects of in-migration were most noticeable on the city. Thus, it is not surprising that he directly related in-migration to urban growth and diversity. Today, however, natural replacement rather than in-migration is the major factor contributing to American metropolitan growth. While cities are no longer inundated by waves of immigrants with their strange and sometimes conflicting ways of life, the cultural impact of immigration can still be seen in most large cities. However, immigration as a source of urban diversity has decreased as a major factor for social change. Aside from unique cases such as the Cuban immigration to Miami, mass foreign immigration is apparently a thing of the past.

Three out of four Americans now are classified as urban residents. Contemporary population movement resembles an urban-to-urban circulatory system. Military, academic, and commercial bureaucracies all require employee movement as a matter of course. This is particularly true of upwardly mobile technocrats, moving from city to city. Even black in-migrants are now most likely to come from other urban areas. Actually, a higher proportion of blacks than whites are now city dwellers, a fact which should help to dispel the stereotype of rural southern black migration to northern centers.

This urban-to-urban pattern does not mean that population changes are no longer a source of urban diversity. Bureau of the Census figures indicate, for example, that one out of five households moves every year. In spite of some arguments to the contrary (that is, *The Organization Man*), population movement in and by itself does result in the circulation of new ideas and life styles. Urban-to-urban spatial mobility reduces the physical and social barriers that insulate people. They become exposed to different ways of thinking and living. Communication technology also aids in the circulation of a new idea. In fact, because of mass communications media, cultural diffusion today is less dependent on population migration than in the past, although we still do not fully understand all the implications of the new technology.

The nature of cities themselves encourages continued diversity. Cities attract large numbers of people, thereby becoming a pool of diverse human resources. The larger the city, the greater will be the opportunity for a wide variety of activities. Jane Jacobs' article in Section Two (2.6) illustrates this by showing the relationship between the size of the city and the potential for new enterprises. Large heterogenous settings are more conducive to small, specialized operations, or, as Jacobs puts it, new ideas need old buildings. She emphasizes population size and urban environment as generators of new social organizational forms.

Others posit a more complicated relationship. John Seeley, whose article closes this volume (5.7), argues that in normal times the city is that place "where the civilization is refined, developed, elaborated, and fed back to the hinterland." This role of the city is called the *orthogenetic* role (Redfield and Singer, 1954), and it takes the form of elaborating, embellishing, and refining existing modes of life. In his article, Seeley also notes that cities play a *heterogenetic* role:

> . . . in abnormal times, the city is that place where its successor is being incubated, nurtured, fostered, or developed. And the conscience of the city lies at that *nucleus nucleorum*, wherever it may be, where most actively, most passionately, most devotedly, most integrally the foundations of the new civilizations are being in action and interaction conceived, incarnated, tested, and worked out.

All cities play both the more conservative orthogenetic and the more radical heterogenetic cultural roles. In transitional times, cities regardless of their long-term cultural roles tend to move in the direction of the more radical role. In other words, in transitional periods cities are likely to serve as havens for new, strange, and even radical ideas and life styles. The city is the place where exotic groups and activities are found, and thus it provides conditions for the generation or at least the incubation of diversity.

However, as Paul Meadows (*see* Article 2.2) seems to suggest, the city's role as a generator of diversity is dependent on general societal patterns. It appears that evolutionary trends are under way which may lead to quite different modes of life. For example, the economy, once predominantly extractive and goods-producing, has become the first service economy in history (Fuchs, 1968:2). Today more than half of all workers in the United States are in occupations not producing goods. While the total number of new industrial jobs increased by four million during the period from 1947 to 1965, the service sector increased by thirteen million (Fuchs, 1968:2), a pattern also identified by Robert Weller in his article (*see* 2.4).

As technology and social organization continue to change, conditions are created which call for new adaptive mechanisms. For instance, the institutionalization of science has necessitated a search for new ideas, which is now one of our most prestigious occupations. Knowledge is being "produced" as a product in its own right, and new ideas are being generated at record speeds. The very lucrative business of opinion sampling has developed toward this end of informing us what we are thinking.

Concomitant with the rapid circulation of ideas has been a change in established value systems. The speed of these social changes has led some to define our era as one of ideological crisis, manifested, for instance, by the hippie/crazie phenomenon and the drug scene. Because ideological changes do not fit well with existing modes of life, old needs often remain unsatisfied while new ones are emerging.

During transitional periods the changing needs of the era may create pressing social problems. For example, throughout history growing urban populations have created problems of safety, welfare, and order. Melvin Webber (*see* Article 2.8) says that today,

> . . . problems of the city place generated by early industrialization are being supplanted by a new array different in kind. With but a few remaining exceptions (. . . air pollution is a notable one), the recent difficulties are not place-type problems at all. Rather, they are the transitional problems of a rapidly developing society. . . .

As a result, new needs are developing, which generate problems that are scarcely recognized until they create a crisis.

Nuclear power and its implications for warfare, economics, and politics is the most obvious contemporary example of how change in one sector such as technology can create major problems not only in social organization but also in environment. The proposed development of the SST jet transport, which with its sonic boom portended environmental as well as auditory damage, similarly illustrates how developments in one realm can create crises in others.

Present problems are partially the result of our heavy reliance on technology. Given technology's past successes in solving the problems of survival in the city, the American reliance on technology is understandable. Medical advances, for example, greatly reduced health hazards, while steam, electricity, and the internal combustion engine alleviated problems of transportation. As solutions in areas of social problems, new organizational forms were devised such as political reform movements, public education, mass communication, labor organization, and city planning. Today, however, technological advances frequently result in population, environmental, and organizational strains.

Seeley points out that philosophers ranging from Mannheim to Marcuse agree that we do best what makes no sense. In Article 5.7 Seeley states:

> What we have perfected is technology, and it is technology on which most men, most places, most times rest such vague hopes as still stir. It is now in or almost in our hand to feed lavishly, clothe, and render "literate" the world. . . . The Universe capitulates. We are everywhere triumphant. But a premonitory smell of cosmic Neroism is in the air, and the cry of "Stop The World; I Want To Get Off" has become, whether absurd or not, pervasive and insistent.

Sociocultural Continuity

Thus, the city is the place where new forms are introduced. But, the city also provides a setting in which diverse forms, once established, can be successfully transmitted from generation to generation. Not all innovations are readily accepted by a society or a community. In this section Gans (3.3), Amory (3.6), and Berger (3.7) all document the persistence of established sociocultural patterns. People generally are selective in their acceptance of alternative beliefs, ideals, or norms. Cleveland Amory, for example, a social critic with a keen eye and sharp tongue, illustrates the importance of tradition and habit among the upper class. Bennett Berger shows that continuity of life styles can be found among working-class in-migrants to suburbia. It is true that both Vice Lords and Boston Brahmins must find physical sustenance and shelter. But, because of class and racial differences, each meets these needs quite differently. And, at the same time, both are part of a larger system that rationalizes and legitimizes the inequities in their lives.

In addition to biological needs, man has developed an expanding array of social needs, suggested in the familiar phrase, *life style.** The term *subculture* is frequently used, and sometimes misused, to characterize the organization of these different ways of life. Subculture, in this context, refers to "the normative systems of groups smaller than the society of which they are a part" (Yinger, 1960:626). According to Gans:

> . . . each subculture is an organized set of related responses that has developed out of people's efforts to cope with the opportunities, incentives, and rewards, as well as the deprivations, prohibitions, and pressures which the natural environment and society—that complex of co-existing and competing subcultures—offer to them. (Gans, 1962:249)

An example of a subculture is the ethnic enclave that Wirth described in his

---

*It is well to distinguish between those requirements which must be met if the individual is to survive and those which must be met if the society is to be viable. These two classes of needs should not be confused. In the evolutionary development of societies, the significance of basic biological needs is noted in the historical emergence of institutional forms. For example, institutions that are related to biological needs emerged very early in human history. The family institution existed in some form in all societies, and religious institutions were also evident relatively early. On the other hand, certain forms of economic and political institutions did not emerge until after the agricultural and urban revolutions. The political state and large-scale armies are two such institutional forms.

classic book, *The Ghetto*. Both Liebow's *Tally's Corner* and Keiser's *The Vice Lords* are contemporary illustrations of groups with distinctive subcultural norms and values. Over a period of time, these different ways of meeting social needs become more or less patterned, or "socially integrated."

Social integration, however, does not describe how sociocultural patterns of life, once established, remain so resistant to change. Basic biological and social needs continue through time, but obviously that is not a sufficient explanation for the continuity of sociocultural patterns. Social attitudes, once formed, are difficult to change; but that also is a partial answer. One approach to the problem of continuity is to examine how norms and values are transmitted from one generation to another, a process called *socialization*. Studies indicate that how norms are learned and who guides the socialization process are in large part determined by one's position in the stratification structure. Lower-class males, such as the Vice Lords, are exposed to different values and norms than the children of either the Boston Brahmins or working-class suburbanites. Even when goals are held in common, the access to the means for achieving these goals is differentially distributed. Within each class, the institutional patterns of socialization are highly structured; and as a result ways of life tend to be perpetuated over time.

However, most sociocultural patterns do eventually change. For example, traditional rural ways of life have largely died out in America; the same is true of many patterns of life based on ethnicity and religion. In America, the passing of each older generation has seen a steady erosion of old traditions. Changes such as intermarriage, increased schooling, and occupational mobility have all contributed to the evolution of new patterns of life.

Article Overview

Wirth's classic article (3.2), which has already been discussed in detail, leads off the reading in this section. The validity of Wirth's analysis is still open to debate, as the two following articles by Herbert Gans (3.3) and Stanley Guterman (3.4) indicate. Wirth, for example, tied social and cultural heterogeneity to increasing population size and density. Yet in recent decades the population and density of major cities such as New York and Chicago have been decreasing without any evidence of decreasing heterogeneity. Perhaps more important, subsequent studies have shown that urban residents maintain kinship and friendship ties, enjoy family life, and are active in neighborhood activities. In retrospect, Wirth's thesis is probably something of an overstatement. The article by Gans is essentially a critique of Wirth's view of urban life styles. Gans' criticism is that Wirth is inaccurate insofar as he viewed the city as being a melting-pot that will inevitably break down existing cultural and social patterns. There is some doubt as to whether Gans accurately interpreted what Wirth actually said about the melting-pot effect. Reread the quote in the first paragraph of this introduction and draw your own conclusions. Wirth emphasizes the value of diversity at the aggregate level in the city. The city as an ecological unit provides a setting where diverse groups can co-exist and even thrive. Diversity is tolerated, indeed even rewarded, in the city. While Wirth applies the idea of melting-pot to the cultures of groups and aggregates, he does not state, as Gans claims, that "the melting-pot effect was far more powerful than the tendency toward segregation."

However, Gans does touch on a very significant point when he distinguishes between the ecological and behavioral-cultural perspectives on city life styles. The ecological view examines behavior patterns as they reflect the social and natural environment, while the cultural view examines the interaction of people as friends and neighbors, thus emphasizing the values and sentiments of individuals in interaction. Gans makes an important contribution at this micro-level by focusing on life styles within particular community or neighborhood areas within the city. His emphasis is on the vitality of neighborhood life within the larger urban setting.

Guterman's article logically follows the pieces by Wirth and Gans. In his defense of Wirth, Guterman first briefly reviews the controversy and suggests weaknesses in the arguments made by Wirth's critics. By so doing he provides a counterpoint to the more common criticisms of Wirth. Guterman then goes on to provide his own data that support Wirth's original position. Guterman's article illustrates, in a relatively modest fashion, how sociologists attempt to interplay theory and research.

The first three pieces stress the issue of diversity and continuity in urban life styles. The remaining pieces in this section bring the urban scene to life. They vividly depict the similarity and diversity of urban patterns of interaction, and they make visible the patterns of choices people make, given their range of alternatives. These alternatives reflect individual class and life style characteristics as will be shown. For example, the extremes of life styles are illustrated in comparing the life of a Vice Lord with that of a "proper" Bostonian.

Anthropologist R. Lincoln Keiser's description of the life of a Chicago Vice Lord (Article 3.5) emphasizes the degree to which the whole pattern of one's life reflects the conditions of his social and physical environment. The influence of social structure upon behavior is also dissected by social critic Cleveland Amory (Article 3.6). His selection on the unique behavior patterns of upper-class Boston Brahmins serves to remind us that unique subcultural patterns are not solely the product of the ghetto. Amory's nontheoretical excerpt also reminds us that social scientists do not by any means have a monopoly on describing and interpreting the social structure.

The selections from *The Vice Lords* and from *The Proper Bostonians* certainly illustrate the range of life-style variations found in the city. The Vice Lords are black, the Bostonians are white. The Lords are poor, the Bostonians are rich. The Lords' mode of dress is modish and highly stylized, while the Bostonians' is traditional and conservative. The Lords are fatalistic in their world view, while the Bostonians are confident of their ability to influence, if not completely control, future events. At the same time, both groups are part of the same larger social system. While the societal integration of these two groups is limited by time, space, culture, and circumstance, both groups use the same general language and both must meet personal physical needs within the limits of the national economic system.

Article 3.7 by Bennett Berger examines the relationship between population movement and life-style continuity. Berger's analysis of working-class suburbs asks if working-class movement from central city to suburb necessarily results in the acquisition of a middle-class way of life. His analysis corrects some popular misconceptions about suburban ways of life. Movement to the suburbs does not necessarily result in upper-middle-class life styles. His article makes clear the tenacity of working-class norms, perceptions, and world views among blue-collar suburbanites. According to Berger, social attitudes and behavior continue to reflect class, ethnic, and life-style factors, regardless of place of residence.

Conclusion

Though there is still continuity of life styles within cities, new forms are also emerging. The threshold of a new era may be reflected in changing values and norms concerning kinship, abortion, space, the environment, and even technology. The material in this section, and in the sections that preceded it, suggest that some of the changes are not of recent origin, but are the continuation of long-term, ongoing changes in population patterns, social organization, environment, and technology.

In the past, the city was the place where new ideas and life styles emerged. Today, the city is increasingly becoming part of the larger national and even international systems, which are themselves increasingly urban. As once-independent suburbs are now city neighborhoods, individual cities are increasingly becoming the neighborhoods of emerging national and international urban systems. Thus it seems reasonable to expect that cities will continue to be the place where things are happening.

REFERENCES

Fuchs, Victor R. (1968) *The Service Economy.* New York: Columbia University Press.

Gans, Herbert J. (1962) *The Urban Villagers.* New York: Free Press.

Redfield, Robert, and Milton B. Singer. (1954) "The Cultural Role of Cities," *Economic Development and Cultural Change,* Vol. III, No. 1.

Sennett, Richard. (1969) *Classic Essays on the Culture of Cities.* New York: Appleton.

Yinger, J. Milton. (1960) "Contraculture and Subculture," *American Sociological Review,* Vol. 25, pp. 625–635.

I. The City and Contemporary Civilization

Just as the beginning of Western civilization is marked by the permanent settlement of formerly nomadic peoples in the Mediterranean basin, so the beginning
of what is distinctively modern in our civilization is best signalized by the
growth of great cities. Nowhere has mankind been farther removed from
organic nature than under the conditions of life characteristic of great cities.
The contemporary world no longer presents a picture of small isolated groups
of human beings scattered over a vast territory, as Sumner described primitive
society.[1] The distinctive feature of the mode of living of man in the modern
age is his concentration into gigantic aggregations around which cluster lesser
centers and from which radiate the ideas and practices that we call civilization.

The degree to which the contemporary world may be said to be "urban"
is not fully or accurately measured by the proportion of the total population
living in cities. The influences which cities exert upon the social life of man
are greater than the ratio of the urban population would indicate, for the city
is not only in ever larger degrees the dwelling-place and the workshop of
modern man, but it is the initiating and controlling center of economic, political, and cultural life that has drawn the most remote parts of the world into
its orbit and woven diverse areas, peoples, and activities into a cosmos.

The growth of cities and the urbanization of the world is one of the most
impressive facts of modern times. Although it is impossible to state precisely
what proportion of the estimated total world-population of approximately
1,800,000,000 is urban, 69.2 per cent of the total population of those countries that do distinguish between urban and rural areas is urban.[2] Considering
the fact, moreover, that the world's population is very unevenly distributed
and that the growth of cities is not very far advanced in some of the countries
that have only recently been touched by industrialism, this average understates
the extent to which urban concentration has proceeded in those countries
where the impact of the industrial revolution has been more forceful and of
less recent date. This shift from a rural to a predominantly urban society,
which has taken place within the span of a single generation in such industrial-

From Louis Wirth, "Urbanism as a Way of Life," *American Journal of Sociology,* Vol.
44 (July 1938), pp. 1–24. Copyright, 1938, The University of Chicago. All rights
reserved. Reprinted by permission of The University of Chicago Press.

ized areas as the United States and Japan, has been accompanied by profound changes in virtually every phase of social life. It is these changes and their ramifications that invite the attention of the sociologist to the study of the differences between the rural and the urban mode of living. The pursuit of this interest is an indispensable prerequisite for the comprehension and possible mastery of some of the most crucial contemporary problems of social life since it is likely to furnish one of the most revealing perspectives for the understanding of the ongoing changes in human nature and the social order.[3]

Since the city is the product of growth rather than of instantaneous creation, it is to be expected that the influences which it exerts upon the modes of life should not be able to wipe out completely the previously dominant modes of human association. To a greater or lesser degree, therefore, our social life bears the imprint of an earlier folk society, the characteristic modes of settlement of which were the farm, the manor, and the village. This historic influence is reinforced by the circumstance that the population of the city itself is in large measure recruited from the countryside, where a mode of life reminiscent of this earlier form of existence persists. Hence we should not expect to find abrupt and discontinuous variation between urban and rural types of personality. The city and the country may be regarded as two poles in reference to one or the other of which all human settlements tend to arrange themselves. In viewing urban-industrial and rural-folk society as ideal types of communities, we may obtain a perspective for the analysis of the basic models of human association as they appear in contemporary civilization.

II. A Sociological Definition of the City

Despite the preponderant significance of the city in our civilization, however, our knowledge of the nature of urbanism and the process of urbanization is meager. Many attempts have indeed been made to isolate the distinguishing characteristics of urban life. Geographers, historians, economists, and political scientists have incorporated the points of view of their respective disciplines into diverse definitions of the city. While in no sense intended to supersede these, the formulation of a sociological approach to the city may incidentally serve to call attention to the interrelations between them by emphasizing the peculiar characteristics of the city as a particular form of human association. A sociologically significant definition of the city seeks to select those elements of urbanism which mark it as a distinctive mode of human group life.

The characterization of a community as urban on the basis of size alone is obviously arbitrary. It is difficult to defend the present census definition which designates a community of 2,500 and above as urban and all others as rural. The situation would be the same if the criterion were 4,000, 8,000, 10,000, 25,000, or 100,000 population, for although in the latter case we might feel that we were more nearly dealing with an urban aggregate than would be the case in communities of lesser size, no definition of urbanism can hope to be completely satisfying as long as numbers are regarded as the sole criterion. Moreover, it is not difficult to demonstrate that communities of less than the arbitrarily set number of inhabitants lying within the range of influence of metropolitan centers have greater claim to recognition as urban communities than do larger ones leading a more isolated existence in a predominantly rural area. Finally, it should be recognized that census definitions are unduly influenced by the fact that the city, statistically speaking, is always an administrative concept in that the corporate limits play a decisive role in delineating the urban area. Nowhere is this more clearly apparent than in the concentrations of population on the peripheries of great metropolitan centers which cross arbitrary administrative boundaries of city, county, state, and nation.

As long as we identify urbanism with the physical entity of the city, viewing it merely as rigidly delimited in space, and proceed as if urban attributes abruptly ceased to be manifested beyond an arbitrary boundary line, we are not likely to arrive at any adequate conception of urbanism as a mode of life. The technological developments in transportation and communication which virtually mark a new epoch in human history have accentuated the role of cities as dominant elements in our civilization and have enormously extended the urban mode of living beyond the confines of the city itself. The dominance of the city, especially of the great city, may be regarded as a consequence of the concentration in cities of industrial and commercial, financial and administrative facilities and activites, transportation and communication lines, and cultural and recreational equipment such as the press, radio stations, theaters, libraries, museums, concert halls, operas, hospitals, higher educational institutions, research and publishing centers, professional organizations, and religious and welfare institutions. Were it not for the attraction and suggestions that the city exerts through these instrumentalities upon the rural population, the differences between the rural and the urban modes of life would be even greater than they are. Urbanization no longer denotes merely the process by which persons are attracted to a place called the city and incorporated into its system of life. It refers also to that cumulative accentuation of the characteristics distinctive of the mode of life which is associated with the growth of cities, and finally to the changes in the direction of modes of life recognized as urban which are apparent among people, wherever they may be, who have come under the spell of the influences which the city exerts by virtue of the power of its institutions and personalities operating through the means of communication and transportation.

The shortcomings which attach to number of inhabitants as a criterion of urbanism apply for the most part to density of population as well. Whether we accept the density of 10,000 persons per square mile as Mark Jefferson[4] proposed, or 1,000, which Willcox[5] preferred to regard as the criterion of urban settlements, it is clear that unless density is correlated with significant social characteristics it can furnish only an arbitrary basis for differentiating urban from rural communities. Since our census enumerates the night rather than the day population of an area, the locale of the most intensive urban life—the city center—generally has low population density, and the industrial and commercial areas of the city, which contain the most characteristic economic activities underlying urban society, would scarcely anywhere be truly urban if density were literally interpreted as a mark of urbanism. Nevertheless, the fact that the urban community is distinguished by a large aggregation and relatively dense concentration of population can scarcely be left out of account in a definition of the city. But these criteria must be seen as relative to the general cultural context in which cities arise and exist and are sociologically relevant only in so far as they operate as conditioning factors in social life.

The same criticisms apply to such criteria as the occupation of the inhabitants, the existence of certain physical facilities, institutions, and forms of political organization. The question is not whether cities in our civilization or in others do exhibit these distinctive traits, but how potent they are in molding the character of social life into its specifically urban form. Nor in formulating a fertile definition can we afford to overlook the great variations between cities. By means of a typology of cities based upon size, location, age, and function, such as we have undertaken to establish in our recent report to the National Resources Committee,[6] we have found it feasible to array and classify urban communities ranging from struggling small towns to thriving world-metropolitan centers; from isolated trading-centers in the midst of agricultural regions to thriving world-ports and commercial and industrial conurbations. Such differences as these appear crucial because the social characteristics and influences of these different "cities" vary widely.

A serviceable definition of urbanism should not only denote the essential characteristics which all cities—at least those in our culture—have in common, but should lend itself to the discovery of their variations. An industrial city will differ significantly in social respects from a commercial, mining, fishing, resort, university, and capital city. A one-industry city will present different sets of social characteristics from a multi-industry city, as will an industrially balanced from an imbalanced city, a suburb from a satellite, a residential suburb from an industrial suburb, a city within a metropolitan region from one lying outside, an old city from a new one, a southern city from a New England, a middle-western from a Pacific Coast city, a growing from a stable and from a dying city.

A sociological definition must obviously be inclusive enough to comprise whatever essential characteristics these different types of cities have in common as social entities, but it obviously cannot be so detailed as to take account of all the variations implicit in the manifold classes sketched above. Presumably some of the characteristics of cities are more significant in conditioning the nature of urban life than others, and we may expect the outstanding features of the urban-social scene to vary in accordance with size, density, and differences in the functional type of cities. Moreover, we may infer that rural life will bear the imprint of urbanism in the measure that through contact and communication it comes under the influence of cities. It may contribute to the clarity of the statements that follow to repeat that while the locus of urbanism as a mode of life is, of course, to be found characteristically in places which fulfill the requirements we shall set up as a definition of the city, urbanism is not confined to such localities but is manifest in varying degrees wherever the influences of the city reach.

While urbanism, or that complex of traits which makes up the characteristic mode of life in cities, and urbanization, which denotes the development and extensions of these factors, are thus not exclusively found in settlements which are cities in the physical and demographic sense, they do, nevertheless, find their most pronounced expression in such areas, especially in metropolitan cities. In formulating a definition of the city it is necessary to exercise caution in order to avoid identifying urbanism as a way of life with any specific locally or historically conditioned cultural influences which, while they may significantly affect the specific character of the community, are not the essential determinants of its character as a city.

It is particularly important to call attention to the danger of confusing urbanism with industrialism and modern capitalism. The rise of cities in the modern world is undoubtedly not independent of the emergence of modern power-driven machine technology, mass production, and capitalistic enterprise. But different as the cities of earlier epochs may have been by virtue of their development in a preindustrial and precapitalistic order from the great cities of today, they were, nevertheless, cities.

For sociological purposes a city may be defined as a relatively large, dense, and permanent settlement of socially heterogeneous individuals. On the basis of the postulates which this minimal definition suggests, a theory of urbanism may be formulated in the light of existing knowledge concerning social groups.

III. A Theory of Urbanization

In the rich literature on the city we look in vain for a theory of urbanism presenting in a systematic fashion the available knowledge concerning the city as a social entity. We do indeed have excellent formulations of theories on such special problems as the growth of the city viewed as a historical trend and as a recurrent process,[7] and we have a wealth of literature presenting insights of sociological relevance and empirical studies offering detailed information on a variety of particular aspects of urban life. But despite the multiplication of research and textbooks on the city, we do not as yet have a comprehensive body of compendent hypotheses which may be derived from a set of postulates implicitly contained in a sociological definition of the city, and from our general sociological knowledge which may be substantiated through empirical research. The closest approximations to a systematic theory of urbanism that we have are to be found in a penetrating essay, "Die Stadt," by Max Weber,[8] and a memorable paper by Robert E. Park on "The City: Suggestions for the Investigation of Human Behavior in the Urban Environment."[9] But even these excellent contributions are far from constituting an ordered and coherent framework of theory upon which research might profitably proceed.

In the pages that follow we shall seek to set forth a limited number of identifying characteristics of the city. Given these characteristics we shall then indicate what consequences or further characteristics follow from them in the light of general sociological theory and empirical research. We hope in this manner to arrive at the essential propositions comprising a theory of urbanism. Some of these propositions can be supported by a considerable body of already available research materials; others may be accepted as hypotheses for which a certain amount of presumptive evidence exists, but for which more ample and exact verification would be required. At least such a procedure will, it is hoped, show what in the way of systematic knowledge of the city we now have and what are the crucial and fruitful hypotheses for future research.

The central problem of the sociologist of the city is to discover the forms of social action and organization that typically emerge in relatively permanent, compact settlements of large numbers of heterogeneous individuals. We must also infer that urbanism will assume its most characteristic and extreme form in the measure in which the conditions with which it is congruent are present. Thus the larger, the more densely populated, and the more heterogeneous a community, the more accentuated the characteristics associated with urbanism will be. It should be recognized, however, that in the social world institutions and practices may be accepted and continued for reasons other than those that originally brought them into existence, and that accordingly the urban mode of life may be perpetuated under conditions quite foreign to those necessary for its origin.

Some justification may be in order for the choice of the principal terms comprising our definition of the city. The attempt has been made to make it as inclusive and at the same time as denotative as possible without loading it with unnecessary assumptions. To say that large numbers are necessary to constitute a city means, of course, large numbers in relation to a restricted area or high density of settlement. There are, nevertheless, good reasons for treating large numbers and density as separate factors, since each may be connected with significantly different social consequences. Similarly the need for adding heterogeneity to numbers of population as a necessary and distinct criterion of urbanism might be questioned, since we should expect the range of differences to increase with numbers. In defense, it may be said that the city shows a kind and degree of heterogeneity of population which cannot be wholly accounted for by the law of large numbers or adequately represented by means of a normal distribution curve. Since the population of the city does not reproduce itself, it must recruit its migrants from other cities, the countryside, and—in this country until recently—from other countries. The city has thus historically been the melting-pot of races, peoples, and cultures, and a most favorable breeding-ground of new biological and cultural hybrids. It has not only tolerated but rewarded individual differences. It has brought together people from the ends of the earth *because* they are different and thus useful to one another, rather than because they are homogeneous and like-minded.[10]

There are a number of sociological propositions concerning the relationship between (*a*) numbers of population, (*b*) density of settlement, (*c*) heterogeneity of inhabitants and group life, which can be formulated on the basis of observation and research.

SIZE OF THE POPULATION AGGREGATE

Ever since Aristotle's *Politics,*[11] it has been recognized that increasing the number of inhabitants in a settlement beyond a certain limit will affect the relationships between them and the character of the city. Large numbers involve, as has been pointed out, a greater range of individual variation. Furthermore, the greater the number of individuals participating in a process of interaction, the greater is the *potential* differentiation between them. The personal traits, the occupations, the culural life, and the ideas of the members of an urban community may, therefore, be expected to range between more widely separated poles than those of rural inhabitants.

That such variations should give rise to the spatial segregation of individuals according to color, ethnic heritage, economic and social status, tastes and preferences, may readily be inferred. The bonds of kinship, of neighborliness, and the sentiments arising out of living together for generations under a common folk tradition are likely to be absent or, at best, relatively weak in an aggregate the members of which have such diverse origins and backgrounds. Under such circumstances competition and formal control mechanisms furnish the substitutes for the bonds of solidarity that are relied upon to hold a folk society together.

Increase in the number of inhabitants of a community beyond a few hundred is bound to limit the possibility of each member of the community knowing all the others personally. Max Weber, in recognizing the social significance of this fact, pointed out that from a sociological point of view large numbers of inhabitants and density of settlement mean that the personal mutual acquaintanceship between the inhabitants which ordinarily inheres in a neighborhood is lacking.[12] The increase in numbers thus involves a changed character of the social relationships. As Simmel points out:

> [If] the unceasing external contact of numbers of persons in the city should be met by the same number of inner reactions as in the small town, in which one knows almost every person he meets and to each of whom he has a positive relationship, one would be completely atomized internally and would fall into an unthinkable mental condition.[13]

The multiplication of persons in a state of interaction under conditions which make their contact as full personalities impossible produces that segmentalization of human relationships which has sometimes been seized upon by students of the mental life of the cities as an explanation for the "schizoid" character of urban personality. This is not to say that the urban inhabitants have fewer acquaintances than rural inhabitants, for the reverse may actually be true; it means rather that in relation to the number of people whom they see and with whom they rub elbows in the course of daily life, they know a smaller proportion, and of these they have less intensive knowledge.

Characteristically, urbanites meet one another in highly segmental roles. They are, to be sure, dependent upon more people for the satisfactions of their life-needs than are rural people and thus are associated with a greater number of organized groups, but they are less dependent upon particular persons, and their dependence upon others is confined to a highly fractionalized aspect of the other's round of activity. This is essentially what is meant by saying that the city is characterized by secondary rather than primary contacts. The contacts of the city may indeed be face to face, but they are nevertheless impersonal, superficial, transitory, and segmental. The reserve, the indifference, and the blasé outlook which urbanites manifest in their relationships may thus be regarded as devices for immunizing themselves against the personal claims and expectations of others.

The superficiality, the anonymity, and the transitory character of urban-social relations make intelligible, also, the sophistication and the rationality generally ascribed to city-dwellers. Our acquaintances tend to stand in a relationship of utility to us in the sense that the role which each one plays in our life is overwhelmingly regarded as a means for the achievement of our own ends. Whereas, therefore, the individual gains, on the one hand, a certain degree of emancipation or freedom from the personal and emotional controls of intimate groups, he loses, on the other hand, the spontaneous self-expression, the morale, and the sense of participation that comes with living in an integrated society. This constitutes essentially the state of *anomie* or the social void to which Durkheim alludes in attempting to account for the various forms of social disorganization in technological society.

The segmental character and utilitarian accent of interpersonal relations in the city find their institutional expression in the proliferation of specialized tasks which we see in their most developed form in the professions. The operations of the pecuniary nexus leads to predatory relationships, which tend to obstruct the efficient functioning of the social order unless checked by professional codes and occupational etiquette. The premium put upon utility and efficiency suggests the adaptability of the corporate device for the organization of enterprises in which individuals can engage only in groups. The advantage that the corporation has over the individual entrepreneur and the partnership in the urban-industrial world derives not only from the possibility it affords of centralizing the resources of thousands of individuals or from the legal privilege of limited liability and perpetual succession, but from the fact that the corporation has no soul.

The specialization of individuals, particularly in their occupations, can proceed only, as Adam Smith pointed out, upon the basis of an enlarged market, which in turn accentuates the division of labor. This enlarged market is only in part supplied by the city's hinterland; in large measure it is found among the large numbers that the city itself contains. The dominance of the city over the surrounding hinterland becomes explicable in terms of division of labor which urban life occasions and promotes. The extreme degree of interdependence and the unstable equilibrium of urban life are closely associated with the division of labor and the specialization of occupations. This interdependence and instability is increased by the tendency of each city to specialize in those functions in which it has the greatest advantage.

In a community composed of a larger number of individuals than can know one another intimately and can be assembled in one spot, it becomes necessary to communicate through indirect mediums and to articulate individual interests by a process of delegation. Typically in the city, interests are made effective through representation. The individual counts for little, but the voice of the representative is heard with a deference roughly proportional to the numbers for whom he speaks.

While this characterization of urbanism, in so far as it derives from large numbers, does not by any means exhaust the sociological inferences that might be drawn from our knowledge of the relationship of the size of a group to the characteristic behavior of the members, for the sake of brevity the assertions made may serve to exemplify the sort of propositions that might be developed.

DENSITY

As in the case of numbers, so in the case of concentration in limited space, certain consequences of relevance in sociological analysis of the city emerge. Of these only a few can be indicated.

As Darwin pointed out for flora and fauna and as Durkheim[14] noted in the case of human societies, an increase in numbers when area is held constant (i.e., an increase in density) tends to produce differentiation and specialization, since only in this way can the area support increased numbers. Density thus reinforces the effect of numbers in diversifying men and their activities and in increasing the complexity of the social structure.

On the subjective side, as Simmel has suggested, the close physical contact of numerous individuals necessarily produces a shift in the mediums through which we orient ourselves to the urban milieu, especially to our fellow-men. Typically, our physical contacts are close but our social contacts are distant. The urban world puts a premium on visual recognition. We see the uniform which denotes the role of the functionaries and are oblivious to the personal eccentricities that are hidden behind the uniform. We tend to acquire and develop a sensitivity to a world of artefacts and become progressively farther removed from the world of nature.

We are exposed to glaring contrasts between splendor and squalor, between riches and poverty, intelligence and ignorance, order and chaos. The competition for space is great, so that each area generally tends to be put to the use which yields the greatest economic return. Place of work tends to become dissociated from place of residence, for the proximity of industrial and commercial establishments makes an area both economically and socially undesirable for residential purposes.

Density, land values, rentals, accessibility, healthfulness, prestige, aesthetic consideration, absence of nuisances such as noise, smoke, and dirt determine the desirability of various areas of the city as places of settlement for different sections of the population. Place and nature of work, income, racial and ethnic characteristics, social status, custom, habit, taste, preference, and prejudice are among the significant factors in accordance with which the urban population is selected and distributed into more or less distinct settlements. Diverse population elements inhabiting a compact settlement thus tend to become segregated from one another in the degree in which their requirements and modes of life are incompatible with one another and in the measure in which they are antagonistic to one another. Similarly, persons of homogeneous status and needs unwittingly drift into, consciously select, or are forced by circumstances into, the same area. The different parts of the city thus acquire specialized functions. The city consequently tends to resemble a mosaic of social worlds in which the transition from one to the other is abrupt. The juxtaposition of divergent personalities and modes of life tends to produce a relativistic perspective and a sense of toleration of differences which may be regarded as prerequisites for rationality and which lead toward the secularization of life.[15]

The close living together and working together of individuals who have no sentimental and emotional ties foster a spirit of competition, aggrandizement, and mutual exploitation. To counteract irresponsibility and potential disorder, formal controls tend to be resorted to. Without rigid adherence to predictable routines a large compact society would scarcely be able to maintain itself. The clock and the traffic signal are symbolic of the basis of our social order in the urban world. Frequent close physical contact, coupled with great social distance, accentuates the reserve of unattached individuals toward one another and, unless compensated for by other opportunities for response, gives rise to loneliness. The necessary frequent movement of great numbers of individuals in a congested habitat gives occasion to friction and irritation. Nervous tensions which derive from such personal frustrations are accentuated by the rapid tempo and the complicated technology under which life in dense areas must be lived.

HETEROGENEITY

The social interaction among such a variety of personality types in the urban milieu tends to break down the rigidity of caste lines and to complicate the class structure, and thus induces a more ramified and differentiated framework of social stratification than is found in more integrated societies. The heightened mobility of the individual, which brings him within the range of stimulation by a great number of diverse individuals and subjects him to fluctuating status in the differentiated social groups that compose the social structure of the city, tends toward the acceptance of instability and insecurity in the world at large as a norm. This facts helps to account, too, for the sophistication and cosmopolitanism of the urbanite. No single group has the undivided allegiance of the individual. The groups with which he is affiliated do not lend themselves readily to a simple hierarchical arrangement. By virtue of his different interests arising out of different aspects of social life, the individual acquires membership in widely divergent groups, each of which functions only with reference to a single segment of his personality. Nor do these groups easily permit of a concentric arrangement so that the narrower ones fall within the circumference of the more inclusive ones, as is more likely to be the case in the rural community or in primitive societies. Rather the groups with which the person typically is affiliated are tangential to each other or intersect in highly variable fashion.

Partly as a result of the physical footlooseness of the population and partly as a result of their social mobility, the turnover in group membership generally is rapid. Place of residence, place and character of employment, income and interests fluctuate, and the task of holding organizations together and maintaining and promoting intimate and lasting acquaintanceship between the members is difficult. This applies strikingly to the local areas within the city into which persons become segregated more by virtue of differences in race, language, income, and social status, than through choice or positive attraction to people like themselves. Overwhelmingly the city-dweller is not a home-owner, and since a transitory habitat does not generate binding traditions and sentiments, only rarely is he truly a neighbor. There is little opportunity for the individual to obtain a conception of the city as a whole or to survey his place in the total scheme. Consequently he finds it difficult to determine what is to his own "best interests" and to decide between the issues and leaders presented to him by the agencies of mass suggestion. Individuals who are thus detached from the organized bodies which integrate society comprise the fluid masses that make collective behavior in the urban community so unpredictable and hence so problematical.

Although the city, through the recruitment of variant types to perform its diverse tasks and the accentuation of their uniqueness through competition and the premium upon eccentricity, novelty, efficient performance, and inventiveness, produces a highly differentiated population, it also exercises a leveling influence. Wherever large numbers of differently constituted individuals congregate, the process of depersonalization also enters. This leveling tendency inheres in part in the economic basis of the city. The development of large cities, at least in the modern age, was largely dependent upon the concentrative force of steam. The rise of the factory made possible mass production for an impersonal market. The fullest exploitation of the possibilities of the division of labor and mass production, however, is possible only with standardization of processes and products. A money economy goes hand in hand with such a system of production. Progressively as cities have developed upon a background of this system of production, the pecuniary nexus which implies the purchasability of services and things has displaced personal relations as the basis of association. Individuality under these circumstances must be replaced by categories. When large numbers have to make common use of facilities and institutions, an arrangement must be made to adjust the facilities and institutions to the needs of the average person rather than those of particular individuals. The services of the public utilities, of the recreational, educational, and cultural institutions must be adjusted to mass requirements. Similarly, the cultural institutions, such as the schools, the movies, the radio, and the newspapers, by virtue of their mass clientele, must necessarily operate as leveling influences. The political process as it appears in urban life could not be understood without taking account of the mass appeals made through modern propaganda techniques. If the individual would participate at all in the social, political, and economic life of the city, he must subordinate some of his individuality to the demands of the larger community and in that measure immerse himself in mass movements.

IV. The Relation between a Theory of Urbanism and Sociological Research

By means of a body of theory such as that illustratively sketched above, the complicated and many-sided phenomena of urbanism may be analyzed in terms of a limited number of basic categories. The sociological approach to the city thus acquires an essential unity and coherence enabling the empirical investigator not merely to focus more distinctly upon the problems and processes that properly fall in his province but also to treat his subject matter in a more integrated and systematic fashion. A few typical findings of empirical research in the field of urbanism, with special reference to the United States, may be indicated to substantiate the theoretical propositions set forth in the preceding pages, and some of the crucial problems for further study may be outlined.

On the basis of the three variables, number, density of settlement, and degree of heterogeneity, of the urban population, it appears possible to explain the characteristics of urban life and to account for the differences between cities of various sizes and types.

Urbanism as a characteristic mode of life may be approached empirically from three interrelated perspectives: (1) as a physical structure comprising a population base, a technology, and an ecological order; (2) as a system of social organization involving a characteristic social structure, a series of social institutions, and a typical pattern of social relationships; and (3) as a set of attitudes and ideas, and a constellation of personalities engaging in typical forms of collective behavior and subject to characteristic mechanisms of social control.

URBANISM IN ECOLOGICAL PERSPECTIVE

Since in the case of physical structure and ecological processes we are able to operate with fairly objective indices, it becomes possible to arrive at quite precise and generally quantitative results. The dominance of the city over its hinterland becomes explicable through the functional characteristics of the city which derive in large measure from the effect of numbers and density. Many of the technical facilities and the skills and organizations to which urban life gives rise can grow and prosper only in cities where the demand is sufficiently great. The nature and scope of the services rendered by these organizations and institutions and the advantage which they enjoy over the less developed facilities of smaller towns enhances the dominance of the city and the dependence of ever wider regions upon the central metropolis.

The urban-population composition shows the operation of selective and differentiating factors. Cities contain a larger proportion of persons in the prime of life than rural areas which contain more old and very young people. In this, as in so many other respects, the larger the city the more this specific characteristic of urbanism is apparent. With the exception of the largest cities, which have attracted the bulk of the foreign-born males, and a few other special types of cities, women predominate numerically over men. The heterogeneity of the urban population is further indicated along racial and ethnic lines. The foreign born and their children constitute nearly two-thirds of all the inhabitants of cities of one million and over. Their proportion in the urban population declines as the size of the city decreases, until in the rural areas they comprise only about one-sixth of the total population. The larger cities similarly have attracted more Negroes and other racial groups than have the smaller communities. Considering that age, sex, race, and ethnic origin are associated with other factors such as occupation and interest, it becomes clear that one major characteristic of the urban-dweller is his dissimilarity from his fellows. Never before have such large masses of people of diverse traits as we find in our cities been thrown together into such close physical contact as in the great cities of America. Cities generally, and American cities in particular, comprise a motley of peoples and cultures, of highly differentiated modes of life between which there often is only the faintest communication, the greatest indifference and the broadest tolerance, occasionally bitter strife, but always the sharpest contrast.

The failure of the urban population to reproduce itself appears to be a biological consequence of a combination of factors in the complex of urban life, and the decline in the birth-rate generally may be regarded as one of the most significant signs of the urbanization of the Western world. While the proportion of deaths in cities is slightly greater than in the country, the outstanding difference between the failure of present-day cities to maintain their population and that of cities of the past is that in former times it was due to the exceedingly high death-rates in cities, whereas today, since cities have become more livable from a health standpoint, it is due to low birth-rates. These biological characteristics of the urban population are significant sociologically, not merely because they reflect the urban mode of existence but also because they condition the growth and future dominance of cities and their basic social organization. Since cities are the consumers rather than the producers of men, the value of human life and the social estimation of the personality will not be unaffected by the balance between births and deaths. The pattern of land use, of land values, rentals, and ownership, the nature and functioning of the physical structures, of housing, of transportation and communication facilities, of public utilities—these and many other phases of the physical mechanism of the city are not isolated phenomena unrelated to the city as a social entity, but are affected by and affect the urban mode of life.

URBANISM AS A FORM OF SOCIAL ORGANIZATION

The distinctive features of the urban mode of life have often been described sociologically as consisting of the substitution of secondary for primary contracts, the weakening of bonds of kinship, and the declining social significance of the family, the disappearance of the neighborhood, and the undermining of the traditional basis of social solidarity. All these phenomena can be substantially verified through objective indices. Thus, for instance, the low and declining urban-reproduction rates suggest that the city is not conducive to the traditional type of family life, including the rearing of children and the maintenance of the home as the locus of a whole round of vital activities. The transfer of industrial, educational, and recreational activities to specialized institutions outside the home has deprived the family of some of its most characteristic historical functions. In cities mothers are more likely to be employed, lodgers are more frequently part of the household, marriage tends to be postponed, and the proportion of single and unattached people is greater. Families are smaller and more frequently without children than in the country. The family as a unit of social life is emancipated from the larger kinship group characteristic of the country, and the individual members pursue their own diverging interests in their vocational, educational, religious, recreational, and political life.

Such functions as the maintenance of health, the methods of alleviating the hardships associated with personal and social insecurity, the provisions for education, recreation, and cultural advancement have given rise to highly specialized institutions on a community-wide, statewide, or even national basis. The same factors which have brought about greater personal insecurity also underlie the wider contrasts between individuals to be found in the urban world. While the city has broken down the rigid caste lines of pre-industrial society, it has sharpened and differentiated income and status groups. Generally, a larger proportion of the adult-urban population is gainfully employed than in the case with the adult-rural population. The white-collar class, comprising those employed in trade, in clerical, and in professional work, are proportionately more numerous in large cities and in metropolitan centers and in smaller towns than in the country.

On the whole, the city discourages an economic life in which the individual in time of crisis has a basis of subsistence to fall back upon, and it discourages self-employment. While incomes of city people are on the average higher than those of country people, the cost of living seems to be higher in the larger cities. Home ownership involves greater burdens and is rarer. Rents are higher and absorb a larger proportion of the income. Although the urban-dweller has the benefit of many communal services, he spends a large proportion of his income for such items as recreation and advancement and a smaller proportion for food. What the communal services do not furnish the urbanite must purchase, and there is virtually no human need which has remained unexploited by commercialism. Catering to thrills and furnishing means of escape from drudgery, monotony, and routine thus become one of the major functions of urban recreation, which at its best furnishes means for creative self-expression and spontaneous group association, but which more typically in the urban world results in passive spectatorism on the one hand, or sensational record-smashing feats on the other.

Being reduced to a stage of virtual impotence as an individual, the urbanite is bound to exert himself by joining with others of similar interest into organized groups to obtain his ends. This results in the enormous multiplication of voluntary organizations directed toward as great a variety of objectives as there are human needs and interests. While on the one hand the traditional ties of human association are weakened, urban existence involves a much greater degree of interdependence between man and man and a more complicated, fragile, and volatile form of mutual interrelations over many phases of which the individual as such can exert scarcely any control. Frequently there is only the most tenuous relationship between the economic position or other basic factors that determine the individual's existence in the urban world and the voluntary groups with which he is affiliated. While in a primitive and in a rural society it is generally possible to predict on the basis of a few known factors who will belong to what and who will associate with whom in almost every relationship of life, in the city we can only project the general pattern of group formation and affiliation, and this pattern will display many incongruities and contradictions.

URBAN PERSONALITY AND
COLLECTIVE BEHAVIOR

It is largely through the activities of the voluntary groups, be their objectives economic, political, educational, religious, recreational, or cultural, that the urbanite expresses and develops his personality, acquires status, and is able to carry on the round of activities that constitute his life-career. It may easily be inferred, however, that the organizational framework which these highly differentiated functions call into being does not of itself insure the consistency and integrity of the personalities whose interests it enlists. Personal disorganization, mental breakdown, suicide, delinquency, crime, corruption, and disorder might be expected under these circumstances to be more prevalent in the urban than in the rural community. This has been confirmed in so far as comparable indices are available; but the mechanisms underlying these phenomena require further analysis.

Since for most group purposes it is impossible in the city to appeal individually to the large number of discrete and differentiated individuals, and since it is only through the organizations to which men belong that their interests and resources can be enlisted for a collective cause, it may be inferred that social control in the city should typically proceed through formally organized groups. It follows, too, that the masses of men in the city are subject to manipulation by symbols and stereotypes managed by individuals working from afar or operating invisibly behind the scenes through their control of the instruments of communication. Self-government either in the economic, the political, or the cultural realm is under these circumstances reduced to a mere figure of speech or, at best, is subject to the unstable equilibrium of pressure groups. In view of the ineffectiveness of actual kinship ties we create fictional kinship groups. In the face of the disappearance of the territorial unit as a basis of social solidarity we create interest units. Meanwhile the city as a community resolves itself into a series of tenuous segmental relationships superimposed upon a territorial base with a definite center but without a definite periphery and upon a division of labor which far transcends the immediate locality and is world-wide in scope. The larger the number of persons in a state of interaction with one another the lower is the level of communication and the greater is the tendency for communication to proceed on an elementary level, i.e., on the basis of those things which are assumed to be common or to be of interest to all.

It is obviously, therefore, to the emerging trends in the communication system and to the production and distribution technology that has come into existence with modern civilization that we must look for the symptoms which will indicate the probable future development of urbanism as a mode of social life. The direction of the ongoing changes in urbanism will for good or ill transform not only the city but the world. Some of the more basic of these factors and processes and the possibilities of their direction and control invite further detailed study.

It is only in so far as the sociologist has a clear conception of the city as a social entity and a workable theory of urbanism that he can hope to develop a unified body of reliable knowledge, which what passes as "urban sociology" is certainly not at the present time. By taking his point of departure from a theory of urbanism such as that sketched in the foregoing pages to be elaborated, tested, and revised in the light of further analysis and empirical research, it is to be hoped that the criteria of relevance and validity of factual data can be determined. The miscellaneous assortment of disconnected information which has hitherto found its way into sociological treatises on the city may thus be sifted and incorporated into a coherent body of knowledge. Incidentally, only by means of some such theory will the sociologist escape the futile practice of voicing in the name of sociological science a variety of often unsupportable judgments concerning such problems as poverty, housing, city-planning, sanitation, municipal administration, policing, marketing, transportation, and other technical issues. While the sociologist cannot solve any of these practical problems—at least not by himself—he may, if he discovers his proper function, have an important contribution to make to their comprehension and solution. The prospects for doing this are brightest through a general, theoretical, rather than through an *ad hoc* approach.

NOTES

1. William Graham Sumner, *Folkways* (Boston, 1906), p. 12.
2. S. V. Pearson, *The Growth and Distribution of Population* (New York, 1935), p. 211.
3. Whereas rural life in the United States has for a long time been a subject of considerable interest on the part of governmental bureaus, the most notable case of a comprehensive report being that submitted by the County Life Commission to President Theodore Roosevelt in 1909, it is worthy of note that no equally comprehensive official inquiry into urban life was undertaken until the establishment of a Research Committee on Urbanism of the National Resources Committee. (Cf. *Our Cities: Their Role in the National Economy* [Washington: Government Printing Office, 1937].)
4. "The Anthropogeography of Some Great Cities," *Bull. American Geographical Society,* XLI (1909), 537–66.
5. Walter F. Willcox, "A Definition of 'City' in Terms of Density," in E. W. Burgess, *The Urban Community* (Chicago, 1926), p. 119.
6. *Op. cit.,* p. 8.
7. See Robert E. Park, Ernest W. Burgess, *et al., The City* (Chicago, 1925), esp. chaps. ii and iii; Werner Sombart, "Städtische Siedlung, Stadt," *Handwörterbuch der Soziologie,* ed. Alfred Vierkand (Stuttgart, 1931); see also bibliography.
8. *Wirtschaft und Gesellschaft* (Tübingen, 1925), Part II, chap. viii, pp. 514–601.
9. Park, Burgess, *et al., op. cit.,* chap. i.
10. The justification for including the term "permanent" in the definition may appear necessary. Our failure to give an extensive justification for this qualifying mark of the urban rests on the obvious fact that unless human settlements take a fairly permanent root in a locality the characteristics of urban life cannot arise, and conversely the living

together of large numbers of heterogeneous individuals under dense conditions is not possible without the development of a more or less technological structure.

11. See esp. vii. 4. 4–14. Translated by B. Jowett, from which the following may be quoted:

"To the size of states there is a limit, as there is to other things, plants, animals, implements; for none of these retain their natural power when they are too large or too small, but they either wholly lose their nature, or are spoiled. . . . [A] state when composed of too few is not as a state ought to be, self-sufficing; when of too many, though self-sufficing in all mere necessaries, it is a nation and not a state, being almost incapable of constitutional government. For who can be the general of such a vast multitude, or who the herald, unless he have the voice of a Stentor?

"A state then only begins to exist when it has attained a population sufficient for a good life in the political community: it may indeed somewhat exceed this number. But, as I was saying, there must be a limit. What should be the limit will be easily ascertained by experience. For both governors and governed have duties to perform; the special functions of a governor are to command and to judge. But if the citizens of a state are to judge and to distribute offices according to merit, then they must know each other's characters; where they do not possess this knowledge, both the election to offices and the decision of lawsuits will go wrong. When the population is very large they are manifestly settled at haphazard, which clearly ought not to be. Besides, in an overpopulous state foreigners and metics will readily acquire the rights of citizens, for who will find them out? Clearly, then, the best limit of the population of a state is the largest number which suffices for the purposes of life, and can be taken in at a single view. Enough concerning the size of a city."

12. *Op. cit.,* p. 514.

13. Georg Simmel, "Die Grossstädte und das Geistesleben," *Die Grossstadt,* ed. Theodor Petermann (Dresden, 1903), pp. 187–206.

14. E. Durkheim, *De la division du travail social* (Paris, 1932), p. 248.

15. The extent to which the segregation of the population into distinct ecological and cultural areas and the resulting social attitude of tolerance, rationality, and secular mentality are functions of density as distinguished from heterogeneity is difficult to determine. Most likely we are dealing here with phenomena which are consquences of the simultaneous operation of both factors.

3.3 URBANISM AND SUBURBANISM AS WAYS OF LIFE: A REEVALUATION OF DEFINITIONS

HERBERT J. GANS

The contemporary sociological conception of cities and of urban life is based largely on the work of the Chicago School, and its summary statement in Louis Wirth's essay "Urbanism as a Way of Life" (40).[1] In that paper, Wirth developed a "minimum sociological definition of the city" as "a relatively large, dense and permanent settlement of socially heterogeneous individuals." (40, p. 50) From these prerequisites, he then deduced the major outlines of the urban way of life. As he saw it, number, density, and heterogeneity created a social structure in which primary-group relationships were inevitably replaced by secondary contacts that were impersonal, segmental, superficial, transitory, and often predatory in nature. As a result, the city dweller became anonymous, isolated, secular, relativistic, rational, and sophisticated. In order to function in the urban society, he was forced to combine with others to organize corporations, voluntary associations, representative forms of government, and the impersonal mass media of communications (40, pp. 54–60). These replaced the primary groups and the integrated way of life found in rural and other pre-industrial settlements.

Wirth's paper has become a classic in urban sociology, and most texts have followed his definition and description faithfully (5). In recent years, however, a considerable number of studies and essays have questioned his formulations (1, 5, 13, 15, 17, 19, 20, 23, 24, 27, 28, 30, 35, 38, 41).[2] In addition, a number of changes have taken place in cities since the article was published in 1938, notably the exodus of white residents to low- and medium-priced houses in the suburbs, and the decentralization of industry. The evidence from these studies and the changes in American cities suggest that Wirth's statement must be revised.

There is yet another, and more important reason for such a revision. Despite its title and intent, Wirth's paper deals with urban-industrial society, rather than with the city. This is evident from his approach. Like other urban sociologists, Wirth based his analysis on a comparison of settlement types, but unlike his colleagues, who pursued urban-rural comparisons, Wirth contrasted the city to the folk society. Thus, he compared settlement types of pre-industrial and industrial society. This allowed him to include in his

From Herbert J. Gans, "Urbanism and Suburbanism as Ways of Life: A Re-Evaluation of Definitions," in Arnold Rose, ed., *Human Behavior and Social Processes*. Copyright © 1962 by Houghton Mifflin Company. Reprinted by permission of the publisher.

theory of urbanism the entire range of modern institutions which are not found in the folk society, even though many such groups (e.g., voluntary associations) are by no means exclusively urban. Moreover, Wirth's conception of the city dweller as depersonalized, atomized, and susceptible to mass movements suggests that his paper is based on, and contributes to, the theory of the mass society.

Many of Wirth's conclusions may be relevant to the understanding of ways of life in modern society. However, since the theory argues that all of society is now urban, *his analysis does not distinguish ways of life in the city from those in other settlements within modern society.* In Wirth's time, the comparison of urban and pre-urban settlement types was still fruitful, but today, the primary task for urban (or community) sociology seems to me to be the analysis of the similarities and differences between contemporary settlement types.

This paper is an attempt at such an analysis; it limits itself to distinguishing ways of life in the modern city and the modern suburbs. A re-analysis of Wirth's conclusions from this perspective suggests that his characterization of the urban way of life applies only—and not too accurately—to the residents of the inner city. The remaining city dwellers, as well as most suburbanites, pursue a different way of life, which I shall call "quasi-primary." This proposition raises some doubt about the mutual exclusiveness of the concepts of city and suburb and leads to a yet broader question: whether settlement concepts and other ecological concepts are useful for explaining ways of life.

The Inner City

Wirth argued that number, density, and heterogeneity had two social consequences which explain the major features of urban life. On the one hand, the crowding of diverse types of people into a small area led to the segregation of homogeneous types of people into separate neighborhoods (40, p. 56). On the other hand, the lack of physical distance between city dwellers resulted in social contact between them, which broke down existing social and cultural patterns and encouraged assimilation as well as acculturation—the melting pot effect (40, p. 52). Wirth implied that the melting pot effect was far more powerful than the tendency toward segregation and concluded that, sooner or later, the pressures engendered by the dominant social, economic, and political institutions of the city would destroy the remaining pockets of primary-group relationships (40, pp. 60–62). Eventually, the social system of the city would resemble Tönnies' *Gesellschaft*—a way of life which Wirth considered undesirable.

Because Wirth had come to see the city as the prototype of mass society, and because he examined the city from the distant vantage point of the folk society—from the wrong end of the telescope, so to speak—his view of urban life is not surprising. In addition, Wirth found support for his theory in the empirical work of his Chicago colleagues. As Greer and Kube (19, p. 112) and Wilensky (38, p. 121) have pointed out, the Chicago sociologists conducted their most intensive studies in the inner city.[3] At that time, these were slums recently invaded by new waves of European immigrants and rooming house and skid row districts, as well as the habitat of Bohemians and well-to-do Gold Coast apartment dwellers. Wirth himself studied the Maxwell Street Ghetto, an inner-city Jewish neighborhood then being dispersed by the acculturation and mobility of its inhabitants (39). Some of the characteristics of urbanism which Wirth stressed in his essay abounded in these areas.

Wirth's diagnosis of the city as *Gesellschaft* must be questioned on three counts. First, the conclusions derived from a study of the inner city cannot be generalized to the entire urban area. Second, there is as yet not enough evidence to prove—nor, admittedly, to deny—that number, density, and heterogeneity result in the social consequences which Wirth proposed. Finally, even if the causal relationship could be verified, it can be shown that a significant proportion of the city's inhabitants were, and are, isolated from these consequences by social structures and cultural patterns which they either brought to the city, or developed by living in it. Wirth conceived the urban population as consisting of heterogeneous individuals, torn from past social systems, unable to develop new ones, and therefore prey to social anarchy in the city. While it is true that a not insignificant proportion of the inner city population was, and still is, made up of unattached individuals (26), Wirth's formulation ignores the fact that this population consists mainly of relatively homogeneous groups, with social and cultural moorings that shield it fairly effectively from the suggested consequences of number, density, and heterogeneity. This applies even more to the residents of the outer city, who constitute a majority of the total city population.

The social and cultural moorings of the inner city population are best described by a brief analysis of the five types of inner city residents. These are:

1. the "cosmopolites";
2. the unmarried or childless;
3. the "ethnic villagers";
4. the "deprived"; and
5. the "trapped" and downward mobile.

The "cosmopolites" include students, artists, writers, musicians, and entertainers, as well as other intellectuals and professionals. They live in the city in order to be near the special "cultural" facilities that can only be located near the center of the city. Many cosmopolites are unmarried or childless. Others rear children in the city, especially if they have the income to afford the aid of servants and governesses. The less affluent ones may move to the suburbs to raise their children, continuing to live as cosmopolites under considerable handicaps, especially in the lower-middle-class suburbs. Many of the very rich and powerful are also cosmopolites, although they are likely to have at least two residences, one of which is suburban or exurban.

The unmarried or childless must be divided into two subtypes, depending on the permanence or transience of their status. The temporarily unmarried or childless live in the inner city for only a limited time. Young adults may team up to rent an apartment away from their parents and close to job or entertainment opportunities. When they marry, they may move first to an apartment in a transient neighborhood, but if they can afford to do so, they leave for the outer city or the suburbs with the arrival of the first or second child. The permanently unmarried may stay in the inner city for the remainder of their lives, their housing depending on their income.

The "ethnic villagers" are ethnic groups which are found in such inner city neighborhoods as New York's Lower East Side, living in some ways as they did when they were peasants in European or Puerto Rican villages (15). Although they reside in the city, they isolate themselves from significant contact with most city facilities, aside from work places. Their way of life differs sharply from Wirth's urbanism in its emphasis on kinship and the primary group, the lack of anonymity and secondary-group contacts, the weakness of formal organizations, and the suspicion of anything and anyone outside their neighborhood.

The first two types live in the inner city by choice; the third is there partly because of necessity, partly because of tradition. The final two types are in the inner city because they have no other choice. One is the "deprived" population: the very poor, the emotionally disturbed or otherwise handicapped; broken families; and, most important, the non-white population. These urban dwellers must take the dilapidated housing and blighted neighborhoods to which the housing market relegates them, although among them are some for whom the slum is a hiding place, or a temporary stopover to save money for a house in the outer city or the suburbs (27).

The "trapped" are the people who stay behind when a neighborhood is invaded by non-residential land uses or lower-status immigrants, because they cannot afford to move, or are otherwise bound to their present location (27).[4] The "downward mobiles" are a related type; they may have started life in a higher class position, but have been forced down in the socioeconomic hierarchy and in the quality of their accommodations. Many of them are old people, living out their existence on small pensions.

These five types all live in dense and heterogeneous surroundings, yet they have such diverse ways of life that it is hard to see how density and heterogeneity could exert a common influence. Moreover, all but the last two types are isolated or detached from their neighborhood and thus from the social consequences which Wirth described.

When people who live together have social ties based on criteria other than mere common occupancy, they can set up social barriers regardless of the physical closeness or the heterogeneity of their neighbors. The ethnic villagers are the best illustration. While a number of ethnic groups are usually found living together in the same neighborhood, they are able to *isolate* themselves from each other through a variety of social devices. Wirth himself recognized this when he wrote that "two groups can occupy a given area without losing their separate identity because each side is permitted to live its own inner life, and each somehow fears or idealizes the other." (39, p. 283) Although it is true that the children in these areas were often oblivious to the social barriers set up by their parents, at least until adolescence, it is doubtful whether their acculturation can be traced to the melting pot effect as much as to the pervasive influence of the American culture that flowed into these areas from the outside.[5]

The cosmopolites, the unmarried, and the childless are *detached* from neighborhood life. The cosmopolites possess a distinct subculture which causes them to be disinterested in all but the most superficial contacts with their neighbors, somewhat like the ethnic villagers. The unmarried and childless are detached from neighborhood because of their life-cycle stage, which frees them from the routine family responsibilities that entail some relationship to the local area. In their choice of residence, the two types are therefore not concerned about their neighbors, or the availability and quality of local community facilities. Even the well-to-do can choose expensive apartments in or near poor neighborhoods, because if they have children, they are sent to special schools and summer camps which effectively isolate them from neighbors. In addition, both types, but especially the childless and unmarried, are transient. Therefore, they tend to live in areas marked by high population turnover, where their own mobility and that of their neighbors creates a universal detachment from the neighborhood.[6]

The deprived and the trapped do seem to be affected by some of the consequences of number, density, and heterogeneity. The deprived population suffers considerably from overcrowding, but this is a consequence of low income, racial discrimination, and other handicaps, and cannot be considered an inevitable result of the ecological make-up of the city.[7] Because the deprived have no residential choice, they are also forced to live amid neighbors not of their own choosing, with ways of life different and even contradictory to their own. If familial defenses against the neighborhood climate are weak, as is the case among broken families and downward mobile people, parents may lose their children to the culture of "the street." The trapped are the unhappy people who remain behind when their more advantaged neighbors move on; they must endure the heterogeneity which results from neighborhood change.

Wirth's description of the urban way of life fits best the transient areas of the inner city. Such areas are typically heterogeneous in population, partly because they are inhabited by transient types who do not require homogeneous neighbors or by deprived people who have no choice, or may themselves be quite mobile. Under conditions of transcience and heterogeneity, people interact only in terms of the segmental roles necessary for obtaining local services. Their social relationships thus display anonymity, impersonality, and superficiality.[8]

The social features of Wirth's concept of urbanism seem therefore to be a result of residential instability, rather than of number, density, or heterogeneity. In fact, heterogeneity is itself an effect of residential instability, resulting when the influx of transients cause landlords and realtors to stop acting as gatekeepers—that is, wardens of neighborhood homogeneity.[9] Residential instability is found in all types of settlements, and, presumably, its social consequences are everywhere similar. These consequences cannot therefore be identified with the ways of life of the city.

The Outer City and the Suburbs

The second effect which Wirth ascribed to number, density, and heterogeneity was the segregation of homogeneous people into distinct neighborhoods[10] on the basis of "place and nature of work, income, racial and ethnic characteristics, social status, custom, habit, taste, preference and prejudice" (40, p. 56). This description fits the residential districts of the *outer city*.[11] Although these districts contain the majority of the city's inhabitants, Wirth went into little detail about them. He made it clear, however, that the sociopsychological aspects of urbanism were prevalent there as well (40, p. 56).

Because existing neighborhood studies deal primarily with the exotic sections of the inner city, very little is known about the more typical residential neighborhoods of the outer city. However, it is evident that the way of life in these areas bears little resemblance to Wirth's urbanism. Both the studies which question Wirth's formulation and my own observations suggest that the common element in the ways of life of these neighborhoods is best described as *quasi-primary*. I use this term to characterize relationships between neighbors. Whatever the intensity or frequency of these relationships, the interaction is more intimate than a secondary contact, but more guarded than a primary one.[12]

There are actually few secondary relationships, because of the isolation of residential neighborhoods from economic institutions and work places. Even shopkeepers, store managers, and other local functionaries who live in the area are treated as acquaintances or friends, unless they are of a vastly different social status or are forced by their corporate employers to treat their customers as economic units (30). Voluntary associations attract only a minority of the population. Moreover, much of the organizational activity is of a sociable nature, and it is often difficult to accomplish the association's "business" because of the members' preference for sociability. Thus, it would appear that interactions in organizations, or between neighbors generally, do not fit the secondary-relationship model of urban life. As anyone who has lived in these neighborhoods knows, there is little anonymity, impersonality or privacy.[13] In fact, American cities have sometimes been described as collections of small towns.[14] There is some truth to this description, especially if the city is compared to the actual small town, rather than to the romantic construct of anti-urban critics (33).

Postwar suburbia represents the most contemporary version of the quasi-primary way of life. Owing to increases in real income and the encouragement of home ownership provided by the FHA, families in the lower-middle class and upper working class can now live in modern single-family homes in low-density subdivisions, an opportunity previously available only to the upper and upper-middle classes (34).

The popular literature describes the new suburbs as communities in which conformity, homogeneity, and other-direction are unusually rampant (4, 32). The implication is that the move from city to suburb initiates a new way of life which causes considerable behavior and personality change in previous urbanites. A preliminary analysis of data which I am now collecting in Levittown, New Jersey, suggests, however, that the move from the city to this predominantly lower-middle-class suburb does not result in any major behavioral changes for most people. Moreover, the changes which do occur reflect the move from the social isolation of a transient city or suburban apartment building to the quasi-primary life of a neighborhood of single-family homes. Also, many of the people whose life has changed reported that the changes were intended. They existed as aspirations before the move, or as reasons for it. In other words, the suburb itself creates few changes in ways of life. Similar conclusions have been reported by Berger in his excellent study of a working-class population newly moved to a suburban subdivision (4).

A Comparison of City and Suburb

If urban and suburban areas are similar in that the way of life in both is quasi-primary, and if urban residents who move out to the suburbs do not undergo any significant changes in behavior, it would be fair to argue that the differences in ways of life between the two types of settlements have been overestimated. Yet the fact remains that a variety of physical and demographic differences exist between the city and the suburb. However, upon closer examination, many of these differences turn out to be either spurious or of little significance for the way of life of the inhabitants (34).[15]

The differences between the residential areas of cities and suburbs which have been cited most frequently are:

1. Suburbs are more likely to be dormitories.
2. They are further away from the work and play facilities of the central business districts.
3. They are newer and more modern than city residential areas and are designed for the automobile rather than for pedestrian and mass-transit forms of movement.
4. They are built up with single-family rather than multi-family structures and are therefore less dense.
5. Their populations are more homogeneous.
6. Their populations differ demographically: they are younger; more of them are married; they have higher incomes; and they hold proportionately more white collar jobs (8, p. 131).

Most urban neighborhoods are as much dormitories as the suburbs. Only in a few older inner city areas are factories and offices still located in the middle of residential blocks, and even here many of the employees do not live in the neighborhood.

The fact that the suburbs are farther from the central business district is often true only in terms of distance, not travel time. Moreover, most people make relatively little use of downtown facilities, other than work places (12, 21). The downtown stores seem to hold their greatest attraction for the upper-middle class (21, pp. 91–92); the same is probably true of typically urban entertainment facilities. Teen-agers and young adults may take their dates to first-run movie theaters, but the museums, concert halls, and lecture rooms attract mainly upper-middle-class ticket-buyers, many of them suburban.[16]

The suburban reliance on the train and the automobile has given rise to an imaginative folklore about the consequences of commuting on alcohol consumption, sex life, and parental duties. Many of these conclusions are, however, drawn from selected high-income suburbs and exurbs, and reflect job tensions in such hectic occupations as advertising and show business more than the effects of residence (29). It is true that the upper-middle-class housewife must become a chauffeur in order to expose her children to the proper educational facilities, but such differences as walking to the corner drug store and driving to its suburban equivalent seem to me of little emotional, social, or cultural import.[17] In addition, the continuing shrinkage in the number of mass-transit users suggests that even in the city many younger people are now living a wholly auto-based way of life.

The fact that suburbs are smaller is primarily a function of political boundaries drawn long before the communities were suburban. This affects the kinds of political issues which develop and provides somewhat greater opportunity for citizen participation. Even so, in the suburbs as in the city, the minority who participate are the professional politicians, the economically concerned businessmen, lawyers and salesmen, and the ideologically motivated middle- and upper-middle-class people with better than average education.

The social consequences of differences in density and house type also seem overrated. Single-family houses on quiet streets facilitate the supervision of children; this is one reason why middle-class women who want to keep an eye on their children move to the suburbs. House type also has some effects on relationships between neighbors, insofar as there are more opportunities for visual contact between adjacent homeowners than between people on different floors of an apartment house. However, if occupants' characteristics are also held constant, the differences in actual social contact are less marked. Homogeneity of residents turns out to be more important as a determinant of sociability than proximity. If the population is heterogeneous, there is little social contact between neighbors, either on apartment-house floors or in single-family-blocks; if people are homogeneous, there is likely to be considerable social contact in both house types. One need only contrast the apartment house located in a transient, heterogeneous neighborhood and exactly the same structure in a neighborhood occupied by a single ethnic group. The former is a lonely, anonymous building; the latter, a bustling micro-society. I have observed similar patterns in suburban areas: on blocks where people are homogeneous, they socialize; where they are heterogeneous, they do little more than exchange polite greetings (16).

Suburbs are usually described as being more homogeneous in house type than the city, but if they are compared to the outer city, the differences are small. Most inhabitants of the outer city, other than well-to-do homeowners, live on blocks of uniform structures as well—for example, the endless streets of rowhouses in Philadelphia and Baltimore or of two-story duplexes and six-flat apartment houses in Chicago. They differ from the new suburbs only in that they were erected through more primitive methods of mass production. Suburbs are of course more predominantly areas of owner-occupied single homes, though in the outer districts of most American cities homeownership is also extremely high.

Demographically, suburbs as a whole are clearly more homogeneous than cities as a whole, though probably not more so than outer cities. However, people do not live in cities or suburbs as a whole, but in specific neighborhoods. An analysis of ways of life would require a determination of the degree of population homogeneity within the boundaries of areas defined as neighborhoods by residents' social contacts. Such an analysis would no doubt indicate that many neighborhoods in the city as well as the suburbs are homogeneous. Neighborhood homogeneity is actually a result of factors having little or nothing to do with the house type, density, or location of the area relative to the city limits. Brand new neighborhoods are more homogeneous than older ones, because they have not experienced resident turnover, which frequently results in population heterogeneity. Neighborhoods of low- and medium-priced housing are usually less homogeneous than those with expensive dwellings because they attract families who have reached the peak of occupational and residential mobility, as well as young families who are just starting their climb and will eventually move to neighborhoods of higher status. The latter, being accessible only to high-income people, are therefore more homogeneous with respect to other resident characteristics as well. Moreover, such areas have the economic and political power to slow down or prevent invasion. Finally, neighborhoods located in the path of ethnic or religious group movement are likely to be extremely homogeneous.

The demographic differences between cities and suburbs cannot be questioned, especially since the suburbs have attracted a large number of middle-class child-rearing families. The differences are, however, much reduced if suburbs are compared only to the outer city. In addition, a detailed comparison of suburban and outer city residential areas would show that neighborhoods with the same kinds of people can be found in the city as well as the suburbs. Once again, the age of the area and the cost of housing are more important determinants of demographic characteristics than the location of the area with respect to the city limits.

Characteristics, Social Organization, and Ecology

The preceding sections of the paper may be summarized in three propositions:

1. As concerns ways of life, the inner city must be distinguished from the outer city and the suburbs; and the latter two exhibit a way of life bearing little resemblance to Wirth's urbanism.
2. Even in the inner city, ways of life resemble Wirth's description only to a limited extent. Moreover, economic condition, cultural characteristics, life-cycle stage, and residential instability explain ways of life more satisfactorily than number, density, or heterogeneity.
3. Physical and other differences between city and suburb are often spurious or without much meaning for ways of life.

These propositions suggest that the concepts urban and suburban are neither mutually exclusive, nor especially relevant for understanding ways of life. They—and number, density, and heterogeneity as well—are ecological concepts which describe human adaptation to the environment. However, they are not sufficient to explain social phenomena, because these phenomena cannot be understood solely as the consequences of ecological processes. Therefore, other explanations must be considered.

Ecological explanations of social life are most applicable if the subjects under study lack the ability to *make choices,* be they plants, animals, or human beings. Thus, if there is a housing shortage, people will live almost anywhere, and under extreme conditions of no choice, as in a disaster, married and single, old and young, middle and working class, stable and transient will be found side by side in whatever accommodations are available. At that time, their ways of life represent an almost direct adaptation to the environment. If the supply of housing and of neighborhoods is such that alternatives are available, however, people will make choices, and if the housing market is responsive, they can even make and satisfy explicit *demands.*

Choices and demands do not develop independently or at random; they are functions of the roles people play in the social system. These can best be understood in terms of the *characteristics* of the people involved; that is, characteristics can be used as indices to choices and demands made in the roles that constitute ways of life. Although many characteristics affect the choices and demands people make with respect to housing and neighborhoods, the most important ones seem to be *class*—in all its economic, social and cultural ramifications—and *life-cycle stage.*[18] If people have an opportunity to choose, these two characteristics will go far in explaining the kinds of housing and neighborhoods they will occupy and the ways of life they will try to establish within them.

Many of the previous assertions about ways of life in cities and suburbs can be analyzed in terms of class and life-cycle characteristics. Thus, in the inner city, the unmarried and childless live as they do, detached from neighborhood, because of their life-cycle stage; the cosmopolites, because of a combination of life-cycle stage and a distinctive but class based subculture. The way of life of the deprived and trapped can be explained by low socioeconomic level and related handicaps. The quasi-primary way of life is associated with the family stage of the life-cycle, and the norms of child-rearing and parental role found in the upper working class, the lower-middle class, and the non-cosmopolite portions of the upper-middle and upper classes.

The attributes of the so-called suburban way of life can also be understood largely in terms of these characteristics. The new suburbia is nothing more than a highly visible showcase for the ways of life of young, upper-working-class and lower-middle-class people. Ktsanes and Reissman have aptly described it as "new homes for old values" (22). Much of the descriptive and critical writing about suburbia assumes that as long as the new suburbanites lived in the city, they behaved like upper-middle-class cosmopolites and that suburban living has mysteriously transformed them (7; 14, p. 154–162; 25; 36). The critics fail to see that the behavior and personality patterns ascribed to suburbia are in reality those of class and age (6). These patterns could have been found among the new suburbanites when they still lived in the city and could now be observed among their peers who still reside there— if the latter were as visible to critics and researchers as are the suburbanites.

Needless to say, the concept of "characteristics" cannot explain all aspects of ways of life, either among urban or suburban residents. Some aspects must be explained by concepts of social organization that are independent of characteristics. For example, some features of the quasi-primary way of life are independent of class and age, because they evolve from the roles and situations created by joint and adjacent occupancy of land and dwellings. Likewise, residential instability is a universal process which has a number of invariate consequences. In each case, however, the way in which people react varies with their characteristics. So it is with ecological processes. Thus, there are undoubtedly differences between ways of life in urban and suburban settlements which remain after behavior patterns based on residents' characteristics have been analyzed, and which must therefore be attributed to features of the settlement (11).

Characteristics do not explain the causes of behavior; rather, they are clues to socially created and culturally defined roles, choices, and demands. A causal analysis must trace them back to the larger social, economic, and political systems which determine the situations in which roles are played and the cultural content of choices and demands, as well as the opportunities for their achievement.[19] These systems determine income distributions, educational and occupational opportunities, and in turn, fertility patterns, child-rearing methods, as well as the entire range of consumer behavior. Thus, a complete analysis of the way of life of the deprived residents of the inner city cannot stop by indicating the influence of low income, lack of education, or family instability. These must be related to such conditions as the urban economy's "need" for low-wage workers, and the housing market practices which restrict residential choice. The urban economy is in turn shaped by national economic and social systems, as well as by local and regional ecological processes. Some phenomena can be explained exclusively by reference to these ecological processes. However, it must also be recognized that as man gains greater control over the natural environment, he has been able to free himself from many of the determining and limiting effects of that environment. Thus, changes in local transportation technology, the ability of industries to be footloose, and the relative affluence of American society have given ever larger numbers of people increasing amounts of residential choice. The greater the amount of choice available, the more important does the concept of characteristics become in understanding behavior.

Consequently, the study of ways of life in communities must begin with an analysis of characteristics. If characteristics are dealt with first and held constant, we may be able to discover which behavior patterns can be attributed to features of the settlement and its natural environment.[20] Only then will it be possible to discover to what extent city and suburb are independent —rather than dependent or intervening—variables in the explanation of ways of life.

This kind of analysis might help to reconcile the ecological point of view with the behavioral and cultural one, and possibly put an end to the conflict between conceptual positions which insist on one explanation or the other (9). Both explanations have some relevance, and future research and theory must clarify the role of each in the analysis of ways of life in various types of settlement (6, p. xxii). Another important rationale for this approach is its usefulness for applied sociology—for example, city planning. The planner can recommend changes in the spatial and physical arrangements of the city. Frequently, he seeks to achieve social goals or to change social conditions through physical solutions. He has been attracted to ecological explanations because these relate behavior to phenomena which he can affect. For example, most planners tend to agree with Wirth's formulations, because they stress number and density, over which the planner has some control. If the undesirable social conditions of the inner city could be traced to these two factors, the planner could propose large-scale clearance projects which would reduce the size of the urban population, and lower residential densities. Experience with public housing projects has, however, made it aparent that low densities, new buildings, or modern site plans do not eliminate anti-social or self-destructive behavior. The analysis of characteristics will call attention to the fact that this behavior is lodged in the deprivations of low socio-economic status and racial discrimination, and that it can be changed only through the removal of these deprivations. Conversely, if such an analysis suggests residues of behavior that can be attributed to ecological processes or physical aspects of housing and neighborhood, the planner can recommend physical changes that can really affect behavior.

A Re-evaluation of Definitions

The argument presented here has implications for the sociological definition of the city. Such a definition relates ways of life to environmental features of the city qua settlement type. But if ways of life do not coincide with settlement types, and if these ways are functions of class and life-cycle stage rather than of the ecological attributes of the settlement, a sociological definition of the city cannot be formulated.[21] Concepts such as city and suburb allow us to distinguish settlement types from each other physically and demographically, but the ecological processes and conditions which they synthesize have no direct or invariate consequences for ways of life. The sociologist cannot, therefore, speak of an urban or suburban way of life.

Conclusion

Many of the descriptive statements made here are as time-bound as Wirth's.[22] Twenty years ago, Wirth concluded that some form of urbanism would eventually predominate in all settlement types. He was, however, writing during a time of immigrant acculturation and at the end of a serious depression, an era of minimal choice. Today, it is apparent that high-density, heterogeneous surroundings are for most people a temporary place of residence; other than for the Park Avenue or Greenwich Village cosmopolites, they are a result of necessity rather than choice. As soon as they can afford to do so, most Americans head for the single-family house and the quasi-primary way of life of the low-density neighborhood, in the outer city or the suburbs.[23]

Changes in the national economy and in government housing policy can affect many of the variables that make up housing supply and demand. For example, urban sprawl may eventually outdistance the ability of present and proposed transportation systems to move workers into the city; further industrial decentralization can forestall it and alter the entire relationship between work and residence. The expansion of present urban renewal activities can perhaps lure a significant number of cosmopolites back from the suburbs, while a drastic change in renewal policy might begin to ameliorate the housing conditions of the deprived population. A serious depression could once again make America a nation of doubled-up tenants.

These events will affect housing supply and residential choice; they will frustrate but not suppress demands for the quasi-primary way of life. However, changes in the national economy, society, and culture can affect people's characteristics—family size, educational level, and various other concomitants of life-cycle stage and class. These in turn will stimulate changes in demands and choices. The rising number of college graduates, for example, is likely to increase the cosmopolite ranks. This might in turn create a new set of city dwellers, although it will probable do no more than encourage the development of cosmopolite facilities in some suburban areas.

The current revival of interest in urban sociology and in community studies, as well as the sociologist's increasing curiosity about city planning, suggest that data may soon be available to formulate a more adequate theory of the relationship between settlements and the ways of life within them. The speculations presented in this paper are intended to raise questions; they can only be answered by more systematic data collection and theorizing.

REFERENCES

1. Axelrod, Morris. "Urban Structure and Social Participation," *American Sociological Review,* Vol. 21 (February 1956), pp. 13–18.
2. Bell, Wendell. "Social Choice, Life Styles and Suburban Residence," in William M. Dobriner (ed.), *The Suburban Community.* New York: G. P. Putnam's Sons, 1958, pp. 225–247.
3. Bell, Wendell, and Maryanne T. Force. "Urban Neighborhood Types and Participation in Formal Associations," *American Sociological Review,* Vol. 21 (February 1956), pp. 25–34.
4. Berger, Bennett. *Working Class Suburb: A Study of Auto Workers in Suburbia.* Berkeley, Calif.: University of California Press, 1960.
5. Dewey, Richard. "The Rural-Urban Continuum: Real but Relatively Unimportant," *American Journal of Sociology,* Vol. 66 (July 1960), pp. 60–66.
6. Dobriner, William M. "Introduction: Theory and Research in the Sociology of the Suburbs," in William M. Dobriner (ed.), *The Suburban Community.* New York: G. P. Putnam's Sons, 1958, pp. xiii-xxviii.
7. Duhl, Leonard J. "Mental Health and Community Planning," in *Planning 1955.* Chicago: American Society of Planning Officials, 1956, pp. 31–39.
8. Duncan, Otis Dudley, and Albert J. Reiss, Jr. *Social Characteristics of Rural and Urban Communities, 1950.* New York: John Wiley & Sons, 1956.
9. Duncan, Otis Dudley, and Leo F. Schnore. "Cultural, Behavioral and Ecological Perspectives in the Study of Social Organization," *American Journal of Sociology,* Vol. 65 (September 1959), pp. 132–155.

10. Enders, John. *Profile of the Theater Market.* New York: Playbill, undated and unpaged.

11. Fava, Sylvia Fleis. "Contrasts in Neighboring: New York City and a Suburban Community," in William M. Dobriner (ed.), *The Suburban Community.* New York: G. P. Putnam's Sons, 1958, pp. 122–131.

12. Foley, Donald L. "The Use of Local Facilities in a Metropolis," in Paul Hatt and Albert J. Reiss, Jr. (eds.), *Cities and Society.* Glencoe, Ill.: The Free Press, 1957, pp. 237–247.

13. Form, William H., *et al.* "The Compatibility of Alternative Approaches to the Delimitation of Urban Sub-areas," *American Sociological Review,* Vol. 19 (August 1954), pp. 434–440.

14. Fromm, Erich. *The Sane Society.* New York: Rinehart & Co., Inc., 1955.

15. Gans, Herbert J. *The Urban Villagers: A Study of the Second Generation Italians in the West End of Boston.* Boston: Center for Community Studies, December 1959 (mimeographed).

16. Gans, Herbert J. "Planning and Social Life: An Evaluation of Friendship and Neighbor Relations in Suburban Communities," *Journal of the American Institute of Planners,* Vol. 27 (May 1961), pp. 134–140.

17. Greer, Scott. "Urbanism Reconsidered: A Comparative Study of Local Areas in a Metropolis," *American Sociological Review,* Vol. 21 (February 1956), pp. 19–25.

18. Greer, Scott. "The Social Structure and Political Process of Suburbia," American Sociological Review, Vol. 25 (August 1960), pp. 514–526.

19. Greer, Scott, and Ella Kube. "Urbanism and Social Structure: A Los Angeles Study," in Marvin B. Sussman (ed.), *Community Structure and Analysis.* New York: Thomas Y. Crowell Company, 1959, pp. 93–112.

20. Janowitz, Morris. *The Community Press in an Urban Setting.* Glencoe, Ill.: The Free Press, 1952.

21. Jonassen, Christen T. *The Shopping Center Versus Downtown.* Columbus, Ohio: Bureau of Business Research, Ohio State University, 1955.

22. Ktsanes, Thomas, and Leonard Reissman. "Suburbia: New Homes for Old Values," *Social Problems,* Vol. 7 (Winter 1959–60), pp. 187–194.

23. Reiss, Albert J., Jr. "An Analysis of Urban Phenomena," in Robert M. Fisher (ed.), *The Metropolis in Modern Life.* Garden City, N.Y.: Doubleday & Company, Inc., 1955, pp. 41–49.

24. Reiss, Albert J., Jr. "Rural-Urban and Status Differences in Interpersonal Contacts," *American Journal of Sociology,* Vol. 65 (September 1959), pp. 182–195.

25. Riesman, David. "The Suburban Sadness," in William M. Dobriner (ed.), *The Suburban Community.* New York: G. P. Putnam's Sons, 1958, pp. 375–408.

26. Rose, Arnold M. "Living Arrangements of Unattached Persons," *American Sociological Review,* Vol. 12 (August 1947), pp. 429–435.

27. Seeley, John R. "The Slum: Its Nature, Use and Users," *Journal of the American Institute of Planners,* Vol. 25 (February 1959), pp. 7–14.

28. Smith, Joel, William Form, and Gregory Stone. "Local Intimacy in a Middle-Sized City," *American Journal of Sociology,* Vol. 60 (November 1954), pp. 276–284.

29. Spectorsky, A. C. *The Exurbanites*. Philadelphia: J. B. Lippincott Co., 1955.

30. Stone, Gregory P. "City Shoppers and Urban Identification: Observations on the Social Psychology of City Life," *American Journal of Sociology,* Vol. 60 (July 1954), pp. 36–45.

31. Strauss, Anselm. "The Changing Imagery of American City and Suburb," *Sociological Quarterly,* Vol. 1 (January 1960), pp. 15–24.

32. Vernon, Raymond. *The Changing Economic Function of the Central City*. New York: Committee on Economic Development, Supplementary Paper No. 1, January 1959.

33. Vidich, Arthur J., and Joseph Bensman. *Small Town in Mass Society: Class, Power and Religion in a Rural Community*. Princeton, N.J.: Princeton University Press, 1958.

34. Wattell, Harold. "Levittown: A Suburban Community," in William M. Dobriner (ed.), *The Suburban Community*. New York: G. P. Putnam's Sons, 1958, pp. 287–313.

35. Whyte, William F. *Street Corner Society*. Chicago: The University of Chicago Press, 1955.

36. Whyte, William H., Jr. *The Organization Man*. New York: Simon & Schuster, 1956.

37. Wilensky, Harold L. "Life Cycle, Work, Situation and Participation in Formal Associations," in Robert W. Kleemeier, *et. al.* (eds.), *Aging and Leisure: Research Perspectives on the Meaningful Use of Time*. New York: Oxford University Press, 1961, Chapter 8.

38. Wilensky, Harold L., and Charles Lebeaux. *Industrial Society and Social Welfare*. New York: Russell Sage Foundation, 1958.

39. Wirth, Louis. *The Ghetto*. Chicago: The University of Chicago Press, 1928.

40. Wirth, Louis. "Urbanism as a Way of Life," *American Journal of Sociology,* Vol. 44 (July 1938), pp. 1–24. Reprinted in Paul Hatt and Albert J. Reiss, Jr. (eds.), *Cities and Society*. Glencoe, Ill.: The Free Press, 1957, pp. 46–64. [All page references are to this reprinting of the article.]

41. Young, Michael, and Peter Willmott. *Family and Kinship in East London*. London: Routledge & Kegan Paul, Ltd., 1957.

NOTES

1. I am indebted to Richard Dewey, John Dyckman, Davis Riesman, Melvin Webber, and Harold Wilensky for helpful comments on earlier drafts of this essay.

2. I shall not attempt to summarize these studies, for this task has already been performed by Dewey (5), Reiss (23), Wilensky (38), and others.

3. By the *inner city,* I mean the transient residential areas, the Gold Coasts and the slums that generally surround the central business district, although in some communities they may continue for miles beyond that district. The *outer city* includes the stable residential areas that house the working- and middle-class tenant and owner. The *suburbs* I conceive as the latest and most modern ring of the outer city, distinguished from it only by yet lower densities, and by the often irrelevant fact of the ring's location outside the city limits.

4. The trapped are not very visible, but I suspect that they are a significant element in what Raymond Vernon has described as the "gray areas" of the city (32).

5. If the melting pot has resulted from propinquity and high density, one would have

expected second-generation Italians, Irish, Jews, Greeks, Slavs, etc., to have developed a single "pan-ethnic culture," consisting of a synthesis of the cultural patterns of the propinquitous national groups.

6. The corporation transients (36, 38), who provide a new source of residential instability to the suburb, differ from city transients. Since they are raising families, they want to integrate themselves into neighborhood life, and are usually able to do so, mainly because they tend to move into similar types of communities wherever they go.

7. The negative social consequences of overcrowding are a result of high room and floor density, not of the land coverage of population density which Wirth discussed. Park Avenue residents live under conditions of high land density, but do not seem to suffer visibly from overcrowding.

8. Whether or not these social phenomena have the psychological consequences Wirth suggested depends on the people who live in the area. Those who are detached from the neighborhood by choice are probably immune, but those who depend on the neighborhood for their social relationships—the unattached individuals, for example—may suffer greatly from loneliness.

9. Needless to say, residential instability must ultimately be traced back to the fact that, as Wirth pointed out, the city and its economy attract transient—and, depending on the sources of outmigration, heterogeneous—people. However, this is a characteristic of urban-industrial society, not of the city specifically.

10. By neighborhoods or residential districts I mean areas demarcated from others by distinctive physical boundaries or by social characteristics, some of which may be perceived only by the residents. However, these areas are not necessarily socially self-sufficient or culturally distinctive.

11. For the definition of *outer city,* see Footnote 3.

12. Because neighborly relations are not quite primary, and not quite secondary, they can also become *pseudo-primary;* that is, secondary ones disguised with false affect to make them appear primary. Critics have often described suburban life in this fashion, although the actual prevalence of pseudo-primary relationships has not been studied systematically in cities or suburbs.

13. These neighborhoods cannot, however, be considered as urban folk societies. People go out of the area for many of their friendships, and their allegiance to the neighborhood is neither intense nor all-encompassing. Janowitz has aptly described the relationship between resident and neighborhood as one of "limited liability." (20, Chapter 7)

14. Were I not arguing that ecological concepts cannot double as sociological ones, this way of life might best be described as small-townish.

15. They may, of course, be significant for the welfare of the total metropolitan area.

16. A 1958 study of New York theater-goers showed a median income of close to $10,000 and 35 per cent were reported as living in the suburbs (10).

17. I am thinking here of adults; teen-agers do suffer from the lack of informal meeting places within walking or bicycling distance.

18. These must be defined in dynamic terms. Thus, class includes also the process of social mobility, stage in the life-cycle, and the processes of socialization and aging.

19. This formulation may answer some of Duncan and Schnore's objections to socio-psychological and cultural explanations of community ways of life (9).

20. The ecologically oriented researchers who developed the Shevsky-Bell social area analysis scale have worked on the assumption that "social differences between the populations of urban neighborhoods can conveniently be summarized into differences of economic level, family characteristics and ethnicity." (3, p. 26) However, they have equated "urbanization" with a concept of life-cycle stage by using family characteristics to define the index of urbanization (3, 18, 19). In fact, Bell has identified suburbanism with familism (2).

21. Because of the distinctiveness of the ways of life found in the inner city, some writers propose definitions that refer only to these ways, ignoring those found in the outer city. For example, popular writers sometimes identify "urban" with "urbanity," i.e., "cosmopolitanism." However, such a definition ignores the other ways of life found

in the inner city. Moreover, I have tried to show that these ways have few common elements, and that the ecological features of the inner city have little or no influence in shaping them.

22. Even more than Wirth's they are based on data and impressions gathered in the large Eastern and Midwestern cities of the United States.

23. Personal discussions with European planners and sociologists suggest that many European apartment dwellers have similar preferences, although economic conditions, high building costs, and the scarcity of land make it impossible for them to achieve their desires.

3.4 IN DEFENSE
OF WIRTH'S "URBANISM
AS A WAY OF LIFE"

STANLEY S. GUTERMAN

It is now thirty years since this journal published Louis Wirth's classic essay stressing the relative weakness of primary relations as among the distinguishing characteristics of the urban way of life. Wirth argued that the city's gigantic size, along with its density and its social and cultural heterogeneity, fosters an absence of personal acquaintanceship among interacting individuals. Interaction is based on segmentalized roles with a corresponding impersonality, superficiality, and transitoriness of social relations. All of these factors weaken, if not destroy, the bonds of sentiment and intimacy among the inhabitants.[1]

The flavor of his analysis is conveyed in the following passage:

> Characteristically, urbanites meet one another in highly segmental roles. . . . Their dependence upon others is confined to a highly fractionalized aspect of the other's round of activity. This is essentially what is meant by saying that the city is characterized by secondary rather than primary contacts. The contacts of the city may indeed be face to face, but they are nevertheless impersonal, superficial, transitory, and segmental. The reserve, the indifference, and the blase outlook which urbanites manifest in their relationships may thus be regarded as devices for immunizing themselves against the personal claims and expectations of others.[2]

Criticisms of Wirth

In the years since Wirth's paper originally appeared, his view of urban social relations has come to be widely questioned. Relying on a wealth of empirical research on ties with friends, neighbors, extended kin, and co-workers, scholars have contended that primary groups lead a vibrant existence and play an important role in the day-to-day lives of urban inhabitants. Wilensky and Lebeaux, for example, interpret the evidence to mean that the "alleged anonymity, depersonalization, and rootlessness of city life may be the exception rather than the rule. The typical city dweller maintains close relations with friends among either neighbors, or people in other parts of the

From Stanley S. Guterman, "In Defense of Wirth's 'Urbanism as a Way of Life,'" *American Journal of Sociology,* Vol. 74:5 (March 1969), pp. 492–499. © 1969 by The University of Chicago. All rights reserved. Reprinted by permission of the author and The University of Chicago Press.

urban area or both." In the opinion of these writers, the available data "suggests that the breakdown of primary group life and informal controls has been greatly exaggerated."[3]

In a review of forty studies on ties among extended kin, Sussman and Burchinal maintain that the "emphasis on the atomistic character of urban families has contributed to incorrect assumptions concerning interaction within the kinship matrix." A more accurate description of kin relations in the city, they believe, is provided by the notion of the "modified extended family" in which there "are mutual aid and social activities among kin related families."[4]

On the idea that areas within a city differ in the degree to which they are urbanized, Scott Greer says, "Although highly urbanized populations are not typical of most city dwellers (they are an extreme of a continuum), those who do exist deviate widely from the stereotype of the atomistic man. They are greatly involved in the family and kinship group, and they participate intensively in friendship and cliques."[5] If the "stereotype" is not descriptive even of the highly urbanized segments of a city, how much less so must it be of the other segments?

Most recently, Tomeh has written that a major criticism of "Wirth and others of the Chicago school is that they exaggerated the degree of secularization and disorganization that supposedly typifies urban communities." Research has disclosed "strong kinship and neighborhood ties in those areas of the city where such relations were often assumed to be quite weak."[6]

The more recent views of social life in the city, then, differ sharply in emphasis from those of Wirth—if, indeed, the two sets of views are not in outright conflict with each other. The proponents of these newer views, moreover, can marshal an impressive array of empirical studies to support the contention that isolation from friends and kind is a rare occurrence in the city.[7]

Weaknesses of the Criticisms

Despite the formidable case that Wirth's detractors appear to have made out, it is the thesis of this paper that they have not done full justice to his conception of urban life. When one examines the studies on which their arguments are based, he discovers that—with two partial exceptions that are discussed toward the end of this paper[8]—these studies are less than adequate for testing Wirth's views. To begin with, the measures employed often deal with the frequency with which an individual interacts, or gets together socially, with his associates.[9] The high rate of interaction that is generally found among city dwellers is thought to refute Wirth's views. The fallacy here is that Wirth was not concerned with the *quantity* of interaction. In one passage, for example, he explicitly remarked, "This is not to say that the urban inhabitants have fewer acquaintances than rural inhabitants, for the reverse may actually be true."[10] His concern, rather, was with the *quality* of interaction. Thus he spoke of the "impersonal, superficial, transitory, and segmental" character of social ties in the city and of "the reserve, the indifference, and the blasé outlook which urbanites manifest in their relationships."[11] Insofar as the measures used in the empirical research do not tap the dimensions implicit in

Wirth's discussion, this research cannot be regarded as truly testing his ideas.

I must immediately concede that there are studies that do use indicators referring to the quality of social relations. But even these investigations leave something to be desired. For they are not comparative. The samples are confined to persons living in large cities, so that they do not permit one to make inferences about differences between urban areas, on the one side, and small towns and rural areas, on the other.[12] As Wirth observed in one passage, "We must . . . infer that urbanism will assume its most characteristic and extreme form in the measure in which the conditions with which it is congruent are present. Thus the larger, the more densely populated, and the more heterogenous a community, the more accentuated the characteristics associated with urbanism will be."[13] To the extent that Wirth intended to depict the ways in which highly urbanized settlements differ from less urbanized settlements, the absence of a comparative design vitiates the existing studies as a test of his theory.[14]

Finally, these studies are limited to relations with kin, friends, neighbors, and the like. To be sure, the studies frequently touch on relations with co-workers, but such relations are invariably viewed in terms of leisure-time, friendship activities. What is wrong here is that the relationships that these studies focus on constitute only a part of any person's network of social relations. Wirth never intended to confine his analysis to that part. On the contrary, his interest was in the total network. Consider his remark that the "distinctive features of the urban mode of life have often been described sociologically as consisting of the substitution of secondary for primary contacts";[15] or his mention of "the number of people . . . with whom they [urban inhabitants] rub elbows in the course of daily life";[16] or his reference to the absence of "sentimental and emotional ties" and to "a spirit of competition, aggrandizement, and mutual exploitation."[17] The language Wirth uses in these and other passages seems to refer in large part to economic and business relationships. Because the existing studies are confined to ties with friends and kin, they fail to deal with the secondary types of interaction that play a large role in most urbanites' day-to-day existence. Thus even if research were to demonstrate that ties with friends and kin are no less "impersonal, superficial, transitory, and segmental" in the city than in small towns and rural areas, it would still not justify rejection of Wirth's ideas inasmuch as it would tell us nothing about the comparative quality of social relations outside of the kin and friendship networks.

Wirth's critics, then, appear to have allowed the deficiencies and limitations of the existing studies to lead them astray.[18] Instead of designing investigations that would come to grips with the subtlety and complexity of Wirth's theory, they implicitly reinterpreted the theory to make it congruent with the procedures that the researchers had used—and in doing so, they stripped it of its trenchant qualities.

Data Supporting Wirth's Views

In addition to these considerations rebutting the critics, I have data which —by showing a negative correlation between the intimacy of friendship ties and the size of the locality in which a person lives—support Wirth's depiction of social relations in the city. A by-product of a study of Machiavellianism among hotel employees, these data avoid two of the pitfalls of previous investigations. For one thing, the index of intimacy employed here seems a reasonably valid measure of the quality of friendship relations. For another, the sample includes residents of both large cities and small towns, thus permitting comparisons between respondents in the two.

Sampling and Fieldwork Procedures

The sample consisted of 483 employees in twenty-six hotels operated by two chains and located in the eastern coastal states between Washington, D.C., and Bangor, Maine. All of the hotels were year-round establishments for transients. The main consideration in deciding which hotels in the two chains would be included in the study was to minimize the amount of travel that would have to be done in the course of the field work. This procedure was necessitated by limitations in the research budget.

Budgetary limitations also dictated the use of a self-administered questionnaire. Because giving such a questionnaire to manual workers would have created insurmountable problems, the sample was confined to employees on the white-collar and managerial levels. Among the types of personnel included were general managers and their assistants, heads of various departments, front-office clerks, switchboard operators, headwaiters, chefs, accountants, bookkeepers, security officers, and secretaries. In twenty-three of the hotels, the sample was simply defined as all white-collar and managerial employees. In the three largest hotels there were too many such employees to include all in the sample, so I stratified the population by the respondent's type of work, set a sample quota for each type, and selected a random sample from each stratum.[19]

The fieldwork was conducted in the autumn of 1963 and the winter of 1964. Each respondent filled out a highly structured self-administered questionnaire, which took on the average an hour and a half to complete. Usually the hotel management set aside a room in which groups of respondents assembled to fill in the questionnaire on company time. The number of respondents filling out the questionnaire at the same sitting varied from one to fifteen. As each respondent completed the questionnaire, I briefly checked it over and had him correct any gross errors.

To maximize the candor of replies to the questionnaire, it was important to convince respondents that no information about individuals would be disclosed to the management. In addition to oral and written assurances of confidentiality and not requiring the respondent to identify himself in the questionnaire, I took several steps to demonstrate my good faith. Accompanying each questionnaire was a letter on university stationery emphasizing the purely academic nature of the research and promising to send each respondent a summary of the preliminary findings. This promise was later kept. On the first page of the instrument, moreover, was an "official acknowledgement" of financial assistance from the United States Department of Health, Education, and Welfare.

Finally, participation in the study was voluntary. Respondents were expressly told that they could refuse to fill out a questionnaire if they so wished. Aside from my probable inability in most instances to make individuals participate, there was an additional pragmatic reason for this practice. Had I been seeking information about individuals in order to turn over such information to management, most respondents would have expected me to permit no refusals. The policy of keeping participation voluntary was thus designed to underscore my independence of management.

Measurement Procedures

The index of the intimacy of friendship ties is based on a section of the questionnaire in which the respondent was asked to list the first names of the "*five* persons (or married couples) *not related* to you, *whom you know best.*" The respondent, in effect, gave five replies to each item, one for each of the friends listed. One item, for example, read "You know the immediate family of this person well." A response consisted of placing a check mark under the name of each friend to whom the statement was applicable.

Four dimensions have been employed in constructing the intimacy index. The first three are taken from Sorokin's modalities of social interaction.[20]

1. Intensity refers to the strength of affect that an individual feels toward another person and the extent to which an individual is psychologically affected by the actions of another person. One of the items intended to tap this dimension asked if the respondent "would feel badly if you happen to lose touch with this person."
2. Extensity, according to Sorokin, is the "proportion of the activities and psychological experiences involved in interaction out of the sum total of the activities and psychological experiences of which the person's whole life process consists." This dimension appears synonymous with what Wirth had in mind when he wrote of segmentalization. The one item designed to measure extensity in the questionnaire inquired about the range of topics the respondent talked about when he was with each friend.
3. The duration of a relationship is simply the length of time that the relationship has existed. To measure this dimension, I have calculated the mean percentage of the respondent's life during which he knew the five friends listed.
4. The interconnectedness of the respondent's circle of friends has been gauged by the extent to which the respondent knew the other associates of each friend.[21] One item asked whether the "two closest friends of this person (not including yourself) are good friends of yours."[22]

To measure the size of the locality, I have relied on an item in the questionnaire which asked the respondent to name the "town (or locality) and state" in which he was living at the time he answered the questionnaire. With this information, it was easy to go to the 1960 Census to obtain the population of the locale. If a respondent raised in an urbanized area, the size variable refers to the population of the urbanized area—not the population of the municipality—in which he lived. Three urbanized areas were included in the study. Two of them, Boston and Washington, had populations of between 1.5 and 2.5 millions; the third, New York City, a population of slightly over 14 million.[23] Of the respondents who lived outside of these three areas, none lived in communities having more than 120,000 inhabitants; over 90 per cent lived in towns having a population of less than 40,000; and over 75 per cent lived in towns having less than 20,000 population.

The Findings and Their Limitations

Table 3.4A[24] examines the relation of intimacy to the size of the locale in which the respondent lived at the time of the fieldwork. The data show a negative correlation: residents of large cities and their suburbs are less likely to have close friendships than residents of small towns. Insofar as this finding evidences the relatively unprimary character of social relations in urban settings, it raises even further doubts about the arguments of Wirth's critics.

Although our data are highly suggestive, they nonetheless have certain distinct limitations. First, the sampling procedures employed make it hazardous to generalize the findings. Aside from the fact that the sample was confined to white-collar and managerial employees in the hotel industry, selection of the hotels for inclusion in the study was not based on probability sampling procedures. Added to this is the fact that in three of the hotels the proportion of the intended sample that refused to participate was exceedingly high (i.e., over 30 per cent). These three hotels were all in urbanized areas of 1.5 million or more inhabitants. That the high refusal rate is not evenly distributed over the range of the independent variable may have biased the findings here.[25]

A second limitation is that the only measure of the quality of a person's social relations used here is that of the respondent's friendship ties. I have presented data neither on relations with extended kin nor on relations with other kinds of associates.

Finally, the index of the intimacy of friendship ties is based solely on the respondent's report. I did not give questionnaires to the five friends named by each respondent in order to check the reliability of his report.

TABLE 3.4A   Intimacy of Friendship Ties by Population of Urbanized Area or Locality (If Outside Urbanized Area) Where Respondent Currently Lives

Intimacy	Population		
	Under 120 Thousand (%)	Between 1.5 and 2.5 Million (%)	14 Million (%)
Low	42	47	58
Medium	24	26	19
High	34	27	23
	100 (131)	100 (185)	100 (145)

NOTE.—$\chi^2 = 8.77$; d.f. = 4; $.10 > P > .05$.

Comparable Data from Previous Studies

Apart from the inconclusiveness of the present data, uncertainties emerge from two studies that offer data comparable to those presented here. Sutcliffe and Crabbe studied five groups—each consisting of eight Australian first-year university students—matched on a number of variables. The first three groups lived in Sydney, the fourth in the suburbs, and the fifth in towns of less than 40,000 population. After listing all of the "various people you know and meet," the respondents answered seven items about their relationship with each such person. On the basis of the replies, the persons named were classified into three categories varying in degrees of friendship—"best friend," "friend," and "acquaintance." The findings of the study unfortunately are equivocal. The respondents who lived in the small towns characterized fewer persons as "best friends" than the respondents who lived in the urban and suburban areas. If, however, one lumps the "best friends" and the "friends" together, it turns out that the findings are just the opposite: the small town residents named a greater number than the urbanites and the suburbanites.[26]

With a Guttman scale measuring participation in the extended family, Key studied 357 individuals who lived in different-sized localities in the Midwest. He failed to find any linear relation between size and participation. His results are thus at variance with those presented here.[27]

The discrepancies between these two studies and the present one can perhaps be explained by examining some differences in the research procedures. First, the studies did not measure the quality of social relations in the same manner. The items in the Sutcliffe and Crabbe study deal with such things as willingness to lend articles, amount of confiding, and willingness to support the other person in the face of criticism. Aside from the fact that Key's measure refers to kin while mine refers to friends, his measure is conceptually impure in that it contains items that gauge both the frequency and quality of interaction. And only a minority of the five items in his scale—one dealing with the frequency of lending and borrowing and the other with the frequency of "favors other than lending"—measure quality. Thus the measures used in these studies seem to be tapping dimensions that are different from those on which the present study is based (intensity, extensity, duration, and the interconnectedness of the social network). In my opinion, the measure used here does a much better job of capturing the nuances of quality as Wirth implicitly conceived it in his essay. In any event, the correlation between urbanism and the quality of social relations could conceivably depend on the dimensions used to measure the latter variable.

In addition, Key's study uses different cutting points for the population variable than those used here. In his data, the category at the high end of this variable consists of metropolitan areas of more than 100,000 population. In my study, by contrast, the medium and high categories consist of urbanized areas having *at least* 1.5 million population. One doubts that most, if any, of the respondents in his high category would fall into the medium or high category in the present study. If so, the discrepancies in our findings could, in part, be due to the fact that we focused on different portions of the population variable. Should this conjecture be true, there may be a relationship between urbanism and the quality of social relations, but it may hold only for the upper portion of the urbanism variable. In other words, it is conceivable that disintegration in the quality of relations does not occur in marked form except in metropolitan areas of several million inhabitants.

Conclusions

In summary, I have argued that the evidence that Wirth's critics rely on to refute his characterization of social relations in the city is inadequate in one or more respects. First, the studies often deal with the quantitative aspect of social relations, ignoring the qualitative aspect that was Wirth's central concern. Second, the studies are not comparative: with few exceptions, they fail to include the residents of both large cities, on the one side, and small towns and rural areas, on the other. Third, their focus is on relations with friends and kin; they ignore other relationships.

In support of Wirth's views, I presented data showing a negative association between the size of the locality a person lives in and the intimacy of his friendship ties.

Given the limitations of my data and given the discrepancies between my findings and those of two previous comparable studies, it would clearly be unwarranted to argue that this discussion has confirmed Wirth's theory of urbanism as a way of life. What this discussion has accomplished is admittedly more modest but nevertheless important: it has demonstrated the need for a fresh look at that theory utilizing research based on adequate measures and adequate design.

NOTES

1. See Louis Wirth, "Urbanism As a Way of Life," *Amercian Journal of Sociology,* XLIV (July, 1938), 1–24.
2. *Ibid.,* p. 12.
3. Harold L. Wilensky and Charles N. Lebeaux, *Industrial Society and Social Welfare* (New York: Russell Sage Foundation, 1958), pp. 122 and 125.
4. Marvin B. Sussman and Lee Burchinal, "Kin Family Network: Unheralded Structure in Current Conceptualizations of Family Functioning," *Marriage and Family Living,* XXIV (1962), 234–35.
5. Scott Greer, *The Emerging City: Myth and Reality* (New York: Free Press, 1962), pp. 92–93.
6. Aida K. Tomeh, "Participation in a Metropolitan Community," *Sociological Quarterly,* VIII (1967), 85.
7. A number of these studies are cited in nn. 9 and 12 below.
8. The partial exceptions are John P. Sutcliffe and B. D. Crabbe, "Incidence and Degrees of Friendship in Urban and Rural Areas," *Social Forces,* XLII (October, 1963), 60–67; and William H. Key, "Rural-Urban Differences and the Family," *Sociological Quarterly,* II (1961), 49–56.
9. For studies dealing with frequency of interaction with associates, see Scott Greer, "Urbanism Reconsidered: A Comparative Study of Local Areas in the Metropolis," *American Sociological Review,* XXI (1956), 19–24; Scott Greer and Ella Kuba, "Urbanism and Social Structure: A Los Angeles Study," in Marvin B. Sussman (ed), *Community Structure and Analysis* (New York: Thomas Y. Crowell Co., 1959), pp. 93–112; Morris Axelrod, "Urban Structure and Social Participation," *American Sociological*

Review, XXI (1956), 13–18; Aida K. Tomeh, "Informal Group Participation and Residential Patterns," *American Journal of Sociology,* LXX (July, 1964), 28–35; and Tomeh, "Participation in a Metropolitan Community" (n. 6 above), pp. 85–102.

10. Wirth, *op. cit.* (n. 1 above), p. 12.

11. *Ibid.*

12. For investigations that contain measures of the quality of social relations but are not comparative in their design, see Wendell Bell and Marion T. Boat, "Urban Neighborhoods and Informal Social Relations," *American Journal of Sociology,* LXII (1956–57), 391–98; Marvin B. Sussman, "The Isolated Nuclear Family: Fact or Fiction," *Social Forces,* VI (1959), 333–40; Nicholas Babchuk and A. P. Bates, "The Primary Relations of Middle-Class Couples," *American Sociological Review,* XXVIII (June, 1963), 377–84; and Nicholas Babchuk, "Primary Friends and Kin: A Study of the Associations of Middle Class Couples," *Social Forces,* XLIII (May, 1965), 483–93. Two reviews of research focusing on the quality of ties among extended kin are Sussman and Burchinal, *op. cit.* (n. 4 above), pp. 231–40; and Joan Aldous, "Urbanization, The Extended Family and Kinship Ties in West Africa," *Social Forces,* XLI (October, 1962), 6–11.

13. Wirth, *op. cit.* (n. 1 above), p. 9.

14. Admittedly there are studies that compare residents of census tracts that vary in their degree of "urbanism" or "family status." But in a given study, these tracts are taken from a single metropolitan area. Whatever the merits of such studies, they are no substitute for research comparing residents of different-sized localities. For examples of research making intrametropolitan comparisons, see Greer, "Urbanism Reconsidered," *op. cit.* (n. 9 above); Greer and Kuba, *op. cit.* (n. 9 above); Tomeh, "Informal Group Participation and Residential Patterns," *op. cit.* (n. 9 above); and Bell and Boat, *op. cit.* (n. 12 above).

15. Wirth, *op. cit.* (n. 1 above), pp. 20–21.

16. *Ibid.,* p. 12.

17. *Ibid.,* p. 15.

18. Let me emphasize that in calling attention to the inadequacies of the studies cited here, I am speaking strictly from the standpoint of their suitability for testing Wirth's theory. From other standpoints, including that of their intrinsic merit, these investigations may be unexceptionable.

19. Following are some of the characteristics of the sample. Almost two-thirds consisted of males. There was a fairly even distribution of respondents on the age variable, those in the "50 and over" age category, however, being somewhat more numerous than those in the other three age categories (18–29, 30–39 and 40–49). Approximately half of the sample came from three giant urban hotels, each of which had no less than 700 personnel. At the other extreme, about 30 per cent worked for units having less than 90 employees each.

20. See Pitirim A. Sorokin, *Social and Cultural Dynamics* (New York: American Book Co., 1937), III, 6–15.

21. The idea for this fourth dimension comes from Elizabeth Bott, *Family and Social Network* (London: Tavistock Pub., 1957).

22. The intimacy index is based on six items, each of which is assigned code values of 0 to 3. A "no answer" to any constituent item results in the respondent being left out of the analysis. The theoretical range is from 0 to 18. The scoring of the first four items is based on the number of friends to whom, according to the respondent, a given statement applies.

1. You would feel badly if you happened to lose touch with this person.

2. You know the immediate family of this person well.

3. This person has given you a gift within the past 12 months (for your birthday, for Christmas, etc.).

4. The two closest friends of this person (not including yourself) are good friends of yours.

5. Write in the number of years you have known each person. [This item was used to compute the mean per cent of the respondent's life that he had known the five friends listed. This proportion determined the score assigned to each respondent.]

6. How about the *number of different kinds* of things you talk about with each of the above persons? *Write in the letters* designating those with whom you discuss:
One or two subjects of mutual interest___
Several subjects of mutual interest___
Quite a few subjects of mutual interest___
A very wide range of subjects of mutual interest___
    (The first alternative was given a score of 1, the last a score of 4, and those in between scores of 2 and 3. The respondent received a score for each friend, and the scores for the five friends were then summed to yield a total score for the item. The latter score determined the code value assigned for this item.)
    The work of Robin M. Williams, Jr., on friendship proved a valuable source of suggestions for item formulation; see Williams, "Friendship and Social Values in a Suburban Community" (Eugene: University of Oregon, 1956 [mimeographed]).
23. The urbanized area is a census concept that refers to a large city—in the 1960 Census, one of 50,000 or more population—and the surrounding suburban territory. The effect of using the urbanized area instead of the town or city as the unit for measuring population is to classify suburbs by the population of the total urban complexes of which they are a part. Use of the urbanized area was dictated by considerations associated with the major study—that on Machiavellianism—from which the data given here are drawn. For a formal definition of the urbanized area, see U.S. Bureau of the Census, *United States Census of Population: 1960*, I: *Characteristics of Population*, Part A: "Number of Inhabitants" (Washington, D.C.: Government Printing Office, 1961), xviii–xix.
24. The *N*'s in the table add up to less than the size of the sample (483). This is due to a lack of information necessary for classifying some respondents on one or the other variable. In coding respondents on the intimacy index; e.g., it was my practice to give no score to those individuals who failed to reply to any of the items in the index.
25. There is some evidence that the effect of the high refusal rates operates against the arguments presented in this paper. We know that the proportion of respondents who are Machiavellian is somewhat lower in the hotels with the high refusal rates than in the other hotels located in the cities of the same size. We also know that there is a slight negative correlation between an individual's Machiavellianism score and the intimacy of his friendship ties. Thus the high refusal rates may have served artificially to raise the percentage in the cities having high intimacy scores and thereby spuriously to lower the correlation between size of locale and intimacy. This is only surmise on my part. But if it is correct, the evidence offered here in support of Wirth would have been even more favorable to his position had the high refusal rates not occurred.
26. See Sutcliffe and Crabbe, *op. cit.* (n. 8 above).
27. See Key, *op. cit.* (n. 8 above).

R. LINCOLN KEISER

My life. I really can't tell about it 'cause I lived it. I was born on 29th and Prairie. I guess I lived there for quite a long time. The first place I can actually remember I lived was on Frontier. We had a little small house over there, and we lived there for about three or four years. Over there there's nothing but killing. It was just a regular routine.

We got a big family. I got six brothers, and I think three sisters . . . I ain't counted lately. You know how it is. If somebody asks you how many, it's hard to say. I was nextest to the oldest. My sister, she older than me. And you know, we was up mellow. Then everything started going bad.

The way things ran down, me and my brother, we actually grew real fast because we had whole lots of family problems. We didn't have the proper clothes to wear, and people used to laugh . . . at the way we was dressed, and this and that. And even the teachers gave us a hard time—which they do to a lot of peoples. We actually had a difficult time going to school 'cause we didn't have the proper clothes. And people would talk about us. You know, it was hard. The teacher even failed me one semester. I was actually ashamed to go home and tell my mother that I had got failed. My problem was I didn't care. See, I never did think about nothing but the family, and because I don't want to fail, that don't mean that I should let myself go. Life still should be lived.

At the same time my father started acting funny too. It seemed like he was separating from the family. He wasn't coming home proper. He was coming home maybe . . . but not like he's supposed to. See, the old man, he didn't have no job, and he left us to ourselves. Many nights we went hungry, and if we didn't go out and get it ourselves, we wouldn't eat. You dig? He wouldn't provide the food. Like many days me and my brother went out and sold boxes and found pop bottles. We actually hustled pop bottles and stuff to get something to eat. If we didn't find different things to sell, we wouldn't eat. The old man, I guess he didn't believe in, you know, growing up. He just didn't want to see us grow up. Maybe he just couldn't realize it, but instead of us growing like normal kids, we had to provide for the family when he wasn't there. Then my mother, she was fixing to have a baby. It was my youngest brother, Jerry. And behind that she was sick. She was pretty sick for about five or six years. She was on the verge of a nervous breakdown, but she had to get up out of the bed and take care of the family. That's how it was for a long time. She was sick pretty close to ten years.

My uncle, he stayed in the penitentiary. Me and him was tight. See, we're the only two black sheep of the family. We didn't know it then, but as it came out we were. His daughter, she a prostitute now. She be out on 63rd. I don't know where he is now. I haven't seen him in maybe ten or twelve years, and I haven't seen my cousin in a long time, but I heard she's on the corner. Don't nobody trusting her in they house neither. She'll take anything from anybody.

You know how things go along. Time pass. I got older, so we moved on the West side. We moved to out to West Jackson. Then we was going to Jefferson. I stayed there 'til I graduated. It was pretty nice over there. I was in a little club called the Vandykes. When we moved in I just saw them on the streets and they saw me. I was a new boy at school, so I just started hanging around with them. They turned out to be pretty mellow. I was in the Midgets. We was small. Still we wasn't as powerful as the Lords because they had the Braves in that hood too, and they were kicking strong. The Braves and the Jew Town Cobras, they had going east on Roosevelt, all that up tight. We just had about three or four blocks from Damen back to Ashland. We didn't have a whole big section like the Lords did. But what was ours was ours. We kept things up tight. Least *they* did. I was too young to do anything. Then came the King Pipers. That was Tiny Tim and them.

We all going to school together and we all lived on the same street. We'd get together and talk, and we got into a lot of little trouble together . . . steal milk and stuff like that. Mostly we used to play baseball or basketball at the playground, or something like that. Sometimes we might fight Tiny Tim and them, and the project boys, they'd come over and we'd run them back. Other than that we didn't have too much to worry about because where we was there wasn't too much over there people wanted anyway. That was around '58 or '59.

After we moved from there, we moved over to Paulina, and I got busted for burglary. I broke into this store next door—me and a cat named James Walker. We had broken into this place two or three times. The last time we broke in we stole a hundred and thirty dollars, and we got a .25 automatic. I cut my hand on that too. So this cat that was with me, he tricked.[1] He got busted or something and he tricked on me. They got me that night about ten o'clock. I was in the bed. My sister, she called and we went to the back door. My mother was in the bed too. My mother was sick. So they came and took me away, and I stayed for a day or two. Then I came home and when I went back to court they sent me to the Audy Home for two weeks. That mother fucking Audy Home is a bad place to be. I guess it's the worst place in the City of Chicago! It not nothing right!! They served us some chicken, it was so salty and so bloody that you couldn't even eat it. Only thing you could actually get full of—if you was lucky—was if you could catch some bread. You know, they used to throw bread and stuff around the room, and if you could catch it you could eat it, and if you didn't, you just didn't eat. I think the welfare had that place on. See, the way we had it, the office really didn't mean anything. Everybody need some kind of leadership, and everybody had just as much say as everybody else. It run something like Congress. That's the way we had it. We didn't have, like a certain officer to run the meeting. And when we were gangbanging, I couldn't say I really led them all because lots of them I missed out on. I wasn't there. You can't be with them all the time 'cause you never know who coming down there at you. The Lords didn't have to look for trouble. Trouble came to them . . . after they got their rep. See, a new club, they wouldn't go out looking for the Cobras. The first one they come looking for is the Lords. This is how the Lords got involved in lots of jive. People looked to them. Sometimes you don't have no reason why to go out and fight because when you get out there anybody might get killed. A small war just as big as a big war. It can become a big thing. Death is death you know. That's how it was.

Since we lived around there, we knew everybody. Everybody from that area know everybody. The majority of the Lords, we all know each other. Lots of them even know our families. So it was just like . . . brothership.

Now we created whole lots of stuff. We did whole lots, you know. We used to rob those peoples on the "L" all the time. We used to have a long sword, maybe three feet long, and we used to rob all those peoples and throw them off the "L." We usually started around Tuesday night. We used to do it from Tuesday to Saturday—go out on peoples and take they money and stuff. And any money we got we'd take and buy wine and get high, or else go down to the restaurant and buy some hamburgers and eat and fool around. Maybe we'd go out and bother somebody else, or go out to fight or something. We'd come back, get drinking, and get high again. That's all we did. It was a regular routine. . . .

You know, nobody know for sure how a gang war starts. You never know if you even involved in a gang war at first. It could get started when you're not around, and you won't know nothing about it. One minute you may be down there, and the next minute you may be fighting. It could get started over a little simple thing. And what everybody really searching for is power. Like if I was to go out and start a fight with a club now. I wouldn't come back and tell my partners 'cause they may be mad at me, and when the humbugging starts they'd think it was this other club. So the Commanches could of started it and the Lords could have started it. Don't nobody know.

Now we was still fighting the Cobras at the same time. This one night we was just out having fun. We weren't out to shoot nobody in particular. I remember I had a .41 Magnum, one of my partners had a .38 special, and a stud had a .32 short. We went down Harding shooting up peoples. I don't know who we were shooting at, or what for, but we were fighting the Cobras, and I guess we were just shooting after everybody. We came back, and there weren't but two of us—me and Ringo.

So Ringo, he yells, "We're Vice Lords, mighty Vice Lords!" He yelling to this man coming up the street.

This stud said, "Well, you all Vice Lords, huh!?"

We said, "Yeah!"

And by the time he was reaching for his back pocket . . . I guess he didn't get out what he wanted to get out before I got what I got out. I shot him in the leg or foot or something, and he ran down the street . . . hollering like a dog! I don't even know if he a Cobra, but it was in the Cobra's hood. It was 13th and Avers, something like that.

But the Cobras came back on us. We was standing in front of the YMCA, and all of a sudden a car came around Polk street and started slowing down. Everybody turned around and looked.

I said to the man, "Go ahead, man! Go ahead!" But the stud wouldn't move his car. All of a sudden maybe about six studs popped out with shotguns, man, and Fool, he ran! He ran into somebody's crib, and he ain't knock on the door or anything! They chased us all the way down back to Independence! . . .

This is when we broke up the Commanches. After this one fight they broke up. It must of happened between nine-thirty and ten o'clock. I was sitting there on 16th and Lawndale, and some dude came down and said the Commanches jumped on Cave Man and some more of the fellows. I forgot who they was.

Somebody said, "Get everybody together!"

So somebody got on the telephone and called the fellows from Maypole —Tankson and them. We told the Vice Ladies to stay back, but they came down there anyway. I remember how this was—how we got down there. We all went on top of this big old truck. We was packed on it! So we came down there, and it seemed like it was really funny. We was down there . . . we was fighting, killing up each other, and all of a sudden we got hemmed up! And the Commanches, they had us! They had us up tight! We was boxed in. And so by some coincidence some of the fellows was coming behind them, but it just seemed like they wasn't getting there fast enough. And all of a sudden we looked up, and here come Tankson and them. So the Commanches, they seen them before we did, and they started running. I'll never forget this. It was King Solomon . . . crazy ass King Solomon. He had one of these little Hookvilles. It's a knife, a linoleum knife. Got a hook on the end. And a stud in the Commanches called Ghengis Khan, he went to run, and that's when Solomon got him . . . with the Hookville. Cut the stud's whole guts out! And two more of their fellows got shot—Big James, one of their top boys, and Big House Willy. We really fucked them up that night. This was the whole Imperial group, Commanches and everybody 'cause this was right on their corner, right where they grew up at, on 16th and Trumbull.

And Ghengis Khan was on the critical list. The paper made a big write-up on it. And they was talking about if Ghengis Khan would die, there was going to be a big war. But see, what they was trying to do was to turn up 16th and Lawndale and take over the corner. Naturally, we wouldn't go for that. And the police was after us that night too 'cause we was coming down the street— marching in the middle of the street with shotguns. It was a humbug. . . .

I'd say Cave Man and them was kind of jealous of us, you know, 'cause at that time we was swinging pretty hard. We was younger than Cave and them. We was little bitty dudes, and they was big, but we used to keep pockets full of money. We used to keep gallons and stuff of wine. We always used to keep money and all stay clean while we had a suit or something on. And we used to have a house to go up to all the time. We had got our own girls. We used to call them the Supreme Queens. They just did they part too. When we fought they was outside. They take our guns and hide them when the police bust us. They used to write to us in jail, and they was really something mellow. Lots of times if a certain fellow break in a store, some of the girls be with him. Just get different stuff. They was just like the boys. They used to drink just like we did . . . and maybe even more. They really came down to be pretty nice. And they used to give dances and stuff. We never did invite Cave and them because actually they was too old. They figured they was too old to be messing with us anyway. So we didn't never run up to them asking them for nothing. Everytime they came down they always wanted us to buy them something to drink, and they wanted our girls too. They were very jealous of our girls. And it all got messed up as soon as they found out about it. They wanted to come over and start tearing up things. They just couldn't let well enough be well enough. If the girls didn't want to go with them they wanted to start knocking them down, tearing up they houses. Pretty soon we didn't have anything anymore. We faced with the same problem, no place to go, and everything started all over again.

Another reason Cave and them was jealous of us was because we was independent, and them, they always wanted to run things. They wanted to be head of everything. Maybe they afraid they might get old. I don't know. But they wanted to run everything, and we didn't like it. So we changed our name to Mighty St. Louis Lords. And the YMCA was all over Cave because he supposed to be the leader and stuff. They gave Cave and them everything they wanted. They'd look to Cave before they'd look to us, and we was the ones out there creating everything. So we cut the YMCA and all them peoples loose, and we set up a kind of independent group. We had a sponsor of our own at the B.B.F.[2] But we was still Lords. Apparently they couldn't dig that. They wanted us to follow after them—you know, Conservative. Which we couldn't see why we should follow them, the Conservative name, when we the only ones be out there doing anything. And we still didn't change our name. We stood up for ourselves, and now a lot more studs call theyselves Mighty Vice Lords too.

So then Cool Fool and King Solomon, they got into it with Cave and them. The same night Cave, Rifleman, and some more fellows, they came down, and they talking about how they going to fall on us 'cause we had got into it with Pole Cat, and we wasn't going by Conservatives. They got kind of hot, but we said we wasn't going to change our name regardless. We would fight anybody! And this was when the Roman Saints had just come out, and they had started coming across—moving north. The Saints had got heavy, and we was the only ones pushing them studs back. We had the Saints broke up. I ain't talking about these little studs around now calling theyselves Roman Saints. We went after their big boys. Their big boys was Kneecaps and them —all they presidents and stuff. They was scared to go to school. Really! If they did go the rest of them would have to come there and walk them home. We chased all of them home! . . .

I remember when we had that .22 rifle. The Saints hadn't been out too long. Like I said, the first time they came out we damn near broke them up 'cause they was scared to come to school. We had a big fight with them. There were three of us. And we whupped them in hand to hand combat. We had whupped them then, so they had broken down. Then the next thing, I heard the Roman Saints were carrying on.

We used to go down there and shoot up two or three of them all the time. They were scared. After meetings we used to go out and do things up in their hood. One night we had a meeting. It was Monday. We all was broke, and we couldn't buy no wine. So we went up there in the alley and started humbugging. I got shot in the leg that night. Yeah! We was coming down Albany, and they was shooting at us. We was running around, just having fun, though. We weren't running 'cause they was shooting. Well, there really wasn't anything else to do. We got in a gangway and hollered out, "Mighty Vice Lords!" and they started shooting at us again. I guess I didn't get out of the way fast enough. I got shot in the leg. Matter of fact I didn't know nothing about it 'til the next day. My mother asked me how come I couldn't get out the bed. I thought I broke my leg or something. So I went to the doctor, and he took out a shell. He said I was pretty lucky.

We used to meet with the Roman Saints. The YMCA set the meetings up. But they didn't mean nothing. See, they never do sets it up for the peoples that're doing it. They always try to set them up with the people they think got the most influence. That's O.K., but the only thing wrong, they forget there's whole lots of jealous people. Everybody trying to be like that person up there. They figure if he goes to the meeting, why can't I go too when I'm out there standing by his side doing as much as he doing. That's what they thinking. But the Y, they just don't see it.

I went to lots of meetings myself. They cooked dinners and stuff. Had nice dinners. They'd dance and talk—talk about their difficulties . . . and that's it. They go back on the streets and go right on doing the old routine. Go back out there and start fighting again. It might last for a week. That's all. It don't last too long. Then they call another meeting. They talk about the same thing again. It's O.K. . . . I guess, but them peoples are not equipped like they should be. They don't have the right kind of anything. Maybe the money's out there, but the YMCA, they so strict. I don't see how you can be strict with a wolf pack. Really! You got to have a place of your own to really tear up something, like a gym or something.

And then lot's of peoples don't want to do one special thing. Like the YMCA, the only thing they want you to do is come up there and play some games or go in the gym and play basketball. Who wants to do that every two or three days? That's all it was. And not everybody can skate, so who wants to go there and skate? We better off everybody sticking together doing shit on the streets 'cause you was too limited to what you could do at the Y.

Then when they did have dances there'd be so many peoples there that you didn't know, trying to get something out of you, you better off not even going. Maybe they're trying to get some information for one of them pictures you see on television—like "Keep it Cool," and all them pictures. Anytime they going to have a dance at the YMCA you could bet after that that the Bell Telephone Company, or some movie outfit going to move in that next summer and try to make a picture of the group. They going to try to go around and meet everybody. Like last year them people come all the way from New York and all over just to meet us. And when we used to be fighting, they'd have peoples running up and down trying to get pictures out of it . . . to show how it was. It don't do no good! Peoples look at it and think you a fool! Those studs out there taking pictures, they don't even know what you doing it for. Actually they don't really care because they ain't going to give away nothing. You not going to get nothing out it! If they do give away something, its just to gain something themselves. To actually give something to somebody else you don't know is kind of foolish. I know I don't do it. I know the next man won't do it . . . especially if he think you not going to use it. Nine out of ten the money being donated, you don't get the proper use out of it anyway. Most of it go to waste.

But if they had just a little more than they have now, there probably wouldn't be many clubs out there. There going to be a club anyplace you go, and there always going to be a bad guy, or somebody that think they bad anyway. But when you got close to six hundred boys think they bad running down the streets carrying guns, that's pretty bad! And all these years they still haven't got no solution for this here problem. When you think of all the money the United States is spending out on other things, and they talking about this is not a major problem. I don't know what is! Something must be wrong. When you look at the future, the way everybody on the streets cutting up each other, there won't be no future! There won't be nobody left by the time they get through . . . to do anything. They killing off everybody! And the peoples, they don't care. Only thing they do is hire more policemen. What's the police doing? The police is killing more than we are! The police are living better than we are! They still driving five or six thousand dollar cars. I don't see how they can afford them. And most of us, we can't even afford a hamburger. They catch us with a quarter, they going to whup our asses up, take our quarter, and put it in they pocket. Yeah! And they say it's not a major problem! It is a major problem. But still when it comes up to the point, they always willing to draft you. You the first one they going to call for to fight. But they don't think they have to give you anything. Give you a decent place to go? Nope! You know, they might build a center or something, but they going to have so many rules there that you just can't enjoy yourself. Like you're going to have only third nights to come. What good is coming on third nights, [when] you can't go every night? Not much good.

Then lots of places you got to pay to go. In some neighborhoods it's O.K. to pay, but in some neighborhoods everybody don't have that kind of money be paying. Around here if you haven't got that money to pay, you just don't go. All these centers just for the good guys anyway—good girls and boys. None of the clubs go in. Miss Love's center[3] is O.K., but she just don't have the money to run it, and the government hasn't given her any money. I guess it's too much like right. Yeah. Somebody might learn something! The more you stay down, the more they can rest. The only thing they think is good for you is being busted. They treat you like animals! You're a savage . . . savage! As long as they can get you any time they want you, draft you and send you to fight something that they started, it's O.K. Huh! They start something they can't handle, they going to call you to go over and handle it. As far as them doing you justice, making sure that you got a decent place to go or a decent place to live, that's too much money they're got to be spending out. They can afford to give away millions of dollars a year to somebody else, but not to us. We got to be satisfied with what we got—making the best of it we can.

And around this Lawndale area there's more people starving than any China, I'll bet you—more people starving around here. Take this whole Lawndale area. I'd say ninety percent of them is on the Aid . . . some kind of welfare. In the morning you go out and there's somebody standing on their porch waiting on the check. That's why probably so many peoples on this ADC, carrying on. They look at everybody else. It's a common thing. Just like going to work now. You look like a fool not being on, and everbody else on, they're living better than you living and staying home. I don't know how they got it arranged, but its kind of foolish. . . .

You'll catch a fool in every crowd, and the Lawndale area is full of fools. Everybody think they know more than everybody else. Nobody know anything . . . no more than somebody else tell them what they might see, or what somebody might hear from their next door neighbor.

And talking about cash, all them fellows working for that Commission on Youth Welfare, all them cats, man . . . that's the the most sickening sight I ever seen. All them sit back there in their office making five to ten thousand dollars a year, running out program after program. They have interviews about what they're doing for the Lawndale area, and one of the biggest well known gangbangers can walk up on them . . . they wouldn't even know who he is. We are strangers to them, but still they going to write, Cupid did this here, or Bull did this here, or Little Lord did this here. I might walk up on them, and they wouldn't know me, Bull walk up on them, they wouldn't know him, Little Lord might walk up on them, they wouldn't know him neither . . . until somebody do something, and then there's a whole lot of bullshit. They shaking hands. Then they want to find jobs for everybody. But as far as them coming out to the streets and want to work on their own, they not going to do that. They don't see no reason why they should do it. It's no use to them. So long as they draw their check it's mellow. When they check stop coming to them, they got to work then. All this is just a thing—a way to make a living. As long as we out on the street and fighting, they got money coming in. But if we want to settle down and just be somebody, they won't accept it then. They say we all savages. But it's not so. Everybody wants to live decent. We not going to be young savages all our life. One day we going to have to be able to vote, and them guys going to be out of a job!

The younger generation coming up, I'm quite sure that they don't want to come up the same way we did. Especially when we get to be part of society, some of those kids going to be ours, and we don't want them going through that same shit we went through—trying to come up being somebody instead of nobody. I guess that's just the way it is. We nobody.

That Youth Commission and all them cats . . . full of shit. Just like they never been. Who know them? Nobody. Who care to know them? Nobody. What they ever did for somebody? Nothing . . . nothing at all. They might interview a couple of peoples when they job's on the line, but come down to cold facts, who they think about? Nobody but themselves. They pass some old exam for this job, so the State decides to give it to them. They living the life of a king. What they got to do? Nothing. What makes their job so easy, the papers do most of they work. All they have to do is hop up and read the papers, ask a couple of questions, and write a report. They might not send it in for six months. That's it. But for them to get down to real problems . . . no good. What I believe the caseworkers should do if they was really out for the peoples is to be really true to they work. But you can't be a true caseworker with so many peoples who all got problems. Like in Lawndale, how many caseworkers do they got? About fifty. Now how in the hell can fifty caseworkers take care of damn near four or five thousand boys, all who got problems?! Half of them ain't got clothes to wear to school, and nowhere to get any from. Half of them are drop-outs, and ain't nobody trying to get no job for them. And out of that fifty caseworkers, maybe about ten is looking out for their job—they're looking out for the fellows—and the other forty just there. They might as well not be there—just a lot of expense, just a way to spend money. It's sickening! . . .

When you on the streets you learn what's what. That's something they don't teach you in school. School don't teach you about life. It teaches you about past life—what somebody had did, and how somebody made something. It don't teach you about how to live. And this is something they can't teach you . . . unless you be in the streets. School put education in you head, but the streets tell you what you going to do when you grown. The streets teach you how to live.

O.K., say a stud got a education. Oh yeah, he give you the right answer for what's two and two, but he couldn't go out in the street and make five dollars like you could . . . or couldn't tell you what's happening. Education, it does mean something, though. You might get a job before me. But the peoples that actually know what they doing, the peoples that're making it . . . what I mean is you can't really make it unless you know what's happening in the streets. I don't care how much education you got, if you don't know how to live in the streets, it don't mean nothing. A fellow like me, I figure well at least I know I'm living in the streets. Anytime I'm out in the streets I can make myself a hustle. You dig? I always can make myself a buck . . . if I want to bad enough. 'Cause there's always somebody on the street, a fool. There's always a fool out there! I don't care what generation you is, you always going to find a fool. And every time the price go up—every time a more intelligent fool come out in the street, then you got to be a little bit more intelligent.

And maybe those people in school be more advanced than me, but on the long run you got to look at this here. The thing will equal up because in order for them to use this knowledge, they got to first come on the street. And half those people with all that education haven't got the stomach to live on the street and go through all that shit. And because their parents put them in school so young, they don't know the first thing about the streets, so they might fall ten or twelve years behind me. While they're trying to learn how to live on the streets, I'll catch up with them. That's where my parents upped theirs . . . 'cause I know what's going on. I know what's out there. They don't know what is what—what's happening. They don't know nothing about nothing. And as much as nine out of ten times they'll get lost . . . or end up a gangster.

What you learn on the streets is how to live. See, you never know who might knock on your door. Iike I say, I might hit you in the head and rob you tonight, and tomorrow I wouldn't know who I hit. Half the time you don't care. I might not remember your face but you might remember mine . . . so you got to be very observant. You learn to do certain things. You learn your senses. You learn to smell things, you learn to control your ways. Out south, out north, or out west there's a whole lot of gangbangers wherever you go. Like out south there're the Rangers, out north the Continental Pimps, and out west there're the Vice Lords and Cobras too. That why I say at least all of them been on the streets and they know what's happening. All them people with that education, they don't even know what's happening.

I could tell them some things they don't know about too—how to get along with peoples. I could get along with some peoples they couldn't. There's certain things I could understand about them peoples that they couldn't. Take the caseworkers. They're all short tempered because they don't have the patience to stake out to what their ideas would be about life. They won't take time out to see how they feel about what is what. And all them caseworkers are always telling, telling! How the hell can you tell somebody something? I can't tell you, or anybody what to do. I can maybe make a suggestion about how you might better yourself about this and that. But life's a funny thing, that's all I can do.

Now I'm not old. I'm in what you call the middle grade. I'm out of my teens. I'm twenty years old, and the five out of the twenty I was out there in the street I learned more than in all the other fifteen . . . because of the different people I run into, and the incidents that happened. Actually I learned how to find myself, how to look up and face responsibility—things that everybody didn't give you. It was always this way in a club. There's somebody always depending on you. Somebody always looking up to you to do something so they could keep on going. This gives you a good feeling. So you do it, and they do it. But everybody in a club got to change and go through a different way of life. You not going to be a gangfighter all your life. People steady advertising you need this, you need that. You need doctors, you need lawyers, undertakers, and you think what you're losing. So you got to change. . . .

I'm out of the Lords. I just got tired of fighting so I got out. You know, you don't stay in a club. Anytime a fellow join a club he grabbing for something. Everybody join a club reaching for a certain goal, and when you reach that goal, that's it. Like maybe you're reaching for something. When you reach for that, when you get it, you're going to start reaching for something else, you know. It's a steady thing. I joined the Lords to gain respect and get known—across the neighborhood. And I gained it . . . in a way—some ways good, and some ways bad because in the way I gained it I did develop more enemies than I did friends. Maybe the first time I turn my back somebody might run up on me. I don't know. All I can say, when you're out there you don't know who's sisters and brothers. You shoot . . . and it could be some of your own peoples. You don't know nothing about that. You know, there's people in you family you don't know, and on occasions you might be fighting them.

So I just got out, that's all. But just because you get out of a club, you still owes certain . . . you don't really owe anything, but you feel . . . like they come around and they ask you for something to drink or something, I mean, you feel that this is only something that you should give it to them. But going out and gangbanging with them, that's no good. I wouldn't even hang around with them much 'cause it shows a certain kind of something. People look at it as you still there. And when you hanging with a group . . . peoples is peoples. Peoples don't understand why you hang with them, who you are, or what. Peoples name you. Peoples name the club. Yeah! That's how peoples react if you're a teenager. Once you a Lord, you branded for the rest of your life.

NOTES

1. Tricked: informed.
2. B.B.F.: A social agency with social centers and street workers.
3. The Tennessee Memorial Community Center: Miss Love, a Black concert singer, donated her money and time to this center. There was no paid staff—only volunteers from the Black community. The center was one of the few places the Vice Lords were welcome. Miss Love was not able to get any funds from the War on Poverty, and the center closed for lack of financing.

CLEVELAND AMORY

The scene is the dining room in the Proper Bostonian home of Judge John Lowell in the suburb of Chestnut Hill. The time is the early morning of half a century ago. The characters are: Mrs. John Lowell, the true Boston dowager type, serene, capable; a maid, also Boston type, ageless, starchy; old Judge John himself—a Lowell.

As the curtain rises, the time is 7:30 by the grandfather clock. The Lowells are at breakfast, Mrs. Lowell at one end of the table, her husband at the other. The judge's face is hidden behind his morning paper. From the pantry the maid enters, comes over close to Mrs. Lowell and says something in a low voice. It is obviously bad news, which Mrs. Lowell is determined to communicate at once to her husband. The cook has burned his cereal. There is no more of such cereal in the house. Lest there be any misunderstanding Mrs. Lowell concludes her speech slowly: "There isn't going to be any oatmeal this morning, John."

This is no minor domestic tragedy. To the best of his wife's knowledge Judge John Lowell has up until this morning had oatmeal every single day of his life. The silence is nerve-racking. Slowly the paper is lowered and the face of the judge appears. Then the reply:

"Frankly, my dear, I never did care for it."

The significance of that story goes beyond the fact that it is gospel truth as handed down in a succeeding generation of the Lowell Family. It is more than the single story of one Lowell going without oatmeal for one morning. It is actually a typical story. Old Judge John Lowell, last of a line of three Judge John Lowells, was a character, but not in the individual sense that, for example, the Father of Clarence Day's *Life With Father* was a character. Day's Father was a breakfast-table tyrant capable of turning every morning repast into a regal ceremony for himself and an ordeal for his wife, children and cook, but one can scarcely imagine his sons or his grandsons carrying on in his tradition. In Boston the tradition of the ceremonial breakfast lives on. At her "Sunrise Farm" home in Westwood, Mrs. Ralph Lowell, wife of Boston's most prominent Lowell today, serves oatmeal every morning. In other Proper Bostonian homes in Chestnut Hill or Dedham or Dover there are also other Lowells or Cabots or Higginsons who eat their oatmeal—and do so, of course, without considering the irrelevant question of whether they like it or not.

Oatmeal is simply a Proper Bostonian custom, and as such it has taken its apparently permanent place alongside such other recognized customs as the morning lecture and the afternoon walk, the trustee meeting and the charity bazaar, the daily tea and the anniversary dinner, the formal call and Friday Symphony. Unfortunately, somewhere along this line, in the Proper Bostonian mind, the mandatory maintenance of all these customs or social conventions would seem to have taken the place of manners or social graces. The poet T. S. Eliot put this in philosophical terms when some years ago he defined Boston Society as "quite uncivilized—but refined beyond the point of civilization." Speaking more specifically, a historian of the Cabot Family summed up his subject briefly. "A strange dynasty," he declared, "with customs but no manners."

Such a phrase, it seems only fair to note, might well have been used for almost any other of Boston's First Families besides the oft-maligned Cabot. Certainly the Forbeses are strange. Their repertoire of customs runs the Boston gamut from bird walking to mahjong. As for their manners, acting what is called "Forbesy" has long been synonymous in Boston with high-hat behavior. The phrase is also applicable to the Adamses. Branded as strange from their insistence on living in Quincy instead of in more socially circumspect territory, they have been practicing their Family customs since 1636. Yet their manners were classified for posterity in the phrase that they alone could say "even a gracious thing in an ungracious way."

It would be possible to go farther down the line. But in the same way that the Lowells' oatmeal stands forth as the typical Proper Bostonian custom it is possible to take the Cabots as typical of Boston Society's lack of manners. The Cabot record of living up to the phrase originally coined for their Family is a strong one. Cabot women, in particular, have been known for their brusque deportment apparently from the time the Family first moved to Boston. An authority on these women, since he himself married one, old Colonel Lee, nineteenth-century lion of Lee, Higginson & Co., was among the first to take cognizance of this. He once declared that not only his Family, but the Lowells, the Jacksons and the Higginsons as well, "came up from Newburyport to Boston, social and kindly people inclined to make acquaintances and mingle with the world pleasantly. . . But they got some Cabot wives who shut them up." In more recent times another Cabot husband has been known to admit that he has often discussed with his wife what he frankly regards as an inherent gracelessness in her Family. Meeting the late Dr. Richard Cabot, he felt free, in view of his wife's kinship, to ask the distinguished doctor and sociologist to dinner. He has never forgotten Dr. Richard's matter-of-fact reply: "Really I have so many people I should like to dine with but never get around to, I should not pretend that I ever would do it."

The redeeming feature of such a remark would seem to lie in its frankness. Cabots are nothing if not forthright. In another Society a Family occupying the same position as the Cabots in Boston would undoubtedly feel it incumbent upon themselves to make at least a pretense in the direction of social polish. The Cabots make none—and Boston Society cherishes them the more for this. The Cabots are in their way the Great Danes, or the mastiffs, of the Boston social breed, and if a Proper Bostonian, proudly pointing out a Cabot home to a visitor, should be greeted at the gate by a Cabot with an assumed show of friendliness, he would feel as foolish in front of his visitor as if, after expounding on the fierceness of his favorite watchdog, the animal should appear on the scene and behave like a lap dog.

Fortunately his Cabots rarely let him down. Occupying close to two pages in the Boston *Social Register,* the most impressive representation in that volume of any First Family in the city, the Cabots, wherever they may live and no matter how remote their connections with one another, all seem to share a magnificent disregard of the minor amenities of life. "My wife's always telling me," explains Judge Charles Cabot, "I can run a community drive but I don't know how to give a Christmas present." Godfrey Lowell Cabot, present-day Family patriarch, is a charming example of social independence. At various gatherings where he is in attendance, conversation must be tailored to suit his presence. Though he was once active in Boston politics himself, politics under a Democratic administration would never be a fit subject for discussion. So bitterly was the patriarch opposed to the liberal policies of Woodrow Wilson—a man, he once said, "who could not run a peanut stand"—that even his closest friends never cared to find out where he stood on Franklin D. Roosevelt. A young man from Philadelphia tells the story of having been invited to Godfrey Lowell Cabot's house on Beacon Street and, knowing nothing of the man's reputation and indeed little about him except his name, proceeded to josh him on the latter point, asking him how it felt to be both a Lowell and a Cabot in Boston. What followed was a silence of such ominousness that he knew at once he had overstepped his bounds. "I'm afraid that's a pretty silly question, Mr. Cabot," he said sheepishly. "Young man," thundered Cabot, "it's the damnedest silliest question I've been asked in ninety years." . . .

BENNETT M. BERGER

In recent years a myth of suburbia has developed in the United States. In saying this, I refer not to the physical facts of the movement to the suburbs; this is an ecological tendency to which all recent statistics on population mobility bear eloquent testimony.[1] I refer instead to the social and cultural ramifications that are perceived to have been inherent in the suburban exodus. Brunner and Hallenbeck, for example, call the rise of suburbia "one of the major social changes of the twentieth century,"[2] and the popular literature especially is full of characterizations of suburbia as "a new way of life."

The significance of the past decade cannot be overestimated since it is only in this period that suburbia has become a *mass* phenomenon and hence prone to the manufacture of modern myth. Suburbanization, however, goes back as far as the latter part of the nineteenth century, when the very wealthy began to build country estates along the way of suburban railroad stations. Improvements in the automobile and the development of good highways after World War I brought greater numbers of wealthy people to suburban areas in the 1920's. The depression of the 1930's slowed the process of suburbanization, but the late 1930's saw the development of some new residential construction at the peripheries of city limits. The big boom in suburban development, of course, came after World War II with the proliferation of "the mass produced suburbs" all over the country, and well within the reach of middle- and lower-middle-income people. And in the last few years, suburbanization of secondary and tertiary industry has followed closely upon residential suburbanization. Carl Bridenbaugh has noted that suburbanization began as far back as the early part of the eighteenth century. "One ordinarily thinks of the suburban movement of the present century as being of recent origin, and it will come as a surprise to many that the flight from the city began in the first half of the eighteenth century—and for the same reasons as today. The differences were in degree only. Just as Londoners moved westward from the City in search of quiet, air, comfort, lower rents, and more room for display, so did Philadelphians cross the northern and southern bounds of the metropolis in a perennial search for the 'green.' . . . That great-

From Bennett M. Berger, *Working Class Suburbs,* University of California Press, Berkeley and Los Angeles, 1960. Reprinted by permission of The Regents of the University of California.

est of townsmen, Benjamin Frankin, even moved from High Street to Second and Sassafra, grumbling that 'the din of the Market increases upon me; and that, with frequent interruptions, has, I find, made me say some things twice over.' "[3]

The literature on suburbanization seems to fall roughly into two categories. Studies of suburbanization by sociologists have been going on for a long time; with few exceptions, however, these have been primarily ecological or demographic in character.[4] On the other hand, studies of and comment on the culture and social psychology of suburban life have, again with a few exceptions, been left largely to popular writers, journalists, and intellectuals.[5] To urban sociologists in general, "suburbs" is a term of ecological reference; ecologists and demographers may often dispute the most useful way of conceiving "suburbs" for the purposes of their work, but the dispute is largely a technical one. "Suburbia," on the other hand, is a term of cultural reference; it is intended to connote a way of life, or, rather, the intent of those who use it is to connote a way of life.[6] The ubiquity of the term suburbia in current popular literature suggests that its meaning is well on its way to standardization—that what it is supposed to connote is widely enough accepted to permit free use of the term with a reasonable amount of certainty that it will convey the images it intends. In the last ten or twelve years, these images have coalesced into a full-blown myth, complete with its articles of faith, its sacred symbols, its rituals, its promise for the future, and its resolution of ultimate questions. The details of the myth are rife in many of the mass circulation magazines as well as in more intellectual periodicals and books; and although the details should be familiar to almost everyone interested in contemporary cultural trends, it may be well to summarize them briefly.

Elements of the Myth

Approaching the myth of suburbia from the outside, one is immediately struck by rows of new ranch-type houses either identical in design or with minor variations in a basic plan, winding streets, neat lawns, two-car garages, infant trees, and bicycles and tricycles lining the sidewalks.[7] Near at hand is the modern ranch-type school and the even more modern shopping center, dominated by the giant supermarket, which is flanked by a pastel-dotted expanse of parking lot. Beneath the television aerial and behind the modestly but charmingly landscaped entrance to the tract home reside the suburbanite and his family. I should perhaps say "temporarily reside" because the most prominent element of the myth is that residence in a tract suburb is temporary; suburbia is a "transient center" because its breadwinners are upward mobile, and live there only until a promotion and/or a company transfer permits or requires something somewhat more opulent in the way of a home. The suburbanites are upward mobile because they are predominantly young (most commentators seem to agree that almost all are between twenty-five and thirty-five), well educated, and have a promising place in some organizational hierarchy—promising because of a continuing expansion of the economy with no serious slowdown in sight. They are engineers, middle-management men, young lawyers, salesmen, insurance agents, teachers, civil service bureaucrats —occupational groups sometimes designated as organization men, and sometimes as "the new middle class." Most such occupations require some college education, so it comes as no surprise to hear and read that the suburbanites are well educated. Their wives too seem to be well educated; their reported conversation, their patois, and especially their apparently avid interest in theories of child development all suggest their exposure to higher education.

According to the myth, a new kind of hyperactive social life has apparently developed in suburbia. This is manifest not only in the informal visiting or "neighboring" that is said to be reft, but also in the lively organizational life that goes on. Associations, clubs, and organizations are said to exist for almost every conceivable hobby, interest, or preoccupation. The hyperactive participation of suburbanites is said to extend beyond the limits of voluntary associations to include an equally active participation in local civil affairs. This active, busy participation by young families is encouraged by the absence of an older generation who, in other communities, would normally be the leaders. The absence of an older generation is said to have an especially strong effect upon the young women of the community who, thrown back upon their own resources, develop a marked independence and initiative in civic affairs. The informal social life revolves around the daytime female "kaffeeklatsch" at which "the girls" discuss everything from the problems of handling salesmen to the problems of handling Susie. In the evening the sociability (made possible by the baby-sitting pool) is continued with rounds of couples dropping in on each other for bridge, a drink, or some conversation.

This rich social life is fostered by the homogeneity of the suburbanites; they are in the same age range and have similar jobs and incomes, their children are around the same age, their problems of housing and furnishing are similar. In short, they have a maximum of similar interests and preoccupations which promote their solidarity. This very solidarity and homogeneity (when combined with the uniformities of the physical context) are often perceived as the sources of "conformity" in the suburbia; aloofness or detachment is frowned upon. The intenseness of the social life is sometimes interpreted as a lack of privacy, and this lack of privacy, when added to the immediate visibility of deviations from accepted norms, permits strong, if informal, sanctions to be wielded against nonconformity. The "involvement of everyone in everyone else's life" submits one to the constant scrutiny of the community, and everything from an unclipped lawn to an unclipped head of hair may be cause for invidious comment. On the other hand, the uniformity and homogeneity make suburbia classless or one-class (variously designated as middle or upper middle class). For those interlopers who arrive in the suburbs bearing the unmistakable marks of a more deprived upbringing, suburbia is said to serve as a kind of "second melting pot" in which those who are mobile upward out of the lower orders learn to take on the appropriate folkways of the milieu to which they aspire.

During the daylight hours, suburbia, in the imagery of the myth, is a place almost wholly given over to child rearing. Manless during the day, suburbia is a female society in which the young mothers, well educated and without the interference of tradition (represented by doting grandparents), can rear their children according to the best modern methods. "In the absence of older people, the top authorities on child guidance [in suburbia] are two books: Spock's *Infant Care,* and Gesell's *The First Five Years of Life.* You hear frequent references to them."[8]

The widely commented upon "return to religion" is said to be most visible in suburbia. Clergymen are swamped, not only with their spiritual duties but with marriage counseling and other family problems as well. The revivified religious life in suburbia is not merely a matter of the increasing size of Sunday congregations; the church is not only a house of worship but a local civic institution also, and as such it benefits from the generally active civic life of the suburbanites.

Part of the myth of suburbia is the image of suburbanites as commuters: they work in the city. For cartoonists and other myth-makers, this mass morning exodus to the city has provided opportunity for the creation of images such as "the race to make the 7:12," getting the station wagon started on a cold morning, or the army of wives waiting at the Scarsdale station for the 5:05 from the city. A good deal has been deduced about the way of life in the suburbs from the fact of commuting. For father, commuting means an extra hour or two away from the family, for example, with its debilitating effects upon the relation between father and children. Sometimes this means that Dad leaves for work before the children are up and comes home after they are put to bed. Naturally, these extra hours put a greater burden upon the mother, and have implications for the relation between husband and wife.

In commuting, the commuter returns in the morning to the place where he was bred, for the residents of suburbia are apparently former city people who "escaped" to the suburbs. By moving to the suburbs, however, the erstwhile Democrat from the "urban ward"[9] becomes the suburban Republican. The voting shift has been commented on or worried about at great length; there seems to be something about suburbia that makes Republicans out of people who were Democrats while they lived in the city. But the political life in the suburbs is said to be characterized not only by the voting shift, but by the vigor with which it is carried on. Political activity takes its place beside other civic and organizational activity, intense and spirited.

Sources of the Myth

The foregoing characterization is intended neither as ethnography nor as caricature. Brief and sketchy as it is, it does not, I think, misrepresent the typical image of suburbia that, by way of highbrow as well as middlebrow periodicals (as well as some recent books), has come to dominate the minds of most Americans, including intellectuals. It takes scarcely more than a moment's reflection, however, for the perplexing question to arise; why should a group of tract houses, mass produced and quickly thrown up on the outskirts of a large city, apparently generate so uniform a way of life? What is the logic that links tract living with "suburbanism as a way of life?"

If the homes characteristic of suburbia were all within a narrow price range, we might expect them to be occupied by families of similar income, and this might account for some of the homogeneity of the neighborhood ethos. But suburban developments are themselves a heterogeneous phenomenon. The term "suburbia" has not only been used to refer to tract-housing developments as low as $7,000 per unit and as high as $65,000 per unit,[10] but also to rental developments whose occupants do not think of themselves as homeowners. The same term has been used to cover old rural towns (such as those in the Westchester-Fairfield county complex around New York City) which, because of the expansion of the city and improvements in transportation, have only gradually become suburban in character;[11] it has been applied also to gradually developing residential neighborhoods near the peripheries of city limits. Clearly, then, the ecological nature of suburbs cannot justify so monolithic an image as that of "suburbia."

If the image of suburbia is limited to the mass-produced tract developments, perhaps it is the fact of commuting that links suburban residence with "suburbanism as a way of life." Clearly, the demands of daily commuting create certain common conditions which might go far to explain some of the ostensible uniformities of suburban living. But certainly commuting is not inherent in suburban living despite the many students of suburbia who have made commuting an essential part of the definitions of suburbs. *Fortune,* for example, says that, "The basic characteristic of suburbia is that it is inhabited by people who work in a city, but prefer to live where there is more open space, and are willing to suffer both inconvenience and expense to live there." Von Rhode says, "The distinguishing aspect of the suburb is, of course, the commuter." And Walter Martin says, ". . . the characteristics essential to suburban status . . . are a unique ecological position in relation to a larger city and a high rate of commuting to that city." These definitions would exclude the community reported on in this study from the category "suburb," but more than twenty-five years ago, Lundberg noted, ". . . perhaps too much has been made of commuting as a phenomenon unique to the suburb. As a matter of fact, comparatively few people in a large city live within walking distance of their work. From this point of view a great number of people living in the city are also commuters . . . commuting can certainly not be stressed as a unique feature or a fundamental distinction of suburban life as contrasted with urban."[12]

It may have been true that the occupations of most suburbanites required a daily trip to and from the central business district of the city; it may still be true, but it is likely to be decreasingly true with the passage of time. The pioneers to the suburban residential frontier have been followed not only by masses of retail trade outlets, but by industry also. Modern mass production technology has made obsolete many two- and three-story plants in urban areas,[13] and today's modern factories are vast one-story operations which require wide expanses of land, which are either unavailable or too expensive in the city itself. Thus with the passage of time, "industrial parks" will increasingly dot suburban areas, and the proportions of suburbanites commuting to the city each day will decrease.[14]

If the occupations of most suburbanites were similar in their demands, this might help account for the development of a generic way of life in the suburbs. Or indeed, if suburbs were populated largely by organization men and their families, then we could understand more readily the style of life that is said to go on. Or, lacking this, if organization men, as Whyte puts it, give the prevailing *tone* to life in the suburbs, then we could more readily understand the prevalence of his model in the literature. But there is no ready hypothesis to explain why the occupations of suburbanites should be so homogeneous. It may be true that the typical organization man is a suburbanite. But it is one thing to assert this and quite another thing to assert that the typical tract suburb is populated by organization men and their families and/or dominated by an "organization" way of life.

Clearly then (and with all due respect for the selective aspects of suburban migration), one suburb is apt to differ from another not only in the price range of its homes, the income characteristics of its residents, their occupational make-up, and the home-to-work traveling patterns of its breadwinners, but also in its educational levels, the character of the region, the size of the suburb, the social-geographical origin of its residents, and countless more indices—all of which, presumably, may be expected to lead to differences in "way of life."

But we not only have good reason to expect suburbs to *differ* markedly from one another; we have reason to expect striking *similarities* between life in urban residential neighborhoods and tract suburbs of a similar socioeconomic make-up. Most residential neighborhoods are "manless" during the day; why not? Husbands are at work, and the only men around are likely to be salesmen and local tradespeople. Even in large cities many men "commute" to work, that is, take subways, buses, or other forms of public transportation to their jobs which may be on the other side of town.[15] Also there are thousands of blocks in American cities with rows of identical or similar houses within a narrow rental or price range, and presumably occupied by families in a similar income bracket.[16] Certainly, urban neighborhoods have always had a class character and a "way of life" associated with them. Certainly the whole image of "conformity" in suburbia closely parallels the older image of the tyranny of gossip in the American small town.

There is, then, apparently no reason to believe, no ready and viable hypotheses to explain why "suburbia" should be the new and homogeneous phenomenon it is usually conceived to be. What are the sources of the alleged new way of life? Why should the occupations of suburbanites be so homogeneous? Why should there be more conformity? Why should the "social life" be so intense? Why should organizational participation be so widespread? Why should the churches be so much busier than elsewhere? Why should educational levels be so much higher than average? Why should the residents vote Republican? In short, why does "suburbia" set off this chain reaction of images, associations, and ideas that have coalesced into a single myth?

Working-Class Suburbs

This is, of course, a large question, and it would be premature to attempt an answer at this point. It is enough for the present to observe that the myth of suburbia flourishes in spite of an apparent lack of logic in its formulation. In continually referring to "the myth of suburbia" I do not mean to imply that the reports on the culture of suburban life have been falsified, and it would be a mistake to interpret the tone of my remarks as a debunking one. I mean only to say that the reports we have had so far are extremely selective; they are based, for the most part, upon life in Levittown, New York; Park Forest, Illinois; Lakewood, near Los Angeles; and, most recently (the best study so far), a fashionable suburb of Toronto, Canada. The studies that have given rise to the myth of suburbia have been studies of *middle-class suburbs,* that is, suburbs of very large cities[17] populated primarily by people in the occupational groups often thought of as making up the "new middle class"—the engineers, teachers, and organization men mentioned earlier.[18] If the phrase "middle-class suburb" strikes the eye as redundant, it is testimony to the efficacy of the myth, for as I have suggested, there is certainly no reason to believe that residence in a new tract suburb in and of itself immediately (or even within a few years) generates a uniquely new middle-class style of life. Nor is there any reason to believe that the self-selective processes of suburban migration are such that suburbs attract an overwhelming majority of white-collar people to them.

These remarks are intended to suggest that the extant image of suburbia may be a distorted one; that its accuracy may be limited to the suburbs of great metropolises which are populated by former residents of the central city who work in its white-collar hierarchies. Thus whereas in most minds, Westchester and Nassau counties in New York, and Park Forest, Illinois, are ideal typical representatives of "suburbia," they may, in fact, be representative only of suburbs of great cities and of a way of life lived by metropolis-bred, well-educated people of white-collar status. If this or something like this is, in fact, the case, then it is clearly a mistake to identify "suburbanism" exclusively with the kind of life that is said to go on in places like these. Large tracts of suburban housing, in many respects indistinguishable from those on Long Island and in Park Forest, have gone up and are continuing to go up all over the country, not only near large cities, but near middle-sized and small ones as well. And if, as is not unlikely, many of the residents of these are rural-bred, with relatively little education, and innocent of white-collar status or aspirations, then we may expect sharp differences between their social and cultural life and that of their more sophisticated counterparts in white-collar suburbs. . . .

The study reported here is in a sense an attempt to test, on a working-class population, the validity of some of the influences that have been attributed to residence in new tract suburbs. The burden of the study has been to call into question certain commonly accepted facts of life in "suburbia," as these facts have been presented to us both by popular writers and by some professional social scientists. Although none of our findings gives us the right to doubt the truth of what many people have said of places like Park Forest and Levittown, they do give us permission to question the right of others to generalize about "suburbia" on the basis of empirical studies of selected samples whose "representativeness" has yet to be demonstrated. In other words, there are good reasons for believing that organization men live as Whyte says they do, and that the "new" middle class lives as others have said *they* do. But there is no reason to believe that what is characteristic of organization men or of the "new" middle class is also characteristic of the mass-produced suburbs. In a way, it is remarkable that, in spite of the efflorescence of the mass-produced suburbs in post-World War II America, references to "suburbia" more often than not cite the examples of Park Forest and Levittown—as if these two communities could represent a nation-wide phenomenon that has occurred at all but the lowest income levels and among most occupational strata.[19] At the same time, it would be arrogant to claim too much representativeness for the sample we have studied here. Auto workers are among the best paid of semiskilled manual workers; our tract is probably somewhat more homogeneous than most because of the circumstances of its occupancy; and, of course, the sample contains a heavy proportion of "Okies" and "Arkies."

It is true that some of our findings may seem to provide grounds for asserting that some social mobility has taken place among the group of suburbanites we studied. They claim, for example, many new friends, an increased interest in politics, and a new feeling of respectability. In addition, the milieu of the women in some ways approximates the female worlds reported as characteristic of white-collar suburbs. But it is important to keep in mind that the correlates of class are always temporary, and that not all correlates of class are equally important to membership in a class. Few people, that is, are mobile in *every* respect, and it is precisely in those respects *least* crucially associated today with the passage into a "suburban" milieu that changes can be noted in our sample. Homeownership in a homogeneous community and high school education can adequately account for just about all the changes we have seen; but whereas at one time, to be a high school educated homeowner constituted important qualifications for membership in the middle class, today they qualify one only for "respectability."

On the other hand, it is precisely in those respects which, from the point of view of status stratification, are most crucial for entrance into a "suburban" milieu that we fail to discern changes in the style of life of the sample we studied. Membership and activity in formal associations are rare; so is semiformal mutual visiting between couples. There is little evidence of pronounced striving, status anxiety, or orientations to the future. They neither give parties nor go to them. Their tastes and preferences seem untouched by the images of "suburbia" portrayed in the mass media.

Although the major point I have tried to make here is that these suburbanites have not, to any marked extent, taken on the patterns of behavior and belief associated with white-collar suburbs, I have also tried to emphasize their new feeling of well-being; they count; they feel like respectable people with a stake in the life of the community. "In Richmond," one respondent said, "we were one of the masses; down here there's community living." Adding this to the suggestion by Kornhauser and his colleagues that the working class can experience vast economic gains without necessarily losing their working-class orientations, it is possible to envision a well-housed and domestically comfortable working class, conscious of their hard won material gains, aware of their concomitant position as responsible, respectable persons, and willing to act to see to it that these gains are not threatened by the unpredictable fluctuations of the economy.

But these "gains" are collective gains, and as such, they do not so much constitute evidence of individual social mobility as they do of the mobility of an entire stratum. In a prosperous society there occurs not only individual mobility between strata in a relatively stable hierarchy; they entire hierarchy is pushed upward by prolonged widespread prosperity, and is rearranged by changes in occupational or income distribution. At the same time, the function of stratification symbols is to maintain viable distinctions among different categories of people, and when criteria which formerly distinguished rank no longer do so because they have become widely available, it is not too much to expect a restructuring of the symbolic aspects of stratification—if, that is, their distinction-maintaining function is to remain viable. . . .

The Functions of the Myth of Suburbia

Why, then, does the myth of suburbia flourish? The appearance of the mass-produced suburbs has been seized upon by the media, mass and otherwise, as a *major phenomenon,* as some sort of fundamental change, not only in ecological structure but in social structure and culture as well—apparently rivaling urbanization and industrialization in the scope of its significance. Suburbia is something to *talk* about—everywhere from the pages of learned journals to best sellers, from academic halls to smoke-filled political rooms to suburban patios and picture-windowed living rooms, and finally now (as if further proof were needed of its significance) to Hollywood. In the movie version of the novel *No Down Payment,* ostensibly a fictional account of life in the new suburbia, Hollywood makes a pointed comment on stratification: the sequence of violence, rape, and accidental death is set in motion by the only important character in the film who is not a white-collar man. Frustrated at being denied the job of police chief (because of his lack of education), the rural, Tennessee-bred service station manager drinks himself into a stupor, rapes his upper-middle class, college-educated neighbor, and then is accidentally killed, symbolically enough, under the wheels of his new Ford. The film closes with his blonde, nymphomaniacal widow leaving the suburb for good on a Sunday morning, while the white collar group is seen leaving the Protestant church (denomination ambiguous) with looks of quiet illumination on their faces.

The flourishing of myths and stereotypes (and, by extension, the image of the age in which they flourish) depends in part upon the availability of visible symbols. The extent, for example, to which the *impact* of juvenile delinquency upon the public consciousness depends not on criminal acts, but on long sideburns, rock and roll, motorcycles, and black leather jackets is worth some research.[20] Similarly, a good part of the peculiar susceptibility of suburbia to the manufacture of myth probably lies in the fact that a large supply of visible symbols are ready at hand. Picture windows, patios and barbecues, power lawn mowers, the problems of commuting, and the armies of children manning their mechanized vehicles down the sidewalks, are only secondarily facts; primarily they are symbols whose function is to evoke an image of a way of life for the nonsuburban public. Presumably, suburbanites know what "suburbia" is like—at least to the extent that the apprehension of such an abstraction is possible. Nevertheless, the myth of suburbia probably also functions to give suburbanites a sense of the "form" of their own lives by dramatically rendering in a public forum the experience of suburbanites, and thus making it historical.[21]

In addition, the visible symbols of suburbia are easily integrated with other aspects of the "spirit" of this "age." Suburbia is the locus of gadgetry, shopping centers, and "station wagon culture"; its grass grows greener, its chrome shines brighter, its lines are clean and new and modern. Suburbia is America in its drip-dry Sunday clothes, standing before the bar of history fulfilled, waiting for its judgment. But like Mr. Dooley's court, which kept its eyes on the election returns, the "judgments" of history are also affected by contemporary ideological currents, and the myth of suburbia flourishes precisely because it is useful as a symbol to widely divergent shades of opinion whose function it is to ship the judgment of history.

Because it is a significant phenomenon, "suburbia" is something upon which men are called to take a stand, much as the "Southern Agrarians" "took their stand" against urbanism and industrialism nearly thirty years ago. To some people suburbia represents the fulfillment of the American middle-class dream; it is identified with the continuing possibility of upward mobility, with expanding opportunities in middle-class occupations, with rising standards of living and real incomes, and the gadgeted good life as it is represented in the full-color ads in the mass-circulation magazines. To less sanguine senses, for example, those of some architects, city planners, estheticians, and designers, suburbia represents a dreary blight on the American landscape, the epitome of American standardization and vulgarization, with its row upon monotonous row of mass-produced cheerfulness masquerading as homes, whole agglomerations or "scatterations" of them masquerading as communities. To these eyes, the new tract suburbs of today are the urban slums of tomorrow. There is a third group to whom the myth of suburbia is also important; I mean sociologists and other students of contemporary social and cultural trends. David Riesman says of the authors of *Crestwood Heights* that they "collide, like Whyte, with a problem their predecessors only brushed against, for they are writing about *us,* about the professional upper middle class and its businessman allies, not about a New England museum for the upper class, such as Yankee City, or a small and rather parochial town in the South or Midwest, such as Jonesville or Elmtown. They are writing, as they are almost too aware, about themselves, their friends, their 'type.' "[22] Added to the fascination of professionally studying people who are much like oneself (a kind of positively sanctioned voyeurism), is the tendency to see in suburbia the convergence of some of the apparently major social and cultural trends of our time (other-direction, social mobility, neoconservatism, status anxiety, and the like), thus making of suburbia a microcosm in which the processes at work in the larger society can conveniently be studied. Finally, the vocabularies of some recent left-wing critics of American society seem to have substituted the terms "suburb" and "suburban" for the now embarrassingly obsolete term "bourgeois" as a packaged rebuke to the whole tenor of American life. What used to be condemned as "bourgeois values," "bourgeois style," and "bourgeois hypocrisy" are now simply designated as "suburban."

Although the myth of suburbia is useful to all these groups, it cannot be written off simply as ruling class propaganda or as an attempt to see only the sunny side of things, or, for that matter, as an attempt to see only the darker side of things—or even as a furtive attempt to peer into a mirror. Too many responsible intellectuals, though accepting the facts of suburbia, are nevertheless extremely critical of what they see.

But precisely *what* is it that they see that they are critical of? Is it conformity? status anxiety? popular culture? chrome? tail fins? gadgetry? gray flannel suits? No doubt, these are symbols powerful enough to evoke images of an enemy. But the nature of this "enemy" remains peculiarly elusive. Surely, there is nothing specifically suburban about conformity, status anxiety, and the rest, and surely there is nothing diabolical about mass-produced domestic comfort and conservatively cut clothes. It is extraordinary that, with the single exception of William Whyte's attempt to trace "the web of friendship" on the basis of the physical structure of the Park Forest "courts,"[23] no one, to my knowledge, has come to grips with the problem of defining what is specifically *suburban* about suburbia. Instead, most writers are reduced to the use of hackneyed stereotypes, not even of suburbia, but of the upper middle class.[24] If, indeed, the images intended to represent suburbia are only symptoms of the commitments of the upper middle class to a way of life whose roots lie conventionally deeper (for example, in the structure of corporate opportunity), then the attack on suburbia may be only a scapegoat phenomenon; suburbia becomes a convenient, safe scapegoat on which to blame the consequences of commitment to chrome idols. Viewed this way, the attack on suburbia has interesting and advantageous consequences for the not-quite-completely-critical intellectual. To heap abuse upon suburbia (instead of upon the ethos of success and the demanding conditions of social and economic mobility) places him comfortably in the great tradition of American social criticism, and at the same time renders him respectable and harmless—because, after all, the critique of suburbia is essentially a "cultural" critique, not a political or economic one rife with agitational implications. The critic identifies himself by his criticism with culture and taste but at the same time he does not expose himself to the retaliations of powerful political and economic interests, precisely because his criticism constitutes no direct threat to them.[25] Indeed, it may be, as Edward Shils has suggested, that a "cultural" critique is all that is possible today from a left-wing point of view, and certainly the critique of mass culture.[26]

But in spite of the string of symbolic epithets that identifies suburbia as the citadel of standardization and vulgarization and conformity, suburbia is testimony to the fact that Americans are living better than ever before. One of the points of this book is to emphasize that this is true not only for white-collar people, but for blue-collar, frayed collar, and turned collar people, also. Today, a family which does not live in a slum is paying upward of 85 or 90 dollars a month in rent, and for this or only slightly more, one can "buy" a new tract home in the suburbs. There is an irony, therefore, in the venom that left-wing cities inject into their discussions of suburbia (as well as of popular culture), not only because Marx himself was aware that a certain level of material satisfaction and leisure were prerequisite to the "leap into freedom," but because, like the criticism of popular culture which Shills has noted, the criticism of suburbia tends to become a criticism of industrialization, "rationality," and "progress," and thus brings these critics quite close to the classic conservatives, whose critique of industrialization was also made in terms of its "cultural" consequences.[27] It is almost as if left-wing social critics feared the seduction of the working class by pie not in the sky, not even on the table, but in the freezer.

By accepting the myth of suburbia, the liberal and left-wing critics are placed in the ideologically weak position of haranguing the suburbanites precisely for the meaninglessness they attribute to the very criteria of their success. The critic waves the prophet's long and accusing finger and warns: "You may *think* you're happy, you smug and prosperous striver, but I tell you that the anxieties of status mobility are too much; they impoverish you psychologically, they alienate you from your family"; and so on. And the suburbanite looks at his new house, his new car, his new freezer, his lawn and patio, and, to be sure, his good credit, and scratches his head, bewildered. The critic appears as the eternal crotchet, the professional malcontent telling the prosperous that their prosperity, the visible symbols of which surround them, is an illusion: the economic victory of capitalism is culturally Pyrrhic.[28] "Middle-class" symbols have for so long been identified with the enemies of the labor movement, socialism, and the working class, that relatively high standards of living may tend to be perceived as evidence of the disappearance of a real working class instead of as *conditions* capable of generating a consciousness of collective achievement which is worth fighting to preserve.

NOTES

1. In 1953, for example, *Fortune* reported that suburban population had increased by 75 per cent over 1934, although total population was increasing by only 25 per cent; between 1947 and 1953 the increase was 43 per cent. See "The New Suburban Market," *Fortune* (November, 1953), p. 234. That this trend is continuing is indicated by a recent Census Bureau report showing that between 1950 and 1956 the population of suburbs increased by 29.3 per cent, although their central cities gained by only 4.7 per cent. For a full discussion of this whole tendency, see Donald Bogue, *Population Growth in Standard Metropolitan Areas, 1900–1950,* especially pp. 18–19, tables 13 and 14, p. 30, and table 19, p. 34.

2. Edmund deS. Brunner and Wilbur C. Hallenbeck, *American Society: Urban and Rural Patterns,* p. 253.

3. See Frederick Lewis Allen's classification of the five stages of suburbanization in "The Big Change in Suburbia, Part I." For some pungent commentaries on the early periods of Suburbanization in this century, see H. A. Bridgman, "The Suburbanite"; Lewis Mumford, "The Wilderness of Suburbia"; H. I. Phillips, "The 7:58 Loses a Passenger"; Christine Frederick, "Is Suburban Living a Delusion?" and Ethel Swift, "In Defense of Suburbia." For the beginnings of suburbanization, see Carl Bridenbaugh, *Cities in Revolt: Urban Life in America, 1743–1776,* p. 24.

4. Some of the more recent work includes: J. Allen Beegle, "Characteristics of Michigan's Fringe Population"; Noel P. Gist, "Developing Patterns of Urban Decentralization"; Chauncey Harris, "Suburbs"; Lewis W. Jones, "The Hinterland Reconsidered"; Leo F. Schnore, "The Functions of Metropolitan Suburbs"; Leo F. Schnore, "Satellites and Suburbs"; Leo F. Schnore, "The Growth of Metropolitan Suburbs." See also Walter T. Martin, *The Rural-Urban Fringe.*

5. See, for example, William H. Whyte's famous series of articles, later revised and reprinted as Part VII of his *The Organization Man;* Harry Henderson, "The Mass-Produced Suburbs, Part I," and "The Mass- Produced Suburbs, Part II: Rugged American Collectivism"; Frederick Lewis Allen, "The Big Change in Suburbia, Part I," and "The Big Change in Suburbia, Part II: Crisis in the Suburbs"; John Keats, *The Crack in the Picture Window;* Carl von Rhode, "The Suburban Mind"; William Newman, "Americans in Subtopia," and Maurice Stein, "Suburbia, A Walk on the Mild Side"; and Phyllis McGinley, "Suburbia, Of Thee I sing." Some of the exceptions, that is, work by sociologists, include John Seeley, *et al.; Crestwood Heights* . . . ; Sylvia Fava, "Suburbanism as a Way of Life"; David Riesman, "The Suburban Dislocation"; Nathan Whetten, "Suburbanization as a Field for Sociological Research"; Ritchie Lowry, "Toward a Sociology of Suburbia"; and the early works by Harlan P. Douglass, *The Suburban Trend,* and George Lundberg, *et al., Leisure: A Suburban Study;* William Dobriner (ed.), *The Suburban Community.* The following references were published too late for consideration here: Andrew M. Greeley, *The Church and the Suburbs,* New York, 1959; Albert I. Gordon, *Jews in Suburbia,* Boston, 1959; Robert C. Wood, *Suburbia, Its People and Their Politics,* Boston, 1959; Thomas Ktsanes and Leonard Reissman, "Suburbia-New Homes for Old Values," *Social Problems,* Winter, 1959–1960.

6. David Riesman comments in a melancholy vein that the ecological work on suburbs and the sociopsychological work do not complement each other: ". . . the characteristic situation in sociology today [is] that research in the macrocosmic and in the microcosmic scarcely connect, scarcely inform each other." David Riesman, *op. cit.,* p. 125.

7. The following characterization is a distillation of the literature cited in footnote 5, above. Since what follows is essentially a sketch, the literature, in general, will not be cited. Detailed and specific references to this literature *will* be made, however, in appropriate places in succeeding chapters. In a sense, what follows is more than a sketch; it is really a *definition* of "suburbia," for though there is no standard definition of "suburb" in any rigorous sense (see Brunner and Hallenback, *op. cit.,* p. 255), "suburbia" almost universally implies a *tract housing development* within commuting distance of a large city. We will use the terms "suburb" to refer to tract housing developments within standard metropolitan areas and "suburbia" to refer to the kind of life that is said to be led in them. We suggest, however, that commuting is an irrelevant aspect of the definition.

8. Harry Henderson, "The Mass-Produced Suburbs, Part II: Rugged American Collectivism," p. 84.

9. William Whyte has a way of making the phrase "urban ward" resound with connotations of poverty, deprivation, soot, and brick—as if "urban ward" were a synonym for "slum."

10. "In a single suburb of Chicago, for example, you can buy ranch houses that cost $10,000 or $65,000 just a few hundred yards apart." Russell Lynes, *The Tastemakers,* p. 253. $7,000 was the original price for homes in Levittown, Long Island.

11. The articles by Carl von Rhode and Phyllis McGinley, cited earlier, clearly evoke the image of a Connecticut town on Long Island Sound. It is perhaps all to the good that this kind of suburb has recently been designated an "exurb." See A. C. Spectorsky's diverting book, *The Exurbanites.*

12. See "The New Suburban Market," p. 129. See also Carl von Rhode, *op. cit.,* p. 294; Walter T. Martin, "The Structuring of Social Relationships Engendered by Suburban Residence"; and George Lundberg, *et al., Leisure: A Suburban Study,* p. 47.

13. In 1954, *Time* reported, ". . . now industry is seeking the country too, looking for large tracts of open land to build efficient one-story plants. Of 2,658 plants built in the New York area from 1946 to 1951 only 593 went up in the city proper." *Time,* "Flight to the Suburbs," (March 22, 1954), p. 102. For more detailed reports of this trend see Evelyn Kitagawa and Donald Bogue, *Suburbanization of Manufacturing Activities within Standard Metropolitan Areas.* For tertiary industry, see Raymond Cuzzort, *Suburbanization of Service Industries within Standard Metropolitan Areas,* and James D. Tarver, "Suburbanization of Retail Trade in the Standard Metropolitan Areas of the U.S., 1948–1954."

14. What this means, of course, is that increasing numbers of factory workers will be living in suburbs—not necessarily satellite industrial cities, but new tract suburbs. Woodbury has noted that the decline in the proportion of production workers in cities has

been matched by increases in suburban areas of the same cities. See Coleman Woodbury, "Suburbanization and Suburbia," p. 7.

15. Webster still prefers to define "commuter" as someone who travels by way of a commutation ticket.

16. The same fears for massification and conformity were felt regarding these urban neighborhoods as are now felt for the mass-produced suburbs. See Riesman, "The Suburban Dislocation," p. 123.

17. Suburbanization, of course, has not only occurred around our largest cities, but around smaller ones as well: ". . . with the exception of a general tendency for SMA's of one million inhabitants or more to grow at a slightly less rapid rate than SMA's smaller than this, there has been no pronounced or consistent trend for rates of total metropolitan growth to vary with size. . . ." Quoted by Woodbury, op. cit., from Bogue, op. cit. David Riesman has observed, "so far as I can see we know almost nothing about the suburbs (old or new) surrounding the smaller cities." David Riesman, op. cit., p. 124.

18. The Toronto study is frankly a study of a wealthy suburb and is, without doubt, quite reliable. The unanimity about well-studied Park Forest also lends credence to its portrayal. However, Levittown, New York, and Lakewood, California, are more ambiguous cases. One sharp resident of Levittown writes me that suburb is not *only* white collar, but contains plenty of "blue collar, frayed collar, and turned collar people also," and that the different groups have different ways of life. The vast Lakewood development is heavily populated with southern California aircraft workers, and there is considerable doubt that *Newsweek's* report on Lakewood, so heavily laden with the mobility motif, took adequate account of them.

19. Why have Park Forest and Levittown been studied and commented on *so much?* Is it only because Chicago and New York are centers of research personnel and facilities? Is it because Chicago and New York are centers of the mass media? Is the myth of suburbia one more example of the identification of "New York culture" with American culture? These are questions worth pursuing.

20. With striking insight, Harold Rosenberg has observed that "What is remarkable about the manufacture of myths in the twentieth century is that is takes place under the noses of living witnesses of the actual events and, in fact, cannot dispense with their collaboration." Harold Rosenberg, *The Tradition of the New*, p. 221.

21. Certainly, suburban self-consciousness is a recent development (together with the myth); as late as 1946, Carl von Rhode was able to say, ". . . the growth of the suburb . . . is one of the remarkable phenomena of our time—and one of which, unfortunately, the suburbanite himself is generally unaware." "The Suburban Mind," *Harper's* (April, 1946), p. 289. Certainly this is no longer true.

22. See David Riesman's Introduction to John R. Seeley, *et al., Crestwood Heights: A Study of the Culture of Suburban Life*, p. vii.

23. See William H. Whyte, Jr., *The Organization Man*, chapter 25.

24. For example, ". . . out on the suburban frontiers, they are creating a new social order of their own. It is a modern, up-to-date social order, tailored with white-button-down oxford shirts, bow ties, and flannel suits." Louis Harris, *Is There a Republican Majority?* p. 137.

25. The "proletarian literature" of the 1930's had, at the very least, a specific and concrete villain. After reading a proletarian novel or poem of this period, one could at least come away hating the bloated and exploiting "capitalist." Much of the art of the "beat generation" is proletarian too, but the villain has become blurred and diffuse. One comes away hating "them," but who "they" are remains indistinct. For this reason, the mass media can afford to be tolerant and mildly satirical of the "beat generation," whereas the frankly revolutionary literature of the earlier period had to be dealt with more harshly. The Luce magazines, for example, have been prominent also in the satirical treatment of the culture of suburbia—though at the same time emphasizing the great advancements in the standard of living it represents.

26. See Edward A. Shils, "Daydreams and Nightmares: Reflections on the Criticism of Mass Culture," pp. 587–608.

27. Exceptions are Disraeli, the early Churchill, and a few other English conservatives, who tried to unite the gentry and the working classes against the middle classes. See,

for example, Peter Viereck's discussion of this in *Conservatism, from John Adams to Churchill,* pp. 42–45.

28. A typical example of this view is Erich Fromm's discussion of Park Forest in *The Sane Society,* pp. 152–162.

ANNOTATED BIBLIOGRAPHY

Brown, Claude. (1965) *Manchild in the Promised Land.* New York: Signet.
An autobiography of growing up in the Harlem of junkies and storefront salvation. Well written.

Gans, Herbert J. (1967) *The Levittowners.* New York: Vintage.
This is a study of the first residents of Levittown, New Jersey, and their organization of the community's political and social systems. A mild defense of bland lower-middle-class life styles.

Gans, Herbert J. (1962) *The Urban Villagers.* New York: Free Press.
A participant-observation of the West End of Boston that emphasizes the persistence of the Italian peasant class, culture, and social life patterns in the heart of the metropolis.

Harrington, Michael. (1963) *The Other America.* New York: Macmillan.
This short volume shocked the affluent society of the 1960s with the realization that the nation had an invisible land of almost fifty million poor. This book has been credited with sparking the development of the war on poverty.

Keller, Suzanne. (1968) *The Urban Neighborhood.* New York: Random House.
A sociological examination of the role of neighbor, the concept of neighboring, and neighborhood activities and relationships written expressly for the urban planner.

Liebow, Eliot. (1966) *Tally's Corner.* Boston: Little, Brown.
Tally's Corner is an anthropologist's short case study of male streetcorner life in the black ghetto of Washington, D.C. Read the selections on the streetcorner men's physical problems with some caution; some street people of Washington claim Liebow was fooled into believing it.

Malcolm X. (1966) *The Autobiography of Malcolm X.* New York: Grove Press.
A strong, passionate statement of what it means to be black in America by one of the most dynamic leaders of the black revolution. Excellent.

Riesman, David. (1950) *The Lonely Crowd.* New Haven, Conn.: Yale University Press.
The now-famous analysis of the new middle class in terms of traditional, inner- and other-directed social character.

Whyte, William Foote. (1955) *Street Corner Society,* Chicago: University of Chicago Press.
This study of the social structure of an Italian slum neighborhood in Boston has become a minor sociological classic. An eighty-two page methodological appendix is even more fascinating than the text itself. The insights on how participant-observation really works should be read by every aspiring sociologist.

Whyte, William H., (1956) *The Organization Man.* New York: Doubleday (Anchor).
The best all-around description of the life styles of the upwardly mobile white-collar worker in the corporation, university, or similar large organization. This book provides an interesting picture of the behavior and aspirations of the so-called silent generation. Part Seven, "The New Suburbia: Organization Man at Home," is particularly relevant.

Wolfe, Tom. (1968) *The Pump House Gang.* New York: Random House.
Wolfe's shrewd and satiric observations on the underside of the social scene. Wildly funny and frighteningly perceptive pieces on status seekers, Hugh Hefner, beach boys, Marshal McLuhan, and automated Hilton hotels.

(Above) Early pollution on the Mississippi River front at Memphis, Tennessee, 1919. Official photograph of the U.S. Army Engineer District, Memphis. (Left) Oceanhill-Brownsville, New York City, 1967. Photo by Ernie Baxter from Black Star.

In the framework of the evolutionary perspective, every social system contains within it strain points capable of erupting into conflict. Traditionally, sociologists consider these strain points as social problems. The readings in this section examine salient social problems in terms of conflict within existing social structures.

The attempt to label something as a social problem, let alone explain why it occurs, raises ideological, philosophical, and theoretical questions. For example, the approach taken by Presidential commissions on riots and violence, and similar groups usually view urban violence and other forms of social conflict as social problems that require solutions. The picture, however, is more complex than this. Conflict sometimes has the socially beneficial result of providing a balancing mechanism for mediating tensions between groups (*see* Coser, Article 4.2).

Lewis Coser (*see* Article 4.2) argues persuasively that conflict is most likely to have a stabilizing or tension-reducing function in loosely structured pluralistic societies. As he states:

> In loosely structured groups and open societies, conflict, which aims at a resolution of tension between antagonists, is likely to have stabilizing and integrative functions for the relationship. By permitting immediate and direct expression of rival claims, such social systems are able to readjust their structures by eliminating the sources of dissatisfaction. (Coser and Rosenberg, 1964:207)

Rigid social systems, on the other hand, are far less likely to experience conflicts that crisscross one another and in this way prevent deep cleavages in society. Poorly integrated subgroups such as urban blacks living in a rigid social system can escalate their conflict into violence. Rigid social systems with limited options do not easily adapt to new situations.

Riots occurred rather frequently in early American cities, especially where inequitable conditions coexisted with sluggish means for reform and change. Early Boston, for example, was known as the Metropolis of Sedition, and the fury of the mobs greatly disturbed propertied persons of quality and breeding. After one "patriotic" meeting in 1765, the mob, shouting "Liberty and Property," sacked the Lieutenant Governor's mansion to the extent of a loss of £25,000 sterling (Bridenbaugh, 1955:307). From the official viewpoint the situation deteriorated to the point at which in 1768 two regiments of British troops were dispatched to Boston—not to be withdrawn until after five protestors were killed in the 1770 Boston Massacre. The riot that culminated in the patriotic destruction of the famous Boston tea is, of course, known to every schoolboy.

Early American violence, however, was not limited to the Bay Colony. Newporters, angered by the use of the Royal Navy to prevent their lucrative molasses smuggling, were in constant conflict with royal authorities. The fury of the people led to a series of confrontations, frequently accompanied by burning and destruction of property.

In the 1970s, as was the case in the 1770s, pleas for a return to peace and tranquillity are misleading. The assumption that all we have to do is solve the present problem and everything will return to peace and quiet is not only naïve, but it is also socially dangerous, or, in Dahrendorf's word, utopian. As Section One illustrates, the normalcy of the past is largely an illusion of the present. The nation was settled by dissenters who resented traditional forms of authority. On numerous occasions, colonial conflict took the form of violence, the Revolutionary War being the ultimate example. Alexis de Tocqueville, a most perceptive early observer of America, was quick to note the relation between city size and potential for conflict. Almost a century and a half ago he wrote:

> The United States have no metropolis, but they already contain several very large cities. Philadelphia reckoned 161,000 inhabitants and New York 202,000 in the year 1830. The lower orders which inhabit these cities constitute a rabble even more formidable than the populace of European towns. They consist of freed blacks in the first place, who are condemned by the laws and by public opinion to a hereditary state of misery and degradation. They also contain a multitude of Europeans who have been driven to the shores of the New World by their misfortunes or their misconduct; and these men inoculate the United States with all our vices, without bringing with them any of those interests which counteract their baneful influence. As inhabitants of a country where they have no civil rights, they are ready to turn all the passions which agitate the community to their own advantage; thus, within the last few months serious riots have broken out in Philadelphia and in New York. Disturbances of this kind are unknown in the rest of the country, which is nowise alarmed by them, because the population of the cities has hitherto exercised neither power nor influence over the rural districts. Nevertheless, I look upon the size of certain American cities, and especially on the nature of their population, as a real danger which threatens the future security of the democratic republics of the New World; and I venture to predict that they will perish from this circumstance unless the government succeeds in creating an armed force, which, whilst it remains under the control of the majority of the nation, will be independent of the town population, and able to repress its excesses. (de Tocqueville, 1961:342)

Today conflict and violence are no less important as elements of social change than they were in the past. Conflict should not always be viewed as a pathology or aberration of the social order, since it has the positive function of preventing ossification of a society by exerting pressure for either adjustment among institutions or innovation of new structural relations. George Simmel, for example, stated:

The sociological significance of conflict (Kampf) has in principle never been disputed. Conflict is admitted to cause or modify interest groups, unifications, organizations. . . . it itself is a form of sociation [sic]. (Simmel, 1955:13)

Both conflict and order are correlative aspects of social reality. H. L. Nieburg, whose work we have included (*see* Article 4.3), explicitly acknowledges this relationship when he says that "conflict is probably inevitable in social life, just as is the search for order and stability."

Violence or the threat of violence should also be anticipated, particularly in urban settings. As black spokesman H. Rap Brown put it, "Violence is as American as cherry pie."

Article Overview

It is extremely difficult to adequately conceptualize the meaning of social conflict. We generally tend to express it in terms of the manifestations a conflict takes, for example, violence. Urban violence is a central concern of contemporary urban dwellers, probably because its potential has been realized on many occasions.

Articles 4.2, 4.3, and 4.4 deal exclusively with urban violence, and, in so doing, attempt to conceptualize the reality of social conflict. Lewis Coser's discussion of social change (Article 4.2) explicitly emphasizes the functional role played by violence. He knowingly plays down its disruptive (dysfunctional) aspects in order to concentrate on such positive functions of violence as a form of achievement, as a danger signal, and as a catalyst. This is a legitimate and useful viewpoint, although it is only one side of the picture. The other side, as we know, is far less attractive; the response that violence often produces is counterviolence and repression.

H. L. Nieburg (Article 4.3) further explores the role played by conflict and violence within the institutional mechanisms of the modern industrial state. He focuses on the political and racially oriented violence of the late 1960s and early 1970s. Conflict between powerful forces, he says, is extant in every community, and the resolution of these conflicts is ultimately summarized in political, legal, and other social institutions. However, the continuing presence of competing forms and the breakdown of arrangements must inevitably raise the question of institutional viability.

Nieburg distinguishes between frictional and political violence. Frictional violence is that which is inherent in all social systems and thus is a normal state of affairs. Political violence, on the other hand, challenges the very system of norms that police power is designed to protect. It emanates from deep grievances that cause protestors to commit spontaneous or even recurring and deliberate acts of violence. Nieburg argues that for political violence to become a normal, inherent form of conflict there must be evidence that it is worth its great risks. If so, then political violence will be a form of social bargaining. While a strong critic of the present system, Nieburg still works within it. Fully recognizing the bankruptcy of current policies, he retains faith in "the ultimate efficacy of political solutions."

The piece by Flaming and Palen (Article 4.4) empirically examines some of the points raised by Coser and Nieburg, and presents a perspective that provides some balance for the various views of violence. In studying the efficacy of violence as a mechanism of social change, the authors attempt to place the thesis of the positive function of violence in a broader historical perspective. They review previous riot studies, and include empirical work of their own regarding the aftereffects of the Milwaukee riot of 1967. Flaming and Palen conclude that negative effects of violence clearly outweigh any positive gains. Thus, the utility of violence as a means of positive social change can be questioned.

Considerations of violence are bound to raise the question of the distribution of power within the urban structure. Power is always unevenly distributed within any organization. Some organizations have greater power than others because (1) they control scarce resources, (2) they occupy organizational positions that facilitate the exercise of authority; (3) they are better organized; (4) they are willing to use force to achieve their ends; and (5) they possess an ideology or belief system that legitimizes their rule.

The questions of what groups have power in the metropolitan area and how it is exercised has become a major interest of both sociologists and political scientists. During recent decades, two schools of thought have emerged regarding community power structure. The first theory describes the pyramidal nature of urban area power relationships, and assigns to the economic sector the dominant position in the decision-making process, hence the powerlessness of elected officials. The second theory usually finds that American community power structures, to the extent that they exist at all, are highly pluralistic. Thus, as the argument goes, the economic sector does not dominate in policy-making, and local political officeholders exert considerable influence.

Edward Banfield and James Wilson (Article 4.5) describe research on the so-called informal power structure; that is, those influentials who occupy no formal governmental office but can change things if they so choose. Banfield and Wilson question the decision-making power and influence of these economic and civic elites, which leads us to describe these authors as conservative, conservatism here being a belief that economic elites play a relatively minor role in community decision-making. (*See* Annotated Bibliography at the end of Section Four for studies arguing community dominance by economic elites.)

The selections by Lowe (4.6), Rainwater (4.7), and Kozol (4.8) are problem-oriented. All three discuss the breakdown of institutional arrangements for meeting basic societal needs. All three imply that unmet needs underlie urban violence. Jeanne Lowe concentrates on the basic problem of housing, detailing the failures of post-World War II urban-renewal and public-housing programs (the power structure's answer to the housing problem for low-income groups). The failure of these programs has caused the poor to place an increasing reliance on direct-action techniques, such as rent strikes and political violence (*see also* Section Five).

Lee Rainwater's article converges on the psychological and social problems created by inadequate housing. He contrasts the housing needs and values of low-income families with those of working- and middle-class families. In the former case, simple physical safety is the overriding concern, while in the latter housing becomes an extension of one's personality and self.

Jonathan Kozol, like Rainwater, concentrates on that segment of the population where basic institutional arrangements have most obviously failed. Kozol's descriptions of the psychological violence done by the Boston school system to inner-city children suggest the bankruptcy of this segment of the public school system as a viable social institution. The school's crumbling and decaying physical facilities closely parallel the deterioration of its social and educational system. Given this shadow of an educational system, it is much easier to understand Cupid's "education" as a Vice Lord (*see* Article 3.5).

Conclusion

Most Americans are accustomed to viewing problems in biographical or psychological terms. This sentiment is voiced by C. Wright Mills: "Men do not usually define the troubles they endure in terms of historical change and institutional contradiction." (Mills, 1959:3). Our perspective, however, views social problems from a structural rather than from a biographical framework.

This approach to the study of social problems means that one is more likely to emphasize change over stability and conflict over equilibrium. Such a perspective is congruent with the evolutionary P.O.E.T. framework. Equally important, it has significant implications for problem solving, covered in Section Five.

REFERENCES

Bridenbaugh, Carl. (1955) *Cities in Revolt*. New York: Knopf.
Coser, Lewis A., and Bernard Rosenberg. (1964) *Sociological Theory*. New York: Macmillan.
Mills, Wright C. (1959) *Sociological Imagination*. London: Oxford.
Simmel, George. (1955) *Conflict and the Web of Group Affiliations*. Translated by Kurt Wolf. New York: Free Press.
de Tocqueville, Alexis. (1961) *Democracy in America*. Translated by H. Reeve. New York: Schocken.

4.2 SOME SOCIAL FUNCTIONS OF VIOLENCE

LEWIS A. COSER

The folklore of psychology has it that animals in experimental studies display systematically different behavioral characteristics depending on the investigator. Rats described by American observers are seen as frenetically active, given to a great deal of motor activity, forever dashing in and out of mazes, always trying to get somewhere—though not always certain of exactly where. In contrast, experimental animals seen through the lenses of German investigators, apes, for example, seem given to long and intense periods of pensive deliberation and musing cogitation.

This jest highlights an important truth. There *are* systematic differences in the ways a particular scholarly community at a given moment in time chooses to approach the manifold data with which it is confronted. In sociology, for example, even if most American social theorists would readily agree in the abstract that conflict as well as order, tension as well as harmony, violence as well as peaceful adjustment characterize all social systems in varying degrees, social theory actually has settled mainly for a remarkably tame and domesticated view of the social world. This is so despite the fact that European social thinkers such as Marx, Weber, and Simmel, upon whose works so much of American theorizing depends for its inspiration, had an entirely different orientation.

It seems as if American social science, developing in a society which, its birth through revolution notwithstanding, has only known one major internal upheaval throughout its history, has failed to be sensitized to the pervasive effects of violence, conflict, and disorder which to the European thinker were facts that they could not but be acquainted with intimately. While to the European thinker the fragility of the social fabric and the brittleness of social bonds seemed self-evident experiences, American social science proceeded from a world view in which social violence was at best seen as a pathological phenomenon. As Arnold Feldman has recently argued:

> Violence is conceived as being *incidental* to the basic character of social structures and processes. Indeed the very conception of social structure ordinarily excludes the source of structural destruction.[1]

From Lewis A. Coser, "Some Social Functions of Violence," *The Annals of the American Academy of Political and Social Science,* Vol. 304 (March 1966). Reprinted by permission of the author and the American Academy of Political and Social Science.

As long as American sociology confined its attention mainly to a limited view of the contemporary American scene, its neglect of conflict and violence was, perhaps, none too disabling, at least until recently. But at present, when sociology has happily awakened to the need of doing comparative studies of social structures in both geographical space and historical time, this domesticated vision of the social world can be severely hampering. In addition, it seems that even the proper study of American society can no longer profit from exclusive emphasis on models and constructs in which conflict and violence are deliberately or unwittingly minimized. Just as analyses of, say, contemporary South Africa, Latin America, or Southeast Asia, or of seventeenth-century England or nineteenth-century France, would be patently unrealistic if they ignored the functions of political violence, so it has become increasingly evident that such ignoring would be just as unrealistic in the study of the current racial scene in the United States.

For a number of years I have urged a correcting of the traditional balance in theoretical and empirical emphasis in studies of social conflict and social order and have suggested that it is high time to tilt the scale in the direction of greater attention to social conflict.[2] Though much of my work was more generally concerned with the wider topic of social conflict rather than with the somewhat narrower area of social violence, a number of propositions previously advanced apply to violence as well. There is no need, therefore, to reiterate them in this paper. Instead, I shall focus selectively on but a few functions of social violence: violence as a form of achievement, violence as a danger signal, and violence as a catalyst. It is to be understood that this is by no means an exhaustive list of the functions of violence, nor will its dysfunctions be dealt with in this paper.

Violence as Achievement

Certain categories of individuals are so located in the social structure that they are barred from legitimate access to the ladder of achievement, as Merton has argued in convincing detail.[3] Moreover, as Cloward and Ohlin[4] have shown more recently, certain categories of persons may find themselves in structural positions which effectively prevent them from utilizing not only legitimate channels of opportunity but criminal and illegitimate channels as well. I shall argue that when all such channels are barred, violence may offer alternate roads to achievement.

Cloward and Ohlin take as a case in point adolescents in disorganized urban areas who are oriented toward achieving higher positions and yet lack access to either conventional or criminal opportunity structures. "These adolescents," they argue,

> seize upon the manipulation of violence as a route to status not only because it provides a way of expressing pent-up angers and frustrations but also because they are not cut off from access to violent means by vicissitudes of birth. In the world of violence, such attributes as race, socioeconomic position, age, and the like are irrelevant; personal worth is judged on the basis of qualities that are available to all who would cultivate them. The acquisition of status is not simply a consequence of skill in the use of violence or

of physical strength but depends, rather, on one's willingness to risk injury or death in the search for "rep."[5]

In the area of violence, then, ascriptive status considerations become irrelevant. Here, the vaunted equal opportunity, which had been experienced as a sham and a lure everywhere else, turns out to be effective. In the wilderness of cities, just as in the wilderness of the frontier, the gun becomes an effective equalizer. Within the status structure of the gang, through a true transvaluation of middle-class values, success in defense of the "turf" brings deference and "rep" which are unavailable anywhere else. Here the successful exercise of violence is a road to achievement.

Nor need we rest consideration with the case of juvenile delinquency. One can make the more general assertion that in all those situations in which both legitimate and illegitimate socioeconomic achievement seems blocked, recourse to aggressive and violent behavior may be perceived as a significant area of "achievement." This may help to explain the ideal of *machismo* in the lower classes of Latin America. Here, as in the otherwise very different violence in disorganized urban areas of American cities, men tend to feel that only prowess in interpersonal violence or in aggressive sexual encounters allows the achievement of personal identity and permits gaining otherwise unavailable deference. Where no social status can be achieved through socioeconomic channels it may yet be achieved in the show of violence among equally deprived peers.

Somewhat similar mechanisms may be at work in the intrafamilial aggression and violence of American lower-class fathers. These men tend to compensate for inadequate rewards in the occupational world at large by an aggressive assertion of male superiority within the little world of the family—as Donald McKinley has recently argued with much cogency.[6] The disproportionately high rate of interpersonal violence among Negro males may yield to a similar explanation. Since Negroes are assigned lowest position in all three major dimensions of the American status system—ethnicity, class, and education—and since their mobility chances are nil in the first and minimal in the second and third, it stands to reason that achievement in the area of interpersonal violence might be seen as a channel leading to self-regard and self-enhancement—at least as long as conflict with the dominant white majority seems socially unavailable as a means of collective action. This does not preclude that violent acting out may not also at the same time call forth a feeling of self-hatred for acting in the stereotypical manner in which the Negro is accused of acting by the dominant white.

Revolutionary violence, both in the classical revolutions of the past and in the anticolonialist liberation movements of the present, can also be understood in this manner. Participation in such violence offers opportunity to the oppressed and downtrodden for affirming identity and for claiming full manhood hitherto denied to them by the powers that be. Participation in revolutionary violence offers the chance for the first act of participation in the polity, for entry into the world of active citizenship. In addition, participation in acts of violence symbolizes commitment to the revolutionary cause. It marks to the actor, but also to his circle, the irrevocable decision to reject the *ancien régime* and to claim allegiance to the revolutionary movement.

This has been well described by the late Frantz Fanon, an active participant in the Algerian movement of liberation and one of its most powerful ideological spokesmen. "For colonial man," he writes,

> violence incarnates absolute *praxis*. . . . The questions asked of militants by the organization are marked by this vision of things. "Where did you work? With whom? What have you done?" The group demands that the individual commits an irreversible deed. In Algeria, for example, where almost all of the men who called for the struggle of national liberation were condemned to death or pursued by the French police, confidence in a man was proportional to the degree of severity of his [police] case. A new militant was considered reliable when he could no longer return to the colonial system. It seems that this mechanism was at play among the Mau Mau in Kenya where it was required that each member of the group strike the victim. Hence everyone was personally responsible for the victim's death. . . . Violence once assumed permits those who have left the group to return to their place and to be reintegrated. Colonial man liberates himself in and through violence.[7]

The act of violence, in other words, commits a man symbolically to the revolutionary movement and breaks his ties with his previous life and its commitments. He is reborn, so to speak, through the act of violence and is now in a position to assume his rightful place in the revolutionary world of new men.

Similar considerations may also account for the otherwise puzzling fact that women, normally much less given to violence than men, have played leading roles in classical revolutionary movements and in such modern liberation movements as that of Algeria. Here one may suggest that situations where the old norms have broken down differ significantly from normatively stable situations. In the latter, women, having internalized the acceptance of their lower status relative to men, tend to have low rates of active violence. Their suicide as well as their homicide rates are much lower than those of men. Being more sheltered in their lower status positions, women tend to have less motivation for aggression whether directed toward self or toward others. The situation is different, however, when the old norms are challenged, as in revolutions. Here many observers have noted high female participation rates in violent crowds and in street riots. In certain key revolutionary events, such as the March to Versailles of October 1790, and in later food riots, women were predominant. Writes the foremost student of revolutionary crowds, George Rudé, "On the morning of October 5 the revolt started simultaneously in the central markets and the Faubourg Saint-Antoine; in both cases women were the leading spirits."[8]

Revolutionary situations topple the status order and allow underdogs to aspire to equal participation. They provide the occasion for women to act like men. It is as if women were to say to themselves:

> If all these extraordinary actions have become possible, then it is perhaps permissible to entertain the extraordinary idea that women need no longer accept their inferior status and can aspire to achieve a hitherto unattainable equality.

Here, as in all the other cases considered, violence equalizes and opens to the participants access to hitherto denied areas of achievement.[9]

Violence as a Danger Signal

The late Norbert Wiener once remarked that cancer is so peculiarly dangerous a disease because it typically develops through its early stages without causing pain. Most other diseases, by eliciting painful sensations in the body, bring forth bodily signals which allow early detection of the illness and its subsequent treatment. Pain serves as an important mechanism of defense, permitting the medical readjustment of bodily balance which has been attacked by disease. It seems hardly far-fetched to apply this reasoning to the body social as well.

A social dysfunction can, of course, be attended to only if it becomes visible, if not to the total community, at least to certain more sensitive and more powerful sectors of it. But the sensitive usually lack power, and the powerful often lack sensitivity. As Merton has phrased the issue, there are latent social problems, "conditions which are . . . at odds with values of the group but are not recognized as being so,"[10] which can become manifest, and hence subject to treatment, only when particular groups or individuals choose to take cognizance of them. Merton urges that it is the task of the sociologist to make latent social problems manifest; at the same time he stresses that

> those occupying strategic positions of authority and power of course carry more weight than others in deciding social policy and so . . . in identifying for the rest what are to be taken as significant departures from social standards.[11]

Granted that the social perceptions of those in power and authority may be influenced by social scientists calling attention to previously neglected problems, it would be an indulgence in unwarranted Comtean optimism to assume that such enlightenment will at times be sufficient to alert them. It is at this point that the signaling functions of social violence assume importance.

Although there are individual, subcultural, and class variations in the internalized management and control of anger in response to frustration, I take it to be axiomatic that human beings—other than those systematically trained to use legitimate or illegitimate violence—will resort to violent action only under extremely frustrating, ego-damaging, and anxiety-producing conditions. It follows that if the incidence of violence increases rapidly, be it in the society at large or within specific sectors of it, this can be taken as a signal of severe maladjustment. I would further suggest that this signal is so drastic, so extremely loud, that it cannot fail to be perceived by men in power and authority otherwise not noted for peculiar sensitivity to social ills. This is not to say, of course, that they will necessarily respond with types of social therapy that will effectively remove the sources of infection. But I suggest that outbreaks of social violence are more apt than other less visible or sensitive indicators at least to lead them to perceive the problem.

To be sure, outbreaks of violence can be seen as mere manifestations of underlying conditions. Yet, perhaps because of this, they may lead power-holders to effect a change in these conditions. Two illustrations will have to suffice. Conventional historical and sociological wisdom has it that the British Chartist movement of the first half of the last century and the often violent and destructive popular movements which preceded it were but manifestations of temporary imbalances brought by the Industrial Revolution upon the British social and political scene. These imbalances, it is argued, were progressively eliminated through a variety of social structural changes, more particularly through an increase in structural differentiation which gradually provided the homeostatic forces that led to the restabilization of British society in the second part of the nineteenth century.[12] In this view, Chartism was a symptom of a temporary pathological condition, and its defeat highlighted the return to equilibrium and stability.

This view seems to be seriously deficient, if for no other reason than that it ignores the impact of Chartism and related movements on the political decision-makers. It ignores, in other words, the determining contribution of this movement. Far from being but an epiphenomenal manifestation of temporary maladjustment, Chartism had a direct impact by leading to a series of reform measures alleviating the conditions against which it had reacted. Violence and riots were not merely protests: they were claims to be considered. Those involved in them assumed that the authorities would be sensitive to demands and would make concessions. And it turned out that they were right.[13]

Historians will hardly deny that the condition of the laboring poor, and more particularly the industrial working class, between the beginning of the Industrial Revolution and the middle of the nineteenth century was appalling. Nor is it subject to debate that for a long time these conditions were barely perceived by those in power. Finally, it is not to be doubted that legislative remedies, from factory legislation to the successive widening of the franchise and the attendant granting of other citizenship rights to members of the lower classes,[14] came, at least in part, in response to the widespread disorders and violent outbreaks that marked the British social scene for over half a century. Let me quote from Mark Hovell, one of the earliest, and still one of the best, of the historians of the Chartist movement. "The Chartists," he writes:

> first compelled attention to the hardness of the workmen's lot, and forced thoughtful minds to appreciate the deep gulf between the two nations which lived side by side without knowledge of or care for each other. Though remedy came slowly and imperfectly, and was seldom directly from Chartist hands, there was always the Chartist impulse behind the first timid steps toward social and economic betterment. The cry of the Chartists did much to force public opinion to adopt the policy of factory legislation in the teeth of the opposition of the manufacturing interests. It compelled the administrative mitigation of the harshness of the New Poor Law. It swelled both the demand and necessity for popular education. It prevented the unqualified victory of the economic gospel of the Utilitarians. . . . The whole trend of modern social legislation must well have gladdened the hearts of the ancient survivors of Chartism.[15]

The often violent forms of rebellion of the laboring poor, the destructiveness of the city mobs, and other forms of popular disturbances which mark English social history from the 1760's to the middle of the nineteenth century, helped to educate the governing elite of England, Whig and Tory alike, to the recognition that they could ignore the plight of the poor only at their own peril. These social movements constituted among other things an effective signaling device which sensitized the upper classes to the need for social reconstruction in defense of a social edifice over which they wished to continue to have over-all command.[16]

My second example concerning violence as a danger signal will be brief since it deals with recent experiences still vivid in social memory: the civil rights movement and the war against poverty. The plight of the American Negro and of the urban poor until recently had a very low degree of visibility for the bulk of the white population and the decision-makers on the American scene. Much of it was physically not visible in the sense that it took place in segregated areas not customarily visited by "good people." Much of it, on the other hand, though physically visible, was yet not socially perceived. The sociology of social perception, a sociology elucidating why people sometimes look and why they sometimes look away, it may be remarked in passing, still is to be written. Be that as it may, the shock of recognition, the jolt to conscience, occurred only when the Negroes, through by-and-large nonviolent action in the South and through increasingly violent demonstrations and even riots in the North, brought the problem forcibly to the attention of white public opinion and the white power structure. To be sure, a whole library of books has been written on the dehumanizing consequences of the racial caste system. Yet all this became a public issue only after a number of large-scale social conflicts, beginning in Montgomery, Alabama, helped to highlight the issue. No doubt, the slow process of structural differentiation might have taken care of the problem some time in the indeterminate future. In fact, something was done about it here and now mainly because Negroes, no longer satisfied with promises and having gained some advances, now raised their level of expectations, indicating in quite drastic a manner that they were no longer prepared to wait, that they wanted *Freedom Now*. (I shall return to the topic in the last part of this paper.) Much as one might deplore the often senseless violence displayed in such racial riots as those in Los Angeles, one cannot help feeling that they, too, constituted quite effective signaling devices, perhaps desperate cries for help after other appeals had been unavailing. They indicated a sickness in the body social which demands immediate remedy if it is not to undermine social order altogether.

Violence as a Catalyst

Marx once remarked: "The criminal produces an impression now moral, now tragic, and hence renders a 'service' by arousing the moral and aesthetic sentiments of the public." Marx here anticipated by many years similar formulations by Durkheim and Mead stressing the unanticipated functions of crime in creating a sense of solidarity within the community.[17] Here I shall argue a related idea, namely, that not only criminals, but law-enforcing agents also, may call forth a sense of solidarity against their behavior. More particularly, the use of extralegal violence by these officers may, under certain circumstances, lead to the arousal of the community and to a revulsion from societal arrangements that rest upon such enforcement methods.

It is common knowledge that the violence used by sheriffs and other Southern officers of the law against Southern Negroes engaged in protest activities and voting-registration drives has had a major impact upon public opinion and federal legislation. The fact is that such methods had been relied upon by Southern police for a very long time without any marked reaction against them. Why, then, did they suddenly become counterproductive? Two major factors seem to account for this reversal. First, modes of control involving the extralegal uses of violence worked well as long as the acts in question could be committed with a minimum of publicity and visibility. They became suicidal when they were performed under the glare of television cameras and under the observation of reporters for national newspapers and magazines.

Everett Hughes, in discussing the Nazi case, has argued that all societies depend for their maintenance on a certain amount of "dirty work" by shady agents of the powers that be, and he added that such dirty work is usually performed far from the sight of "good people."[18] Indeed, the usefulness of those doing the "dirty work" may well come to an end when it must be performed in full view of "good people." If, as Hughes argues, those who do the dirty work "show a sort of concentrate of those impulses of which we are or wish to be less aware," then it stands to reason that they cease to be useful if they have to operate in full view. The solid middle-class citizen of Nazi Germany seems, by and large, to have been unconcerned with what was being done to the Jews; even the early public degradation of Jews in city streets seems to have left them unaffected. But the Hitler regime showed very good judgment indeed in carefully hiding and camouflaging its later murderous methods. One may doubt that the death camps could have been operated except in secret. Similarly, solid middle-class citizens in both North and South may have been aware of the extralegal uses of violence habitually resorted to by Southern sheriffs and police. Yet as long as such knowledge did not intrude too much in their visual field, they remained unconcerned. Matters changed drastically when these inhuman methods were fully exposed to the public at large. Now visibility could no longer be denied. Had these officials become conscious of the changed circumstances under which they were now forced to operate, they might well have abandoned these methods in favor of more subtle means of intimidation. As it turned out, they were subject to the "trained incapacity" upon which Veblen and Kenneth Burke have commented. They adopted measures in keeping with their past training —and the very soundness of this training led them to adopt the wrong measures. Their past training caused them to misjudge their present situation.[19] The very exercise of violence which had been productive of "order" in the past now produced a wave of public indignation which undermined the very practice.

The matter of publicity, powerfully aided by the recent "communication revolution," though crucially important, is not the only one to be considered here. It is equally relevant to observe that violent tactics of suppression tend to be much less successful when used against people who are publicly committed to the principle of nonviolence. Violence by the police, even extralegal violence, may be approved, or at least condoned, when it can be justified by reference to the supposed actual or potential violence of the offending criminal. That is, such behavior seems to be justified or condoned when there exists, or seems to exist, a rough equivalence between the means used by both sides. A tooth for a tooth tends to be a maxim popularly applicable in these cases. But the matter is very different when the presumed offender is committed in principle to a politics of nonviolence. The nonviolent resisters in the South, as distinct from other cases where nonviolence was not based on principle, had consciously assumed the burden of nonviolence. That is, they had made a commitment to the public not to have recourse to violence. When violence was used against them, this hence came to be seen as a breach of a tacit reciprocal commitment on the part of those they opposed. What is ordinarily perceived as a multilateral relationship in which both sides actually or potentially use violence, came now to be perceived as unilateral violence. This impression was still accentuated when acts of official or semiofficial violence were being directed against ministers, that is, against men who enjoy specific mandates and immunities as men of peace.

For these reasons, extralegal violence habitually used in the South to maintain the caste system turned out to be a most effective triggering device for measures to abolish it. One need, perhaps, not go so far as to argue, as Jan Howard has recently done,[20] that the very effectiveness of the nonviolent methods used depended on the assumption or expectation that it would encounter violent reactions that would arouse the public conscience. The violent reactions did not have to be anticipated. But it was nevertheless one of the latent functions of Southern violent response to the nonviolent tactics used to lead to the arousal of a previously lethargic community to a sense of indignation and revulsion.

Nor is the Southern case unique. Even in earlier periods extralegal violence on the part of law-enforcement agencies has often been suicidal. The Peterloo Massacre of 1819 in Manchester, when a crowd of listeners to speeches on parliamentary reform and the repeal of the Corn Laws was charged by soldiers who killed ten and injured hundreds, became a rallying cry for the reformers and radicals. The wholesale massacre of participants in the French Commune of 1871 created a sense of intimate solidarity, but also of alienation from society at large, among large sectors of the French working class. In these latter cases the impact was not on the total society but only on particular sectors of it, but in all of them the show of violence on the part of officialdom was suicidal in so far as it transformed victims into martyrs who became symbols of the iniquity and callousness of the rulers.

Lest it be understood that I argue that unanticipated and suicidal uses of violence are limited to cases involving law-enforcement agents alone, let me remark, even if only in passing, that there are clearly other groups within society whose resort to violence may under specifiable circumstances bring forth similar suicidal consequences. In particular, when minority groups appeal to the public conscience and attempt to dramatize the fact that they are treated with less than justice and equity, their resort to violence may effectively hamper their cause. They must depend in their appeal on winning to their side previously indifferent and unconcerned sectors of the public. Resort to violence, however, even though it may serve as a danger signal, is also likely to alienate precisely those who are potential recruits for their cause. Hence groups such as the Black Muslims and other extremist Negro organizations may, if they resort to violence, bring about suicidal results by turning previously indifferent or potentially sympathetic bystanders into hostile antagonists.

Conclusion

The preceding discussion has identified and examined a series of cases in which violence may perform latent or manifest functions. The approach was meant to be exploratory and tentative rather than exhaustive and systematic. It is hoped, however, that enough has been said to show that the curiously tender-minded view of the social structure which has generally predominated in American social theory is seriously deficient and needs to be complemented by a more tough-minded approach.

NOTES

1. Arnold S. Feldman, "Violence and Volatility: The Likelihood of Revolution," *Internal War,* ed. Harry Eckstein (New York: Free Press of Glencoe, 1964), p. 111. See also, Ralf Dahrendorf, *Class and Class Conflict in Industrial Society* (Stanford, Calif.: Stanford University Press, 1959) and a series of later papers collected in the author's *Gesellschaft und Freiheit* (Munich: R. Piper, 1961).

2. Lewis A. Coser, *The Functions of Social Conflict* (Glencoe, Ill.: Free Press, 1956); Lewis A. Coser, "Social Conflict and the Theory of Social Change," *British Journal of Sociology,* VIII, 3 (September 1957), pp. 197–207; Lewis A. Coser, "Some Functions of Deviant Behavior and Normative Flexibility," *American Journal of Sociology,* LXVIII, 2 (September 1962), pp. 172–181; Lewis A. Coser, "Violence and the Social Structure," *Violence and War,* Vol. VI of *Science and Psychoanalysis,* ed. Jules Masserman (New York: Grune and Stratton, 1963).

3. Robert K. Merton, *Social Theory and Social Structure* (rev. ed.; Glencoe, Ill.: Free Press, 1957), chaps. 4 and 5.

4. Richard A. Cloward and Lloyd E. Ohlin, *Delinquency and Opportunity* (Glencoe, Ill.: Free Press, 1960).

5. *Ibid.,* p. 175.

6. Donald G. McKinley, *Social Class and Family Life* (New York: Free Press of Glencoe, 1964).

7. Frantz Fanon, *Les Damnés de la Terre* (Paris: Francis Maspero, 1961), pp. 63–64.

8. George Rudé, *The Crowd in the French Revolution* (Oxford: Clarendon Press, 1959), p. 73.

9. I have dealt with this in a somewhat different framework in "Violence and the Social Structure," *op. cit.*

10. Robert K. Merton, "Social Problems and Social Theory," *Contemporary Social Problems,* ed. Robert K. Merton and Robert A. Nisbet (New York: Harcourt and Brace, 1962), p. 709.

11. *Ibid.,* p. 706.

12. Cf. Neil J. Smelser, *Social Change in the Industrial Revolution* (Chicago: University of Chicago Press, 1959) and the same author's *Theory of Collective Behavior* (New York: Free Press of Glencoe, 1963). In the latter work, social movements are seen as always involving the "action of the impatient" who "short-circuit" the process of social readjustment by "exaggerating reality," see pp. 72–73. In this perspective one might be justified in concluding that had impatient Christians not short-circuited the adjustment process in ancient Israel, the Jews would have readjusted in time—and spared the world the spectacle of much later impatient religious action.

13. Eric J. Hobsbawm, *The Age of Revolution* (London: Weidenfels and Nicholson, 1962), p. 111.

14. Cf. T. H. Marshall, *Class, Citizenship and Social Development* (New York: Doubleday Anchor Books, 1965).

15. Mark Hovell, *The Chartist Movement* (London: Longmans, Green, 1918), pp. 210–211. See also Edouard Dolléans, *Le Chartisme* (Paris: Marcel Rivière, 1949).

16. On the politics of rioting and crowd action see, among others, George Rudé, *The Crowd in History* (New York: John Wiley & Sons, 1964); *The Crowd in the French Revolution* by the same author, also his *Wilkes and Liberty* (Oxford: Clarendon Press, 1962); Eric J. Hobsbawm, *Labouring Men* (London: Weidenfels and Nicholson, 1964) and his earlier *Social Bandits and Primitive Rebels* (Glencoe, Ill.: Free Press, 1959).

17. For the relevant quotations from Marx, Durkheim, and Mead, see Coser, "Some Functions of Deviant Behavior," *op. cit.*

18. Everett C. Hughes, "Good People and Dirty Works," *Social Problems,* X, 1 (Summer 1962), pp. 3–11.

19. Kenneth Burke, *Permanence and Change* (New York: New Republic, 1936), p 18.

20. In *Dissent* (January–February 1966).

4.3 PATTERNS OF VIOLENCE

H. L. NIEBURG

"He who slays a king and he who dies for him are alike idolators."——*G. B. Shaw*

Events of this century have done much to shatter our confidence. An attitude of despair, however, is just as unhelpful as one of self-righteous virtue. The best response to present troubles is an unsentimental and unruffled perspective, one that recognizes both the problems and the still formidable resilience of our people and our institutions. The wrong attitude can itself generate a self-fulfilling prophesy. The disorders that threaten us are far from apocalyptic. We must approach them as psychiatrists approach mental illness, "in its biographical setting." Similarly, violent political behavior must be studied in the context of the social system in which it occurs. Knowledge of morbid conditions depends upon our knowledge and definition of health.

In some sense, a widespread appeal to violence represents a strain toward re-integration and legitimacy. We must seek knowledge not only of how and why the social barriers against extremism are breached, but also of how society can constructively assimilate demands for change. Dark and ugly acts flicker in the interstices and at the perimeters of the stable social systems. Institutions must localize, contain, repress, and redirect such isolated threats. They are probably ineradicable and are not the problem. It is not the presence of violence, but rather its degree and kind, its effects in inhibiting political leadership from a creative role, the imminent deadlock of escalated and counterescalated force, the general loss of legitimacy of normative institutions, and the danger of contagion. Even the loss of a popular leader to a lone assassin's bullet is not the problem; rather it is the danger of divisive conditions which fomented it, which make it a pattern, and which attack and undermine the recuperative powers of the society. The problem of political violence raises virtually every other major issue in political sociology and political theory, as well as every major unresolved issue of public policy and the social system.

Many studies demonstrate that social stress is a factor of cohesion rather than division. Under the discipline of external war, the rate of both suicide

Reprinted with the permission of the author and publisher. H. L. Nieburg, "Patterns of Violence," *The UWM Magazine,* Winter, 1969 (The University of Wisconsin—Milwaukee Bureau of Publications, Milwaukee, Wisconsin).

and murder fall (although suicide falls at a sharper rate than murder). The real test of social cohesion occurs under conditions of relative stress/relief. Latent divisive forces are suddenly discharged; long deferred demands for social change suddenly assert higher priorities than those of discipline and unity. Stress is not uniformly distributed in society and thus endows bargaining relationships with differential commitment and urgency. If the main function of government is defined as "allocating values," then the negative of that function is "the allocation of stress." Groups without access to the formal process of values always get more than their share of stress and forms of direct action and political protest may be viewed as an effort to re-allocate stress. Langston Hughes: "Seems like what makes me crazy has no effect on you/ I'm gonna keep on doing until you're crazy too."

In analyzing contagion and precipitating events, we must look to conditions that endow them with efficacy. To comprehend and deal with a pattern of political assassination, we must ask: how is assassination learned and reinforced? Why and for whom does such behavior become adaptive and functional: if indeed assassination should become a fad or a tradition, this would suggest conditions of deeply divided legitimacy, including incipient or actual warfare between large social groups. Once such a pattern is established, it suggests that less provocative forms of political action have lost efficacy and that only sensational political murders are still potent as rallying symbols for some and an attack on the social viability of others.

Among current diagnoses of conditions and events that generate violence, four factors are frequently mentioned. One encompasses the rapidity and magnitude of social change, uprooting of populations, obsolescence of institutions and capital investments, deepening relative deprivation, and unfulfilled expectations. The requirements and tasks of war and diplomacy which generate and legitimize patterns of violence and the use of formal restraint as a means of social control is another factor.

The Vietnam war is seen both as a condition and a precipitant because of the unsuccess of U. S. policies and arms, the bitter issues raised by the draft, economic inflation and other social costs, and more important, the loss of legitimacy of national government. Finally, the Black Revolution or rebellion provides the model and the inspiration of extreme political tactics, because of the proven efficacy of such tactics in achieving Negro demands, in pilloring the guilty conscience of White America, and in challenging the tokenism and evasion which characterized the response to non-violent methods.

All of these factors are pertinent to the increasing incidence of political violence in America. However, the uprooting by social change, war and diplomacy, and Vietnam are judged to be largely background factors capable of inducing a variety of non-violent outcomes. Rather, it is the pattern and history of black militancy that is judged the active ingredient and most salient precipitant. It is this factor that has catalyzed and directed new norms of political behavior, endowing them with legitimacy, demonstrating their bargaining value to other groups, and eliciting retaliatory behavior.

The uprooting and turbulence of the modern age, the breakup of the family as a social group, working mothers, moonlighting fathers, the increase in all forms of crime, the vast movement and mixing of populations due to industrial development and war, urbanization, mental illness, permissiveness, secularism, dope addiction, etc., all are part of the diagnosis of the pathologies of our times. Along with the weakening of the family, informal and internalized controls, comes a compensatory increase in reliance upon formal external controls by all institutions, social, economic, and political. Large impersonal corporations, government bureaucracies, faceless, hostile, and unfamiliar policemen strive to contain the exploding disruptions of social change and by their very method, generate resistance and challenges.

The violence of a Mike Hammer or a James Bond becomes an adaptive fantasy and a model for self-defense against a heartless and dehumanized society. Violence is glorified in all of the media of popular culture, and Gestapo-types become the "Good Guys." As in the turbulence of nineteenth century European revolutions, the criminal becomes a romantic hero and the social misfit a prophet. The children of the middle classes adopt the tradition of the slums that jail is not only honorable but a necessary stopping place in personal development and peer recognition. Sexual intercourse in public, nudity, illegal traffic of dope, and attacks on policemen become forms of neo-Romanticist revolutionary action.

Manipulations of people "as though they are things" has been cited by Martin Luther King and others as being as much responsible for the perpetuation of grief and misery in our cities as the absence of wealth. We are baffled by the *drop-out* from Establishment values by vast numbers of peoples of all social classes and age groups, especially those who are beneficiaries of the comforts, conveniences, and wealth generated by an expanding economy. Lewis Mumford, always the incisive diagnostician, sees "a pathology that is directly proportionate to the overgrowth" of the metropolis, "its purposeless materialism, its congestion, and its insensate disorder . . . a sinister state" that manifests itself in the enormous sums spent on narcotics, sedatives, stimulants, hynotics and tranquilizers, not alone by the hippie generation, but by a great mass of middle class adults, an adjustment to the vacuous desperation and meaningless discipline of their daily lives.

Hiding behind palace guards of computer punch cards and automated production lines, giant authoritarian corporations, systems engineers and managers create a spiritually empty drive for production and gadgetry, mobilizing all of our lives to tasks that are meaningless, generating alienation and estrangement. Droves of people withdraw defensively into the trance of drugs and television or strike back wildly at the faceless social distance that destroys the possibility of creative human confrontation. The soldier activating electronically-controlled missiles has no basis for empathy with his target; the industrial manager prefers to automate rather than deal with union grievance committees; state legislators delegate the problems of traffic control and waste disposal to systems engineering firms rather than deal face-to-face with the refractory human element of county boards, mayors, aldermen, and citizens. Thus, modern society imposes an unbearable burden on human empathy, generating personal *anomie,* attempts to contrive new principles of community, and extremes of political action. Alienation and a denial of the legitimacy of the whole society become a necessary defense mechanism. New sub-cultures search for first-hand experience, personal integrity, and real refreshment in a world destroyed by suffocating abundance.

Thus, the United States faces some curious paradoxes: the most productive economy in history stagnates at a high level and intensifies, rather than allays, social cleavages; the most democratic society witnesses political opportunities rejected in favor of violent protest; a high level of abundance and material well-being generates anger in the poor and terrible anxieties for the middle classes, especially the young; a sophisticated, advanced civilization re-enacts the dilemmas of a Banana Republic and makes a mockery of fondest doctrines of economic development and political stability.

War and diplomacy represent a cluster of variables having two impacts upon the norms of political behavior. They intensify the rapidity of social change and the uprooting of established institutions discussed above. War, Cold War, and permanent international crisis thrust upon us the unavoidable tasks and priorities of defense preparedness and international responsibility. In the atmosphere of tension and crisis, all elements of spatial and social mobility are accelerated, solid social structures are dismantled and new ones jerry-built. Populations and life situations are scattered by the winds of international events. Insistent demands of national security disrupt the order of personal life and hang the whole social balance upon the shifting center of each new foreign problem.

War and diplomacy also provide a pattern of national behavior which by its very nature legitimizes violence in all its forms. This cannot help but inflame private behavior, raise the level of social irritability, and weaken inhibitions against personal violence. In addition to the great World Wars of this century, the world since 1945 has seen twelve limited wars, forty-eight *coup d'etats,* seventy-four rebellions for independence, one hundred sixty-two social revolutions, and vast numbers of racial, religious, and nationality riots. The respectable men in the highest offices of the land play the game of "Chicken" with nuclear diplomacy, and the same sport tends to become normative for all kinds of domestic political purposes. Guns become status symbols and elemental protection for homeowners and shopkeepers, just as missiles do for nations. Ministers, teachers, and leaders urge the people to peaceable conduct and love while simultaneously supporting mutilation and murder abroad. Confrontation diplomacy pursued in the national interest cannot help but proliferate confrontation politics among interest groups at home. Gestapos, GPUs, CIAs, espionage, subversion, and all forms of official undergrounds facilitate and legitimize an underground at home.

Such facts of life, indisputable and honored, make it easy for many people, especially those whose interest it serves and those who are young, to accept uncritically the scenario of an international assassination chain carried out under official auspices. The script reads from Lumumba to Diem, Diem to John F. Kennedy, John F. Kennedy to Malcolm X (who commented on the former's death that the "the pigeons have come home to roost!"), Malcolm X to George Lincoln Rockwell, to Martin Luther King, to Robert F. Kennedy . . . and the next act in the series is already under preparation. So the series is legitimized. So it becomes reasonable and necessary that the next great political sensation requires another major assassination. So the pattern is generalized and escalated as other groups and individuals, aspirants to political attention and efficacy, deliberate which victim deserves and will best serve their purpose to get into the act.

The lingering unsuccess of Vietnam is frequently cited as the most immediate precipitating event in the whole pattern of violence sustained and legitimized by contemporary war and diplomacy. Much of the so-called "moral issue" which surrounds the war is the result of the failure of policy to achieve minimal U.S. objectives at acceptable risk/cost within a tolerable time, rather than the substance of U.S. national interest in Southeast Asia. Be that as it may, the so-called "credibility gap" is essentially a way of describing the loss of legitimacy of national government and the incumbent administration. All kinds of unresolved issues, some related, others remote to Vietnam, share in the collapse. The critics and opponents generalize their assault, exploiting the disaster of official policy as a means to attack and weaken "The Establishment." Every disaffected group sings the unsuccess of Vietnam in order to advance and argue their own values and to assert their own new principles of re-integration and legitimacy.

Certainly major failures of national policy have the effect of weakening the legitimacy of institutions and leaders. However, the direction of the revolt reflects all kinds of conflicts that preceded Vietnam and do not require a major foreign policy failure for validation. This is not to minimize the fact that the Vietnam War has intensified all of the elements of an uprooted society. The requirements of military service, the tremendous mobilization of national resources and money, the wave of inflation with the dislocation of lives and values for vast numbers of middle class Americans, and the postponement of positive public programs to deal with competing priorities, all have embellished existing tensions and tendencies with a galloping fire. In this sense, Vietnam may be considered both a precipitating event and a background condition.

None of the factors or conditions noted above taken separately or together are sufficient causes for extreme political behavior and violence. The normalization of violence requires something more—a demonstration of its efficacy as a form of social bargaining. In the Black Rebellion such tactics have emerged as most efficacious. Here they have achieved a degree of legitimacy which invites imitation by every excluded social group, ranging from the Students for a Democratic Society to American Indians, Puerto Rican high school students, and teachers. A specific coincidence of historical circumstances has made the time ripe for Negro self-consciousness and concerted social action and has also predisposed other claimants for political access to emulate Negro success.

One does not require an hypothesis of "organized conspiracy" and "outside agitators" to explain the clear pattern of escalated violence and counter-violence that has accompanied the search for identity, organization, and leadership by the black community. Nor is the theory of relative or absolute deprivation a satisfactory explanation. Rather, the direction of the Black Power Movement has been largely a result of the response by dominant white power groups to early low-risk tactics of non-violence. The process by which radical militants achieved legitimacy and entered the mainstream of Negro leadership has been largely dependent on the tokenism, evasion, and resistance which discredited the legalistic approach of the NAACP and the non-violent methods of Martin Luther King. To the shame of the white community and its leadership, riots and insurrectionary sniping are accomplishing breakthroughs that seemed impossible prior to the long hot summers of the early 1960's. Even backlash and the rise of white extremism confirm and augment the efficacy of black militancy, endowing it with a defensive justification and raising the level of cost/risk for the whole society, thereby forcing the Middle to seek real social adjustments as the only means of isolating, limiting, and containing the dangers of continued escalation.

Like the decades of violence that accompanied the organizing phase of the labor movement, the initial series of confrontations between the black community and the police represented an organizing phase, whose primary function was to unite the Negro community and discredit both white liberals and Uncle Toms who had previously claimed to act on its behalf. "Black is beautiful," Black Power, and Black Separatism are tactics of unification, rather than program goals.

In its initial response, white policemen sought to punish the whole community, treating all Negroes, including bystanders, as rioters and looters, as if by terrorism to teach the whole black community the futility of violence. This was a test of legitimacy which the white policemen lost; instead they aided and abetted the organizing process. Training programs were put into effect to teach police and the national guard to deal with rioters selectively, in an effort to isolate the law breakers. Policemen inclined to terrorize were removed from ghetto assignments and efforts were made to legitimize anti-riot measures, such as new forms of token participation in policy making, poverty programs, and police review boards for some black leaders.

To a certain extent these measures succeeded. They forced black militants into more extreme tactics which divided the Negro community. However, these actions were not all of one piece, and by and large, the conditions of social exclusion and isolation for most Negroes remained in force. Police action based upon limited force is difficult to implement and ineffective against snipers and guerilla tactics. Thus, a trend toward such tactics followed. There are extremists in every community. By reacting against a whole community in dealing with isolated acts of provocation, the power structure endows extremists, both black and white, with a power over events they can attain in no other way. Any irresponsible black teenager holds in his hands the power to start an incident at any time. Escalation and counter-escalation are built into the situation and the Negro community is forced to support acts of its own extremists. For decades police have responded to the acts of Negroes (including children) as though a state of undeclared war existed between the two communities. They interpreted their duty to intimidate and terrorize at every opportunity, creating an automatic riot syndrome which could be triggered by any claimant to leadership, irresponsible youth, or irresponsible policeman. It is now impossible for policemen to arrest one man without having to deal with all the bystanders as though they were equally guilty. Lynching and the murder of civil rights workers lost its efficacy in the South in the early stages of the struggle. If three civil rights workers were murdered today, ten more would appear tomorrow. If one "uppity nigger" were lynched, ten more would aggressively taunt their white masters the next day. Police terrorism has equally lost its efficacy in the cities of the North.

The characteristic pattern of contemporary riots has shown a tendency toward violent counter-escalation against police action by elements of both Negro and white communities. While the white violence has been limited, the Negro violence escalates in response to police action, often with general support from the black community and with enhanced responsiveness, organization, and danger of future outbreaks. This phenomena is different in kind from frictional violence, the ever-present margin of anti-social acts by individuals and groups. The capability of infinite escalation heightens the risk and increases the cost to society beyond acceptable levels; most important, it destroys the efficacy of normal methods of police power. This kind of violence must be termed "political." It addresses itself to changing the very system of social norms which police power is designed to protect. It focuses grievances in recurring, deliberate, or spontaneous acts of violence, even at great risk and cost to the actors. The peaceable procedures of political adjustment fail to divert the escalation, whether because they be closed, discredited, halting, or simply untried.

We witness the phenomena each year anew and more perilous as imitative outbreaks proliferate not only in summer and by race, but throughout the seasons and as a model for disruptive action by other groups. Many observers of the dilemma recognize the distinctive element of political confrontation and crisis which rioters themselves seem instinctively to feel. A Dutchman who rioted against Nazi occupation during World War II noted that, like the American Negroes, the Dutch rioters were "filled with elation by the fact that they were doing something." There was a community feeling that combined hope, impatience, and impulsiveness. They looted "to obtain trophies, not to get merchandise they could use profitably. Loot has to have symbolic value; strictly utilitarian goods are set on fire!"

Two tendencies are now at work for other groups: an effort to exploit the potential black violence for their own purposes, and an imitation of the pattern of black protest as a means of unifying other claimant groups and winning attention for their demands. Just as every energetic pressure group capitalized for decades on the Cold War, the Soviet Sputnik triumph, the Space Gap, the Chinese Peril, the International Communist Conspiracy; just as educators, scientists, industrialists, and military men all offered special-interest formulas to save the nation; so the explosion of the Black Ghetto has provided a new self-serving slogan for all groups. A massive black army of potential seditionists, saboteurs, and Mau Mau terrorists is evoked for a wide variety of ends. Prevailing power groups exploit the urban tragedy to maintain their own advantages, reiterating that the path to progress is more money invested in scientific and technical innovation, new government contracts to renew the slums, to operate job camps, to train and rehabilitate black workers, to maintain an expanding economy based on government subsidies and tax advantages, all of which will bring about a painless solution without curtailing existing property rights, righting social inequities, or modifying the disparities of political power. So too, teachers and public employees escalate the use of strikes and demonstrations. The welfare poor and the college youth exploit the methods and summon the image of the Black Rebellion, suggesting that denial of their claims will lead to the escalation of which only the numbers and solidarity of the black community is so far capable. A violent confrontation between Vietnam protestors and police raises the threat of even more dangerous uprisings in the black ghetto, now no longer disorganized and self-destructive, but galvanized under paramilitary organizations like the Black Panthers, and aiming not at random property damage, but rather at guerilla warfare, and sabotage against key industries and white suburbs.

In this setting, violent confrontation becomes more frequent. All kinds of groups seek organization and legitimacy by probing and testing the established authorities, while searching for opportune issues around which to rally and extend their leadership. The escalation of sensation will, they hope, win political efficacy by evoking the dangers of reciprocal extremism. The traditional "rites of spring" of white youth, the rituals of mischief (panty raids, love-ins, etc.) cross the line to become institutionalized beer riots in La Crosse, Wisconsin, beach riots at Fort Lauderdale, and holiday harassment of police. Assassination and counter-assassination of college student leaders, as well as government officials, has long been a feature in many Latin American countries. It can happen here! Just as strikes and property damage are filtering down through the high schools and grade schools, so extreme forms of escalated violence can similarly spread throughout the society, if we are imprudent enough to let it happen. The power to direct and control these events lies more in the hands of the powerful than it does in the rallying cries and ambitions of the powerless.

The attempt to obliterate all occasions and possibilities of political and personal violence is unrealistic and even dangerous. Any effort by the state to obtain an absolute monopoly over violence leads inexorably to complete totalitarian repression of all activities and associations which may, however remotely, create a basis of anti-state or anti-establishment action. The logic of such attempts generates a strong counter reaction. In addition to forcing opposition into the most extreme channels (the very thing the state seeks to eliminate), a repressive system threatens the freedom and safety of every citizen. A democratic system must preserve the right of organized action by private groups and accept the risk of the implicit capability of violence. By permitting a pluralistic base, the democratic state enables potential violence to have a social effect and to bring social accommodation with only token demonstration, facilitating a process of peaceful political and social change.

The good society must learn to manage constructively some degree of violence and potential violence. Communities can endure even with murder societies in their midst, providing the institutions of the whole maintain their legitimacy and are able to isolate and control the effects of anti-social actions. One can never hope to completely eliminate the ubiquity of anonymous telephone or letter threats to authors, public personalities, and people who get their names in the paper. Political assassination cannot be eliminated once and for all by any preventive measures which are not even more dangerous to the health and survival of the nation. Attempts to make assassination impossible are incompatible with a free political process and may in fact enhance the probability of *coup d'etat*. The most anxious man in a totalitarian system is the dictator, just as the most anxious man in prison is the warden.

However, it is possible for society to manage its problems in such a way that no single man can change history with a single bullet. The inefficacy of political assassination is the best safeguard against the danger that an isolated act can begin a self-perpetuating series and provide a pattern for political success.

At all times, even in a healthy society, the whole spectrum of political options is occupied by claimants for leadership and legitimacy. The best way to keep the extremes of the spectrum from overwhelming the center is to improve the efficacy and legitimacy of such modes of political action and leadership as will de-escalate latent threats of violence, facilitate social change and political integration of new groups. The very success of peaceable modes of bargaining constitute a prediction of futility for extremist actions. When these do occur, the vast multitudes of the nation will support the actions of the state in limited and reasonable deterrence, localization, and when necessary containment by appropriate and measured, rather than over-reactive, means of force. George Wallace's threat to run his car over demonstrators tends to escalate and legitimize political violence. Mayor Daley's instruction to police to "shoot-to-maim" looters has the same effect. Government must learn the value of non-violence as an appropriate tactic of control in certain conditions where violence, even the superior violence of the state, will not work.

It is a simple matter to diagnose theoretically the conditions of and causes of political violence. It is much more difficult as a matter of practical policy to know how to avoid social trials by ordeal. How does government terminate and stabilize a period of search behavior and confrontation? How to conserve and integrate adaptive social innovations? The way a social process starts and spreads has been much more studied than the question of how it terminates. A process may cease because it has exhausted itself, or because a point of termination is institutionalized as part of the process itself. Some processes may go on indefinitely, ceasing only with the disappearance of the groups whose interests they served or opposed. In some cases, a process provides built-in opportunities at which it can be deliberately stopped or redirected. What do you do in a situation where high risk political confrontation is already well-established and seemingly irreversible?

It is easy to formulate verbal generalities that seem to answer these questions. One can create counter-tendencies to dampen extreme oscillations. This calls for highly creative political action and leadership, not only from the leaders of prevailing cadres and groups, but on every level of social and political organization in both the formal and informal polity. This may not be as difficult as it appears. There is a strong tendency in social life toward humanizing power, toward creating conditions of predictability and order in the midst of change, and avoiding the danger created for all by efforts to apply overly extreme penalties and measures to some. One of the great facts of American response to the recent series of political assassinations has been the tendency of the community to unite against all varieties of extremism, to seek new routes of conciliation and social reform. This is a built-in corrective which, with a little luck, can see us through grave situations.

The nation-state is a complex living organism whose growth tends to respond to the interests and desires of those who exercise political, social, and economic power. Most of the great political problems that confront us arise from the emergence of a new capability for social bargaining on the part of previously submerged groups. To serve only established and prevailing power groups will always leave basic social equations to fester and writhe beneath the surface, ultimately to break through and deface the grand facade of established power. Our institutions must aim at the discovery of new constituencies and new routes of access by which they can generate their own leadership. This is a very real challenge to our ingenuity and inventiveness as political innovators.

In terms of political power, there are no abstract issues, only "who gets what, when, and how?" and "who's doing what to whom?" All situations, however desperate they may be to some, are manageable and purblindly tolerable for those who do not suffer them. Therefore, they are not recognized or defined as social problems. It is a political fact that has defined, for example, the crisis of the cities as "a problem." So long as slum occupants confined their crimes to the ghettoes, internalized the disarray of their lives through mental disease or buffered it with narcotics, there was no problem for most of the society. However, with the arrival of self-consciousness, militancy, and incipient organization, the heat is on. Metropolitan pathology ceases to be an abstract issue to be safely exploited, studied, and pacified; but it has become a confrontation, urgent, inescapable, and perilous. The same might also be said of many other new groups that are winning self-identity and organization. When this happens, cheap fixes and evasions no longer serve. Even counter-insurgency and police repression become provocative, ineffective, and self-defeating. Postponement, tokenism, all the old political bag of tricks are bankrupt and outworn culturally, morally, economically, and politically. Those who are already articulate and enjoy some assets of social bargaining have a responsibility to save themselves by saving all.

On the other hand, I reiterate the futility of sentimentalizing over both problems and remedies. Conflict is probably inevitable in social life, just as is the search for order and stability. When the priorities of one conflict are somehow terminated, we can be certain others will take their place, as dangerous and insoluble as the last. To live is to grow, to grow is to strive, to strive is to struggle. We must be sophisticated enough to understand the imperfect justice of all human relations, past, present, and future. It is the unfinished nature of our task and the imperfections of ourselves that generate the dynamics of politics and give individual freedom its meaning. Justice is not to be had for any except as the rigors of political bargaining give it status and degree for those who prevail in the shifting compromises of the bargaining process. In regard to the problems of race, like other problems, they may be genuinely insoluble in the short run. The best we can hope for is to create a sense of movement and a faith in the ultimate efficacy of political solutions. A sense of movement toward solutions is the great thing that generates excitement and interest and nourishes hope. It is the ultimate means of preserving the legitimacy of a whole society.

4.4 URBAN VIOLENCE: A QUESTION OF EFFICACY

KARL H. FLAMING and J. JOHN PALEN

This article focuses on one particular type of urban violence, the inner-city racial riots of the last decade. Our attention is not on the riots themselves, for that has been done many times over; but, rather, we will consider the possible social and economic consequences that may have resulted from the violence. In particular, we will examine several hypotheses concerning the positive functions of violence in producing change. Data on the aftermath of the 1967 riot in Milwaukee are compared with the limited information on other major urban riots (McCord, *et al.,* 1969).

A number of theorists have speculated on the functions and consequences of violence. Lewis Coser, for example, explicitly deals with this question (Coser, 1966). Coser treats social violence as a subcategory of social conflict.

Harold Nieburg takes Coser's arguments further by hypothesizing that political violence is most likely to occur when institutional processes break down (Nieburg, 1968).

Strong emphasis on the positive functions of violence is apparently shared by many black ghetto residents, who also see riots as having positive effects. A survey for *Newsweek* magazine in 1966 found that more than one-third of rank-and-file Negroes thought that Watts-style rioting helped the Negro cause more than it hurt it. On the other hand, 20 percent believed that it hurt, and the remainder felt it made no difference (Brink and Harris, 1966:264). A 1969 *Newsweek* study found that approximately one-third of the blacks interviewed thought riots profited their cause, and one-fifth thought Negroes could not win their rights without violence (*Newsweek,* June 30, 1969:23). Another study of Negro opinions after the Los Angeles riot found that Negro respondents believed the riot called white attention to Negro problems, provided a way of expressing resentment against oppressors, and brought help to the black population from whites (Sears and Tomlinson, 1968:502).

Our study examines the degree to which violence does bring about positive results for ghetto blacks. Particular attention is given to empirical examination of changes in basic conditions for blacks following the 1967 riot in Milwaukee, Wisconsin. Based on the findings in this one urban area,

Adapted especially for this book from Flaming, 1970, Chapter V.

some possible reformulation of the hypothesis of the positive function of violence is suggested.

Historical Evidence

Allen Grimshaw's 1959 study of major United States riots prior to the 1960s states that riots had both negative and positive effects. The negative effects he cites include human casualties, property damage, polarization of the races, curtailment of social work agencies, and out-migration of Negroes from riot communities. Positive effects include improved physical conditions for minority groups, civil rights legislation, improved administration of rights under the law, and public conferences to promote rights for minorities (Grimshaw, 1959).

A discussion of negative effects of more recent civil disturbances is provided by a 1967 report of the McClellan Commission. This survey of 128 mayors indicated that, from March 1965 to September 1967, 12 law officers and 118 civilians were killed; 1199 law officers and 2242 civilians were injured; 7985 cases of arson were reported; and there were 28,932 arrests and 5434 convictions (*Riots, Civil and Criminal Disorders,* 1967: foldout). In addition, the mayors of the 128 cities estimated $210.6 million dollars in property damage and $504.2 million dollars in economic losses. However, the latter estimates may be unreliable since some mayors (for example, Milwaukee's) did not attempt to estimate property and economic losses. In his study of the Watts riots, Paul Jacobs states bluntly that:

> Since the August 1965 revolt in Los Angeles a few meaningful improvements have taken place. A few hundred residents of the Barrios and the ghettoes have had an opportunity to learn some things about organization and political action through the use of anti-poverty funds. A few dozen new organizations of the poor and minority groups are beginning to make some demands upon society. Yet there has been no important fundamental change in Los Angeles or in any other American city. (Jacobs, 1966:286)

Another study of the aftermath of the Watts riot supports Jacob's conclusions. Howard and McCord point out that 25 percent of the homes in Watts are considered deteriorated or dilapidated, as opposed to 7 percent in the county as a whole; and between 1959 and 1965, a time of growing prosperity for the nation, the median income for Los Angeles Negroes dropped 8 percent (McCord, *et al.,* 1969:53–54). During this period the unemployment rate among Watts Negroes rose from 12.6 percent to 19.7 percent; male unemployment in Watts was 30 percent in 1965 (McCord, *et al.,* 1969:54). Data indicated little change since the 1965 riot. Joblessness stayed at about the same level as it was before the riot. The Chamber of Commerce attempted a crash program to produce more jobs, but, according to the County Human Relations Commission, they came up with perhaps 200 to 300 jobs and job-training opportunities when at least 5000 were needed to have a serious impact on the problem (McCord, *et al.,* 1969: 65–66).

A national assessment of the aftermath of recent riots was a short monograph entitled *One Year Later,* prepared by the staffs of Urban America, Incorporated, and the Urban Coalition. The thrust of the report was that great numbers of Negroes were still, as of 1969, excluded from the benefits of economic progress as a result of discrimination in employment, and continue to be confined to segregated housing and schools. Also noted was the growing concentration of impoverished Negroes in major cities and the seriousness of police-community problems. As stated by the report itself:

> The Commission's description of the immediate consequences of the present policies choice sounds strikingly like a description of the year since its report was issued: some change but not enough; more incidents but less full-scale disorders because of improved police and military response; a decline in expectations and therefore in short-run frustrations. If the Commission is equally correct about the long run, the nation in its neglect may be sowing the seeds of unprecedented future disorder and division. For a year later, we are closer to being two societies, black and white, increasingly separate and scarcely less equal. (Urban America, Inc. and Urban Coalition, 1969:118)

The Milwaukee Case

Before analyzing the aftermath of the Milwaukee riot, some demographic data on the city and historical information on the riot itself are in order. The city of Milwaukee at the time of the riot had a population of approximately 750,000 and the Milwaukee Standard Metropolitan Statistical Area had over 1,400,000 inhabitants, which places Milwaukee among the largest cities that were hit by riots during the late 1960s. The Negro Population of Milwaukee has grown rapidly from in-migration in recent decades. As of 1950, blacks numbered only 21,000 or 3.4 percent of the city population, but by 1960 the figure jumped to 62,458 or 8.4 percent. According to 1969 estimates, the black population numbered 90,000 or 12 percent of the city's total population.

Milwaukee experienced one of the most serious riots of the 1960s (Wanderer, 1968). The city was one of just a few to report deaths; it ranked near the top in number of arrests and in total community disruption. The Milwaukee riot did not occur as the result of any single incident, such as was reported for Watts, Newark, and Detroit. Rather, tensions that had been high broke into overt violence on Sunday, July 31, 1967.

Major violence continued through the night and into the following morning. Early Monday morning a twenty-four-hour city-wide curfew was put into effect by law-enforcement and city officials. The Inner Core North was cordoned off by Milwaukee police and the National Guard was called in. Major crowd activity continued, although arrests, arson, and sniping continued for another three days. Four persons died; approximately 1500 were arrested, more than 90 percent being convicted of some charge, of which 197 were for serious offenses.

We will examine information on the aftermath of the Milwaukee riot under four headings: (1) police practices; (2) employment; (3) housing; and (4) education. These areas of concentration were not selected at random, but on the basis of a probability survey of 125 black and 259 white Milwaukeans' opinions concerning the cause of the riot (Flaming, 1968).

The Police

Major riot studies invariably document black anger with the police. The Kerner Commission Report cites this factor as the single most important Negro grievance (National Advisory Commission on Civil Disorders, 1968:143). There is deep resentment over the behavior of police in black communities—not only during riots, but throughout the year. McCord and Howard found that the proportion of blacks who felt police were abusive ranged from 56 percent in Oakland to 31 percent in Houston (McCord, et al., 1969:82). A 1966 Newsweek poll found that 33 percent of the Negroes interviewed felt that the police were harmful to Negro rights. By 1969 a follow-up Newsweek poll found that the figure had jumped to 46 percent (Newsweek, June 30, 1969:19).

A 1968 Milwaukee survey of black inner-city residents found that blacks cited police brutality and anger with police among the major causes of the riot (Slesinger, 1968:10). Well over half of the blacks sampled believed that police frequently insult blacks, unnecessarily frisk and search blacks, and use unnecessary force in arrest. In addition, more than one-third of the blacks believed that the police unnecessarily stop and search cars and frequently beat people up. Milwaukeans' responses regarding police appear typical of black opinions across the country.

The deteriorating relationship between the Milwaukee police department and the black community following the riot can be seen in the problem of recruiting black police officers. The police chief publicly stated before the riot that harassment from a small group of clergy and some organizations had hindered his recruitment program (Milwaukee Journal, January 19, 1966). Whatever the reason, the police department had only token black representation at the time of the 1967 riot. In 1967 there were 50 blacks on a 1800-man force; in 1969 there were only 42 blacks out of 2256 men. This number was considerably below the 6.6 percent average black representation on police forces in United States cities over a half million (Urban America, Inc. and Urban Coalition, 1969:79). As of 1970, the Milwaukee department had made little effort to directly recruit black and other minority groups onto the force. If anything, black enlistments were discouraged (Feit, 1970:12–14). Thus Milwaukee is rather unique in having had an actual decrease in the proportion of Negroes on the police force. For example, during this same period Washington, D.C., went from one-third to one-half black recruits, and Detroit doubled the number of blacks it hired (Urban America, Inc. and Urban Coalition, 1969:79).

Employment Opportunities

Milwaukee area unemployment rates have generally paralleled the nation at large. Unemployment rates of minority groups in the Milwaukee area are estimated to exceed white unemployment rates by two to two-and-one-half times. As of July 1970, the estimated unemployment rate among blacks ages sixteen to thirty was 30 percent. This compared with an estimated 6.8 percent unemployment rate for all Negroes in the Milwaukee area for July 1967, at the time of the riot. Increasing black joblessness reflected national as well as strictly local conditions. It is the national economy that largely determines general employment rates.

Education

There was little overt change in Milwaukee public school policies as a result of the 1967 civil disturbance. In the words of the Wisconsin Advisory Committee:

> Milwaukee, from all observable signs, has not begun to address itself to developing viable programs that would stimulate racial integration of children dren. As a matter of fact, evidence of Milwaukee's resistance can be seen in refusal of the board of school directors to discontinue intact bussing of children. (Wisconsin Advisory Committee, 1969)

Prior to the violence, the pattern was one of de facto segregation and ignoring racial questions. Neither policy nor pattern changed in the three years following the riot. Most inner-city schools, already overwhelmingly black in 1967, were almost totally black in 1970.

Housing

Studies done after the 1967 riot document black dissatisfaction with housing conditions in Milwaukee. Open housing was the most publicized issue in the Milwaukee area civil rights struggle. The first proposal for an open-housing ordinance was made in 1963 by a black city council member; it was rejected 17 to 1. In the following years, repeated ordinances were voted down. Following the riot, the NAACP Youth Council, led by the militant Fr. James Groppi, resumed the open-housing marches that had already resulted in numerous confrontations with white citizens and with the Milwaukee police. These marches were responsible for the organization of the police tactical squad. Even after the riot, the marches were not able to obtain passage of a city open-housing ordinance. Only after passage of a federal law in the spring of 1968 did the Milwaukee Common Council pass open-housing legislation, and it largely duplicated existing federal law.

After the riot, low-income Milwaukee area residents saw no relief in long-term needs. This issue was dramatized in 1969 by a take-over of abandoned Army barracks by the Milwaukee Tenants' Union. The ratio of new housing starts to the destruction of existing housing documents the problem.

> According to Milwaukee department of building inspection reports, during the years 1960 through 1967 a total of 14,219 dwelling units were razed in the city of Milwaukee. Of these units, 8723 were in the inner city. During those same years, a total of 29,383 dwelling units were built in the city. Of these 1423 were built in the inner city. Of those built in the inner city, 1052 were dwelling units for the elderly, 254 for low-income persons, and 117 private houses. (Wisconsin Advisory Committee, 1969:88)

The inner city thus lost six times more units than it added. The majority of the dwellings were razed as a result of highway and urban renewal programs. Low-income housing projects completed since the riot have been for the elderly.

In general, the period following the riot saw the passage of open-housing legislation, the continued dislocation of Negroes by urban renewal and highway programs, little new housing whether private or public, and some rat control. Today, overall objective housing conditions remain approximately the same as in 1967.

Implications

To what extent did the urban rioting of the 1960s serve as a form of achievement or as a catalyst for further changes? Our findings cast doubt on the hypothesis that riots serve as a warning or message to the larger community. For example, analyses of opinion after the Milwaukee riot showed that whites tended to view it as a breakdown of social control rather than the culmination of long-held grievances. According to the Milwaukee survey:

> In contrast to blacks, whites placed more emphasis on behaviorial problems (the failure of parents to control their children, rebelliousness of youth, and irresponsible persons in search of kicks and excitement), forces from without (outsiders coming into the city and stirring up trouble, part of the Black Nationalism movement, and part of a national Communist conspiracy), and civil rights agitation at the local level (local civil rights leaders stirring up unrest). As noted earlier, the black community continues to define the meaning of the disturbance in terms of the tangible, real-life problems they face on a day-to-day basis. (Slesinger, 1968:11–12)

These data indicate that whites continued to ignore or reject the message of the riot, just as they had ignored decades of studies documenting problems in the areas of health, rat control, housing, jobs, and law enforcement.

The function of violence as a form of achievement is also open to serious question. Milwaukee data are limited insofar as nothing can be said about the immediate psychological function of riot violence as a type of individual emotional achievement. However, information is available regarding the degree to which riot violence serves as a catalyst for reform. It is difficult to see where the Milwaukee riot has resulted in any major breakthroughs for the Negro community.

Taken as a whole, riot violence failed to serve as a warning, to open previously denied areas for achievement, or to trigger significant reform. A tenable alternative hypothesis is that civil rights activism, not the violence of the riot, had already alerted the community to black grievances, and that the community had chosen to ignore or reject these warnings. It is also worth speculating as to the relative efficacy of violence as opposed to other noninstitutionalized means of bringing about social change. Saul Alinsky's techniques, for example, suggest one possible alternative.

Finally, it should be noted that we have used Coser's argument as a point of departure and hypothesis. Further studies on the efficacy of violence no doubt will bring more definitive answers to the important issues raised by this and earlier studies. Obviously there is need for change in many areas. Equally evident is the lack of effective mechanisms for change.

REFERENCES

Brink, William, and Louis Harris. (1966) *Black and White.* New York: Simon and Schuster.

Coser, Lewis A. (1966) "Some Social Functions of Violence," *The Annals of the American Academy of Political and Social Science,* Vol. 304, March, pp. 8–18.

Feit, Kenneth. (1970) *The Milwaukee Police Department: An In-Depth Study.* An unpublished report distributed in the bimonthly report of the Council on Urban Life, Room 308, 2200 North Third Street, Milwaukee, Wisconsin.

Flaming, Karl H. (1968) "Who Riots and Why? Black and White Perspectives in Milwaukee." (Milwaukee, Wisconsin: Milwaukee Urban League, 1968—litho.)

Flaming, Karl H. (1970) "The 1967 Milwaukee Riot: A Historical and Comparative Analysis." Unpublished Ph.D. Dissertation, Syracuse University, Syracuse, New York.

Grimshaw, Allen D. (1959) "A Study in Social Violence: Urban Race Riots in the United States." Unpublished Ph.D. Dissertation, University of Pennsylvania.

Jacobs, Paul. (1966) *Prelude to Riot: A View of Urban America from the Bottom.* New York: Vintage.

McCord, William, John Howard, Bernard Friedberg, and Edwin Harwood. (1969) *Life Styles in the Black Ghetto.* New York: Norton.

Milwaukee Journal. January 19, 1966.

National Advisory Commission on Civil Disorders. (1968) *Report of the National Advisory Commission on Civil Disorders.* Washington, D.C.: U.S. Government Printing Office; also New York: Bantam.

Newsweek. June 30, 1969, pp. 17–35.

Nieburg, H. L. (1968) "Violence, Law, and the Social Process," *American Behavioral Scientist,* Vol. 2, March-April, pp. 17–19.

Riots, Civil, and Criminal Disorders. (1967) Hearings before the Permanent Subcommittee on Investigations (McClellan Commission), Committee on Government Operations, U.S. Senate. Washington, D.C.: U.S. Government Printing Office.

Sears, David O., and T. M. Tomlinson. (1968) "Riot Ideology in Los Angeles: A Study of Negro Attitudes," *Social Science Quarterly,* Vol. 49, December, pp. 485–503.

Slesinger, Jonathan A. (1968) "Community Opinions Regarding the Summer, 1967, Disturbances in Milwaukee." Unpublished.

Urban America, Inc., and Urban Coalition. (1969) *One Year Later: An Assessment of the Nation's Response to the Crisis Described by the National Advisory Commission on Civil Disorders.* Washington, D.C.: Urban Coalition.

Wanderer, Jules J. (1968) "1967 Riots: A Test of the Congruity of Events," *Social Problems,* Vol. 16, Fall, pp. 193–198.

Wisconsin Advisory Committee. (1969) *Final Report of the Wisconsin Advisory Committee on the Report of the National Commission on Civil Disorders.* State of Wisconsin.

4.5 CITY POWER STRUCTURES

EDWARD C. BANFIELD and JAMES Q. WILSON

Power Structure

The term "power structure" was popularized by the sociologist, Floyd Hunter, who found in a study of "Regional City" (Atlanta, Georgia) that about forty "power leaders," most of them businessmen, "set the line on policy" in city affairs while an "understructure" of about several hundred persons, including the principal elected and appointed city officials, merely carried out the policies decided upon by the very few at the top of the power pyramid. "The structure," Hunter wrote, "is that of a dominant policy-making group using the machinery of government as a bureaucracy for the attainment of certain goals coordinate with the interests of the policy-making group."[1]

Later investigators, using other research methods and studying cities that were doubtless very different from Atlanta, found power structures which, if they deserved to be called that at all, were entirely unlike that described by Hunter. In New Haven, for example, Robert A. Dahl found a highly pluralistic system, characterized by "stubborn and pervasive ambiguity," in which both leaders and led, drawn from many strata of the community and occupying diverse roles, both led and were led, and in which it was necessary to distinguish "direct" influence (possessed by relatively few) from "indirect" (possessed by a great many).[2] In Chicago, one of the present authors found that the heads of the Democratic party machine had ample power to decide almost any matter. For various reasons they preferred to "ratify" proposals put before them by affected interests, when the interests agreed among themselves, rather than to initiate proposals themselves. When the affected interests disagreed among themselves, the elected officials followed the strategy of delaying a decision as long as possible while at the same time encouraging those concerned to put pressure upon them. From the amount and nature—especially the "representativeness"—of this pressure they found cues by which to form an estimate of how the matter was viewed by the public at large. The elected official, according to this account, "feels that it is his duty to do what 'a broad cross-section of the community' wants"; efforts to influence him help him sense what the community wants.[3]

Despite such very important differences from city to city—differences that may be explainable largely but not entirely in terms of methodology[4]—one thing is common to all: persons not elected to office play very considerable parts in the making of many important decisions. The differences among cities in this regard (especially if Atlanta be left out of account) are more in degree than in kind. Public affairs in New Haven and Chicago, although not "run" by tiny, informal "power elites," are nevertheless much influenced by persons who occupy no official position.

Those who exercise power unofficially (we will call such people "influentials") do so for ends that range from self-serving or business-serving to group-serving or community-serving. A group of businessmen, for example, may urge an urban renewal project upon the city for no other purpose than to make money. Or again such a group may urge a project out of concern for the welfare of some part of the city's population ("the better class of people") or from concern for the welfare of the city as a whole ("restoring the central city will be good for everybody"). Almost always motives in such matters are extremely mixed. The Urban League may be supported by some contributors who do so for purely business reasons, by others who think "the community needs it," and by still others whose motives are of both sorts. Distinctions along these lines, despite the impossibility of applying them unambiguously in many concrete cases, are indispensable in a discussion of influence in the city. We shall distinguish exercises of influences that are "business-serving" from those that are "public-serving." Civic activity and civic leadership, as we shall use the terms, consist only of exercises of influence that are largely, or mainly, public-serving. Thus, insofar as a banker member of a housing improvement association seeks to serve the interests of his bank he is an "interest group representative" and insofar as he seeks to serve the interests (as he sees them) of the whole public, or of some considerable sector of it, he is a "civic leader."

American Political Culture and Private Influence

The active participation of private parties in the conduct of public business, whether as interest group representatives or as civic leaders, is a peculiarly American phenomenon. In many other free countries, it is taken for granted that public affairs are to be managed solely by those who have been elected or appointed to office; no others may participate in the management of them, although they may, of course, make their views known and, when an election is held, give or withhold consent. In London, for example, there is not even a chamber of commerce or a taxpayer's association, and no businessman would dream of "giving leadership" to a local council from behind the scenes. If he wanted to take part in local government he would stand for election, and if he won a seat he would regard himself as the representative of a public, not of the "business community."[5]

The presence of the influential on the American civic scene is to be accounted for on several grounds. The most important of these, perhaps, is the decentralization of authority that is so characteristic of the American political system. In Europe, the formally constituted authorities have ample power to carry out whatever schemes they may decide upon. In our country, by contrast, authority is almost always fragmented. Accordingly, the businessman (or anyone else) finds it easy to "get in on the act." Because he can check the public official, he can also bargain with him; as it is usually expressed, the official "needs his cooperation." Businessmen are active in American civic affairs, then, because the nature of the political system encourages them to get and use influence.

Another reason for the influential's presence in civic affairs is that the community (or at least some sections of it) often has more respect for his judgment and integrity than for those of the politician or bureaucrat. Rightly or wrongly, local politicians and bureaucrats are seldom held in very high regard; the politician is often considered an "opportunist" at best and the bureaucrat is usually thought to lack enterprise and imagination. As the mayor of Minneapolis recently explained,

> It is apparent that we have not yet evolved in America an understandable and acceptable role or status for the politician. The rewards of our economy and of our society are attached to other pursuits, notably to the professions and to business generally. "Success" is still identified with the amassing of wealth and the acquiring of economic "position." To some extent we now attach status to the leaders of the clergy and in higher education, but for the politician status is variable and uncertain. We do not have a tradition that regards the role of the civil servant or of the public official as involving a form of "calling" or dedicated service, such as religious or educational leadership.[6]

Since it is success in other than public service pursuits, especially business, that distinguishes the man of great capacity in our culture, it is not surprising that when a city wants assurance that its affairs are being managed efficiently it often turns to a businessman for "expert" opinion. In some cities politicians almost routinely exhibit to the electorate some "seal of approval" given by business and other civic leaders.[7] In others (Boston, for example) there are formal arrangements by which lay bodies are given powers to make continuing investigations of the conduct of city affairs.

The influential is often valued as much for his status attributes as for his judgment. One of the functions of much civic activity is to give some people an opportunity to "rub elbows" with others and by so doing to demonstrate that they and the institutions and causes they represent are worthy and statusful. Businessmen "keep score" on one another's prestige, and on the prestige of one another's firm, by noting who serves on the board of this or that civic association. For them and for others, sitting at the head table with "important" people may be a very rewarding experience.

The influential also serves a symbolic function in civic affairs. One who presides on public occasions must "represent" something to which the whole community aspires or gives allegiance. In England this is always the person closest to the throne. Lord So-and-So is the chairman of the committee to raise funds for the new hospital because in some mysterious way he partakes of the charisma attaching to royalty. Americans have to select their human symbols on a different basis, and often they select one who partakes of the charisma attaching to wealth. This need not mean that Americans are more materialistic than the British—only that it is much harder for Americans to symbolize what they have in common. According to Peter B. Clark, the businessman civic leader symbolizes a complex of widely held values, not only wealth but also achievement, efficiency, respectability, soundness, public-spiritedness, and the qualities that make for local growth and expansion.[8]

Still another reason for the influential's role is that he shares with the general public the view that he owes the community a debt of service. He may not make any payments on this debt; indeed, he may even serve himself at the expense of the public. Nevertheless, he agrees in principle that he is under a moral obligation to "serve." This is an idea which businessmen in many other cultures, even the British, would find quixotic and which is seldom entertained even by members of "old" and "noble" families.

Finally, businessmen and other influentials are encouraged to participate in civic affairs because they and their fellow citizens think that they ought to help promote the economic growth and prosperity of the city. For generations Americans have been making money from the rise in land values and the increase in commercial and industrial activity that have accompanied urban expansion; even those people who have not owned land or had other direct economic interest in growth have enjoyed a psychic income from living in cities that are "going somewhere." Americans, in short, are natural-born civic boosters, and the more influential they are the more powerfully they are expected to boost.

The Variety of Civic Authority

Peter B. Clark divided the universe of civic activity in Chicago into five subject matter fields which differ in personnel, style of operation, and significance for public policy.[9] Although based on one very large city, Clark's findings are, we think, reasonably representative of a pattern that exists in most large and (in abbreviated form) many small ones. His fields of civic activity are these:

1. *Race relations and inter-faith activities.* The welfare of the Negro, and to a lesser extent of the Jew and the Catholic as well, is the special concern of one set of civic leaders. The leaders in this field are not the most influential, wealthy, or prestigious ones. They tend to be Jewish and Catholic businessmen or lawyers or else to be second-level corporation executives assigned to race-relations work by their companies. Much of their activity is behind the scenes. Civic associations in this field issue press releases on what are for them particularly important issues; for the most part, however, they work through private discussions with employers, politicians, and others whose cooperation is wanted. Big businessmen tend to steer clear of this field because they consider it controversial.

2. *Good-government activities.* In Chicago there are three principal associations in this field. One of them analyzes the records of local candidates for election and makes recommendations to the voters; another sponsors panel discussions of city and metropolitan problems and proposes new policies and changes in the structure of government; and the third keeps track of criminal activities and the operation of law enforcement agencies. Most of the civic leaders in this field are Protestants who have a religious, or quasi-religious, concern for "improving public morality"—a motive, incidentally, that is not conspicuous in the other fields of civil activity. Their tactic is to carry on "a constant but low-keyed harassment of politicians through the newspapers"; the effect of this, if any, is by its very nature hard to identify. Partly for this reason, perhaps, the most influential, wealthy, and prestigious civic leaders find the good-government field "uninteresting" when it is not "too controversial."

3. *Welfare and fund-raising activities.* Chicago raises about $250,000,000 a year by public subscription for charitable purposes. Organizing the various "drives" to collect money and giving general policy direction to the welfare professionals who spend it are what civic leaders in this field do. These leaders are of two general types: men of great wealth who contribute generously and representatives of the large corporations which put up most of the money in practically all "drives." Corporations take turns assigning their executives to service on civic fund-raising committees. Being on such a committee is, both for a wealthy family and for a corporation, a way of meeting a "civic responsibility" and of carrying on "good public relations." Civic leaders in this field do not, however, have much influence in public affairs by virtue of these activities.

4. *Cultural, university, and hospital work.* Those at the very pinnacle of civic prestige—people who have great inherited wealth or who are the heads of large corporations—are the trustees and officers of universities, hospitals, and art and other museums. These institutions have big real estate holdings in the city and are in many other ways sensitive to political and other changes; therefore their trustees are frequently called upon to exercise influence on their behalf.

5. *Business promotion, construction, and planning activities.* Decisions affecting the growth and prosperity of the central city, and above all of the downtown business section, particularly decisions about urban renewal, expressway routes, port developments, airport improvement, and the location of major public buildings, are a field of civic activity in which bankers, real estate men and department store owners and other businessmen are prominent. There are, of course, always differences of interest and opinion among those who are concerned with these matters. To a large extent, therefore, civic activity in this field consists of efforts by civic leaders to reach agreement among themselves with regard to the recommendations that are to be made to the public authorities and, when agreement cannot be reached,

of competitive efforts by the various factions of civic leaders to get their plans accepted and those of their opponents rejected or delayed.

Clark found that most Chicago civic leaders usually confine most of their civic activity to one or another of these fields, and that they are poorly informed about the fields in which they are not actually involved. The preoccupation of the wealthiest "old families" and of the heads of the largest corporations with cultural, university, and hospital work tends to make them unavailable for participation in the other fields of civic activity and therefore to leave civic leadership in these other fields to persons in the second rank of wealth and prestige.

The Civic Association

Much (but by no means all) civic activity takes place through the medium of voluntary associations—"the characteristic social unit of the modern city," as Oscar Handlin has called them.[10] Few cities are too small to have at least one or two associations devoted to the cause of civic welfare, and in the larger cities there are scores or even hundreds. Not many associations take the whole range of city affairs as their domain; most are highly specialized, confining themselves to some sector of one of the subject matter fields listed above. Some have long histories, large memberships, and big budgets, and others are no more than names on a letterhead. Some are ceaselessly active in governmental affairs; others are active only intermittently.[11]

A civic association is held together largely, or even entirely, by general, nonmaterial (intangible) inducements, especially the opportunity to enjoy mutual association and to serve the community.[12] Having no specific, material inducements to offer, the association cannot put its members under a strict discipline; it may entice or persuade them but it cannot order them, and it must always be on the lookout for "program material" that will attract their interest and create enthusiasm for the organization and its purposes. What Wallace Sayre and Herbert Kaufman say of New York City civic associations —that they are "run by relatively small inner cores of activists"—may be said also of the associations in other cities.[13] Even the activists, though they often spend much of their time on association drives, have no vital personal stake in them (no one entrusts his vital interests to an organization he cannot control). The nonactivists' connection is often entirely nominal.

The "voluntary" character of the civic association greatly influences its choices of activities—those it does not engage in as well as those it does. For one thing, it is constantly under the necessity of convincing its members that they are accomplishing something worthwhile through it. But it must do this without touching anything controversial; even though a large majority of its membership approves its stand in a controversial matter, it risks losing the support of the minority who do not. Usually it deals with this dilemma in one or both of two ways: it gives the members prestige, publicity, and other such satisfactions in lieu of a sense of accomplishment, and it substitutes evidence of accomplishment of means for evidence of accomplishment of ends. The Philadelphia Housing Association, for example, cannot show accomplishment in terms of its ultimate end, the improvement of housing, but it can show that it is doing many things that presumably further that end. Thus, according to a recent issuance:

> the Association undertakes research and data analysis in fields of concern; sponsors publications, public meetings, filmstrips, tours, and other educational and informational activities; regularly publishes ISSUES; provides counseling and assistance to individuals and groups; evaluates public programs and confers with public officials; operates two area committees; and organizes extensive committee activities. In all of its efforts, the Association works closely with other social agencies and with public agencies responsible for carrying out housing and renewal programs.

A civic association is in a particularly advantageous position if its activity is believed to be instrumental to the attainment of *several* ends. Even if the ends are mutually incompatible, it will be supported by those who entertain the ends, provided, of course, that it does not foolishly specify which of the incompatible ends it is trying to attain. The Community Service Organization in Los Angeles, for example, has had extraordinary success in registering Mexicans as voters: turnout among Mexicans, many of whom are low-income immigrants, is now among the highest of any group in the country. The organization's supporters (competing politicians, labor unions, and church groups) have different and in some cases opposed interests in getting out the Mexican vote; they support the organization *because* its goal is purely instrumental.

Selecting ends that are both very vague and very worthy makes it especially easy for a civic association to claim accomplishment. It can make its claims "without fear of contradiction" because the very vagueness of the end guarantees that the specific activities it engages in cannot be shown to be ineffective.

Civic associations often impress their members with their prestige, power, and accomplishment by establishing their right to be consulted by public officials. A politician who wants an association's "support" (not necessarily a declaration by it in favor of his candidacy; perhaps nothing more than a favorable reference to him in its newsletter or an invitation to sit at the head table at its annual dinner) may defer publicly to its views before making important appointments or policy proposals in the subject-matter field that is of particular concern to it. The consultative role of the civic association has in many places been given legal, or quasi-legal, standing. For example, the mayor of New York, in making appointments to the board of education, is required by state law to consider the recommendations of "representative associations, civil, educational, business, labor and professional groups active or interested in the field of education and child welfare." Whether formal or informal, such arrangements give an association something to point to with pride when the time comes to report some accomplishment to its members. To be sure, the politician may ignore the association's recommendation when he gets it and, even if he acts on the recommendation, the appointee does not necessarily take the policy positions that the association would like him to take. Nevertheless, it can claim—often with justice—that it has had some influence, albeit indirect, on events.

The Influence of the Professional Staff

A large and well-established civic association employs a professional staff to do research, maintain relations with government officials, the press, and other civic associations, put out press releases and publications, and prepare program material for the membership. Because the association represents a job to the professionals and only an avocation to the officers, and because the professionals are necessarily in much closer touch with the details of the association's affairs, *de facto* control is usually in the hands of the staff. By making recommendations as to who should be put on the board and "groomed for leadership," by "training" new board members to the organizational (i.e., staff) point of view, by selecting program material, by using "research" to influence policy, by writing speeches and press releases for uncritical and often uninterested officers and board members, the staff may—and indeed often must—play a principal part in deciding the association's character, style, and strategy. The civic leaders who are the nominal heads of the association can hardly prevent this if they try: they are too busy with more important (private-serving) activities to take charge and, moreover, they realize that the staff must have a considerable degree of freedom if it is to serve the association effectively.

The staff man, having a large personal stake in the maintenance and enhancement of the organization, is particularly sensitive to the dangers of controversy. He avoids doing anything that might split the association or impart to it an "unfavorable image." If a point is reached where some substantial achievement in terms of the association's ends can be made only at the cost of losing some membership support, he is likely to forego the achievement. Not to do so, he would say, would destroy the "effectiveness" of the organization in the long run.

The ideological bent of the staff man is often different from that of the civic leaders who comprise his board of directors. He is selected, usually on the recommendation of other staff people, for his ability to assemble facts, write memoranda on policy matters, get along with people (especially those in government, academic, and professional circles), and for his commitment to public-serving, as distinguished from private-serving, ends.[14] He is apt, therefore, to share the views—conventional wisdom, it may be—of the occupational groups in which he was trained, with which he works, and to which he looks for approval. Consciously or otherwise, he often "feeds" to the officers and members of the association a policy line which is different from the one they would choose for themselves and which may even run directly counter to their interests and views. In Boston, for example, an association of conservative Republican businessmen undertook to make recommendations with regard to local tax policy. The staff they employed—liberal Democrats, as it happened—submitted a report which recommended (among other things) a graduated income tax. The businessmen signed the report and published it as a matter of course, although none of them favored an income tax and although there were no grounds for supposing that the staff's view of what "the public interest" required was any more defensible than the businessmen's.

The Ineffectiveness of Associations

Civic associations are rarely effective in terms of their stated ends. Several reasons for this must be apparent from what has already been said. The civic leader has no vital personal interest at stake; the association cannot give him orders; its ends must be vague or instrumental to give him the illusion at least of accomplishment. These circumstances tend strongly to prevent any concrete accomplishment. Even more important is the association's deeply ingrained fear of controversy. The larger and more "powerful" (prestigious and well-financed) an association and—what often goes with this—the more completely it is controlled by its staff, the less likely it is to risk any loss of support by taking up a cause that its members consider controversial. In his study of civic activity in Chicago, Clark found that the large, permanent civic associations were generally ineffective because, even in the matters that concerned them most, they would not do anything that might alienate some of their support. In some instances, Clark found, they "took ambiguous positions; they could not influence politicians because the politicians did not know what the associations actually wanted. On other issues the associations took no stands at all; they withdrew. In still other issues, when they did take positions they used ineffective tactics."[15]

Associations which make their appeal to some highly homogeneous—and therefore relatively small—sector of the public are in a very different position in these respects from associations which make their appeal to the whole public or to some large—and consequently heterogeneous—sector of it. For example, the Parent-Teacher Association, which wants a large membership drawn from all walks of life, must avoid anything deeply controversial. On the other hand the National Association for the Advancement of Colored People, which wants a membership that will fight for racial justice, must have an uncompromising commitment to ends that (from the standpoint of the community, but not of its membership) are "extreme" and controversial. The controversy that is poison to the large, broadly based association is the staff of life to the small, narrowly based one. The very smallness of an association tends to become a cause of its remaining small; for in order to maintain itself it must appeal to extremists or deeply committed persons, and by doing this it condemns itself to remain small. And smallness usually means that it is relatively poor and ineffectual as well.

A circumstance which has further tended to make civic associations ineffective is the practice, now widespread, of financing many of them partly from the receipts of united community fund drives. Since this money is given by the public at large, organizations receiving it are required to refrain from "political" (i.e., controversial) activities. Although the rule is probably seldom enforced, its effect is undoubtedly to make the recipient associations even more wary of controversy than they would otherwise be.

Civic associations could often accomplish more in terms of their stated ends if they worked together harmoniously. In fact they very rarely do. What Sayre and Kaufman say about civic associations in New York can be said about them elsewhere as well, that "they are incurably pluralistic, competitive, specialized in their interests, jealous of their separate identities."[16] This is to be explained by their peculiar maintenance needs. Since they must compete for resources (money, prestigious names, volunteer effort) and for program material ("safe" issues, workable projects), they are usually more concerned with establishing and preserving their separate identities than with achieving something by joint action. Organizational rivalry is most intense among associations with similar objectives, clienteles, and memberships. Many large cities, for example, have four different Jewish "defense" agencies—the Anti-Defamation League, the American Jewish Congress, the American Jewish Committee, and the Jewish Labor Committee. With memberships and goals that overlap to a great extent, much effort is put forth to maintain the identity of each association and to resist efforts at consolidation or joint action. Usually such agencies can make a good case for separateness. A merger, by reducing competition, would reduce the total amount of resources (members and funds) that they could raise without giving any assurance that the resulting unified association would be more influential than the several competing ones together.

More Effective Civic Activity

The civic leader, when he does not have to take account of the maintenance needs of an organization, that is, when he acts "as an individual," is less reluctant to take a stand on controversial matters. For this reason and others, he may exercise a considerable influence when "on his own" apart from a civic association. He is likely then to be in one or another of three quite distinct roles: (1) He may advise the mayor on some particular subject matter, such as downtown redevelopment, and act as a go-between for the mayor and some group or sector of the public, such as downtown businessmen. (2) He may negotiate the terms on which conflicting interests will agree to some specific undertaking (e.g., the main outline of an urban renewal program) that will then be presented to the public authorities for action. (3) He may promote, publicize, or "sell" to the larger public some undertaking that has already been agreed upon by a small group of activists; he does this by arranging meetings, giving after-dinner speeches, and issuing statements to the press.[17] In order to be effective in any of these capacities a civic leader must have the respect of the leading politicians and businessmen, something which is fairly rare because of the differences in point of view and background between those two groups. Usually such a civic leader has little or no *partisan* political weight.

Civic leaders are also relatively effective when they act through *ad hoc* civic associations. Because it is brought into being for a particular purpose and is expected to pass out of existence when that purpose has been accomplished, the *ad hoc* association is not as preoccupied with its own maintenance as is the permanent association and therefore lacks the permanent association's motive to avoid controversy. Its membership and leadership, moreover, are recruited with its particular purpose in mind, and they are therefore relatively cohesive and highly motivated. Because it either has no staff or has one that has been recruited for temporary service, the *ad hoc* association is less likely than the permanent association to fall under staff control.

The limitations of the permanent association being what they are, it is not surprising that when "important" (and hence controversial) issues arise the almost invariable practice is to create *ad hoc* associations to do what the permanent ones cannot, or will not, do. There are scores of permanent associations concerned with housing in New York, but when some people wanted to persuade the City Housing and Redevelopment Board to build a middle-income cooperative apartment instead of a rental project in Brooklyn, they organized the Cadman Plaza Civic Association and required that each member deposit fifty dollars as evidence of his interest. With just one well-defined purpose to serve and with a membership that had a tangible stake in its affairs, the association was almost certain to be more effective than any of the big, well-staffed associations would be. The necessity of taking a stand in favor of cooperative and against rental housing would have paralyzed them.[18]

The Civic Participation Movement

Citizen participation, which as we have shown has always been characteristic of the highly decentralized governmental institutions of American cities, has in recent years come to be regarded in many quarters as a normative principle inseparable from the idea of democracy itself. Indeed, the spread of the doctrine that there *ought* to be "grass roots" participation in local affairs has largely coincided with a reduction in real opportunities for ordinary citizens to exercise influence in the matters of importance to them; for example, opportunity to "participate" in planning urban renewal projects has taken the place of opportunity to "fix" traffic tickets. Some efforts to stimulate "grass roots" community organization arise out of the need felt by elected officials to establish lines of communication with voters which will serve some of the functions formerly served by ward and precinct organizations. The decay or destruction of precinct organization has left the officeholder unable to mobilize neighborhood opinion in support of his program.[19]

Citizen participation has also been encouraged by certain national reform organizations. The National Municipal League and the American Council to Improve Our Neighborhoods (ACTION), for example, have published pamphlets telling how to start civic associations and how to lead them to success. Some advocates of citizen participation justify it on the theory, popularized by the TVA, that there ought to be "a democratic partnership" between government agencies and the people's institutions.[20] This view appeals at once to the popular opinion that government ought to be kept subject to constant citizen control and surveillance. It also appeals to the desire of the government agencies themselves to demonstrate the democratic character of their activities; the agencies, which are of course confident that they will be the senior members in any "partnership," like to have groups that will share with them, or take from them, responsibility for decisions that may be otherwise indefensible.

Thus, federal housing policy requires that before a city can receive federal funds for urban renewal projects, a local citizens' association must participate in and endorse the final plan. The law requires that this involvement include not only ready acceptance of the plans by the organized public but also the active participation by the public in the planning activity.

The one elaborate study that has been made of a civic association created to give citizens opportunities to participate in planning affords little basis for encouragement about such ventures. The study, by Peter Rossi and Robert Dentler, concerns the part played by the Hyde Park-Kenwood Community Conference in the development of a thirty-million-dollar renewal project in the neighborhood of the University of Chicago.[21] The Conference put the "democratic partnership" doctrine to the test under highly favorable circumstances. It had a public that was used to community-serving activities, for the neighborhood had a high proportion of university professors, professional workers, and other upper-middle-class people. It could draw almost without limit on the services of experts in planning, law, architecture, community organization, and other related fields. By every standard except one the Conference turned out to be a great success; it was ably led, it raised an adequate budget and employed a competent staff, and it had genuine "grass roots" support, for there was widespread support for the idea of improving the neighborhood and for the idea of keeping it genuinely interracial. Nevertheless, "citizen participation . . . played a relatively negligible role in determining the contents of the Final Plan," Rossi and Dentler concluded, although it played a considerable role in winning acceptance for the plan. If, as seemed likely to them, the Conference represented the upper limit of possible citizen participation in such an enterprise, then the "maximum role to be played by a citizen movement in urban renewal is primarily a passive one."[22]

One body was effective in determining the content of the plan. This, it is instructive to note, was a pseudo-civic association, the South East Chicago Commission, established, financed, and used as a kind of "secular arm" by the University of Chicago, which had a large, direct, material interest in the future of the neighborhood. The Commission did not have a mass membership, was not internally democratic, was not much interested in general principles; it was remarkably effective precisely because it was run by a man who knew exactly what he wanted and did not have to consult a membership. The Conference was in exactly the opposite position: its functions were mainly to bring about agreement by affording citizens opportunities to learn of the details of the proposed plan; to serve as a "lightning rod" to attract and ground dissent; and to impart to the plan a legitimacy which the Commission and the University, being "selfish" and "undemocratic" organizations, could not give it.

In New York, where Columbia University sought to rehabilitate its decaying neighborhood around Morningside Heights, no effective citizens' organization on behalf of the plan could be created at all. There a normal pattern was followed: The citizens organized on an *ad hoc* basis to *oppose* specific plans of the University as soon as these plans became known.

NOTES

1. Floyd Hunter, *Community Power Structure* (Chapel Hill: University of North Carolina Press, 1953), p. 102.

2. Robert A. Dahl, *Who Governs?* (New Haven: Yale University Press, 1962). The quoted phrase is on p. 102.

3. Edward C. Banfield, *Political Influence* (New York: Free Press of Glencoe, 1961), p. 287. For critical discussions of many other studies of influence and power, see Nelson

W. Polsby, "Power in Middletown: Fact and Value in Community Research," *Canadian Journal of Economics and Political Science,* November 1960, pp. 592–603.

4. The method of Hunter and others is to ask presumably well-informed people ("judges") to rank according to relative "power" the "top leaders" of the city. Those nominated are then asked about their activities, associations, and friendships. The patterns thus revealed—"sociometric choices"—are assumed to describe "who really runs things" in the city. The method of Dahl, Banfield, and others is to discover who initiates, modifies, or blocks action on controversial matters. Attributions of power or influence, as distinguished from evidence of its exercise in concrete cases, are not relied upon. For discussion of the methodological question, see, in addition to the books already cited in this chapter, Herbert Kaufman and Victor A. Jones, "The Mystery of Power," *Public Administration Review,* Summer 1954, pp. 205–212; Nelson W. Polsby, "How to Study Community Power; the Pluralist Alternative," *Journal of Politics,* vol. XXII (1960), pp. 474–484; Polsby, "Three Problems in the Analysis of Community Power," *American Sociological Review,* December 1959, pp. 796–803: Raymond E. Wolfinger, "Reputation and Reality in the Study of Community Power," *American Sociological Review,* October 1960, pp. 636–644; Peter H. Rossi, "Community Decision-Making," *Administrative Science Quarterly,* June 1956, pp. 415–554; and Rossi, "Power and Community Structure," *Midwest Journal of Political Science,* November 1960, pp. 390–401; Howard J. Ehrlich, "The Reputational Approach to the Study of Community Power," *American Sociological Review,* December 1961, pp. 926–927; William V. D'Antonio and Eugene C. Erickson, "The Reputational Technique as a Measure of Community Power: An Evaluation Based on Comparative and Longitudinal Studies," *American Sociological Review,* June 1962, pp. 362–376.

5. See Delbert C. Miller's two articles: "Industry and Community Power Structure: A Comparative Study of an American and an English City," *American Sociological Review,* February 1958, pp. 9–14, and "Decision-Making Cliques in Community Power Structure: A Comparative Study of an American and an English City," *American Journal of Sociology,* November 1958, pp. 299–310.

6. Arthur Naftalin, in *The City,* a pamphlet published by the Center for the Study of Democratic Institutions (Santa Barbara, Calif., 1952), p. 34.

7. See Banfield, *op. cit.,* p. 276 ff.

8. Peter B. Clark, "Civic Leadership: The Symbols of Legitimacy," paper delivered before the annual meeting of the American Political Science Association, New York City, September 1960.

9. Peter B. Clark, "The Chicago Big Business as a Civic Leader," unpublished dissertation, Department of Political Science, University of Chicago, 1959. See also Wallace S. Sayre and Herbert Kaufman, *Governing New York City* (New York: Russell Sage Foundation, 1960), pp. 76–80 and chap. xiii.

10. In Lloyd Rodwin (ed.), *The Future Metropolis* (New York: George Braziller, 1961), p. 22.

11. The variety of nongovernmental groups in New York is well described by Sayre and Kaufman, *op. cit.,* pp. 76–80.

12. Peter B. Clark and James Q. Wilson, in their "Incentive Systems: A Theory of Organization," *Administrative Science Quarterly,* September 1961, pp. 129–166, distinguish three types of voluntary association: the *material,* which exists primarily to get tangible benefits for its members (e.g., a taxpayers' association); the *purposive,* which exists primarily to get intangible or ideological benefits (e.g., the National Association for the Advancement of Colored People); and the *solidary,* which exists primarily to afford the members the satisfactions of mutual association (e.g., B'nai B'rith). Their analysis of the significance of these differences in incentive systems for the role and strategy of associations in civic affairs is drawn upon in what follows.

13. Sayre and Kaufman, *op. cit.,* p. 481.

14. For example, in the fall of 1962 the Philadelphia Housing Association was seeking an assistant director for its professional staff of four (managing director, assistant director, research director, and community worker). The position paid $6,700 to $10,000, depending upon the experience of the person chosen. The qualifications were as follows:

Graduate study, preferably in government or public administration. At least three years of experience in a public or private agency involved in some aspect of urban renewal.

Commitment to the public interest and the objectives and program of the Housing Association.

General interest in urban problems and some knowledge of the literature.

Ability to gather information on specific topics quickly and accurately, and relate it to over-all policy considerations.

Ability to write easily and to speak with facility.

Ability to get along well with people of varying backgrounds and viewpoints.

15. Clark, *op. cit.*, p. 119.
16. Sayre and Kaufman, *op. cit.*, p. 80.
17. See Banfield, *op. cit.*, pp. 279–283.
18. For other examples, see the cases described at length in Banfield, *op. cit.*
19. See, for example, A Theodore Brown's account of the efforts of the reform administration in Kansas City to establish neighborhood councils, in Banfield (ed.), *Urban Government* (New York: Free Press of Glencoe, 1961), pp. 543–553.
20. For a discussion of TVA's doctrines and practice, see Philip Selznick, *TVA and the Grass Roots, A Study in the Sociology of Formal Organization* (Berkeley: University of California Press, 1949). For an application of the doctrines to urban affairs, see Coleman Woodbury (ed.), *The Future of Cities and Urban Redevelopment* (Chicago: University of Chicago Press, 1953), chap. iv. It is interesting that Woodbury refers specifically to the TVA experience.
21. Peter H. Rossi and Robert A. Dentler, *The Politics of Urban Renewal* (New York: Free Press of Glencoe, 1961). See also Julia Abrahamson, *A Neighborhood Finds Itself* (New York: Harper, 1959).
22. Rossi and Dentler, *ibid.*, pp. 5–12.

4.6 THE HOUSING DILEMMA

JEANNE R. LOWE

Sooner or later, one must get to the root question of where and how people live, and whether there is enough housing to meet their needs.

It bears stating that urban renewal—although part of the Housing Act of 1949—has not been, and is not of itself, a housing program. From the time that Title I began until June 1965, 311,197 dwelling units were demolished on urban renewal project sites and only 166,288 were built or are planned in their place.[1] Moreover, 35 per cent of all Title I funds now go to predominantly nonresidential projects. Rehabilitation and code enforcement, while they improve the housing stock that remains, tend to further reduce the net supply available to present tenants.

Add to such official renewal efforts other concurrent public improvement programs: highways often cut a path through cities' deteriorated areas; private activities—clearance for office buildings, parking lots, plant expansion—rip out housing but do not replace it. The total decrease in living space is formidable. Officials estimate that each year, nationally, as many as 300,000 dwelling units are demolished for all such purposes. Further, private demolition activities outweigh all public programs in volume, three to one.

In this total picture, urban renewal is relatively insignificant—although it has received the lion's share of blame by the public for destroying and not replacing low-income housing. Yet, because of its legal relocation requirements, the renewal program must concern itself with an adequate standard local housing supply, priced within reach of the dislocated, and it must compete with many others for such suitable vacancies as exist.

There has been much talk on the national level about the amount of new units that must be created annually in order to house adequately the 13,400,000 households living in substandard or overcrowded dwellings (as of the most recent national census); to keep up with the needs of the country's expanding population; and to retire obsolete housing. The consensus is that some 2,000,000 dwelling units must be produced a year, as compared to the average annual production during the past few years of only 1,500,000.

There is a vagueness, however, about what kind of housing should be produced for whom, at what cost, and where; how much government and private enterprise should or can be expected to do; and what localities can and might do to make up this deficit. We lack the machinery to make sure that enough housing exists to meet the needs of various unserved or under-served groups, especially at middle- and lower-income levels. The federal housing programs are a congeries of devices put together since 1934 to meet special needs (not all of them housing) and to accommodate special interests, pressures and ideologies. The special assistance programs that have been added since 1961 still do not implement the idealistic national housing policy enunciated in the preamble to the Housing Act of 1949—"a decent home and a suitable living environment for every American family."

Primarily, we have relied on the profit motive offered by private enter-prise, with some cushioning by the Federal Housing Administration. This has not proved to be a reliable mechanism for generating adequate housing, espe-cially for moderate- and low-income city families. We have an annual pro-duction gap of 500,000 dwelling units, and between 1950 and 1960 the number of substandard units in use in cities decreased by only 10 per cent. (While many slum buildings were demolished, other housing deteriorated.)

The point is that special-assistance housing is produced not nationally, but locally, where the lack of machinery becomes strikingly clear. Few states have housing agencies or programs. Cities just have pieces of programs vested in separate empires. One of these, the urban renewal agency (which may or may not be an independent authority), has the responsibility for tearing down obsolete buildings or encouraging their rehabilitation, and for getting private investors or owners to build on a specified site or to repair—hopefully with the cooperation of the FHA and local banks—according to official plans.

The public housing authority, another local but independently constituted body, also clears slums. It, however, has direct government financing available to build or rehabilitate low-rent housing. Federal law requires that priority be given in these low-rent projects to people eligible by income who have been displaced by urban renewal and by public housing itself. But this requirement does not insure the dislocates' admission. It does not guarantee that the units will be built and ready when families are to be dislocated several years hence, or even that the units will be of the right size to accommodate those displaced.

Of the 126,632 families on the urban renewal relocation workload since Title I began who were eligible for public housing, only one third have been rehoused in low-rent units. (Only a handful of renewal sites have been used for public housing, though during the past few years the numbers planned have been on the rise.) Gaining construction of new city housing specifically priced for middle-income families who earned too much for admission to low-income projects but not enough to afford decent private housing was almost impossible until passage of the Housing Act of 1961.[2]

Yet even public housing, for reasons we shall explore, fails to serve its market. By 1966, all the units built since the program began could house only 605,000 families, or 2,290,000 people, but some 11,000,000 urban fam-ilies had incomes below the median maximum admission limits of public housing.

The Federal Housing Administration is the only national public agency which has the means for encouraging the production of housing for the middle-income market in cities. But it is constituted to serve the private builder, not the public, and FHA and the urban renewal agency have often been on opposite sides of the fence. Moreover, cities do not have agencies specifically set up to program the FHA aids, a gap which urban renewal agencies are only beginning to fill as new housing assistance is legislated.

The Filter Process and Discriminatory Practices

Central cities usually have to rely on what is known in the housing field as the filter process to create vacancies in standard housing for families of lower incomes.

Filter process describes the way in which the normal housing market should work. According to the theory, as new housing is built, families who can afford to pay more vacate older units which then become available to families of a somewhat lower income who are on their way up the economic ladder and who in turn move out of still less desirable quarters. The oldest and worst housing will then be taken off the market voluntarily by its owners since there is no longer a demand for it and it should no longer be profitable, as rents are reduced to the level of new tenants' pocketbooks. The filter process does work, but only to a point.

First, not enough new housing is being built, especially for moderate- and low-income families, to create the full supply upon which the filter theory is predicated and the voluntary retirement of dilapidated or obsolete housing depends.

Secondly, where vacancies exist, families too often cannot afford the rentals at legal occupancy standards. Many must pay far more than one quarter of their income for shelter. Owners, in order to accommodate the new market and still squeeze their usual annual return from properties which have probably been depreciated several times, will divide larger living units into smaller ones. They convert old single-family homes into multiple-family use, allow more people to live in an apartment than should according to the law, or lease space in structures which should be torn down. Landlords also cut costs by reducing maintenance on such buildings.

They may thus solve the immediate shelter problem of the families, and even do so legally if a city's code specifications are not too exacting or systematically enforced. Such practices, however, prolong the life of unfit housing, create newly overcrowded housing (not to overlook the schools and neighborhoods which serve them) and spread the blight and decay which comprehensive urban renewal is supposed to eliminate.

A closely related and increasingly significant reason for the failure of the filter process is that the private housing market does not work freely for the growing non-white portion of the urban population. Instead, it excludes this sector from a substantial part of the housing supply and then exploits their situation.

The effect of discriminatory practices by the real estate, home building and mortgage lending industries was authoritatively studied and documented for the first time during the late 1950's and early 1960's by two sets of nationwide investigations—one conducted under the auspices of the Ford Foundation-sponsored Commission on Race and Housing, the other by the United States Commission on Civil Rights.[3] Although they found differences between regions and among some cities, and although the studies for the Commission on Race and Housing were undertaken prior to the 1960 census, the situation has remained so unchanged (the census corroborated the general findings) for the vast majority of non-whites—who have since grown in number in cities— and it is sufficiently similar in cities across the country that the basic facts should concern anyone who is interested in the future of American cities.

The studies found that the typical non-white family receives less for its rental dollar than the white family, whatever its income level or social position. And since the large majority of non-white families are renters, the ramifications are serious. They must pay a higher proportion of family income, as much as 50 per cent more, to obtain smaller, inferior accommodations[4] and are forced into significantly more overcrowding. Three times as many Negroes live in structurally substandard housing, in inferior neighborhoods, and over-crowding is four times more common than among white families.

Generally the quality of housing occupied by non-white families has improved markedly since 1950—as has that of white families. But the big gap separating the standard of accommodations occupied by the two groups has remained substantially unchanged. (A 1963 report on *Our Non-White Population and Its Housing* published by the Housing and Home Finance Agency revealed that the number of overcrowded white families decreased by 200,000 while the number of overcrowded units occupied by non-white families during the 1950's increased from nearly 1,000,000 to 1,300,000, even though the total proportion decreased.)

Because Negroes can often get more for their housing as homeowners than as renters, they purchase at much lower incomes than do whites. But this impulse to homeownership is exploited by realtors who capitalize on the fear they have inculcated in white property owners about minority groups' allegedly depressing effect on property values. By engaging in "block-busting," the realtor scares white families into selling their homes at panic prices by bringing a Negro family into a street. He then exploits the pent-up demand of Negroes for decent homes in better neighborhoods by selling them houses he has acquired at deflated values at inflated prices. Mark-ups by blockbusters as high as 112 per cent were revealed in hearings conducted in 1962 by the New York City Commission on Human Relations.

But the lending institutions really determine who lives where, because they hold the key to financing home purchase. The U.S. Commission on Civil Rights found that banks operated "on the premise that only a homogeneous neighborhood can offer an economically sound investment," and banks thus would withhold mortgages for a "first purchase" by a Negro in a white neighborhood. Once a neighborhood began to change, however, the Commission found that the banks would do "everything they can to expedite" the trend, including withholding mortgages from prospective white purchasers in those areas. Moreover, even when a Negro was fully qualified as a credit risk, lenders might charge him a higher discount on his loan or not issue one at all.

Such practices perpetuate the fear of white families that when a Negro family moves into their neighborhood, the area will inevitably become predominantly non-white. Professor William Grigsby of the University of Pennsylvania's Institute for Urban Studies has pointed out: "It is the pattern of market segregation which itself causes the inundation that whites observe and fear. In other words, since only a few areas are available to the expanding non-white population, when a new section 'opens up,' non-white demand tends to focus at this point of limited supply. In such a situation, a quick transformation from white to Negro occupancy frequently occurs."

The suburban "white noose" is another major reason the normal market process does not work. Housing is a metropolitan commodity and almost all new housing since the war has been put up in the suburbs. But scarcely any of it has been sold to non-whites. It is held that the tract developers, who put up most new housing, fear the effect that an open-sales policy would have upon their white customers.

Suburban pressures have discouraged new interracial housing tracts. A builder who endeavors to put through such a development against the opposition of local property owners finds that town and village governments can employ a host of subterfuges—large-lot zoning, the withholding of building permits, failure to install necessary water and sewer lines, even condemnation of a proposed building site for a park or other public use—without excluding him directly. Also, his usual sources of financing may dry up. At the same time, suburban realtors, like those in cities, refuse to show homes to Negro house hunters unless these are in "changed" areas.

Even new homes built privately with government mortgage guarantees or insured loans have not served the Negro market in proportion to its size. Only one percent of the government-insured homes constructed since World War II was purchased by non-whites, although Negroes comprised 10 per cent of the population. Generally, this one per cent was located in segregated developments, or substandard locations to which white families did not have to resort. In addition, most suburban housing was and is priced beyond the Negro market; this is a matter to which we shall return.

For many years, the Federal Housing Administration itself contributed to these patterns of residential segregation. It actually recommended restrictive covenants until the Supreme Court outlawed them in 1948, and before 1949, its underwriting manual, which governs insuring practices, warned against "adverse influences from lower-class infiltration and inharmonious racial groups." Although the FHA officially changed its policies, during the big postwar suburban building boom the home building industry still acted on the former basis and the federal agency did little to police them; thus the FHA allowed the suburbs to become more lily-white, and deprived the growing number of potential Negro home purchasers of the attractive terms of supposedly color-blind government insurance.

As white families left the drab older sections of cities for new and better homes in the suburbs, Negro families moved into these areas. In effect, these Negro families made possible the departure of the white families and the volume of new construction in suburbs to be sustained, although they could not benefit from it directly. The growing Negro middle class has, in fact, been denied a status symbol of major significance in the American way of life.

The metropolitan schism that has developed as a result can be seen at its extreme in the Washington, D.C. area, which has a total of 2,150,000 people. The District of Columbia itself, with a population of 801,000, is 63 per cent Negro; the suburbs, with more people than the metropolitan area, is 93 per cent white.

The effect of all these forces on the Negro's housing has been that the neighborhood where he may buy is usually older and lower in value, as is his home, which is thus a poorer lending risk. His down payment must be larger in proportion to what he buys, his repayment period is shorter, and interest charges are often higher. Refusal by banks to lend in some older or changing neighborhoods has frequently forced minority home purchasers to resort to loan sharks who charge outrageous terms, and to buy on insecure contract sales that do not give the owner title to a property until it is fully paid for. If he defaults one payment, he loses the house and his whole investment. Moreover, the non-white has less money left to spend on the higher cost of maintaining such an older property.

So lending, building, realty and even government practices have increased segregation and perpetuated the stereotypes of the Negroes as poor homeowners and neighbors who have a depressing effect on property values. They also have encouraged the deterioration of properties and neighborhoods to the detriment of entire communities, and furthered the segregated use of schools and other public facilities.

Yet the findings of a landmark study, *Property Values and Race,* undertaken for the Commission on Race and Housing refuted the time honored myth about racial intrusion deflating property values. This ten-year study of twenty middle-aged neighborhoods in seven cities, carried out by Luigi Laurenti and published in 1960, was the first to isolate the effect on the price of homes of non-white entry into a formerly white neighborhood. Laurenti's authoritative work concluded that minority purchasers, far from depressing values, tended to stabilize or even to raise them.

His research has since been corroborated by other studies, the most extensive being a ten-city survey of the *Midwestern Minority Housing Market* for the Advance Mortgage Corporation. Its 1963 report stated: "Property values in neighborhoods in racial transition generally held their own or rose above the neighboring norm, thus refuting a long-held stereotype." Price declines occurred in contiguous white neighborhoods which had been "written off by one market and not yet entered by another." . . .

Urban Renewal and Income Restraints

Where does urban renewal fit into this picture? A number of the earlier Title I redevelopment projects replaced generations-old slum ghettos with developments that offered the best values in private rental housing marketed without discrimination. As a result, these have been outstanding showcases for integrated living in central cities. The value of this achievement depends on a person's class and perspective. (We will come to the newer neighborhood conservation projects later in this chapter.)

In 1950, when part of the decaying "Black Belt" on Chicago's South Side was being cleared for redevelopment, the action was met with demonstrations and cries against racial discrimination. Yet a decade later, white and Negro families lived next door to each other in Lake Meadows and Prairie Shores, the first and second new housing developments in the area, and even had cocktails and dinner together in the project's new community center.

In fact, the first group of buildings in Lake Meadows were tenanted primarily by Negroes; yet the sponsor of Prairie Shores found no resistance on the part of white families moving into his apartments, although they knew the housing was to be racially integrated, and that Lake Meadows was predominantly Negro in occupancy. No doubt the fact that Prairie Shores' sponsor, Fred Kramer, a well-known mortgage banker and civic leader, resided in the development himself and personally showed apartments to prospective tenants, was an important contributing factor. So was the proximity of Michael Reese Hospital, with its built-in market of white nurses and doctors. (Again, the number of families with school-age children was limited.) Kramer's rent schedule of $30 a room—achieved by bringing in equity partners who were willing to accept a reasonably moderate return on their money, acquiring the land for fifty cents an acre, and winning the city's cooperation on taxation—made Prairie Shores the best new rental value in town. The attractive layouts of the apartments and the conveniences serving them helped to make the development desirable for white families with wider housing alternatives.

In fact, Kramer's apartments were an excellent demonstration of the common denominators in housing developments successfully integrated from the start that were found by Eunice and George Grier; their analysis, *Privately Developed Interracial Housing,* was another study carried out for the Commission on Race and Housing. The best way of insuring white demand for residence and ownership in an integrated community, the study showed, was to create a development outstandingly attractive in appearance, location and facilities and excellent in value.

Yet, despite its central location and unusual open-occupancy policy in the "most segregated" city in the country, Prairie Shores was far from overwhelmed by Negro applicants, even though virtually no new private housing was available for them elsewhere in the metropolitan area. The developer said that he had to go out of his way to find non-white tenants to achieve even a 20 per cent ratio. He attributed the limited demand primarily to lack of income on the part of Chicago's Negro population. The original portion of Lake Meadows seemed to have absorbed the bulk of the non-white market for rental housing in the $30-to-$35 a-room range. Here, as in other urban renewal projects built without special government financial assistance to lower housing costs (and also in suburban developments), the high price of new housing itself placed a ceiling on the degree of integration.[5]

The "thinness" of the non-white market for both new sales and rental housing throughout the country has been reported by builders and lenders. Economics is one of, if not *the,* major barriers. In fact, the report on the *Midwest Minority Housing Market* found that "the spread between white and non-white incomes remains so great, they would have to be treated as distinct markets even if no other limiting factors existed."

When the Griers undertook their study in the late 1950's, they found that "if all new private housing were open to Negroes, only a few would take advantage of it"—about 5 per cent. "And only a slight and statistically unimportant degree of integration would result." The Advance Mortgage Corporation's survey of midwestern cities revealed that under 5 per cent of the homes bought by Negroes were new.

Since the time of these surveys, there has been an increase in the number of Negro families in the middle-income bracket, and it is estimated that since those surveys the number of Negroes in the new home market has doubled. (A minimum income of $7,000 a year is considered necessary to purchase a new home on the most favorable terms. By 1964, 12.7 of the non-white urban families were in that category, although various circumstances precluded all from actually being in the market.)

But the Griers point out that the overall situation has not changed significantly. While there is a great proportionate increase at the upper levels, there is "no real narrowing of the gap between white and Negro in the new home market." (The median income of the non-farm *white* family in 1964 was $7,045—$3,000 more than that of the non-white, and much of the latter was attributable to multiple wage earners in a family.)

This is a matter of particular importance to integration; experience shows that it is much easier to establish a new integrated neighborhood or development than to prevent transition to segregation in an old neighborhood.

But fair-housing committees have found that, in spite of the recent "spectacular rise" in Negro homeownership, more homes in established white neighborhoods are available to Negro purchasers than there are applicants. Part of this surprisingly weak demand is due to the high cost of the housing. But it is also attributable to the reluctance of many Negros to be "pioneers" —to subject their family to rebuffs, insults and even physical violence in potentially hostile neighborhoods, and to the human desire to live near family and friends. Karl and Alma Taeuber point out in *Negroes in Cities* (1965) that "it seems impossible to separate coercive and voluntary components of racial segregation." Evidently personal factors have outweighed a desire on the part of many Negroes to escape segregated living; this underlines the need for programs to encourage and inform, within both ghetto areas and white communities.

"Minor gains must be measured against tremendous losses": the situation was thus described by the 1965 Fair Housing Conference.[6] Although there is more movement into mixed or previously white communities, and although the number of new interracial city and suburban developments grows, segregation is growing faster, and Negro concentration in central cities is steadily increasing.

The magnitude of the trend can be seen in an estimate of what would be necessary to reverse it in Washington D.C. made by George Schermer,[7] a national expert in the human relations field.

In the Washington metropolitan area, he reported non-white families have been increasing at the rate of 6,000 annually, and the ratio is accelerating so quickly that between 1960 and 1980 it will average 8,800 a year.

But no more than 100 non-whites a year are finding houses on a truly integrated basis throughout the metropolitan area.

Schermer found that if the area were to simply freeze ghettos at their present size and integrate only the additional families, it would be necessary to accommodate 8,800 non-white families annually in suburban areas. But if the District of Columbia were to reestablish a fifty-fifty racial balance by the year 2000, some 12,000 non-white families would have to be accommodated in the suburbs every year for the next thirty-five years; 4,000 white families annually would have to be attracted into the District.

"Of course, the numbers bit is only part of it," Schermer added. "There must [also] be equalization of buying power, restructuring of community and service facilities in suburban areas to meet the needs of low and moderate income families, and the revitalization of central city areas to attract middle class families."

The 1965 Fair Housing Conference, believing that the fair-housing movement had failed to make more of an impact largely because of its "middle-class nature," decided that first priority must be given to "a sharp increase in the supply of low- and middle-income housing located especially in areas which are predominantly white." The National Committee Against Discrimination in Housing began working in 1966 with local anti-poverty groups to encourage low-income Negroes to move out of ghettos.

But since private industry produces almost nothing for families with incomes under $7,000—and about 87 per cent of the urban Negro families fit into that category—publicly assisted housing is required.

More than prohibitory laws are needed, and financial assistance from government is required if the pattern of growing central city ghettos is to be reversed or even reduced. But the big problem, after getting the necessary housing programs, is how to put them to use in the larger metropolitan area.

New Housing Tools and Government Assistance

A major step in filling the cost gap between housing produced by the private market and public housing was taken by Congress in 1961 with a new FHA program, Section 221(d)3, more familiarly known as (d)3. This was the first federal housing program specifically created to encourage private construction of rental or cooperative housing priced for the low-middle-income market, within or outside of urban renewal areas.

Although it was not legislated specifically for the non-white market, (d)3 housing has inevitably met that market's needs to a much greater extent than had earlier FHA programs like 220. Moreover, with the signing of the President's order in 1962 banning discrimination in federally assisted housing, units built under this program were all to be marketed on an open-occupancy basis.

Section 221(d)3 lowers the cost of housing by making the below-market interest rate the government pays—which varies from 3 to 4 per cent —available to finance construction, with sponsorship restricted to non-profit or limited-profit corporations and cooperatives. The program does not require private financing beyond the small 2 per cent cash equity required from the sponsor. Congress authorized the Federal National Mortgage Association[8] to buy all the (d)3 permanent mortgages. The program thus reduces the single largest item in shelter cost, the debt service, by as much as one third, and it results in monthly savings to the tenant or cooperator of between $15 and $25 an apartment. Occupancy is limited by law to moderate-income families.

In the first four years of the program, 45,000 units of (d)3 housing were contracted for—a marked improvement over earlier FHA special-assistance programs. For a number of urban renewal projects initiated under higher-rental programs such as 220, it made the difference between success and failure.[9] In many renewal neighborhoods, it would be impossible to build for the market without (d)3. In fiscal 1966 applications were made for 30,000 new units, and the Housing Department estimated there would be 45,000 in fiscal 1967.

Still, (d)3 presents certain difficulties. One of these is finding qualified sponsors. Church groups, settlement houses, foundations and other groups which typically sponsor such non-profit housing lack the necessary skills for developing and managing such real estate undertakings, and the FHA does not have the staff to compensate for this lack. Local offices drag processing; they worry about defaults and Congress. In some cities, the local urban renewal agency helps guide these new housing sponsors. A national technical advisory service on the local level for this so-called "third force" in housing is also being offered through Urban America, Inc., a private non-profit urban improvement group.

One problem, the rising federal interest rate, was met in 1965 when Congress pegged the rate for this program at a flat 3 per cent. Another constriction, the need for a locality to have a "workable program," makes it presently impossible to build (d)3 housing in many suburbs. Other limits are the funds that Congress makes available to FNMA and the low per-unit construction costs; family income ceilings fixed by Congress make it difficult to use 221(d)3 in metropolitan areas with high construction, land and living costs.

In such high-cost areas, some abatement of the real estate tax in conjunction with (d)3 housing is necessary to build housing priced low enough for the low-middle-income market. In fact, localities could all do much more by using two potent local tools, real estate tax abatement and low-interest government loans, without federal aid. It would, however, require enabling action by their state legislatures.

New York, since 1955, has had the outstanding example of this type of locally assisted middle-income housing under its Mitchell-Lama or Limited Profit Housing Companies program. Under this act, the city or state can make low-interest, long-term loans of up to fifty years' duration to sponsors of limited-profit housing. Cities are also allowed to grant abatement of real estate taxes on up to 50 per cent of the assessed valuation of the property prior to its improvement for a thirty-year period. The ceiling on rents or carrying charges is set by official policies at $30 a room.[10] Some 30,000 Mitchell-Lama units have been built in New York City. As the cost of construction continues to outpace the rise in the cost of living and in the incomes of certain groups, such kinds of local assistance appear to be necessary in order to provide the middle third—the teachers, civil servants, nurses, policemen and bus drivers—with standard shelter.

But these public aids should be used judiciously, in the context of desired goals, and with a recognition of comparative yields and benefits. When potentially high-yield land is pre-empted for tax-abated housing, as has happened on some Manhattan sites, it might be cheaper and more efficient to raise municipal salaries or to provide families with direct housing assistance.

Moreover, experience with Mitchell-Lama has not proved that housing priced specifically for the middle-income market can, of itself, hold in the city the average white or non-white middle-class family with several children —nor can it bring them back from the suburbs. In neighborhoods where public schools are poor, these publicly assisted middle-income apartments generally do not attract families with children, and many of the larger apartments remain vacant. Families with two or three children who could afford the down payment on a cooperative seem to prefer to spend a little more and buy a house, generally in the suburbs, where public schools are better.

A study of the non-white market for the Mitchell-Lama cooperatives in New York City found that only 36 per cent of the families could afford the monthly carrying charges and the initial down payment, or the similarly modest rents charged in such city- and state-aided housing. Only 5 per cent could afford non-aided new private apartments. The rest, in order to have standard homes, would have to accept low-rent public housing.

Nationally, although the majority of white families in metropolitan areas have the income and freedom to buy or rent standard housing within their means, non-white urban families are not only restricted in choice, but half have incomes of $4,000 or less. Moreover, 44 per cent of the Negroes in cities live in substandard housing, compared to 13 per cent of the whites. Of the families displaced by urban renewal, 59 per cent of the non-white families (who comprise the majority) have been eligible by income for public housing.

Given these circumstances, and the fact that Negroes must spend more for less housing, it is hardly surprising that half of all the residents in public housing today are Negro. Yet there are far more poor white people than there are poor Negroes in cities. And here we run into the basic dilemma that has hounded city rebuilders in recent years: *who wants public housing? . . .*

What seems to have been glossed over by many appraisers of public housing is that when the program was making its public record of achievement in the late 1930's and the early 1940's, the program did not, by and large, reach the lower socioeconomic class. During the depression years the ill-housed and low-income families were not necessarily lower-class families. Tenants in the PWA projects were mostly skilled laborers and the lower-income segment of clerical and white-collar workers. The communal projects seemed to work very well for the middle-class but low-income family and for the upwardly mobile lower class (as well as for veterans going to college on the GI Bill).

Those who had pointed with pride to formerly disturbed slum dwellers whose social habits were allegedly improved or whose problems were reduced by moving to public housing, underestimated the influence of public housing management, newly available services and other important non-shelter variables. It seems likely that the improvement resulted from a combination of factors: among them a decent, uncrowded home; a responsible landlord; new attention from health and social agencies; and many years of hard work by management.

Finally, one cannot underestimate the importance of new opportunities and motivations that low-income families derived from the different and better jobs becoming available nationally in the post-depression and early postwar years. Given a financial lift by the expanding economy and union wage demands, elevated from working to middle class by the changes taking place within the private economy, the ill-housed "worthy" poor of the depression, or their children, became part of the postwar middle-income bulge and headed for the suburbs. Soon they were organizing PTA's, Cub Scouts, hobby clubs, coffee klatches and improvement associations in the new developments. "When people move from . . . the city to the . . . suburb, their participation and associational life increases deeply," Max Lerner wrote in *America as a Civilization* (1957), using phrases strikingly similar to the early public housing chronicles of the transition from slum to housing project.

But people can also be found participating busily in the beehive, highrise, middle-income cooperative housing developments in New York City. The difference in behavior appears to stem from class and cultural factors rather than from residential environment and its design.

In cities, meanwhile, portions of the neglected lower class, along with many urban newcomers, have been uprooted from slums and moved to projects designed by and largely for the middle class; they have brought with them very different family patterns, values and needs.

We have only begun to study the orientations and values attached to place of residence, environment and neighbors by working- and lower-class families. These new insights call for a reconsideration of slum clearance criteria, the design of housing for low-income families, the criteria and methods of tenant selection in public housing, and the kinds of personnel needed in projects.

Some directors are bothered because so many of today's poor are not like the old public housing tenants. Some have even blamed urban renewal and other public improvement programs for foisting on the projects all those large, socially troubled, often apathetic and increasingly non-white families, who, left on their own, would probably not have applied for admission and who also scare off "normal" low-income families.

Is public housing intended to house the needy, or to create "healthy" communities? Can it do both? Two different schools of thought emerged. The first, and more pervasive, is obsessed by the poor image of public housing. This group has wanted to reconstitute projects into socially "normal," racially integrated communities with a "better cross-section" of low-income families, more white families, and a minimum of problem families, the "rotten apples" that spoil a project.[11] They have blamed income ceilings for depriving projects of leaders; they contend that these limits rob families of the initiative to earn more money because, it is said, they will then have to pay more rent, and when their earnings reach a certain level, move out. Ceilings are also unnatural and stigmatizing, it is suggested, and they make the public housing project, in the words of the National Federation of Settlement Houses and Neighborhood Centers, into "the modern symbol of the poor-house."

This group advocated that tenants whose incomes rise be allowed to remain and pay full economic rent; they could eventually buy their project apartment or house. Smaller units in scattered sites, or rehabilitated housing are proposed as an alternative to projects. These would be preferably outside of slum-ghetto areas. Some preferred to give rent supplements or direct subsidies so the needy can live in standard, privately owned housing. The goal seems to have been well summarized by one big city planning director: make public housing "invisible."

The second, less prevalent school was exemplified by the National Capital Housing Authority. It accepted early the relocation challenge of urban renewal, and programmed all its units to facilitate the end of slums in the District. The Authority believed, as the NCHA's former director James Ring had stated, that the uprooted and disorganized families were "more acutely in need of public housing's services than other families who have taken the initiative and are eager to break away from the slums." The Washington public housing officials tried to marshal all possible community resources to meet such tenants' immediate needs and then help them graduate to the private housing market. As far back as 1954, the annual report of the National Capital Housing Authority stated that "Public housing would not be performing its job if it retained in tenancy [over-income families] in preference to low-income families who are waiting for a chance to live in decent housing."

Yet even in Washington, by the early 1960's, it was evident that the conventional approach was not keeping pace with the pressing needs of large low-income families. If some dent were to be made in just the long list of displaced families which had been waiting for admission to public housing— some for ten and twelve years—supplementary housing resources would have to be found beyond the usual projects.

Washington, like other cities, was running into two practical obstacles. One was trying to construct large enough apartments for big low-income families within the cost limits set by the Public Housing Administration. The other was finding sites on which to build. . . .

. . .[E]xclusionism, compounded by the increasing shortage of open land in central cities, has forced local authorities to rely more and more on the clearance of congested slum areas to obtain sites, or not to build at all.

Experience in public housing management has shown that it is easier to handle social problems in row houses or projects of limited size. Keeping down gross densities in projects was a major goal of public housing from its inception.

But the necessity for the authorities to use slum land, and consequently to absorb the high cost of slum clearance into project development,[12] or to make the most use of limited open land, combined with ever-rising construction costs, resulted in the proliferation of the high-rise project—a gross caricature of the community unit of the 1930's. It provided more decent low-rent dwelling units and gave tenants more light, air and living space per dwelling than in the slum. But it also put large families into unfamiliar elevator buildings at densities they had never experienced. The supervision of children became more of a problem, housing management became more difficult, and social problems more disruptive, while the project, the "modern symbol of the poor-house," became more visible than ever to the rest of the community.

Large-scale projects built on former slum land have many additional "hidden" costs, the first being a social one—the enormous disruption of the former residents and their communities. Then, many more personnel are needed. Elaborate police protection is required to patrol the grounds of a publicly owned facility in the middle of a slum. High-rise buildings need more managerial and supervisory staff per capita. These costs must be paid out of tenants' rent. This is particularly important because operating expenses in public housing are not subsidized; they are financed out of rent receipts. The higher these costs, the fewer really low-income families can be housed.

The one city that for many years moved ahead, largely undeterred by the implications of these trends, was New York City, where Construction Coordinator Robert Moses leadership gave the local program much of its thrust. As a result, New York built enough public housing to relocate the city of Buffalo, and in the process contributed disproportionately to the bad national image of public housing. But politicians could boast that they had helped the poor without offending homeowners and taxpayers.

Public housing also suffers from an esthetic dilemma. Architects who have been frustrated in attempts to improve the bleak and institutional design of public housing tend to blame government red tape, the low fees and rigid standards imposed by the Low Rent Housing Manual, and bureaucratic resistance to anything that looks attractive. However, Public Housing Commissioner Marie McGuire, who has done much to improve project design, pointed out: "If, in the interest of economy—and in my judgment false economy—we build conventional box-type apartments, we arouse the esthetic ire of the community. But when we build architecturally attractive dwellings, we are told we are squandering the taxpayer's money."

Design has been most institutional and most out of context with its surroundings where there has been the most, and thus the most conspicuous, public housing—in big cities. An inverse ratio appears to exist between quantity and quality of appearance. (Use of the same building design over and over again was encouraged in New York as a cost-saving device and created that city's barracks-like projects.)

In small communities or in western cities, where densities are lower and cost factors and political pressures milder—and where most public housing has been built—there are small-scale projects with neighborhood orientation. Even in larger cities, as in Pittsburgh or Philadelphia, where the executive director had a sense of mission, the housing authority and local architects joined to overcome inhibiting government regulations; low-rent housing in these areas displayed considerable ingenuity, sensitivity to neighborhood and site, and amenity of design, suggesting that the fault has not been entirely with federal laws, or with realtor and community harassment. However, much less housing got built.

Still, even New York's level of project design has improved considerably under new progressive leadership since the 1958 local reorganization. The Housing Authority has shown unusual initiative in obtaining private foundation financing of attractive facilities, such as plazas, which the federal formula does not finance. This seems to support a veteran federal administrator's claim that "the Achilles heel of the program has been the boy from City Hall who is given the job on the basis of party loyalty rather than ability."

What little empirical evidence there is about consumer preferences, however, suggests that project design affronts certain middle-class observers more than the low-income tenants. In a nine-city survey carried out by the federal public housing agency to learn why tenants voluntarily move from low-rent projects, "nothing was so often praised as the structural quality and general attractiveness of the projects." What bothered the respondents most of all about the physical quality and environment was the surrounding slum neighborhood—which remained unchanged.

More New Tools and New Dilemmas

The Housing and Urban Development Act of 1965 presented an assortment of alternative means for housing the urban poor and, hopefully, for overcoming the many obstacles that have recently blocked public housing's traditional approach. The three major programs are all designed to avoid monster projects and sharp distinctions between public and private housing by making use of existing privately owned structures or newly built private housing for low-income families.

One new provision enables local housing authorities to either lease or purchase, and rehabilitate, private structures under somewhat shorter terms than public housing's usual forty years for new buildings, and to rent these units to low-income families under the usual formula. Another provision allows authorities to contract for the use of up to 10 per cent of the apartments in private buildings on one-to-three-year renewable leases; the tenants may be selected by the owners, who are required by contract to bring buildings up to code standards. Tenant charges and rentals are on the same basis as in conventional public housing.

The most unorthodox approach is the rent supplement program, which departs entirely from the public landlord and project approach. The supplements make it possible for low-income families to live in privately owned, FHA-assisted middle-income housing built by nonprofit or limited-profit sponsors using the (d)3 program, but at full market interest rate. The Federal Housing Administration pays the difference between 25 per cent of the tenants' incomes and the economic rents required in such housing. The law also authorized that the traditional projects be continued along with these new experimental programs.[13]

With such a variety of publicly assisted programs for both low- and middle-income families, it should be possible not only to move ahead with the task of housing the urban poor, but also to avoid the many objections raised to both public housing and urban renewal. Perhaps the new social end results, which people are coming to expect of renewal, may be realized along with physical improvements.

Among the principal objections raised are mass dislocation of the poor (often non-white) and destruction of communities; ghettoization by income and segregation by color. The main new social goals are planned renewal with the participation of the residents; community preservation and on-site rehousing of dislocatees; elimination of ghettos and integration of communities; economically and socially heterogeneous neighborhoods. (According to proponents of the latter view, socioeconomic distance can be bridged through residential proximity; middle-class patterns transmitted to the lower class through neighborhood interaction; ghettos, low incomes and prejudices can thus be eliminated. Talk about renewal in terms other than diversity, not merely of building types but also of racial and economic groups, has come to be regarded here as heretical and undemocratic.)

One cannot challenge the validity of these goals, taken separately. But it soon becomes obvious that realization of one goal may be detrimental or antithetical to others. Dilemmas and conflicts inevitably arise, not just between physical and fiscal versus social goals, but also among the social objectives, and hard choices must be made, both by residents and by public officials. Once we have accepted this fact, certain questions arise. Whose objectives are more representative and valid? Who will benefit? If social goals become predominant, how many of the poor will get decent housing, and how soon will cities be renewed? The fact is that people of good will are not in agreement on how to proceed.

There are, for example, strong differences between the views of proponents of desegregation and ghetto dispersion through public actions, and the practices and apparent desires of many who live in so-called Negro ghettos.

At a national conference on programs for "breaking up the ghetto" held in the spring of 1966 by the National Committee Against Discrimination in Housing in cooperation with the federal Office of Economic Opportunity, the sharp disagreement expressed by some members of the audience was a shock to the sponsors. One California representative stated that it is unpopular in the Negro community to move into a white area, and that dispersion is called "political castration." A San Franciscan said of her community, Hunter's Point, "Some want to stay and some want to go. We know what he want— decent facilities. But we don't know how to get the money to get them." This viewpoint was echoed by the anti-poverty program director from Los Angeles. "People in Watts aren't clamoring to get out," he said. "They want more buses, quality housing and the freedom to get out, if they want." A New Orleans representative pointed out that in his city, there had always been racial dispersion, but "on a master and servant basis, not among equals. Aren't we confusing race and culture?" he asked. The dilemma several speakers raised was: do we have to strengthen the ghetto before we can disperse it?

There is deep confusion, even within civil rights ranks, about urban renewal. Title I projects that entail massive clearance and family dislocation in Negro slums have been criticized as "Negro removal." Yet integrationists condemn the newer kinds of projects which instead emphasize housing rehabilitation and improvement of Negro neighborhoods; they call this "embalming a ghetto." If one were to heed these critics, urban renewal could not win on racial grounds. . . .

Chicago's Hyde Park—Kenwood

In Chicago's physically deteriorating Hyde Park–Kenwood area, one of the country's earliest and largest Title I conservation projects, the main renewal goal was to improve and thus maintain the only racially integrated community in "the most segregated" city. This required some very difficult choices.

Hyde Park–Kenwood is an area of one square mile and 75,000 people bordering Lake Michigan, located between the black belt to the south of center city and the University of Chicago. An attractive, well-located and once fashionable community, with a strong liberal tradition and a high percentage of homeownership, its residents included many professional people and a large number of the city's civic leaders.

In 1948, when the Supreme Court ruled that restrictive covenants were unenforceable, the community did not fight as Negro families spilled over into it from the bursting ghetto next door. The variety of housing in the area offered suitable dwellings for many income levels and family types. Negro professionals and businessmen bought substantial homes alongside white neighbors, who welcomed them. But as block-busters crowded low-income non-whites into the area's big old-fashioned mansions, and converted apartment houses into one-room slums, block by block, many white families fled. Schools became crowded with pupils from lower cultural backgrounds, and many whites were scared away by the crime wave that was sweeping the district. By the time that renewal planning began in the mid-1950's, over one third of the area's population was non-white, and it was generally predicted that in ten years Hyde Park–Kenwood—like other changing Chicago neighborhoods—would be a slum.

The rape of a faculty wife in 1949 precipitated the formation of a citizen organization, the Hyde Park–Kenwood Community Conference, which soon achieved national renown and a membership of 4,000. They early set their goal: "to establish and maintain a stable inter-racial community of high standards." They recognized that their community had been deteriorating physically for many years due to zoning variances, the wartime housing squeeze, inadequate city services, and postwar illegal overcrowding. They also recognized that their community could be neither interracial nor stable unless community standards and facilities were made to be competitive with those in the suburbs to which white middle-class families were fleeing.

The Conference requested designation for Title I aid, and the University retained a planner to devise the renewal proposal. Over a two-year period, the plan, which laid heavy emphasis on enhanced livability and institutional expansion to stabilize the area, was hammered out—with some 400 meetings among the planner and Conference committees, block groups, neighborhood hearings, and after endless soul-searching.

At best the plan was a compromise, and no one was really happy. In order to achieve the enhanced livability and facilities—enlarged playgrounds and schools, better traffic patterns, densities reduced to prewar levels, and expansion of the community's various institutions—20 per cent of the dwelling units would have to be cleared. Some were standard homes occupied by white families, including faculty members. But the vast majority of homes were substandard, and 60 per cent were occupied by Negroes, most of whom were too poor to afford any standard shelter except low-rent public housing.

Originally, the Conference pressed for 600 units of public housing, some to be small, scattered projects and others rehabilitated. (An eighty-four-unit project for the elderly was already scheduled by the Housing Authority.) But as the city's mortgage market began warning that the private millions necessary to construct 2,000 units of new housing called for in the plan (and to rehabilitate many deteriorated buildings) would not be forthcoming with so much public housing nearby, even the Conference watered down its demands to 120 units. (After the clearance called for in the plan, one quarter of the families in the community would still be low income.) The final plan submitted to the city by the area's Mayor-appointed Community Conservation Council—which included representatives of business, residents, institutions in the area, and white and Negro members—proposed only sixty low-rent units.

No protest came from the comparatively well-off Negro residents of Hyde Park–Kenwood. (The lower-income residents, white and non-white, rarely attended neighborhood meetings or participated in planning.) As one Negro civic leader declared, "I think we should take the same position as the white people. It's a class position, really. . . . You can't create a homogeneous community out of heterogenous elements."

Some non-white homeowners felt that *they* had the most to lose if Hyde Park–Kenwood followed the course of racial turnover of other Chicago neighborhoods. As one expressed it to a white neighbor in Kenwood (which by 1960 was so successfully integrated that residents held a formal ball for one hundred couples of both races), "You have some place to go. We haven't. If you leave, city services and police protection will go down. Will the schools stay as good?"

The uncomfortable conclusion was that to maintain stable racial integration, the number of low-income Negro families in public housing would have to be very limited. Former Hyde Parkers Elaine May and Mike Nichols, appearing at a Conference benefit, quipped, "Here's to Hyde Park–Kenwood, where Negro and white stand shoulder to shoulder against the poor."

NOTES

1. These official figures include only committed land in Title I projects.

2. Until the 1961 Act, the only tool available for such middle-income families was the now discarded Section 221, under which FHA offered insurance for private builders who put up minimal relocation housing in ordinarily questionable sites. So few builders were interested in this unprofitable housing that it produced only 5,342 multiple-family units and 21,988 home units—most of the latter were rehabilitated, not new, and, due

to the problems of timing, very few were actually occupied by displaced families. The 1961 Act also eased admission of those with incomes slightly in excess of the public housing limits.

3. *Report of the U.S. Commission on Civil Rights 1959* and *1961 Commission on Civil Rights Report, Book 4: Housing,* Superintendent of Documents, Government Printing Office, Washington, D.C. The major studies prepared for the Commission on Race and Housing and the Commission's final report, *Residence and Race,* were published by the University of California Press, 1960.

4. The lowest-income centers, who form the bulk of urban non-whites, commonly have to pay a much larger percentage of their income for shelter than do whites of similar economic status. It is not uncommon for big city landlords to charge and obtain a bonus for allowing non-whites to rent their substandard accommodations.

5. A Chicago human relations leader asserts that the Negro market for such rents is greater than the units available and that "occupancy controls" are used to maintain balance. But he does not dispute that where the metropolitan housing market is not open, a developer who wants meaningful integration must make special efforts to keep substantial white occupancy. The fact is sophisticated civil rights groups believe it important for Chicago to have a showcase for integration.

6. Held by the National Committee Against Discrimination in Housing and the Phelps Stokes Fund Inc.

7. In a report made for a 1966 conference held by the National Committee Against Discrimination in Housing.

8. The Federal National Mortgage Association (FNMA) is an instrument of the federal government intended to provide a "secondary" mortgage market for government-insured or guaranteed programs. Under Congressional mandate, it may also buy mortgages for such housing in urban renewal areas or for other specific types of housing designated by Congress or deemed to be in the public interest by the President where the private mortgage market does not fill the need.

9. One such early project, Park Town in Cincinnati, provides an interesting case. When originally marketed by its sponsor, the Reynolds Metals Company, as a cooperative at full market interest rates, only 20 per cent of the units were sold. One reason for such poor sales was the relatively undesirable location. But after (d)3 was enacted and the sponsor shifted the project to this lower-cost financing, sales in the project rapidly went up to 80 per cent of occupancy.

The change in financing also brought about a market shift in the racial composition of the tenancy. Park Town had been marketed on an open-occupancy basis from the start, but the higher-cost 220 housing was 40 per cent white, and the lower-cost (d)3 housing 16 per cent. The portion of whites has not gone over 20 per cent since.

The change in racial composition was believed to be due in good part to the low-income ceilings Congress imposed on (d)3 housing. Granted the project remained integrated, but many more Negro families were now eligible than before. Conversely many of the original white tenants were now excluded. And Negro families, having fewer housing choices available to them than white families, were far more likely to move in there.

10. Every 10 per cent cut in taxes is reflected in savings of about $1.15 to $1.30 per room, or about $5.75 to $6.50 per two bedroom apartment. When in 1966, the city's borrowing rate was forced about 5 per cent due to municipal fiscal problems, charges in Mitchell-Lama projects were forced several dollars above the $30 ceiling.

11. The New York City Housing Authority in 1961 developed a list of social eligibility requirements for applicants as a way of keeping out undesirables and potential trouble-makers. In this policy, eight "clear and present dangers" to other tenants are cited as making a family ineligible for admission. These include "grossly unacceptable house-keeping," and a "record of unreasonable disturbance or destruction of property." In addition, twenty-one conditions indicative of "potential problem" families are to be considered before a final decision on admission is made. These include "irregular work history," "two or more separations of husband and wife in the past five years," "out-of-wedlock children," "lack of parental control" and "retardation of any family member."

Recently, pressures from civic groups and City Hall have forced a re-examination of these policies. The Housing Authority applied to the Office of Economic Opportunity for a $1,100,000 grant to pay for extra caseworkers, teachers and other personnel to work with problem families in urban renewal areas so they can qualify for public housing.

12. The write-down which permits Title I sites to be rebuilt at desirable densities is not available to public housing unless it is built in renewal areas. The low-rent housing project must absorb the entire cost of acquiring and demolishing slum property. In order to spread the high initial acquisition cost within the limits set by Congress for per-unit development costs—it has been found that acquisition costs average $2,285 per unit in a former slum area compared to $589 in a non-slum area—the low-income project usually must be built high-rise.

13. Other new federal housing aids which are not part of the public housing program but will help low-income owners improve their housing include: direct grants of up to $1,500 for rehabilitation to families with incomes under $3,000 in urban renewal areas, and 100 per cent loans for rehabilitated housing owned by families with somewhat higher incomes.

LEE RAINWATER

Men live in a world which presents them with many threats to their security as well as with opportunities for gratification of their needs. The cultures that men create represent ways of adapting to these threats to security as well as maximizing the opportunities for certain kinds of gratifications. Housing as an element of material culture has as its prime purpose the provision of shelter, which is protection from potentially damaging or unpleasant trauma or other stimuli. The most primitive level of evaluation of housing, therefore, has to do with the question of how adequately it shelters the individuals who abide in it from threats in their environment. Because the house is a refuge from noxious elements in the outside world, it serves people as a locale where they can regroup their energies for interaction with that outside world. There is in our culture a long history of the development of the house as a place of safety from both nonhuman and human threats, a history which culminates in guaranteeing the house, a man's castle, against unreasonable search and seizure. The house becomes the place of maximum exercise of individual autonomy, minimum conformity to the formal and complex rules of public demeanor. The house acquires a sacred character from its complex intertwining with the self and from the symbolic character it has as a representation of the family.[1]

These conceptions of the house are readily generalized to the area around it, to the neighborhood. This fact is most readily perceived in the romanticized views people have about suburban living.[2] The suburb, just as the village or the farm homestead, can be conceptualized as one large protecting and gratifying home. But the same can also be said of the city neighborhood, at least as a potentiality and as a wish, tenuously held in some situations, firmly established in others.[3] Indeed, the physical barriers between inside and outside are not maintained when people talk of their attitudes and desires with respect to housing. Rather, they talk of the outside as an inevitable extension of the inside and of the inside as deeply affected by what goes on immediately outside.

When, as in the middle class, the battle to make the home a safe place

From Lee Rainwater, "Fear and the House-as-Haven in the Lower Class." Reprinted by permission of the *Journal of the American Institute of Planners,* Vol. 32, No. 1 (January 1966).

has long been won, the home then has more central to its definition other functions which have to do with self-expression and self-realization. There is an elaboration of both the material culture within the home and of interpersonal relationships in the form of more complex rituals of behavior and more variegated kinds of interaction. Studies of the relationship between social class status and both numbers of friends and acquaintances as well as kinds of entertaining in the home indicate that as social status increases the home becomes a locale for a wider range of interactions. Whether the ritualized behavior be the informality of the lower middle class family room, or the formality of the upper middle class cocktail party and buffet, the requisite housing standards of the middle class reflect a more complex and varied set of demands on the physical structure and its equipment.

The poverty and cultural milieu of the lower class make the prime concern that of the home as a place of security, and the accomplishment of this goal is generally a very tenuous and incomplete one. (I use the term "lower class" here to refer to the bottom 15 to 20 percent of the population in terms of social status. This is the group characterized by unskilled occupations, a high frequency of unstable work histories, slum dwellings, and the like. I refer to the group of more stable blue-collar workers which in status stands just above this lower class as the "working class" to avoid the awkwardness of terms like "lower-lower" and "upper-lower" class.) In the established working class there is generally a somewhat greater degree of confidence in the house as providing shelter and security, although the hangovers of concern with a threatening lower class environment often are still operating in the ways working class people think about housing.[4]

In Figure 4.7A, I have summarized the main differences in three orien-

FIGURE 4.7A.   Variations in Housing Standards within the Lower and Working Classes

Focus of Housing Standard	Core Consumer Group	Most Pressing Needs in Housing	
		Inside the House	Outside Environs
Shelter	Slum dwellers	Enough room Absence of noxious or dangerous elements	Absence of external threats Availability of minimum community services
Expressive elaborations	Traditional working class	Creating a pleasant, cozy home with major conveniences	Availability of a satisfying peer group society and a "respectable enough" neighborhood
All-American affluence	Modern working class	Elaboration of the above along the line of a more complex material culture	Construction of the all-American leisure style in terms of "outdoor living" "Good" community services

tations toward housing standards that are characteristic of three different consumer groups within the lower and working classes. I will elaborate below on the attitudes of the first group, the slum dwellers, whose primary focus in housing standards seems to be on the house as a shelter from both external and internal threat.

Attitudes toward Housing

As context for this, however, let us look briefly at some of the characteristics of two working class groups. These observations come from a series of studies of the working class carried out by Social Research, Inc. over the past ten years. The studies have involved some 2,000 open-ended conversational interviews with working class men and women dealing with various life style areas from child rearing to religion, food habits to furniture preferences. In all of this work, the importance of the home and its location has appeared as a constant theme. These studies, while not based on nationally representative samples, have been carried out in such a way as to represent the geographical range of the country, including such cities as Seattle, Camden, Louisville, Chicago, Atlanta, as well as a balanced distribution of central city and suburban dwellers, apartment renters, and home owners. In these studies, one central focus concerned the feelings working class people have about their present homes, their plans for changes in housing, their attitudes toward their neighborhoods, and the relation of these to personal and familial goals. In addition, because the interviews were open-ended and conversational, much information of relevance to housing appeared in the context of other discussions because of the importance of housing to so many other areas of living.[5] In our studies and in those of Herbert Gans and others of Boston's West End, we find one type of working class life style where families are content with much about their housing—even though it is "below standard" in the eyes of housing professionals—if the housing does provide security against the most blatant of threats.[6] This traditional working class is likely to want to economize on housing in order to have money available to pursue other interests and needs. There will be efforts at the maintenance of the house or apartment, but not much interest in improvement of housing level. Instead there is an effort to create a pleasant and cozy home, where housework can be carried out conveniently. Thus, families in this group tend to acquire a good many of the major appliances, to center their social life in the kitchen, to be relatively unconcerned with adding taste in furnishings to comfort. With respect to the immediate outside world the main emphasis is on a concern with the availability of a satisfying peer group life, with having neighbors who are similar, and with maintaining an easy access back and forth among people who are very well known. There is also a concern that the neighborhood be respectable enough—with respectability defined mainly in the negative, by the absence of "crumbs and bums." An emphasis on comfort and contentment ties together meanings having to do with both the inside and the outside.

Out of the increasing prosperity of the working class has grown a different orientation toward housing on the part of the second group which we can characterize as modern instead of traditional. Here there is a great emphasis on owning one's home rather than enriching a landlord. Along with the acquisition of a home and yard goes an elaboration of the inside of the house in such a way as not only to further develop the idea of a pleasant and cozy home, but also to add new elements with emphasis on having a nicely decorated living room or family room, a home which more closely approximates a standard of all-American affluence. Similarly there is a greater emphasis on maintenance of the yard outside and on the use of the yard as a place where both adults and children can relax and enjoy themselves. With this can come also the development of a more intense pattern of neighborhood socializing. In these suburbs the demand grows for good community services as opposed to simply adequate ones, so that there tends to be greater involvement in the schools than is the case with traditional working class men and women. One of the dominant themes of the modern working class life style is that of having arrived in the mainstream of American life, of no longer being simply "poor-but-honest" workers. It is in the service of this goal that we find these elaborations in the meaning of the house and its environs.

In both working class groups, as the interior of the home more closely approximates notions of a decent standard, we find a decline in concerns expressed by inhabitants with sources of threat from within and a shift toward concerns about a threatening outside world—a desire to make the neighborhood secure against the incursions of lower class people who might rob or perpetrate violence of one kind or another.

As we shift our focus from the stable working class to the lower class, the currently popular poor, we find a very different picture. In addition to the large and growing literature, I will draw on data from three studies of this group with which I have been involved. Two studies deal with family attitudes and family planning behavior on the part of lower class, in contrast to working class couples. In these studies, based on some 450 intensive controversial interviews with men and women living in Chicago, Cincinnati, and Oklahoma City housing was not a subject of direct inquiry. Nevertheless we gained considerable insight into the ways lower class people think about their physical and social environment, and their anxieties, goals, and coping mechanisms that operate in connection with their housing arrangements.[7]

The third study, currently on-going, involves a five year investigation of social and community problems in the Pruitt-Igoe Project of St. Louis. This public housing project consists of 33 11-story buildings near downtown St. Louis. The project was opened in 1954, has 2,762 apartments, of which only some 2,000 are currently occupied, and has as tenants a very high proportion (over 50 percent) of female-headed households on one kind or another of public assistance. Though originally integrated, the project is now all Negro. The project community is plagued by petty crimes, vandalism, much destruction of the physical plant, and a very bad reputation in both the Negro and white communities.[8] For the past two years a staff of ten research assistants has been carrying out participant observation and conversational interviewing among project residents. In order to obtain a comparative focus on problems of living in public housing, we have also interviewed in projects in Chicago (Stateway Gardens), New York (St. Nicholas), and San Francisco (Yerba Buena Plaza and Westside Courts). Many of the concrete examples which follow come from these interviews, since in the course of observation and interviewing with project tenants we have had the opportunity to learn a great deal about both their experiences in the projects and about the private slum housing in which they previously lived. While our interviews in St. Louis provide us with insight into what it is like in one of the most disorganized public housing communities in the United States, the interviews in the other cities provide the contrast of much more average public housing experiences.[9] Similarly, the retrospective accounts that respondents in different cities give of their previous private housing experience provides a wide sampling in the slum communities of four different cities.

In the lower class we find a great many very real threats to security, although these threats often do seem to be somewhat exaggerated by lower class women. The threatening world of the lower class comes to be absorbed into a world view which generalizes the belief that the environment is threatening more than it is rewarding—that rewards reflect the infrequent of good luck and that danger is endemic.[10] Any close acquaintance with the ongoing life of lower class people impresses one with their anxious alienation from the larger world, from the middle class to be sure, but from the majority of their peers as well. Lower class people often seem isolated and to have but tenuous participation in a community of known and valued peers. They are ever aware of the presence of strangers who tend to be seen as potentially dangerous. While they do seek to create a gratifying peer group society, these groups tend to be unstable and readily fragmented. Even the heavy reliance on relatives as the core of a personal community does not do away with the dangers which others may bring. As Walter Miller has perceptively noted, "trouble" is one of the major focal concerns in the lower class world view.[11] A home to which one could retreat from such an insecure world would be of great value, but our data indicate that for lower class people such a home is not easy to come by. In part, this is due to the fact that one's own family members themselves often make trouble or bring it into the home, but even more important it is because it seems very difficult to create a home and an immediate environment that actually does shut out danger.[12]

Dangers in the Environment

From our data it is possible to abstract a great many dangers that have some relation to housing and its location. The location or the immediate environment is as important as the house itself, since lower class people are aware that life inside is much affected by the life just outside.

In Figure 4.7B, I have summarized the main kinds of danger which seem to be related to housing one way or another. It is apparent that these dangers have two immediate sources, human and non-human, and that the consequences that are feared from these sources usually represent a complex amalgam of physical, interpersonal, and mortal damage to the individual and his family. Let us look first at the various sources of danger and then at the overlapping consequences feared from these dangers.

There is nothing unfamiliar about the non-human sources of danger. They represent a sad catalogue of threats apparent in any journalist's account of slum living.[13] That we become used to the catalogue, however, should not

FIGURE 4.7B.   A Taxonomy of Dangers in the Lower Class Home and Environs: Each of These Can Involve Physical, Interpersonal, and Moral Consequences

Source of Danger	
Non-Human	*Human*
Rats and other vermin	Violence to self and possessions
Poisons	Assault
Fire and burning	Fighting and beating
Freezing and cold	Rape
Poor plumbing	Objects thrown or dropped
Dangerous electrical wiring	Stealing
Trash (broken glass, cans, etc.)	Verbal hostility, shaming, exploitation
Insufficiently protected heights	Own family
Other aspects of poorly designed or	Neighbors
deteriorated structures (e.g., thin walls)	Caretakers
Cost of dwelling	Outsiders
	Attractive alternatives that wean oneself
	or valued others away from a stable life

obscure the fact that these dangers are very real to many lower class families. Rats and other vermin are ever present companions in most big city slums. From the sense of relief which residents in public housing often experience on this score, it is apparent that slum dwellers are not indifferent to the presence of rats in their homes. Poisons may be a danger, sometimes from lead-base paints used on surfaces which slum toddlers may chew. Fires in slum areas are not uncommon, and even in a supposedly well designed public housing project children may repeatedly burn themselves on uncovered steampipe risers. In slums where the tenant supplies his own heating there is always the possibility of a very cold apartment because of no money, or, indeed, of freezing to death (as we were told by one respondent whose friend fell into an alcoholic sleep without turning on the heater). Insufficiently protected heights, as in one public housing project, may lead to deaths when children fall out windows or adults fall down elevator shafts. Thin walls in the apartment may expose a family to more of its neighbor's goings-on than comfortable to hear. Finally, the very cost of the dwelling itself can represent a danger in that it leaves too little money for other things needed to keep body and soul together.

That lower class people grow up in a world like this and live in it does not mean that they are indifferent to it—nor that its toll is only that of possible physical damage in injury, illness, incapacity, or death. Because these potentialities and events are interpreted and take on symbolic significance, and because lower class people make some efforts to cope with them, inevitably there are also effects on their interpersonal relationships and on their moral conceptions of themselves and their worlds.

The most obvious human source of danger has to do with violence directed by others against oneself and one's possessions. Lower class people are concerned with being assaulted, being damaged, being drawn into fights, being beaten, being raped. In public housing projects in particular, it is always possible for juveniles to throw or drop things from windows which can hurt or kill, and if this pattern takes hold it is a constant source of potential danger. Similarly, people may rob anywhere—apartment, laundry room, corridor.

Aside from this kind of direct violence, there is the more pervasive ever-present potentiality for symbolic violence to the self and that which is identified with the self—by verbal hostility, the shaming and exploitation expressed by the others who make up one's world. A source of such violence, shaming, or exploitation may be within one's own family—from children, spouse, siblings, parents—and often is. It seems very likely that crowding tends to encourage such symbolic violence to the self but certainly crowding is not the only factor since we also find this kind of threat in uncrowded public housing quarters.[14] Most real and immediate to lower class people, however, seems to be the potentiality for symbolic destructiveness by their neighbors. Lower class people seem ever on guard toward their neighbors, even ones with whom they become well-acquainted and would count as their friends. This suspiciousness is directed often at juveniles and young adults whom older people tend to regard as almost uncontrollable. It is important to note that while one may and does engage in this kind of behavior oneself, this is no guarantee that the individual does not fear and condemn the behavior when engaged in by others. For example, one woman whose family was evicted from a public housing project because her children were troublemakers thought, before she knew that her family was included among the twenty families thus evicted, that the evictions were a good thing because there were too many people around who cause trouble.

Symbolic violence on the part of caretakers (all those whose occupations bring them into contact with lower class people as purveyors of some private or public service) seems also endemic in slum and public housing areas. Students of the interactions between caretakers and their lower class clients have suggested that there is a great deal of punitiveness and shaming commonly expressed by the caretakers in an effort to control and direct the activities of their clients.[15]

The defense of the client is generally one of avoidance, or sullenness and feigned stupidity, when contact cannot be avoided. As David Capolvitz has shown so well, lower class people are subjected to considerable exploitation by the commercial services with which they deal, and exploitation for money, sexual favors, and sadistic impulses is not unknown on the part of public servants either.[16]

Finally, outsiders present in two ways the dangers of symbolic violence as well as a physical violence. Using the anonymity of geographical mobility, outsiders may come into slum areas to con and exploit for their own ends and, by virtue of the attitudes they maintain toward slum dwellers or public housing residents, they may demean and derogate them. Here we would have to include also the mass media which can and do behave in irresponsibly punitive ways toward people who live in lower class areas, a fact most dramatically illustrated in the customary treatment of the Pruitt-Igoe Project in St. Louis. From the point of view of the residents, the unusual interest shown in their world by a research team can also fit into this pattern.

Finally, the lower class person's world contains many attractive alternatives to the pursuit of a stable life. He can fear for himself that he will be caught up in these attractive alternatives and thus damage his life chances, and he may fear even more that those whom he values, particularly in his family, will be seduced away from him. Thus, wives fear their husbands will be attracted to the life outside the family, husbands fear the same of their wives, and parents always fear that their children will somehow turn out badly. Again, the fact that you may yourself be involved in such seductive pursuits does not lessen the fear that these valued others will be won away while your back is turned. In short, both the push and the pull of the human world in which lower class people live can be seen as a source of danger.

Having looked at the sources of danger, let us look at the consequences which lower class people fear from these dangers. The physical consequences are fairly obvious in connection with the non-human threats and the threats of violence from others. They are real and they are ever present: One can become the victim of injury, incapacitation, illness, and death from both non-human and human sources. Even the physical consequences of the symbolic violence of hostility, shaming, and exploitation, to say nothing of seduction, can be great if they lead one to retaliate in a physical way and in turn be damaged. Similarly there are physical consequences to being caught up in alternatives such as participation in alcohol and drug subcultures.

There are three interrelated interpersonal consequences of living in a world characterized by these human and nonhuman sources of danger. The first relates to the need to form satisfying interpersonal relationships, the second to the need to exercise responsibility as a family member, and the third to the need to formulate an explanation for the unpleasant state of affairs in your world.

The consequences which endanger the need to maintain satisfying interpersonal relations flow primarily from the human sources of danger. That is, to the extent that the world seems made up of dangerous others, at a very basic level the choice of friends carries risks. There is always the possibility that a friend may turn out to be an enemy or that his friends will. The result is a generalized watchfulness and touchiness in interpersonal relationships. Because other individuals represent not only themselves but also their families, the matter is further complicated since interactions with, let us say, neighbors' children, can have repercussions on the relationship with the neighbor. Because there are human agents behind most of the non-human dangers, one's relationships with others—family members, neighbors, caretakers—are subject to potential disruptions because of those others' involvement in creating trash, throwing objects, causing fires, or carrying on within thin walls.

With respect to the exercise of responsibility, we find that parents feel they must bring their children safely through childhood in a world which both poses great physical and moral dangers, and which seeks constantly to seduce them into a way of life which the parent wishes them to avoid. Thus, childrearing becomes an anxious and uncertain process. Two of the most common results are a pervasive repressiveness in child discipline and training, and, when that seems to fail or is no longer possible, a fatalistic abdication of efforts to protect the children. From the child's point of view, because his parents are not able to protect him from many unpleasantnesses and even from himself, he loses faith in them and comes to regard them as persons of relatively little consequence.

The third area of effect on interpersonal relations has to do with the search for causes of the prevalence of threat and violence in their world. We have suggested that to lower class people the major causes stem from the nature of their own peers. Thus, a great deal of blaming others goes on and reinforces the process of isolation, suspiciousness, and touchiness about blame and shaming. Similarly, landlords and tenants tend to develop patterns of mutual recrimination and blaming, making it very difficult for them to cooperate with each other in doing something about either the human or nonhuman sources of difficulty.

Finally, the consequences for conceptions of the moral order of one's world, of one's self, and of others, are very great. Although lower class people may not adhere in action to many middle class values about neatness, cleanliness, order, and proper decorum, it is apparent that they are often aware of their deviance, wishing that their world could be a nicer place, physically and socially. The presence of nonhuman threats conveys in devastating terms a sense that they live in an immoral and uncontrolled world. The physical evidence of trash, poor plumbing and the stink that goes with it, rats and other vermin, deepens their feeling of being moral outcasts. Their physical world is telling them they are inferior and bad just as effectively perhaps as do their human interactions. Their inability to control the depredation of rats, hot steam pipes, balky stoves, and poorly fused electrical circuits tells them that they are failures as autonomous individuals. The physical and social disorder of their world presents a constant temptation to give up or retaliate in kind. And when lower class people try to do something about some of these dangers, they are generally exposed in their interactions with caretakers and outsiders to further moral punitiveness by being told that their troubles are their own fault.

Implications for Housing Design

It would be asking too much to insist that design per se can solve or even seriously mitigate these threats. On the other hand, it is obvious that almost all the nonhuman threats can be pretty well done away with where the resources are available to design decent housing for lower class people. No matter what criticisms are made of public housing projects, there is no doubt that the structures themselves are infinitely preferable to slum housing. In our interviews in public housing projects we have found very few people who complain about design aspects of the insides of their apartments. Though they may not see their apartments as perfect, there is a dramatic drop in anxiety about nonhuman threats within. Similarly, reasonable foresight in the design of other elements can eliminate the threat of falling from windows or into elevator shafts, and can provide adequate outside toilet facilities for children at play. Money and a reasonable exercise of architectural skill go a long way toward providing lower class families with the really safe place of retreat from the outside world that they desire.

There is no such straightforward design solution to the potentiality of human threat. However, to the extent that lower class people do have a place they can go that is not so dangerous as the typical slum dwelling, there is at least the gain of a haven. Thus, at the cost perhaps of increased isolation, lower class people in public housing sometimes place a great deal of value on privacy and on living a quiet life behind the locked doors of their apartments. When the apartment itself seems safe it allows the family to begin to elaborate a home to maximize coziness, comfortable enclosure, and lack of exposure. Where, as in St. Louis, the laundry rooms seem unsafe places, tenants tend to prefer to do their laundry in their homes, sacrificing the possibility of neighborly interactions to gain a greater sense of security of person and property.

Once the home can be seen as a relatively safe place, lower class men and women express a desire to push out the boundaries of safety further into the larger world. There is the constantly expressed desire for a little bit of outside space that is one's own or at least semiprivate. Buildings that have galleries are much preferred by their tenants to those that have no such immediate access to the outside. Where, as in the New York public housing project we studied, it was possible to lock the outside doors of the buildings at night, tenants felt more secure.

A measured degree of publicness within buildings can also contribute to a greater sense of security. In buildings where there are several families whose doors open onto a common hallway there is a greater sense of the availability of help should trouble come than there is in buildings where only two or three apartments open onto a small hallway in a stairwell. While tenants do not necessarily develop close neighborly relations when more neighbors are available, they can develop a sense of making common cause in dealing with common problems. And they feel less at the mercy of gangs or individuals intent on doing them harm.

As with the most immediate outside, lower class people express the desire to have their immediate neighborhood or the housing project grounds a more controlled and safe place. In public housing projects, for example, tenants want project police who function efficiently and quickly; they would like some play areas supervised so that children are not allowed to prey on each other; they want to be able to move about freely themselves and at the same time discourage outsiders who might come to exploit.

A real complication is that the very control which these desires imply can seem a threat to the lower class resident. To the extent that caretakers seem to demand and damn more than they help, this cure to the problem of human threat seems worse than the disease. The crux of the caretaking task in connection with lower class people is to provide and encourage security and order within the lower class world without at the same time extracting from it a heavy price in self-esteem, dignity, and autonomy.

NOTES

1. Lord Ragland, *The Temple and the House* (London: Routledge & Kegan Paul Limited, 1964).

2. Bennett M. Berger, *Working-Class Suburb* (Berkeley: University of California Press, 1960) and Herbert Gans, "Effect of the Move From the City to Suburb" in Leonard J. Duhl (ed.), *The Urban Condition* (New York: Free Press, 1963).

3. Anselm L. Strauss, *Images of the American City* (New York: Free Press, 1961).

4. In this paper I am pulling together observations from a number of different studies. What I have to say about working class attitudes toward housing comes primarily from studies of working class life style carried out in collaboration with Richard Coleman, Gerald Handel, W. Lloyd Warner, and Burleigh Gardner. What I have to say about lower class life comes from two more recent studies dealing with family life and family planning in the lower class and a study currently in progress of social life in a large public housing project in St. Louis (being conducted in collaboration with Alvin W. Gouldner and David J. Pittman).

5. These studies are reported in the following unpublished Social Research, Inc. reports: *Prosperity and Challenging Working Class Life Style* (1960) and *Urban Working Class Identity and World View* (1965). The following publications are based on this series of studies: Lee Rainwater, Richard P. Coleman, and Gerald Handel, *Workingman's Wife: Her Personality, World and Life Style* (New York: Oceana Publications, 1959); Gerald Handel and Lee Rainwater, "Persistence and Change in Working Class Life Style," and Lee Rainwater and Gerald Handel, "Changing Family Roles in the Working Class," both in Arthur B. Shostak and William Gomberg, *Blue-Collar World* (New York: Prentice-Hall, 1964).

6. Marc Fried, "Grieving for a Lost Home," and Edward J. Ryan, "Personal Identity in an Urban Slum," in Leonard J. Duhl (ed.), *The Urban Condition* (New York: Free Press, 1963); and Herbert Gans, *Urban Villagers* (New York: Free Press of Glencoe, Inc., 1962).

7. Lee Rainwater, *And the Poor Get Children* (Chicago: Quadrangle Books, 1960), and Lee Rainwater, *Family Design: Marital Sexuality, Family Size and Family Planning* (Chicago: Aldine Publishing Company, 1964).

8. Nicholas J. Demerath, "St. Louis Public Housing Study Sets Off Community Development to Meet Social Needs," *Journal of Housing*, XIX (October, 1962).

9. See, D. M. Wilner, *et al., The Housing Environment and Family Life* (Baltimore: Johns Hopkins University Press, 1962).

10. Allison Davis, *Social Class Inflences on Learning* (Cambridge: Harvard University Press, 1948.

11. Walter Miller, "Lower Class Culture as a Generating Milieu of Gang Delinquency," in Marvin E. Wolfgang, Leonard Savitz, and Norman Johnson (eds.), *The Sociology of Crime and Delinquency* (New York: John Wiley Company, 1962).

12. Alvin W. Schorr, *Slums and Social Insecurity* (Washington, D.C.: Department of Health, Education and Welfare, 1963).

13. Michael Harrington, *The Other America* (New York: Macmillan Co., 1962).

14. Edward S. Deevey, "The Hare and the Haruspex: A Cautionary Tale," in Eric and Mary Josephson, *Man Alone* (New York: Dell Publishing Company, 1962).

15. A. B. Hollinghead and L. H. Rogler, "Attitudes Toward Slums and Private Housing in Puerto Rico," in Leonard J. Duhl, *The Urban Condition* (New York: Free Press, 1963).

16. David Caplovitz, *The Poor Pay More* (New York: Free Press of Glencoe, 1963).

The room in which I taught my Fourth Grade was not a room at all, but the corner of an auditorium. The first time I approached that corner, I noticed only a huge torn stage curtain, a couple of broken windows, a badly listing blackboard and about thirty-five bewildered-looking children, most of whom were Negro. White was overcome in black among them, but white and black together were overcome in chaos. They had desks and a teacher, but they did not really have a class. What they had was about one quarter of the auditorium. Three or four blackboards, two of them broken, made them seem a little bit set apart. Over at the other end of the auditorium there was another Fourth Grade class. Not much was happening at the other side at that minute so that for the moment the noise did not seem so bad. But it became a real nightmare of conflicting noises a little later on. Generally it was not until ten o'clock that the bad crossfire started. By ten-thirty it would have attained such a crescendo that the children in the back rows of my section often couldn't hear my questions and I could not hear their answers. There were no carpetings or sound-absorbers of any kind. The room, being large, and echoing, and wooden, added resonance to every sound. Sometimes the other teacher and I would stagger the lessons in which our classes would have to speak aloud, but this was a makeshift method and it also meant that our classes had to be induced to maintain an unnatural and otherwise unnecessary rule of silence during the rest of the time. We couldn't always do it anyway, and usually the only way out was to try to outshout each other so that both of us often left school hoarse or wheezing. While her class was reciting in unison you could not hear very much in mine. When she was talking alone I could be heard above her but the trouble then was that little bits of her talk got overheard by my class. Suddenly in the middle of our geography you could hear her saying:

"AFTER YOU COMPARE, YOU HAVE GOT TO BRING DOWN."

Or "PLEASE GIVE THAT PENCIL BACK TO HENRIETTA!"

Neither my class nor I could help but be distracted for a moment of sudden curosity about exactly what was going on. Hours were lost in this way. Yet that was not the worst. More troublesome still was the fact that we did not ever *feel* apart. We were tucked in the corner and anybody who wanted could peek in or walk in or walk past. I never minded an intruder or observer, but to notice and to stare at any casual passer-by grew to be an irresistible temptation for the class. On repeated occasions I had to say to the children: "The class is still going. Let them have their discussion. Let them walk by if they have to. You should still be paying attention over here."

Soon after I came into that auditorium, I discovered that it was not only our two Fourth Grades that were going to have their classes here. We were to share the space also with the glee club, with play rehearsals, special reading, special arithmetic, and also at certain times a Third or Fourth Grade phonics class. I began to make head-counts of numbers of pupils and I started jotting them down:

Seventy children from the two regular Fourth Grades before the invasion.

Then ninety one day with the glee club and remedial arithmetic.

One hundred and seven with the play rehearsal.

One day the sewing class came in with their sewing machines and then that seemed to become a regular practice in the hall. Once I counted one hundred and twenty people. All in the one room. All talking, singing, yelling, laughing, reciting—and all at the same time. Before the Christmas break it became apocalyptic. Not more than one half of the classroom lessons I had planned took place throughout that time.

"Mr. Kozol—I can't hear you."

"Mr. Kozol—what's going on out there?"

"Mr. Kozol—couldn't we sing with them?"

One day something happened to dramatize to me, even more powerfully than anything yet, just what a desperate situation we were really in. What happened was that a window whose frame had rotted was blown right out of its sashes by a strong gust of wind and began to fall into the auditorium, just above my children's heads. I had noticed that window several times before and I had seen that its frame was rotting, but there were so many other things equally rotted or broken in the school building that it didn't occur to me to say anything about it. The feeling I had was that the Principal and custodians and Reading Teacher and other people had been in that building for a long time before me and they must have seen the condition of the windows. If anything could be done, if there were any way to get it corrected, I assumed they would have done it by this time. Thus, by not complaining and by not pointing it out to anyone, in a sense I went along with the rest of them and accepted it as something inevitable. One of the most grim things about teaching in such a school and such a system is that you do not like to be an incessant barb and irritation to everybody else, so you come under a rather strong compulsion to keep quiet. But after you have been quiet for a while there is an equally strong temptation to begin to accept the conditions of your work or of the children's plight as natural. This, in a sense, is what had happened to me during that period and that, I suppose, is why I didn't say anything about the rotting window. Now one day it caved in.

First there was a cracking sound, then a burst of icy air. The next thing I knew, a child was saying: "Mr. Kozol—look at the window!" I turned and looked and saw that it was starting to fall in. It was maybe four or five feet tall and it came straight inward out of its sashes toward the heads of the children. I was standing, by coincidence, only about four or five feet off and was able to catch it with my hand. But the wind was so strong that it nearly blew right out of my hands. A couple of seconds of good luck—for it was a matter of chance that I was standing there—kept glass from the desks of six or seven children and very possibly preserved the original shape of half a dozen of their heads. The ones who had been under the glass were terrified but the thing that I noticed with most wonder was that they tried very hard to hide their fear in order to help me get over my own sense of embarrassment and guilt. I soon realized I was not going to be able to hold the thing up by myself and I was obliged to ask one of the stronger boys in the class to come over and give me a hand. Meanwhile, as the children beneath us shivered with the icy wind and as the two of us now shivered also since it was a day when the mercury was hovering all morning close to freezing, I asked one of the children in the front row to run down and fetch the janitor.

When he asked me what he should tell him, I said: "Tell him the house is falling in." The children laughed. It was the first time I had ever come out and said anything like that when the children could hear me. I am sure my reluctance to speak out like that more often must seem odd to many readers, for at this perspective it seems odd to me as well. Certainly there were plenty of things wrong within that school building and there was enough we could have joked about. The truth, however, is that I did not often talk like that, nor did many of the other teachers, and there was a practical reason for this. Unless you were ready to buck the system utterly, it would become far too difficult to teach in an atmosphere of that kind of honesty. It generally seemed a great deal easier to pretend as well as you could that everything was normal and okay. Some teachers carried out this posture with so much eagerness, in fact, that their defense of the school ended up as something like a hymn of praise and adoration. "You children should thank God and feel blessed with good luck for all you've got. There are so many little children in the world who have been given so much less." The books are junk, the paint peels, the cellar stinks, the teachers call you nigger, and the windows fall in on your heads. "Thank God that you don't live in Russia or Africa! Thank God for all the blessings that you've got!" Once, finally, the day after the window blew in, I said to a friend of mine in the evening after school: "I guess that the building I teach in is not in very good condition." But to state a condition of dilapidation and ugliness and physical danger in words as mild and indirect as those is almost worse than not saying anything at all. I had a hard time with that problem—the problem of being honest and of confronting openly the extent to which I was compromised by going along with things that were abhorrent and by accepting as moderately reasonable or unavoidably troublesome things which, if they were inflicted on children of my own, I would have condemned savagely.

A friend of mine to whom I have confided some of these things has not been able to keep from criticizing me for what he thinks of as a kind of quiet collusion. When I said to him, for example, that the Reading Teacher was trying to do the right thing and that she was a very forceful teacher, he replied to me that from what I had described to him she might have been a very forceful teacher but she was not a good teacher but a very dangerous one and that whether she was *trying* to do the right thing or not did not impress him since what she *did* do was the wrong thing. Other people I know have said the same thing to me about this and I am certain, looking back, that it is only the sheer accident of the unexpected events which took place in my school during the last weeks of the spring that prompted me suddenly to speak out and to take some forthright action. I am also convinced that it is that, and that alone, that has spared me the highly specialized and generally richly deserved contempt which is otherwise reserved by Negro people for their well-intending but inconsistent liberal friends.

After the window blew in on us that time, the janitor finally came up and hammered it shut with nails so that it would not fall in again but also so that it could not open. It was a month before anything was done about the large gap left by a missing pane. Children shivered a few feet away from it. The Principal walked by frequently and saw us. So did supervisors from the School Department. So of course did the various lady experts who traveled all day from room to room within our school. No one can say that dozens of people did not know that children were sitting within the range of freezing air. At last one day the janitor came up with a piece of cardboard or pasteboard and covered over about a quarter of that lower window so that there was no more wind coming but just that much less sunshine too. I remember wondering what a piece of glass could cost in Boston and I had the idea of going out and buying some and trying to put it in myself. That rectangle of cardboard over our nailed-shut window was not removed for a quarter of the year. When it was removed, it was only because a television station was going to come and visit in the building and the School Department wanted to make the room look more attractive. But it was winter when the window broke, and the repairs did not take place until the middle of the spring.

In case a reader imagines that my school may have been unusual and that some of the other schools in Roxbury must have been in better shape, I think it's worthwhile to point out that the exact opposite seems to have been the case. The conditions in my school were said by many people to be considerably better than those in several of the other ghetto schools. One of the worst, according to those who made comparisons, was the Endicott, also situated in the Negro neighborhood and like my own school, heavily imbalanced. At Endicott, I learned, it had become so overcrowded that there were actually some classes in which the number of pupils exceeded the number of desks and in which the extra pupils had to sit in chairs behind the teacher. A child absent one day commonly came back the next day and found someone else at his desk. . . .

Perhaps a reader would like to know what it is like to go into a new classroom in the same way that I did and to see before you suddenly, and in terms you cannot avoid recognizing, the dreadful consequences of a year's wastage of real lives.

You walk into a narrow and old wood-smelling classroom and you see before you thirty-five curious, cautious and untrusting children, aged eight to thirteen, of whom about two-thirds are Negro. Three of the children are designated to you as special students. Thirty per cent of the class is reading at the Second Grade level in a year and in a month in which they should be reading at the height of Fourth Grade performance or at the beginning of the Fifth. Seven children out of the class are up to par. Ten substitutes or teacher changes. Or twelve changes. Or eight. Or eleven. Nobody seems to know how many teachers they have had. Seven of their lifetime records are missing: symptomatic and emblematic at once of the chaos that has been with them all year long. Many more lives than just seven have already been wasted but the seven missing records become an embittering symbol of the lives behind them which, equally, have been lost or mislaid. (You have to spend the first three nights staying up until dawn trying to reconstruct these records out of notes and scraps.) On the first math test you give, the class average comes out to 36. The children tell you with embarrassment that it has been like that since fall.

You check around the classroom. Of forty desks, five have tops with no hinges. You lift a desk top to fetch a paper and you find that the top has fallen off. There are three windows. One cannot be opened. A sign on it written in the messy scribble of a hurried teacher or some custodial person warns you: DO NOT UNLOCK THIS WINDOW IT IS BROKEN. The general look of the room is as of a bleak-light photograph of a mental hospital. Above the one poor blackboard, gray rather than really black, and hard to write on, hangs from one tack, lopsided, a motto attributed to Benjamin Franklin: "*Well begun is half done.*" Everything, or almost everything like that, seems a mockery of itself.

Into this grim scenario, drawing on your own pleasures and memories, you do what you can to bring some kind of life. You bring in some cheerful and colorful paintings by Joan Miro and Paul Klee. While the paintings by Miro do not arouse much interest, the ones by Klee become an instantaneous success. One picture in particular, a watercolor titled "Bird Garden," catches the fascination of the entire class. You slip it out of the book and tack it up on the wall beside the doorway and it creates a traffic jam every time the children have to file in or file out. You discuss with your students some of the reasons why Klee may have painted the way he did and you talk about the things that can be accomplished in a painting which could not be accomplished in a photograph. None of this seems to be above the children's heads. Despite this, you are advised flatly by the Art Teacher that your naïveté has gotten the best of you and that the children cannot possibly appreciate this. Klee is too difficult. Children will not enjoy it. You are unable to escape the idea that the Art Teacher means herself instead.

For poetry, in place of the recommended memory gems, going back again into your own college days, you make up your mind to introduce a poem of William Butler Yeats. It is about a lake isle called Innisfree, about birds that have the funny name of "linnets" and about a "bee-loud glade." The children do not all go crazy about it but a number of them seem to like it as much as you do and you tell them how once, three years before, you were living in England and you helped a man in the country to make his home from wattles and clay. The children become intrigued. They pay good attention and many of them grow more curious about the poem than they appeared at first. Here again, however, you are advised by older teachers that you are making a mistake: Yeats is too difficult for children. They can't enjoy it, won't appreciate it, wouldn't like it. You are aiming way above their heads . . . Another idea comes to mind and you decide to try out an easy and rather well-known and not very complicated poem of Robert Frost. The poem is called "Stopping By Woods on a Snowy Evening." This time, your supervisor happens to drop in from the School Department. He looks over the mimeograph, agrees with you that it's a nice poem, then points out to you—tolerantly, but strictly—that you have made another mistake. "Stopping By Woods" is scheduled for Sixth Grade. It is not "a Fourth Grade poem," and it is not to be read or looked at during the Fourth Grade. Bewildered as you are by what appears to be a kind of idiocy, you still feel reproved and criticized and muted and set back and you feel that you have been caught in the commission of a serious mistake.

On a series of other occasions, the situation is repeated. The children are offered something new and something lively. They respond to it energetically and they are attentive and their attention does not waver. For the first time in a long while perhaps there is actually some real excitement and some growing and some thinking going on within that one small room. In each case, however, you are advised sooner or later that you are making a mistake. Your mistake, in fact, is to have impinged upon the standardized condescension on which the entire administration of the school is based. To hand Paul Klee's pictures to the children of this classroom, and particularly in a twenty-dollar volume, constitutes a threat to this school system. It is not different from sending a little girl from the Negro ghetto into an art class near Harvard Yard. Transcending the field of familiarity of the administration, you are endangering its authority and casting a blow at its self-confidence. The way the threat is handled is by a continual and standardized underrating of the children: They can't do it, couldn't do it, wouldn't like it, don't deserve it . . . In such a manner, many children are tragically and unjustifiably held back from a great many of the good things that they might come to like or admire and are pinned down instead to books the teacher knows and to easy tastes that she can handle. This includes, above all, of course, the kind of material that is contained in the Course of Study.

Try to imagine, for a child, how great the gap between the outside world and the world conveyed within this kind of school must seem: A little girl, maybe Negro, comes in from a street that is lined with car-carcasses. Old purple Hudsons and one-wheel-missing Cadillacs represent her horizon and mark the edges of her dreams. In the kitchen of her house roaches creep and large rats crawl. On the way to school a wino totters. Some teenage white boys slow down their car to insult her, and speed on. At school, she stands frozen for fifteen minutes in a yard of cracked cement that overlooks a hillside on which trash has been unloaded and at the bottom of which the New York, New Haven and Hartford Railroad rumbles past. In the basement, she sits upon broken or splintery seats in filthy toilets and she is yelled at in the halls. Upstairs, when something has been stolen, she is told that she is the one who stole it and is called a liar and forced abjectly to apologize before a teacher who has not the slightest idea in the world of who the culprit truly was. The same teacher, behind the child's back, ponders audibly with imagined compassion: "What can you do with this kind of material? How can you begin to teach this kind of child?"

Gradually going crazy, the child is sent after two years of misery to a pupil adjustment counselor who arranges for her to have some tests and considers the entire situation and discusses it with the teacher and finally files a long report. She is, some months later, put onto a waiting-list some place for once-a-week therapy but another year passes before she has gotten anywhere near to the front of a long line. By now she is fourteen, has lost whatever innocence she still had in the back seat of the old Cadillac and, within two additional years, she will be ready and eager for dropping out of school.

Once at school, when she was eight or nine, she drew a picture of a rich-looking lady in an evening gown with a handsome man bowing before her but she was told by an insensate and wild-eyed teacher that what she had done was junk and garbage and the picture was torn up and thrown away before her eyes. The rock and roll music that she hears on the Negro station is considered "primitive" by her teachers but she prefers its insistent rhythms to the dreary monotony of school. Once, in Fourth Grade, she got excited at school about some writing she had never heard about before. A handsome green book, brand new, was held up before her and then put into her hands. Out of this book her teacher read a poem. The poem was about a Negro—a woman who was a maid in the house of a white person—and she liked it. It remained in her memory. Somehow without meaning to, she found that she had done the impossible for her: she had memorized that poem. Perhaps, horribly, in the heart of her already she was aware that it was telling about her future: fifty dollars a week to scrub floors and bathe little white babies in the suburbs after an hour's streetcar ride. The poem made her want to cry. The white lady, the lady for whom the maid was working, told the maid she loved her. But the maid in the poem wasn't going to tell any lies in return. She knew she didn't feel any love for the white lady and she told the lady so. The poem was shocking to her, but it seemed bitter, strong and true. Another poem in the same green book was about a little boy on a merry-go-round. She laughed with the class at the question he asked about a Jim Crow section on a merry-go-round, but she also was old enough to know that it was not a funny poem really and it made her, valuably, sad. She wanted to know how she could get hold of that poem, and maybe that whole book. The poems were moving to her . . .

This was a child in my class. Details are changed somewhat but it is essentially one child. The girl was one of the three unplaced special students in that Fourth Grade room. She was not an easy girl to teach and it was hard even to keep her at her seat on many mornings, but I do not remember that there was any difficulty at all in gaining and holding onto her attention on the day that I brought in that green book of Langston Hughes.

Of all of the poems of Langston Hughes that I read to my Fourth

Graders, the one that the children liked most was a poem that has the title "Ballad of the Landlord." The poem is printed along with some other material in the back part of this book. This poem may not satisfy the taste of every critic, and I am not making any claims to immortality for a poem just because I happen to like it a great deal. But the reason this poem did have so much value and meaning for me and, I believe, for many of my students, is that it not only seems moving in an obvious and immediate human way but that it *finds* its emotion in something ordinary. It is a poem which really does allow both heroism and pathos to poor people, sees strength in awkwardness and attributes to a poor person standing on the stoop of his slum house every bit as much significance as William Wordsworth saw in daffodils, waterfalls and clouds. At the request of the children later on I mimeographed that poem and, although nobody in the classroom was asked to do this, several of the children took it home and memorized it on their own. I did not assign it for memory, because I do not think that memorizing a poem has any special value. Some of the children just came in and asked if they could recite it. Before long, almost every child in the room had asked to have a turn.

All of the poems that you read to Negro children obviously are not going to be by or about Negro people. Nor would anyone expect that all poems which are read to a class of poor children ought to be grim or gloomy or heart-breaking or sad. But when, among the works of many different authors, you do have the will to read children a poem by a man so highly renowned as Langston Hughes, then I think it is important not to try to pick a poem that is innocuous, being like any other poet's kind of poem, but I think you ought to choose a poem that is genuinely representative and then try to make it real to the children in front of you in the way that I tried. I also think it ought to be taken seriously by a teacher when a group of young children come in to him one morning and announce that they have liked something so much that they have memorized it voluntarily. It surprised me and impressed me when that happened. It was all I needed to know to confirm for me the value of reading that poem and the value of reading many other poems to children which will build upon, and not attempt to break down, the most important observations and very deepest foundations of their lives.

ANNOTATED BIBLIOGRAPHY

Dahl, Robert A. (1961) *Who Governs?* New Haven, Conn.: Yale University Press.
A case study of community power structure in New Haven, Connecticut. The volume argues strongly against the existence of a socioeconomic elite and for a pluralistic theory of community power.

Hunter, Floyd. (1963) *Community Power Structure.* New York: Doubleday (Anchor).
First published in 1953, Hunter's seminal study of community decision making in Atlanta, Georgia, spurred many other social scientists to do their own empirical research of community power structures, if only to prove him wrong. Hunter suggested that Atlanta was controlled by a pyramidal power structure dominated by economic elites.

Jacobs, Paul. (1966) *Prelude to Riot.* New York: Vintage.
A well-written account of Los Angeles and the reasons for the Watts riot. Jacobs is a competent journalist and social critic. His dismembering of the McCone Commission Report as a case of doctoring evidence is particularly effective.

Mills, C. Wright. (1966) *The Power Elite.* New York: Oxford.
A fascinating and controversial study of the interlocking web of corporation, military, and political power and the men who wield it. Mills' volume has become a new left classic. Its thesis has provided the underpinning for much political-economic theory.

National Advisory Commission on Civil Disorders. (1968) *Report of the National Advisory Commission on Civil Disorders.* Washington, D.C.: U.S. Government Printing Office (also New York: Bantam).
The official report on the disorders of the 1960s, and an excellent source. It reviews the history of violence in America by making use of extensive research data, and reports the data in raw form. It identifies the central problem as one of racism, and offers strategies for solution.

Rudé, George. (1964) *The Crowd in History.* New York: Wiley.
An excellent examination of crowd behavior in terms of its social characteristics, activities, causes, and consequences. Rudé's analysis provides both a historical perspective and a social analysis of crowd behavior from another area, but it is of immediate value to the understanding of violence in contemporary American life.

(Above) A radical approach to the housing crisis. Operation Move-In taking over a building, New York City. Photo by Marco Vega. (Left) A reformist approach—the planned city. Artist's rendering of Columbia, Maryland. Photo by United Press International.

The previous three sections have dealt primarily with the social organizational aspects of the developing urban ecosystem. Section Two emphasized how the use of physical space reflects an urban population's social organization. Section Three examined the diversity of life-style patterns found within the various physical and social areas of the urban setting. The discussion of social organization, its structure and characteristics in Sections Two and Three led to Section Four's consideration of selected social problems and their manifestation in urban social structures.

The books ends as it began, with a broader wholistic approach to urban structures. If we learn anything from the study of America's urban development it is that responses to urban problems require a system-wide approach. While focusing on social organization as a single dimension of the ecosystem is useful for drawing conceptual boundaries, such a highly concentrated perspective cannot provide broad practical solutions. Urban problems have population, technological, and environmental as well as social organizational components; therefore any solution must take these variables into account. An illustration using the P.O.E.T. framework will help to concretize the value of a broad approach to planning and problem solving. Time has proven that programs limited to affecting only one variable generally fail, as the following example of the efforts to solve the urban housing crisis illustrates.

By the end of the 1940s urban areas were suffering from severe housing shortages, due largely to war-stimulated in-migration to the city plus increasing urban birth rates. One approach to the housing crisis was to employ new building techniques that made possible the development of mass suburban housing tracts. This technological response was facilitated by important social organizational changes in financing, such as the G.I. Bill and liberalized F.H.A. loans. And, the lack of established local governmental regulations within emerging suburbs—such as lenient building codes and minimal requirements for sewers, fire protection, lights, and so on—also facilitated extremely rapid housing growth.

The impact on the physical environment of rapid suburban development is not hard to discern. Indiscriminate land clearance destroyed the existing physical ecology while shortcuts, such as lack of sewers, polluted even distant areas. Burgeoning suburban population growth, almost exclusively dependent on the technology of the automobile, resulted in the proliferation of highways. Increased reliance on the automobile, together with the emphasis on single-family unit construction, resulted in the massive disappearance of open space surrounding the central city. Thus, the immediate housing crisis was met largely by turning to technology with little consideration of the effects of rapid population growth on the environment and social organization.

From these kinds of experiences we have learned that there are no simple solutions. In fact, there are not even simple problems. Many of the disputes over approaches to solving problems of racism, violence, poverty, and the environment begin with disagreement over the nature of the problem itself. We are continually reminded that what one individual considers a problem, or how serious he believes a problem to be, is related to his ideology, or point of view.

A wide variety of problem-solving approaches have been advocated, ranging from the use of existing social mechanisms in conventional ways to the restructuring of the entire system. Figure 5.1A illustrates various responses to problems based upon the assumptions one makes about problem solving and one's approach to planning. The figure provides a format for studying a number of currently proposed solutions for urban problems. It also provides a heuristic device for locating responses along a conventional-to-radical continuum.

The upper-left-hand cell identifies some conventional responses often

FIGURE 5.1A   Probable Strategies and Actions for Addressing Social Problems by Alternative Assumptions Regarding Problem Solving and General Approaches to Planning

	General Approaches Social Planning		
Assumptions Regarding Problem Solving	Conventional Approaches (System needs minor modification and/or "fine tuning.")	Reformist Approaches (System needs some major modification.)	Radical Approaches (System needs major revision or replacement.)
Most, if not all, problems can be solved by existing mechanisms.	New leadership Better administration Shift priorities New legislation		
Some problems cannot be solved by existing mechanisms.		Mobilize political power outside existing party structures Quasi-legal protest Civil disobedience Urban rioting of the sixties	
Most, if not all, problems cannot be solved by existing mechanisms.			Rejection of societal goals Counter Culture movements Bombings and other forms of planned violence Revolution

used by established power structures. These responses are based on the assumption that if there is in fact a problem it can be handled in terms of available mechanisms. The viability of the system itself is not questioned; rather, problems tend to be defined in terms of the inadequacy of individuals and thus can be solved by conventional social planning. This approach often criticizes those within the system responsible for the administration of programs and policies. One of the traditional responses, therefore, is to replace personnel with new faces. For example, criticism of the draft during the late 1960s led to the replacement of the Director of Selective Service.

Another closely related response falling within the conventional range (upper-left-hand cell of Figure 5.1A) is the reassessment of existing priorities. Conventional responses generally emphasize the allocation of priorities and resources within the system, rather than the system's structural modification through the political process. During the late 1960s, for example, the increasing fiscal demands of the Vietnam War resulted in the relative de-emphasis of poverty programs.

The second cell on the diagonal identifies typical reformist responses. Reformist responses can generally be characterized by ideological commitment to the goals and ideals of the society, but not to the conventional means for achieving these goals. Reformers have less confidence than traditionalists in the value of established social planning mechanisms for dealing with social problems. Reformers are also more likely to see the system itself as a source of problems. Thus they are more likely to accept or actively originate methods that fall outside the traditional system. The civil rights movement of the 1960s was an example of a reformist response. It was committed to making the system honor its own ideals. Since the movement identified the system as part of the problem, its methods such as street demonstrations and civil disobedience were often quasi-legal.

The radical response described in the third cell on the diagonal is characterized by at least an implicit rejection of many goals of the society as well as the accepted means of their implementation. Existing social structures are viewed as being so flawed that it is thought easier simply to start over. Radical responses include overt ideological as well as programmatic dimensions. Thus, acts of violence can be legitimized in terms of ideological premises. The logical end-product of the radical approach may be countercultures and revolution.

The authors in this section can be located at different points in Figure 5.1A. In the discussion that follows we will generally progress from those authors who tend to fall in the upper left-hand quadrant of the figure to those whose approaches would place them in the lower right-hand quadrant. This reflects a continuum from more conventional to more radical approaches.

The lead piece by Daniel P. Moynihan, a former counsellor to President Nixon, clearly assumes that most if not all problems facing urban areas can be solved within the system. The crisis of the cities according to Moynihan is that:

> The tumult of the times arises, in essence, from a crisis of authority. The institutions that shaped conduct and behavior in the past are being challenged or, worse, ignored.

The crisis is one of lack of public confidence in existing systems. Thus what Moynihan proposes is an overall national urban policy to restore confidence in the system. As he notes: "When authority systems collapse, they are replaced by power systems that are coercive."

He also feels that:

> The sense of general community is eroding, and with it the authority of existing relationships; simultaneously, a powerful quest for specific community is emerging in the form of ever more intensive assertions of racial and ethnic identities.

Moynihan takes as an assumption the basic soundness of the system itself. His proposals emphasize how to work within the system to make it more responsive and effective. His national urban policy as spelled out in his ten points stress three general themes. The first is a call for a shift in priorities. The second is a call for greater co-ordination between different levels of government and the public which hopefully will lead to greater efficiency. Third is an appeal for a heightened esthetic commitment to the city and its values.

> Moynihan's proposal regarding the reorganization of local government dovetails with Henry Schmandt's approach.

Schmandt starts from the premise that:

> The large central city is obsolete as a political entity. It is a failing leviathan that can no longer function effectively. . . .

Schmandt lucidly details both the structural rigidity and irrelevancy of present urban political boundaries. What he proposes is governmental restructuring to create more meaningful political units. This would be accomplished by establishing a metropolitan government covering the entire Standard Metropolitan Statistical Area. This new government unit would be divided into smaller suburb-size political units that would handle local problems.

Schmandt is proposing a general restructuring of the political system at the metropolitan level. The essentials of the approach have been discussed by planners for decades. The appeal of such approaches is that they are attempts to solve critical problems through rational reform. Historically, such approaches have received little serious policy consideration.

Another approach to rational planning is James W. Rouse's New Town of Columbia, Maryland (Article 5.4). Columbia is not just another suburb, it is a completely planned new city that will have an eventual population in excess of 100,000. The New Town's concept is in many respects a rejection of the possibility of solving problems within existing structures. As Rouse says:

> The simple fact is that, with the powers and processes that now exist in local government and in the home building industry, it is impossible to provide in an orderly and intelligent way, for the metropolitan growth which we know lies just ahead.

A major criticism of New Town's approach is that it does not offer any solutions for existing central-city problems. Some critics claim that, rather than attacking problems, New Town's approach simply sidesteps issues, particularly those of poverty and race.

An author who certainly does not sidestep these issues is the controversial community organizer, Saul Alinsky. Charles E. Silberman's article on Alinsky (5.5) details how Alinsky gets things done by *not* working within the power structure. Alinsky organized poor blacks in a run-down area of Chicago so that they could stop being bulldozed out. To do this he built a neighborhood organization with a power base strong enough to wring concessions from the local establishment. His pragmatic approach to power enabled the neighborhood organization to defeat the combined efforts of The University of Chicago and the mayor's political machine. Alinsky's techniques are based on the assumption that playing by establishment rules foredooms the organization to failure. He understands that one must know the power system and its weaknesses if it is to be successfully modified.

Alinsky stands out from the previous planners insofar as he is willing to use nonconventional and controversial techniques to obtain essentially conventional goals. He does not seek to overthrow the system, but rather to more equitably distribute its rewards. (It might be mentioned that The University of Chicago has changed most of the policies described by Silberman and now is attempting to work with the local community.)

The absence of power to affect one's own fate, particularly among low-income blacks, is generally given as a major cause of the urban riots of the 1960s. James Geschwender (Article 5.6) argues that the inner-city disturbances of recent years must be seen not as relatively spontaneous outbursts, but as part of a "social movement which is developing along potentially revolutionary lines." Geschwender implies that as earlier riots appeared to bring results ghetto residents became aware of riots as a potentially successful political tactic.

Dissatisfaction does not, of course, always result in revolution. Our own urban history illustrates the more typical response of apathy resulting from oppression. The lower classes of colonial Charles Town had more reason than most citizens to rebel, but they remained fairly docile. In part, the reason for this was that half of Charles Town's population were slaves. The white artisans and craftsmen were caught between the pretensions of the upper-class gentry and the increasing skill level of their slaves. This effectively prevented the community from developing a large, stable middle-class population as found in other colonial cities. Fear of being classified with slaves was effectively used by the upper class to dampen cries of lower-class whites for redress of wrongs. After a brief insurrection was attributed to the report that some Negroes had mimicked their betters in crying "Liberty," lower-class whites ceased agitating for equal rights. Similarly, contemporary low-income whites more frequently support the system rather than join forces with dissatisfied blacks.

The concluding article (5.7) by John Seeley calls into question the problem-solving ability of our entire system. Seeley puts the issue of changing urban culture into a broad evolutionary perspective. He suggests that the western city has reached its climax and is destined to be swept away, at least in its present form. According to Seeley, "the city is the locus of the civilization's conscience. . . ," but in the near future the city will be "the province and backwoods filled with and ruled by provincials and back-woodsmen attempting to learn and undo." He argues that existing theory and concepts of planning are not adequate to cope with these events. Most dysfunctional, from his perspective, is the search for solutions, especially attempts to plan for the future. The way to the future, he suspects, is not by planning but by finding oneself and reorienting—without reintegrating into the old system.

Given our emphasis on evolutionary development, Seeley's piece provides an appropriate concluding article for the volume. Not only does he provide a fresh approach to urban history but he also challenges many of our assumptions regarding the relationships among technology and other components of the ecosystem.

Conclusion

We believe that Seeley's analysis supports our general theme that too much attention is given to contemporary processes without relating them to our past and our future. The P.O.E.T. framework as an integrating scheme alerts one to the evolutionary implications of contemporary developments. It is our hope that students will feel encouraged to pursue their studies of urban society with a fuller appreciation of historical and evolutionary patterns.

DANIEL P. MOYNIHAN

In the spring of 1969, President Nixon met in the Cabinet room with ten mayors of American cities. They were nothing if not a variegated lot, mixing party, religion, race, region in the fine confusion of American politics. They had been chosen to be representative in this respect, and were unrepresentative only in qualities of energy and intelligence that would have set them apart in any company. What was more notable about them, however, was that in the interval between the invitation from the White House and the meeting with the President, four had announced they would not run again. The mayor of Detroit who, at the last minute, could not attend, announced *his* noncandidacy in June.

Their decisions were not a complete surprise. More and more, for the men charged with governance of our cities, politics has become the art of the impossible. It is not to be wondered that they flee. But we, in a sense, are left behind. And are in trouble.

At a time of great anxiety—a time that one of the nation's leading news magazines now routinely describes as "the most serious domestic crisis since the Civil War," a time when Richard Rovere, writing of the 1972 elections, can add parenthetically, "assuming that democracy in America survives that long"—these personal decisions may seem of small consequence; yet one suspects they are not.

All agree that the tumult of the time arises, in essence, from a crisis of authority. The institutions that shaped conduct and behavior in the past are being challenged or, worse, ignored. It is in the nature of authority, as Robert A. Nisbet continues to remind us, that it is consensual, that it is not coercive. When authority systems collapse, they are replaced by power systems that *are* coercive.[1] Our vocabulary rather fails us here: the term "authority" is an unloved one, with its connotations of "authoritarianism," but there appears to be no substitute. Happily, public opinion is not so dependent on political vocabulary, certainly not on the vocabulary of political science, as some assume. For all the ambiguity of the public rhetoric of the moment, the desire of the great mass of our people is clear. They sense the advent of a power-based society and they fear it. They seek peace. They look to the restoration of legitimacy, if not in existing institutions, then in new or modified ones. They look for a lessening of violent confrontations at home, and, in great numbers, for an end to war abroad. Concern for personal safety on the part of city dwellers has become a live *political* fact, while the reappearance— what, praise God, did we do to bring this upon ourselves?—of a Stalinoid rhetoric of apocalyptic abuse on the left, and its echoes on the right, have created a public atmosphere of anxiety and portent that would seem to have touched us all. It is with every good reason that the nation gropes for some means to weather the storm of unreason that has broken upon us.

It would also seem that Americans at this moment are much preoccupied with the issue of freedom—or, rather, with new, meaningful ways in which freedom is seen to be expanded or constrained. We are, for example, beginning to evolve some sense of the meaning of group freedom. This comes after a century of preoccupation with individual rights of a kind which were seen as somehow opposed to, and even threatened by, group identities and anything so dubious in conception as *group* rights.

The Civil Rights Act of 1964 was the culmination of the political energies generated by that earlier period. The provisions which forbade employers, universities, governments, or whatever to have any knowledge of the race, religion, or national orgin of individuals with which they dealt marked in some ways the high-water mark of Social Darwinism in America; its assumption that "equality" meant *only* equal opportunity did not long stand unopposed. Indeed, by 1965 the federal government had already, as best one can tell, begun to require ethnic and racial census of its own employees, and also of federal contractors and research grant recipients. To do so violated the spirit if not the letter of the Civil Rights Act, with its implicit model of the lone individual locked in equal—and remorseless—competition in the market place, but very much in harmony with the emerging sense of the 1960's that groups have identities and entitlements as well as do individuals. This view is diffusing rapidly. In Massachusetts, for example, legislation of the Civil Rights period, which declared any public school with more than 50 per cent black pupils to be racially "imbalanced" and in consequence illegal, is already being challenged—by precisely those who supported it in the first instance. In so far as these demands have been most in evidence among black Americans, there is not the least reason to doubt that they will now diffuse to other groups, defined in various ways, and that new institutions will arise to respond to this new understanding of the nature of community.

In sum, two tendencies would appear to dominate the period. The *sense of general community is eroding,* and with it the authority of existing relationshops; simultaneously, a powerful *quest for specific community is emerging* in the form of ever more intensive assertions of racial and ethnic identities. Although this is reported in the media largely in terms of black nationalism, it is just as reasonable to identify emergent attitudes in the "white working class," as part of the same phenomenon. The singular quality of these two tendencies is that they are at once complementary and opposed. While the ideas are harmonious, the practices that would seem to support one interest are typically seen as opposing the other. Thus, one need not be a moral philosopher or a social psychologist to see that much of the "crisis of the cities" arises from the interaction of these intense new demands, and the relative inability of the urban social system to respond to them.

Programs Do Not a Policy Make

Rightly or otherwise—and one is no longer sure of this —it is our tradition in such circumstances to look to government. Social responses to changed social requirements take the form, in industrial democracies, of changed government policies. This had led, in the present situation, to a reasonably inventive spate of program proposals of the kind the New Deal more or less began and which flourished most notably in the period between the presidential elections of 1960 and 1968, when the number of domestic programs of the federal government increased from 45 to 435. Understandably, however, there has been a diminution of the confidence with which such proposals were formerly regarded. To say the least, there has been a certain nonlinearity in the relationship between the number of categorical aid programs issuing forth from Washington and the degree of social satisfaction that has ensued.

Hence the issue arises as to whether the demands of the time are not to be met in terms of *policy,* as well as program. It has been said of urban planners that they have been traumatized by the realization that everything relates to everything. But this is so, and need paralyze no one; the perception of this truth can provide a powerful analytic tool.

Our problems in the area of social peace and individual or group freedom occur in urban settings. Can it be that our difficulties in coping with these problems originate, in some measure, from the inadequacies of the setting in which they arise? Crime on the streets and campus violence may mark the onset of a native nihilism: but in the first instance they represent nothing more complex than the failure of law enforcement. Black rage and white resistance, "Third World" separatism, and restricted neighborhoods all may define a collapse in the integuments of the social contract: but, again, in the first instance they represent for the most part simply the failure of urban arrangements to meet the expectations of the urban population in the areas of jobs, schools, housing, transportation, public health, administrative responsiveness, and political flexibility. If all these are related, one to the other, and if in combination they do not seem to be working well, the question arises whether the society ought not to attempt a more coherent response. In a word: ought not a national urban crisis to be met with something like a national urban policy? Ought not the vast efforts to control the situation of the present be at least informed by some sense of goals for the future?

The United States does not now have an urban policy. The idea that there might be such is new. So also is the Urban Affairs Council, established by President Nixon on January 23, 1969, as the first official act of his administration, to "advise and assist" with respect to urban affairs, specifically "in the development of a national urban policy, having regard both to immediate and to long-range concerns, and to priorities among them."

What Happened

The central circumstance, as stated, is that America is an urban nation, and has been for half a century.

This is not to say Americans live in *big* cities. They do not. In 1960 only 9.8 per cent of the population lived in cities of 1 million or more. Ninety-eight per cent of the units of local government have fewer than 50,000 persons. In terms of the 1960 census, only somewhat more than a quarter of congressmen represented districts in which a majority of residents lived in central city areas. The 1970 census will show that the majority of Americans in metropolitan areas in fact live in suburbs, while a great many more live in urban settlements of quite modest size. But they are not the less urban for that reason, providing conditions of living and problems of government profoundly different from that of the agricultural, small town past.

The essentials of the present "urban crisis" are simple enough to relate. Until about World War II, the growth of the city, as Otto Eckstein argues, was "a logical, economic development." At least it was such in the northeastern quadrant of the United States, where most urban troubles are supposed to exist. The political jurisdiction of the city more or less defined the area of intensive economic development, that in turn more or less defined the area of intensive settlement. Thereafter, however, economic incentives and social desires combined to produce a fractionating process that made it ever more difficult to collect enough power in any one place to provide the rudiments of effective government. As a result of or as a part of this process, the central area ceased to grow and began to decline. The core began to rot.

Two special circumstances compounded this problem. First, the extraordinary migration of the rural southern Negro to the northern city. Second, a postwar population explosion (90 million babies were born between 1946 and 1968) that placed immense pressures on municipal services, and drove many whites to the suburbs seeking relief. (Both these influences are now somewhat attenuating, but their effects will be present for at least several decades, and indeed a new baby boom may be in the offing.) As a result, the problems of economic stagnation of the central city became desperately exacerbated by those of racial tension. In the course of the 1960's tension turned into open racial strife.

City governments began to respond to the onset of economic obsolescence and social rigidity a generation or more ago, but quickly found their fiscal resources strained near to the limit. State governments became involved, and much the same process ensued. Starting in the postwar period, the federal government itself became increasingly caught up with urban problems. In recent years resources on a fairly considerable scale have flowed from Washington to the cities of the land, and will clearly continue to do so. However, in the evolution of a national urban policy, more is involved than merely the question of programs and their funding. Too many programs have produced too few results simply to accept a more or less straightforward extrapolation of past and present practices into an oversized but familiar future. *The question of method has come as salient as that of goals themselves.*

As yet, the federal government, no more than state or local government, has not found an effective *incentive* system—comparable to profit in private enterprise, prestige in intellectual activity, rank in military organization—whereby to shape the forces at work in urban areas in such a way that urban goals, whatever they may be, are in fact attained. This search for incentives, and the realization that present procedures such as categorical grant-in-aid programs do not seem to provide sufficiently powerful ones, must accompany and suffuse the effort to establish goals as such. We must seek, not just policy, but policy allied to a vigorous strategy for obtaining results from it.

Finally, the federal establishment must develop a much heightened sensitivity to its "hidden" urban policies. There is hardly a department or agency of the national government whose programs do not in some way have important consequences for the life of cities, and those who live in them. Frequently —one is tempted to say normally!—the political appointees and career executives concerned do *not* see themselves as involved with, much less responsible for the urban consequences of their programs and policies. They are, to their minds, simply building highways, guaranteeing mortgages, advancing agriculture, or whatever. No one has made clear to them that they are simultaneously redistributing employment opportunities, segregating or desegregating neighborhoods, depopulating the countryside and filling up the slums, etc.: all these things as second and third order consequences of nominally unrelated programs. Already this institutional naïveté has become cause for suspicion; in the future it simply must not be tolerated. Indeed, in the future, a primary mark of competence in a federal official should be the ability to see the interconnections between programs immediately at hand and the urban problems that pervade the larger society.

The Fundaments of Urban Policy

It having been long established that, with respect to general codes of behavior, eleven precepts are too many and nine too few, ten points of urban policy may be set forth, scaled roughly to correspond to a combined measure of urgency and importance.

1. The poverty and social isolation of minority groups in central cities is the single most serious problem of the American city today. It must be attacked with urgency, with a greater commitment of resources than has heretofore been the case, and with programs designed especially for this purpose.

The 1960's have seen enormous economic advances among minority groups, especially Negroes. Outside the south, 37 per cent of Negro families earn $8,000 per year or more, that being approximately the national median income. In cities in the largest metropolitan areas, 20 per cent of Negro families in 1967 reported family incomes of $10,000 or over. The earnings of *young* married black couples are approaching parity with whites.

Nonetheless, certain forms of social disorganization and dependency appear to be increasing among the urban poor. Recently, Conrad Taeuber, Associate Director of the Bureau of the Census, reported that in the largest metropolitan areas—those with 1 million or more inhabitants—"the number of black families with a woman as head increased by 83 per cent since 1960; the number of black families with a man as head increased by only 15 per cent during the same period." Disorganization, isolation, and discrimination seemingly have led to violence, and this violence has in turn been increasingly politicized by those seeking a "confrontation" with "white" society.

Urban policy must have as its first goal the transformation of the urban lower class into a stable community based on dependable and adequate income flows, social equality, and social mobility. Efforts to improve the conditions of life in the present caste-created slums must never take precedence over efforts to enable the slum population to disperse throughout the metropolitan areas involved. Urban policy accepts the reality of ethnic neighborhoods based on free choice, but asserts that the active intervention of government is called for to enable free choice to include integrated living as a normal option.

It is impossible to comprehend the situation of the black urban poor without first seeing that they have experienced not merely a major migration in the past generation, but also that they now life in a state almost of demographic seige as a result of population growth. What demographers call the "dependency ratio"—the number of children per thousand adult males—for blacks is nearly twice that for whites, and the gap widened sharply in the 1960's.

TABLE 5.2A. Children per 1000 Adult Males

	1960	1966
White	1,365	1,406
Negro	1,922	2,216

It is this factor, surely, that accounts for much of the present distress of the black urban slums. At the same time, it is fairly clear that the sharp escalation in the number of births that characterized the past twenty-five years has more or less come to an end. The number of Negro females under age five is now exactly the number aged five to nine. Thus the 1980's will see a slackening of the present severe demands on the earning power of adult Negroes, and also on the public institutions that provide services for children. But for the decade immediately ahead, those demands will continue to rise— especially for central city blacks, whose median age is a bit more than ten years below that for whites—and will clearly have a priority claim on public resources.

2. Economic and social forces in urban areas are not self-balancing. Imbalances in industry, transportation, housing, social services, and similar elements of urban life frequently tend to become more rather than less pronounced, and this tendency is often abetted by public policies. A concept of urban balance may be tentatively set forth: a social condition in which forces tending to produce imbalance induce counterforces that simultaneously admit change while maintaining equilibrium. It must be the constant object of federal officials whose

programs affect urban areas—and there are few whose do not—to seek such equilibrium.

The evidence is considerable that many federal programs have induced sharp imbalances in the "ecology" of urban areas—the highway program, for example, is frequently charged with this, and there is wide agreement that other, specifically city-oriented programs such as urban renewal have frequently accomplished just the opposite of their nominal objectives. The reasons are increasingly evident. Cities are complex social systems. Interventions that, intentionally or not, affect one component of the system almost invariably affect second, third, and fourth components as well, and these in turn affect the first component, often in ways quite opposite to the direction of the initial intervention. Most federal urban programs have assumed fairly simple cause and effect relationships that do not exist in the complex real world. Moreover, they have typically been based on "common sense" rather than research in an area where common sense can be notoriously misleading. In the words of Jay W. Forrester, "With a high degree of confidence we can say that the intuitive solution to the problems of complex social systems will be wrong most of the time."

This doubtless is true, but it need not be a traumatizing truth. As Lee Rainwater argues, the logic of multivariate analysis, and experience with it, suggest that some components of a complex system are always vastly more important than others, so that when (if) these are accurately identified a process of analysis that begins with the assertion of chaos can in fact end by producing quite concise and purposeful social strategies.

3. At least part of the relative ineffectiveness of the efforts of urban government to respond to urban problems derives from the fragmented and obsolescent structure of urban government itself. The federal government should constantly encourage and provide incentives for the reorganization of local government in response to the reality of metropolitan conditions. The objective of the federal government should be that local government be stronger and more effective, more visible, accessible, and meaningful to local inhabitants. To this end the federal government should discourage the creation of paragovernments designed to deal with special problems by evading or avoiding the jurisdiction of established local authorities, and should encourage effective decentralization.

Although the "quality" of local government, especially in large cities, has been seen to improve of late, there appears to have been a decline in the vitality of local political systems, and an almost total disappearance of serious effort to reorganize metropolitan areas into new and more rational governmental jurisdictions. Federal efforts to recreate the ethnic-neighborhood-based community organization, as in the poverty program, or to induce metropolitan area planning as in various urban development programs, have had a measure of success, but nothing like that hoped for. Meanwhile the middle class norm of "participation" has diffused downward and outward, so that federal urban programs now routinely require citizen participation in the planning process and beyond; yet somehow this does not seem to have led to more competent communities. In some instances it appears rather to have escalated the level of stalemate.

It may be we have not been entirely candid with ourselves in this area. Citizen participation, as Elliott A. Krause has pointed out, is in practice a "bureaucratic ideology," a device whereby public officials induce nonpublic individuals to act in a way the officials desire. Although the putative object may be, indeed almost always is, to improve the lot of the citizen, it is not settled that the actual consequences are anything like that. The ways of the officials, of course, are often not those of the elected representatives of the people, and the "citizens" may become a rope in the tug-of-war between bureaucrat and representative. Especially in a federal system, "citizen participation" easily becomes a device whereby the far-off federal bureaucracy acquires a weapon with which to battle the elected officials of local government. Whatever the nominal intent, the normal outcome is federal support for those who would diminish the legitimacy of local government. But it is not clear that the purposes are typically advanced through this process. To the contrary, an all round diminishment rather than enhancement of energies seems to occur.

This would appear especially true when "citizen participation" has in effect meant putting indignant citizens on the payroll. However much these citizens may continue to "protest," the action acquires a certain hollow ring. Something like this has already happened to groups that have been openly or covertly supported by the federal government, seeking to influence public opinion on matters of public policy. This stratagem is a new practice in American democracy. It began in the field of foreign affairs, and has now spread to the domestic area. To a quite astonishing degree it will be found that those groups that nominally are pressing for social change and development in the poverty field, for example, are in fact subsidized by federal funds. This occurs in protean ways—research grants, training contracts, or whatever—and is done with the best of intentions. But, again, with what results is far from clear. Can this development, for example, account for the curious fact that there seems to be so much protest in the streets of the nation, but so little, as it were, in its legislatures? Is it the case, in other words, that the process of public subsidy is subtly debilitating?

Whatever the truth of this judgment, it is nevertheless clear that a national urban policy must look first to the vitality of the elected governments of the urban areas, and must seek to increase their capacity for independent, effective, and creative action. This suggests an effort to find some way out of the present fragmentation, and a certain restraint on the creation of federally-financed "competitive governments."

Nathan Glazer has made the useful observation that in London and Tokyo comprehensive metropolitan government is combined with a complex system of "subgovernments"—the London Boroughs—representing units of 200,000–250,000 persons. These are "real" governments, with important powers in areas such as education, welfare, and housing. In England, at all events, they are governed through an electoral system involving the national political parties in essentially their national postures. (Indeed, the boroughs make up the basic units of the parties' urban structure.) It may well be there is need for social inventions of this kind in the great American cities, especially with respect to power over matters such as welfare, education, and housing that are now subject to intense debates concerning "local control." The demand for "local control" is altogether to be welcomed. In some degree it can be seen to arise from the bureaucratic barbarities of the highway programs of the 1950's, for example. But in the largest degree it refects the processes of democracy catching up with the content of contemporary government. As government more and more involves itself in matters that very much touch on the lives of individual citizens, those individuals seek a greater voice in the programs concerned. In the hands of ideologues or dimwits, this demand can lead to an utter paralysis of government. It has already done so in dozens of urban development situations. But approached with a measure of sensitivity— and patience—it can lead to a considerable revitalization of urban government.

> 4. A primary object of federal urban policy must be to restore the fiscal vitality of urban government, with the particular object of ensuring that local governments normally have enough resources on hand or available to make local initiative in public affairs a reality.

For all the rise in actual amounts, federal aid to state and local government has increased only from 12 per cent of state-local revenue in 1958 to 17 per cent in 1967. Increasingly, state and local governments that try to meet their responsibilities lurch from one fiscal crisis to another. In such circumstances, the capacity for creative local government becomes least in precisely those jurisdictions where it might most be expected. As much as any other single factor, this condition may be judged to account for the malaise of city government, and especially for the reluctance of the more self-sufficient suburbs to associate themselves with the nearly bankrupt central cities. Surviving from one fiscal deadline to another, the central cities commonly adopt policies which only compound their ultimate difficulties. Yet their options are so few. As James Q. Wilson writes, "The great bulk of any city's budget is, in effect, a fixed charge the mayor is powerless to alter more than trivially." The basic equation, as it were, of American political economy is that for each one per cent increase in the Gross National Product the income of the federal government increases one and one-half per cent while the normal income of city governments rises half to three-quarters of a point at most. Hence both a clear opportunity and a no less manifest necessity exist for the federal government to adopt as deliberate policy an increase in its aid to urban governments. This should be done in part through revenue sharing, in part through an increase in categorical assistance, hopefully in much more consolidated forms than now exist, and through credit assistance.

It may not be expected that this process will occur rapidly. The prospects for an enormous "peace and growth dividend" to follow the cessation of hostilities in Vietnam are far less bright than they were painted. But the fact is that as a nation we grow steadily richer, not poorer, and we can afford the government we need. This means, among our very first priorities, an increase in the resources available to city governments.

A clear opportunity exists for the federal government to adopt as a deliberate policy an increase in its aid to state and local governments in the aftermath of the Vietnam war. Much analysis is in order, but in approximate terms it may be argued that the present proportion of aid should be about doubled, with the immediate objective that the federal government contribution constitute one-third of state and local revenue.

5. Federal urban policy should seek to equalize the provision of public services as among different jurisdictions in metropolitan areas.

Although the standard depiction of the (black) residents of central cities as grossly deprived with respect to schools and other social services, when compared with their suburban (white) neighbors, requires endless qualification, the essential truth is that life for the well-to-do is better than life for the poor, and that these populations tend to be separated by artificial government boundaries within metropolitan areas. (The people in between may live on either side of the boundaries, and are typically overlooked altogether.) At a minimum, federal policy should seek a dollar-for-dollar equivalence in the provision of social services having most to do with economic and social opportunity. This includes, at the top of the list, public education and public safety. (Obviously there will always be some relatively small jurisdictions— "the Scarsdale school system"—that spend a great deal more than others, being richer; but there can be national or regional norms and no central city should be allowed to operate below them.)

Beyond the provision of equal resources lies the troubled and elusive question of equal results. Should equality of educational opportunity extend to equality of educational achievement (as between one group of children and another)? Should equality of police protection extend to equality of risks of criminal victimization? That is to say, should there be not only as many police, but also as few crimes in one area of the city as in another? These are hardly simple questions, but as they are increasingly posed it is increasingly evident that we shall have to try to find answers.

The area of housing is one of special and immediate urgency. In America, housing is not regarded as a public utility (and a scarce one!) as it is in many of the industrial democracies of Europe, but there can hardly be any remaining doubt that the strong and regular production of housing is nearly a public necessity. We shall not solve the problem of racial isolation without it. Housing must not only be open, *it must be available*. The process of filtration out from dense center city slums can only take place if the housing perimeter, as it were, is sufficiently porous. For too long now the production of housing has been a function, not of the need for housing as such, but rather of the need to increase or decrease the money supply, or whatever. Somehow a greater regularity of effective demand must be provided the housing industry, and its level of production must be increased.

6. The federal government must assert a specific interest in the movement of people, displaced by technology or driven by poverty, from rural to urban areas, and also in the movement from densely populated central cities to suburban areas.

Much of the present urban crisis derives from the almost total absence of any provision for an orderly movement of persons off the countryside and into the city. The federal government made extraordinary, and extraordinarily successful, efforts to provide for the resettlement of Hungarian refugees in the 1950's and Cuban refugees in the 1960's. But almost nothing has been done for Americans driven from their homes by forces no less imperious.

Rural to urban migration has not stopped, and will not for some time. Increasingly, it is possible to predict where it will occur, and in what time sequence. (In 1968, for example, testing of mechanical tobacco harvesting began on the east coast and the first mechanical grape pickers were used on the west coast.) Hence, it is possible to prepare for it, both by training those who leave, and providing for them where they arrive. Doubtless the United States will remain a nation of exceptionally mobile persons, but the completely unassisted processes of the past need not continue with respect to the migration of impoverished rural populations.

There are increasing indications that the dramatic movement of Negro Americans to central city areas may be slackening, and that a counter movement to surrounding suburban areas may have begun. This process is to be encouraged in every way, especially by the maintenance of a flexible and open housing market. But it remains the case that in the next thirty years we shall add 100 million persons to our population. Knowing that, it is impossible to have no policy with respect to where they will be located. *For to let nature take its course is a policy.* To consider what might be best for all concerned and to seek to provide it is surely a more acceptable goal.

7. State government has an indispensible role in the management of urban affairs, and must be supported and encouraged by the federal government in the performance of this role.

This fact, being all but self-evident, tends to be overlooked. Indeed, the trend of recent legislative measures, almost invariably prompted by executive initiatives, has been to establish a direct federal-city relationship. States have been bypassed, and doubtless some have used this as an excuse to avoid their responsibilities of providing the legal and governmental conditions under which urban problems can be effectively confronted.

It has, of course, been a tradition of social reform in America that city government is bad and that, if anything, state government is worse. This is neither true as a generalization nor useful as a principle. But it is true that, by and large, state governments (with an occasional exception such as New York) have *not* involved themselves with urban problems, and are readily enough seen by mayors as the real enemy. But this helps neither. States *must* become involved. City governments, without exception, are creatures of state governments. City boundaries, jurisdictions, and powers are given and taken away by state governments. It is surely time the federal establishment sought to lend a sense of coherence and a measure of progressivism to this fundamental process.

The role of state government in urban affairs cannot easily be overlooked (though it may be deliberately ignored on political or ideological grounds). By contrast, it is relatively easy to overlook county government, and possibly an even more serious mistake to do so. In a steadily increasing number of metropolitan areas, it is the county rather than the original core city that has become the only unit of government which makes any geographical sense. That is to say, the only unit whose boundaries contain most or all of the actual urban settlement. The powers of county government have typically lagged well behind its potential, but it may also be noted that in the few—the very few— instances of urban reorganization to take place since World War II, county government has assumed a principal, even primary role in the new arrangement.

    8. The federal government must develop and put into practice far more effective incentive systems than now exist whereby state and local governments, and private interests too, can be led to achieve the goals of federal programs.

The typical federal grant-in-aid program provides its recipients with an immediate reward for promising to work toward some specified goal—raising the education achievement of minority children, providing medical care for the poor, cleaning up the air, reviving the downtown business district. But there is almost no reward for actually achieving such goals—and rarely any punishment for failing to do so.

There is a growing consensus that the federal government should provide market competition for public programs, or devise ways to imitate market conditions. In particular, it is increasingly agreed that federal aid should be given directly to the consumers of the programs concerned—individuals included—thus enabling them to choose among competing suppliers of the goods or services that the program is designed to provide. Probably no single development would more enliven and energize the role of government in urban affairs than a move from the *monopoly service* strategy of the grant-in-aid programs to a *market* strategy of providing the most reward to those suppliers that survive competition.

In this precise sense, it is evident that federal programs designed to assist those city-dwelling groups that are least well off, least mobile, and least able to fend for themselves must in many areas move beyond a *services* strategy to an approach that provides inducements to move from a dependent and deficient status to one of independence and sufficiency. Essentially, this is an *income* strategy, based fundamentally on the provision of incentives to increase the earnings and to expand the property base of the poorest groups.

Urban policy should in general be directed to raising the level of political activity and concentrating it in the electoral process. It is nonetheless possible and useful to be alert for areas of intense but unproductive political conflict and to devise ways to avoid such conflict through market strategies. Thus conflicts over "control" of public education systems have frequently of late taken on the aspect of disputes over control of a monopoly service, a sole source of a needed good. Clearly some of the ferocity that ensues can be avoided through free choice arrangements that, in effect, eliminate monopoly control. If we move in this direction, difficult "minimum standard" regulation problems will almost certainly arise, and must be anticipated. No arrangement meets every need, and a good deal of change is primarily to be justified on grounds that certain systems need change for their own sake. (Small school districts, controlled by locally elected boards may be just the thing for New York City. However, in Phoenix, Arizona, where they have just that, consolidation and centralization would appear to be the desire of educational reformers.) But either way, a measure of market competition can surely improve the provision of public services, much as it has proved an efficient way to obtain various public paraphernalia, from bolt-action rifles to lunar landing vehicles.

Here, as elsewhere, it is essential to pursue and to identify the *hidden* urban policies of government. These are nowhere more central to the issue than in the matter of incentives. Thus, for better than half a century now, city governments with the encouragement of state and federal authorities have been seeking to direct urban investment and development in accordance with principles embodied in zoning codes, and not infrequently in accord with precise city plans. However, during this same time the tax laws have provided the utmost incentive to pursue just the opposite objectives of those incorporated in the codes and the plans. It has, for example, been estimated that returns from land speculation based on zoning code changes on average incur half the tax load of returns from investment in physical improvements. Inevitably, energy and capital have diverted *away* from pursuing the plan and *toward* subverting it. It little avails for government to deplore the evasion of its purposes in such areas. Government has in fact established two sets of purposes, and provided vastly greater inducements to pursue the implicit rather than the avowed ones. Until public authorities, and the public itself, learn to be much more alert to these situations, and far more open in discussing and managing them, we must expect the present pattern of self-defeating contradictions to continue.

9. The federal government must provide more and better information concerning urban affairs, and should sponsor extensive and sustained research into urban problems.

Much of the social progress of recent years derives from the increasing quality and quantity of government-generated statistics and government-supported research. However, there is general agreement that the time is at hand when a general consolidation is in order, bringing a measure of symmetry to the now widely dispersed (and somewhat uneven) data-collecting and research-supporting activities. Such consolidation should not be limited to urban problems, but it must surely include attention to urban questions.

The federal government should, in particular, recognize that most of the issues that appear most critical just now do so in large measure because they are so little understood. This is perhaps especially so with respect to issues of minority group education, but generally applies to all the truly difficult and elusive issues of the moment. More and better inquiry is called for. In particular, the federal government must begin to sponsor longitudinal research— i.e., research designed to follow individual and communal development over long periods of time. It should also consider providing demographic and economic projections for political subdivisions as a routine service, much as the weather and the economy are forecast. Thus, Karl Taeuber has shown how seemingly unrelated policies of local governments can increase the degree of racial and economic differentiation between political jurisdictions, especially between cities and suburbs.

Similarly, the extraordinary inquiry into the educational system begun by the U.S. Office of Education under the direction of James S. Coleman should be established on an on-going basis. It is now perfectly clear that little is known about the processes whereby publicly-provided resources affect educational outcomes. The great mass of those involved in education, and of that portion of the public that interests itself in educational matters, continue undisturbed in its old beliefs. But the bases of their beliefs are already thoroughly undermined and the whole structure is likely to collapse in a panic of disillusion and despair unless something like new knowledge is developed to replace the old. Here again, longitudinal inquiries are essential. And here also, it should be insisted that however little the new understandings may have diffused beyond the academic research centers in which they originated, the American public is accustomed to the idea that understandings do change and, especially in the field of education, is quite open to experimentation and innovation.

Much of the methodology of contemporary social science originated in clinical psychology, and perhaps for that reason tends to be "deficiency-oriented." Social scientists raise social *problems,* the study of which can become a social problem in its own right if it is never balanced by the identification and analysis of social *successes.* We are not an unsuccessful country. To the contrary, few societies work as hard at their problems, solve as many, and in the process stumble on more unexpected and fulsome opportunities. The cry of the decent householder who asks why the social science profession (and the news media which increasingly follow the profession) must be ever preoccupied with juvenile delinquency and never with juvenile decency deserves to be heard. Social science like medical science has been preoccupied with pathology, with pain. A measure of inquiry into the sources of health and pleasure is overdue, and is properly a subject of federal support.

10. The federal government, by its own example, and by incentives, should seek the development of a far heightened sense of the finite resources of the natural environment, and the fundamental importance of aesthetics in successful urban growth.

The process of "uglification" may first have developed in Europe; but, as with much else, the technological breakthroughs have taken place in the United States. American cities have grown to be as ugly as they are, not as a consequence of the failure of design, but rather because of the success of a certain interaction of economic, technological, and cultural forces. It is economically efficient to exploit the natural resources of land, and air, and water by technological means that the culture does not reject, albeit that the result is an increasingly despoiled, debilitated, and now even dangerous urban environment.

It is not clear how this is to change, and so the matter which the twenty-second century, say, will almost certainly see as having been the primary urban issue of the twentieth century is ranked last in the public priorities of the moment. But there *are* signs that the culture is changing, that the frontier sense of a natural environment of unlimited resources, all but impervious to human harm, is being replaced by an acute awareness that serious, possibly irreparable harm is being done to the environment, and that somehow the process must be reversed. This *could* lead to a new, nonexploitive technology, and thence to a new structure of economic incentives.

The federal establishment is showing signs that this cultural change is affecting its actions, and so do state and city governments. But the process needs to be raised to the level of a conscious pursuit of policy. The quality of the urban environment, a measure deriving from a humane and understanding use of the natural resources, together with the creative use of design in architecture and in the distribution of activities and people, must become a proclaimed concern of government. And here the federal government can lead. It must seek out its hidden policies. (The design of public housing projects, for example, surely has had the consequence of manipulating the lives of those who inhabit them. By and large the federal government set the conditions that have determined the disastrous designs of the past two decades. It is thus responsible for the results, and should force itself to realize that.) And it must be acutely aware of the force of its own example. If scientists (as we are told) in the Manhattan Project were prepared to dismiss the problem of long-lived radioactive wastes as one that could be solved merely by ocean dumping, there are few grounds for amazement that business executives in Detroit for so long manufactured automobiles that emitted poison gases into the atmosphere. Both patterns of decision evolved from the primacy of economic concerns in the context of the exploitation of the natural environment in ways the culture did not forbid. There are, however, increasing signs that we are beginning to change in this respect. We may before long evolve into a society in which the understanding of and concern about environmental pollution, and the general uglification of American life, will be both culturally vibrant and politically potent.

Social peace is a primary objective of social policy. To the extent that this derives from a shared sense of the aesthetic value and historical significance of the public places of the city, the federal government has a direct interest in encouraging such qualities.

Daniel J. Elazar has observed that while Americans have been willing to become urbanized, they have adamantly resisted becoming "citified." Yet a measure of "citification" is needed. There are perhaps half a dozen cities in America whose disappearance would, apart from the inconvenience, cause any real regret. To lose one of those six would plunge much of the nation and almost all the immediate inhabitants into genuine grief. Something of value in our lives would have been lost, and we would know it. The difference between these cities that would be missed and the rest that would not, resides fundamentally in the combination of architectural beauty, social amenity, and cultural vigor that sets them apart. It has ever been such. To create such a city and to preserve it was the great ideal of the Greek civilization, and it may yet become ours as we step back ever so cautiously from the worship of the nation-state with its barbarous modernity and impotent might. We might well consider the claims for a different life asserted in the oath of the Athenian city-state:

> We will ever strive for the ideals and sacred thing of the city,
> both alone and with many;
> We will unceasingly seek to quicken the sense of public duty;
> We will revere and obey the city's laws;
> We will transmit this city not only not less, but greater, better
> and more beautiful than it was transmitted to us.

NOTE

1. "The Twilight of Authority," *The Public Interest,* no. 15, Spring 1969.

HENRY J. SCHMANDT

Thomas Jefferson based his hopes for American democracy on the proposition that we would not live in cities, that we would all be self-employed, that we would be so well-educated that we could meet any new difficulties, and that we would be trained in civic virtue through local government. Now we live in cities, we are all employed by others, our educational system is partly custodial and partly technical, thus unfitting us to meet new difficulties, and anybody who connects civic virtue with local government would be sent to a psychiatrist.[1]

The transformation described here evolved over a long span of our national history, but the changes which are taking place today are almost contemptuous of time in the rapidity with which they occur. It requires little reflection to realize that the urban world at the beginning of the 1970s is a far cry from the one we knew just ten years ago. We have witnessed a decade of acute social ferment marked by intensifying conflicts over poverty, race, resource allocation, and the use and distribution of social power. No segment of the community—from the ghetto to the university campus—has been left untouched. The decade has left us uneasy, tense, angry, protestful, and, above all, perplexed.

Although our major social and economic problems are national in scope, the cities are the battlegrounds, the locus of our domestic difficulties as well as of our future. It is here that we will either succeed or fail, for it is in the urban areas that the bulk of the nation's resources, human and material, are concentrated—a simple fact, yet one that many of our state and national lawmakers seem unable to comprehend. For if we are really concerned with our urban problems, how can we explain a national policy which in 1969 allocated almost a half billion dollars to the development of biological and chemical warfare devices and less than $10 million for the subsidization of interest rates to enable low-income families to purchase homes?

The "urban crisis," however defined, is less a lack of material resources and expertise than an absence of will and determination. It is as much as anything an attitudinal problem; an unwillingness to come to grips with reality, a tendency to opt for a romanticized past, a desire to avoid personal

From an unpublished paper by Henry J. Schmandt, "Solutions for the City as a Social Crisis." Reprinted by permission of the author.

involvement and responsibility, and a readiness to find scapegoats for our troubles. We are not lacking in programmatic suggestions for coping with the social and physical ills of our cities—literally thousands are presented each year to the legislative chambers and administrative arms of our local, state, and national governments. Nor are we lacking in technological know-how. It will be a cause of bewilderment to future historians as they search through the chronicles of this century that a nation which can send astronauts to the moon is unable to move the traffic on its city streets or clear its air and water of pollution, or that can produce a gross national product soon to exceed a trillion dollars annually cannot remove the huge pockets of poverty in its midst.

The urban political system, that which we are primarily concerned with here, has traditionally acted only in response to crisis. It has demonstrated little ability to innovate or take the lead in guiding social change. One is constantly reminded of this fact as he considers ways of redesigning or updating the system to make it more relevant to the needs of the time. Certainly—we try to convince ourselves—there must be a better way for the political and social institutions of our large urban complexes to function than lurching from crisis to crisis. As Winnie the Pooh reflected:

> Here is Edward Bear, coming downstairs now, bump, bump, bump, on the back of his head, behind Christopher Robin. It is, as far as he knows, the only way of coming downstairs, but sometimes he feels that there really is another way, if only he could stop bumping for a moment and think of it. And then he feels perhaps there isn't.

My objective in this paper is to sketch out in broad outline, from the perspective of a political scientist, some of the elements of a rational approach to the "City as a Social Crisis." This analysis will first touch on the assumptions underlying the approach and on several major trends in the society that are conditioning the quality of urban life and precipitating its problems. It will then suggest a set of general strategies and structural changes in the governmental organization of the metropolitan community to accommodate these forces and channel them toward the achievement of societal goals.

Assumptions

Seven assumptions are implicit in this presentation and form the basis for shaping the proposals to be discussed later.

1. A significant and influential segment of the population—albeit a minority—takes seriously the major goals of American society as set out in our basic legal and political documents and enunciated by our leading spokesmen for almost two centuries. These include respect for the dignity of all men regardless of their race, religion, ethnic, origin, point of view, or the haircut they wear; equality of opportunity for all, whether in education, housing or employment; and maximum freedom of choice and action commensurate with the rights of others.

2. The United States in general and urban communities in particular, will face a series of continuing crises in the immediate years ahead until the gross disparities which now exist in the society are eliminated. Correlative with this premise is the clearly demonstrated proposition that the best opportunities for institutional change occur during and immediately following crises.

3. Moral exhortations about the rights of man will do little to stimulate social reform. Such exhortations provide legitimacy to actions aimed at remedying inequalities; they do not in themselves modify attitudes or behavior when power and resource distribution are at stake. To accomplish significant change, strategies must be devised which will appeal to the self-interests of all segments of the society.

4. The most critical problems facing urban communities today are those related to race and poverty: unemployment, welfare, inadequate housing and schooling, maldistribution of resources, discrimination, and unequal opportunity. To say this is not to be unmindful of the serious physical problems of our large metropolitan agglomerations: pollution of the environment, traffic congestion, unsightly and inefficient developmental patterns, and the other difficulties which inconvenience the urban dweller and detract from the quality of his surroundings. For the first time in history, man is in a position to control almost completely his physical environment; yet this capability will remain unrealized until he is able to design means of effectively coping with the social problems that threaten to tear his cities apart.

5. The metropolis constitutes an economic entity that must be treated as such. It is a common labor market, a common housing market, and a common transportation network.

6. Solution to the major problems of our large urban areas has long since passed beyond the capacity of the local communities. Their resolution will require action at all levels of public authority, together with greatly increased involvement on the part of business and industry, organized labor, and the nation's educational institutions.

7. It is psychologically sound, as well as in accord with the democratic creed, for human beings to have some direct control over the institutions which have a major effect on their daily lives. As the Coleman report, *Equality of Educational Opportunity,* found with respect to the young, "a sense of control of their own fate" is more highly related to achievement than any other factor in their background or school.[2] The same may be said of the urban population at large. Dysfunctional consequences inevitably follow when segments of the community feel powerless to affect the system.

Trends

From assumptions we move next to the identification of relevant trends or forces in the society, a task which necessitates some arbitrary exclusions in the interest of simplification. Numerous such trends, ranging all the way from continued cybernation of the work world to new forms of artistic expression, help condition social behavior. The three which are singled out here as particularly important for our present purposes relate to the bureaucratization of the society, the location of power and decision-making authority, and specialization.

In response to the increase in societal scale and the growing complexity of running the public establishment, we have developed a set of bureaucratic management institutions which often seem impersonal and alien to human feelings. As Suzanne Langer has said: "Our technological civilization . . . seems to overtake and overwhelm us as though it were something foreign coming in on us." Most individuals at one time or another have experienced the feeling of being overpowered by the social apparatus, and many have felt an acute sense of futility in trying to affect it. The reaction can lead, as it did some time ago in Boston, to the strange sight of Birchites and Students for a Democratic Society sharing the same picket line in protest against an urban renewal project—both groups speaking from widely different ideological perspectives for a resurgence of individualism against "the system."[3]

Inadequately structured size can create serious problems by discouraging participation and involvement and by destroying spontaneity and creative diversity. It can push individuals and groups into seeking devices and strategies as a protection against bigness, overcentralized government, and paternalism. Political manifestations of the reaction to impersonal bureaucratization may be found, for example, in the changing style of urban politics: from one of brokerage or mediation among competing interests to one of conflict. More and more, the traditional channels of access to the policy-making and value-allocating centers of local government are being bypassed in favor of such techniques as crisis precipitation and confrontation politics. The use of these strategies, moreover, is not limited to racial minorities or the poor: they are being increasingly employed by other more "respectable" groups in the society as evidenced in strikes by teachers, work slowdowns and demonstrations by police, and uprisings by students. This process has been hastened, if not triggered, by the seeming rigidity of the bureaucratic structure, its continued—although predictable—unwillingness to risk any diminution of its powers, and the insensitivity of many local public administrators to the new challenges in the society.

Along with bureaucratization, technology and increasing scale have continuously pushed the centers of power upward so that the fate of the modern urban community rests less on its own decisions than on those which are made at the national and state capitols and in the corporate board rooms of the industrial and banking giants. We have become a nation of dependent cities, increasingly reliant upon the funds supplied by higher levels of public authority to keep the system minimally functional. Federal and state grants-in-aid to local units, to cite one indication, now exceed $20 billion annually.

Increasingly also, our cities have become dependent on outside intervention to ameliorate their critical problems, social as well as physical. Not until the national government acted did either the cities or states make any concerted efforts to take care of their unmet social needs; nor, in fact, did many of them move to abate air and water pollution until federal legislation made it mandatory for them to do so. The stimulus for change has consistently come from outside; seldom has the local community acted to reshape its local institutions or practices—whether in the field of open housing or school district reorganization—as a result of internally generated pressure. In more recent years, its repeatedly demonstrated incapacity to effect local settlements in socially and politically controversial areas of concern has further hastened the erosion of its powers.

The third major trend, specialization, is manifested both functionally in the kinds of tasks that are performed and spatially in the geographical distribution of economic activities and social types. Just as sections of an urban community are identified with particular commercial and industrial uses, so are whole neighborhoods given over to groups socially differentiated by age, socioeconomic status, ethnicity, and race. Specialization of either variety pulls in two directions. On the one hand, it divides the system into numerous parts, each distinguished by its own interests and objectives and each anxious to build up protective walls around its sphere of concern. On the other hand, it creates a counterforce to bring the separate but highly interdependent components back into a coordinated operation.

The segregation of social types in space is especially relevant to the problem before us. The urban dweller has two sets of interests: one associated with the notion of place, the other spatially undefined.[4] The first includes those activities which relate to the quality of the neighborhood he lives in, the character of his neighbors, the security of his person and home, and the public services which affect his social and physical surroundings. A large majority in the population regard the immediate environment in which they reside as a haven for protecting and maintaining their life styles. People tend to shy away from the threat of social diversity, from living in the same neighborhood or belonging to the same club with others of different values and ways of life. Each family-oriented group demands that others conform to its values and accept its priorities. In the process, as Herbert Gans points out, each group seeks to prevent others from shaping the institutions that must be shared, such as the schools, for otherwise the family and its culture are not "safe."[5] Thus the movement of hippies into an area of single-family dwellings or of blacks into white neighborhoods arouses intense opposition precisely because the move is perceived by the residents as a threat to their way of living and their values.

Alongside these spatially-defined concerns is a whole set of other interests that are not a function of location. In both the social and work world, technology and wealth have permitted the geographical range of intercourse to expand phenomenally, thereby freeing interactions of many types from the requirement of physical proximity and multiplying the ties and interests which transcend space. Work, friendship, and professional contacts, for example, are not bounded by the individual's residential environs. Neither are the problems of poverty, deprivation, and unemployment territorially defined—a fact which places them beyond the scope of effective neighborhood or local action.

This division of interests has certain implications for government. Local control is particularly sought by residents over those activities which they perceive as conducive to the preservation of their life styles. These include the provision of child-rearing facilities (the schools in particular), protection from miscreant neighbors, and the "gate-keeping" functions or the exclusion of people with "strange" cultural attributes or conflicting values. These spatially related concerns have in many ways become more important to the lower-middle class than to those higher on the status scale. The former are more intimately bound to their neighborhoods by an equity in a home which often represents their life's savings, by lower mobility, by feelings of insecurity, and by fewer ties to the outside world. Efforts at social change which disregard these deeply ingrained feelings are not likely to go far.

Proposals and Strategies

It is within this broad setting and against the backdrop of these various forces that proposals and strategies for change must be fashioned. As the foregoing discussion suggests, these must be designed to:

1. Effect a more equitable distribution of social goods while appealing to the self-interests of all groups in the society;
2. Prevent crises, yet be prepared to take advantage of them when they do arise;
3. Promote a genuine multi-racial community, yet provide wide opportunity and freedom for individuals and families to enjoy the life styles compatible with their values and desires;
4. Move away from solutions which challenge head-on the place-related interests of individuals; and
5. Facilitate the centralization of those functions necessary to maintain the metropolitan system while at the same time developing approaches to political decision-making at the sub-community or neighborhood level. Gargantua and Grassroots need not be dichotomous alternatives; both are indispensable to a democratic society.

REDISTRIBUTION

To proceed within this general framework will require new redistributive policies on the one hand, and a restructuring of local political institutions on the other. In regard to the former it is important at the outset to distinguish analytically between the distribution and delivery systems of government.[6] The first is the principal means of tempering the inequities which inevitably arise in a competitive society; it is accomplished principally through income redistribution in the form of public assistance programs, housing subsidies, and other types of transfer payments. The second, or delivery system, consists of the organizational mechanisms through which public goods and services are furnished to the citizen consumers; it serves as a redistributive agent only to the extent that its output, such as education, is not paid for equally by all the recipients.

Local governments are not effective redistribution agencies because of the circumscriptions on their ability to tap resources and the intense opposition that redistributive issues generate among members of the community.

Such units, whether municipalities or school districts, have a built-in tendency to segregate access to public goods and the opportunity structure. As the evidence clearly shows, the traditional politics of brokerage functions best at the local level when the redistributive objective is minimal; it does not work well when local government is called upon to effect significant transfer payments (principally in the form of services) from the "haves" to the "have nots." We can see this fact illustrated when redistributive policies of the national government, such as the poverty program, are channeled through the local delivery system, thus thrusting the latter into a major allocative role which it is ill-equipped to play.

This suggests that our strategy should be designed to relieve local units of their redistributive function by shifting substantially more of this responsibility to higher levels of public authority. Such an objective could be accomplished in two ways: one by moving from the present heavy reliance on public assistance to national policies that emphasize direct income-transfer payments to the disadvantaged through such devices as the negative income tax, liberalized social security payments, and rent supplements; the other by transferring to the state primary responsibility for the financing of those services, particularly public education, which involve a large income-redistributive element. An approach of this nature would enable the local polity to operate in a less tense environment and would open the way for institutional changes which are not possible under existing arrangements.

INSTITUTIONAL RESTRUCTURING

Along with the modification of reallocation policies, we should also concentrate on the task of reshaping our local political and social institutions to accommodate the emerging trends and forces in the society. For this purpose two broad lines of attack are proposed here: one involving governmental restructuring; the other the mobilization of private talents and resources in a collateral and complementary thrust to the activities of the public sector. Both are long-range objectives that can be accomplished only by a series of steps over time. Both pose numerous problems and involve calculated risks; but both seek to preserve and promote the basic values and norms of the society by broadening the opportunity structure for all its members. They are by no means novel—although I believe they are presented in a new light—and they will be considered unrealistic by many. For as Machiavelli observed: "There is nothing more difficult to carry out, nor more doubtful of success nor more dangerous to handle than to initiate a new order of things." Yet as indicated earlier, constructive change is possible in an age of constant crisis, provided we are ready and prepared to move with substantive and procedural programs as the opportunities arise.[7] Moreover, two forces are now converging which enhance the possibilities of meaningful change: the newly found activism of racial minorities and the poor; and the increasing federal and state intervention in the affairs of the nation's urban areas.

GOVERNMENTAL RESTRUCTURING

The proposal for reorganizing the local governmental system starts from the premise that the large central city is obsolete as a political entity. It is a failing leviathan that can no longer function effectively because it has neither the power or resources to sustain itself nor an environment favorable to its existence. For similar reasons, the central city mayor is an outmoded political figure, shouldered with immense responsibilities but with little effective power or means to execute them. To attempt to strengthen either the core municipality as a political organ or the office of mayor as a metropolitan political leader is like trying to redesign a hand abacus to make it competitive with the electronic computer. So long as the central city continues in its present political form, it is neither relevant to the needs of large-scale society nor conducive to the kind of local participatory democracy that is one of the nation's avowed goals. The disputes over the model cities program as well as over relocation and housing, to mention but a few examples, reveal the inherent weaknesses in the existing political structures of our metropolitan areas.

What is necessary, therefore, is to move in two directions. One is to create the kind of urban governmental mechanism that is capable of handling the major maintenance functions of a metropolitan aggregation, playing the coordinating role essential to a specialized and large-scale community, and guaranteeing the "openness" of the opportunity structure. The other is to establish local governmental units of such size that the individual will have meaningful opportunity to participate in and control those public activities which directly and immediately affect his neighborhood and his life style. The first objective will require the creation of a metropolitan or regional government with territorial jurisdiction over the entire urbanized area; the second will necessitate the division of the central city into smaller political units of 100,000 to 150,000 population, each with governmental structures and power similar to those of the suburban municipalities. Under this plan, the counties and all special districts within the urban region would be abolished as governmental entities; the other local units—the suburban municipalities and suburban school districts—would continue in existence as at present, although some consolidation would be in order. The central business district and the major industrial concentrations, because of their importance to the total community, would be placed under the jurisdiction of the larger government. Elections to the regional council would be by district, with the chief executive selected at large.

The argument might be made that a metropolitan or regional government could be created, as it has in several Canadian areas, without dismantling the central city. My response to this is two-fold. First, the establishment of such a government in the large S.M.S.A.'s of this country will continue to be a virtual impossibility so long as the core city remains a political entity. The existence of a disproportionately large political body among units much smaller in size but equal in legal powers and authority is not conducive to the harmonious negotiation and settlement of issues. Decentralization of the large

unit, on the other hand, can open the doors to a regional approach by neu-
tralizing suburban fears of central city domination and destroying once and
for all the city-suburban dichotomy. It is also likely to win the support of
various groups within the city itself that would otherwise look upon the establishment of a regional government as a further dilution of their power and
influence. Political decentralization of the core city could, in other words, be
converted into a key bargaining issue to precipitate a metropolitan or regional
settlement.

Second, leaving the central city political structure intact with do nothing
to solve the critical problem of bureaucratic scale and of citizen involvement
and control. The poorer sections of the city will continue to be regarded and
dealt with as underdeveloped colonies rather than as emerging nations. The
rhetoric of participation will flourish but the devolving of power to the neighborhoods or subcommunities will remain an illusion as it now is. The white
middle classes will become more and more disenchanted with the internal
political strife generated by the inadequately structured system, while the disadvantaged and minority groups will grow increasingly resentful of the efforts
of the local political and bureaucratic establishment to protect its power and
control.

The crucial question in a governmental restructuring, such as proposed
here, is the assignment of functional responsibilities to each of the two levels.
Such an allocation must be highly sensitive to the self-interests of the localities
and their constituencies if the plan is to serve its purpose and meet with a
measure of acceptance. To provide a conceptual basis for making this determination, it is helpful to divide the functions into three categories: place-
related, non-place-related, and mixed. The first pertains to those activities
which directly impinge on the life styles, values, and amenities of individuals
and families within a given urban space.[8] These are the functions that most
concern the citizen in his place of residence. They include education, building
and housing code enforcement, regulation of taverns, refuse collection and
sanitation, and neighborhood recreational facilities.

The second group involves those functions that are essential to the maintenance of the overall urban system and are only incidentally associated with
space and life styles. Among these are the control of air and water pollution,
utility services such as water supply and waste disposal, expressways and ar-
terial streets, areal planning and development, central facilities such as museums, public hospitals, airports, major recreational facilities which require
large parcels of land, conservation of open space and other natural resources,
and the traditional county functions.

The third category consists of those functions which have both place
and non-place related aspects. As such, they affect both neighborhood life
styles and the maintenance of the total urban system. Housing and redevelopment, for example, fall into this category. Economically, the metropolis or
region constitutes a single housing market. At the same time, however, housing and redevelopment are intimately related to the quality of one's neighborhood and the life style values he is seeking to protect or promote. The same
is true, in a somewhat different sense, of the police function. Law enforcement is of area-wide import; yet certain aspects of it, routine patrolling in

particular, affect the mode of living of a neighborhood and are of peculiar concern to its residents.

The first two categories present few conceptual difficulties in determining the allocation of responsibilities. If the debilitating effects of bureaucratic bigness on civic attitudes and behavior are to be countered, functions in the life style group must be kept within a scale where meaningful involvement, participation, and control by the residents are possible and feasible. The question here is less one of efficiency and economy than how compatible the administration of these activities is with the norms and goals of the affected individuals and perceived needs. Primary jurisdiction in this functional area therefore properly rests with the local units or subcommunities.

Activities in the second, or systems maintenance, category logically belong in an area-wide or regional agency since they serve to bind together the specialized but highly interdependent segments of the metropolis into an effective operating unit. They become dysfunctional or extremely costly and inefficient when supplied by numerous political units. More importantly, it is only at this level that an urban area can aggregate sufficient political power to deal realistically with its environment and with the higher centers of public and private authority.

The third, or mixed, category involves greater difficulties in determining functional allocations. Zoning is a case in point. It can be used as a tool for shaping the kind of neighborhood the residents want, and in this respect it logically belongs at the local level. Yet it can also be used to thwart the larger interests of the total community through unreasonable exclusionary practices. Like law enforcement, it is a type of activity that can only be partially decentralized. Control over certain aspects of the function must rest with the area-wide authority, with the reminder that the sensitivity of the local units to the needs of the larger community can best be cultivated by building incentives into the system rather than by coercive means.

Obviously the breaking up of the central city into smaller units would intensify the existing disparities in resources among local governments unless accompanied by modifications in the method of financing services. Among the steps which will be taken sooner or later, regardless of whether we move toward the kind of governmental restructuring proposed here, are: (1) the shifting of financial responsibility for public education to the state or a regional taxing authority; (2) the assumption by the county or larger unit of government of responsibility for providing the local share for federal grant-in-aid programs such as urban renewal and model cities; and (3) special allotments by the state or regional government to the poorer units on a need formula basis to meet their special service requirements. These devices would involve only a modicum of income redistribution on the part of the local system and, if made part of a larger settlement, they would not generate the degree of opposition usually associated with such efforts.

Human Mobilization Corporation

Collateral with governmental restructuring, the second major thrust in equipping the urban community with adequate problem-solving mechanisms would be directed at mobilizing the private resources of the area to play a complementary but vital part in this process. Creation of a regional or metropolitan government would greatly strengthen the ability of the overall community to cope with its problems. However, as a public body, such an agency would not have the freedom of a private organization to innovate, take calculated risks, act with dispatch, and move in certain directions. What I am suggesting, therefore, is the formation of a quasi-public instrumentality, a Human Mobilization Corporation, to engage in and stimulate activities in areas of physical and social concern where local governments have proved peculiarly inept. The overarching goal of such a corporation would be the continuous enlargement and development of the opportunity structure for all segments of the metropolitan community.

The Human Mobilization Corporation would be established as a nonprofit organization under state or federal enabling legislation. Its board of directors would be chosen by the participating groups and would be widely representative of all major interests in the community, including business, labor, government, the poor, and racial minorities. It would have authority to engage in a broad range of developmental activities such as the construction of housing for low-income families, the building of new towns or settlements in the urban region, the operation of experimental schools, and the recruitment and training of managerial talent among deprived groups. Through close working arrangements with the higher educational institutions and industries of the area, it would engage in R and D programs related to the human needs of the community's population and would seek to stimulate utilization of the findings.

A corporation of this nature could be particularly influential in the housing field. For despite open housing laws and other legislation against discrimination, it is highly unlikely that the existing suburbs will be opened up to low income and minority groups on more than a token scale. Nor is it at all certain that many of those now disadvantaged would want to live in surroundings where life styles are incompatible with their own cultural traits and where attitudes are unfriendly if not overtly hostile. Assuming that national policy will continue to move in the direction of making home-ownership possible for all segments of the population, the Human Mobilization Corporation could become the principal mechanism for seeing that full advantage is taken of these programs. Rather than attempting to challenge the place-related interests of the majoritarian society, it could in cooperation with builders, private investors, and neighborhood development corporations (such as envisaged under bills now pending in Congress and in some state legislatures), move to assemble and develop land in the outer sections of the metropolis as well as in the deteriorating inner neighborhoods. As we have seen to our great dismay, urban redevelopment operated by central cities has not and, in fact, cannot provide the answer to the housing needs of the urban disadvantaged or open up opportunities for them to move to other parts of the area. A metropolitan or regional government would be in a far better position to discharge this responsibility but it too would be circumscribed by political realities unless supported and supplemented by vigorous and independent action in the private sphere.

The question of financing such a corporation presents, as always, a key problem. Its initial capital would have to come from federal and state grants and loans, private foundations, and the sale of bonds to the general public. The last source is particularly important, since one of the objectives of this approach would be to get wide citizen involvement in the cause of human development. By issuing "Human Opportunity Bonds," individuals, organizations, and businesses could be enlisted in a major effort to upgrade the life and well-being of the community and activate its vastly underutilized resources: human and material. Many of the activities of the corporation would be self-liquidating and others ancillary to the investment by business and industry in development projects. In addition, the corporation would be able to draw upon a largely untapped reservoir of volunteer assistance. Many businessmen and professional personnel, as well as students and other segments of the society, would be willing to donate a portion of their leisure time to socially significant projects if provided with meaningful opportunity. The possibilities here, in an age when affluence is beginning to trouble the social conscience of many individuals, are unlimited if only we can generate the imagination and mechanisms to capitalize on them.

Conclusion

These proposals admittedly have something of a utopian ring. Yet they are designed to take advantage of the emerging and predominant forces within the society rather than run counter to them. As such, they are not beyond the realm of accomplishment if we take the longer view. It is becoming increasingly clear that our large metropolitan communities are on a collision course with chaos. We have long since passed the stage when small doses of cure will suffice; the response must be equal to the challenge. The events of recent years have shaken our complacency but have not generated the level of response the urban crisis demands. This failure is not surprising given the general well-being and growing affluence of the nation and the propensity to avoid the true issues by venting our frustrations on whatever scapegoats seem to serve our purposes.

Rhetoric aside, we are entering into a critical period of our urban existence. The steps that we take during the next decade may well determine whether we shall have perpetual social war in our cities, or whether we shall be able to devise an urban system capable of accommodating the conflicting interests which are the inevitable hallmark of a diverse and pluralistic society. Major changes are inevitable; the question is what direction they will take—and that choice is ours. As Sir Francis Bacon warned: "He that will not apply new remedies must expect new evils; for time is the greatest innovator."

NOTES

1. Robert Hutchins, Annual Report of the President, Center for the Study of Democratic Institutions, 1968.
2. James S. Coleman et al., Equality of Educational Opportunity (Washington, D.C.: U.S. Government Printing Office, 1967).

3. See in this connection Lisa Peattie, "Reflections on Advocacy Planning," *Journal of the American Institute of Planners,* XXXIV (March 1968), pp. 80–88.

4. Melvin M. Webber, "The Urban Place and the Nonplace Urban Realm," in Melvin M. Webber *et al., Explorations into Urban Structure* (Philadelphia: University of Pennsylvania Press, 1964), pp. 79–137.

5. *The Levittowners* (New York: Pantheon Books, 1967), p. 414.

6. See in this connection Henry J. Schmandt and John Goldbach, "The Urban Paradox," in Henry J. Schmandt and Warner Bloomberg, Jr. (eds.), *The Quality of Urban Life* (Beverly Hills: Sage Publications, 1969).

7. See Donald N. Michael, "Urban Planning and Policy Problems," in *Urban America: Goals and Problems* (Washington, D.C.: U.S. Government Printing Office, 1967), p. 79.

8. See Oliver P. Williams, "A Framework for Metropolitan Political Analysis," in Thomas R. Dye (ed.), *Comparative Research in Community Politics* (Athens: University of Georgia Press, 1966), pp. 41–56.

5.4 NEW TOWNS:
COLUMBIA, MARYLAND

JAMES W. ROUSE

The simple fact is that, with the powers and processes that now exist in local government and in the home building industry, it is impossible to provide, in an orderly and intelligent way, for the metropolitan growth which we know lies just ahead.

Our cities grow by accident—by whim of the private developer and public agencies. A farm is sold and begins raising houses instead of potatoes—then another farm—; forests are cut; valleys are filled; streams are buried in storm sewers; kids overflow the schools—here a new school is built—there a church. Then more schools and more churches. Traffic grows; roads are widened; service stations, Tastee Freez, hamburger stands pockmark the highway. Traffic strangles. An Expressway is cut through the landscape—brings clover leafs—which bring shopping centers, office buildings, high-rise apartments. Relentlessly, the bits and pieces of a city are splattered across the landscape. By this irrational process, non-communities are born—formless places, without order, beauty or reason; with no visible respect for people or the land. Thousands of small, separate decisions—made with little or no relationship to one another, nor to their composite impact—produce a major decision about the future of our cities and our civilization—a decision we have come to label "suburban sprawl."

Sprawl is dreadfully inefficient. It stretches out the distances people must travel to work, to shop, to worship, to play. It fails to relate these activities in ways that strengthen each and, thus, it suppresses values that orderly relationships and concentration of uses would stimulate. Sprawl is ugly, oppressive, massively dull. It squanders the resources of nature—forests, streams, hillsides—and produces vast, monotonous armies of housing and graceless, tasteless clutter. But worst of all, sprawl is inhuman. It is anti-human. The vast, formless spread of housing, pierced by the unrelated spotting of schools, churches, stores, creates areas so huge and irrational that they are out of scale with people—beyond their grasp and comprehension—too big for people to feel a part of, responsible for, important in. The richness of real community—in both its support and its demands—is largely voided. Variety and

Partial Statement on HR 1296, Title II, Land Development and New Communities, before Housing Sub-Committee, Banking and Currency Committee, House of Representatives, March 25, 1966.

choice are reduced to a sort of pre-packaged brand-name selection of recreation, culture and education. The individual is immersed in the mass. What nonsense this is. What reckless, irresponsible dissipation of nature's endowment and man's hopes for dignity, beauty, growth.

This Sub-committee can plan better than we are building the American city. It requires no vast program of research, no technological breakthrough, no huge subsidy, no army of technicians or crusading volunteers to build better American cities. We know the rough measurements of our future growth—how many people we must provide for; what they will require in houses and apartments, schools and colleges, churches, hospitals, offices and factories, retail stores, lumber yards and service stations. Our task is simply to provide now for what we can calculate will be required to accommodate our future growth; to provide rationally now for what we know is going to occur; to arrange the pieces in a constructive way with a decent respect for man and nature instead of improvising frantically and impulsively with each new thrust of growth as if it were a gigantic surprise beyond our capacity to predict or to manage.

Why, in a nation with such enormous capacity for organization and production, is there such bewilderment about producing the environment in which we grow our people? The answer is easy but frightening. We simply have no machinery, no process, no organized capacity in the United States to put to work the knowledge that exists among us about planning for the future growth of our cities. Is there any other aspect of American life in which the gap is so wide between our knowledge and our performance as in the growth of the American City?

The building of the city is nobody's business—neither government nor industry. We have assigned a vague responsibility to local government to provide for orderly growth but have given it neither the power, the process, nor the financial capacity with which it can fulfill that responsibility. The most advanced planning and zoning concepts in America today are inadequate to preserve our forests and stream valleys and maintain open spaces. They cannot produce well formed communities with a rich variety of institutions and activities and a wide range of choice in housing density, type, price and rent. As a matter of fact, zoning has become almost a guarantee of sprawl rather than protection against it. Frightened communities, with no alternative process available, leap to the illusion that low density zoning will preserve a way of life and protect against rising taxes. The one to three acre zoning that results simply extends a thin coat of suburban sprawl over an ever widening area.

Nor have we developed the capacity in the home building industry for producing well planned large scale urban development. Although the business of city building is the largest single industry in America, there is no large corporation engaged in it. City building has no General Motors or General Electric—no IBM, no Xerox; no big capital resources to invest in the purchase of large land areas; no big research and development program unfolding new techniques to produce a better environment. There are no large corporations engaged in the end-product production of the American City. City building—the development of houses and apartments, stores and offices

—is the business of thousands of very small corporations, no one of which has within its own resources the financial capacity to invest millions of dollars in land holdings to be planned and developed over, say, 10–15 years. Thus, except for the occasional accident of a large land holding remaining in single ownership on the threshold of urban growth, there is no vehicle, public or private, by which planning and development occurs on a scale sufficiently large to provide sensitively for nature or for man.

We face the addition of 70,000,000 people to our cities over the next 20 years—a new Toledo each month or a Denver, a Dallas and an Atlanta each year. Yet, not one single metropolitan area in the United States has plans to match the growth it knows it must face; and, if it had the plans, it would lack the powers and processes to execute them. This is the state of our nation and the prospect of our civilization as we convert over 1,000,000 acres of land each year from agricultural to urban use; as we move forward to produce, over the next 40 years, in our urban centers, the equivalent of everything we have built in our cities and suburbs since Plymouth Rock. Urban growth should be our opportunity, not our enemy. It invites us to correct the past; to build new places that are infused with nature and stimulating to man's creative sense of beauty; places that are in scale with people and so formed as to encourage and give strength to real community which will enrich life; build character and personality; promote concern, friendship, brotherhood.

Is it too much for such a nation to expect that we will substitute, for aimless sprawl, places of scale and beauty that are felicitous for the growth of our people? Certainly not, but to do it we must equip our severely undercapitalized home building industry to acquire, plan and develop land on a larger scale than is now possible. That is the purpose of the FHA Insurance Program. Furthermore, we must equip our local governments to assemble land for large scale planning and development; to serve it with public utilities and roads; and then market it to private developers for construction of houses, apartments, stores, offices, industry and all the components of a sound community. That is the purpose of the loans to local land development agencies.

The City of Columbia

May I illustrate what such a local land development agency might accomplish by sketching what we are doing in Columbia. And we are doing here what in many, if not most, metropolitan areas of the United States can only be done by local government.

We have assembled, at a cost of $23 million, 165 farms and parcels into 15,600 acres of land lying midway between Baltimore and Washington in Howard County, Maryland. Here we have planned the City of Columbia, which begins development this fall and is scheduled by 1980 to have a population of over 100,000 people. It will not be just a better suburb, but a complete new city.

It will employ 30,000 people in its plants, offices, stores, and institutions; provide housing for 31,000 families ranging from high-rise apartments to 10-acre lots, and priced to serve the company janitor as well as the company president. It will have 70 schools, 50 churches, a college, a hospital, a library system. It will be a city consisting of nine small towns of 10,000 to 15,000 each with their own schools, churches, stores, and services centered at a village green. The towns will be separated by 3,500 acres of permanent open space. Five lakes (which we will build), stream valleys, forests, 26 miles of riding trails, parks, and recreation areas will interlace the entire city.

At the center will be a lively downtown with department stores, offices, hotels, restaurants, theatres, concert halls, galleries, central library, college, hospital. Downtown will have an 80-acre lake as its front yard and a 50-acre forest at its side. The towns will be connected to one another, to downtown, and to employment centers by a bus system running on its own own right-of-way.

And will Columbia hurt the City of Baltimore? Why, of course not. Would the City of Baltimore be better off with irrational, piecemeal, inefficient sprawl reaching out from its borders than it will be if the same growth is accommodated within complete, well-planned new communities? Baltimore has enormous opportunities that are not available to Columbia or any other outlying new community. It has a massive employment center at its core, strong retail facilities; the graduate schools of the University of Maryland, the Peabody Conservatory of Music, the Central Branch Library, the center of Government, a magnificent harbor. The center of Baltimore is, and always will be, closer to more people in the metropolitan area than any single outlying location. Baltimore's task, and that of every other American City, is to correct its obsolescence; get rid of its slums; to address itself to the urban renewal opportunity through comprehensive planning large enough to re-form the center of the City into a beautiful, efficient, powerful economic force, and to reshape the older areas around downtown into a system of healthy, slum-free communities. Any new community developer would be off and running if he had the advantages that are now held by the central city. A city's job is to make itself work for its people and its purposes. It cannot benefit by aimless, irrational, sprawling suburbs, nor will it be hurt by the encouragement of well-planned, well-formed new communities.

The Mayors have been misled and they will see that this is so. But the country cannot wait these precious years, when the growth is rolling in on our cities, and stand aimlessly wringing our hands in anguish about our inability to handle the demands of urban growth. We owe it to our country to make our civilization the best that we know, and not hold it back to something much less than the best, in order to avoid unhappy contrast with the worn-out, old inner cities which we know we must renew.

And what about the home builder? The home building industry is one of the largest industries in America, and yet there are no large corporations engaged in it. It is a proliferation of small enterprises that, individually, lack the capital to engage in large-scale development. There are very few, if any, home builders in America who could have, out of their own resources, invested $23,000,000.00 to acquire the land that will be Columbia. And without such large-scale land assembly, comprehensive planning and good community development is almost impossible. Let me illustrate:

1. We were able to preserve the three major stream valleys in our area —and over 3,000 acres of forest—because our land holdings were large enough to transfer development out of these areas on to the land most suitable for development. We have thus been able to establish lakes, bridle paths and an open space system which will serve the entire City of Columbia. Our first two lakes will cost over $1,500,000. A builder acquiring a few hundred acres or even a thousand acres could not possibly have absorbed this cost. But spread over 15,000 acres it adds only $100 per acre to our land cost—less, we believe, than the value added.

2. We have provided for a public transportation system in Columbia— a bus system, running on its own right-of-way, separated from the roads and the pedestrian walkways; connecting all the village centers, downtown, and major employment centers. 40% of the population will live within a two-minute walk of a bus stop. Buses will run every five minutes at 10 cents a ride for adults and a nickel a ride for kids, and, according to our engineering projections, be fully economic. But the success of this system depends upon a wide variety of uses—major employment centers, retail stores, offices, hotels, schools, etc., and a large population of prospective users. A development of a few hundred, or even a few thousand acres, could not hope to provide such a system.

3. We have been able, in Columbia, to relate the schools to the communities they serve—an elementary school at the heart of each neighborhood; a junior high school and a high school at the heart of each village. All kids will be able to walk or ride a bike to school. At the present cost of school busing in Howard County, it is possible that the County will save more than a million dollars a year in school busing alone. And the schools will be part of the communities where the kids and their parents live. We have been able to lay out, with the approval of the School Board and the local Planning Commission, more than 50 school sites to meet the school needs in Columbia over the next 15 years. All of this is only possible because of very large land holdings and large scale planning.

4. We were able to acquire the ugly commercial islands along US 29, where it runs through the heart of Columbia, and we will be able to extinguish these commercial uses. Thus, instead of having these ugly beginnings of commercial blight extend like a cancer along the main road through our town, we have been able to establish Columbia Pike (US 29) as a landscaped parkway for the five miles it passes through Columbia. We will strengthen the commercial use and the service to customers by concentrating business in attractive, well-planned business centers off the Parkway. We paid premium prices for some of this land, as high as $75,000 an acre in some instances, and we could afford to do it only because we could spread the excess cost over our large land holdings. A developer of a few hundred, or even a few thousand acres, could not have assumed this burden.

5. Washington's National Symphony has reached an agreement with us to provide 30 concerts a season in a Summer Music Festival in Columbia each year for the next 20 years. Thirteen Protestant denominations have joined together to form a Religious Facilities Corporation and a cooperative ministry. The Catholic Archdiocese and the Jewish faith are represented as participant observers on this Church Committee and are working closely with the Protestant churches to achieve the maximum interfaith cooperation. This is one of the most remarkable demonstrations of cooperation among the churches that we have seen in our country. The State Department of Education has obtained a grant and completed a study for a library system for Columbia that contemplates resourceful use of modern technology, including computers and information storage and retrieval systems. The C & P Telephone Company has made a special study of communications systems in Columbia and has proposed the most advanced system of community-wide communications that has been made available to any community in America. All of these developments and many others in which we are involved are possible only because we are planning a complete new community on a large enough scale to spread individual cost items that would otherwise be unacceptable, and to support education, cultural, health, recreation and business systems, that small, piecemeal, unplanned growth could not justify.

6. Most remarkable—and perhaps most important of all: we obtained our zoning. Howard County is essentially rural. It has resisted urbanization because it despises the bits and pieces of sprawl, as do nearly all rural counties that are perched on the edge of urban growth. Zoning was the major issue in the 1962 election for County Commissioners. The winning ticket promised to protect Howard County against the ravages of urban growth. You can imagine that the announcement, one year later, of our assembly of 15,000 acres of land for the purpose of building a city was greeted with skepticism, anxiety, and perhaps a touch of hostility. It must be significant to you, as elected representatives of your people, to know that when we completed our plans for a whole new city, presented them to the people of Howard County and requested a change in the County zoning laws to create a new zoning classification known as a "New Town District," not a single person in Howard County opposed this zoning request. The same people who abhorred and fought the invasion of urban sprawl, accepted, and supported the development of a whole new city that would preserve the stream valleys and the forests; provide recreation, culture, entertainment, convenient, well-planned business, and public transportation. They are willing to accept high-rise apartments, garden apartments, townhouses, the very land uses they were fighting when they were gathered together in a rational, beautiful, human, well planned new city.

But now, surely, you are asking: "If you have been able to do this at

Columbia and finance it privately, are the Federal programs proposed in Title II necessary?" Clearly, I think they are, or I would not be here now.

Let me remind you that I am a private developer and a private mortgage banker. I believe in the private enterprise system. The home building industry in America is the most productive in the world. But there are some things it cannot do without assistance—the very assistance it now resists. There is absolutely no means whatsoever by which the home building industry, as it is now constituted in America, can develop the sensibly organized new communities that America needs to accommodate its future growth. The special vitality of the home building industry derives from its enormous number of individual operators, and this very fact guarantees—unless some new form of assistance is provided—that we will continue to build our cities in little bits and pieces, irrationally, unrelated to one another. The home building industry lacks the capital among its individual enterprises to undertake large-scale land assembly, planning, and development. It lacks the financial capacity and organization required to attract financial investment from life insurance companies and savings banks on the scale required to handle the growth of the American metropolis. Of course, there are exceptions. There is a handful— perhaps two handsful—of developers around the country who can attract the capital to undertake a Columbia. And such new towns will unfold. But the overwhelming preponderance of American home builders are left to the limitations of piecemeal development.

The hope of the FHA Insurance Program is that small builders will be able to undertake middle-size developments, and that middle-size builders will undertake larger developments than would otherwise be possible. And we must stimulate planning and development over larger land areas if we are to preserve our natural resources and provide communities that serve and dignify a man, his wife, and family.

The FHA financing program has provided the underlying support for the growth of the home building industry in America. It has raised housing and subdivision standards and pointed the way to steady improvement in the quality of new housing.

It is specially appropriate that its insurance program now be used to permit the private banking and building industries to improve the neighborhood—the environment—in which our housing is built. The enormous growth of our Cities calls for the planning and development, not just of houses, but of new communities. This FHA Insurance Program will be an important aid to private industry in making it possible.[1]

But in addition to enlarging the capacity of the home builder, we must make it possible for local government to take the initiative in acquiring land and planning community development, in the path of urban growth, where, but for such action, piecemeal, fractured suburban sprawl is the alternative. This is no threat to the private home building industry but an asset. It means that local government by initiating, planning and development over a larger area than the small builder could possibly handle on his own, can create an environment in which the small builder has a vastly improved opportunity to compete with the large community developer. We are performing exactly this role in Columbia and will make the land available to home builders to build individual houses for sale to the market. But we will have supplied parkways, lakes, open spaces, community halls, school sites, swimming pools, tennis courts, employment centers, stores and offices to strengthen his environment and support his market.

The Country needs to enlarge the application of the process by which a Columbia is built. It cannot afford to rely on the capacity or the whim of the private developer alone. We have a national interest in seeking better communities to accommodate our urban growth. A program of loans to local land development agencies can be an important, perhaps indispensable, stimulant to the growth of this process.

NOTE

1. Passed as Title IV, "Land Development and New Communities," of the Demonstration Cities and Metropolitan Development Act of 1966.

CHARLES E. SILBERMAN

By 1960, Woodlawn had become a virtually all-Negro slum.[1] Although nearly 25 per cent of the area's residents receive some form of welfare, they pay an average of $84 a month in rent—more than $10 *above* the city average—for which they occupy an average housing unit of 2.2 rooms. A birth rate 25 per cent above the city's average has put pressure on the capacity of the local public schools. There is a flourishing traffic in gambling, narcotics, and prostitution, especially in one stretch under the elevated subway tracks; the commercial business district is active but declining, with large numbers of stores vacant. In short, Woodlawn is precisely the sort of obsolescent, decaying, crowded neighborhood which social workers and city planners assume can never help itself—the sort of neighborhood in which even such advocates of social action as S. M. Miller assume that "directed, concerted action toward political or any other kind of goals is extremely unlikely."

But Woodlawn *is* helping itself; it is taking concerted action toward a wide variety of goals. The impetus for TWO came from three Protestant ministers and a Catholic priest who had come together through their concern with the spiraling decline of their neighborhood and the indifference of both the city and the University of Chicago, located just to the north of Woodlawn. The clergymen had "worn out the seats of several good pairs of trousers attending an uncountable number of meetings held to 'do something about Woodlawn' "—meetings which seemed only to lead to still more meetings. "We were watching a community dying for lack of leaders, a community that had lost hope in the decency of things and people," one of the founders, Dr. Ulysses B. Blakeley, co-pastor of the First Presbyterian Church and Moderator of the Chicago Presbytery, explains. "Outsiders consider a place like this a kind of zoo or jungle; they may mean well, but they choke us. It seemed to us that any effort would be futile unless our own people could direct it, choose their own goals, and work for them, grow in the process, and have a sense again of the rightness of things."

After investigating various approaches to community organization, therefore, the clergymen "took the plunge," as Dr. Blakeley and his co-pastor, Dr. Charles T. Leber, Jr., described it in *Presbyterian Life:* they called on Saul D.

Alinsky, executive director of the Industrial Areas Foundation, and invited him to help organize the Woodlawn community. A sociologist and criminologist by training, Alinsky is a specialist in creating mass organizations on a democratic basis "in order that the so-called 'little man' can gather into his hands the power he needs to make and shape his life." His organizing career began in the late 1930s, when he was one of the principal architects of Chicago's much admired Back of the Yards Neighborhood Council, which turned the stockyards area—the locale for Upton Sinclair's *The Jungle*—into one of the most desirable working-class neighborhoods in Chicago.[2] When his success in organizing the Back of the Yards evoked requests to do the same in other cities, Alinsky organized the Industrial Areas Foundation, a non-profit institution which has organized some forty-four groups across the country. The most notable of these, until the formation of The Woodlawn Organization, were in California, where the IAF organized some thirty communities of Mexican-Americans and welded them together in the Community Service Organization. The Industrial Areas Foundation's President is Dr. George N. Shuster, retired president of Hunter College and now assistant to the president of Notre Dame University; the board of directors includes, among others, Mrs. Valentine E. Macy, whose husband is a power in New York Republican politics; Ralph Helstein, president of the Packinghouse Workers Union; Cecil North, former president of Metropolitan Life Insurance Company; Rev. Ralph Abernathy, second-in-command under Rev. Martin Luther Knig; and Meryl Ruoss, chairman of the Institute of Strategic Studies of the Board of National Missions of the Presbyterian Church.

"Took the plunge" is an apt way of describing what the Woodlawn ministers did in approaching Alinsky, however—for he is nothing if not controversial. Indeed, he delights in controversy; one of his basic premises, he likes to say, is that *all* important issues are controversial. Alinsky's opponents (few of whom have bothered to read *The Prince*) see him as Machiavelli reincarnated; Alinsky has been attacked, at various times, as a communist, a fascist, a dupe of the Catholic Church, the mastermind of a Catholic conspiracy (Alinsky in Jewish), a racist, a segregationist, and an integrationist seeking to mongrelize Chicago. His supporters are equally immoderate in their praise; as Drs. Blakeley and Leber wrote, "No one in the city is as detested or as loved, as cursed or as blessed, as feared or as respected." Certainly no one in recent memory has had as great an impact on the city of Chicago; and none in the United States has proposed a course of action or a philosophy better calculated to rescue Negro or white slum dwellers from their poverty or their degradation. For Alinsky is that rarity of American life: a superlative organizer, strategist, and tactician who is also a philosopher (or a superlative philosopher who is also an organizer, strategist and tactician).

The essential difference between Alinsky and his enemies is that Alinsky really believes in democracy: he really believes that the helpless, the poor, the badly-educated can solve their own problems if given the chance and the means; he really believes that the poor and uneducated, no less than the rich and educated, have the right to decide how their lives should be run and what services should be offered to them, instead of being ministered to like children. "I do not believe that democracy can survive, except as a formality," he has written, "if the ordinary citizen's part is limited to voting—if he is incapable of initiative and unable to influence the political, social and economic structures surrounding him."

The individual can influence these structures only if he has power, for power means nothing more or less than the capacity to make one's interests felt in the decisions that affect him. There are two sources of power, in Alinsky's view: money and people. Since the residents of Woodlawn and of areas like it obviously have no money, their only source of power is themselves— which is to say the creation of an effective organization. Alinsky's frankness about power is upsetting to a good many people who regard open discussion of power as somehow lacking in taste—the equivalent, almost of discussing one's marital life in public. For power, as John Kenneth Galbraith has written, plays a curious role in American life. The privilege of controlling the actions or of affecting the income and property of others is something that no one of us can profess to seek or admit to possessing. No American ever runs for office because of an avowed desire to govern. He seeks to serve . . . The same scrupulous avoidance of the terminology of power," Galbraith adds, "characterizes American business. The head of the company is no longer the boss—the term survives only as an amiable form of address—but the leader of the team. No union leader ever presents himself as anything but a spokesman for the boys."[3]

Alinsky takes delight in violating this etiquette. "The only reason people have ever banded together," he baldly states, "and the only reason they ever will, is the fact that organization gives them the power to satisfy their desires or to realize their needs. There never has been any other reason." In his view, people join a trade union to develop enough power to force a change in their working conditions; they join a political party in order to have a power instrument that can win an election and carry out their political objectives; they organize a church as a power instrument to convert others to their religious belief. "Even when we talk of a community lifting itself by its bootstraps," Alinsky says, "we are talking of power. It takes a great deal of power to lift oneself by one's own bootstraps."

To create such a power structure in an area like Woodlawn, however, requires enormous skill and effort, and a break with convention. The reason most efforts at organizing slum neighborhoods fail, Alinsky argues, is not the nature of the community but the objectives of the organizers and of the methods they use. Most approaches to community organization, as Professor Dan W. Dodson has written, involve "more of an emphasis on how to get the different vested interests together to slice up areas of 'service' than . . . a consideration of how to get people genuinely organized in fighting for the things which would bring them dignity and respect." The conventional appeal to homeowners' interests in conserving property values is useless in a community in which the majority of people rent, and in which the homeowners would have to sell if forced to comply with the building code. A call for civic pride falls flat in a community which hates its neighbors and which is convinced it is going to be bulldozed out of existence sooner or later; neighborhoods like Woodlawn are too drab and dismal to cause anyone to rally around them. Even civil rights is too much of an abstraction. "The daily lives of Woodlawn people," an early Alinsky memo on Woodlawn suggested, "leave them with little energy or enthusiasm for realizing principles from which they themselves will derive little practical benefit. They know that with their educational and economic handicaps they will be exceptions indeed if they can struggle into a middle-class neighborhood or a white-collar job." Instead of these appeals of the conventional neighborhood organizer and group worker, Alinsky uses the classical approach of trade union organization: he appeals to the self-interest of the local residents and to their resentment and distrust of the outside world, and he seeks out and develops a local, indigenous leadership.

While indigenous leadership is crucial if the organization is to mean anything in the lives of its members, the initial impetus must come from the outside, and the mean and difficult job of building the organization must be handled by full-time organizers who know how to conquer the apathy of the slum and how to weld its disparate fragments into a unified whole. For the indigenous leaders of the slum area are not in touch with each other; without training, they lack the skills needed to keep a large organization running; and in most cases it has never occurred to any of them to lead a mass organization. (If any one thing is known in the Negro slum—or the white slum, for that matter—it is that you can't fight City Hall.) Just as no factory would ever be organized without stimulus and guidance from the outside, so no slum can be organized without a good deal of help.

But the Industrial Areas Foundation insists that help be used to make the local community self-sufficient, not to keep it dependent. Alinsky will not enter a community unless he is invited by something like a cross-section of the population, and he usually insists, as a condition of entering, that the community itself, no matter how poor, take over the full responsibility for financing the new organization within a period of three years.[4] Alinsky has a standard way of dramatizing the importance of financial independence at the convention at which a new group formally approves its constitution. The audience is usually full of enthusiasm and terribly proud of the constitution, which local citizens have hammered out over a long period of time. Alinsky takes a copy of the document, looks at it briefly, and then tosses it to the floor, announcing to the startled audience: "This constitution doesn't mean a damned thing. As long as the IAF organizers are on my payroll they'll do what I damn well tell them to do and not what it says on any paper like that." After a shocked silence, someone in the audience invariably calls out, "I don't understand. I thought you were on our side!" "I am," Alinsky answers back. "But think of the number of people who've come down here telling you the same thing, and how many turned out to be two-timing, double-crossing S.O.B.s. Why should you trust me? The only way you can be sure that the aims in that constitution are carried out is to get the organizers off my payroll and onto your payroll. Then *you* can tell them what to do, and if they don't do it, you can fire them and get someone who will."

Once the Industrial Areas Foundation enters a community, the process of building an organization follows a fairly standard pattern:

Organizers from the Industrial Areas Foundation filter through the neighborhood, asking questions and, more important, listening in bars, at street corners, in stores, in peoples' homes—in short, wherever people are talking—to discover the residents' specific grievances;

At the same time, the organizers try to spot the individuals and the groups on which people seem to lean for advice or to which they go for help: a barber, a minister, a mailman, a restaurant owner, etc.— the "indigenous" leaders;

The organizers get these leaders together, discuss the irritations, frustrations, and problems animating the neighborhood, and suggest the ways in which power might be used to ameliorate or solve them;

A demonstration or series of demonstrations are put on to show how power can be used. These may take a variety of forms: a rent strike against slum landlords, a cleanup campaign against a notorious trouble spot, etc. What is crucial is that meetings and talk, the bedrock on which middle-class organizations founder, are avoided; the emphasis is on action, and on action that can lead to visible results.

In this way, the new organization begins to take form as a supergroup comprising many existing member groups—churches, block clubs, businessmen's associations—and of new groups that are formed purely as a means of joining the larger organization. As the organization begins to move under its own steam, the IAF men gradually phase themselves out and local leaders take over. This does not mean that volunteers take over the whole work load, however. One of the cardinal principles of the IAF is that a full-time paid staff is necessary if a community organization is to continue to function; volunteers, especially in a slum neighborhood, simply do not have the time. But the local leaders take on the responsibility for making decisions and for meeting the budget; sometimes they hire one of the IAF organizers as a permanent staff head, sometimes they come up with their own organizers.

So much for general principles and procedures. The actual work of creating The Woodlawn Organization was begun in the spring and summer of 1960, eighteen months after the four ministers had called on Alinsky for help. (He had told them he would not come to Woodlawn until a representative committee had extended the invitation.) By this time, the invitation was being extended by the Greater Woodlawn Pastors Alliance with support from most other organized groups in the community. The organizing effort was made possible by grants from the Catholic Archdiocese of Chicago, the Presbyterian Church of Chicago, and the Schwarzhaupt Foundation, a private philanthropy which has supported Industrial Areas Foundation projects elsewhere in the United States.

How do you begin to organize an area like Woodlawn? As Nicholas von Hoffman, then chief organizer for the IAF (now a reporter of a Chicago daily) put it with studied casualness, "I found myself at the corner of Sixty-third and Kimbark and I looked around." It did not take much looking or listening to discover, as might be expected in a Negro slum, that one of the things that "bugged" residents the most was cheating and exploitation by some of the businessmen of the area. In most low-income areas, credit-purchasing is a trap; naïve and semi-literate customers are high-pressured into signing installment contracts without reading the fine print or having it explained. According to Dr. Leber, there were instances of customers being charged effective interest rates as high as 200 per cent; second-hand merchandise was represented as new; and prices bordered on outright piracy: a $6 diamond chip in a gaudy ring setting would be sold for $250 with a "Certificate of Guarantee" that it was a real diamond. (It *was* a real diamond—but one worth only $6.) Credit-purchasing aside, many merchants took unfair advantage of their customers' ignorance; food stores, for example gave short weight, overcharged, and in a few cases actually rigged their cash registers to give false totals.

Hence, when the IAF organizers started fanning through the community, complaints began to pile up. Here was an issue, moreover, on which the legitimate businessmen in the area could unite with the consumers, for the crooked merchants hurt business for everyone else. As a result, TWO—bringing together the leaders of the Businessman's Association, some of the ministers, and some of the indigenous leaders who were being turned up—worked out a Code of Business Ethics covering credit practices, pricing, and advertising. To implement the Code, TWO set up a Board of Arbitration consisting of four representatives from the Businessman's Association, four from consumer groups, with an impartial chairman from outside the community elected by the eight Board members.

If this had been all, however, TWO would have been stillborn. To publicize the Code, and to publicize the new organization, a big parade was staged in which nearly a thousand people marched through the business section carrying signs, singing, and creating enough of a stir to make the front pages of most Chicago newspapers. The next Saturday, a registered scale was set up at a nearby Catholic church along with an adding machine; people who shopped at the markets suspected of giving false weights and improper totals brought their packages directly to the church, where they were weighed, and cash register slips checked and the false weights and false totals publicized. Most of the offending merchants quickly agreed to comply with the "Square Deal" agreement. To bring recalcitrant merchants to terms leaflets were distributed through the community accusing them of cheating and urging residents to stay away.

The Square Deal campaign served its purpose. It eliminated a considerable amount of exploitation and chicancery on the part of Woodlawn merchants. More important, it made the residents of Woodlawn aware of the existence of the new organization and drove home the fact that through organization they *could* improve some of the circumstances of their lives. Two years later, a TWO vice-president recalled that it was the Square Deal campaign that brought him into the organization, and that really put TWO on a solid footing. "We showed people that they don't have to accept everything, that they can do something about it," he said—"but that they have to be organized to do it."

To capitalize on the enthusiasm this campaign created, the IAF staff men moved next to organize rent strikes in a number of Woodlawn buildings. Wherever a substantial majority of the tenants could be persuaded to act together, a tenants' group was formed which demanded that the land-

lord, within some stated period of time, clear up physical violations that
made occupancy hazardous or uncomfortable—broken windows, plumbing
that did not work, missing steps from staircases, inadequate heat, etc. When
the landlords ignored the ultimatum, TWO organized a rent strike: rents
were withheld from the landlord and deposited in escrow in a special bank
account. To dramatize the strike on one block where several adjoining
buildings were involved, residents spelled out "This Is A Slum" in huge
letters on the outside of the building. If the landlord remained recalcitrant,
groups of pickets were dispatched to march up and down in front of the
landlord's own home, carrying placards that read "Your Neighbor Is A
Slumlord." The picketing provided a useful outlet for the anger the tenants
felt, and gave them an opportunity, for the first time in their lives, to use
their color in an affirmative way. For as soon as the Negro pickets appeared
in a white suburban block, the landlord was deluged with phonecalls from
angry neighbors demanding that he do something to call the pickets off.
Within a matter of hours landlords who were picketed were on the phone
with TWO, agreeing to make repairs.

Landlords were not the only ones who were picketed; over-crowded
and segregated schools became a target, too. When William G. Caples, president of the Board of Education, refused to meet with TWO to discuss their
complaints—he denounced the organization as "the lunatic fringe"—a delegation of eighteen Protestant and Catholic pastors staged a sit-in at the executive offices of Inland Steel, where Caples was public relations vice-president;
at the same time, TWO rank-and-filers circled the building on the outside,
carrying placards denouncing Caples as a segregationist. (Caples resigned
the following month "because of the pressure of company business.") And
when Superintendent of Schools Benjamin Willis denied that overcrowding
could be relieved by transferring Negro students to all-white schools, TWO
sent "truth squads" of mothers into neighboring white schools to photograph
empty and half-empty classrooms. (In one elementary school, which was
81.5 per cent Negro, classes averaged 48.4 students per room; a school
nine blocks away, but 99 per cent white, had an average of 28.4 pupils per
room.) TWO members also staged a "death watch" at Board of Education
meetings: a large group would attend each meeting wearing long black capes,
to symbolize the "mourning" of Negro parents over the plight of their children.

It is precisely this sort of tactic that leads some of Alinsky's critics to
denounce him as an agitator who deals in hate and who incites to conflict,
a troublemaker whose stated goal is to "rub raw the sores of discontent,"
as an early TWO memorandum put it. "The fact that a community may be
stirred and organized by 'sharpening dormant hostilities' and 'rubbing raw
the sores of discontent' is not new," says Julian Levi, executive director of
the South East Chicago Commission and mastermind and director of the
University of Chicago's urban renewal activities. "The technique has been
proved in practice in the assembling of lynch mobs." (Levi and the University have been trying alternately to discredit Alinsky and to ignore him
since he began organizing Woodlawn.) As an example of the methods to
which he objects, Levi cites a TWO leaflet naming a local food store and

warning people to "watch out" for short weights, spoiled food, and short-changing. "If this is what this merchant is really doing," Levi says, "he should be punished by the court—but with all the safeguards the law provides. This is not the way people should be taught to protect themselves," he argues; they should be taught to register complaints with the Department of Health (about spoiled food), and Department of Weights and Measures (about short weights), and the Police Department (about short change). Levi similarly deplores the use of rent strikes. If landlords were violating the building code, he argues, TWO should have brought action through the Building Department, the way the South East Chicago Commission does, instead of taking the law into its own hands.

But slum dwellers, as Levi surely knows, have been complaining to the Building Department and to other city agencies for years, to no avail. The reason the South East Chicago Commission is able to get rapid action on complaints it registers with the Building Department or any other city agency is that it has what politicians call "clout": the Commission is the urban renewal arm of the University of Chicago, whose board of trustees includes some of the most influential businessmen and politicians in the city. As Professors Peter H. Rossi and Robert A. Dentler said in their study of the University's urban renewal program in the Hyde Park-Kenwood area, Levi "could in effect represent the most powerful community interests in demanding protection from the Chicago Department of Buildings and the Mayor's Housing and Redevelopment Coordinator. Pressure on real estate speculators was also channeled through the University's strong connections with the business community. Banks and insurance companies were warned that their funds were in jeopardy when invested as mortgages on illegally converted property in the area. Insurance companies were persuaded to suspend policies written on badly maintained properties. Publicity about the ownership of notorious slum properties was given to the press, which published unflattering accounts of the abuse of housing decency."[5] TWO had none of these gentlemanly weapons at its disposal—hence its need to use cruder tactics.

For all their self-righteous indignation over Alinsky's tactics, moreover, the University of Chicago and its South East Chicago Commission have never shrunk from the blunt and naked use of power when their interests seemed to require it. Consider this account by Rossi and Dentler:

> When a real estate speculator purchased a six-family apartment house and promptly moved in nine Negro families, the local block group of the Hyde Park-Kenwood Community Conference spotted the move . . . The day after the nine families moved in, Julian Levi visited the speculator, threatened him with legal action for violating the housing code, and confronted him with evidence of overcrowding; at the same time a generous offer to buy was made by the University real estate office. The speculator sold the apartment dwelling to the University on the next day and one day later the nine Negro families were moved out by the University's real estate managers. *Had this purchase and eviction not been possible, legal action through municipal channels would at best have achieved the levying of fines against the speculator—months and possibly even years after the conversion occurred. Thus, it is one matter to threaten prosecution via the courts and another to be able to buy up properties which are in violation of the law.* [Emphasis added]

In any case, Levi's criticisms miss the point—that the tactics he deplores are designed to serve more than one end. In the case of the fledgling Woodlawn Organization, the most urgent need was to persuade the local population that it could solve some of its problems through organization. It is impossible to understand Alinsky's tactics, in fact, without understanding the basic dilemma inherent in organizing any slum area, and particularly a Negro slum. The basic characteristic of the slum—its "life style" so to speak—is apathy; no organization can be created unless this apathy can be overcome. But slum residents will not stir unless they see a reasonable chance of winning, unless there is some evidence that they *can* change things for the better. This reluctance to act is perfectly understandable; it is not true that the very poor have nothing to lose. Quite the contrary. In some respects, they have more to lose than the middle class; they face the danger of having their relief checks cut off, of losing an unskilled patronage job, of having a son on probation remanded to jail—of suffering any one of a host of reprisals a politically-oriented bureaucracy can impose. (One of the differences between the lower-class Negro communities and middle-class white communities is that the latter clamor for more protection *by* the police, while the former frequently demand—and need—protection *from* the police. Certainly the traffic in narcotics, gambling, and illicit sex that is omnipresent in every Negro slum could not go on without the active cooperation of the local police.)

Quite frequently, therefore, the apathy that characterizes the slum represents what in many ways is a realistic response to a hostile environment. But realistic or not, the adjustment that is reached is one of surrender to the existing conditions and abdication of any hope of change. The result is a community seething with inarticulate resentments and dormant hostilities repressed for safety's sake, but which break out every now and then in some explosion of deviant or irrational behavior. The slum dwellers are incapable of acting, or even of joining, until these suppressed resentments and hostilities are brought to the surface where they can be seen as problems—*i.e.,* as a condition you can do something about.

And so Alinsky pleads guilty to the charge of being an agitator, of arousing dormant hostilities or rubbing raw the sores of discontent: that is precisely the point of what he is doing! "The community organizer," he writes, "digs into a morass of resignation, hopelessness, and despair and works with the local people in articulating (or 'rubbing raw') their resentments." In telling them over and over again, " 'You don't have to take this, and you can do something about it,' he becomes a catalytic agent transmuting hidden resentments and hostilities into open problems." His job is to persuade the people to move—to be active, to participate, in short to develop and harness the power necessary to change the prevailing patterns. "When those prominent in the status quo turn and label you an agitator, they are completely correct, for that is, in one word, your function—to agitate to the point of conflict."

But agitation by itself is not enough; the inhabitants of a slum like Woodlawn must be convinced not only that a solution is possible but also that it is probable; they must see some tangible evidence that banding together will give them the capacity to alter the circumstances of their lives.

To use the language of war (for that is what it is), the only way to build an army is by winning a few victories. But how do you gain a victory before you have an army? The only method ever devised is guerila warfare: to avoid a fixed battle where the forces are arrayed and where the new army's weakness would become visible, and to concentrate instead on hit-and-run tactics designed to gain small but measurable victories. Hence the emphasis on such dramatic actions as parades and rent strikes whose main objective is to create a sense of solidarity and of community.

Once this guerila warfare begins, the best organizing help of all frequently comes from "the enemy"—the established institutions who feel themselves threatened by the new organization. What really welded the Woodlawn community together, for example, was the University of Chicago's announcement, on July 19, 1960, that it planned to extend its "South Campus" into Woodlawn by annexing an adjacent strip a block wide and a mile long. Woodlawn pute was coming to a head, "and it needs more land if it's going to continue to be first rate." Levi's job, as he defined it, was to get the land the University needed, and if possible, to create a compatible community as well. But getting the land came first. A certain degree of conflict seemed inevitable—for the University, as Levi explained it, would be there thirty, fifty, a hundred years from now, whereas the people in the surrounding community would long since have departed. It was understandable that the local residents might want to put their short-run interests first; but the University had to keep its eyes fixed on the long run.

The University may have kept its eyes fixed firmly on the long run, but its knee was in its opponent's groin. In February of 1961, for example, Carl Larsen, the University's Public Relations Director, together with Julian Levi and another P.R. man, called on several Chicago dailies to warn them against "the evil forces" of Alinsky, the Industrial Areas Foundation, the Catholic Church, and TWO. They brought with them a dossier on Alinsky and his foundation containing a number of items: the main one was a copy of the Industrial Areas Foundation's income tax return showing various Catholic groups as its principal source of financial support in the year in question. (How the University happened to have a copy of the Foundation's tax return has never been explained.) The same income tax return was included in a dossier which the University sent to this writer in the fall of 1961, via a friendly reported, in the hopes of dissuading me from including a section on TWO in an article I was preparing for *Fortune* Magazine. When I asked the reporter what the income tax return was supposed to demonstrate, other than support of the IAF by the Catholic Church, he replied that that *was* the point. In his opinion, which reflected that of the University's spokesmen, Catholic support was itself enough to discredit the IAF and TWO.[6]

When the Chicago dailies balked at running the proposed article, Larsen, Levi, and company persuaded the editor of the University's weekly student paper, the Chicago *Maroon,* to take up the cudgels. They also arranged for the Law School to check the article; as a result, it was copyrighted under the name of the writer—a rarely used procedure which guaranteed the University immunity against any possible suit for libel. The article, which attracted a great deal of attention—University P.R. men were still distributing copies nine months later—ran in the March 3, 1961, issue under a banner headline reading CHURCH SUPPORTS "HATE GROUP." It continued as follows:

> An organization now working in Woodlawn and dedicated to "sharpening dormant hostilities" received over $56,000 last year from the Chicago Catholic Bishop and the National Conference of Catholic Charities.
>
> The *Maroon* has learned that the controversial Industrial Areas Foundation (IAF), which is now helping the Temporary Woodlawn Organization to "organize" the south side community, also received approximately $43,000 from the two Catholic groups in 1958.
>
> In recent months, the TWO has attempted to organize residents of Woodlawn in opposition to the University of Chicago's plans for building a "South Campus" between 60th and 61st, Cottage Grove to Stony Island.

The article went on to quote Rev. Walter Kloetzli, a Lutheran minister who has been carrying on a vendetta against Alinsky for some years, to the effect that the Catholic-IAF-TWO conspiracy was designed to keep Negroes locked into Woodlawn in order to preserve the all-white parishes in the areas southwest and southeast of Woodlawn. "These people are trying desperately to maintain the White-Negro status quo in areas south of Woodlawn," Reverend Kloetzli argued, "and they anticipate that redevelopment in Woodlawn will cause an influx of Negroes into areas southwest and southeast of Woodlawn."

The fact of the matter was that Kloetzli's charges had been aired two years previously, and found to be unsubstantiated, at a meeting of some thirty Presbyterian, Lutheran, and Catholic representatives called to discuss the IAF's intervention in Woodlawn. Alinsky had answered the charges to the satisfaction of virtually everyone present, and afterwards had submitted to them a twenty-four-page memorandum replying to fourteen questions raised by the churchmen. In a letter to the editor of the *Maroon,* the distinguished Lutheran theologian Joseph Sittler, a member of the faculty of the University of Chicago's Divinity School, called the March 3 article "irresponsible" and formally protested its publication. "The Roman Church," Dr. Sittler added, "has, indeed, enumerated through an extended statement of Cardinal Archbishop Meyer, a wise and charitable policy" regarding integration.

The Archdiocese in fact has been one of the most outspoken advocates of integration in the city of Chicago. Indeed, it was the Archdiocese's position on race relations and housing that brought it into conflict with the University. University officials apparently have regarded the Church as an enemy ever since 1958, when Monsignor John Egan, Executive Director of the Cardinal's Committee on Community Organization and Urban Renewal, criticized the then-pending Hyde Park-Kenwood urban renewal program. Monsignor Egan saw the program, quite rightly, as a venture in Negro removal; he pointed out that plans called for demolition of a great deal of adequate housing occupied largely by Negroes, and that few of these residents would be able to afford the new apartments and houses that were to be erected. Monsignor Egan also criticized what he considered inadequate provisions for relocation and insufficient safeguards for property owners whose homes were not torn down in the first wave of bulldozing; the plans permitted acquisition of homes later on for such reasons as "obsolete layout" of a building.

In any event, the Woodlawn Organization certainly was not the product of any Papist conspiracy. On the contrary, the organization represents one of the most meaningful examples of Protestant-Catholic co-operation to be found anywhere in the United States. (Dr. Sittler described the meeting at which Alinsky answered the Kloetzli charges as one of the most hopeful instances of Protestant-Catholic amity to have occurred in four centuries.) As we have seen, the organization was created as a result of close collaboration between Father Martin Farrell, paster of Woodlawn's largest Catholic church, and the Reverend Drs. Blakeley and Leber, co-pastors of Chicago's oldest Protestant congregation, the First Presbyterian Church of Chicago; financial support came from both Presbyterian and Catholic sources. This collaboration extended down to the church members; when Father Farrell's church gave him a testimonial dinner on the occasion of his twenty-fifth anniversary as pastor, tickets to the event were sold in a number of Protestant churches in Woodlawn, and almost as many Protestants as Catholics attended. Equally important, this ecumenical spirit affected Chicago's Protestant and Catholic church leaders, too. Cardinal Meyer, for example, is a staunch proponent of inter-church co-operation on social problems, believing that joint social action rather than dialogue provides the soundest basis for an ecumenical movement. The result has been collaboration of the Archdiocese, the Chicago Presbytery, and the Church Federation of Chicago. The involvement of church leaders of all denominations in social action to improve the Negro's lot is TWO's most enduring contribution. The example is spreading to other cities. In Kansas City, Missouri, for example, Presbyterians, Catholics, and Methodists are collaborating in an attempt to develop a TWO-type program, while Catholics, Presbyterians, and Lutherans are working together in Gary, Indiana.

The controversy over the South Campus plan has been revealing in another respect. There has been a great deal of talk, in recent years, about ways of increasing "citizen participation" in city planning, especially urban renewal planning; federal legislation now requires local citizen participation in the formulation of renewal plans as a condition of federal aid. The Woodlawn experience indicates that "participation" means something very different to planners and to the academic researchers on whom they lean, than it does to the people being planned for. To the former, "citizen participation" means that the local residents are given a chance to air their views *after* the plans have been drawn, not before; planning, in this view, is a matter for experts, and "participation" is really thought of as "acquiescence." Thus Rossi and Dentler hail the Hyde Park-Kenwood Community Conference as the outstanding example of citizen participation in urban renewal planning—but they also point out that the organization did not play a significant role in influencing the specific details of the plan. Its achievement was to create popular acceptance for a plan which, at least in part, was inconsistent with the organization's stated objectives. Hence the two scholars conclude that "the maximum role to be played by a citizen-participation movement in urban renewal is primarily a passive one." Professor James Q. Wilson is even more blunt: "If one's goal is urban renewal on any really large scale in our cities," he writes, planners would be well-advised to eschew any real citizen participation. For "the higher the level of indigenous organization in a lower-class neighborhood, the poorer the prospects for renewal in that area . . . Perhaps this explains," Professor Wilson adds, "why most local urban renewal directors made no effort to encourage citizen participation except on a city-wide basis—with little or no representation from the affected neighborhood."[7]

Certainly the Chicago city planners showed no eagerness to engage the Woodlawn residents in any active role. Indeed, the planners' response to Woodlawn's demand that it be given responsibility and allowed to exercise initiative in planning for its own future was a proposal to inundate the area with paternalism. Thus, the City Plan Commission, in March of 1962, presented a comprehensive plan for Woodlawn which included a huge program of urban renewal clearance, conservation, and rehabilitation; a massive investigation of illiteracy, ill-health, crime and unemployment; and a pilot attack on these problems to be financed by large government and foundation grants. In response to a question as to whether the planning committee had been guided by opinions from the community, the committee's Coordinating Consultant replied, "There is nobody to speak for the community. A community does not exist in Woodlawn." And Professor Philip Hauser, another consultant, volunteered his view that "The people there have only one common bond, opposition to the University of Chicago," and added gratuitously, "This is a community that reads nothing."

The two consultants were quickly disabused of their view. TWO responded with rhetoric ("We don't want to be planned for like children"; "We're tired of being pawns in sociological experiments"). But it did something unique in the annals of urban renewal: in conjunction with the Businessman's Association, it hired a firm of city planners to make a detailed critique of the city's proposal and to come up with alternate proposals. The critique pointed out a number of glaring contradictions between the City Plan Department's evaluation of Woodlawn in 1946, when it was all-white, and in 1962, when it was virtually all-Negro; for example, the 1946 report found that "land coverage in the community is not excessively high," while the 1962 report complained of dangerous overcrowding of both land and buildings, although no new construction had taken place in the interim. The critique also pointed out that the city's program would demolish a substantial number of attractive, well-kept homes in an area of relatively high owner-occupancy, but left untouched the bulk of the area classified as the most blighted.

To the discomfiture of the planners, TWO attacked the city's "social planning" as vigorously as it attacked the urban renewal planning. "Self-determination applies in the field of social welfare," the organization resolved at its 1962 convention. "Therefore the best programs are the ones that we develop, pay for and direct ourselves . . . Our aim is to lessen burdens in practical ways, but in ways that also guarantee we will keep our personal and community independence. We go on record as unqualifiedly opposing all notions of 'social planning' by either government or private groups. We will not be planned for as though we were children." Far from pleasing them, Woodlawn's desire for independence seemed only to anger the planners, whose "Papa knows best" attitude was being attacked on all sides. "Some of their resolutions against welfare are singularly unfortunate," Professor Hauser observed. "What would they do without welfare?" Others called the resolutions "revolutionary" and even "subversive." The Woodlawnites were puzzled. "They've been calling us 'welfare chiselers' and 'dependent' and everything else in the book," said one TWO Negro. "Now they distrust us for trying things for ourselves." "Do you think it's possible," a TWO organizer asked Georgie Ann Geyer, a reporter for the *Chicago Daily News,* "that someone other than the Negro has a vested interest in welfare?"

The distinguished University of Chicago sociologists and the professorial planners may not have gotten the message (they have scrupulously ignored TWO's existence), but the politicians did. Concerned for his political life, Mayor Richard Daley forced the reluctant Chancellor of the University of Chicago to meet with TWO representatives in the Mayor's office; the negotiators agreed on a compromise which called for construction of low-income housing on vacant land *before* any existing buildings were torn down. For the first time in the history of urban renewal in the United States, people displaced by demolition will have new homes waiting for them in the same neighborhood. Instead of the usual wholesale replacement of lower-class housing by "middle-income" units, Woodlawn will be renewed in steps. Only houses beyond salvage will be torn down; units to be rehabilitated will be repaired without evicting tenants. And city officials agreed to give TWO majority representation on the citizens planning committee that will draw up further plans and supervise their execution. Mayor Daley personally called Dr. Blakeley to ask him to serve as chairman.

Forcing the University of Chicago and the city planners to take account of the desires of the community is not the only victory The Woodlawn Organization has won. Before TWO was formed, every school in Woodlawn save one was on either double shift or overlapping session, and Board of Education members had announced that they saw no possibility of eliminating the double shift in their lifetime. By the spring of 1963, the double shift had been dropped and overcrowding substantially reduced. TWO has persuaded a number of Chicago firms to open up jobs for Negroes; it has stimulated a number of local block organizations to clean up and maintain their neighborhoods, and has forced landlords to repair their property. TWO's attacks on "the silent six" Negro aldermen of the Dawson machine has forced an unaccustomed militancy on them, and thereby changed the whole complexion of Chicago politics. In the process, TWO's president, Rev. Arthur M. Brazier, has become the principal spokesman on civil rights for Chicago Negroes; before TWO was organized, Reverend Brazier had been on obscure minister of a Pentacostal church concerned almost exclusively with the next life. The leadership and organization strength TWO has provided is the only thing that has kept Chicago's civil rights coalition together, and Brazier has the eloquence and ability to go on to become a major figure in the national civil rights movement.

What makes The Woodlawn Organization significant, however, is not so much what it is doing for its members as what it is doing *to* them. "The most important thing to me about the forty-six busloads of people who went to City Hall to register," Alinsky commented at the time, "was their own reaction. Many were weeping; others were saying, 'They're paying attention to us'; 'They're recognizing that we're people.' " Eighteen months later, an active member observed, "City Hall used to be a forbidden place, but we've made so many trips there and seen so many people that it's beginning to feel like a neighborhood store." Other members expressed themselves in much the same way: "We've lost our fear of standing up and expressing ourselves"; "We don't have to go hat in hand, begging, anymore. It's a wonderful feeling." What is crucial, in short, is not what the Woodlawn residents win, but that *they* are winning it; and this makes them see themselves in a new light— as men and women of substance and worth.

Besides giving its members a sense of dignity and worth, the Woodlawn Organization has given a good many people a sense of direction and purpose and an inner discipline that has enabled them to overcome the "floundering phenomenon." "This has been the most satisfying and rewarding period of my life," one TWO officer remarked in the spring of 1963. 'The organization has given me a real sense of accomplishing something—the only time in my life I've had that feeling." Indeed, activity in TWO has completely reshaped this man's life; he remembers the date and even the hour of the first TWO meeting he attended; he dates events from that time, the way a happily married couple dates events from their wedding day. But TWO has done more than just give purpose and meaning to his life, important as that is. Like so many other Woodlawnites, he had been accustomed to waste enormous amounts of time and energy through sheer inefficiency, *i.e.,* personal disorganization. This made the initial organizing work more difficult than anything the organizers had ever encountered in white slums; at first, every little venture seemed to fail because the personal disorganization. Even such an apparently simple matter as rounding up a half-dozen people to hand out leaflets at a particular time loomed as a major task: the six selected would turn up at different times, the leaflets would be lost or misplaced, the volunteers would get bored before they had finished distributing the leaflets, etc., etc., etc. Bit by bit, however, the members learned how to accept orders, how to carry out a simple task and follow through on it; then they began to learn how to give orders, how to organize a rent strike or a rally, how to handle a meeting, how to talk on their feet and debate an issue, how to handle opposition. The result, for those who have been actively involved in the organization, has been to transform their existence, for the discipline of the organization gradually imposes itself on their own lives. And as the individual learns to organize his own life, he learns how to relate to others. "We've learned to live together and act as a community," another TWO activist says. "Now I know people all over Woodlawn, and I've been in all the churches. Two years ago I didn't know a soul."

It would be inane to pretend that Woodlawn has become a model community; it remains a poverty-stricken, crime-ridden slum, though a slum with hope—a slum that is developing the means of raising itself by its own bootstraps. Most of the problems that make Woodlawn what it is—high unemployment, lack of education, family disorganization, poor health, bad housing

392 PLANNING FOR THE URBAN CRISIS

—cannot be solved by a community organization alone. Help is needed; enormous resources must be poured into Woodlawn in the form of compensatory education, job retraining, advice on child-rearing, preventive medicine, etc. But experience in every city in the nation demonstrates that any paternalistic program imposed from above will be resisted and resented as "welfare colonialism." *TWO's greatest contribution, therefore, is its most subtle: it gives Woodlawn residents the sense of dignity that makes it possible for them to accept help.* For help now comes (or seems to come, which amounts to the same thing) not as the result of charity but as the result of their own power; they have decided what services they need and what services they would like to have. Hence programs which the community, in the past, would have avoided with contempt as one more instance of "Mr. Charlie's brainwashing," are now eagerly sought after. Thus, negotiations between TWO and the University of Chicago have led to development of a nursery school program designed to reverse the effects of cultural deprivation. Negotiations between TWO and a team of psychiatrists enabled the latter to set up some promising experiments in group therapy; the psychiatrists and social workers work through TWO's network of block clubs to bring people into the program. When a program enters Woodlawn with TWO's endorsement and recommendation, it carries a cachet that greatly multiplies its chances of success.

NOTES

1. The change in the color of Woodlawn's residents seems to have changed the area's history as well; thus, a 1962 city report on "Key Social Characteristics of the Woodlawn Community" suggests, in contradiction to the 1946 report, that as a result of "almost planless growth since the 1893 Columbia Exposition," the community had been deteriorating for more than a half-century.
2. Critics of Alinsky now point to Back of the Yards and suggest that *anyone* could have organized the area, since the residents are virtually all Catholics. But when Alinsky began his organizing work, the stockyards area quite literally was a jungle. The residents were Catholic, all right—but they belonged to an incredible number of churches, each representing a different nationality or ethnic group at war with all the others. Animosity between them was so great that Catholic priests ministering to one ethnic group literally were not on speaking terms with priests from other ethnic backgrounds: Alinsky managed to unite all the Catholics—and then to forge a working alliance between the local Churches, the Chicago Archdiocese, and the Packinghouse Workers Union—at the time (though no longer) under communist domination. Paradoxically, the Back of the Yards organization has become very conservative in recent years: *e.g.,* it has been quite effective in keeping Negroes out of the neighborhood.
3. John Kenneth Galbraith, *American Capitalism,* Boston: Houghton Mifflin Company, 1956.
4. Because of the poverty of Woodlawn, and even more because of the long tradition of Negro dependence, Alinsky has found it necessary to stretch that period by a year or two. TWO is on its way to financial independence, however; as of January, 1964, it had $10,000 in its treasury.
5. Peter H. Rossi & Robert A. Dentler, *The Politics of Urban Renewal,* Glencoe, Ill.: The Free Press, 1961.
6. Among the other items in the dossier was a photostat of a *New York Times* article of January 24, 1960, reporting the split-up of the Chelsea Community Council, which Alinskiy had helped organize on a part-time basis. The Hudson Guild, a settlement house whose director had served as the community's spokesman until the broader-based organization was formed, led a number of groups in withdrawing from the organization

when its will was thwarted. The *Times* suggested that trouble in the Council arose from two fundamental questions: "Should an indigent section of the community be allowed to block desirable development just because it can muster a majority vote?" "Has a community house, or any other small group, the right to impose its will on the majority of the area's population even if it is for the good of the community?" (The "good of the community," in this instance, was an urban renewal plan designed to tear down the low-income housing in the area and replace it with middle-income co-operatives). The groups pulling out of the Council, the *Times* reporter indicated, answered "yes" to the second question. So, presumably, did the University of Chicago administration.

7. *Cf.*, James Q. Wilson, "Planning and Policies: Citizen Participation in Urban Renewal," *Journal of the American Institute of Planners,* November, 1963.

5.6 CIVIL RIGHTS PROTEST AND RIOTS: A DISAPPEARING DISTINCTION

JAMES A. GESCHWENDER

The civil rights movement has dominated much of the American scene from 1954 to the present, with urban disorders pretty well taking over center stage since 1963. The liberal segment of white America has generally had a positive image of the civil rights movement but has viewed big city riots with a mixture of fear and disgust. A number of social scientists also view civil rights activities and riots as two different and contradictory types of phenomena. This paper will take the assumption of difference as a hypothesis rather than a postulate. In this discussion sociologists' conceptualizations of social movements and riots will be examined, characteristics of recent urban disorders will be evaluated, and conclusions will be drawn.

It must be emphasized that the problem to be examined is not one of mere labeling. This paper is concerned with the proper label for recent urban disorders, but only because the question has broader implications. First, there are important theoretical considerations. The nature of the concepts used, the theories invoked, and the hypotheses drawn all will be influenced by the correct classification of the disorders as riots or as parts of a developing social movement, for the problem cannot be understood accurately by using an invalid classificatory scheme. If predictions of the future are to be accurate, we must start with a valid base.

The second implication—the application of sociological principles—is closely related to the need for accurate prediction. Social scientists cannot make useful recommendations for action to politicians or segments of society unless they have a correct image of the current expressions of black unrest, a correct image of the depth and intensity of unrest, a perception of the extent to which this unrest has crystallized into a prerevolutionary movement, and some reasonably accurate predictions for the future. The type of societal changes that will ameliorate conditions producing hostile outbursts will not be sufficient to change the direction of a social movement which is developing along potentially revolutionary lines.

From James A. Geschwender, "Civil Rights Protest and Riots: A Disappearing Distinction." Reprinted with permission from the *Social Science Quarterly,* Vol. 49 (December 1968), pp. 474–484.

Hostile Outbursts and Social Movements

Neil J. Smelser has developed a highly elaborate conceptual framework for the analysis of collective behavior.[1] He uses a value-added approach in which six determinants (necessary conditions) of collective behavior combine to specify the nature and characteristics of any particular collective episode. The six determinants are structural conduciveness, structural strain, growth and spread of a generalized belief, precipitating factors, mobilization of participants for action, and the operation of social control.[2] Any particular form of collective behavior produced by these determinants may be analyzed in terms of four basic components of social action: values, norms, mobilization of motivation for organized action, and situational facilities.[3] Each component of social action is categorized into seven levels of specificity, but present purposes do not require a detailed exposition of the theory.

For Smelser, the crucial distinction between hostile outbursts (riots) and norm-oriented movements (that category of social movements which includes the civil rights movement) lies in the area of growth and spread of generalized beliefs. The value-added analysis of the development of hostile outbursts begins by examining ambiguity and anxiety. Anxiety is fused with the mobilization series to produce a generalized belief that some agent, or agents, is responsible for the anxiety-producing situation. This suspicion of agents is short-circuited to the selection of a particular kind of agent. A desire to punish, restrict, damage, or remove the agent then emerges, and wish-fulfillment beliefs of two types manifest themselves. They take the form of an exaggerated belief in the ability to punish agents of evil and to remove the evil ascribed to the agents. This belief is basically a generalized sense of omnipotence which is short-circuited to specific results.[4]

The early stages of the development of a norm-oriented movement are identical to those in the development of a hostile outburst. The norm-oriented movement, too, begins with ambiguity, anxiety, the attachment of the anxiety to some agent, and the exaggeration of the threatening nature of that agent. At this point, however, its development diverges. A belief develops that the normative control of the agent is inadequate and this belief becomes directed toward a particular set of laws or customs. Thus it comes to be accepted that the problem can be solved by changing the normative structure. This expectation becomes channeled into a decision about the particular type of normative change that would be expected to immobilize or destroy the agent, eliminating the source of the problem.[5]

The distinction between hostile outbursts and social movements focuses attention on the belief system. If the episode of collective behavior is seen as a direct attempt to attack or punish the agents of evil (in this case, police and white businessmen), then it is classed as an hostile outburst (a riot). However, if the episode of collective behavior is seen as a means of bringing about normative change to prevent the agents from working their evil, then it is termed a social movement. The presence or absence of scapegoating and/or violence does not determine the classification of a particular episode, because violence and scapegoating are elements of both hostile outbursts and norm-oriented movements. Smelser states that

> hostile outbursts are frequently adjuncts of larger-scale social movements. On certain occasions reform movements . . . may erupt into violence. Revolutionary movements . . . are frequently accompanied by violence. The primary difference among terms such as "riot," "revolt," "rebellion," "insurrection," and "revolution" all of which involve hostile outbursts—stems from the scope of their associated social movements.[6]

The task, then, is to determine whether the recent urban disorders are isolated outbursts of pent-up hostility directed against perceived oppressors, such as police and white businessmen in the black ghetto, or part of a larger movement aimed at bringing about fundamental alterations in the normative order of American society. Probably a majority of white liberals and many social scientists have decided on the former alternative.[7]

Characteristics of the Disorders

Research reports suggest that three aspects of the disorders contribute most to the labeling of the disorders as riots. First, the prime activity of most participants was looting.[8] Second, the disorders were spontaneous, relatively unorganized, and leaderless.[9] Third, the participants apparently did not attempt to seize permanent control of an area or specify political demands.[10] These objections will be examined one at a time.

LOOTING

First, the existence of looting, per se, should be investigated. Oberschall makes two points with regard to looting. He suggests that many petty thieves and small-time professional crooks came into the Watts area to engage in looting but left prior to the major waves of arrests. He indicates further that looting is a frequent occurrence in all disasters, natural or otherwise.[11] Both of these points may be well taken. Fires, floods, tornadoes, and riots all represent periods of upheaval. At such times, the burden upon police and other agents of social control is greatly increased. They are not in a position to enforce all aspects of the law and many persons take this opportunity to improve their lot temporarily by acquiring a ham, a television set, furniture, or liquor. Looting during a riot may be, as Lee Rainwater describes it, "a kind of primitive attempt at an income redistribution."[12] In other words, the "have-nots" temporarily increase their possessions, without seriously attacking the distributive system.

This view must be balanced with an alternative one, for theft of any sort may be considered an act of rebellion. Hobsbawm has documented the fact that banditry in peasant societies has often been a form of social protest and represents an archaic form of social movement.[13] In such a case, the bandit who followed the Robin Hood model of stealing from the privileged and redistributing a portion of his gains to the underprivileged often had the support and affection of the peasantry. American history has its counterparts.

Jesse James, Pretty Boy Floyd, and Babyface Nelson are only a few of the many American bandits who have been renowned in song and legend for their fights against the propertied and their generosity toward the needy. Theft, when directed against the right targets, may be seen as a direct attack upon the exploiter and upon the whole system of exploitation.

There is evidence that looting during the recent urban disorders was so directed. Rustin indicates that in the Watts riot the victims of looting and arson were whites rather than blacks.[14] He further points out that not all whites were victims; the white-owned businesses that had reputations for fair dealing and nondiscriminatory practices were spared. In Detroit some black-owned businesses were also targets.[15] These however, were black merchants who had the same reputation for exploitation as did many whites.[16] There is, incidentally, some indication that in Detroit a group of individuals provided leadership in looting without participating in it themselves.[17]

A more basic criticism of the Oberschall interpretation of looting must be made, however. Dynes and Quarantelli state that looting rarely occurs in natural disasters and the little that does occur differs in many significant respects from that which occurs in urban disorders.[18] They cite one example of major looting in a natural disaster (the Chicago snowstorms of January and February, 1967) but suggest that the similarity in area of incidence may mean that this looting was a continuation of the looting during the disorder of 1966.[19]

If looting is characteristic of the current urban disorders but rarely occurs in natural disasters, it cannot be explained in the same terms in both cases. It is doubtful that the Dynes-Quarantelli interpretation in terms of property redefinition is adequate.[20] Looting appears to be more than simply a protest against the prevailing definition of property rights. The selection of white and black exploiters as targets of looting and arson suggests that it is an attack upon the system of distribution of property and that it also provides an opportunity to acquire property. In short, looting constitutes an attack upon exploitation rather than upon exploiters—an act more characteristic of social movements than of hostile outbursts.

ORGANIZATION

Second, the fact that the disorders were spontaneous rather than the result of conspiracy is informative. The Kerner Commission saw no evidence of conspiracy, of deliberate incitement, or of organization in the disorders.[21] This is, however, no reason to conclude that they are not part of a social movement. To make such a statement is to misunderstand the nature of a social movement.

The treatment of social movements by Lang and Lang provides instructive insights.[22] They define a social movement as a "large-scale, widespread, and continuing, elementary collective action in pursuit of an objective that affects and shapes the social order in some fundamental aspect."[23] A social movement is seen as having organized associations at its core that provide general direction and focus; but it also includes large, unorganized segments pushing in the same direction but not integrated with the core associations.

Lang and Lang specifically state that "unless we are able to distinguish between the core group and a larger mass of supporters not formally joined, we are not dealing with a social movement."[24]

Not all participants in every social movement need to have identical definitions of goals, strategy, and tactics; it is only necessary that they share the same general objectives. The degree of mutual cooperation and coordination of activities is, in fact, problematic in any given social movement. Lang and Lang state:

> One group working for a cause . . . may appear to be so involved in its quarrels with another group sharing its objective that members of both groups hardly seem to be participants in the same movement. Yet, however riddled by factional disputes a movement may be, the knowledge that other groups are working toward the same ends gives each unit a sense of participation in it. They compete to see which is the purest representative of the doctrine.[25]

Thus it would seem that any definition of the civil rights movement must be broad enough to include such disparate organizations as the Urban League, National Association for the Advancement of Colored People, Southern Christian Leadership Conference, Student Nonviolent Coordinating Committee, and the Congress on Racial Equality, provided they are all working for the same general objectives, such as the furthering of the position and rights of the black American. The definition must also be broad enough to include the unorganized participants of demonstrations, boycotts, and even urban disorders, provided, again, that the participants have the same general goals.[26] The lack of organization does not, *ipso facto,* exclude looters, snipers, and arsonists from the civil rights movement. Their motives must be examined, which will be done later in this paper.

TACTICS

Third, does the absence of stated political demands and/or any attempt to seize permanent control of a geographic area exclude urban disorders from the category of social movements? The answer to this question requires a comprehensive analysis of the nature and role of tactics in a social movement.

The reluctance to treat urban disorders as a segment of the civil rights movement very likely stems from the tendency to define the movement in terms of its organized core associations and to define its tactics in terms of the more respectable ones of court suits, nonviolent direct action, and voter registration drives. Killian and Grigg note, however, that each of the above tactics emerged when previous modes of behavior proved inadequate in bringing about sufficiently broad results as rapidly as desired.[27] It is plausible to assume that segments of the black community have become dissatisfied with the slow, token changes brought about by the respectable tactics and are developing more drastic ones to increase the speed and scope of change. Oberschall lends support to this interpretation when he states:

> The collective significance of these events, however, is that the civil rights gains made by the Negro movement in the last few years, which have bene-

fitted the Southern Negro and middle-class Negroes, have not altered the situation of the lower-class urban Negroes outside of the South and have not removed the fundamental sources of grievances of a large proportion of the Negro population in the U.S.[28]

The historical role of urban mobs in controlling ruling elites and in attempting to bring about changes is well documented. Hobsbawn states:

> Provided the ruler did his duty, the populace was prepared to defend him with enthusiasm. But if he did not, it rioted until he did. . . . The treatment of perennial rioting kept rulers ready to control prices and to distribute work or largess, or indeed to listen to their faithful commons on other matters.[29]

> Nevertheless, such a symbiosis of the "mob" and the people against whom it rioted was not necessarily the fundamental factor about its politics. The "mob" rioted, but it also sometimes made revolutions. . . . It was poor; "they" were rich; life was fundamentally unjust for the poor. These were the foundations of its attitude. . . . The implicit revolutionism of the "mob" was primitive; in its way it was the metropolitan equivalent of the stage of political consciousness represented by social banditry in the countryside.[30]

Thus, a plausible assumption is that the civil rights movement has undergone an evolution of tactics. As one tactic proves inadequate to the task it is replaced by another seen as more adequate. In the recent past, accommodation gave way to court suits. The orderly tactics gave way to the less orderly tactics of direct action, which Waskow analyzes under the concept of "creative disorder."[31] "Creative disorder" may now be giving way to "creative rioting."[32] Ghetto riots may be an attempt to use violent disorder creatively to bring about change. This does not mean that all individuals involved in the civil rights movement are now, or will be, participating in riots. There always has been a tactical division of labor: some civil rights adherents use court suits; others engage in nonviolent direct action; others, however, may have moved on to creative rioting.[33]

The stating of political demands and the attempts to permanently occupy and control a given territory are tactics which are likely to appear in a fully developed insurrection or revolution. The tactic of creative rioting represents a move in this direction developing from creative disorder. It is an intermediate tactic which does not go as far as revolution. That is, it may appear in prerevolutionary situations—situations which have the potential for developing into revolutions but which will not necessarily do so.

Oberschall may not be entirely accurate when he states that political demands are missing in the current urban disorders. The Kerner Commission report states:

> In 21 of the 24 disturbances surveyed, discussion or negotiation occurred during the disturbances. These took the form of relatively formal meetings between government officials and Negroes during which grievances and issues were discussed and means were sought to restore order.[34]

These meetings usually were with "established leaders" but youths were involved in 13 discussions. The combination of discussion of grievances and the presence of the more militant youths indicates the presence of some sort of political demands even though no attempt to occupy territory permanently may have been made. Urban disorders, therefore, may be a new civil rights tactic which stops short of revolution.

The case for creative rioting—ghetto riots as an integral part of the civil rights movement—has not yet been fully demonstrated. The nature and pattern of looting lend more support to this interpretation than they do to the alternative interpretation of urban disorders as hostile outbursts. The lack of deliberate instigation or organization in the disorders is neutral, as it is equally consistent with either interpretation. The lack of an attempt to assume permanent control of a given territory does not prevent the current ghetto riots from being a step in the evolution of tactics within the civil rights movement just short of full-blown insurrection. Due to the inconclusive nature of the foregoing, one must analyze the characteristics of riot participants prior to drawing final conclusions. The prime source of data will be the recent surveys of riot participation conducted in Detroit and Newark.

Characteristics of Riot Participants

A number of characteristics of self-identified rioters or riot supporters correspond to those noted in the sociological literature as characterizing individuals who are prone to participate in social movements or revolutions. Both Lyford P. Edwards and Crane Brinton state that individuals who perceive their legitimate aspirations for mobility to be blocked are especially prone to engage in revolutionary behavior.[35] The Kerner Commission report notes that the self-identified rioters in Newark were significantly ($p < .05$) more likely than the self-reported noninvolved individuals to believe that their level of education entitled them to a job with more income and responsibility than the one they presently possessed.[36] The Newark rioters were also less likely than the noninvolved to perceive that there was an opportunity for them to acquire their desired job ($p < .06$) and significantly more likely ($p < .025$) to believe that discrimination was the factor preventing them from so doing.[37] No comparable data from Detroit are available. Taken jointly, these characteristics indicate the existence of the blocked-mobility syndrome that Edwards and Brinton find typical of potential revolutionaries.

Status inconsistency also has been interpreted as a characteristic that predisposes individuals toward participation in social movements or revolutions.[38] Evidence suggests that rioters tend to be status-inconsistent. The Detroit rioters were significantly *better educated* than the noninvolved ($p < .05$) and the Newark rioters, too, tended to be better educated than the noninvolved ($p < .06$).[39] Both Newark and Detroit rioters tended to have *lower incomes* than the noninvolved, although neither difference is statistically significant.[40] The Newark rioters also tended to have lower job status than the noninvolved ($p < .06$).[41] No data on occupational status are available from Detroit. While there is no difference between rioters and the noninvolved in terms of current rate of unemployment, the Newark rioters were significantly more likely to have been unemployed for a month or longer within the past year ($p < .05$).[42] No comparable data are available from Detroit.

These data together indicate that rioters were considerably less likely to be able to bring their occupational status, income, or employment status up to a level comparable to their level of education. When this observation is combined with the fact that Negroes are more likely than whites to have their levels of occupation and income lag behind their educational level, then there can be no doubt that active rioters are status inconsistent—and inconsistent to a greater degree than the noninvolved.[43] More important, the rioters' "profiles" are inconsistent, with high education–low income or high education–low occupation profiles, which are precisely the ones most likely to produce participation in extremist social movements of leftist inclinations.[44]

The fact that rioters exhibit status inconsistency and possess thwarted aspirations does not in itself demonstrate that riots are part of a social movement. One additional factor, however, lends credence to this interpretation. Ransford found that Watts Negroes who were socially isolated from whites were significantly more willing to use violence than were those with greater contact with whites.[45] This conclusion agrees with the suggestion by Marx that the isolation of an aggrieved category of persons into an interacting collectivity is likely to produce a conflict group with a high degree of group consciousness and an awareness of a common enemy.[46] The likelihood that racially isolated blacks may develop "black consciousness" and a hostility toward whites which could manifest itself in rioting as a revolutionary activity gains support from data on the Detroit and Newark rioters. Both Newark and Detroit rioters were significantly more likely than the noninvolved to believe that Negroes are more dependable than whites (p < .05 and <.001, respectively) and that Negroes are "nicer" than whites (p < .025 and <.001, respectively).[47] Newark rioters were significantly more likely than the noninvolved to describe themselves as "black" (p < .025) and were more prone to believe that all Negroes should study African history and languages (p < .06).[48] No comparable data are available from Detroit. Newark rioters were significantly more likely than the noninvolved to believe that presently integrated civil rights groups would be more effective without whites (p < .005) and to admit that sometimes they hated whites (p < .001).[49] While there are no data on the likelihood that Detroit rioters hated whites, they, also, were more likely than the noninvolved to say that integrated civil rights groups would be more effective without whites (p < .10).[50]

These data strongly suggest that rioters are individuals largely isolated from whites, that they interact with blacks who share common grievances, that they develop a high level of hostility toward whites, combined with a high level of black consciousness, and that they subsequently participate in riots as a means of attacking the "system." In short, they are participating in a social movement that may or may not reach revolutionary proportions.

The suggestion presented above—that urban riots may represent an evolution of tactics from the more respectable to the more violent—gains support from the following facts. Newark rioters were significantly more likely than the noninvolved to participate in discussions of Negro rights (p < .025), to participate in activities of civil rights groups (p < .05), to identify political figures (p < .205), to be politically knowledgeable (p < .025), and to not trust the Newark government to do what is right (p <

10).[51] While there are no directly comparable data from Detroit, the rioters there were significantly more likely than the noninvolved to feel that anger toward politicians (p < .05) and toward the police (p < .05) had much to do with causing the riots.[52]

Conclusion

The rioters discussed above are not the normally apathetic, noninvolved individuals who participate in hostile outbursts. They tend to be politically knowledgeable and active in civil rights activities. Many of them have apparently come to the conclusion that traditional political and civil rights tactics cannot bring about desired results and thus they have shifted to newer tactics. This interpretation is supported by the desire of a large number of rioters to exclude whites from civil rights organizations. The theoretically relevant characteristics of thwarted aspirations and status inconsistency suggest, but do not demonstrate, this conclusion. The factor of racial isolation, though, pushes further in the direction indicated. Political knowledgeability, civil rights activities, black consciousness, hostility toward whites, and mistrust of government "put the icing on the cake" and make the conclusion emphatic.

The earlier discussion of looting strongly suggested that current urban disorders were a developing part of the civil rights movement. The discussions of degree of organization of riots and of tactics were consistent with the interpretation of urban disorders as either hostile outbursts or segments of a social movement. The discussion of the characteristics of rioters, however, removed remaining doubts. The present author no longer questions that the urban disorders are, in fact, creative rioting. Creative rioting falls clearly within the evolutionary pattern of the civil rights movement, a social movement which may or may not eventually become revolutionary.

This thesis should not be misconstrued; this paper does not contend that all urban disorders were creative rioting. The outbreaks of 1964 in Harlem, Rochester, Jersey City, and Philadelphia may have been simple hostile outbursts, although they did bring about a response on the community, state, and national levels. As subsequent riots continued to bring about real, if limited, results, individuals may have become aware of riots as a potentially successful tactic. This is not to say that the riots were deliberately instigated. Rather, a potential riot situation may have made some individuals aware of the utility of rioting, which in turn stimulated riot behavior. Once a riot was underway, other individuals were motivated to continue and direct it. Thus, rioting shifts from the category of a hostile outburst to that of a creative force in the civil rights movement.

NOTES

1. Neil J. Smelser, *Theory of Collective Behavior* (New York: The Free Press of Glencoe, 1963).
2. *Ibid.*, pp. 14–17.
3. *Ibid.*, pp. 23–28.
4. *Ibid.*, pp. 101–103.

5. *Ibid.,* pp. 111–112.

6. *Ibid.,* p. 227.

7. See, for example, Allen D. Grimshaw, "Civil Disturbance, Racial Revolt, Class Assault: Three Views of Urban Violence," paper presented before the American Association for the Advancement of Science, New York, December 28, 1967; and Anthony Oberschall, "The Los Angeles Riot," *Social Problems,* 15 (Winter, 1968), pp. 322–341. For examples of sociologists taking positions similar to the one presented herein, see Lewis M. Killian, *The Impossible Revolution* (New York: Random House, 1968); and Robert Blauner, "Whitewash over Watts," *Transaction,* 3 (March–April, 1966), p. 9.

8. See, for example, Tom Parmenter, "Breakdown of Law and Order," *Transaction,* 9 (Sept., 1967), pp. 13–21; Oberschall, "Los Angeles Riot," p. 327; and *Report of the National Advisory Commission on Civil Disorders* (New York: Bantam Books, 1968), p. 93.

9. See, for example, Oberschall, "Los Angeles Riot," p. 341; *Report on Civil Disorders,* pp. 201–202; and Arthur I. Waskow, *From Race Riot to Sit-In* (Garden City, N.Y.: Doubleday-Anchor, 1967), p. 260.

10. Oberschall, "Los Angeles Riot," p. 340.

11. *Ibid.,* pp. 335–338.

12. Lee Rainwater, "Open Letter on White Justice and the Riots," *Transaction,* 9 (Sept., 1967), p. 25.

13. E. J. Hobsbawm, *Primitive Rebels* (New York: W. W. Norton, 1959), esp. Ch. 2.

14. Bayard Rustin, "The Watts 'Manifesto' and the McCone Report," *Commentary,* 41 (March, 1966), pp. 29–35.

15. *Report on Civil Disorders,* p. 88.

16. Private interviews with observers of the disorder.

17. Louis E. Lomax, "Seeds of Riot Planted Here by Salesmen," *Detroit News,* August 6, 1967, pp. 1–2.

18. Russell Dynes and E. L. Quarantelli, "What Looting in Civil Disturbances Really Means," *Transaction,* 5 (May, 1968), pp. 9–14.

19. *Ibid.,* p. 12.

20. *Ibid.,* pp. 13–14.

21. *Report on Civil Disorders,* pp. 201–202.

22. Kurt Lang and Gladys Engel Lang, *Collective Dynamics* (New York: Crowell, 1961), pp. 489–544.

23. *Ibid.,* p. 490.

24. *Ibid.,* p. 497.

25. *Ibid.,* p. 496.

26. Although probably clear from the context, the term "civil rights movement" is not here used in the narrow sense of attempts to acquire legal rights and legal equality through normative means. It is used in the broader sense of all attempts to gain legal rights and legal equality as well as those attempts to translate legal rights into actual functioning rights and equality.

27. Lewis Killian and Charles Grigg, *Racial Crisis in America* (Englewood Cliffs, N.J.: Prentice Hall, 1964), pp. 18–23.

28. Oberschall, "Los Angeles Riot," p. 341.

29. Hobsbawm, *Primitive Rebels,* p. 116.

30. *Ibid.,* p. 118.

31. Waskow, *From Race Riot to Sit-In,* pp. 225–290.

32. "Creative rioting" as used herein refers to a particular tactical type of behavior aimed at bringing about societal change. It involves the conscious and deliberate use of violent attacks against property and/or persons. The violence against property may be either of a destructive or of a confiscatory (theft) nature. Violence against persons usually is not directed randomly against persons as individuals or members of a group; rather, it is frequently directed against persons as symbols of authority or oppression. It tends to be incidental to attacks upon property or the system of exploitation.

Thus, creative rioting differs from creative disorder in that the latter is nonviolent and, while disruptive of societal processes, is not destructive of property. Creative rioting also differs from revolution in that it tends to be too short-lived, less organized, and less coordinated than required for a full-scale, violent attempt to seize control of society.

33. Similarly, there may be a division of labor within a rioting mob. Some participants may consciously use rioting as a tactic to promote change, while others simply attempt to improve their personal well-being by acquiring more possessions, and still others try to avenge real or alleged wrongs. The latter two groups are not, strictly speaking, using creative rioting, but by swelling the numbers of rioters—thereby increasing the duration and intensity of the disorders—they contribute to the overall effect of the creative rioters.

34. *Report on Civil Disorders,* pp. 126–127.

35. Lyford P. Edwards, *The Natural History of Revolution* (Chicago: The University of Chicago Press, 1927), p. 30; and Crane Brinton, *The Anatomy of Revolution* (New York: W. W. Norton, 1938), p. 78.

36. *Report on Civil Disorders,* p. 127, n. 130. Henceforth, self-reported rioters and self-reported noninvolved will be referred to, respectively, as rioters and noninvolved.

37. *Ibid.,* p. 175, nn. 131 and 132.

38. For a summary of such literature see James A. Geschwender, "Continuities in Theories of Status Inconsistency and Cognitive Dissonance," *Social Forces,* 46 (Dec., 1967), pp. 160–171.

39. *Report on Civil Disorders,* p. 174, n. 126.

40. *Ibid.,* p. 174, n. 124.

41. *Ibid.,* p. 175, n. 129.

42. *Ibid.,* p. 175, nn. 127 and 128.

43. James A. Geschwender, "Negro Education: The False Faith," *Phylon* (forthcoming); and James A. Geschwender, "Social Structure and the Negro Revolt: An Examination of Some Hypotheses," *Social Forces,* 43 (Dec., 1964), pp. 248–256.

44. Geschwender, "Continuities in Theories," pp. 169–171.

45. H. Edward Ransford, "Isolation, Powerlessness, and Violence: A Study of Attitudes and Participation in the Watts Riot," *American Journal of Sociology,* 73 (March, 1968), p. 586.

46. Reinhard Bendix and Seymour Martin Lipset, "Karl Marx' Theory of Social Classes," in Reinhard Bendix and Seymour Martin Lipset, eds., *Class, Status and Power* (New York: Free Press of Glencoe, 1953), pp. 26–35.

47. *Report on Civil Disorders,* p. 175, n. 134.

48. *Ibid.,* p. 175, n. 135.

49. *Ibid.,* p. 175, n. 136.

50. *Ibid.*

51. *Ibid.,* pp. 177–178, nn. 140, 139, 141.

52. *Ibid.,* p. 178, n. 142.

5.7 REMAKING
THE URBAN SCENE:
NEW YOUTH IN AN OLD ENVIRONMENT

JOHN R. SEELEY

I

There is something fatal to the understanding of urban problems in the means by which we seek it. The means are, conventionally, the orderly presentation of facts as complete, accurate, and sure as possible, in the context of argument as lucid and precise as possible, with a view to the persuasion or conviction of "rational" minds that think that way. We all know, I think, the roles, rules, and skills involved. But if this procedure has brought us to the present sorry pass, it is ironic that it should be held that necessities of communication require that the fatal process be continued in order to persuade any of its fatality.

Let no one fail to appreciate the difficulty. Imagine a patient in psychoanalysis whose central defense is "intellectualization." His analyst would like him for his own benefit to appreciate the harm he thus does himself. The patient might sense, intuit, appreciate what is lost to him *if* he will not abandon the defense enough to enter as a whole man (as nearly as he can) into the drama that he and his doctor (as representative of "the world") are playing out. But before he will engage, he says: "Prove it to me. Marshal your arguments. Show me a fourfold table of harms and goods cross-classified by intellectualization and whatever is the alternative." If the analyst yields, he and the patient are probably lost in one of two ways: Either it cannot be shown intellectually that intellectualization is as bad for this patient as it actually is, or, if it can, that this would be the worst possible way for him to reach that conclusion, since at the very least it would deepen his reliance on what he already over-relies on.

We cannot reach to the question of "the conscience of the city" by means of a conscience that I hold to be in a radical sense false. It is ironic (and probably self-defeating) to seek to secure conviction on that point by the very methods that the argument impugns.

It might be noted as an intellectual *curiosum* that each of the two courses open *is* subject to and the object of attack. If a psychoanalyst maintains that there is no way to the understanding of analysis except by the experience

From John R. Seeley, "Remaking the Urban Scene: New Youth in an Old Environment." Reprinted by permission from *Daedalus,* Journal of the American Academy of Arts and Sciences, Boston, Massachusetts, Vol. 97, No. 4 (Fall 1968), pp. 1124–1139.

of it—that, in effect, the abstraction and "precision" characterizing scientific speech about it inevitably falsify and misrepresent its nature—he is accused of practicing mysticism, magic, or mumbo-jumbo. If, on the other hand, a McLuhan—no matter what the merit of his contentions—argues by means of a linear logic sequentially presented against "linear logic," books, and sequential as against simultaneous presentation, his critics hold that he cannot believe what he asserts since his practice is incompatible with his theory. The two arguments, taken together, seem to substantiate the conclusion of the dean of an eminent medical school: "There is no learning," he said, "among doctors; only biological replacement by those with new ideas." They might also make intelligible the distress of the young at the difficulties or impossibilities of communication with "anyone over thirty."

In any case, what is here undertaken is a self-contradictory attempt to marshal an over-ordered argument against over-order, an attack on the undue reliance on logic relying unduly on logic, a managerial-type assault on management, a prosaic *demarche* against prosaism, an attempt to convince some colleagues by these methods that they cannot be convinced by such methods, and that failing such conviction they will mistake the future because, so restricted, they misapprehend the present in its most vital particulars.

II

The West (in which must now be included the Westernized or Westernizing nations) has reached a climax. The climax refers both to personal and institutional practices and to those reflective methods by which "adaptation" is secured and operability maintained. By a "climax" I mean that point of highest development precedent to fission, explosion, or exhaustion and replacement by another form. By "another form," I no more mean a minor modification of the old form than the so-called Dark Ages represented in relation to the preceding Roman Empire.

We may discern some intimations as to the probable shape of that successor form by attending to two classes of facts: those connected with alienation and those connected with such alternative and separate integrations as we see beginning. Alienation here means the dissolution of a civilization—not some untoward cause or consequence of it—since civilization exists in attachment, devotion, as community exists (to quote John Dewey) in communication.

If this is what is afoot, and if it can by no means—or at least not much or for very long—be contained, any treatment of "the conscience of the city" must take this development at least for its context or, if approved, for its aim. If the view is correct, there is something tragicomic about sitting around "planning" to secure, extend, and improve what is to be shortly swept away —like Roman generals plotting reparative wars abroad and placatory redistribution of bread and amusement at home, just as a double, irresistible assault striking at the roots of the very idea of Rome was being mounted by "barbarians" abroad and "riff-raff" in catacombs in the heart of the heartland at home.

Just as the city is in normal times that place where the civilization reaches the high point of its gradient, where the civilization is refined, developed, elaborated, and fed back to the hinterland, so in abnormal times the city is that place where its successor is being incubated, nurtured, fostered, or developed. And the conscience of the city lies at that *nucleus nucleorum,* wherever it may be, where most actively, most passionately, most devotedly, most integrally the foundations of the new civilizations are being in action and interaction conceived, incarnated, tested, and worked out.

Most of the thoughts and plans for the future of the city are exacerbation or mere mitigation or fond folly: mitigation if we agree to give cups of water to thirsty children while the world shifts seismically in its shape and center of gravity; folly, if we imagine that we are doing more, or that we are dealing at all with the main and significant flow of events; exacerbation if the plans perfect exactly that which leads the list of *repudianda.*

III

The crisis of the West, the great movement (or drift) toward universal alienation, is attested to by the absence of response appropriate to the very idea of crisis despite or because of endless discussion and attendant hand-wringing. If your patient, child, or colleague talked endlessly of a crisis or series of crises in his life, of a growing feeling of depersonalization, while over some very long period the crisis grew worse and the depersonalization greater, surely you would begin to suspect that the crisis lay at another, a different, a deeper level: that perhaps the talk about crises or that way of talking about crisis was intrinsic and contributory to the crisis and its exacerbation. You would be forced to conclude that the talk (and the action "based" upon it) was insufficient as remedy; you might suspect it was unnecessary (and hence diversionary); you might well entertain the idea that that way of analyzing and dealing with crisis was at or near the core of what generates it. It is not enough to "recognize" and plan against the Kafkaesque—indeed, by now, ultra-Kafkaesque—quality of modern life, if it is precisely the kind of recognition and response that we give to the quality of life that is the source supreme of its increasingly Kafkaesque character. Some people, even if they allow that we have thought our way into the crisis, evidently believe we can think ourselves out of it. Even where they will allow that our way of conceiving and perceiving the world has brought us to this pass, they seem to hold that some continuation of the same or some relatively minor modification will see us through or out. That the whole set of ways of thinking and their attendant ways of acting themselves constitute the crisis is evidently, for them, hard to believe.

It seems evident to me and many that the world may be loosely divided, like Caesar's Gaul, into three parts: a relatively "affluent" part more or less conscious of, more or less disgusted with, and alienated from the "good life" they have finally achieved; a moderately well-off part, some still coasting on the momentum of getting there, but most more or less numbed and indifferent; a needy part desperately struggling by every means to get into the desperate straits of the other two. Such a distribution characterizes not only any single nation (this one especially), but the relations among nations as well. By a developing or an underdeveloped nation, we mean one aspiring or being pressed or maneuvered to get into the state we are in. Those who have qualms about getting them into that state console themselves by supposing that the "beneficiary" nations can at one and the same time commit themselves to our major ways of doing, being, thinking, feeling in the world, and save and preserve "the best of their culture." For people who believe that cultures are or ought to be in a profound and pervasive sense wholes, such a prescription is very strange—so strange, in fact, that one is driven to wonder what vital irrationality the proposal is meant to protect and conceal. Surely if someone had suggested we might graft the business practices of Manchester in the 1890's onto, say, Periclean Greek culture and thus have the double virtue of "cheap goods" (whatever that would have meant to our neo-Pericleans) and high-minded balance (whatever that could have meant to our neo-entrepreneurs), one would have judged the proposing someone crazy. That one or another cultural logic would have had to pervade and prevail, giving everything its ulterior significance and destroying or eliminating whatever was radically incompatible, is as certain as anything human can be, and, if not implicit in the notion of culture, most definitely confirmed by everything we know about it.

Thus the dream of a pluralism in essentials is idle. We are destined, I think, to a cultural unity. And that unity to be achieved in some historically brief interval, a virtual next instant, is unity under the sign of affluence and emptiness, plenitude of "means" and vacuum of satisfactions, satiation, disgust, "power," and nausea that now marks and distinguishes some considerable portion of our own society and a lesser portion of all Western ones.

I can hardly avoid "talking past" those who believe that the source of the deep and pervasive disgust, the *nausée générale,* has to do with "our failures." To be sustained, this view requires either a special meaning for the word "failure" or the recognition that what disgusts us is our success. The alienation, the misery, the nausea are intrinsic to our culture and its essence, implicit in its organizing principles, and most present, most visible, most palpable when and where it is most perfected.

Does anyone have serious difficulty identifying the arch-achievements and most characteristic products of our civilization? Surely some unique supremacy would have to be accorded our "production," our characteristic social organization, our "educational system," our "middle-class way of life" —as much a climax and a hallmark for us this hour as the "gentleman" was for England in the age just past. But a deeper supremacy would have to be our science and technology—now a technology of men as well as of things. And behind and below these are the ways of thinking, being, and acting of which they are the product. Those surely are our grand achievements— indeed, they are us in our distinct us-ness, in motion. These are not our aberrations, but our essential and crowning glories. Indeed they are that to which we do look when we wish or think we wish to correct what we truly consider aberrations: minor departures from expectation, such as air pollution or ghetto "housing." When Rap Brown said, "Violence is as American as cherry pie," he too was trying to get us to cease pretending that an endemic condition connected with our dearest aims and efforts may (for the sake of self-deceit and in order *not* to deal with real problems) be ignored or relegated to special, extraordinary, and disclaimed status. Our violence, both in its "spontaneous" and organized forms, I would have to list also among our arch-achievements: Mace, napalm, and person-shredding devices are as much our lovingly labored products, responsive in use to our deepest needs, as the Lincoln Memorial, the Medical Corps, or the Library of Congress. Indeed, not these severally, but their bonding or welding or wedding is what interests us here.

It would be idle to deny that a variety of responsive opinion obtains even among those who see "the phenomena" with distress or disgust. There are those who regard the phenomena as expressions of human nature, rather than our particular civilizational nature, and who look hence to resignation, "realism," or minor mitigatory measures as appropriate. These are those "reformers"—for want of a better word—who regard what presents itself as evidence of the *immaturity* of a system that is essentially good or potentially viable, and their remedy, of course, is to press on to more of the same planning, control, "education," "resource-utilization," correction of blatant injustice, and the like. There are those who profess and call themselves "radicals," who look to such remedies as new laws—or constitutions even— redefinitions of property or redistribution of titles thereto, the substitution of one elite for another (the inauguration of "meritocracy," for instance). These three seem so much alike as to appear bedfellows squabbling familiarly within the standard Western family. A fourth opinion holds that none of these views touches that which gnaws at the very marrow of the civilization, renders it intrinsically dehumanizing, inevitably corrupting of man and nature. The view ought not to be thought entirely novel even in modern times. Freud seriously raised and left open (in *Civilization and Its Discontents*) the question whether any civilization—viewed as a system protecting people from the threats of nature, the body, and one another—did not of its nature so empty life of pleasure and the possibility of pleasure that the motive for and capacity to sustain the civilization must be in time undercut and destroyed. Not necessarily civilization generally, but certainly *this* civilization is, in a rapidly mounting crescendo, showing itself to be a Moloch at its heart and core.

The evidence lies not in our peccadilloes, sins, and deviations, but in our central and crowning achievements: the most basic kinds of relations among the kinds of persons we have most basically made ourselves. The allegation that we are all "plastic people" loses too much in translation to carry the force, richness, or meaning that belongs to it.

IV

If I try to bring back out of the rich and allusive "language"—words, acts, musics, postures, gestures, shaded and subtle ways of being, breathing, reaching, touching—whatever I can put into "straight" language, what shall I say? How shall I locate in "our" language the source of a *dégoût total,* a *nausée générale,* a large part of which stems from the very nature of that language and the uses to which it is put, the only uses to which it *can* be put since it was developed for just such use?

The central thrusts of the civilization are clearly conquest, control, mastery, subordination, domestication, domination, the bending of all to what is taken to be the human will. It is the apotheosis of willfulness. We appear in the Universe as Conquistadores—no matter what minor modifications we may in our odd moments permit ourselves. Agency is all; patience nothing, except as another way of mastery in rare circumstances, such as terminal cancer. We prefer in practice (whatever we may say abstractly) the effective to the harmless. Nazi soldiers were to Americans part of the family, perhaps in misconduct or error; Balinese non-soldiers are quaint or a mystery, but not serious human beings. All is reduced to the test of use—use in the peculiar "military" sense of the conqueror looking for further conquest. We sometimes smile when the claim is made explicitly that music is to be used to "tame the savage breast" or religion to maintain mental health or serve social solidarity, but in fact we can hardly accredit either comfortably until the claims (or analogical ones) have been made. To be in the world in the mode of lovers or children is so nearly unthinkable a thought that we should reject it, if we could imagine what it implied, as certainly un-American and non-Western and, perhaps, not fully human. We are the society of the girded loin, and what is in our hand is the crook at best and the sword at worst, the two being in our scheme so closely connected anyway as to represent phases in one act, the appropriate act, our paradigm-universal. The questions that divide men politically—the few capable of causing cold wars, of threatening hot ones, and generally of promoting passion—are not about the *whether* of appropriation, but the *whom*. Who is to take title to and exercise dominion over the farthest reaches of space and the uttermost depths of the sea has become an urgent question for us. Our highest imaginative flights suggest "all of us" as the answer, but a non-proprietary, non-possessory relation is outside the ambit of our imagination or beyond the pale of our political practice. The Universe is "ours"—either distributively or collectively. Indeed property, propriety, and the proper (*propre à moi,* the essence of the egoid) are so closely connected conceptually and practically, psychologically and etymologically that it is impossible to think at all in our thought-system without implying (assuming) the relations as given. Freedom is even defined as the condition under which "I am my own man," a statement that on its face seems to imply that slave and slaveholder, owner and owned, are one. We cannot, dare not, would not leave ourselves unconquered, uncontrolled, unowned. We speak severally of "myself" and "my self," and the practice seems so close to common sense, to something given in the nature of things, that any alternative formulation, even a silence before the ineffable, appears needless or misleading or both. The notion that your self is not yours, nor anyone else's, and not in the order of things to which possessory ideas or feelings are appropriate is so patently violative of our ideas, attitudes, practices, and assumptions that it can barely be appreciated as a serious and radically transforming perception. Indeed, it is in a sense an untrue, a false statement. Starting with the assumption with which we all start, we have evolved—or, rather, involuted—selves so truncated, trivialized, narrowed, and ill-nourished that they probably *are* nearly capable of being "owned," used, and held in fee.

The controlling, mastering, conquering, subordinating set is so built into our practices, our psychology, our psyches, our epistemology, our ways of "knowing," and our language that extrication or escape by means of these is actually or virtually barred. Had I prefaced the preceding sentence by saying, "I think that. . . ," the very "I" used would have evoked inevitably in the mind of the reader exactly that controlling, mastering "I," engaged in one more act of control and mastery. That "I"—overly, formally, totally disjunctive from every we, actual and virtual, from every they, from all its and the It—is the condition, cause, consequence, and beginning of the Conquistadorial set and the conquest. It is a particular way of being in the world. Since of its nature it drives toward its own logical conclusion, it progressively bars all other ways totally.

This set, now reaching its climactic elaboration in thought and practice, has given us victory, but victory of the most Pyrrhic kind. Not the unexamined life, but the life of conquest turns out to be not worth living. The stars and the atom's powers and secrets are now ours; the biosphere is our family farm. With every promise of "success," we turn upon ourselves and one another, through "social science," the scopes (whether tele- or micro-) that bid fair to bring our own refractory selves, severally and collectively, also into our service in our severalty or collectivity. The heady hope of a "social science" that will let us truly know ourselves and one another, conjoined to a "planning" that will allow this us in effect to manage that us, is the epitomic expression of the Western dream.

The disease or dream is variously seen: by a Mannheim as a virtually limitless increase in "functional rationality" accompanied by and based upon a virtually limitless decrease in "substantive rationality"; by a Freud as the sacrifice of all pleasures to the point where the will to live is itself overcome by the elaboration of those "defenses" which this civilization represents; by others as the ever more dangerous, ever more irrepressible return of the repressed moves to aggression, the genocidal-suicidal super-achievements of our age; by a Marcuse as the topological transformation of many-sided, multiform man into "one-dimensionality." These men agree that we do ever better what makes no sense, that joy and bliss are dead on the altar of armor, that we are other and strange to all including "our own selves," hellbound to wed death, already all but dead, reduced to a single, last dimension. Those professionals who hear these voices, however, seem dominantly to respond to the vision they evoke with a heightening of the activity which is the cause and expression of the state that the vision recognizes. They seem to hold that either more of the medicine that caused the sickness or a minor variant of the same must be the source of its cure. That senselessness, joylessness, alienation, limitless aggression, the basic alliance with death, and the final reduction of all to nothing are built into the primordial roots and presuppositions of our culture is rarely concluded and still less acted upon. We rely most desperately on what has failed us first. We cannot believe that a world conceived, organized, and related to as we have done may be finally uninhabitable, and the selves correspondingly cast over and over against such a world empty and inoperable. Even when the problem is "located" within the self, we make of that self a "that" in order to "deal with" the problem in our customary fabricant fashion. Our answer to the problems that arise is further and finer fragmentation (so that conquest can continue even as its fruits taste ever more ashen in our mouths). Dissevered each from himself, everyone from everyone else, all from nature, and each more and more from the All, we seek our salvation in one more analytic effort to be followed by one more organizational thrust, a new battle plan for triumph when what is killing us is war.

What we have perfected is technology, and it is technology on which most men, most places, most times rest such vague hopes as still stir. It is now in or almost in our hand to feed lavishly, clothe, and render "literate" the world, to live in virtually instantaneous, universal, continuous, ubiquitous "communication," to annihilate nearly all physical distance, to command more energy than we can use, to engineer mood and perhaps perception at will, to write such genetic prescriptions as we wish, to make such men as whim may dictate. The Universe capitulates. We are everywhere triumphant. But a premonitory smell of cosmic Neroism is in the air, and the cry of "Stop The World; I Want To Get Off" has become, whether absurd or not, pervasive and insistent.

V

There cannot, in the nature of the case, be a well-articulated theory of such things. A way would have to be found to "get out of the culture" in order to find as a new person a new and different direction. Indeed, since some sort of "opening" is of the essence, and since what will follow such opening is unforeknowable, a programmatic specification would be a double contradiction in terms. The first problem is to find the meaning of getting out and the means to do so; the second is to begin to "find one's head" in what then is opened to one; the third is to prevent one's reintegration and re-assimilation; and the fourth is to live in relation to oneself, others, nature, in such fashion as to preserve and enhance the new person in the new related-ness. To look for a formula for a quest is to fail to understand what is implied in either term.

Some faint forecast of what may be before us may be provided by an ideal-typical appreciation of what was till recently known as the "hippie" phenomenon. Being "a hippie," largely a news-media invention, is itself very nearly a contradiction in terms; being "hippie" is a way of being in the world, of being in a different way, a mood, a social movement, a movement of re-ligions, a quest at once personal, social, and transcendent.

The ontogeny of hippieness is as easy to abstract as it is fatal to ade-quate appreciation. The onset is marked by disaffection, disaffiliation, and disgust in the full and literal sense of those terms. What was libidinally in-vested is disendowed; one is orphaned. What had been nurturant is sensed to be poisonous to one's previously barely apprehended deeper being. These sentiments move toward repudiation, more or less clearly articulated, more and more massive. Escape and extrication from the whole fast-woven web of activities, connections, and expectations become paramount necessities, touched with the desperate character of a struggle for survival. Co-emergent is the urgency of finding an adequate experience sufficient at least to suggest or to intimate what in the self and the world has been so radically denied, distorted, and filtered out from the rich life of the rich child of the rich West. What is begun is a long, slow, agonizing quest that moves over a territory having few general and still fewer particular landmarks. Its criteria, recognized in treasured "highs," are the unitive experiences with self, others, nature, the All that depend upon and give rise to some diffusion of the already overbounded ego. The "incidentals" of location, drug-adjuvants, music, fatigue, fasting, costume, style, special language of word, touch, gesture are each less than essential, but more than adventitious. They promote and support, as do the endless but not tightly connected talks in pad and commune, the wandering, tentative searching for one's roots and flower. Finding one's thing and doing one's thing mark stages and are intrinsic; they attest and contribute to a far-reaching transformation of the personality, whose inward signs are growth into gentleness, trust, and grace. No longer—or radically less—atomized, deracinated, homogenized, constricted, and truncated, no longer modeled on mastery, but wedded to wisdom, a recognizable new population emerges not merely bearing a new culture, but being in a new way and manifesting even in mien and posture what it is to be in that Way. For the first time since the history of the West became distinctly Western, a powerful movement emerges whose way is wisdom and whose hero is the sage. No more powerful transformation or revolution can be imagined for a society or a culture than a shift in the type of hero and the mode of self-modeling. From tycoon and bureaucratic-in-chief to sage, from conquest of whatever is to participation in it—these are great distances and direly different directions, dire at least for a civilization so singularly set as ours on so narrow and mean a course.

The first question commonly put to anyone asserting the power of the movement—"How many hippies, exactly, are there?"—attests to a culture lost in mindless counting, computation, calculation, and coping-with or conquering designs and devices. Not only do we instinctively turn to this counting device—to measure magnitude which then becomes undistinguishable from the greatness of something—but the externality, the management set, is implicit in the question. The question means "How many of *them* are there," so that "I" may know whether or how to modify my plans for containing them.

The kindest question asked will often be "How can we plan *for* them?" Dylan's answer—"Get out of the way, if you don't understand, For the times, they are a-changin' "—is evidently incomprehensible, for even the word "understand" is only "understood" by us in characteristic, fatal fashion. We think we understand something when we "grasp" it, have hold of those particulars that permit us to put it in its place. That the vital is only "understood" as it grasps you—or, more exactly, as embrace occurs—is not, it appears, except fleetingly in our understanding.

The question "How can we plan for them?" is so wrong in its every word that no answer is possible. There is an error in the word "them": It is a movement of the spirit, a genuine "change of mind" variously incarnated now in various degrees in various people, that requires a response; it is not some new "subpopulation" or sect. There is an error in the word "we": The likelihood that any intellectual-managerial "we" will be able (failing the advent of fascism) to plan or control underlying populations much longer is negligible, as dramatically attested by the progress of "pot," the development of new sex relations and gender definitions, the "troubles" in school and university and other prisons and ghettos in the last decade. There is error in the word "plan," unless its meaning is so stretched as to include voluntary abdication of the whole scheme of arranging conditions by forethought as to have pre-decided outcomes specified with some particularity. "Planning for Freedom"—the conciliatory slogan—somehow turns out in practice mostly to mean the mere imposition of order *in the name of freedom*.

VI

Even if the foregoing is correct, even if our civilization is about to founder in nuclear fire (or facism) or to become something that "hippieness" foreshadows and forecasts, what has all this to do with "the conscience of the city"?

What is significant about the city is not that it is a "population center" or a place of intersection of roads, rail lines, waterways, or whatnot. A city is that place where whatever is highest in the civilization is being most actively, most vividly, most truly carried on. The city is the locus of the civilization's conscience. Failing that, the city is a population trap, a behavioral sink.

We must remind ourselves of the "hippie" insistence that "finding your head" and finding the appropriate supportive and promotive relation for doing so are co-emergents. No one has as yet gone beyond pad or commune scale in such a search and not abandoned the one half-aim or the other—though a loose commune of communes, not spatially concentrated, seems emerging. Most of these communes are now physically located by choice, not necessity, in the clefts of mountains, on the not-economically-arable plains, in the deserts and waste places generally, in the niches and interstices left free or sparse by the present ecological organization. At least for a while, the conscience of the city and therewith the city may well have its dwelling place anywhere but there.

Indeed, there are other reasons to think that for the near future the city will be literally the province and backwoods, filled with and ruled by provincials and backwoodsmen attempting to learn and do what the advance guard of the civilization is striving to unlearn and undo. It seems perfectly clear that the internal proletariat at home, like the external one abroad, is bound and determined to go through all the stages we have gone through in our miserable quest of this now potentially happy place. Those most external to our society want most the goods and powers, the games and their yield in differential deference, the penalties and rewards, the conquests and controls that are so bitter in our mouths. Just as the poor took on, step by step, the city's abandoned neighborhoods and mansions, so now they seem about to seize the city and with it the city ways that epitomize our maladies and miseries. It will be a "learning environment" of a sort, a learning environment to ease the learning of what we must in agony unlearn, a place to acquire the major diseases one did not have in the vain hope of curing the minor ones one had.

VII

The views and visions earlier adverted to carry with them altogether different implications for the "life of learning" (all life), the manner of learning (all modes), and the environment of learning.

Whatever else is true, the learning must come bearing the personal signature of some fully credible teacher—which is to say someone much more like a guru than our present technicians of skill or information conveyance. No mass process comparable to our present "knowledge" factories in the universities or person and "skill" factories in the schools could fill any part in any congruous "process of education." Something more reminiscent of, though not identical with, discipleship and apprenticeship must supervene. Unitive experiences—or even precessory experiences to these—may be sought, even cultivated, but not engineered. The very notion of putting soul-sustenance and soul-deepening into the grip of a vast machine, organized like an army, standardized, bureaucratized, governed, purporting to derive its authority from the state will seem among the more tragicomic departures in the tragicomic history of man.

We must take it that all large systems—except for the supply of minimum needs at the cost of minimum effort—will largely disappear. What we have to imagine, apart from this minimum, is virtually a nonsystem, and that is, of course, for us, almost beyond imagining. To picture the undesigned is almost as difficult as to design it.

Let us try, however, to imagine a situation—"a scene"—in which the immediate objectives are not so much to learn about something, as to "dig it" or to alter it so that it can be dug. The scene thus defined (to confound Burke's distinctions) includes the action and the actors and the agency. To add to confusion, the purpose—at least the immediate purpose—is to "make the scene" (in a double sense), if it is worth making. The indissoluble double sense of "making the scene" is on the one hand being there and (thereby or otherwise) making it other than it would have been. Digging what there is also implies a double process, but with a tremendous preponderance of emphasis on its first element: It is both unitive and disjunctive or discriminative; it is both to be lost in and to absorb, to be comprehended and to comprehend, to be integrated into and to integrate, to yield to and not master, but embody. It is, in fact (to use Kurt Wolff's terms), to surrender in order to return transformed in order to surrender otherwise.

What is to be dug is more nearly a totality than a convenient working abstraction, though occasionally a peculiarly groovy element may be abstracted. Thus if, for instance, a mathematics lesson should survive as a scene worth making, it is barely possible (and only under peculiar leanings and circumstances) that the beauty of the mathematics will be the principal element dug. The scene (in Burke's sense), the act (as likely as not seen as the funny, pathetic, possibly interesting, peculiarly subtle interplay of personalities), the actors (including oneself, with special attention to the deeper levels of value and significance), and the agency (also dug in its fullness, rather than narrowly as means to an act of narrowly defined purpose) are to be simultaneously dug and in a special sense played into—thus altering all. The special sense of "played into" is that what is meant must have no element of "playing games."

To play games is to be governed by a trinity of *repudianda:* to be acting only or dominantly out of consciousness or forethought (instead of *aus ganz Natur*), for one's advantage, and in the light of other's conscious (especially predetermined and narrowed) expectations. A particular game that has to be avoided is the game of not playing games. The knife edges are very, very fine.

Let there be no question that if "skills" are not "acquired," there will be insufferably little to dig. I have had to put both words in quotation marks because they will be—can be—no longer the same things. "Acquisition," in virtue of its active, aggressive, prehensile, and possessory overtones is the wrong word; and "skills" is unduly connotative of the narrow and the "useful," the narrowly useful. But rhetoric, music, poetry, pictorial and plastic art, not to mention domestic arts, the bread and wine of life, philosophizing and testing of philosophy in dialogue and action—all these are already in process of exceedingly rapid elaboration and development. But whatever corresponds to "skills" will appear as natural emergents from activities and experiences, creditable and valuable in their own general (total) terms, rather than as the results of a self- or other-governed rationalized process of skill production (a series of lessons or a curriculum). Put another way, the way of life will engender the skills that enhance it.

Implicit in all this is a necessity that all men, or most, be teachers (and gurus) in a way for which history affords no example. That transformation can by no means be achieved overnight, for implicit in that implication is another: that "teaching" must, in effect, become a "voluntary," "natural," amateur, continuing function of the life of many, most, or all, rather than, as at present, an involuntary, artificial, intermittent job or trade of an essentially reluctant and, of course, incompetent few. The need, place, and, indeed, possibility for "teaching" as it is presently surviving will be minuscule. The nature of the society contemplated and the likely increase in the tempo of discovery ensure that learning can no longer occur, except marginally, in any situation of unilateral expertise. Increasingly it will be the case that the relative newcomer being taught will have information required for this learning that the relative oldcomer simply cannot have. Because that information will become more and more indispensable, all teaching-learning will have to have the structure of mutuality and the character essentially of a conference. Such doctors—teachers—as remain must be doctors of dialogue. In any case, the bulk of the activity entailed will fall increasingly to the siblingship. And the siblingship will no longer be, solely or primarily, the intense tiny group of "natural" (biological) brothers and sisters nor the non-intense "peers" (friends and acquaintances), but something in between the sibs of the extended families, small "tribes," and such that now begin to dot and will presently fill the landscape.

Very little will need planning—just enough control over the spread of cities and their ways to permit the conscience of the city to find itself chiefly outside these centers, to spread through the society which, by then, may be ready, having reached its fevered climax, to abandon its delirium and search out its new way. That new way, I am confident, will not be, cannot be, in content, organization, aim, or spirit, anything like a continuation or culmination of what we have hitherto nurtured and known.

ANNOTATED BIBLIOGRAPHY

Alinsky, Saul. (1946) *Reveille for Radicals*. Chicago: University of Chicago Press; and Marion K. Sanders. (1970) *The Professional Radical: Conversations with Saul Alinsky*. New York: Harper & Row.

Reveille for Radicals is the original how-to-do-it volume by the master of the craft. *The Professional Radical,* containing more recent thoughts, indicates that Alinsky has not mellowed a bit over the years.

Bollens, John C., and Henry J. Schmandt. (1965) *The Metropolis, Its People, Politics and Economic Life*. New York: Harper & Row.

A balanced view of the metropolis as a dynamic system with discussion of social characteristics and trends, economic developments, physical land-use considerations, and government and politics. The volume discusses a variety of approaches to the problems of metropolitan growth.

Eldridges, H. Wentworth. (1967) *Taming Megalopolis*. New York: Doubleday (Anchor).

Taming Megalopolis is a two-volume set of readings on the problems and promise of planning for the urban future. Volume I, *What Is and What Could Be* provides a general background, while Volume II, *How To Manage an Urbanized World* discusses specific planning approaches and techniques.

Marris, Peter, and Martin Rein. (1967) *Dilemmas of Social Reform*. New York: Atherton.

This book examines some principles, dilemmas, and frustrations with which social reformers in America must contend. It describes the Ford Foundation and federally funded social action programs and their successes and failures. Most important is its discussion of different strategies of reform.

Michelson, William H. (1970) *Man and His Urban Environment: A Sociological Approach,* Reading, Mass.: Addison-Wesley.

A well written, thorough synthesis of available literature on the relationship between urban environments and urban social life. This book provides the basis for Michelson's approach to urban planning.

Mills, C. Wright (1959) *The Sociological Imagination*. New York: Oxford.

Mills provides a lucid analysis of the distinction between biographical and social structural perspectives on social problems. This book must be read.

Moore, Wilbert E. (1963) *Social Change*. Englewood Cliffs, N.J.: Prentice-Hall.

A readable introduction to the whole question of social change. The last chapter provides a summary of evolutionary theory, its early problems, and contemporary revival among change-oriented theorists.

INDEXES

NAME INDEX

SUBJECT INDEX

H

Heterogeneity, in the city, 176–177
Hippie world, 412–413, 414
Historical data, need for, 70–71
History, and the city and technology, 95–104
Housing, 366, 382–383
    attitudes toward, 313–315
    Chicago, Hyde Park–Kenwood, 307–308
    design of, 319–320
    federal aid to, 299–307
    filter process, 293–296
    and Milwaukee riots, 274–275
    problem of, 291–310
    public, esthetics of, 304–305
    public tenants, 302–303
    rent supplement program, 305
    and social class, 311–321
How the Other Half Lives, 26
Human ecology, 84–87
    concentric zonal hypothesis, 85–87
    multiple-nuclei theory, 87
    sector theory, 87
Human Mobilization Corporation, 365–367
Humanitarianism, and the city, 35

I

Ideology, and social organization, 23–25
Incentive systems, federal, 351–352
Individualism, 177
    versus group membership, 180–182
    versus social responsibility, 31
Industrial Areas Foundation, 378, 380–381
Industrialism, 62–67
Industrialization, and social mobility, 73–77
Infant Care, 228
Influentials, 278–280

Inner city, 185–188
    residents of, 186–187
Institutional restructuring, 362
Integration, residential, 128–131
Intellectual life, nineteenth century, 35–36
Intellectualization, 405–406
Intermetropolitan interdependence, 107–111
Internationalization, 144–145
Inter-urbanism, 98–103
Intra-urbanism, sociology of, 95–97
Introduction to Economic History, 105

J

The Jungle, 378

K

Knowledge explosion, 144–146

L

Labor movement, 35, 62–67
Learning, 415–416
Levels, data, 4–5
Life styles
    ecological explanations, 194–195
    upper class, 222–224
    urban, eighteenth century, 31
    youth gangs, 211–221
Looting, as property redistribution, 396–397

M

Machismo, 251
Man Makes Himself, 98
Market strategy, 351
Megalopolis, 91, 105, 107–111
Melting-pot effect, 164–165, 185